TECHNOLOGY OF GUMS, ADHESIVES AND SEALANTS WITH FORMULATIONS

TECHNOLOGY OF GUMS, ADHESIVES AND SEALANTS WITH FORMULATIONS

Written By :-

EIRI BOARD OF CONSULTANTS & ENGINEERS

ENGINEERS INDIA RESEARCH INSTITUTE

4449, Nai Sarak, Main Road, Delhi - 110 006 (India)

Ph: 011- 23918117, 23916431, 23840361

Fax: 91-11- 23916431, 23918117

E-Mail : eirisidi@bol.net.in

Website : http://www.eiriindia.org

Sole Distributor :

INDIAN INSTITUTE OF CONSULTANTS, 4/27, ROOP NAGAR, DELHI-110 007

PRINTED & PUBLISHED BY

ENGINEERS INDIA RESEARCH INSTITUTE

4449, Nai Sarak, Main Road, Delhi - 110 006 (India)
Ph: 011-23918117, 23916431, 23840361
Fax: 91-11-23916431, 23918117
E-Mail : eirisidi@bol.net.in
Website : http://www.eiriindia.org

DISTRIBUTED BY

SMALL INDUSTRY RESEARCH INSTITUTE
INDIAN INSTITUTE OF CONSULTANTS

ISBN : 81-86732-73-X
Printed in New Delhi (INDIA)

Rs. 950

Printed & Published by Sudhir Gupta for " Engineers India Research Institute"
4449 Nai Sarak, Main Road, New Delhi-110 006

Preface

The book " **Technology of Gums, Adhesives & Sealants with Formulations**" covers almost all the basic and advanced details to setup own Adhesive Industry. The book covers Introduction, Mechanism of Adhesive Bonding, End users of Adhesive, Adhesive and Bonding of substrates, Animal Glue, Casein and Mixed Protein Adhesives, Starch Based Adhesives, Neoprene (Polychloroprene) Based Solvent and Latex Adhesive, Acrylic Adhesives, Gum Arabic, Guar Gum, Aerobic Acrylic Adhesive, Acrylic Adhesive and Sealants, Amino Resin Adhesive, Bonding of plastics (Adhesive for Plastics), Carboxylic Polymers in Adhesive, Cyanoacrylate Adhesives, Epoxy Resin Adhesives, Phenolic Resin Adhesive, Polychloroprene Adhesives : Solvent and Latex, Polyester Adhesives, Polythyleneimine in Adhesives, Polysulfide Sealants and Adhesives, Polyurethane Adhesives, Polyurethane Dispersions, Polyvinyl Acetal Adhesives, Polyvinyl Acetate Emulsions and Polyvinyl Alcohol for Adhesives, Resorcinolic Adhesives, Thermoplastic Resin Adhesives, Vinyl Acetate Ethylene Copolymer Emulsion Adhesives, Butyl Rubber and Polyisobutylene Adhesives, Natural Rubber and Reclaimed Rubber Adhesives, Nitrile Rubber Adhesives, Pressure Sensitive Adhesives, Resin for Rubber Based Adhesive, Rubber Adhesives, Styrene Butadiene Rubber Adhesives, Soybeen Adhesives, Starch Adhesives, Animal Glues, Blood Albumen Glues, Casein Glues and Adhesives, Fish Glues etc.

Frankly speaking - the book is also quite indispensable for those who have also setup their industry.

The book has been written for the benefit and to prove an asset and a handy reference guide in the hands of new entrepreneurs and well established Industrialists.

Director
ENGINEERS INDIA RESEARCH INSTITUTE
Nai Sarak, New Delhi (India)
E-mail : eirisidi@bol.net.in

Contents Cum Subject Index

1.

Introduction

Adhesives are social substances. They unite materials creating a whole that is greater than the sum of its parts. They are small in volume compared to the metals, glass, wood, paper, fibres, rubber and plastic that they join together. Just as enzymes, hormones and vitamins, adhesives can be recognised as essential to the health of our industrial society. An adhesive may be described as a substance which is capable of holding materials or adherents together by surface action. This process of joining the two or more surfaces is known as adhesion. The substances loosely covered by this definition of adhesive are cement, sealers, mucilages, pressure and heat sensitive adhesives etc.

The basic function of an adhesive is to fasten the components of an assembly together and maintain the joined parts together under the service conditions. But the two parts can be bonded by other methods also. The adhesives for bonding assumes importance, because the process is fast, easy and economic.

History of adhesives goes back to the vedic periods in India and Pyramid age in Egypt, and also in Crete during 1500 to 500 B.C. Usually naturally accruing gums, animal glues, egg, acacia, tagarcanth, etc. natural gums were in use. Till 1930 before discovery of Phenol Formaldehyde resin synthetic adhesives were not known. After that adhesives science and technology have developed fast and sophisticated, general and specific adhesives have been formulated to join almost everything on this earth. Adhesives have been so designed as to have bond strength as powerful as almost welded joints. Adhesives with predesigned creep characteristics, co efficient of thermal expansion, thermal conductivity have been formulated.

Adhesives are advantageous over other methods of joining materials. Thin films, fibres and small particles that cannot be combined satisfactorily by other techniques are readily bonded by adhesives. Typical examples are laminates of films of various high polymers and plastics, aluminium foil paper, glass wool for insulation, abrasive wheels, paper, type cord with tyres, corrugated boards,paper bags, labels, tapes, safety glass, particle board, plywood etc.

In adhesive bonding stresses are distributed over wider areas making possible lighter and stronger assemblies compared to other methods of fastening. Examples are glued floors, room modules etc. The strength to weight ratios and dimensional stability of anisotropic materials can be improved by cross bonding. Thus wood is converted to water resistant plywood, fibres are made into non woven fabric.

The glue line provides electrical insulation in capacitors, printed circuits, motors etc. The glue line is a moisture barrier, like in laminates and sealants. Dissimilar materials can be joined, aluminium to paper, iron to copper. When two metals joined with adhesives with creep, the metals are not bent on thermal expansion or in contraction. Finally adhesive bondings are faster and cheaper that other methods of fastening or joining.

An ideal adhesives should have : Maximum mechanical strength of the bond, minimum setting time or quick development of bond strength, ease and rapidity of application, resistance to moisture, ability to with-stand temperature variations, produce a flexible bond, resistance to the deterioration by ageing, should be chemically inert to the adherents and should have freedom from objectionable odour, freedom from fire and toxicity hazards.

However, no single adhesive can have all the above desirable properties. Adhesives for particular industrial application is selected according to the more important service conditions required. Modifying agents like plasticizer, stiffeners, driers and fillers etc are incorporated in the adhesive to get the desirable properties. Blends are used to combine the desirable properties of one or more of the adhesive components.

Adhesives are used for bonding of surfaces, where the mechanical bonding methods results in distortion, discolouration, corrosion and other limitation. Adhesive bonding is used to reduce cost and performance improvement. Adhesive bonding is also used to reinforce other fastening methods in an assembly. Adhesives may be used for bonding of dissimilar materials, such as combinations of metals, rubbers, plastics, foamed materials, fabrics, wood etc. and for metals which may constitute a corrosion couple e.g. iron to copper or brass. There are used for bonding of heat sensitive materials like thermoplastics glass etc. Fragile Components such as instrument components, metallic, plastic and glass foils, and delicate parts of cameras and watches are joined by adhesive. Bonding is used in temporary fastenings, where the bond is required to be dismantled later on. Pipe joints, capsules of components, containers, seams etc. are easily sealed with adhesives. Reinforced structure like stiffeners for wall panelling, boxes and containers, partitions, chassis parts of automobiles, aircraft body parts etc. are also now-a-days being bonded using adhesives.

Structural applications of adhesives include load bearing structures in the aircraft fuselage, automotive and civil engineering industries, e.g., clutch facings and brakelinings where adhesives are being used now-a-days. Adhesive applications in laminated structures include sandwich constructions based on honey comb materials of aluminium, foamed plastic, porcelain enamel skins etc. heat exchanger, sheet laminates of plywood, timber beams, plastics, metals, vinyl to steel, copper to phenolic printed circuit boards, wood to metal and rubber sheet to metal, core laminates of electrical dynamos, transformers and motors etc.

Bonded inserts, e.g. plug inserts, studs, rivets, concentrics and shafts, tubes, window frames, furniture assembly, shaft-rotor joints of motors and gears etc., tools, reinforced plastic with metal inserts and paint brush bristles are also some of the applications of adhesives.

Classification

A large variety of adhesives are available in industry, and therefore, their proper classification becomes necessary. The most widely used method of classification is in accordance with their origin or the materials employed in their manufacture. The adhesives may thus be broadly classified as that of animal origin (animal glue, fish glue and casein), of vegetable origin (starch, cellulose-derivatives, rubber and gums etc.) and of synthetic origin (phenolics, vinyls,

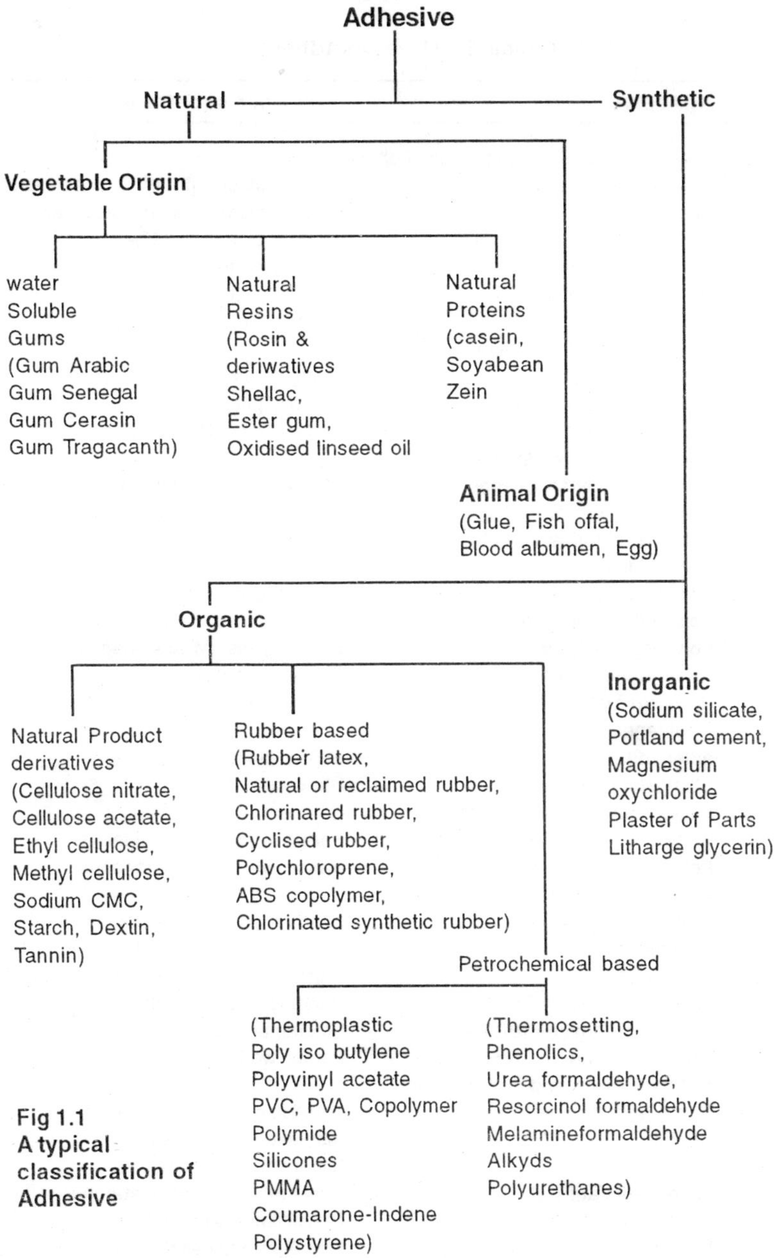

Fig 1.1 A typical classification of Adhesive

epoxies etc.). The other system of classification is based on the mode of adhesion, e.g. pressure sensitive, hot melt, chemical setting and solvent release type etc.

Table 1.1

Typical End Uses of Adhesives

	Adhesive	End User substrate
1.	Thermosetting Synthetic Resin Adhesive :	
	Phenol-formaldehude	Woods, cloths, paper, miscellanious
	Phemol-fururaldehyde	Woods, cloths, paper, miscellanious
	Resorcinol-formaldehyde	Woods, plastics, rubbers
	Urea-formaldehyde	Woods, textiles
	Milamine formaldehyde	Woods, textiles
	Furance	Plastics, rubbers, miscellaneous
	Polyster Resin (including alkyds and allyls)	Cloth, glass fabrics, insulation
	Aniline formaldehyde	Woods, plastics
	Polyurethanes	Woods, miscellaneous
2.	Thermoplastic Synthetic Resin	
	Adhesive Polyisobutylene	Tapes, foils, miscellaneous
	Polyvinyl acetate	Metals, paper, miscellaneous
	Polyvinyl chloride acetate	Miscellaneous
	Polyamides	Metals, woods, miscellaneous
	Silicones	Insulating materials
	Polymethacrylic and Polyacrylic esters	Safety glass, Miscellaneous
	Coumarone Indenes	Rubber, plasticizer
	Polyvinyl bytyral	Safety glass, miscellaneous
	P-toluenesulphonamide-aldehydes	Safety glass, plasticezer
	Plystyrene	Shoe cements
	Maletic Snhydride adducts-glycerol fatty acid resins	Paper, wood, miscellaneous
	Polyvinyl ethers	Paper, wood, miscellaneous
3.	Cellulosic and Srarch Derivatiwes	
	Cellulose nitrate	Leather, paper, miscellaneous
	Cellulose acetate	Leather, paper, miscellaneous
	Ethylcellulose	Paper, cloth, miscellanous
	Methyl cellulose	Paper, modifier, thickener
	Sodium carboxymethyl cellulose	Thickener, paper
	Srarch, dextrin	Paper, wood, textiles
4.	Natural Resins and in Adhesive	
	Rosin and rosin esters	Plasticizers and modifiers
	Shellac	Insulation, miscellaneous
	Asphalts	Minerals, miscellaneous
	Gum tragacanth	Thecker for proteins starch
	Ester gum	Plasticizer and modifier
	Linseed oil (oxidized)	Linoleum, miscellaneous

	Sulphite waste liquors	Linoleum
5.	Water Soluble Gums in Adhesive	
	Gum arabic	Postage paper, miscellaneous
	Gum senegal	Paper, miscellaneous
	Cerasin gum	mixtures
6.	Protein Adhesive	
	Casein	Wood, paper, miscellaneous
	Soyabean protein	Plywood
	Zein	Paper, miscellaneous
7.	Adhesive of Animal or Fish Origin	
	Glue (hide, extracted bone green)	Wood, tapes, miscellaneous
	Fish offal	Wood, miscellaneous
	Blood Albumen	Modifiers for symthetic resin
8.	Adhesive from Rubber or Synthetic Rubber	
	Rubber latex	Cloth, paper, miscellaneous
	Natural or reclaimed rubber	
	Chlorinated rubber & rubber hydrochloride	Miscellaneous, rubber, metals
	Cyclized rubber	Miscelslaneous, rubber, metals, paper
	Polychloroprene	Leather, miscellaneous
	Butadiene-acrylo-mitrile co-polymer	Paper, metals, miscellaneous
	Symthetic resin-rubber combination	Metals, plastics, miscellaneous
	Chlorinated synthetic rubber	miscellaneous
9.	Inorganic Adhesive	
	Sodium silicate	Corrugated paper, paper product
	Portland cement	Mineral aggregates
	Magnesium oxychloride	Ceramics
	Plaster of paris	Miscellaneous
	Litharge-glycerin	Ceramics, plumbing

Another system of adhesive classification is based on their physical state, e.g. liquid, paste, solid forms etc. The liquid based may be further divided into water-based and organic solvent based types. Apart from this there are other miscellaneous methods of classification based on practical applications.

Several classification have been put forward for adhesives. However, each one marginally differs, from the others. A typical classification is given on next page with sets of examples (Fig. 1.1)

The scheme of various types of classification will reveal a lot about adhesives, hence the classification aspect is being dealt with in detail in this chapter.

The typical end-uses of these different classes of adhesives are given in table 1.1

The physical state of adhesive determines its method of application. Liquid adhesives can be easily applied by spreading by mechanical spreaders for flat surfaces and by spraying or brushing for curved or irregularly shaped surfaces. The liquid adhesives can be water emulsions, solvent dispersed or polymerizable liquids. Water emulsions are inexpensive, fire hazard is eliminated and their consistency is adjusted by water, but the adhered surfaces should be porous enough to remove water efficiently. Solvent based liquid adhesives permit a broad variety of formulations and are readily controlled by viscosity measurements. The liquid adhesives are useful, if solvent can be evaporated efficiently. The solution fills the cavities and smoothens the surfaces, this is sometimes a desirable effect.

Liquid based adhesives may be broadly classified into two groups, namely, water based and organic solvent based. Sometimes solvent and water both may be present. All adhesives must be fluid enough to wet the substrates prior to bond formation.

Water based	*Organic solvent based*
Casein Lignin & Tannin Sodium silicate Starch & dextrin Gums Polyvinyl alcohol Sodium carboxy methylcellulose etc.	Cellulose nitrate Cellulose acetate butyrate Cyclised rubber Polyisobutylene nitrate etc.

Some adhesives are made as water dispersions by emulsion polymerization; sometimes the solid polymers are dispersed in the form of emulsions. Thus the following resins etc. are frequently used in the form of emulsion:

Asphalts Coaltar resins MF & UF resins Synthetic rubbers based on polychloroprene, SBR Nitrile and others	Reclaimed rubber Natural rubber Polyacrylates

Vinyl polymers and copolymers, e.g. polyvinyl acetate polyvinyl chloride, polyvi-nyl ether and polyvinyldienes chloride etc.

Advantages and disadvantages of water based vs. solvent-based liquid adhesives are given in Table 1.2.

Table 1.2
Advantages and Disadvantages

Factor	*Water based*	*Solvent based*
1. Cost of production	Cheaper and easier to manufacture	Medium cost
2. Inflammability	Non-inflammable	Hazardous
3. Toxicity	Usually non-toxic	Usually toxic
4. Drying rate	Slow-drying	Quick drying
5. Bond strength	Poor tack, with slow build up	Good, rapid. tack build up
6. Water resistance	poor	good
7. Cold resistance	Subject to freezing with embrittlement to adhesive	Good retention of resilience when frozen

8.	Electrical properties	poor	good
9.	Substrate compatibility	Unsuitable for hydrophobic surfaces eg. inadequate wetting Causes shrinkage of me substrates e.g. textile, paper, and cellulosics, corrosive action to-wards some metals, suitable for porous substrates including foamed plastics	Suitable for even hydrophobic substrate. Good wetting proper-ties. sually unsuitable for plastic forms due to solvent attack. Compatible with metallic surfaces. Basic for contact dhesives.

Pastes may be softened by warming or extruding, under light pressure, on to the adherent surfaces. Due to their high viscosities, they are useful for vertical surfaces also. They may be packed in collapsible tubes. They may be applied with a trowel.

Foam adhesives have been specially and more recently developed for wood industry. The defect, of 'starved' glue line, with low viscosity adhesives, when used with porous surface, has been eliminated in this case of adhesives. The presence of gas bubbles permits broader distribution and less tendency to give a starved glue line.

Adhesives may also be used in the form of tapes, rods and films also. Pressure sensitive marking and sealing tapes are quite frequently used in industry.

Rubber based adhesives are usually used in tapes. Adhesive films may be made by depositing a layer of adhesive on cloth or paper; and sometimes a thin cast or calendered sheet of adhesive may be used by itself. Gummed paper tape and labels are applied by moistening with water while phenolic resin films are used in hot pressed plywood.

Powdered or granulated adhesive may be used at the glue line: heat and pressure is applied to produce flow and uniform distribution. This type of adhesives is particularly useful for metal bonding.

As indicated at the beginning of this chapter, the most widely used classification for adhesives is on the basis of their origin viz. vegetable, animal and synthetic. These are then further classified into sub-groups e.g. cellulosic, protein, organic, inorganic etc. To a great extent the mechanical properties depend on the thermosetting or thermoplastic nature of the bond. This aspect of the adhesives is described below.

Thermoplastic Adhesives

Thermoplastic adhesives are characterised by permanent fusibility and solubility. They will soften with heat and exhibit greater degree of creep under sustained stress. They are thus useful for low-load assemblies of metals, ceramics, plastic and porous materials such as wood paper and textiles etc. which are not exposed to severe conditions of use. Unlike the thermosetting resin adhesives, they do not change chemically in establishing a bond.

These adhesives may be broadly classified into thermoplastic resin adhesives and thermoplastic rubber adhesives. Thermoplastic resin adhesives are based on various synthetic materials e.g. polyamides, vinyl and acrylic polymers and cellulose derivatives etc., and also on natural resins such as rosin, shellac and mineral waxes etc. Hot-melt adhesives come under this category, and are finding use in packaging and plastic film laminate making. Such hot melt adhesives are usually compounded from polythene, vinyl polystyrenes, polycarbonates and polyamides etc. Required plasticizers, fillers and reinforcing materials are incorporated for certain desirable properties. These adhesives are available as solids, films, rods, emulsions etc.

Thermoplastic rubber adhesives are usually based on natural, reclaimed and synthetic rubbers such as neoprene, butyl, SBR and nitriles etc. These adhesives are made in the form of solutions and dispersions. Fillers, plasticizers and other compounding ingredients are incorporated according to requirements.

Thermoplastic adhesives in the form of films may be applied using heat or solvent. The solid adhesives sets on cooling giving the bond.

Thermosetting Adhesives

The thermosetting adhesives through the action of heat, catalysts or both may be converted to a substantially insoluble state. The final material after setting is of high molecular weight an cross-linking is present. These adhesives show good creep resistance and are useful under high load conditions and sever service involving heat, cold, humidity and even chemical exposures. Thermosetting adhesives include animal glues, soyabean and vegetable proteins, case in and water based adhesives, and synthetics based on epoxy, phenolic, polyester, polyaromatic and other thermosetting polymers.

These adhesives are available as liquids, pastes and solids such as films. Liquid types are generally supplied in two-component systems, which become solid on reaction due to catalytic action with or without heat. Sometimes two parts thermosetting rubber resin adhesives are vulcanised at room temperature or under heat and pressure. Structural film adhesives require heat and pressure to achieve maximum mechanical properties. Curing temperatures may be as high as 150-250°C. The bonding pressures may be even up to 100 kg/cm^2. Sometimes for better strength post cure is necessary.

Rubber Resin Blends

A combination of resins and rubber gives the combination of desired properties of both type of materials. Blends of thermosetting resins and synthetic rubber are used for structural bonding of metal and other rigid materials; examples of such adhesives are phenolic neoprene and phenolic nitrile adhesives. Thermosetting resins give brittle bonds but presence of rubber component imparts flexibility and impact or shock resistance. Presence of resins improves tack, cohesion, heat resistance and specific adhesion to surfaces.

Such blend type adhesives are used for bonding of textiles, fabrics to metal and wood, tiles, lamination of paper, metal foil and plastic films, floorings and other industrial applications. These adhesives are available as films, tapes or solvent solutions. The films are cured at elevated temperatures up to 200 and at pressure about 30 to 100 kg/cm^2. Liquid types are dried to remove solvent and then processed as film adhesives.

After this basic information chemical classification of adhesives and their typical end uses can now be given (Table 1.3)

Table 1.3

Chemical classification and end uses of adhesives

Adhesive Classes	*Uses*
1. **Animal Adhesives**	
1. Hide and Bone Glue	Wood, tapes, miscellaneous
2. Fish Glue	Wood, miscellaneous
3. Blood albumin	Modifier for synthetic resin and cellulosic and proteins
4. Shellac	Insulation. Miscellaneous
5. Casein	Wood, paper, miscellaneous
2. Mineral Adhesives	
a. *Inorganic Adhesives*	
1. Sodium silicate	Corrugated paper, paper products
2. Portland Cement	Mineral aggregates
3. Magnesium oxychloride	Ceramics
4. Plaster of parts	Miscellaneous, ceramics
5. Litharge-glycerin	Ceramics, plumbing
b. Organic Adhesives	
1. Asphalts	Insulation, Miscellaneous
3. Vegetable Adhesives	
a. Gums	
1. Gum Arabic	Postage, paper, miscellaneous
2. Gum tragacanth	Thickener for proteins, starch
3. Rosin, rosin esters	Plasticizers and modifiers
4. Ligntn & Tannin	Modifier
b. Proteins	
1. Soybean protein	Plywood
c. Starch Dextrin	Paper, wood, textiles
4. Synthetic Adhesives	
a. Thermoplastic Adhesives	
1. Cellulose nitrate	Leather, paper, miscellaneous
2. Cellulose acetate	Leather, paper, miscellaneous
3. Ethyl cellulose	Paper,cloth,miscellaneous
4. Sodium CMC	Thickener, paper

5.	Polyisobutylene	Tapes, foils miscellaneous
6.	Polyvinyl Acetate	Metals, paper, miscellaneous
7.	Polyvlnyl chloride acetate	Miscellaneous
8.	Polyamides	Metals, wood, miscellaneous
9.	Silicones	Insulating materials
10.	Polymethacrylic and Polyacrylic esters	Safety glass, miscellaneous
11.	Coumarone-indene resin	Rubber, plasticlzer
12.	Polyvlnyl butyral	Safety glass, miscellaneous
13.	Polystyrene	Shoe cements
14.	Polyvinyl ethers	Paper, wood, miscellaneous
b.	*Thermosetting Adhesives*	
1.	Phenol-formaldehyde	Wood, cloth, paper, miscellaneous
2.	Phenol-furfuraldehyde	Wood, cloth, paper, miscellaneous
3.	Resorcinol-formaldehyde	Wood, plastic, rubber
4.	Urea-formaldehyde	Wood, textile
5.	Melamine-formaldehyde	Wood, textile
6.	Furanes e.g. phenol furfural	Plastic, rubber, miscellaneous
7.	Polyester resins e.g. alkyds and allyls	Cloth, glass fabrics, miscellaneous
8.	Aniline formaldehyde	Wood, plastics
9.	Polyurethanes	Wood, miscellaneous
c.	*Elastomer Adhesives*	
1.	Rubber latex	Cloth, paper, miscellaneous
2.	Natural or reclaimed rubber	Rubber,metal, miscellaneous
3.	Chlorinated rubber and rubber hydrochloride	Miscellaneous, rubber, metal
4.	Cyclised rubber	Miscellaneous, rubber, metal, paper
5.	Polychloroprene (neoprene)	Leather, miscellaneous
6.	Butadiene-acrylonitrile rubber	Paper, metal miscellaneous
7.	Synthetic resin-rubber blends	Metal, plastic, miscellaneous
8.	Chlorinated synthetic rubber	Miscellaneous

Other Methods of Classification : The classification of adhesives given above were based on the nature, physical or chemical, of the various adhesives. Practical usage angle may also be made the basis of adhesive classification; and one such method of adhesive classification based on practical use is that of dividing them into two brand categories, viz. Primary Bonding Adhesives and Secondary Bonding Adhesives.

In primary bonding, the assembly and lamination of thin sheets of material into flat or curved structures is carried out with the aid of pressure and warm or hot-setting resin adhesives. The secondary bonding means the assembly of solid components or sections already laminated with the aid of adhesives or other similar components. For an example, attachment of fittings or assembly of reinforcing stringers or ribs to plywood skins constitutes secondary bonding.

The adhesives may also be classified according to their end use viz. paper adhesive, metal adhesive, textile adhesive, rubber cements etc. This classification has some importance to the craftsman or the user but has little use to the formulator. Some such classes of adhesives are given below to clarify the point. Metal adhesives usually have a rubber or chlorinated rubber base. The volatile matter is usually evaporated before the bonding is complete.

Wood adhesives usually have an animal or vegetable material as base; sometimes synthetic materials are also employed. Volatile vehicle is absorbed by the porous wood surface. When used for exterior wood application, adhesive should be weather resistant.

Paper adhesives are usually based on starch, dextrins and proteins. They are used in stamps, labels, corrugated boxes, books etc.

Textile adhesives are usually based on starches and dextrins. Rubber base adhesives may be employed for laminating operations, while synthetic resins are more suitable for sizing of textiles.

Though a large number of adhesives have been in the classifications give above, the list could not be said to be complete, and there are numerous less important adhesives also. Sometimes an adhesive can claim its place in more than one class of adhesives; this particularly happens in the case of blends. In a blend the adhesive is put into category according to the property of the major constituent; the minor constituent simply acts as a modifier.

2.
Mechanism of Adhesive Bonding

When two dissimilar materials are brought into intimate contact, a new interface is formed at the expense of the original two free surfaces in air. The nature of the interaction at the interface (and the condition of the surfaces) determines the strength of the bond that forms between the materials. A wide range of interactions are possible. At one extreme these reactions may prevent formation of a strong bond; at the other extreme they may form such a strong bond that failure of the joint occurs cohesively in one or another of the phases. In both cases, the wettability of one phase by the other is crucial in determining the extent of interfacial interaction.

Generally the more important technological need is for the formation of permanent strong bonds between materials where it is usual for the adhesive to be applied to the substrate as a mobile liquid phase. The adhesive subsequently solidifies as a result of evaporation of solvent, a chemical cross-linking reaction, cooling to below the melting temperature or a combination of the above.

These mechanisms of adhesives include mechanical adsorption (through molecular or ionic attraction, e.g. through electrostatic, covalent or metallic primary bonds or through secondary bonds, such as Vander Waals forces); electrostatic forces (electrical double layer), diffusion (e.g. solvent cementing, heat welding); and weak boundary layer.

All of this work endeavour to explain adhesion phenomena on the basis of liquidity, wetting, spreading, surface tension, contact angles and the eventual cure or change of stage of the adhesive in contact with the adherends. The contact angle is a powerful means of determining adhesion tendencies. There is an unsymmetrical force distribution at the interface between two materials (solids, liquids, vapors or gases) that gives rise to surface tension effects.

Surface tensions of solvents and liquids of interest in adhesives are listed in Table 2.1. Solubility parameters are also listed. As indicated below, these have a relationship to wetting and adhesion.

The solubility parameter (SP) of a solvent or polymer is a function of the cohesive energy density, CED. It is equivalent to the square root of (ΔE divided by *V)* (measured in hilderbrands), where ΔE=energy of vapo- rization, V= molar volume and $\Delta E/V$ = CED (or internal molecular pressure).

SP can be considered as a vector of dipole-dipole forces, hydrogen bonding forces (significant effect) and dispersion forces. Figure 2.2 shows this association between critical surface tension and SP for 14 polymers.

Table 2.1
Surface tensions and solubility parameters of solvents

solvent	Surface tension (dyns / cm)	Temp of test (0C)	Solubility parameter —total (hidebrands)	H-bond index
Hexane	20.0		7.3	2.2
Isopropanol (anhydrous)	20.8	25	11.4	8.9
Ethanol (anhydrous)	22.1	25	12.8	8.9
Acetone	22.6	25	10.0	5.7
n-propanol	23.8	20	11.9	8.9
Isopropyl acetate	24.5	25	8.6	5.2
Methyielthy Ketone	24.6	20	9.3	5.0
n-Butanol	24.6	20	11.2	8.9
I,I,I-Trochloroethane	25.1	20	8.5	2.2
Tributtyl Phosphate	26.7	25		
Ethylene glycol monobutyl ether	27.4		9.8	15.5
n-Butyl acetate	27.6	27	8.7	5.4
Propylene glycol monomethyl ether	27.7		10.2	14.6
Toluene	28.0		8.9	3.8
Xylence (meta))	28.0		8.9	3.8
Ethylene glycol monoethyl ether (2-ethoxy ethanol)	28.2		1.06	15.5
Ethyiene glycol monotethyl	28.6		11.4	15.3
Dimethyl formanmide	37.3	20	12.4	6.4
Tricresyl phosphate	40.7			
Ethylene glycol	48.4	20	17.1	
Formamide	58.2	20	19.2	
Propylene glycol	72.0	25	15.0	
Water (distilled)	72.8	20	23.5	20.7

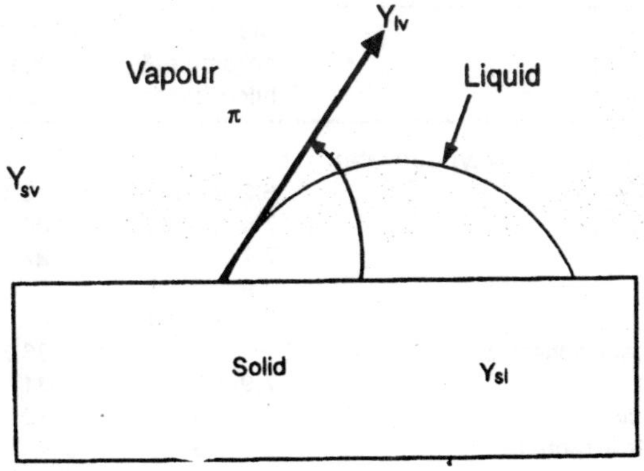

Fig. 2.1

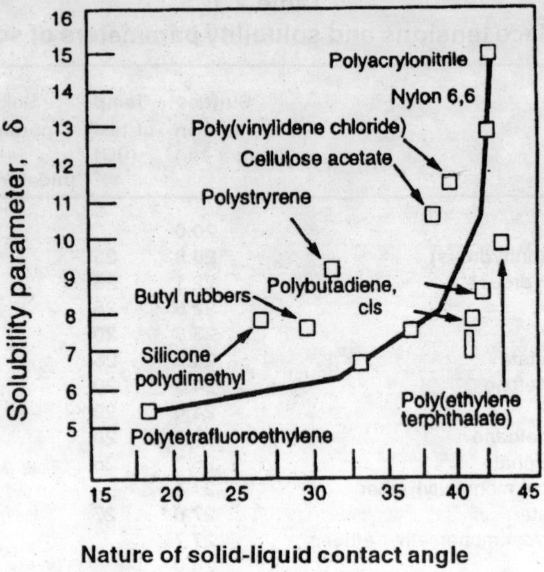

Fig. 2.2
Polymers: Critical Surface Tension vs. Solubility Parameter

Table 2.2
Polymers : Critical surface tension us solubility parameter

	Slubility parameter& hildevrands	Critical surface tension, *Yc* (dyne cm[1])
Poly(1H, 1H-pentadecafluoroctyl acrylate)		10.4
Polytetrafluoroethylene	6.2	18.5
Silicone, polydimethyl	7.6	24
Butyl rubber	7.7	27
Polyethylene	7.9	31
Natural rubber	7.9-8.3	-
Natural rubber rosin adhesive		36
Polyisoprene, cis	7.9-8.3	31
Polybutadience, cis	8.1-8.6	32
Butadience-styrene rubbers	8.1-8.5	-
Polysobutylene	8.0	-
Polystyrene	9.1	32.8
Polystyrene Polysulfide rubber	9.0-9.4	-
Neoprene (chloroprene)	8.2-9.4	38
Butadience-acrylonitrily rubbers	9.4-9.5	-

Poly (vinyl acetate)	9.4	-
Poly (methyl methacrylate)	9.3	39
Poly (vinyl chloride)0	9.5-9.7	39
Urea-formldehyde resin	9.5-12.7	61
Epoxy	9.7	10.9
Polyamide-epichlorohydrin resin	-	52
Ethyl cellulose	10.3	-
Poly (vinyl chloride-acetate	10.4	-
Poly (ethyl..terephthalate)	10.7	43
Cellulose acetate	10.9	39
Cellulose nitrate	10.6-11.5	-
Phenolic resin	11.5	-
Resorcinol adhesives	-	51
Poly(vinylidene chloride) saran	12.2	40
Nylon 6,6	13.6	43
Polyacrylonitrile	15.4	44
Cellulose, from wood pulp	-	35.5, 42
Cellulose, from cotton linters	-	41.5
Cellulose, regenerated	-	44
Starch	-	39
Casein	-	43
Wool	-	45

Surface

Adhesive bonding involves chemistry, physics, rheology, material behaviour, surface behaviours & thermodynamics of materials. The basic concepts of surfaces, bond formation, bond properties and bond failures are discussed.

Solid surfaces have a texture which is characterised by waviness, roughness, and indentations such as scratches and pits. They have little effect on adhesive spreading, but effect bond strength if the peaks are sharp-edged and act as stress concentration points. Such stress risers are less effective with adhesives pliable enough may explain the effect of surface roughness on bond strength, shown in figure 2.3.

Fig. 2.3
The effect of surface roughness on bond strength

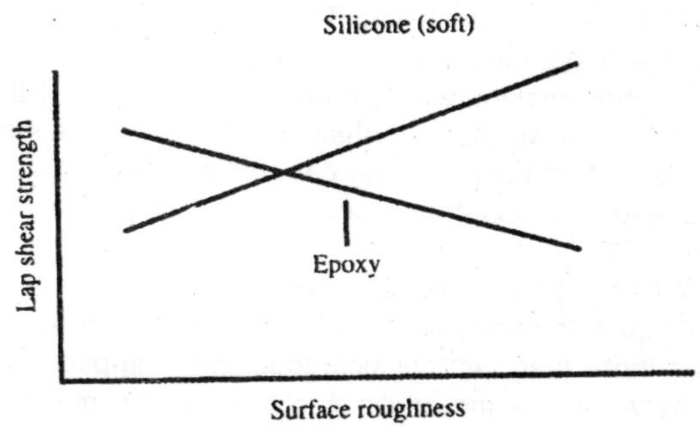

Surface indentations interfere with wetting if they retain trapped air or selectively concentrate solvents from the adhesive. Such air or solvent pockets may result in expansion pressure stresses when the bond is cured or used at high temperatures. Gross indentations of this type are usually easily detected with the eye or under low magnification.

If the oxide on metal surface is tightly held and cohesively strong, it provides better base for bonding than the metal itself. Aluminium is often oxidized (anodized) for this purpose. Water adsorption occurs with virtually every metal surface. Thus, adhesives are selected for their ability to spread over and wet highly polar water-rich surfaces.

Bond Formation

The nature of adhesion has been explained as surface chemical reaction, interdiffusion, dipole-dipole attractions, Van der Waal's forces, and mechanical interlocking. However, none of these explanations alone fits every situation, and more than often several of them appear to play a role in bonding.

A useful theory of adhesion, is suggested on the basis of electrical attractions. These electrical attractions called bonds which result from uneven electron distributions on surfaces, are listed in table 2.3 with their strength.

Table 2.3
Strengths of various Bond Types

Bond *Type*	*Bond strength*
Covalent	80-100 Kcal/mole
Dipole-dipole	8-10 Kcal/mole
Hydrogen	2-12 Kcal/mole
Dispersion	1-2 Kcal/mole

The bond strengths expressed as bond energies range in strength from less than 1 Kcal/mole (weak van der Waal's forces) to more than 100 Kcal/mole (strong chemical bonds). The low strength of many of these attractions and the short distance over which they are effective is offset by the large number of possible bonds per unit area. Theoretically as many as 2 x 10^{63} bonds could exist per square centimeter.

Surfaces not normally considered "electrical" participate easily in attractive interactions if adhesives wet them. The reason for substances such as polyethylene's difficult bonding is because of thermodynamical stability of available adhesives if their molecules attract one another than if they interact with low energy surfaces. The key to the adhesion is to modify the surfaces of difficult to bond materials so that they become capable of manifesting strong electrical attraction. A number of proprietary processes are routinely used industrially for this purpose.

Wetting : Wetting is essential to adhesive bonding. It refers to the intimate association of a liquid (the adhesive) with a solid (the substrate). This intimacy of contact involves more than just physical touching. It implies a sort of "electron cloud mixing" between the materials. A clean surface makes the water molecules in the molecular attractive forces to direct to the substrate, without the wetting. strong bonds are impossible. Wetting results from a chemical affinity between the liquid and the solid. To a first approximation this affinity is explained by molecular polarity. Molecules of low polarity liquids are more likely to break away from each other and establish attractive forces with highly polar surfaces. Even highly polar water will not wet (and thus spread) over the surface when it covered with less polarity contaminants such as grease or oil.

Industrially, a considerable amount of effort is spent in cleaning and otherwise modifying surfaces so that wetting will occur. Time and temperature both favour wetting. As a result, slowly heat cured adhesives often give stronger bonds than room temperature rapidly cured products of similar compositions.

Shrinkage : Adhesives often shrink during cure primarily because solvents in the adhesive escape, leaving less mass in the bondline. Even 100% reactive products experience some shrinkage because their solid polymerised products occupy less volume than the liquid reactants. Hot melts experience shrinkage as a result of cooling. Table 2.4 illustrates the range of shrinkage involved for typical adhesive.

Table 2.4
Typical Percent Cure Shrinkage for Various Adhesives

Adhesive Tapes	*% Shrinkage*
Acrylic	5-10
Anaerobics	6-9
Epoxles	4-5
Urethanes	3-5
Polyamides (hot melts)	1-2
Silicones (curable)	<1

The shrinkage leads to appearance of stresses at the adhesive substrate surface and the possible formation of cracks and voids within the bond line itself. Adhesive with creep are better able to adjust to shrink stresses than rigid products. Formulators are often able to adjust the final creep of their product to the desired level if their customer's curing schedule is known.

Bond Properties

The cohesive strength of an adhesive is equally important as its adhesiveness. Bond strength is often not limited by adhesion. Even when bond failure appears the failure often occurs at a weakly bonded substrate surface layer and is not prevented by a stronger adhesive.

Expansion Coefficients : Differences in expansion between adhesive and substrate can lead to serious stresses at the bond interface. Figure 2.4 illustrates this situation for a phenolic epoxy steel bond. The seven fold plus difference in expansion coefficient between the epoxy and the steel means that the adhesive must move more than seven times as far as the steel when the temperature changes. The interfacial shear stresses that arise because of expansion differences sometimes make particular bonds risky or impossible. The problem is sometimes compounded if low temperature impact resistance is required.

Fig. 2.4
Differences in expansion coefficients

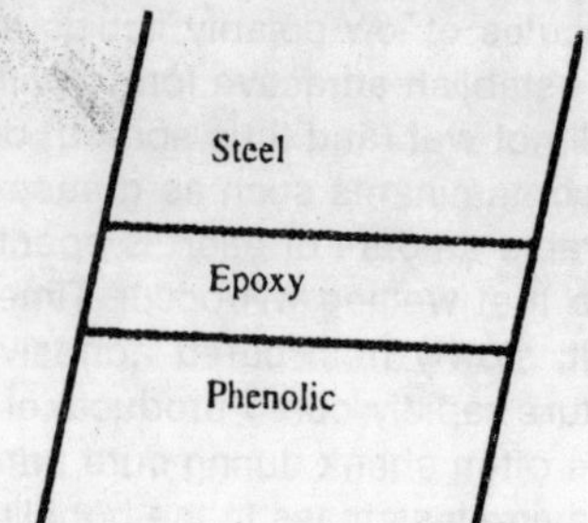

There are several solutions to the expansion mismatch problem. One is to use a resilient adhesive which expands and contracts with temperature change. The penalty here is a possible creep problem and lower ultimate bond strength. Another approach is to adjust the expansion coefficient of the adhesive to a point which is midway between the substrate values. This isn't always possible, but when it can be achieved the adhesive may act as a very satisfactory bridge between the shifting substrate surfaces. A third possibility is to coat one or both of the substrates with a primer or coupling agent. This substance usually is either resilient or of intermediate expansion behaviour itself. The fibreglass reinforced polyester resin industry depends heavily on the coupling agent approach to assure the durability of glass to resin bonds.

Stress Distribution : Stress distribution within an adhesive bond under the load are anything but uniform. Figure 2.5 illustrates approximate stress distributions which result when bonds are loaded in shear and cleavage.

The most undesirable situation occurs in the case of cleavage and peel. In these instances the failing force is concentrated at the edge of the bond and may result in an unzippering type of failure. Total bond length will have little effect in resisting failure of this type.

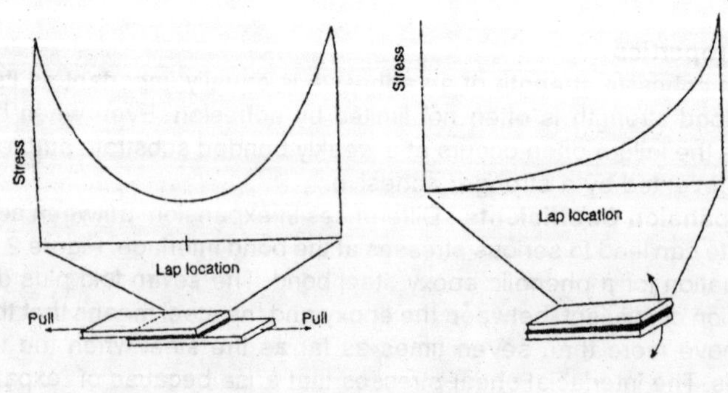

Fig. 2.5
Stress distribution within a bond

Figure 2.5 also indicates that although lap bonds distribute shear stresses over their entire area, the distribution is not uniform. Indeed the middle three quarters of the bond may carry only one quarter of the load. Since the ends of lap bonds absorb most of the stress, it is wise to make the bond as wide as possible. This effect is clearly shown in Table 2.5.

Table 2.5
The Effect of Bond Length and Width on Lap Shear Strength
Using a Commercial Epoxy Adhesive
To Bond 0.317 cm (0.1250in) Steel Plate

Bond Area	*Length.*	Width	Strength
6.45 cm^2 (1.0 in^2)	6.45cm^2 (1.0 In^2)	2.25cm(1.01n)	1.27 cm (0.5 In)
1.27 cm (0.5 In)	2.54 cm (1.0 in)	432 kg (950 lb)	510 kg (1.121 lb)

Motion : Like all organic polymers, adhesive molecules undergo constant thermally induced vibration in several directions at once. The amplitude of these vibrations is determined primarily by temperature, chain flexibility, and cross linking, *and* to a lesser extent by fillers and physical stresses. A certain amount of *chain* flexibility or "wiggle" is desirable since it imparts resiliency and toughness to the adhesive film. Too much flexibility, however, may lead to progressive creep, i.e. plastic flow under load, resulting in ultimate bond failure.

Adhesive formulators use the glass transition temperature, Tg,, as a practical basis for compounding products with the appropriate amount of internal motion. Tg is the temperature as which the slope of a temperature volume plot undergoes a sudden upward change as shown in figure 2.6. Structural adhesives must have a Tg higher than their use temperature in order to avoid being rubbery and experiencing creep. On the other hand, if the adhesive is used far below its glass transition temperature, brittleness may become a problem since the chain segments are so effectively "frozen" in the solid state that they can not deform under impact and absorb applied energy. Typical Tgs for adhesive resins are shown in Table 2.6.

Table 2.6
Typical Tgs for adhesive resins

Resin	*Tg*
Silicone	-90' C (-130' F)
Rubber (natural)	-70' C (-94' F)
Polyamide	60' C (140° F)
Epoxy	100'C (212' F)

An adhesive undergoes a rapid increase in volume at the glass transition temperature (Tg)

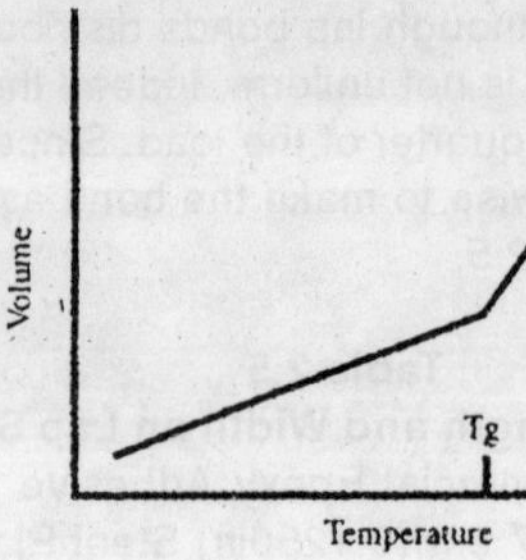

Fig. 2.6
Volume increase at glass transition temperature (Tg)

Bond Failure : Bond durability is greatly reduced by stress, particularly cyclic stress. Potentially harmful bond stresses may be mechanical, thermal, or chemical origin. They result in strain on a bond beyond its ability to resist. Failure results.

All solids and mechanical assemblies have finite abilities to resist stress. The cumulative effect of cyclic stresses, particularly if more than one type is also harmful. Temperature variation combined with cyclic loading, for instance, can greatly reduce adhesive durability compared with simple ambient condition aging of the same sample. Figures 2.7 and 2.8 clearly illustrate the influence of stress on bond strength retention.

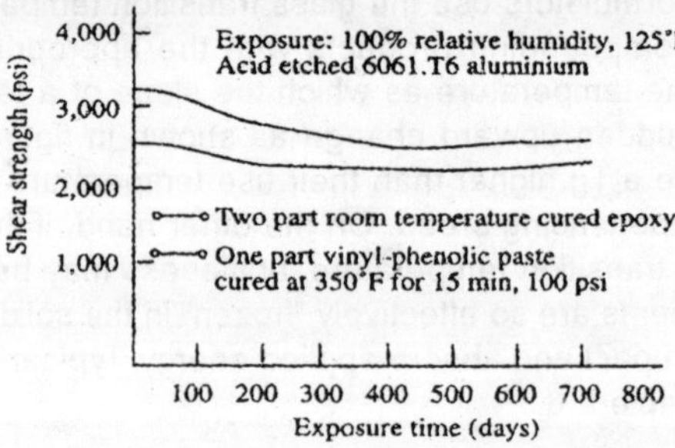

Fig. 2.7

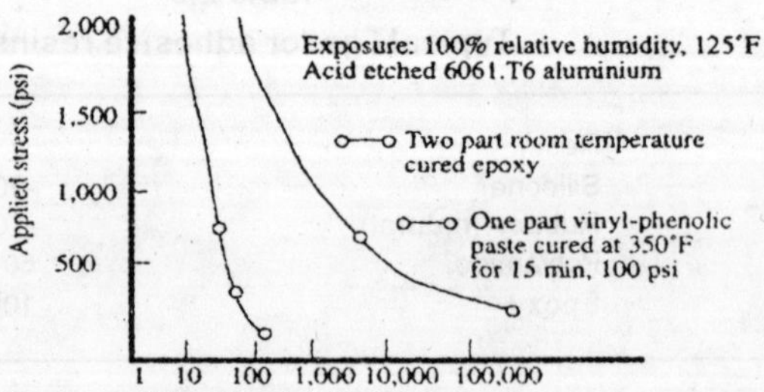

Fig. 2.8

Fig. 2.7 & 2.8
Influence of stress on bond strength retention

Fig. 2.7 and 2.8 show that strength retention differs greatly for stressed and unstressed bonds. Initial shear strength for stressed specimens: epoxy — 2800 psi, vinyl phenolic — 3400 psi.

The phenomena of creep and cracking as a mechanism of bonding failure are understood. While they may be accelerated by temperature changes, they are essentially mechanically induced failure modes. There are times, however, when a properly cured unstressed bond failure occurs for no apparent reason. It may exhibit apparent adhesive failure, sometimes under no load at all after extended ageing.

When behaviour of this type is encountered, the cause is often desorption, i.e. displacement of the adhesive from the surface by a chemical from the environment or from within the substrate. Attachment to substrate sites involves a dynamic equilibrium between the adhesive and other molecules which may be present. Water, solvent, plasticizer, and various gases and ions may all compete for surface attachment sites.

Moisture is by far the most effective desorbing substance commonly available. Most surfaces have a tightly bound water layer when the bond is made. This water layer may act as a willing receptor for moisture which diffuses into the adhesive film.

Bonds are able to resist desorption only if the attacking substances are unable to penetrate the film or if the substrate adhesive bond is thermodynamically or kinetically favoured over the substrate-desorber interaction. Some widely used coupling agents form thin films between the substrate and the adhesive which have very high affinities for each material.

3.

End Users of Adhesive

Adhesives are pervasive in our industrial society, indispensable in the vehicles we drive and fly, our clothes and shoes, our books, our homes. This chapter reviews the commercial aspects of the adhesives.

Uses in Construction Indusry

Adhesives and sealants are employed in construction for many structural and decorative applications, e.g., for gluing doors, installing carpets, wallpaper, panels, making doors, etc. The construction industry is probably the largest user of adhesives and sealants in the developed world. In India use of adhesives are picking up in construction industry.

Glued Floors, Wood Frames, etc.

In recent years, the housing industry has begun the adhesive bonding of subfloors to joints in the prefabrication of prestressed skin or sandwich floor components, in the manufacture of modules, or at the building site itself. To a lesser extent, walls and roofs also are being made by gluing plywood boards to studs. This type of construction has brought improved strength, freedom from squeaking, as well as two savings: thinner studs and joists, and the separation of framing members, widening from 16 to 24 in.

Since the adhesives are required to be gap-filling, viscous mastics are preferred. Most of these are based on rubbers; neoprene, sbr, styrene-butadiene-styrene block copolymer, natural rubber and reclaim. Other systems include urethane, resorcinol-phenol formaldehyde, casein, and vinyl acetate copolymers.

Gypsum Board

Wallboard is a gypsum composition sandwiched between two sets of kraft paper., Dextrin or starch is the binder for the hydrated calcium sulphate.

Adhesives are being utilized in bonding gypsum wallboard to wooden studs, with or without nails. Advantages of glued wallboard are the elimination of nails on prefinished surfaces, lower noise level, and added strength of components of modular homes and prebuilt panel homes which must resist the trauma of transportation.

Joint sealing and taping is required for vertical and exposed horizontal joints. Usually this is accomplished with rubber based pressure sensitive tapes. Also used are "ready mix" products based on a polyvinyl acetate emulsion and "joint compounds" based on starch and casein. All these systems are highly filled Some gypsum board is laminated, using neoprene or natural rubber contact cements.

Class Fibre Insulation

Glass fibres provide thermal insulation in houses, and in ducts, pipes, and other process equipment. Phenol formaldehyde is the most common binder. Some fibreglass butts are faced on one side with kraft paper to which aluminium foil has been laminated with sodium silicate to serve as a heat reflector and moisture vapor barrier. Where the insulation must be bonded, e.g. for duct work and mobile homes, neoprene and asphalt emulsions containing SBR are used.

Insulation Board and Acoustical Tile

A small percentage of these materials are installed with adhesives, mainly mixture of rosin with reclaim rubber and asphalt.

Concrete Adhesives

Latex additives improve the strength of concrete. The most popular of these is acrylic; others include SBR and PVAc.

PVAc adheslves are employed for bonding new concrete to old. Patching and adhering concrete also is accomplished with epoxies. Epoxy and polyester are used as matrices for terrazzo flooring.

Panels

Sandwich panels require adhesive bonding effacing to cores. Foam core panels, primarily polystyrene, are prebuilt by manufacturers of curtain walls, movable partitions and components for commercial refrigeration. The cellular core is adhered with neoprene cement or latex, avoiding solvents which may attack the polystyrene.

For refrigerated warehouses, adhesive systems include a highly filled PVAc and styrene-butadiene resin. Curtain wall panels permit the rapid enclosure of high-rise buildings, so that work can continue during the winter months. They have an outside surface of glass, plastic or metal. The interior face usually is galvanized steel, but may also be porcelain enamel. Adhesives mainly neoprene cement, are employed to bond the composite.

Wooden Doors

Plywood, particle board and phenolic-impregnated paper honeycomb, the principal components are assembled with amino resins or PVAc.

Vinyl Film Laminates

PVC film is bonded to gypsum board, plywood to make prefinished wallboard and to paperboard for ceilings in mobile homes. Almost all of these vinyl acetate copolymers are favoured as laminates; some acrylic is also utilized.

Ceramic Tile Adhesives

Ceramic tiles are used for walls and floors; they may be decorative as well as functional. For wall tiles, the adhesive is solvent or water-based styrene butadiene resin plus SBR. SBR and cellulose ethers are additives for dry-set mortar, with which dry tiles can be applied to floor or wall. Epoxy and furnace resins are important as grouting compounds.

Wall paper Pastes

Adhesives for paper wall coverings, purchased as dry powders to be diluted with water, are based on wheat flour or carboxymethyl cellulose. Heavy weight PVC wall coverings generally are applied with a paste based on polyvinyl acetate and formulated with polyvinyl alcohol, plasticizers, preservatives and starch as a thickener.

Resilient Flooring

It may be either yard goods or tiles 9" or 12" squares made of vinyl asbestos, homogenecus vinyl or vinyl foam. While the contractor utilizes inexpensive adhesives such as asphalt emulsion, asphalt cutback and lino (ligninsulphonate, the do-it-yourselfer installs tiles with a higher priced product based on SBR latex. For convenience, the homeowner-applicator is now turning more and more to tiles, to the underside of which the manufacturer has applied, from hot-melt, a pressure-sensitive styrene-isoprene-styrene block polymer. The pressure-sensitive masscoat is covered with release paper which is peeled off just before application.

Carpet-Installing Adhesives

The use of adhesives for installing carpeting has been increasing and this method of application has become a strong competitor to mechanical fasteners. An SBR system is commonly used. Neoprene-based mastics are preferred in commercial installations where it is known that the carpeting will be replaced frequently. After a period of time, the neoprene reacts with the rubber foam backing, so that when the carpet is removed, the adhesive layer will come with it. Hot-melt seaming tapes employ polyethylene as the adhesive.

Plastic Pipe Cement

PVC and ABS based cement are utilized to joint PVC and ABS pipes.

Sealants

Sealants are consumed for a variety of residential and industrial construction application such as glazing, siding, doors, bath tubs, metal and concrete joints. The systems are based on: oleoresinous, polybutene, butyl, hypalon, acrylic, polyvinyl acetate, polysulfide, polyurethane and silicones. The construction industry is by far the largest consumer of sealants.

Table 3.1
Construction Adhesives and Sealants

Application	Type
Mobile homes	PVAc
Glued floors & other wood frames	Neoprene, SBR/SBS Natural and reclaim rubber Polyurethane Resorcinol-phenol formaldehyde Casein, PVAc
Gypsum board	PVAc, Starch Casein, Neoprene

	Rubber
Glass fibre insulation	Phenol-formaldehyde Sodium sdilicate, Neoprene Asphalt
Insulation board and acoustical tile	Rosin, Asphalt
Concreate	Acrylic, SBR, PVAc Epoxy, Ployester
Panels	Neoprence Cement &latex PVAc, SBR/SB
Wooden doors	Amino, PVAc
Vinyl film laminates	PVAc, Acrylic
Ceramic tile	SB/SBR. SBR Cellulose ethers, Epoxy Furane
Wallpaper pastes	Starch, Carboxy-methyl cellulose PVAc
Resillient flooring	Asphalt emulsoin, Asphalt cutback Linoleum aste, SBR Styrene isoprene-styrene (hot-melt) Acrylic (hot-melt)
Carpet installing	SBR, Neoprene Polyethylene (hot-metal)
Pipe cements	ABS, PVC
Sealants	Oleoresinous, Polybutene Butyl, Hypalon Acrylic, PVAc Polysulfide, Polyurethane, Silicone

Uses in Packaging

One of the visible signs of an affluent society is the degree of packaging of consumer goods. In a few countries e.g. the US most products are individually wrapped. As packaging becomes more sophisticated, utilizing coated stocks and high speed equipment, the adhesive industry has had to develop products which adhere to a variety of substitutes while meeting machine conditions.

Corrugated Board

More than 90% of all packaged freight in this country is in corrugated paper-board containers. This type of stock is desirable because of its high strength-to-weight ratio and low cost. Several types of board are available, varying in numbers of liners (facings) and fluted corrugating mediums:

Table 3.2
Corrugated Board Types

Board type	*Numbers of liners*	*Number of liners*	*Use*
Double-face	2	1	Most common
Single-lined	1	1	Wrapping
Double- wall	3	2	Greater strength
Triple-wall	4	3	Replace plywood

The corrugating medium is heavy kraft paper which is steamed, passed through corrugating rolls, coated at the tip with adhesive and bonded to the liners. The adhesive must provide a strong and permanent bond while running the machines at speeds of 500 fpm.

Sodium silicate adhesives were used for this operation for three quarters of a century. This system is ready to use, with long shelf life and does not require heat for the adhesive to set. But it has a tendency to stick on hot metal surfaces, thus requiring frequent clean-ups; its alkalinity may affect printing inks and paper dyes; it is sensitive to high humidity conditions and it does not provide good adhesion on a wide range of stock.

Starch adhesives based on the Stein-Hall process are now predominant. Advantages of corn starch over silicate include: ability to run with high-speed equipment, better bond and greater flexibility of application. Some of the disadvantages are: heat is required to run the system properly, the adhesive is prepared in plant and starch is susceptible to bacterial growth.

Water-resistant adhesives consist of starches modified with urea-formaldehyde or resorcinol-formaldehyde resins. The system provides a water-resistant bond which may withstand 24 hours of immersion in water without delamination.

Newer systems have been Introduced for special purposes. Polyvinyl alcohols and polyvinyl acetate are being used as cold-set adhesives In combining liners coated on one side with polyethylene or other thermoplastic materials which are unable to withstand exposure to heat. Hot-melts exhibit' high wet tack, low creep and rapid development of viscosity. They are considered in applications involving exposure to adverse moisture conditions.

Solid Fibre Laminated Board

These are built up from laminates, two or more webs of paper fed to a roll laminator. The tapes may be kraft, chipboard, or news board. To make the common three ply board, the center ply is run through an adhesive bath which coats both sides with polyvinyl alcohol clay, starch or silicate adhesive. The three plies come together through a series of pressure rolls, and then the laminate is exposed to heat. Main application is beer cartons.

Paper to Paper Laminates

Binder and box-board laminates are usually two-ply components made of chipboard, kraft and cylinder board, used in the production of set-up boxes, books etc. The main adhesive are silicate and starch.

Cap Liners

Paper board is laminated with glassine, greaseproof kraft or plastic-coated paper. The lamination is die-cut in to bottle cap liners for packaging of drugs, food, and beverages. The adhesive is based on polyvinyl acetate and should be resistant to water, alcohol, oil etc. These laminated are giving way to plastisol cap liners.

Glassine and moisture vapor proof carton laminates are used in breakfast cereal and bakery products. A paraffin wax product dominates.

Sheet or Parry liner laminates consisting of chipboard covered with a decorative paper are used by set-up box producers, book manufacturers, etc. The lamination is performed on a sheet basis rather than a continuous web. The most popular adhesive is based on starch.

Case Sealing

Corrugated cartons, the most common shipping containers, may have their top and bottom flaps sealed by taping or stapling, but over two thirds are sealed with adhesives. Dextrin products have been the leading adhesive. Despite the advent of newer machinery capable of running at faster speeds, thus demanding shorter compression times, the industry decided to stay with dextrin products with the aid of hot melts instead of switching to the more expensive polyvinyl acetate resin emulsions. In the two-component system, the hot-melt is applied in small dots, very sparingly, to provide an almost instantaneous bond, thus allowing enough time for the dextrin adhesive to set to a strong and permanent bond. PVAc adhesives are used on specialties such as frozen food cases, citrus and vegetable cases, etc. The volume of silicate adhesives has been decreasing because machines with long compression time are being replaced.

Folding Cartons

There are two kinds of folding cartons. One type resembles a rectangular tube : the other is like a tray. There are two gluing operations: side seam and bottom. PVAc controls the largest share; the resin is extended with starch and polyvinyl alcohol. Dextrin and hot-melt are also important, and some SBR latex is employed in specially folding cartons. Heat sealed plastic coated cartons, such as milk containers, are in competition with adhesives. The heat seal serves as a side seam. The growth of prepackaged institutional foods and the expansion of foods served through vending machines have contributed to the expansion of the folding carton industry.

Carton Sealing

Many food products, such as pastries and frozen foods, are packaged in folding cartons with top and bottom flaps that are either tucked or glued. The tendency has been toward an increased share of glued flaps. Older adhesives systems, based on dextrin or polyvinyl acetate, have been largely superseded by hot-melts, especially for heavily waxed or coated surfaces. The adhesive is applied in stripes or dot patterns to reduce cost.

Set-up Boxes

Set-up boxes are employed to package shoes, jewellery, cosmetics, and toys. The box is wrapped with a decorative cover paper which provides information about its contents. This paper may be laminated to the box or merely bonded around the edges. Except for small quantities of dextrin, the market is dominated by animal glue.

Multi-wall Bags

These bags consist of three or more plies of paper and plastic. The exterior wall is kraft while the inner plies could be plastic film or coated paper. These heavy-duty bags utilize an adhesive for ply laminations, side seam, and depending on the construction, the bottom.

The inner plies are laminated with starch: PVAc or SBR. The side seam and bottom are glued with starch adhesives. The latter operation required a heavy paste.

Grocery Bags

Grocery and speciality variety bags are made from bleached or unbleached sulphate kraft stock. Starch products are often used for side and bottom seams. The smaller bags have encountered a strong rival in the polyethylene bag.

Speciality Bags

These bags include paper, foil and plastic film combinations for packaging coffee, potato chips, flour, sugar, etc. The bags are normally two-ply constructions. The outer ply is bleached kraft, overprinted and decorated. While the inner ply may be polyethylene, foil, saran, or other.

Hot-melts have the brightest future because of the production speeds of new equipment. Polyvinyl acetate is important because it exhibits good adhesion to a variety of substrates. Starches and SBR also are utilised.

Gummed Tape

Water-activatable tapes can be reinforced with glass fibres or unreinforced. Nearly all gummed tape has a kraft paper backing. The reinforced tape is manufactured by apply a layer of asphalt adhesive to the kraft and embedding a layer of glass scrim, then passing through a nip roll with a second layer of kraft. The two principal gumming adhesives are animal glue and dextrin. The industry has been moving away from bone glue toward dextrin products. Small quantities of SBR and PVAc also are employed.

Foil Lamination

Laminates of foil-to-paper or to plastic films such as polyester, saran, cellophane, and polyethylene are used for a variety of structural and non-structural applications. Among the latter, bonded with silicate, are wrapping paper, tobacco liners, cigarette wrapping, etc. The former are heavier laminates requiring heat and oil resistance, e.g., biscuit can liners and back-and-serve trays laminated with SBR casein, or, sometimes, polyester or PVAc.

Paper to Film

Paper to film laminations are employed as protective package overwraps, record albums, maps, textbook covers, etc. The film is usually polyethylene or polypropylene, sometimes cellophane, vinyl,saran, etc. Adhesive systems are PVAc, butyl rubber, nitrile latex and SBR.

Film to Film

A variety of films are laminated for food and other types of packaging. Polyethylene and cellophane lead the list, followed by vinyl, polypropylene, saran, polystyrene, nylon, and polyester. Polyurethane adhesives are most widely utilized. Other systems include nitrile, polyesters, PVAc, butyl, SBR, and epoxy.

Paper Cups

Nearly all the paper cup adhesives currently in use are based on polyvinyl acetate emulsions. The foamed polystyrene cup has, to a considerable extent, replaced the traditional paper hot cup. Many of the paper cups have a heat seal coating which also functions as the adhesive.

Envelopes

Three gluing operations are performed in the manufacture of envelopes; front seal, back seal, and window adhesives. The front seal is the adhesive applied to the remoistenable flap, and is normally based on dextrin. The back seal is applied to the seams of the envelope as it is manufactured. The adhesive is also a dextrin. One of the objectives of this operation is that the adhesive should not strike through. Window adhesives of PVAc bond the glassine or coated cellophane window patches into window envelopes.

Paper Tubes

The tubes are used as cores for tape, paper, and textile products. They are spiral-wound or convolute-wound. In the former process, the plies are turned on a stationery mandrel. The paper moves continuously in a helical pattern along the mandrel. The strips of paper pass over a glue roll where the adhesive is picked up and the paper is fed into the winder. The other method consists of feeding a specific width of paper over a glue roll to a moving mandrel, where it is rolled up and discharged from the mandrel. The principal adhesives are starch, sodium silicate, and PVAc. Other systems include polyvinyl alcohol, animal glue, and casein.

Fibre Cans

A fibre can consists of a tube with a top and bottom of metal or plastic and lined with an impermeable layer of aluminium foil or plastic film. The adhesives employed for the construction of fibre cans are animal glue, hot-melts (polyamide and EVA), dextrin, neoprene-casein, and PVAc.

Fibre Drums

A fibre drum is a shipping container that can range in capacity from one half gallon to 100 gallons. It is made by convolutely winding fibreboard layers. The tops and bottoms are fibreboard or steel. Sodium silicate is generally used. When moisture resistance is required, a polyvinyl alcohol-clay formulation is utilized.

Bottel Labeling

There are two main types of adhesives employed in fixing labels to bottles: "iceproof and "non-iceproof or "jelly". The former kind is used primarily on beer bottles where water resistance is required. The adhesive is based on casein. The other type is applied to a variety of glass bottles and the system is starch. Polyvinyl acetate is used on plastic bottles. Label adhesives are expected to exhibit excellent mechanical stability. The viscosity is upwards of 50,000 cps.

Metal Can Labeling

Labels are placed only on cans that are not printed. Can labeling required two adhesives. The first is a wood rosin based product known as "hot pickup gum" . The gum is applied by a series of rollers which transfer strips of gum to the can surface. The "lap paste," normally a starch but sometimes PVAc, is used to glue the label stock to itself.

Metal Can Sealing

Some cans are fabricated with an organic extruded side seam based on a polyamide resin, usually nylon 11 or nylon 12. The edges and seam cement are heated to 500° F for a fraction of a second. The can is released from the clamp and allowed to cool. The polyamide cures within five seconds. The end seam compound is an SBR rubber. A hot-melt based on polyamide is used as a can seaming compound in the Miraseam can. The Conoweld utilizes epoxy and polypropylene powder coatings for the inside and outside stripe, respectively.

Uses in Textile Industry

Adhesives are employed in a variety of textile applications. In tufted carpeting, they have become an integral part of the operation. They provide added strength and stability to fibrefill and other non-wovens. Flocking adhesives enable fabrics to look like suede. Laminated fabric facilitates apparel manufacture.

Carpeting

The fantastic growth of carpeting made by the tufting process has created a new market for adhesives. Tufted carpets account for almost 90% of the yardage produced. The carpet is made as follows; the face yarn in needled through a primary backing which can be jute, woven polypropylene, or spun bonded polypropylene. The yarn forms a loop as the needle returns from its next stroke. To insure that the loops are anchored tightly to the primary backup, the backing is coated with a latex. A secondary backing (jute or foam) also is applied with an adhesive to provide additional weight to the finish product. Carpets that are placed in public entrances must be washed or dry cleaned. In those instances, the preferred adhesive is nitrile rubber because of its superior durability. Automotive carpeting is backed with polyethylene powder which is subsequently fused to metal floors by infrared.

The adhesives are based on carboxylated styrene-butadiene copolymers. In the past, natural latexes and conventional SBR were used for these operations. The earlier systems were vulcanised with sulphur, which caused some discoloration. The carboxylated styrene butadiene latexes do not require sulphur to cure. The latex adhesives are dried and cured in an air-heated oven. The ethylene-vinyl acetate copolymer hot-melt system has been introduced to eliminate the expensive drying operation, speed production, and improve the bond to polypropylene fibre. However, hot melts have not been able to overcome the industry's inertia.

Another system being used is polyvinyl chloride. PVC plastisol is applied to the primary backing and then coated with a mechanically foamed plastisol. The PVC can be used with existing equipment, which is an advantage over the hot-melt. An additional plus for the plastisol is the improved fire retardancy of the carpet.

Fibrefill

Fiberfill is used in mattresses, ski jackets, furniture, sleeping bags, and a number of other applications. The fibres (polyester staple) are carded or garnet-fed, lapped, sprayed from the top with the binder, turned over, sprayed again and cured in an oven. The most common adhesive or binder is acrylic latex; however, vinyl-acetate emulsions also are employed. The latex gives stability and strength to the web.

Bonding

The bonding operating consists of combining two fabrics by means of an adhesive. The exterior of face substrate could be a knit or woven; the backing usually is an acetate or nylon tricot. The adhesive is formulated with acrylic (water-based) or polyurethane (solvent based) polymers which must cross-link to impart resistance to laundering and dry cleaning. The backing and the adhesive provide added stability and weight to the face fabric. The bonded goods must pass wash and dry clean cycles without delamination or shrinkage. Main advantage of the composite is that it saves steps in the manufacture of the apparel, sometimes eliminating the need for a lining. Women who are allergic to wool may wear woolen garments providing they are bonded to a synthetic fibre inner layer.

Laminating

Vinyl and polyurethane coated fabrics use an adhesive, sometimes known as a tie coat, to adhere the film to the fabric. This type of lamination is being employed in numerous end uses; e.g., upholstery, wall covering, tablecloth, luggage, etc. A variety of adhesives are utilized; polyurethanes, acrylics, vinyl acetates, and plastisol. The sometimes popular "wet look" is made by this process.

Flocking

A flocked fabric consists of short fibres adhesive bonded to a substrate, usually a woven textile, to obtain a velvety, sued like structure. Flocking can be accomplished by mechanical means alone beater bars or with the aid of electrostatics. In the first method, the adhesive coated fabric, held tightly, travels on top of rotating square bars which cause the tacky fabric to vibrate rapidly.

Some of the fibre flock, fed from a hopper, adheres to the adhesive coated portions of the fabric; the excess flock is removed by suction. The fabric is oven-cured. Alternatively, two high voltage electrodes are employed; one in the hopper to induce a positive charge to the fibres, and the other under the fabric. Because of electrostatic repulsion, the fibres tend to orient themselves better, thus obtaining a more evenly and densely flocked fabric/. Excess fibres are removed by electrostatic suction; then the composite is oven cured. The fibres have been treated with cationic antistatic finished to become more conductive and minimize fibre entanglement. The fibres may be rayon, acrylic, or nylon, and random cut or precision cut. The resultant suede or velvet fabrics go into such products as apparel, upholstery, or shoes. Among the nontextile uses are wallpaper, gift boxes, greeting cards.

The most common adhesive system is based on acrylic latex, but vinyl acetate, alkyds, polyurethane, and neoprene also are employed. The adhesive must have good abrasion resistance, and in textile applications, resistance to washing and dry cleaning.

Non-woven

Non wovens bonded with adhesives include diapers and other disposable, blankets, interlining for apparel, wipe cloths, filters, scouring pads, ribbons and tapes, and coated fabrics. Depending on the particular requirements of the non woven, the binder can be acrylic, vinyl acetate, vinyl chloride, styrenebutadiene, or butadiene-acrylonitrile.

Table 3.3
Textile Adhesives

Application	*Adhesive Type*
Carpeting	SBR. Natural rubber. Nitrile rubber, PVC (plastilsol), EVA (hot metals). Polyethylene (powder)
Fibrefill	Acrylics. Polyurethane
Bonding	Acrylics. Polyurethane
Laminating	Polyurethane. Acrylics, Vinyl Acetate. PVA (plastisol)
Flocking	Acrylics. Vinyl Acetate. Alkyds. Polyurethane. Neoprene
Non-Woven	Acrylics. PVC. SBR. Nitrile rubber. Vinyl acetate

Uses for Wood and Furniture

Adhesives are essential to the manufacture of softwood plywood, hardwood plywood, particleboard, and hardboard. These products, especially softwood plywood and particle board, go mainly into construction and furniture. The wood industry is one of the largest consumers of adhesives which must meet rigorous requirements at low cost. Economics dictate that the adhesives be made captively or bought on long term contact.

Softwood Plywood

Softwood Plywood is made with phenolic resins, aided by blood and flours (wheat, soy, and wood). Wheat flour goes into exterior plywood; soy and wood flours into interior grades. Urea-formaldehyde is the main system utilized to produce hardwood plywood. Other adh esives are wheat flour, walnut shell flour, and blood. Particleboard and hardboard use urea-formaldehyde and phenolic resin, respectively. For lumber laminating, the adhesives are resorcinol phenol formaldehyde, walnut shell flour, and casein.

Table 3.4
Wood and Furniture Adhesives

Application	*Type*
Wood	
Softwood plywood	Phenolic, Blood, Wheat flour. Soy flour. Woodflour
Hardwood Plywood	Urea-formaldehyde. Wheat flour. Walnut shell flour. Blood
articleboard	Urea-formaldehyde
Hardwood	Phenolic
Lumber laminating	Resorcinol-phenol formaldehyde, Walnut shell flour. Casein
Furniture	
Wood veneering	Urea-formaldehyde, EVA (hot-melt), PVAc
High Pressure laminates	PVAc. Urea-formaldehyde, Neoprene, EVA (hot-melt)
Furniture assembling	Urea-formaldehyde, PVAc. Animal glue
Edge Gluing	Urea-formaldehyde. Animal glue, PVAc
PVAc film	Polyester, Urethane, Epoxy
Vinyl Strip	Polyester (hot-melt)

Wood Veneering

Wood Veneering, to make doors and furniture, is dominated by urea-formaldehyde. The bonding, with particleboard as the core material, is performed under pressure at about 275°F for 3 min. Small amounts of ethylene vinyl acetate hot melts and PVAc also are used.

High Pressure Laminates

High pressure laminates are essentially composites of paper with phenolic resin, sometimes with melamine resin facings. In the factory, they are bonded with vinyl acetate based adhesives, or sometimes EVA hot melts, which are increasingly replacing the traditional urea-formaldehyde. Neoprene cement is preferred for on the site lamination, as in counter tops.

Furniture Assembly

Furniture Assembly, traditionally the domain of animal glue, is now accomplished mostly with vinyl acetate copolymers. Edge gluing is performed primarily with urea-formaldehyde. Animal glue and PVAc also are used. PVC film is laminated to particleboard or hardboard with polyester, urethane, or epoxy. Polyester hot melt is utilised to bond vinyl strips.

Uses in Automotive Industry

During the last two decades, the number of adhesive types used by Detroit increased by almost 75%. Typically, automobiles contain more than 20 lb of adhesives and sealants.

Original Equipment Market (OEM)

Vinyl Plastisol

Vinyl plastisol is the most widely used type of adhesive and sealant. A plastisol is a fine dispersion of PVC resin in liquid plasticizer. stable at room temperature, but fused by heat. To improve the adhesion of the plastisol to metal, adhesive promoters such as phenolics, epoxies, and silanes are incorporated. The resin is dissolved in the plasticizer and thus fused during the paint bake operation.

Plastisol strengthens the body by bonding the inner and outer panels of the front hood as well as the roof bow reinforcing members to the underside of the roof panel. Plastisol seals exterior body joints such as roof drip rail seal, fender to body, rear deck lid drain through, quarter panels, and others. Also, this system is replacing lower cost asphalt floor pan sealers in visible areas.

Neoprene

Neoprene adhesives are sometimes preferred to plastisols, e,g, for the bonding of hoods. This adhesive also is used to adhere vinyl roofs.

Nitrile Rubber

Nitrile rubber can be modified with phenolic resins to make either thermosetting structure or contact adhesives. The former type, high in resin content, is used for bonding brake linings and automatic transmission friction elements to metal. The nitrile phenolic contact adhesives, in which the elastomer component dominates, are utilized in bonding vinyl roofs and a variety of trim applications.

SBR Adhesives

SBR adhesives, either solvent or water based, are employed for bonding cloth headliners, floor pans, insulation on roofs, etc. Reclaimed rubber adhesives and sealants are used for adhering carpets and jute pads onto car floors and also for applying trunk gaskets.

Asphalt based Sealants

Asphalt based sealants are found as floor pan sealers, metal/metal underhood joints, and in other applications where staining is not a problem. Polybutene and butyl sealants are employed in a variety of seaming *and* glazing uses. Polysulfides and polyurethane compete in windshield glazing applications. Silicone sealants also are used.

Aftermarket

For the repair of crumpled fenders and other bodywork, lead-based solder has been replaced by highly filled thermosetting resins, predominantly polyester. In the after market, as in OEM (Original Equipment Market), nitrile phenolic adhesives are best for bonding brake linings.

Safety Glass

Laminated glass windshields are required by law. A well plasticized polyvinyl butyral film, bonding the two layers of glass, serves to hold glass fragments upon fracture.

Tyre Adhesives

Adhesives have two main applications in tyres: bonding tire cord to rubber, and adhering plies of rubber to each other. The first operation utilizes RFL, a mixture of resorcinol formaldehyde and a latex which usually contains vinyl pyridine in the polymer. Isocyanate or epoxy may be utilised. Sometimes in a preliminary dip, to improve adhesion to hydrophobic fibres. To build the tire from the calendered plies, natural rubber cement is preferred.

Table 3.5
Automotive Adhesives

Application	*Type*
OEM	PVC (plastisol) Neoprene Nitrile SBR Reclaimed rubber Asphalt Plybutene Butyl Polysulfide Polyurethane Silicone
Aftermarket	Polyester
Safety glass	Polyvinyl butyral film
Tyre adhesives	Resorcinol formaldehyde
latex Natural rubber	

Adhesives for Domestic and Office Uses

The home is a rapidly expanding area of adhesives usage. Homemakers, "do-it-yourselfers," and children seek convenience. The teacher, florist, and many artisans also purchase adhesives.

Polyvinyl Acetate

Polyvinyl acetate adhesives (PVAc), more commonly known as "white glues" are by far the most popular consumer glue. They are easy to work with, are adequate for bonding wood, paper, and most fabric, and require neither mixing not heat. The general purpose white glue is a plasticized polyvinyl acetate homopolymer compounded with additives that provide wet tack, antifreeze and mildew protection. A water washable "school glue," developed to facilitate laundering of children's clothes after spillage, is plasticized vinyl acetate copolymer formulated with additional partially hydrolyzed polyvinyl alcohol, and humectants such as propylene glycol.

Library Pastes

Library pastes, based on starch and dextrin, and mucilages from starch, gun arabic, and bone glue, have declined in popularity, especially in schools, with the advent of the "school glue" mentioned above.

Epoxy Adhesive Cements

Epoxy adhesives cements are usually two parts systems. Since they must be mixed before application, and then have limited pot life, there is much waste. The cement is utilized to bond a variety of non-porous substrates such as metal, ceramic, glass.

Rubber Cements

Rubber cements are solutions of natural rubber in volatile solvents. They are utilized for arts and crafts and in the home.

Cellulose Cements

Cellulose Cements, based on nitrocellulose, may be "non structural" or "structural", the latter contain polystyrene for improved strength. Cellulose cements are used in hobbies, toys and games.

Table 3.6
Consumer Adhesives

Type	Type
White glue	PVAC
Library paste	Starch, Dextrin
Epoxy	Epoxy
Rubber Cement	Natural rubber
Cellulose cement	Nitrocellulose
Contact cement	Neoprene
Pressure Sensitive	Natural rubber, SBR, Acrylic

Contact Cements

Contact cements are based on neoprene. They are used by the building craftsman for applying decorative laminates and other jobs. The do-it-yourselfer finds neoprene cements useful for wood, leather, metal, rubber etc.

Pressure Sensitive Tapes and Labels

Pressure sensitive tapes and labels are applied on a variety of substrates, especially paper, but also cellophane, cloth, vinyl, foil, and, of course, skin. The three major adhesive types are natural rubber, SBR, and acrylic.

Abrasives and Friction Materials

Coated abrasives consist of a single layer of granules bound to a substrate such as paper, cloth, or plastic film. The grains can be sand, flint, emery, garner, or aluminium oxide. The binder is usually animal glue, but phenolic resin is preferred in industrial applications where heat is generated or where water cooling of the abrasive surface is required. Other binders include polyurethane (for flexibility), epoxy, urea-formaldehyde, and alkyds.

Bonded abrasives contain multiple layers of granules, usually in the form of grinding wheel. The product consists of grain plus binder, and sometimes cloth reinforcement. Phenolics, the leading bonding agent, provide high internal strength, good adhesion to the grain, good heat resistance. Sodium silicate may be used for grinding edge tools where generation of heat must be kept down. Shellac wheels provide soft grinding action for polishing. Rubber bonded wheels, usually thin, are run at high speeds as cutoff wheels, or for slicing applications. Polyamides are suggested for bonding diamond wheels. Alkyds, epoxies, and polyurethanes are also used.

Friction materials are made from asbestos cotton tape or asbestos fibres plus an organic binder. They are used as brakes and clutches in automotive and construction equipment, brakes in elevators and automatic washing machines, etc. Phenolic and modified phenolic resins are the principal binders, followed by oleoresinous and rubber (nitrile and natural), which generally have lower heat-resistance and are found mainly in products for the automotive aftermarket.

Table 3.7
Binders for Abrasives and Friction Materials

Application	*Type*
Coated abrasives	Animal glue. Phenolic. Polyurethane. Epoxy Urea-formaldehyde
Bonded Abrasives	Sodium silicate. Shellac. Natural rubber Nitrile rubber, SBR, Phenolic
Friction materials	Phenolic,oleoresinous, Natural rubber Nitrile rubber

Adhesives for Shoes

Almost half the shoes sold in the United States are now imported; but domestic shoe production continues to demand and impressive array of adhesives. These materials are needed to make various shoe components and to attach the soles. either permanently (cemented shoes) or temporarily (preparatory to stitching). In recent years, high performance polyester and polyamide hot melts have achieved acceptance for many operations.

Paramount sole attaching produces a cemented shoe in which the outsole is attached to the shoe bottom with an adhesive. This form of shoemaking accounts for about on half of U.S. domestic production. Most commonly, the cement is applied to both the upper and the sole, after the mating surfaces have been roughened. Neoprene contact cement is predominant; however, thermoplastic polyurethane cement has penetrated the market significantly, especially for bonding PVC shoe uppers and soles. Polyester hot-melt, also in use, is a more expensive material but saves labour, as it is applied to one side only, the sole.

Canvas shoes, or "sneakers," have the sole injection molded or vulcanised. The soles of more than half are injection molded to fabric uppers. Only the autoclave vulcanised shoe employs an adhesive which is a natural rubber latex.

Temporary sole attaching is practiced when the sole is to be attached to the shoe by mechanical means such as stitching. The strength requirements are low. Neoprene cements and, to a lesser extent. Polyester hot melts are used. Among the types of stitched and stapled shoes are Goodyear Welt, Lock-stitch, McKay, and Stitchdown.

Lasting is the process for shaping and assembling the upper portion of the shoe. At one time, the lasting was accomplished with natural rubber cement, but polyamide and polyester hot-melts have taken over.

Folding is the operation whereby the skived edge of the leather is cemented and folded back on itself. This results in a finished topline of the shoe upper. Polyamide hot-melt is used. Doubling is the process in which a fabric functioning as an interliner is placed between the lining and upper. Combining is adhering the lining to the upper when a doubler is not used. It either case, natural rubber is utilized.

Box toes are the stiffening parts that gives shape to the toes. Made of plastic, fabric, or leather, they are impregnated with natural rubber latex or coated with polyamide hot melt, and placed between the doubler and the lining. Counters, also stiffening components, are placed between the lining and doubler around the heel. In welted shoes the counters are impregnated with natural rubber, while in work shoes starch is used for greater stiffness. Other shoes have preformed counters. Sock lining and heel pads are adhered with natural rubber. Heel covering is attached with neoprene cement.

Aftermarket.— Neoprene cement predominates here. The volume has shrunk as the ratio of the cost of repairing shoes to the price of new shoes has increased.

Table 3.8
Shoe Adhesives

Application	*Type*
Permanent sole attaching	Neoprene. Thermoplastic Polyurethane Polyester hot-melt. Neoprene. Natural rubber
Temporary sole attaching	Neoprene, Polyester hot-melt
Shoe Components Lasting	Polyamide hot melt. Polyester hot melt Polyester hot melt
Folding	Polyamide hot-melt
Doubling	Natural rubber
Combining	Natural rubber
Box toes	Natural rubber, Polyamide
hot-melt	
Counters	Natural rubber. Starch
Sock lining	Natural rubber
Heel Pads	Natural rubber
Heel covering	Neoprene
Aftermarket	Neoprene

Adhesives for Electricals and Electronics

Adhesive usage In the electrical industries can be considered in three categories: appliances, electrical equipment, and electronics communications. In the first classification, only small amounts of adhesive are required per unit, yet the volume is great. The adhesives must usually provide good electrical as well as mechanical properties.

Appliances—New designs of refrigerators and freezers have eliminated some adhesives. In today's models, SBR is used as insulation adhesive, asphalt as construction sealant, and vinyl plastisol as drip-pan sealer, respectively.

An epoxy adhesive is employed to bond thermal relays in food disposers. In air conditioners, the polyethylene or polystyrenes foam which acts as a heat and sound insulator is bonded with neoprene. Some units make use of epoxy to join metal tubing. Vinyl plastisol seals the space between the well and the pump in dish washers. Portable models utilize neoprene contact adhesive to mount the counter top to the unit. Home laundry appliances require an adhesive to bind brake elements. Nitrile phenolic and epoxy phenolic films are common systems for washers and dryers, respectively. The oven window in ranges is mounted with the aid of RTV silicone. TV sets employ polyesters for laminating the safety shield on colour units. Epoxy adhesive is used often in the construction of tubes. Some polyvinyl alcohol is utilized as a temporary binder. A variety of adhesive systems are employed in the manufacture of small appliances, e.g. epoxy, silicone. cyanoacrylate, etc.

Many appliances carry nameplates or trim mounted with a pressure sensitive or solvent activated system, usually based on nitrile phenolic film.

Table 3.9
Adhesives for Electrical Applications

Application	Type
Application	
Refrigerator-freezer	SBR, Asphalt, PVC (Plastisol)
Food Disposers	Exoxy
Air conditioner	Meoprene, Exoxy
Wasting machines	Nitril-phenolic film
Dryers	Epoxy-phenolic film
Ranges	Silicone
TVs	Polyester, Epoxy, Polyvinyl alchohol
Small appliances	Epoxy, Silicone, Cyanoacrylate
Decorative uses	Nitrile phenolic film
Electrical Equipment	polyester film, Epoxy coal tar, Silicone Epoxy
Electronics/Communications	polyvinyl butyral-phenolic film, polyester Epoxy, Polyvinyl bytyral, Butyral-modified epoxy

Electrical Equipment–Various types of adhesives are used in the manufacture of generators, motors, transformers, and other electrical equipment. In fractional horsepower motors, stack laminations are made by coating electrical grade steel sheets with epoxy, stacking to the desired thickness, then wiring with heat and pressure. The epoxy serves both as an adhesive and as an insulating layer.

Polyester film is found in electrical applications such as motors, electromagnets, transformers, and electrical components.Epoxy coaltar systems are useful for sealing automotive batteries. The bonding of mica products for insulation of motor and generator rotating components may be accomplished with epoxy. Epoxy, polyester, and silicone resins are used to impregnate glass, asbestos, and polyester tapes and function as wrapping insulation.

Electronics and Communications— These industries consume a wide variety of adhesives, but usually in minute quantities per item. Important applications include polyvinyl butyral-phenolic film in telephones, polyester and epoxy for printed circuits, polyvinyl butyral and butyral modified epoxies for electronic coils. Western Electric uses a few hundred different types of adhesives , many developed by Bell Laboratories, for their communication equipment.

Book Binding Adhesives

It required at least five gluing operations to bind this Handbook. In hardcover books, the printed pages are folded into signatures of 16 or 32 pages. The signatures that make up the book are collated and sewn, then squeezed together and sometimes given an application of starch paste for stability.

In the next step, gluing off, a PVAc based emulsion is placed over the signatures. The adhesive must be flexible and compatible with animal glue (which was formerly used for gluing off as well as lining). Its viscosity determines the amount picked up. The book is then rounded.

The lining operation follows; the crash (scrim fabric) is glued to the signature, then kraft paper liner is glued to the crash. The adhesive employed is a hide type animal glue.

Ajoint resin based on vinyl acetate emulsion polymer is used to adhere the fold of the cover to the end sheet. The final operation is casing-in, which is mounting the book in the case by binding the end sheets of the outside pages to the cover. The casing in paste is formulated with PVAc emulsion extended with starch.

Proceeding the latter step is case making, the manufacture of the rigid outer cover of the book. This is accomplished by lamination of paper or plastic-coated fabric to binder board with animal glue. The glue contains humectants to prevent warping of the cover. The softcover book (paperback) industry has added new dimension to our culture. It has made available information and entertainment at a fraction of the price of hardcover books. The purchase and discard of paperbacks has become casual, and the industry has grown to a production in the United States of close to one billion books a year. Machinery, as well as adhesives, were needed to reduce cost by increasing production speeds.

The adhesive employed is a hot-melt based of EVA. Animal glue was used previously, but with hot-melts it is feasible to run at 30% higher speeds. The method used to bind soft cover books is known as "perfect binding". The operations of assembling the book sections, trimming the back, applying the hot-melt, fastening the cover, and trimming the remaining sides of the book - all these together require less than 10 seconds. At such high speeds, it is imperative that the hot-melt be controlled to meet machine specifications. The adhesive must flow so that : (1) the application is uniform and even; (2) enough adhesive is applied to insure the structural stability of the book; but (3) setting is sufficiently rapid to avoid build-up of adhesive on the equipment.

Table 3.10
Bookbinding Adhesives

Application	Type
Hard-cover books	
Sewing machine paste	Starch
Gluing-off	PVAc
lining	Animal glue
Joint	PVAc
Casing-in	PVSc
Case-maling	Animal glue
Soft cover books (Paper backs)	EVA (hot-melt)
Magazines	EVA (hot-melt) Animal glue
Telephone Directories	Animal glue
Mail-order catalogs	Animal glue EVA (hot-melt)

At the time of the publication of the first edition of this book, only one third of magazines were bound with the use of adhesives; the balance were stapled. The adhesive was predominantly animal glue. At present, the proportion is reversed; about two thirds of magazine production uses adhesives. Hot-melt "perfect binding" accounts for the lion's share of the total, although animal glue is still being used.

Telephone directories are made with animal glue. Mail order catalogs are bound with animal glue and hot-melts; the latter type is becoming more predominant.

Adhesives for Air Craft

This industry does not use large quantities of adhesives. However, the products are expensive, as they are highly specialized and must meet strict specifications. The adhesives are for both structural and non-structural applications. Films are the most prevalent form.

Structural Films

Adhesive films have been adopted by the aircraft industry because they offer various advantages; (1) ease of handling, do not require mixing equipment, and there are no problems with viscosity; (2) composition of product is uniform; (3) even thickness is assured throughout the operation. The components are assembled and held tightly with clamps; then the film is cured in an oven. Four types of films are employed, but epoxy-nitrile takes the lion's share.

Epoxy nitrile films

Epoxy nitrile films combine the toughness of nitrile-butadiene rubber with the strength of epoxies. They have good water-resistance, are flexible at low temperatures, and cure at about 275°F The greatest application is for bonding. Nomex core honeycombs used in the interior of jumbo jets like the Boeing 747.

Epoxy nylon films

Epoxy nylon films show excellent strength properties. They are utilized to bond aluminium facings to aluminium honeycomb cores. The film cures at 350°F, water-resistance is improved by priming the metal surface with phenolics or phenolic-nitriles.

Nitrile phenolic films

Nitrile phenolic film *was* formerly *used* extensively to bond honeycomb skins to cores, but this application has been taken over by newcomers such as epoxy-nitrile and epoxy nylon. Nitrile phenolics are employed principally when both elevated temperature resistance is needed and the peel strength requirement is not critical. Curing temperature is 350°F.

Structural Liquid Adhesives. These are mainly two-part epoxies. They are employed in small quantity for both construction and repair of aircraft.

Non structural films

Non structural Films these pressure sensitive, solvent and heat activated films are used for a variety of decorative applications, such as mounting signs and nameplates.

Non-structural Liquid Adhesives

In the manufacture of tires for aircraft, as for other vehicles, the tire cord dip is based on resorcinol formaldehyde latex, and tires are built and recapped with rubber cement.

A number of rubber-based adhesives (nitrile phenolic, SBR, neoprene, etc) are used in various applications in the construction of planes.

In the manufacture of honeycomb cores, nitrile phenolic adhesives are employed. Adhesive bonded aluminium honeycomb is found in helicopter blades, flays, wings, fairings, and trailing and leading edges.

Table 3.11
Aircraft Adhesives

Type	Type
Structural	Epoxy-nitrile, Epoxy-nylon, Nitrile-phenolic, Epoxy-phenolic
Structural liquid adhesive	Epoxy
Non-structural films	Nitrile-phenolic
Nos-structural liquid adhesive	Nitrile phenolic, SBR, Neoprene, resorcinol formaldehyde latex

4.

Adhesive and Bonding of Substrates

The final adhesive bond depends on the type of the adhesive used, nature of substrate and the care with which the bonding operation is conducted. Because of the great complexity and diverse nature of adhesive compositions, adherends and service requirements, the exact bonding conditions for any given application is prescribed by the adhesive supplier with adequate knowledge of the intended use. Every type of adhesives are not compatible to every kind of substrates. Usually adhesives are designed for substrates and the surfaces are many a time prepared specially. An adhesive which bonds wood well may not be suitable for joining metals or plastics.

Preparation of substrate

In many adhesive applications, such as the use of pressure-sensitive cellophane tapes for wrapping packages, the adherend is bonded without any previous surface treatment. In such cases, the adhesive is so formulated that it has the necessary specific adhesion to the adherend without such treatment. In many other applications, however, the adherend must be modified by mechanical or chemical treatment prior to bonding. Machining of rigid adherends, such as metals or wood, may first be necessary to provide flat and true surfaces for proper mating of the two surfaces. Machining also permits the desired wetting by the adhesive so that a thin adhesive film can adequately bridge over both surfaces. Such mechanical surfacing may also remove surface oxides or various types of contamination that might interfere with adhesion. Light sanding of plastic surfaces, particularly those molded or pressed under high temperatures and pressures, is often of great value in improving adhesion. This is probably due to exposure of a fresh surface of higher surface energy for better specific adhesion rather than to mechanical roughening to improve mechanical adhesion, or keying as was once supposed to occur. Other special means of activating certain adherend surfaces for bonding include ultraviolet irradiation, flame treatments and electron bombardment.

Many adherend surfaces, such as metals, can be improved for adhesive bonding by some chemical treatment. This may be simple removal of grease, oil and other contamination by solvent immersion, vapour degreasing, or detergent baths, or it may involve acid or alkaline etching or electrolytic procedures that chemically modify the metal surface. These chemical modifications may promote better specific adhesion and improve the properties of the adherend by removal of metallic oxide coatings of low cohesive strength or by increasing the corrosion resistance of the metal at the adhesive interface. The metal surface preparation, such as by chemical treatments, also influences the resistance of certain adhesive systems to heat ageing at elevated temperatures.

Certain species of wood, particularly those containing appreciable amounts of oily or resinous extractives, may be improved in gluing ability by solvent or alkaline surface treatments prior to gluing. All such surface treatments must be carefully chosen to avoid undesirable interferences in subsequent bonding, such as effects on the catalyst systems used with chemically reactive adhesives.

An interesting recent application of chemical treatment is one devised for adhesive bonding of polytetrafluoroethylene plastic surfaces by treatment with sodium. Solutions of sodium metal in liquid anhydrous ammonia have been used and more recently a treatment in a 1:1 molar complex of sodium and naphthalene in an excess of tetra-hydrofuran has been described.

Surface Preparation

The methods for the surface preparation of adherends is divided into sections concerned with pretreatment for metals, plastics, rubbers, fibre products. Inorganic materials, wood and painted surfaces. The strength of ajoint depends not only on the cohesive strength of the adhesive (or adherends), but also on the degree of adhesion to the bonding surfaces. Adhesion at the adhesive-adhered interface occurs within a layer of molecular dimensions and the bond strength can be reduced to nothing by surface contaminants which are themselves weakly adherent and which prevent contact between adhesive and substrate. For optimum adhesion, the surfaces to which any adhesive is applied must be cleaned or converted to a suitable condition before bonding and this is the main purpose of all surface pretreatments.

Where high bond strengths are required, the surface preparation must be thorough. With structural adhesives it is important to note that the surface preparation employed may be critical for the fabrication of permanent bonds and therefore, a careful evaluation is required. Similar considerations apply to structural adhesives intended for high temperature and other extreme service conditions. Non-structural adhesives, such as the rubbers and pressure-sensitive materials, usually perform satisfactory if the surface is given a solvent cleaning treatment. It should be noted that where the load bearing requirements are less exacting it may be possible to dispense with pretreatment processes.

Mechanical treatments are useful when the number of assemblies to be bonded is small or where the state of the bonding components forbids the use of chemical agents. Typical techniques include abrasion with sand or emery paper, grit or vapour blasting and steel wool abrasion. Chemical treatments are preferable where the production quantity justifies the installation of necessary equipment. Chemical procedures vary widely with the type of material and normally involve the immersion of degreased surfaces into one or more baths containing solutions of suitable reagents, which may be hot, after which the surfaces are washed in water and dried. When aqueous solutions are used in pretreatments and rinse baths, for best results they should be prepared from distilled water (de-ionised water is satisfactory provided non-ionic organic impurities are absent) in order to avoid deposition of residues of soluble salts on drying the substrate. Clean gloves or tools should be used to handle treated parts and the bonding areas should not be touched.

Mechanical and chemical treatments have recently been supplemented by physical methods which include flame treatments, ionic bombardment in a vacuum (corona discharge) and electric discharge. These techniques have proved successful with inert plastics like PE, PP and polytetrafluoroethylene which are difficult to bond effectively without some kind of pretreatment. The nature of the surface changes brought about by these processes is not fully understood but there is evidence that electrical methods change the molecular structure of the substrate and effect oxidation of the surface in the case of PE.

Degreasing

Metal surfaces are invariably contaminated with oils and greases and an essential pretreatment is degreasing either with steam or by wiping the surface with solvent wetted cloths (until fresh cloths show no signs of soiling) or more effectively by vapour degreasing.

Commonly used organic solvents are trichloroethylene or perchloroethylene. Solvent degreasing is a preliminary treatment for any more extensive pretreatment processes which follow, though it is normally sufficient for joints which will not be subject to abnormal service conditions (e.g. high stresses or severe service environments). Alkaline cleaners and/or detergent solutions are usually employed, after solvent treatments, to remove dirt and inorganic soils. Uninhibited (etching type) strong alkaline solutions are used for ferrous metals, titanium and certain copper alloys, but aluminium generally requires inhibited solutions if etching is to be avoided. The alkaline cleaning process is usually followed by a chemical or mechanical treatment because it leaves surfaces incompatible with most adhesives. The surface must be dried with hot air before bonding.

With dry abrasive blasting the best results are obtained with sharp, jagged grits, with good cutting edges, based on hard materials such as alumina, silica quartz or carborundum. It is important to degrease the surface before and after abrasion and to ensure that the grit particles are free from contamination likely to soil the surface. A final solvent or water rinse serves to remove abrasive dust which would otherwise weaken adhesion at the adhesive-adherend interface.

Chemical methods—Chemical and electrochemical treatments are preferable to mechanical methods where economic processing and easier control of reproducibility or surface (and joint) quality are important. In addition to cleaning action, these treatments may also produce a chemically resistant surface layer which improves bond strength retention in service. The treatment involve immersion in reagents (which range from dilute to concentrated acid or alkaline solutions) at room or elevated temperatures. The acids and bases attack surface oxides more rapidly than the base metal and in the case of acids, inhibitors may be added to enhance this effect in the removal of heavy oxide scales where abrasive blasting is unsuitable.

After the thicker oxide films are removed by pickling, the metal is usually treated under controlled conditions with milder solutions, such as acid-dichromates, to produce thin oxide layers of controlled structure and thickness.

The final rinse is done with high purity water. Epoxy adhesives have a lower tolerance for acids than some other adhesive types and are more tolerant towards alkalinity and chlorides than phenolic-nitrile adhesives. Rinse water temperatures can be critical and should not exceed 70°C.

Pretreatment is mandatory for many plastic which are among the most difficult materials to bond. Apart from substrate roughening by abrasion to improve mechanical adhesion, surface treatments for plastics are basically concerned with the removal of release agents and the formation of higher energy surfaces with a greater affinity for polar adhesives.

Their removal may be achieved by various means, e.g. solvent action, abrasion, gentle heat treatment of the plastic to promote syneresis or by their absorption into an adhesive with which they are compatible.

Plastic Surfaces

Plastics substrates have lower surface energies than materials such as glass, and oxides and minerals and this can prevent the adhesive from wetting the adherend surface sufficiently for good adhesion. Untreated polyethylene and fluorinated polymers and other non-polar materials, present bonding difficulties because their surface energies are below those of solvents or adhesives. Chemical and physical treatments for these materials are designed to promote adhesion by converting the substrate to a higher energy surface. The surface modification may be brought about by diverse means such as:

- Abrasion to remove weakly adherent surface material (of low molecular weight) to expose more adherent bulk material (high molecular weight),
- Reagents which chemically modify and/or etch the substrate,
- Bombardment with ions in a gaseous discharge,
- Exposure to oxidising flames.

Foamed plastics are sufficiently porous to permit the easy absorption of adhesive and rarely require pretreatment. Spongy materials are primed with the adhesive (possibly diluted) which is then partially cured. This technique forms a rigid glue-line foundation and avoids the danger of joint starvation by absorption. Rigid foams are usually cut to expose fresh surface and freed from cutting debris with an air jet. The interlocking of the glue-line with the adherend provides adequate fastening for foamed polymers which are not often subject to high loading.

The modification of raw polymer materials with fillers, pigments and plasticisers etc. has resulted in a variety of plastics displaying significant differences in adhesion properties. Consequently, a particular surface pretreatment which is suitable for a selected plastics material may not be the best one for the same material in modified form.

Chemical oxidation and glow discharge treatments are generally superior to abrasion for increasing the shear and peel strengths of plastics. Combination of treatments is also an effective method of improving the adhesion obtained with a single treatment.

Fibres

Fibre products are based on a wide range of organic and inorganic materials and are used extensively in filament or fabric form for the manufacture of textiles, plastics-laminates and resin composites. For many applications the mechanical adhesion obtained by saturating the adhesive into the fabric interstices is sufficient. Adhesive penetration of the yarn filaments is another factor which favours adhesion to low twist rather than high twist yarns. Certain fabrics fail to give adequate mechanical adhesion regardless of their construction and chemical or physical treatments are then necessary to reinforce specific adhesion at the interface.

Natural fibres, such as cotton, wool and cellulosic materials, contain sufficient polar sites for adhesives to be employed satisfactorily, whereas synthetic fibre materials based on polyacrylonitriles, polyamides, polyesters and polyolefins, tend to have low surface energies which may limit the adhesion obtainable. The surface finish of many, synthetic materials is irregular and not conductive to bonding and chemical modification of the substrate is necessary whenever performance requirements are critical.

Reinforced composites and laminates generally have a thin surface layer of the polymer component so that adhesion to a fibrous substrate is not involved; the adherend is treated as it would be for an unreinforced polymer material. Special pretreatments have been devised to promote specific adhesion in polyester fibre in which no easily reactive site is available. The most widely used system for polyester fibre involves a two-stage process. The fibre is first treated with an adhesive primer based on isocyanates, epoxies, polyvinylchloride and amines in appropriate combinations. This is followed by the application of an adhesive based on a resorcinol-formaldehyde-latex system (RFL) which is then dried. The enduse requirements determine the extent of curing given to the treated fabric. An alternative one-stage process involves the addition of an isocyanate compound to the aqueous RFL adhesive. The composition and solids content of the RFL system are varied to suit particular applications of fibres and rubbers. The treatment is applicable for adhesion to natural, neoprene, butyl, acrylonitrile, styrene butadiene, reclaim and other types of rubber.

The treatment of fibrous substrates with activated species of inert gases, such as helium, has been employed to effect the direct bonding of rubber to nylon. High bond strengths are not usually required of textile bonds since the fabric strength is generally low and large bonding areas are involved and consequently, pretreatments often need not be elaborate. The selection of adhesives for these materials is more concerned with the retention of fabric flexibility and durability when cleaned with solvents and detergent washes.

Paper consists of a random arrangement of short cellulosic fibres. The high porosity of paper combined with its weak but relatively rigid structure makes it a suitable adherend for almost any adhesive without pretreatment, provided it has not been subjected to previous waterproofing treatment with waxes or silicones. Processing and end use generally determine the choice of adhesive for paper.

Non-woven fabrics resemble paper, although the fibres are larger in size and can be considered as a reinforcement for the selected bonding materials. The selection of the bonding material is important to the final performance of the fabric although most non-woven fabrics are bonded with adhesive systems based on aqueous latices and polymeric rubber arid plastic dispersions.

Inorganic fibres are extensively used as a constituents of reinforced composites. Thus, chlorosilane primer pretreatment has been used to increase the specific adhesion of asbestos, quartz and glass fibres, where these are used for plastics laminate fabrication. Carbon fibres, formed by decomposing organic filaments (such as rayon) at high temperatures, are really composites that consist of high modulus graphite crystals in a carbon-graphite matrix. Pretreatment in concentrated nitrie acid (60-70%) followed by immediate coating with the adhesive polymer, is an effective means of improving interfacial adhesion.

Inorganic Material Surfaces

Ceramics and glasses do not usually possess weak surface layers so that substrate modification is not required. Hot acid-chromate solutions (60°C) provide a more effective means of removing surface contamination than solvents. Glass for optical and electronic assemblies may require special treatment where the performance reliability of a finished assembly is important and which is frequently dependent on the preparation of its component parts. A reproducibly clean surface is produced by the cleaning procedure outlined below (Glass methods); the method has proved to be suitable for the preparation of glass substrates intended for subsequent thin-film metal plating by electroless or vacuum deposition techniques and would appear to be worth considering where adhesive bonding to the metal film on glass is envisaged. Chlorosilane priming of glass substrates considerably improves adhesion and is widely employed as a pretreatment for glass-fibre fabrics in plastics laminate composites. For other inorganic materials or minerals, solvent degreasing treatments are sufficient. Silicate minerals such as mica, quartz and gem stones may be treated like glass.

Wood and Allied Materials

Wood surfaces are often contaminated with dust, dirt and exuded natural oils and resins which have an adverse effect on the wettability by adhesives. Improvements are effected when the surface is sanded or planed. Sanded surfaces, with an increased surface bonding area derived by roughening, do not always produce glued joints of high strength, since the surface imperfections are filled with wood dust which may prevent good contact between adhesive and substrate. Planed surfaces bonded with thin glue-lines produce the highest strength joints, but with care sawn joints can be as strong as planed ones. The method effectively removes the top surface and any contaminant material which may have been absorbed below the surface. The porous, cellular structure of wood limits the degree of smoothness which is attainable. Some species of timber absorb adhesive solvents to the extent that starved glue-lines result, primers or high viscosity adhesives may be used to overcome the drainage problems occurring with porous or high moisture woods. It should be noted that ink-bottle pits in the surface also prevent good contact between glue and wood. This type of defect arises where the ends of cells have become burred over during surface preparation. Occluded air in glue-lines from score marks, grooves, pits open-ended cells, is another cause of poor interfacial contact and leads to the presence of stress centres which can promote bond failure on loading.

Wood should be glued as soon as possible after preparation to ensure adequate wetting. Manufacturing standards require that bonding should take place within 48 hours of preparation or within 12 hours if the wood has been pretreated with free-retardants or preservatives. Hydrophilic (polar) adhesives, such as the urea and phenolic resins make goodjoints with wood by virtue of the chemical affinity between them which leads to good wetting properties. High quality glue-lines are more easily achieved with softwoods (e.g. ash, aspen, beech, birch, elm) than with hardwoods (e.g. cypress, cedar, fir, hemlock, larch, pine, redwood, spruce) which are less easily wetted. Wetting properties can be affected where timber has been chemically pretreated with preservatives and fire-retardant materials and further treatment with chemicals such as caustic soda, detergents or solvents may be required before satisfactory glue-lines can be made.

In general, the application of an adhesive to a painted surface is not to be recommended, since the adhesive bond will be only as strong as the bond of the paint to the substrate. Moreover, the migration of adhesive constituents into some types of paint film can lead to early failure at the paint-substrate interface. For improved performance it is desirable to remove the paint film, by abrasion or solvent action and apply the adhesive to the exposed substrate after a suitable pretreatment. Adhesive bonding of foamed rubbers and plastics to painted metal surfaces with contact adhesives is widely practised in certain industries (e.g. automobile). These applications usually require a low adhesive strength well below the bond strength of the paintmetal bond. Pretreatment in such applications need be no more than cleaning the paint surface with detergent followed by abrasion with a medium emery cloth. A final wash with detergent removes the fine dust.

Application Methods

Adhesive may be applied to the adherend surfaces by brushing, roller coating or spraying of liquid adhesives; by roller or knife coating of molten adhesives; by simply laying on a film or sheet of dry adhesive; or in the form of pressure-sensitive tapes. The supplier's recommended amount of adhesive should be applied uniformly over the entire area. Special chemically reactive adhesive systems may require application of one component, such as a thermosetting resin, to one surface and another component, such as a catalyst or a reactivating solvent, to the other surface so that the mixing will occur when the two surfaces are assembled. Some reactive systems, such as highly exothermic epoxy-resin formulations, may best be applied by combining the resin and catalysts from separate containers just at the point of application to the adherend or by double-spray application of the two components directly to the adherend surface so that mixing occurs at the very moment of application. This process permits the use of reactive mixtures that would otherwise harden almost immediately in the pot. .

Adhesive that develop strength rapidly, require immediate assembly of the two adherends after application of the adhesive. Other adhesives may require fairly long periods of open assembly or air drying to permit solvents to volatilize. This may be necessary to develop the tackiness required to produce adhesion on contact with pressure-sensitive liquid adhesives or avoid esters and blowups in the resultant assembled bonds when subsequent hot pressing is done. Many conventional woodworking adhesives require a certain period of delayed assembly after the adhesive has been applied and before bonding pressure is applied during which time the two adherends are placed together in direct contact. This permits some partial loss of solvent into the wood and some chemical reaction in the case of thermosetting-resin adhesives. It results in an increase in consistency of adhesive layer and helps prevent excessive squeezeout when pressure is applied. The actual length of such assembly and air-drying periods is generally decreased as temperatures of the air and the adhesive layer increase due to acceleration of the reaction involved and greater volatility of the solvents at higher temperatures.

With some metal-bonding adhesives the release of solvent is so slow at normal shop temperatures that coated adherends are heated in ovens or on press platens before or after assembly and before pressure is applied. With certain adhesives such preheating is also useful to cure partially or to polymerize the adhesive for more desirable flow during subsequent bonding under pressure. This technique is often referred to as precuring.

After the liquid adhesive has reached the optimum consistency on the adherends, bonding pressure must be applied to the assembled joint. The pressure must be adequate to cause the two surfaces to come together in uniform contact, to permit liquid adhesives to flow out uniformly over the surfaces and to work out air bubbles in the film. With pressure-sensitive or other fast-setting adhesives, pressure can then be immediately released. In slow-setting adhesives, such as certain thermosetting-resin adhesives, pressure must be maintained until chemical reactions, cooling, or other processes have proceeded to the point where adequate bond strength has been developed.

Certain fusible adhesives that are hot-pressed, such as thermoplastic resins, may require cooling below a certain temperature before release of pressure. Many thermosetting resin and nonresin adhesive systems may not have developed full strength when pressure is removed. These systems must be conditioned for an additional period to permit further strength development before machining or other later operations that might otherwise damage the partially completed bond. With certain thermosetting resins, bonded panels may be tightly stacked on removal from the hot press so that the residual heat continues the curing while some pressure is retained from the weight of the stack of panels. This technique, known as hot stacking is commonly used with phenol-resin adhesives in the plywood industry. Conditioning of bonded joints at normal shop conditions also permits equalization of temperature and moisture in adherends and adhesive films and thus relieves internal stresses before subsequent manufacturing operations.

Bonding of Plastics

Thermoplastics may be bonded by many techniques. Heat sealing or heat welding is often convenient for PE film and PVC pipe. Dielectric sealing, effective for materials with high loss factors, is utilized for the fabrication of PVC film into raincoats and household items. Ultrasonic bonding can be used for hard thermoplastics such as polycarbonate. Extruder lamination is a low-cost method for bonding polyethylene film to paperboard or aluminium foil. In other cases, thermoplastics are combined with other materials with the aid of solvent cements or dopes. Thermosets require a polymeric adhesive for its bonding.

Scores of adhesives are useful for the bonding of a large number of plastics. It is noteworthy that treatment of PE, PP, CTFE and PTFE makes them bondable by epoxy or phenolic adhesives which would be ineffective for the untreated plastics. The various treatments for these four plastics have the effect of raising the surface energy, so that they can be wetted by adhesives of higher surface tension.

Polyethylene and polypropylene are difficult to bond without melting unless pretreated. The surface can be etched with a sodium dichromate-sulphuric acid solution for 10 min at 70 to 80°C. Flame treatments and corona discharge are also used, especially for film. More esoteric treatments include nitric acid, aqua regia, UV and x-ray radiation and plasma. In this last technique, helium or other inert gas is excited with the aid of low power radio frequency coil, microwaves or corona discharge. Alternatively, the gas can be oxygen or nitrous oxide.

Treated PE can be bonded with epoxies, nitrile-phenolic or polyvinyl butyral -phenolic adhesives. Polypropylene is bonded similarly. Ionomers - carboxyl-containing ethylene copolymers partially neutralized with sodium or zinc also are utilized. Polyolefin film is laminated to aluminium or cellophane with polyester, polyurethane and nitrile rubber solution adhesives.

Polytetrafluoroethylene and other fluorinated polymers do not respond to conventional etching procedures. The surface is treated instead with metallic sodium, sodium naphthalene or other sodium aryls. They can be prepared by dissolving e.g. metallic sodium and naphthalene in tetrahydrofuran (THF). Also ionized gases (plasma treatment) can be used. Subsequently, fluoropolymers can be bonded with conventional two-part liquid epoxy or nitrile-phenolic adhesives. Polyisobutylenes and silicones function as pressure sensitive adhesives.

Untreated PTFE can be adhesive bonded at elevated temperature with a copolymer of 50-95% tetrafluroethylene with 5-50% hexafluoropropylene.

Polyvinyl chloride, a cement for rigid fittings is prepared by dissolving 10 to 15% of PVC resins in a solvent blend of cyclohexanone, tetrahydrofuran and dimethyl formamide. Epoxy-based adhesives can be formulated for bonding rigid vinyls. For plasticized PVC film, solution acrylic adhesives are utilized. These are prepared from acrylic ester copolymers, often containing carboxylic groups, in ester and ketone solvents. Thermoplastic urethanes in ketone and THF (tetrahydrofuran) solvent blends as well as two-part, nonsolvent reactive urethane systems, composed of polyol and isocyanate-terminated prepolymer, yield excellent results for lamination of vinyl film to itself, leather or textile. Other vinyl film laminating adhesives include solutions of thermoplastic polyesters e.g. butylene terephthalate-isophthalate copolymers and nitrile-butadine rubber. Vinyl and vinyl asbertos tile is adhered to concrete floors with mastics based on SBR, natural and reclaimed rubber. Vinylidene chloride polymers are bonded with many of the same adhesives, especially acrylics and urethanes.

Moulded solid polystyrene (PS) parts can be easily cemented with aromatic hydrocarbon solvent or dope cement. The latter can be a 15% solution of PS in toluene. Unsaturated polyester resins, which usually contain some 30% of styrene monomer, are also good adhesive. For bonding of PS or IPS furniture, e.g. cabinets, hot-melt thermolpastic adhesives are suitable including dimer acid-based polyamides. For PS foam, aromatic hydrocarbon solvent adhesives would result in collapse of the cellular material; hence, it is advisable to use either 100% solids adhesives such as epoxies, urethanes, amino resins or water-based emulsions adhesives such as vinyl acetate and acrylate copolymer emulsions. Polystyrene can be bonded with vinyl acetate/vinyl chloride solution adhesives and acrylics.

ABS pipe is conventionally bonded with dope cement containing 10-15% ABS in a blend of ketone solvents, e.g. acetone, methyl ethyl ketone and methylisobutyl ketone. ABS is relatively easy to bond and a variety of commercial adhesives do it well, including epòxies, urethanes, unsaturated polyester, nitrilephenolics, acrylics and cyanoacrylates.

Nylon plastic parts as well as fibres can be bonded with phenolic and resorcinol-formaldehyde resins, epoxies and polyamide hot-melts. Nitrile rubber, nitrilephenolics and urethanes are also utilized. Pretreatment of the surface with aqueous phenol (80% concentration) is helpful. Nylon film can be laminated with either two component or thermoplastic urethane adhesives.

The most popular way of adhering Polycarbonate (PC) parts is through solvent bonding. The solvent cement is either 100% of methylene chloride or a blend with up to 40% of ethylene chloride. Also PC can be bonded ultrasonically without adhesives. When adhesives are applied, these are usually epoxies or urethanes; but even with pretreatment by abrading and solvent cleaning; the adhesive bond strengths may be inferior to those obtained through methylene chloride cementing.

Polyacetal homopolymer resins is rather difficult to bond and usually requires pretreatment. This is accomplished with sulphuric chromic acid followed by a solvent wipe. Epoxies, nitrile and nitrile-phenolics can be used as adhesives. Plasma treatment also has been shown to improve the epoxy bond significantly on polyacetal-to-steel specimens. Cyano-acrylate adhesives are also good in its performance.

Phenylene oxide-based resin (PPO, Noryl) can be joined by solvent e.g. a blend of 95% chloroform with 5% carbon tetrachloride. Epoxies and urethanes yield satisfactory results on abraded and solvent cleaned surfaces. The Noryls with their oxide-based resin also utilize chlorinated aliphatic solvent blends. These include ethylene dichloride and its blend with up to 15% of trichloroethylene, as well as chloroform or its 95/5 blend with carbon tetrachloride. Dope cements containing 1 to 7% of Noryl in these solvents are suitable too. Epoxies and urethanes can be used on Noryl parts after pretreatment of the surface with chromic-sulphuric acid for 1 min at 80°C. Aromatic hydrocarbons should be excluded to avoid stress cracking.

Thermoplastic polyesters : The surface often is pretreated by alkaline etch, abrading or solvent cleaning. Polyester film can be laminated to itself, aluminium or paper with thermoplastic polyester solution adhesives. Thermoplastic and two-part urethanes, nitrile rubber and solution acrylics, polyisobutylene and vinyl chloride/vinyl acetate copolymer solutions also have been used.

Polymethylmethacrylate cast sheets and parts can be readily solvent-bonded using ketone solvents or acrylic solution dope cement. Alpha-cyanoacrylate adhesives yield excellent bond strengths in excess of 4000 psi. Nitrile/phenolics epoxies and urethanes are also suitable.

Polyamide molded parts can be adhered to themselves or to aluminium with epoxy adhesives. Pretreatments include abrasion and solvent cleaning.

Phenolics, ureas and melamine products are usually bonded to themselves or other substrates with thermosetting adhesives. These include epoxies and their modifications, phenolic and resorcinol-formaldehyde, nitrile-phenolic, butyral-phenolic and urethanes. Cyanoacrylates are also suitable here. Surface pretreatment is usually abrasive e.g. sand blast. In the case of reinforced laminates, an entire ply might be peeled off to expose an inner face of the lamination.

Unsaturated polyester, glass-reinforced is best bonded with modified acrylic solution adhesives and with urethanes. The latter are usually 100% solids, twopackage systems. Unsaturated polyester, nitrile-phenolic and epoxy adhesives are others that are also used.

Plastic bonded to metal

In choosing a suitable adhesive for bonding a plastic part to metal, rubber, ceramics, glass, etc. adequate adhesion to both substrates is required. If the adhesive itself bonds inadequately to one of the substrates, its surface can be primed to enhance the adhesion.

Since metals and other inorganic substrates have lower coefficients of thermal expansion than plastics, it is desirable to minimize stress by choosing adhesives with sufficient elasticity to undergo creep with the changing temperatures.

Methods of Surface preparation of metals include acid etch, sand blasting and surface cleaning. Aluminium can be anodized prior to bonding. Steel can be etched with nitric/hydrofluoric acid or with other mineral acids. Titanium requires a nitric/HF treatment. The surface of metal can be primed with nitrile/ phenolic, vinyl butyral/phenolic, or urethane. Primers are usually low-solids, formulations which leave a thin film of about 1/2 mil thickness. The best adhesion to metal is shown by epoxies and their hybrid modifications - epoxy/ nylon, epoxy/nitrile, epoxy/phenolic often supplied in film form. Nitrile/ phenolics are also widely used.

Excellent adhesion to glass is shown by polyvinyl butyral, acrylics, epoxies and Unsaturated polyester. Primers include silane coupling agents and chromium complexes.

Leather is bonded readily with neoprene and nitrile rubber cements as well as urethane adhesives. In addition, hot-melt adhesives such as thermoplastic polyester and polyamide are suitable.

Structural bonds to wood can be obtained with thermosetting adhesives such as phenolics, urea-formaldehyde, melamine and epoxies. Furniture assembly adhesives include polyvinyl acetate, animal glue and hot-melt formulations based on EVA copolymers, polyester and polyamide.

Ceramics are most readily bonded with epoxies. Neoprene contact cements are also utilized.

Bonding Textiles to Rubber

The largest uses for rubber products are in transportation items such as tyres for automobiles, trucks, airplanes, bicycles and industrial machinery and in industrial products such as belts, hoses or packings. For these purposes elastomers are combined with some type of textile cord or fabric to form composites.

It is important to realize that these composites would not have the required mechanical properties if the textile components were not intimately bonded to the rubber matrices.

When synthetic rubber began to replace natural rubber, the greater speed and load requirements of tyres made necessary the use of the higher strength textiles such as rayon and nylon. These newer types were spun in long, smooth, continuous filaments which did not provide the advantages of mechanical bonds. It is necessary to turn to the use of an adhesive in order to obtain the necessary composite strength.

Rayon and nylon cords are generally treated with the commonly known RFL adhesives, i.e. the resorcinol-formaldehyde-latex dips. Commonly they are prepared by the manufacturer of the treated fabric just prior to dipping. Many formulations are in current use, but the main differences is in whether they are made by in situ reaction of resorcinol with formaldehyde, or from a previously prepared resin.

By careful ageing of the resin master prepared from resorcinol and formaldehyde colloidally dispersed resole molecules or micelles are formed whose composition is dependent upon time, temperature, pH and concentration. However, only low molecular weight types will be obtained under usual ageing conditions.

The properly aged resin master is then combined with a styrene-butadiene latex. In the case of nylon adhesives, the latex will generally consist of a 70:15:15 butadiene-styrene vinylpyridine terpolymer. With rayon adhesives small amounts of this vinylpyridine terpolymer latex may be added in order to promote tackiness of the treated cord, so that the plies will give better adherence during tyre assembly.

Sufficient latex is added to the resin master with good stirring so that five to ten parts of rubber solids are present for each part of resin solids. Although higher values of static adhesion may be obtained at even lower ratios of rubber latex, it has been found that dynamic adhesion is poor at such ratios.

The properties of these resin-rubber molecules are such that they are capable of combining with the functional groups on textile surfaces through residual methylol groups. Later on, when the treated cord is molded into the rubber stock, the remainder of the unsaturated groups in the elastomer portion of the particles are available for reaction with sulphur and eventually combine with the surface of this substrate through direct covalent linkages.

Polyester has become a strong competitor of nylon and rayon tyre cords during the past decade. This only became possible when practical methods for bonding this textile to rubber were finally discovered.

The chord is first treated with a light primary dip in order to convert the surfaces of the outer fibres to a more adherent state with respect to RFL treatment. This first dip is a dilute dispersion mainly consisting of a finely-ground, insoluble disocyanate powder, together with a water-soluble epoxy resin.

When the polyester cord or fabric, is treated with this dip, a coating of particles is deposited on the outer surface. Upon drying to a temperature of about 440°C, the particles coalesce and since they are not capable of wetting the fibre surfaces, flow around and between the outer fibrils of the cord to a depth of 3 to 5 fibrils to form a completely resin-treated outer zone around the periphery of the cord. At this temperature the isocyanates unblock to give off free phenol vapours and to present active isocyanate groups. These immediately react with the epoxy resin and probably with the end groups of the polyester cord surface to form a cured resinous coating on the cord.

Subsequently the cord is treated with a regular RFL dip in the same manner as that used in treating nylon. Since the surface of the chord was rendered chemically reactive by the primary coating, the resorcinol resin is now capable of wetting and reacting with it. Satisfactory bond strengths are obtained when the cords thus treated are piled and vulcanized in regular rubber plystocks.

In another process single dip system in which an RFL type adhesive is modified by the addition of a special type of preformed resin. This resin is a resorcinol-chlorophenol condensation product, which improves the wetting, flow and penetration characteristics of the dip coat.

When a resorcinol-formaldehyde resin is intimately mixed with rubber, the surface properties of the calendered sheets have higher adhesion and the physical properties of the vulcanizate are greatly improved. This improves bonds between rubber and various substrate materials such as steel wire tyre cords, fibre glass and organic textiles with active surfaces, such as nylon, rayon and sized polyesters, without the agency of an adhesive.

By means of this principle, nylon and rayon tyre cords have been vulcanized into rubber composites with bond strengths several times as great as nonmodified rubber.

This system has been developed extensively for improvements in adhesion to various types of treated and untreated textiles and to steel wire. It is based on the addition of three materials: Hi-Sil (hydrated silica), resorcinol and hexamethylene - tetramine (hexa).

Wood Adhesion

In order to effect an optimum glue bond for wood, the adhesive must be capable of penetrating to the level of solidly-attached fibres and adhering thereto by means of specific adhesion. Adequate adhesion may be accomplished if the adhesive can establish a molecular toe-hold on some wood constituent in the cell wall of the solidly attached fibres. Intimate contact is desirable between the opposite wood surfaces. Alternatively, in a thick glue line the glue must be capable of developing cohesive strength at least as strong as the adhesive strength of the glue-wood interface. Such joints will be as strong as the adjacent wood in shear or in tension normal to the glue line.

One of the most important process variables is assembly time. Assembly times interacts with glue spread, moisture content, species and other factors. If assembly time is too short, the adhesive may be too fluid to stay in place sufficiently to create optimum conditions for bonding. If it is too long, so much water may have moved into the adjacent wood that the mobility of the adhesive is greatly reduced and insufficient penetration may occur. If the adhesive is spread on one surface only and too much moisture is lost to that surface before pressure and flow occur in the pressing operation, there may be insufficient mobility of the adhesive to adequately penetrate and wet the unspread surface.

In the case of lumber laminating, if open assembly time is particularly long, it may be exceedingly difficult for the adhesive to wet the unspread surface.

Spread variation is inherent in all rubber-rolled spreaders, independent of veneer thickness variation, but the average spread required differs for the quality of surface being spread and the relative permeability of the wood to the adhesive.

A indicated spread interacts with assembly times. Greater than normal spreads are preferred for rough veneer and lower than normal spreads for unusually smooth veneer. Highly permeable species or surfaces generally require higher average spreads.

Rotary-cut veneer varies remarkably in thickness across the width of the sheet with little variation occurring along the length of the sheet. The thickness of a plywood panel is the result of the chance combination of veneer thickness at any point in the panel, together with the influence of:

1. The average unit pressure
2. The moisture content of the species
3. The time of pressing
4. The compressibility of the species involved.

Due to thickness variation, if a thin veneer of narrow width falls between two unusually thick veneers in the core layer, the unit pressure on the thin veneer may be negligible while that on the adjacent thick veneer may be in excess of 20 kg/cm^2. Veneer thickness variation, thought to affect glue spread, apparently has little effect on spread variation.

The moisture content of individual pieces of wood (veneer of lumber) varies after similar drying treatment. Gluing difficulties may be experienced when extremes in moisture content exist as the result of the chance selection of pieces. A blow in a hot-press plywood panel could result from the chance combination in a single panel of two or more veneers containing moist streaks. The problems arising in a panel in this condition would be worsened with heavy spreads and short assembly time.

It has been established that for most plywood adhesives, the quality of the glue bond goes down as the drying temperature of the veneer goes up, other things being equal. In gas fired dryers which operate in the vicinity of 250 °C, it is sometimes virtually impossible to provide a suitable exterior bond.

The quality of the glue bond goes down as the time after the preparation of the fresh surface increases. In cut cell walls, at least, the surface can be expected to approach a new state of equilibrium with time. The change could involve the absorption of gasses as well as liquids, such as the natural resins of the wood itself.

The rate at which the glue line temperature increases to the point where the minimum time-temperature requirements for the adhesive have been met differs even within a single panel. In establishing the minimum time required to adequately set the adhesive, pressing schedules take into account veneer thickness, species and distances to the most remote glue line.

Pressure required in gluing is dependent upon several factors with which it interacts. They are:

1. The relative roughness of the surface.
2. The surface area of the work.
3. The compressibility of the wood (including both species, moisture content and grain orientation influences)
4. The gap-filling capability of the adhesive, together with the amount of glue spread.
5. Assembly of the laminate - parallel or cross laminated.

Slight pressure would be required for gluing together small, carefully machined blocks of dense wood; whereas high pressure (to a tolerable compression level) is required in gluing large, flat surfaces of very rough wood, as in softwood plywood manufacturing.

In light of the variations in the chemical and physical properties of wood surfaces, as well as the added variation imposed by process variables, the general requirement of wood adhesives is that they be tolerant of the kind of variation encountered in a particular kind of gluing process, such as hot-press plywood, coldpress plywood or lumber laminating.

Penetration at the minimum level must be to the extent of solidly attached wood fibres and it must not destroy the continuity of the adhesive remaining in the glue line. Wetting must occur between the adhesive and the solidly attached fibres reached thereby. This mans that the adhesive must be molecularly compatible with the three basic kinds of interfaces with which it is likely to contact wood.

Some adhesives form a gel when water is lost to the wood after the glue is spread and before the assembly is pressed. Being thixotropic, the gel breaks under pressure and penetration, wetting'and limited diffusion will occur on the opposite surface. In a cold-setting protein adhesive, such as animal glue, the gel is re established under pressure as further water is lost to the wood.

In a phenolic film glue, where no solvent is involved, penetration, wetting and diffusion must occur during that brief interval when the glue melts and becomes a liquid prior to the completion of the chemical reaction.

In hot-press phenolic resins, the gel may be established rather rapidly after spreading and before pressing. Not only does the gel break under pressure, but the entire glue line becomes somewhat fluid during the melt stage of the resin after heat is applied to the panel during pressing.

Process variables, which are subject to some degree of control, at least include:

1. Grain orientation of the wood.
2. Species used and species combinations glued.
3. Moisture content.
4. Drying temperature.
5. Quality of the wood surface.
6. Thickness.
7. Glue spread.
8. Assembly time and conditions.
9. Pressing cycle, pressure, time and temperature.
10. Treatment after pressing, e.g. hot stacking and storage.

Many of these variables can be periodically determined by random sampling. This permits the use of statistical quality control.

The important physico-chemical characteristics of cured adhesives are water resistance, heat resistance and resistance to biological attack.

Bonded and Coated Abrasives

While coated abrasive products are planar, consisting essentially of a single layer of abrasive attached to a flexible backing, bonded abrasives have a three-dimensional structure consisting of abrasive, a bonding material and a varying amount of porosity. Bonded abrasives are used in the form of sticks for hand-held use and segments for mounting on rotating holders or chucks; but by far the greater usage is in the form of wheels. Whereas the coated abrasive produce is discarded when its single abrasive layer loses its sharpness, bonded products, being three-dimensional, operate sacrificially during use with retention of sharpness until all the usable portion has worn away.

The grinding quality of a bonded product in a given application is determined both by the choice of the abrasive and of the bond. Since this is a discussion of adhesives, other sources should be consulted for information about abrasives.

In a bonded abrasive product, the prime role of the bond is that of a structural adhesive. The function is to hold the abrasive in some desired spatial r elationship and to provide mechanical strength and integrity to the composite. Other functions may be designed into the bond, however; it is upon these other functions that the complexity of bonded abrasive technology depends. The bond may be required to provide a strong, tough, thermally resistant wheel for very difficult grinding jobs when rugged durability is needed. Again it may need to be friable or thermally sensitive or weak for free and fast curing action, good finish or low metallurgical damage to the work. It may need to resist water or alkaline coolants.

In the grinding of many metals, reaction of the freshly cut metal surface with air forms an oxide layer which can effectively prevent adhesion of the metal surface to the abrasive, the bond or to itself. This facilitates the abrasive process. Substances which can react more rapidly with fresh metal surfaces than does air or which can melt and cover the surface with a protective layer are called active grinding aids. The most common method for applying such substances to the grinding operation is to use them as fillers in the bond. Through careful selection of fillers, the grinding quality of the bonded product ma)' be greatly improved. Fillers known to be effective are cryolite, fluorospar, fluoborates, sulphur, iron disulphide, polyvinylidene chloride, polyvinylchloride, tin and compounds of lead and antimony. Active fillers cannot be incorporated into metal or vitrified bonds because of the nature of these bonds and their processing. However, wheels which contain accessible and interconnecting porosity may be impregnated after manufacture with various materials to strengthen them, to provide lubrication or to provide active grinding aids. Thus epoxy resins, fats, waxes, graphite and sulphur are frequently incorporated into vitrified wheels and occasionally into organic bonded wheels.

Commercially available organic bonds include ones based on phenolic and modified phenolic resins, alkyds and polyesters, shellac, polyurethane, epoxies and polyimides (for diamond). Additionally, rubber bonds include natural, synthetic natural, GRS, neoprene and acrylonitrile rubber.

These various bonds provide a very wide range of composition and of thermo-mechanical properties. The relatively low curing temperatures range up to about 225°C except for those very few bonds containing refractory polymers like the polyimides, which may reach approximately 400°C. This permits inclusion of thermally sensitive agents which could not survive the processing conditions for metal bond (650°C) or vitrified bond (1250°C). Moreover, the hot vs cold strength of cured organic bonds can be manipulated through choice of composition and curing conditions in such a way that grinding properties can be separated from mechanical strength. Additionally, the strength-to-weight ratio of organic bonds can be very favourable compared with vitrified bonds. This permits the use of organic bonds at very high and efficient centrifugal speeds not economically or technically feasible for either vitrified or metal bond systems.

Organic bonds contain varying amounts of finely divided (usually mineral) filler dispersed in a thermoset polymer matrix. The matrix is derived from combination which may include liquid resins or monomers, rubbery or plastic intermediates and particular solid resins. Additives such as cataylsts, accelerators, plasticiz-ers, co-reactants and processing aids are frequently included and various mixing techniques are used both for bond and mix preparation. Usually the main bond components are blended first, after which the abrasives and bond are combined into a mix for moulding.

In a typical procedure for making a mix, the abrasive is wetted in a mixer with a liquid wetting agent which may be either a coreactant, a plasticizer or a solvent for the resin. Then a powdered resin bond is added and the mixture stirred so that the powder may be coated onto the wetted abrasive particles to form a dry mixture. The degree of pick-up of the powder onto the wetted granules is determined by the proportions of liquid and powder used. Such a mix is relatively free-flowing and can readily be distributed in a cold compression mold.

Plastic or ruboery ingredients for bonds require more vigorous mixing than simple stirring can provide. For this, kneaders, banbury mixers or roll mills are used to blend bond ingredients and to prepare the abrasive mix. Mixes which cannot be spread or packed into a mold readily may be rolled out into sheets, much like the sheeting of rubber compounds, from which product shapes may be cut. Some few bonding systems are liquid and these may be poured into moulds with or without vacuum treatment to remove bubbles.

Compression moulding is virtually universal for the preparation of organic products. Mixes for cold moulding must be formulated to provide green ware strength for product between moulding and curing and to allow the porous green wheel to be cured without becoming distorted through evolution of volatiles. Such swelling could deteriorate strength, change the volumetric composition and change the dimensions of the product.

Stronger and more dense products are obtainable by hot cc pression moulding, usually in a flash mould. For phenolics, a press platen temperature of about 165°C is usually used. Such a hot moulding cycle can be used either to fix the wheel geometry into a partially cured condition for subsequent oven cure, or it can be used to provide the sole curing cycle for the product.

Shellac—The toughness and good adhesive properties of shellac, along with its high heat sensitivity, provides a very fast and free-cutting action. This gives quality of cut, absence of heat damage and high lustre finish unmatched by any other bond system. Its fast wear characteristics and limited strength range are causing it to be replaced by rubber and other organic bonds.

Rubber—Rubber products combine many of the cutting characteristics of shellac with the greater strength, water and heat resistance available in the rubber bond. Physical properties ranging from soft and comfortable elasticity to very high tensile strength and high modulus, are available through appropriate choice of polymers, coreactants and fillers. The rubber system lends itself readily to the incorporation of active grinding aids either as fillers or as integral components of the polymer structure (such as organic halogen and sulphur compounds).

Phenolic—Although substituted phenols and agents other than formaldehyde occasionally find use in resins for phenolic bonds, the backbone of the phenolic abrasive bond system is the phenol-formaldehyde reaction product, either as a resole or as a powdered novolak crosslinked with hexamethylene tetramine. For maximum strength and rigidity over a broad range of temperature, this polymer system has had little competition. No other system has been able to match its structural and thermo-mechanical properties on a cost-performance basis.

The high compatibility of both the phenolic resin intermediate and of the crosslinked material with a wide range of organic and polymeric substances has permitted further wide variation to be built into bonded abrasive products. Materials such as epoxies, various rubbers, polyvinyl chloride, polyvinyl formal and polyvinyl butyral may be combined with the phenolic material either in the resin kettle or later in preparing the abrasive bond or mix. Such modifiers can provide greater toughness and water resistance and can impart a softer grinding action and higher bond quality while rotational strength and break resistance are retained.

Speciality bonds—The polyurethane system can be formulated over a wide range of crosslinking densities and mechanical and thermal properties. Little use has been found, until recently, for this system is bonded abrasives. A bond based on this system has been commercialised for an application in the rough grinding of large milling rolls where deep cuts high wheel speeds and high stock removal rates are found.

Other bond systems have been based on alkyds, unsaturated polyester resins and epoxies. Although such bonds can be formulated to be very strong and thermally resistant, they have usually found application where a very mild or free-cutting action is required. Examples are the finishing of milling and rotogravure rolls, the cutting-off of sensitive or very difficult-to-cut materials and knife grinding.

The great variety of high performance polymers now available, especially those designed for use at temperature beyond the range of ordinary organic materials, has encouraged much effort in evaluation of these for bonded abrasive application. Of these, only the polyimide family has found its way into abrasive usage. The polyimides and polyamide=imides have many useful properties such as high strength and strength retention at high temperatures, toughness, resistance to a wide variety of solvents and abrasive resistance or lubricity. Because of the high cost and difficult fabrication requirements these materials have found only very specialised application where their unique properties can be used to advantage. Two such applications are polimide bonded diamond wheels used in can and in drill flute grinding.

Miscellaneous—The bonded abrasive article, after it is formed and fired, may still be incomplete or unusable in that state. The use of adhesive materials to bond such articles together or to other materials is common and a wide variety of adhesive systems are used.

Such adhesives are frequently room temperature curing, not only for simplicity of use but also because the adherends may be of very dissimilar materials such as vitrified bonded abrasive and steel. The product may be used in a wet environment or be exposed to high temperature during use, so a water resistant and/or heat-resistant cement may be chosen.

Probably the largest adhesive operation for bonded products is the cementing of abrasive wheels, especially vitrified wheels, to a steel plate for mounting on specially adapted grinders. Such an adhesive joint may need to withstand complex thermochemical and environmental stresses during use. One common method for this adhesive application has been to use a rubbery bond based on a rubber compound. Such a bond has largely been replaced by the use of resilient cements based on epoxy resins. The epoxy system can be formulated to provide very elastic bonds either with use of an external plasticizer or preferably, through internal plasticization with epoxy or hardener components. For plate mounting of wheels when a very rigid and/or heat-resistant bond is required, specially formulated filled phenolic adhesives are used. Both epoxy and phenolic adhesives, when properly formulated and cured, can provide adhesive bonds superior to the bond in the bonded abrasive itself.

The second largest use of adhesive is probably that for mounted wheels and abrasive points. Small abrasive shapes are frequently fitted with metal mandrels for mounting in chucks like a drill bit. Although organic bonded materials may have metal mandrels moulded in, the high firing temperatures for vitrified products preclude this technique and the metal mandrels must be inserted and cemented in place afterward. These products may be exposed to severe mechanical abuse and high temperatures during use. Copper oxide-phosphoric acid cement has been widely used here. Other cements have included low melting alloys, phenolic resins and epoxies.

Room temperature curing system such as unsaturated polyesters and epoxies are frequently used to cement threaded bushings into wheels. Inorganic materials such as litharge and sulphur cements and low melting metals are used for anchoring and bonding operations.

Injection moulding compounds are occasionally used to form bushings and mounting pads on abrasive wheels.

Rubber and cellulosic type solvent cements are used for attaching gaskets and blotters and water based adhesives such as sodium silicate, starch and dextrin and latex are used for a variety of applications such as labelling.

Grinding wheels with accessible porosity may be impregnated with liquid curable resins to strengthen the product or to reduce abrasive action on machine mounts. Such a treatment of the hole region of a vitrified wheel, for example, with an epoxy resin, can greatly increase the rotational bursting speed of the wheel and allow higher operating speed to be specified.

Every coated abrasive article consists of at least two basic parts: (1) a backing, which is generally not abrasive itself but provides mechanical continuity to the article and at least some degree of shape flexibility (compared with a generally rigid bonded abrasive); and (2) the abrasive grain and bond composite which does the finishing work. Present methods for manufacturing coated abrasives require that the adhesive bond be further subdivided into two parts: (a) the maker, which is coated directly on the backing and serves Initially to adhere the grain to the backing and (b) the size, which is coated over the grain and maker after partially setting the latter. The reason for this two-part manufacturing process is that better orientation of the abrasive grains can be achieved if relatively little adhesive is used in the first step, while if no additional adhesive were added later, the grains would have insufficient resistance to breaking or being picked out of the backing during use.

Outstanding among the resins used in coated abrasives are phenol-formaldehyde resins of the resole (base catalysed cure) type. The excellent heat-resistance and great tensile strength of cured phenolic resins are strong factors in preferring them. Because of the nature of coated abrasive manufacturing processes, resins must be liquid at the time abrasive grain is applied. Resole resins are commercially available in both aqueous and organic solutions in a wide variety of compositions to give the specific adhesion and mechanical properties required in the final product. In general relatively slow-curing phenolic resins re used for coated abrasives to give stronger bonds to the grain and backing. As with glue, fillers are quite commonly used to improve mechanical properties.

Phenolic resins are now commonly used for the bonds in waterproof coated abrasives, as well. Traditionally, such materials as varnishes and other drying oil-based formulations were used for this purpose, but the relatively high cost of such materials now tends to restrict their use to speciality products which require exceptionally great flexibility.

As a broad and perhaps oversimplified, generalization it can be stated that the five or six adhesive layers required in a coated abrasive composite range from flexible and tough at the backing side to hard and heat-resistant at the grinding surface.

Biological Adherend

The application of adhesives in medical, dental or veterinary practice is unique in that the substrate is living, vital animal tissue. Of the many properties of living tissue with which adhesives technology must cope, the main factor is that adhesion is sought in a water-based system; yet of greatest concern is that this tissue is alive and must be kept alive and unimpaired.

The tissue substrate is elastic, growing and in many cases, of minimal thickness. To stand the test of use and clinical practice, an adhesive selected for biological applications must meet, to some degree, the simultaneous requirements: (1) that its handling properties be suitable for use without excessive difficult by the medical, dental or veterinary practitioner in office or operatory; (2) that the physical properties of the adhesive be satisfactory at body temperatures and under biological conditions, the adhesive be of adequate strength, comparable coefficient of expansion and of course, efficacious in actual use; (3) that its clinical properties be acceptable i.e. the adhesive fulfill its function over a required period of time, from short periods for tapes and bandages, to half a century for tooth restorations. Adhesives sometimes serve as interim aids during growth and repair and thereafter, the adhesive should be degraded biologically and removed by healing processes. The products of such degradation should not be toxic. In application for tooth and bone, adhesives are required to remain intact for prolonged periods of time, years and in these instances, degradation must not occur; (4) however, satisfactory the properties of the adhesive may be, it must also meet rigid standards of safety; its adverse effects must be minimal. Tests for toxicity, both long and short term, must be performed before the adhesive can be admitted to therapeutic practice.

Surface preparation of the living tissue substrate is an important factor in the use of adhesives. Drying, removing of loose debris (debridement), cleaning and removal of greases and oils and on occasion, chemical treatments to prepare for the application of the adhesive, are procedures which require a certain delicacy to maintain living tissue in a vital conditions. The properties of cell membranes, the surfaces of cells, are still largely unexplored and unresolved and in this respect no specific guidelines can be laid down.

The hard tissues of the body are tooth and bone. Two types of bone are distinguished, spongy (cancellous) and dense (compact). The three hard tissues of the tooth are cementum, dentin and enamel. The rigid nature of hard tissue and its limited capacity for regrowth are factors in the frequent necessity for repair and prosthetic replacement. All hard tissues are composites having a keratin-like component and an inorganic component, hydroxyapatite. Bone has a higher fracture energy at low strain rates, characteristic of metals; however, on impact, it behaves like a brittle plastic. Consequently, it will be difficult to find an adhesive with matching properties. Dentin and enamel have similar physical properties although they are more heavily calcified.

Sealants have been proposed as a covering for topical applications of fluoride (sodium fluoride, stannous fluoride or sodium fluorozirconate) to retain the fluoride in situ to permit sufficient time for the formation of a surface layer of enamel with a higher percentage of fluoropatite an enamel more resistant to caries. Fluoride sealants based on acrylate, a cyanoacrylate and polyurethane (Epoxylite 9070) have been tested in recent years.

Time and expense for applying such treatment to a sizeable percentage of the population precludes widespread use. The question remains whether a sealant for caries prevention is necessary at all, since preventive measures such as fluoriation are inherently superior. Comparable efficacy to sealants was shown in 1920's for grinding and polishing, thus smoothing out the pits and fissures (prophylactic odontotomy) or for placing metal fillings in pits and fissures. Sealant technique has undergone several years of testing. It is anticipated that reapplication will be required at periodic intervals. The adhesive sealant technique may fall into disuse because of the necessity of reapplication and of course, because the expense mitigates against widespread use. A single effective application would still reach only a small percentage of the population.

Bone cement, sealants

Methylmethacrylate has found application as a bone cement. In such use, the acrylic is retained by the mechanical interlocking of its extensions into the channels and apertures of the hard tissue substrate. Replacement of damaged hip joints in younger victims, as well as in older persons, has been accomplished with remarkable results, using fast setting methylmethacrylate in a technique first suggested in 1953. A high density polyethylene socket is fastened to the acetabulum with methacrylate cement. The ball end of the femur is replaced by a stainless steel prosthesis which is cemented inside the hollowed out femur previously filled with quick setting acrylate. The ball end mates with the concavity prosthesis in the hip bone. A 3:2 polymer-monomer mix speeds a cold cure set. The activator in the monomer is dimethyl p-toluidine; the polymer powder contains the peroxide catalyst. To insure firm cementation of the socket, all spaces in the spongy bone of the acetabulum are filled by coining i.e. tapping, prior to setting to drive polymer into the channels and apertures of the surrounding bone. The bone is roughened and drilled prior to application of the acrylic cement. The current technique, with simple improvements, has been in use for some 10 years and results re satisfactory.

These operations must be performed under strictly aseptic conditions. Bacteria introduced during surgery forms isolated colonies within the bone which subsequently spread and require removal of the infected bone. No bone growth into the acrylic has been noted. No detectable monomer has been noted in blood or urine down to 10 ppm. The FDA announced approval of a NDA (New Drug Application) for methylmethacrylate for these purposes (Surgical Simplex P Bone Cement and Surgical Simplex P Radiopaque Bone Cement, Howmedica).

Skull injuries have been repaired with methylmethacrylate implants, filling in bone defects due to shell injury or accident and also, to repair orbital fractures and for splints to immobilize mandibular (jaw) fractures, in the search for a low temperature cure adhesive, the use of a polyamide-epoxy resin formulation to cement prothetic bone implants has been reported. The ratio of 5:2 epoxy resin to polyamide by weight is fluid and malleable for 35-40 min and has been tested in prosthetic bone implants for elderly people.

Bone wax is a sealant to stop bleeding in bones (hemostasis); Ethicon Bone Wax W-31G, which contains beeswax and isopropyl palmitate, plugs blood vessels, has minimal foreign body reaction and is degraded subsequent to effecting hemostasis.

In recent years, polymeric materials have been used for restorations on the more readily visible teeth, the prostheses being referred to as anterior restorations. Thus, a distinction is made between restorations which repermanent and can bear mechanical and thermal loads and other restorations which fulfill a cosmetic purpose, formulated as composites to match the colour and texture of natural teeth. Epoxy resins have shown poor attachment to tooth tissue. Improvement has been sought through surface preparation procedures and silane primers preparatory to the bonding of epoxy to tooth surface. An adhesive strength approaching 1000 psi after 24 hr. in water at 37°C. Patrick has investigated rubbery liner materials (acrylic rubber) adhered with a low toxicity epoxide and an amine adduct curing agent. A bonding liner, y-aminopropyltriethoxysil -ane, was reported to increase short-term adhesive strength.

Polymethylmethacrylate has found considerable use as restorative material, but lacks adhesive properties in the presence of oral fluid is and moisture. Addent (3M) uses lithium aluminium silicate as a filler in the acrylate. Inorganic materials are compounded with the methacrylate to obtain reduced shrinkage for a cold curing resin, to reduce the coefficient of thermal expansion and to provide matching hues for teeth. They are prepared for rapid setting in a monomer-polymer mix. Dimethyltoluidine is incorporated in the monomer as an activator and benzoyl peroxide in the polymer acts as the initiator. When, mixed these additives react to liberate free radicals which measurably speed up the polymerization reaction. In some preparations, methacrylic acid is the monomer to which the amine is added, used mostly to reduce subsequent discolouration.

Etching of the cavity surface with phosphoric acid provided greater retention of the acrylate restoration by virtue of the microscopic tags of the acrylate into the etched pits.

Polyurethanes have been evaluated as liners for acrylic resins under research contracts with the NIDR. Joint strength depends more upon the means of preparing the tooth surface than by the choice of adhesive moieties. Higher bond strengths are obtained with polyurethane from castor oil (triglyceride of ricinoleic acid) crossljnked with a poly-phenylene isocyanate.

Soft tissue adhesives

The repair of soft tissue, due to injury, deterioration or disease, may require a close approximation of one tissues mass to another, sealing of blood vessels or fistulas (openings) or the attachment of instruments to tissue. Sutures or other mechanical devices have served this function in the past and still do so. A biological adhesive glue, it was hoped, would eliminate the need for mechanical retention and give the surgeon a material with high adhesive properties which would behave like living tissues. The ideal adhesive would of course, be biologically degradable, be absorbed and/or all away as the living tissues grew back and healed.

The most likely adhesive available at present, the cyanoacrylates, approach satisfaction only for some of the desired properties. Cyanoacrylates were hailed as inaugurating an era of sutureless surgery a promise from polymers. Though they offer a significant tool to the surgical armamentarium a truly great contribution, it is emphasized that the clinical application of this adhesive should not be routine. These flus will serve as an adjunct to surgical techniques, but do not yet render existing procedures obsolete.

Cyanoacrylates

Wounds glued with cyanoacryulates appear to have greater strength when higher homologues of cyanoacrylates are employed. Biodegradability occurs more rapidly for the methyl homologue and is less likely to occur as we ascend the homologous series. Metabolites produced in the degradation of methyl 2-cyanoacrylate are soluble cyanoacrylates and formaldehyde, the latter of which is histotoxic (harmful to the tissues) which probably accounts for tissue destruction and inflammations observed with its us.

Another polycyanoacrylate was selected for development by 3M. Their MBR 4197, hexafluoro isopropyl cyanoacrylate, is comparable in properties to isobutyl cyanoacrylate in bond strength, flexibility and low tissue toxicity.

Cyanoacrylate adhesives have been used to rejoin blood vessels (vascular anastomoses). This adhesive cannot replace sutures. Although the flue can close cardiotomies and aortotomies, the introduction of tissue adhesive directly into the lumen is a hazard which must be avoided. In any event, the patency or success rate, for primary suture anastomosis (joining together) was greater than that for primary cyanoacrylate anastomosis. The glue is indicated only as an adjunct to suturing. Consequently, cyanoacrylates are not recommended for intestinal or other anastomoses when used alone.

Cyanoacrylates have been used successfully in pulmonary surgery to seal a resected lung, to aid in kidney and liver surgery (nephrotomy and nephrectomy) and for brain and nerve repair. Cyanoacrylate adhesives are useful in sealing fistulas, e.g. corneal, cerebrospinal fluid, esophogeal and a variety of intestinal and urinary fistulas.

Under some circumstances, skin injuries, wounds and surface repairs can be treated with advantage by cyanoacrylate adhesives. Skin tissue regrowth renders it likely that trapped cyanoacrylate polymer will ultimately be shed by extrusion from the skin surface. Nevertheless, since polycyanoacrylate fragments definitely delay wound healing by preventing proliferation of fibroblasts and microcirculation, caution must be observed i.e. the cyanoacrylate should be reserved for emergency measure when response to other procedures fails.

Skin incisions closed only by alkyl cyano acrylates demonstrated higher tensile strength than sutured control wounds after one day, but less after four weeks. Further, cyanoacrylate-treated incisions developed maximal wound strength much later than sutured wounds. Consequently, cyanoacrylate adhesives should be used with discretion and as a companion technique to suturing. Cyanoacrylate adhesives, when compared to sutures, produce less edema," inflammation and granulation. In the fixation of skin grafts, the tissue adhesive should be applied circumperiphally to the recipient's skin around the wound. Application to the dermis (the lowest layers of the skin) of either the graft or graft bed may produce local damage, resulting in the eventual sloughing of the involved tissue. Surfaces to be bonded should be approximated as rapidly as possible, not only to maintain a dry field, but to obtain correct positioning before polymerization is initiated. The absence of suture wounds is a desirable cosmetic effect and healing is not impaired when a minimum amount of the cyanoacrylate adhesive is used. Sutures can be eliminated only when minimal strain will be applied to the wounded area and sufficient time can be allowed for healing to approach maximal strength about the 14th day.

Cyanoacrylates find application as a soft tissue adhesive in dentistry. Used on oral tissue, the adhesive is, in effect, applied to an external area and will, in time, be sloughed off. In periodontal surgery, spray application of the adhesive will serve as an excellent hemostatic agent, the gingival wounds being dressed with ease and healing occurring uneventfully. For tooth extraction sites, ulcerations and retention of free mucosal grafts, a cyanoacylate spray application provides an adhesive protective cover while healing occurs. As a dental filling material, mixed with inert hardening fillers, cyanoacrylate lost its retentive properties. It did not afford an effective marginal seal.

Sealants and caulks

Sealants and caulks are important consumer, architectural, construction and engineering compounds; they are used to fill gaps or joints between two or more similar or dissimilar surfaces or contours. Common applications involve the function of sealing, waterproofing and weatherproofing. In addition, sealing materials are required to adhere tenaciously to the mating joint surfaces over a wide range of temperatures, joint movement and environmental stress conditions. Many types of building materials come in contact with the sealant or caulk e.g. glass, concrete, masonry, wood, steel and aluminium. The surfaces must be clean and dry, Primers are applied if needed.

The highest quality materials are the elastomeric sealants and the extruded pre formed and post-formed sealing tapes. Then come the architectural caulking compounds, putties, glazing compounds, bedding compounds, construction mastics and nondrying sealants. Bulk compounds are industrial packs applied by knife. Two components materials such as polysulphide and polyurethanes are supplied in bulk.

Extruded tapes are preformed ribbons or profiles of butyl rubber, neoprene or polyvinyl chloride and may be either solid or expanded. They may be supplied as composite structures with built in rubber cores or rubber rod spacer shims surrounded by an adhesive or pressure-sensitive layer. In addition, hot-melt, field-extruded butyl sealants have been introduced, e.g. for construction and insulated glass.

Sealants are essential to the success of curtainwall construction, for high rise office buildings, apartments and institutional structures. The joints must compensate for foundation settling; temperature changes and wind create stresses and strains in curtainwall panels. The cured sealant must therefore possess good resiliency, elasticity and adhesion as well as resistance to the deteriorating effect of temperature extremes water and sunlight.

The uneven settling of building foundations causes curtainwall panels to shift relative to one another; the resulting stresses must be absorbed by the sealant. Stresses may be shearing, twisting and peeling. Settling of the structure is probably greatest during the first two years after construction.

Thermal expansion and construction of materials used in curtainwalls vary widely; the sealant must compensate. Wind is another important problem. Wind pressure tends to bend glass (or other panels), thus exerting a skewed squeezing and pulling effect on the sealed joint.

The sealant also must have good water resistance and a low moisture vapour transmission rate. The joint must be essentially airtight, because most new curtainwall buildings are air conditioned. Therefore, the sealant should be nonporous and completely fill the seam without shrinking or cracking.

The sun's ultraviolet rays (in concert with atmospheric oxygen and moisture) cause most sealants to discolour, lose their resilience, crack and eventually delaminate from the surfaces being sealed. To avoid costly maintenance and resealing operations, the sealant must be designed for maximum long term UV resistance.

In general, sealants should adhere only at opposite surfaces; the free surfaces should be concave. Most of the strain in a bead of this shape occurs in its central portion; here the cohesive properties of elastomeric sealants are usually good. However, the best performance is achieved when the cohesive strength of the sealant is less than its adhesive strength to the mating surface.

Primers are used particularly on porous masonry surfaces which may be weakened by moisture absorption and by the presence of loose, friable aggregates which would interfere with positive adhesion. Primers overcome this problem by penetrating and reinforcing the porous surface; in addition, a moisture barrier is formed. Wood, metal, glass and porcelain enamel joint surfaces are also primed where extreme wet conditions or unusual joint movement is anticipated.

Primers are normally low solids, fast drying solutions of materials such as chlorinated rubber, urethanes or polyvinyl butyral. (for improved adhesion to glass, ceramics and some masonry surfaces, these primers are often modified with organo-silane agents). They are applied by brush or wiping after adjacent edges have been protected with masking tape.

After the primer dries (usually less than 30 min) the sealant is forced in so that it fills the space and wets the surfaces to which it is to adhere. This is best done using caulking guns (manual or pressure-pump activated) with nozzle tips appropriate to the joint dimension. To fill the joint (or reglet) properly, some of the sealant must be forced to flow in the joint in advance of the gun nozzle.

Tooling (or striking) the joint after application ensures smooth surface and further compresses the sealant against the substrates. Tooling is accomplished with putty knife or stiff brush wet with water, or sometimes mineral spirits. Water is particularly effective in promoting the cure of moisture-curing polysulphides, urethane and silicones.

Excess sealant should be removed from joint faces, tools, equipment etc. immediately after application, e.g. with solvents such as toluol or methyl ethyl ketone. Finally masking tape is stripped off.

Sealants, caulks and glazing compounds are normally highly pigmented (40—80%) compositions based on a wide variety of polymetric vehicles. Some 15 families of polymers are utilized singly or in polyblends to achieve the storage characteristics, application properties, physical performance and durability required for each application at minimum cost. They are discussed here in order of increasing cost:—

Airfield joints

For PCCP airfield runways, both civilian and military, sealant compositions must have fuel resistance, particularly to kerosene-based jet fuel. Consequently the asphalt or pitch is modified by 10-15% nitrile rubber or vinyl chloride vinyl acetate copolymer. Federal spec. SS-S-00167 applies. For parking ramps and areas requiring even higher resistance to jet fuel, 2-component coal-tar-modified polysulphides are preferred, but are more costly.

Automotive

Low cost asphaltic compositions are utilized as floor pan sealers, concealed metal-metal joints under the hood and in other gap-filling uses where staining is not a problem. Sometimes, the filled asphalts also function as adhesives, undercoatings or sound deadness.

Other applications include on-site construction, prefabricated housing, pipe seals and marine use. Asphalt is also a low-cost extender for sealing tapes based on polybutenes or butyl rubber.

Vegetable oils are used as the binder for putties, elastic glazing compounds, architectural caulking compounds

Putties used in the glazing of wood sash, are generally based on linseed oil, filled with calcium carbonate.

Putties are supplied as bulk compounds for knife application to wood or metal sash. Most putties are used in industrial, commercial and maintenance glazing. However, significant quantities continue to be used by homeowners in residential glazing.

Table 4.1
Linseed oil putties (% wt)

	Type I	Type
Calcium carbonate (max.)	88	79
White lead (min.)	-	10
Linseed oil (min.)	12	11
Total	100	100
wt./gal(lb)	18.3	19.6
Nonvolatile (%)	99+	99+

Elastic glazing compounds are based on blown soya or linseed oils. They are formulated with selected calcium carbonates and fibrous fillers, plus small amounts of fatty acids, for easy working properties (knifing) on large glazing installations. Most of these materials are used in industrial and commercial construction and maintenance.

Table 4.2
Elastic glazing compound

	% (Weight)
Clarfked raw soybean oil	7.0
Aged linseed oil (blown)	2.0
Soya fatty acids	0.2
Mineral spirits	1.8
Calcium carbonate - fine	30.0
Calcium carbonate - coarse	55.5
Fibrous talc	3.5
Total	100.0

Architectural caulking compounds—These materials also called oil-based caulking compounds, contain 15-20% blown or heat-bodied vegetable oil, usually soya, plus 5-8% fatty acids and polybutenes. Since these latter polymers do not harden on aging, they prevent embrittlement of the compound. Pigmentation is usually high in calcium carbonate, with fibrous talc or asbestos fibres to provide non-slump characteristics. Solvents up to 3-4% are often added to improve working.

Table 4.3
Architectural caulking compound
(Drying oil caulk - gun grade - neutral shade)

	Lb	Gal
Blown soybean oil	245	30.0
Polybutene (920-950 MW)	110	15.0
Soya fatty acids	16	2.0
Calcium carbonate, fine	800	35.6
Fibrous talc	200	8.4
6% cobalt naphthenate	4	0.5
Mineral spirits	55	8.5
Total	14330	100.0

Wt/ gal = 14.33 lb. Non volatile = 96%

Oil-based caulks are lower in viscosity than glazing compounds, consequently can be applied from caulking cartridges rather than by knife.

Polybutene

The C olefins go into three types of sealants: polybutenes, butyl rubber and polyisoburylene. Polybutenes are largely linear, low molecular weight homopolymers of butene-1, used in sealants either as prime vehicles or as modifying polymers. They are relatively low cost, nondrying tacky polymers. They are used in the formulation of three types of compounds:

Non-drying mastic sealers for concealed metal-metaljoints, where elasticity and resitance to staining are not essential, e.g. hidden joints in curtain-wall construction, acoustical sealants, hidden automotive panel sealants and gap fillers.

Rope caulks and extruded tapes, for non-critical glazing and weather-stripping applications or for bedding compounds in small window frames.

Platicizing modifiers, for oleoresinous caulks, butyl caulks and tapes and for certain elastomeric sealants.

Table below illustrates a typical rope caulk. A knife-applied mastic sealer would have about the same percentage of a lower molecular weight polybutene. Rope caulks and polybutene tapes are sold in rolls of up to 100 ft. length and in various cross-sections. The automotive industry uses heavy cross-section polybutene tapes.

Table 4.4
Polybutene-based sealant (rope caulk)

	% (Wt.)
Polybutene (1300 - 1500 MW))	27.4
Petrolatum	3.2
Tall oil fatty acid	00.6
Asbestos fibre - %R	34.4
Calcium carbonate	32.6
Titanium dioxide, rutile	1.8
Total	100.0

Wt./ gal = 13.8 lb. Non volatile = 99+ %

Butyl rubber and polyisobutylene

Polyisobutylene, PIB is a homopolymer of high molecular weight. The butyl elastomers are copolymers of isobutylene with sufficient isoprene (0.5-2.5%) to permit crosslinking. Most butyl compositions are one-component, e.g. tapes or liquid, gun-grade caulks. They may be modified with plasticizers such as polybutene or tackifiers and fillers such as calcium carbonate and fibrous talc. Two component curing butyl sealants are also available.

Premasticated butyl cutbacks for the sealant industry are also available as are a aeries of depolymerized butyls to improve compounding and processing ease. Chlorobutyl rubbers are also produced; these have found limited use in sealant formulations, mostly in tapes.

One-component butyl caulks— These are superior to oleoresinous caulks in weather resitance, ozone resistance and impermeability to gases and vapours.

Although not truly elastomeric, they can be used safely in joints with movement of up to 10-15%. They are solvent solutions of uncured butyl elastomers with 17-20% polymer and solids content of about 75-85%, NV. They shrink significantly; nevertheless, they can be formulated with fillers and plasticizers, they can be formulated with fillers and plasticizers. A few per cent of drying oils, e.g. 3% dehydrated castor oil, encourage skinning and resistance to dirt pick-up. They are applied by gun. A typical composition is shown in the table below:

Table 4.5
Butyl caulking compound
(Gun grade - aluminium shade)

	lb	Gal.
Buyty rubber (0.35 grade - 50% NV in mineral spirits)	388	55.0
Petroleum resin (60% NV in mineral spirit)	74	10.0
Hydrogenated ethyl alcohol	8.5	1.0
Denatured ethyl alcihol	1.33	0.2
Amine-mldified bentonete	25	1.7
Calcium carbonate fine	400	17.8
Fibrous talc	100	4.2
Aluminum paste (73.5%, NV in mineral spirits)	34	2.5
mineral spirits	50	7.6
Total	1080.8	100.0

Wt/ gak = 11 lb, Non - volatile = 74%.

Two-components sealants— Butyl LM-430 is a 2-component, chemically curing, room temperature-vulcanizable butyl introduced by Enjay Chemical in 1967. Low in moisture-vapour-transmission and easy working because of its low molecular weight and semi-liquid form, it is utilized as a sealant for insulated glass and in electrical as well as other applications. It is filled with calcium carbonate and titanium dioxide, plasticized with polybutene and may be modified with epoxy and silane adhesion promoters. The cure system is p-luinone dioxime activated with lead peroxide.

Preformed tapes— Preformed tapes of butyl, usually vulcanized are extruded, semi-solid sections with pressure-sensitive adhesion. Since they are 100% solid, there are no problems of shrinkage or solvent evaporation. Sold in rolls interlinked with release paper, they are often used together with liquid sealants or solid spacers, shims, etc. They vary from low cost, highly polybutene-extended tapes for trailers and mobile homes, to partially or fully vulcanized butyl rubbers with little polybutene content, for high rise glazing and automotive windshield sealants.

High performance, elastomeric butyl tapes are available for large window-lite glazing in high-rise structures and for windshield sealing. These usually contain crosslinked butyl elastomers (20-40%) plus, polybutenes, resinous tackifiers and reinforcing fillers such as carbon black and platey talc. Chlorobutyl rubber compositions are available for faster and more thorough vulcanization.

Several butyl raw material manufacturers and sealant producers have recently introduced a new concept in butyl tapes. These are premasticated, high viscosity thermoplastic compositions that are fed as talced ribbons into a PSA (polymeric sealant applicator). Within the PSA, the compound is heated and extruded into the joint opening to form a smooth joint that cools rapidly, with excellent adhesion claimed, even to oily or otherwise poorly prepared surfaces.

Table 4.6
Butyl rubber architectural sealing tape (light grey)

	lb	%Wt.
Butyl rubber (268 grade)	100	21.2
Calcium carbonate, surface coated	200	42.4
Silica, hydrated, precipitated	50	10.6
Zinc oxide, surface treated	10	2.1
Antioxidant, phenolic type	2	0.4
Polybutene (1300 MW))	110	23.3
Carbon black, funance type, FEF	0.1	0.2
Total	472.1	100.0

Wt./ gal = 13 lb. Non volatile = 99+%

These hot-applied, post-formed butyl tapes have been successfully used to real insulated glass units, automotive windshields, curtain walls, concrete pipes, precast concrete structural joints and as bedding compounds in combination glazing.

As the homopolymer, polyisobutylene (PIB) is permanently tacky. Most of the PIB used in sealants is employed in the modification of other sealants or tapes, primarily of the butyl type. The remainder is used in bedding compounds in the glazing industry, usually as part of a combination glazing system.

The lower molecular weight grades of PIB are used to modify butyl caulks, the higher molecular weight grades with butyl elastomers in butyl tapes. Both grades go into PIB bedding compounds. Small amounts of PIB are used in the formulation of insulated glass sealants.

Table 4.7
Butyl hot-melt sealant (black - hot applied)

	lb	%
Butyl rubber crosslinked	100	27.0
Carbon black (Statex RH)	100	27.8
Naphthenic rubber process oil	120	33.3
Terpene-phenolic	40	11.1
Total	360	100.0

Wt./ gal = 9.5 lb. Non-volatile = 99+ %

Cured neoprene compositions have excellent elastomeric properties as well as good oil, chemical, ozone, oxidation and heat-resistance, modulus, exterior durability, abrasion resistance; but poor initial colour and colour stability and extended cure time, when compounded for gunning. Applications are usually related to oil and chemical resistance, e.g. chemical plant service, automotive, marine, concrete pipe seals and to a limited extent, lubricant-adhesives for preformed neoprene highway joint seals.

Both one-part and two-part neoprene sealants are made, most commonly using general purpose neoprenes of the GN and W types. Two-part compositions contain from 25 to 30% neoprene, plasticized with materials such as dioctyl sebacate or resinous plasticizers, stabilized with phenolic antioxidants, filled with reinforcing pigments such as carbon black and hard clays and modified with cure-rate regulators and acid acceptors such as zinc oxide, magnesium oxide or litharge. Cure accelerators such as polyamines (i.e. tetra-ethylene pentamine) are used at 5-10 phr based on neoprene. Heat-reactive phenolic resins are also effective. One such compositions is shown in the Table 4.8.

One-part composition up to 35% neoprene. Storage life is extended by reducing the levels of curing agent and by dilution with solvents such as xylol, down to as low as 55% NV.

Other types of neoprene-containing sealants include a neoprene-hypalon gun-grade caulk and a pressure-sensitive neoprene foam tape for mounting molding and trim on autos, boats and trailers.

Elastomers used to a minor extent as the principal binder in sealants include styrene-butadiene rubber (SBR), nitrile rubber and reclaim rubber.

Table 4.8
Neoprene-based sealant

component A	(Parts by wt)
Neoprene (Type W)	100
Magnesium oxide	4
Antioxidant	2
Calcium carbonate	150
Petroleum process oil	30
Amine-modified bentonite	3
Zinc oxide	5
Total	294
Component B	
Butyl phenol-fomaldehyde resin (heat reactive)	45
Xylol	115
Zinc oxide	7
Total	167

Wt/ gal (blended) = 11.5 lb. Non-volatine (blended) = 85%

SBR provides good tack and ease of compounding when used. Formulation is in the 12-15% range, along with modified rosins for increased tack and stabilizers for UV-and ozone-resistance. Because of the high solution viscosity of SBR, large quantities (35-40%) of solvents, such asxylol, are required to achieve satisfactory extrusion properties in a gun-grade compound. Consequently, the resulting sealant has considerable shrinkage. Weathering characteristics are poor. An SBR sealant composition is shown in Table 4.9.

Table 4.9
Styrene-butadiene-based sealant

	% weight
Sturene butadiene rubber	12
Polymerized rosin	19
Hydrogenated rosin, methyl ester	2
Aromatic plasticizer	2
Clay	17
Fibrous talc	100
Tolulol	26
Xylol	12
Total	100

wt / gal = 9.5 lb. Non-volatile = 60%

Nitrile rubbers require high solvent levels to produce gunnable sealants, hence, are little used. Reclaim rubber goes into asphaltic sealants.

Thermoplastic elastomers may have utility in hot-melt sealants. These styrene-butadiene-styrene block copolymers, treated at length in another chapter, process more easily than conventional SBR.

Acrylic solution caulks have been used in glazing and small-joint industrial sealing for over 15 years. The original compounds (at 90% NV) were extremely difficult to extrude at room temperature; cartridge had to be warmed to 120°F before gunning. However, this acrylic sealant has excellent adhesion to common construction surfaces without primers, is non-staining has excellent durability and colour permanence. While extensibility is good, recovery is poor as the polymer is not elastomeric. Later acrylic sealants have been formulated at lower solids so as to allow extrusion at temperatures of 50-60°F. This feature is beneficial to applications, but, if overdone can adversely affect shrinkage and durability properties.

Table 4.10
Acrylic solution sealant
(Room temperature application - gun grade, natural shade)

	Lb	Gal
Acrylic silution polymer (83% NV)	545	62.8
Xylol	75	10.8
Pine oil	6	0.6
Ethylene glycol	9	1.0
Calcium carbonate-fine	422	18.7
Asbestos fibre	17	0.8
Talc	96	4.3
Silica-pyrogenic	28	1.6
Total	1198	100.1

Wt / gal = 12 lb. Non-valatile = 84.5%

Acrylic emulsions are easy to apply, adhere well to most construction joint surfaces, clean up readily, are nonbleeding and nonstaining and dry rapidly so that they can be painted soon after application. They have low shrinkage, excellent flexibility, fair recovery, excellent UV resistance and colour retention.

Rohm and Haas was the principal promoter of acrylic emulsion caulks with its introduction of Rhoplex LC40. LC-40 is a 100% acrylic emulsion copolymer (55% NV). It forms soft, thermoplastic films (Tg = -9 degree). Union carbide and other latex producers have introduced similar polymers for caulks. Newer e mulsions, internally plasticized, have higher solids, improved adhesion and water resistance.

Liquid polysulphide polymers are the base of polysulphide sealants, the workhorse elastomeric sealants used in construction, glazing, marine and aircraft applications for over 25 years.

Polysulphide sealants are now available in one-component as well as two and as gun-grade materials, packed in cartridge or bulk. When they are elastomers, expanding and contracting with joint movement, adhesion is good, with satisfactory resistance to water, dust, chemicals and other contaminants or aggressive atmospheres. Hardness can be varied from that of soft rubbers (Shore A = 20) for curtain-wall sealing and high-rise glazing, to hard rubbers (Short A = 50+) for pour-in-place floor joints and concrete pavement joints which must resist penetration and standing water. Performance life of 20 years or more can usually be expected.

Table 4.11
Polysulphide-based sealant
(Single component - gun grade, white)

	% weight
Polysulphide liquid polymer (Lp-32)	50
Epoxidized soya oil	4
Pyrogenic silica	2
Calcium carbonate - surface treated	5
Titanium dioxide - rutile	22
Hydrated lime	2
Synthetic zeolite	2
Calcium peroxide	4
Chlorinated terphenyl (Aroclor 5432)	2
Gamma-aminopropyl triethoxy silane	1
Toluol	4-6
Total	100

Polyurethanes are the most versatile polymer systems used to formulate elastomeric sealants. To date, however, materials have not reached the potential expected earlier.

Potyurethane sealants are sold both as two-component and one-component gun-grade compositions, packed in cartridge or in bulk. Applications are similar to those of the polysulphides; however, because of problems with hydrolysis and discolouration, insulated glass markets have not yet been etrated.

Modern compounds are finding a place in automotive windshield sealing.

Urethane sealants have good elongation and recovery, excellent abrasion resistance, tear strength and the resistance to indentation needed for floor joint compounds, highway and airfield joint materials make them the preferred compounds for preformed gasket sals in clay and concrete pipe. Low temperature performance (to below -40°C) is superior to that of the polysulphides.

Two-component urethane sealants are difficult to formulate for nonslumping vertical joints. Most of their applications in industrial construction are pourable, self-levelling compounds used in horizontal or floor joints, where their hardness, toughness, abrasion resistance and resistance to indentation are important. They are not suitable for insulated glass sealants because they must be used with primers to achieve adequate glass adhesion and moisture impermeability of the composite is inferior to present materials.

Rapid-cure characteristics make the urethanes excellent candidates for windshield sealants. They are also used in highway and airfield sealing, aircraft construction and in marine applications.

Isocyanate prepolymers are used in the formulation of one-component urethane sealants. A typical gun-grade compound may contain 50-60% of prepolymer, pigmented with titanium dioxide, calcium carbonate and silica, with up to 5% of dry toluol for easier gunning. Compounds may also contain molecular sieves to absorb unremoved water for improved compound stability. As with one-component polysulphide sealants, manufacture of the compound is carried out with dry ingredients, under vacuum and heat so as to eliminate all traces of water.

Table 4.12
Polyurethane-based sealant
(Two-component - gun grade - white)

	Parts (weight)	%
Component A		
Polyethylene glycon-isocyanate Prepolymer (2.6% free isocyanate)	100	100
Comonent B		
Polyhpropylene glycol (MW = 2000)	62	47.3
Titanium dioxide - rutile	15	11.5
Fibrous talc	47	35.8
Calcium oxide	6	4.6
Dibutyl tin di-2-ethylhexoate	1	0.8
Sub-total	131	100.0

wt / gal (blended)) = 11.5 lb. Non-volatile = 99+%

5.

Animal Glue

Animal glue has been used as an aqueous adhesive and size for thousands of years, and in more recent times has also found acceptance as a protective colloid, flocculant, and adhesive composition.

Commercial manufacture dated back to 1690 in Holland, 1700 in England, and the early 19th Century in the United States. By 1900 there were at least 60 producers of animal glue in the United States; now there are only two.

Glue is derived from collagen, the major proteinaceous component of animal and fish skins, as well as tendons and the proteinaceous matrix of bones. In recent times the important commercial raw materials for making animal glue come from tanneries, which supply limed splits and chrome tanned pieces, and from slaughter houses, which furnish fleshings, bide pieces and bones.

The terms gelatin, technical gelatin, and animal glue refer to similar materials obtained from approximately the same stock but through different treatments. Edible gelatin and photographic gelatin are produced under more stringent conditions, producing a product of excellent colour and clarity, low ash and low grease, combined with a very low bacteria count. These gelatins, because of manufacturing costs, sell for considerably more than technical gelatin and animal glues. Edible and photographic gelatins have tended to keep market share and have been the subject of continuing research.

Technical geltin and animal glue, on the other hand, have seen their market share considerably eroded in the last 25 years. This decline has been brought about by the advent of synthetic polymers, which have taken over the sizing of synthetic fibers and the binding of paperback books. (But telephone books and catalogs have stayed with animal glue because of its superior durability and flexibility as well as lower cost.)

Because of the recent demise of a number of glue factories in the western world, there is currently a worldwide shortage of glue, particularly in the highest test grades. At this time there are only two manufacturers in the United States: Milligan & Higgins Division, Hudson Industries Crop., of Johnstown, New York, who make hide glue; and Swift Adhesives (Div. of Reichhold Chemicals), St. Joseph, Missouri, who make bone glue. Cattle are the major source, with rabbits and sheep contributing to a much lesser degree. A substantial amount of hide and bone glue is imported from Brazil, Chile, China, and other countries, and finds its way primarily into compounded adhesives and protective colloids. Leading importers of animal glue are Hudson Industries Corp., Olympic Adhesives, Inc., Nicholson & Co. Transatlantic By-Products Corp., and Swift Adhesives (Div. of Reichhold Chemicals).

CHEMISTRY

Animal glue is essentially the hydrolytic product of collagen, the main protein in animal skins and bones. Collagen as its exists in its natural state is water-insoluble and resistant to mild acids and alkalies as well as proteolytic enzymes other than the collagenases. Veis and Cohen discuss the structure of collagen:

A collagen fibril may thus be pictured as... segments varying in length and cross-section area due to differences in the cross-link distribution and the lateral ordering of the polypeptide chains... The segments are chain networks held together by sets of the acid-stable or B bonds. These segments contain and are held in the gross structure by the acid-labile A bonds and physical forces.

The conversion of collagen to soluble polypeptides involves the breaking of covalent bonds and the disruption of physical forces through the use of either acid and heat or alkali and heat. Acid and heat cause selective disruption of some bonds plus selective peptide bond hydrolysis, yielding tightly coiled lateral aggregates of peptide chains. Alkali and heat bring about a much more complete cross-link-age breakdown, resulting in randomly coiled peptide chains.

Veis describes the collagen-gelatin transition as a stepwise process involving the melting of a trihelical network to an amorphous from, followed by the sequential hydrolysis of various types of covalent bonds.

Collagen from different species and even different parts of the same species varies in stability to acids, alkalies and heat because of differences in intramolecular and intermolecular organization. Glue molecules may be considered to be polypeptide chains containing amino acid sequences of varying lengths depending upon the treatment. The amino acid analysis done by Eastoe, and corroborated by others, on an ox hide gelatin indicated that there are 18 separate amino acids present in varying amounts.

Table 5.1 agrees within tolerable limits with that of Eastoe but also characterizes the ionic nature of the R-radicals on each amino acid.

Later analyses of calfskin collagen show two additional amino acid residues, glutamine and asparagine, each present in about 2% concentration (by number of residues). The distinctive groups have been added to the table.

Amino acid residues are amphoteric, containing both amine and carboxyl groups that are reactive and ionizable.

Amide groups may be hydrolyzed to carboxyl and amine by either alkaline treatment (leading to Type B gelatin) or extended acid degradation (Type A). This loss of amide groups and its relation to the isoionic point has been studied by Eastoe with the results shown in Table 5.2.

Because glues are amphoteric, they may react *as* cations or as anions depending upon the *p*H of the medium and the isoionic point of the glue. Prepared by the alkaline process, glues have *a pI* close to *p*H 4.8, while those processed in acid will have a *pI near pH* 9.0. The former react as cations, the latter as anions.

Gelation involves both intramolecular and intermolecular reorientation upon cooling the system. Veis, among others, concludes that the collagen fold stability is influenced by solvent dicated. Gel formation involves the creation of random primary and secondary bonding; but intermolecular organization or network formations of gels is stabilized by secondary forces such as hydrogen bonding rather than primary covalent bonding. These bonds show a strong dependence upon solvent and temperature. Hydrogen bonding results in a sharp melting temperature whose value depends upon the number of these bonds that have formed.

Table 5.1
Amino Acids in Animal Glue.

Amino Acid	*Residues Per 1000 Total of All Residues*	*Character of R-Radical*	
		Distinctive Groups	*Ionic Character*
Glycine	335.0	-	Neutral
Praline	128.0	Pyrrolidine in the chain	Neutral
Alanine	113.0	-	Neutral
Hydroxyproline	94.5	Hydroxypyrrolidine in the chain	Neutral
Glutamic acid	72.0	Carboxyl	Acid
Arginine	47.0	Guanido	Basic
Aspartic acid	46.5	Carboxyl	Asid
Serine	35.0	Hydroxyl	Neutral
Lysine	27.0	Amine	Basic
Leucine	23.0	-	Neutral
Valine	20.0	-	Neutral
Threonine	18.0	Hydroxyl	Neutral
Phenylalanine	13.0	Phenyl	Neutral
Isoleucine	12.0	-	Neutral
Methionine	5.0	Thiomethyl	Neutral
Hydrocylysive	5.0	Amine, Hydrocyl	Basic
Histidine	4.5	Imidazole	Basic
Tyrosine	4.4	p-Phenylene, Hydroxyl	Very weakly acid
Additional amino acids: Glutamine	20	Primary Amide	Netural
Asparagine	20	Primary Amide	Netural

Table 5.2. Relation Between pi and Amide Nitrogen.

Material	Treatment	*PI*	Amide Nitrogen[a]
Calfskin	Unknown—Eastman Kodak	4.82	1.3
Hide	Lime	4.9	6.8
Hide	Lime	4.94	7.9
Calfskin	Lime and caustic	5.15	14.3
Ossein	Acid	7.8	35.6
Pigskin	Acid	9.4	43.7
Pigskin	Acid	9.4	42.9

[a]mmole/100g protein

The intrinsic viscosity is a measure of the average volume occupied by the individual polymers molecules in dilute solution, where they are in their most random configuration.

Stainsby examined the viscosities of molecules of an alkali-processed gelatin at various *p*H's. At the isoionic point in the absence of salt, the net charge on a glue molecule is zero and the molecule is in a compact from corresponding to its lowest viscosity in normal *p*H ranges. Alteration of the *p*H through the use of add or base results in a net charge that will make the molecule either anionic or cationic. The ionic repulsive charges at these *p*H values prevent the chain from assuming a compact shape, thus causing higher viscosity. Subsequent additions of acid or alkali produce enough counter-ions to eventually neutralize the molecular repulsive charges, and the viscosity begins to collapse below pH 3 or above pH 10.

Manufacturing

Animal glue is the water-soluble product of the hydrolytic degradation of water-insoluble collagen fibers. The products of hydrolysis vary greatly in molecular weight (approx. 10,000 to over 250,000), and measurements of viscosity and gel strength are necessarily average.

The approximate chemical composition of glue is:

Carbon	50.7%
Hydrogen	6.5%
Oxyge	24.9%
Nitrogen	17.9%

Only minor variations on the above composition are found in glues extracted from dissimilar stocks and different methods of manufacture.

Glues in aqueous warm solutions undergo hydrolysis to lower molecular weights. The rate is dependent upon the *pH* and the temperature.The further the *pH* is from 7.0 in either direction, the more rapid will be the hydrolytic activity. Glue manufacturers recommend that dissolved glue solutions not be kept at temperatures above 140-150°F for extended periods, as this would cause thermal degradation.

Glues are subject to enzymatic as well as bacterial attack. Particular care must be taken in manufacturing to reduce these effects through good manufacturing procedures and the use of preservatives. The preservatives currently preferred in the industry are phenols and phenol derivatives, zinc sulfate, and other types as indicated by particular industries.

The two categories of animal glue are hide glue and bone glue. *Hide glue* raw materials may include fleshings, limed or pickled splits, cattle pieces, and chrome-tanned hides and pieces. The producer of either hide glue or bone glue strives for greatest yield and cost efficiency, resulting in optimum test properties, including viscosity, gram strength (jelly), *pH,* moisture, foam, grease, ash, colour, clarity, and odour.

Until very recently a high percentage of hide glue was derived from chrome-tanned skins. Reductions became necessary due to ERA constraints on chrome effluent. The tanning agent is largely removed by the application of caustic and then acid, after which the stock is washed. This process generally takes 24 hours. The stock is then soaked for a number of days in magnesium hydroxide and again washed, maintaining a slightly alkaline *p*H. The retention of a slight excess of magnesium hydroxide during the cook causes any remaining tanning agent in the skin to be precipitated as an insoluble hydroxide. The resulting glue is very light in colour, almost transparent, with a grease content well below 1%.

A shorter method of chrome glue production uses much less water and greatly reduces the chemical effluent. Even though glue yields and tests are lower, this method tends to be cost-efficient in areas of high sewage rates. The method involves starting with a magnesium hydroxide soak as discussed and then cooking in the usual manner (in four steps *as* described below). The final product is similar to that obtained by the previous method, except for higher ash content (4½% versus 3%)

Hide pieces and pickled splits as received must be thoroughly washed in cold water over a number of hours to remove salts, acids, offal, blood, etc. The stock is then soaked in cold milk of lime for a number of days or weeks, after which the lime is washed out. The pH is then adjusted with a small quantity of acid such as hydrochloric, sulfuric, or phosphoric, which should completely permeate the swollen hide. The stock is next backwashed with water until the desired *fM* is reached of 6-7 in the finished product. Then the stock is transferred to cooking tubs containing perforated steam coils and water. The cook involves usually four extractions of approximately four hours each, at progressively higher temperatures. Drawdowns ranging from 2% to 9% glue solids are extracted and filtered. Finally, the glue liquor is evaporated to 20-50% solids, depending upon its viscosity.

In some countries glue continues to be dried in tunnel driers using heat and air which is passed over jelled sheets, stacked on wire nets with air spaces between. Modern driers feed jelled noodles, chips or beads on a continuous traveling screen through heat staged, filtered and conditioned hot air, until the moisture content is approximately 10-15%.

Limed splits may be placed in soaking vats directly for additional liming time, or processed as received depending upon the economics involved. It is cheapest to cook immediately, but the product has lower gram strength.

Fleshings, which contain as much grease as glue, are not a significant factor in domestic glue manufacturing at this time.

Bone gluesare extracted from the collagenous matrix which is the chief organic constituent of all bone. Bone glues fall into two categories, extracted bone and green bone. Extracted bone glues are prepared from bones that have been solvent-extracted to remove by-product grease. Green bones are processed as received from slaughter houses. The bones are crushed, washed and processed in mild acid in pressure vessels. A series of extractions, alternating steam pressure in the jacket and sparging with hot water, removes the dilute glue liquor, which is then filtered or centrifuged to remove by-product grease. The glue is finally concentrated and dried. The residual to produce bonemeal fertilizer, which contains approximately 85% calcium phosphate. Bone china derives its name from the fact that purified bone residue is incorporated into its manufacture.

Properties

Dry animal glues are hard, nearly odourless materials ranging from pale yellow to dark amber. At approximately 260-270°C glue begins to decompose with swelling and charring, evolving dense smoke. Glue retains'its characteristics unaltered if kept dry. Films heated above 100°C for relatively short periods become water resistant. Normal unmodified dry glue will absorb 6-8 times its weight of cold water, remaining in a jelled from until heated. The higher the test (viscosity/grams) the higher the melting point. An extremely useful property of aqueous glue solution is its ability to form a reversible gel upon cooling. This property can be modified to advantage by altering concentrations and/or adding modifiers.

The approximate specific gravity of glue is 1.27. The moisture content is normally 10-15%, ash 2.0-5.0%, pH 5.5-8.0, grease content 0.2%-3.0%.

Glues are soluble in water and insoluble in oils, waxes, organic solvents and absolute alcohol, but emulsification can be achieved in both water-oil and oil-water systems. Glue emulsions serve as encapsulating agents.

Glues can be precipitated in the laboratory by absolute alcohol, tannic acid, picric add, phosphotungstic acid, or a saturated solution of zinc sulfate. Aluminum, ferric, chromic, and magnesium sulfate thicken, coagulate, or precipitate glue from solution; mild tannage and melting point increases can be achieved with the proper use of these compounds.

Numerous patents have been granted for systems involving the insolubilization (cross-linking, tanning) of glue. Formaldehyde and aldehyde donors are effective.

Glue gives a positive reaction to the biuret test and also Molisch's test. In the absence of other nitrogen containing materials, the percentage of glue is, by commercial agreement, the Kjeldahl nitrogen multiplied by the factor 6.25.

Dried films deposited from solutions are continuous, resilient, and noncrystalline, and develop shear tensile strength in excess of 3000 psi on glue-bonded wooden blokes; indeed, tensile strengths as high as 10,000 psi have been reported for glue films.

Glue can be modified by a variety of chemical reactions, including acetylation of the hydroxyl groups, alcoholysis to yield amino acid esters, and aryl sulfonation to give complexes insoluble in water but soluble in organic solvent. Reaction with fatty amines improves water resistance. Quaternization yields cationic molecules. The literature abounds with ideas for modification.

Animal glue has been compounded with many materials, e.g., starches, dex-trins, sugars, various salts, sulfonated oils, emulsions of oils, polyvinyl alcohol, poly-vinyl acetate; plasticizers such as glycols, glycerine, and sorbitol; as well as some water-soluble organic solvents such as butylacrbitol acetate. Viscosities can be modified by compounding with compatible natural gums, alginates, and synthetic thickeners such as carboxymethylcellulose.

Glue manufactured by an acid process, whose PI is approximately 9.0, possesses a jelly strength-to-viscosity ratio of 4-5:1; while alkaline-treated glue whose *pL* is approximately 4.8 has *a* ratio of 2½-3:l.

The melting point of glue and glue compositions can be varied from below room temperature to over 120°F by altering the test of the glue, changing the glue-water ratio, and the addition of specific chemicals. Viscosities are controlled by glue strength, glue-water ratio, total solids, and temperature; glues have good working characteristics from water-thin to approximately 70,000 cps.

Test Grades

Animal glue manufacturers grade their production according to gram strength or jelly strength, which increases with viscosity. Peter Cooper Corp., one of the earliest and largest manufacturers of animal glue and gelatin in the United States, developed the grading system about 1844. Procedures and equipment evolved over the years and did not become standardized until well into the 20th Century.

Table *5.3* cross references the now closed Peter Cooper's code designation with the of Milligan & Higgins. This table takes into consideration only alkaline-extracted glue, which accounts for the greatest proportion of hide glue production.

Table 5.3. Glue Test Grades (Hide Glues).

Pater Cooper Sttandard Grade	Milligan & Higgins Standard Grade	Bloom Grams Range	mid-Point	Millipoise Value (minimum)
5A Extra	8A 495-529	512	191	
4A EXtra	6A	461-494	477	175
3A Extra	5A	428-460	444	157
2A Extra	4A	395-427	411	145
A Extra	2A	363-394	379	131
#1 Extra	A	331-362	347	121
#1 Extra Special	X	299-330	315	111
#1	2XA	267-298	283	101
1XM	2X	237-266	251	92
1X	3XA	207-236	222	82
1¼	3X	1788-206	192	72
1⅜	4X	150-177	164	62
1½	5X	122-149	135	57
1⅝	6X	95-121	108	52
1¾	7X	70-94	82	42

Bone glues differ from hide glues in method of extraction, and have smaller ranges of jell strength and viscosity. The gram strength-viscosity ratio is quite different, particularly in the medium to high test range where bone glues tend to have higher ratios of gram strength-to-viscosity, on the order of 4:1. (Swift bone glue seems to be an exception, with ratios closer to those of hide glue.) In addition, bone glues tend to have slightly lower *pH* values (5.5) than hide glue (6.3).

The price of glue increases with test grade. The higher the test grade, the higher the glue's viscosity, water absorption, and melting point, the faster it sets to a gel, the more aggressive the tack, and the stronger the dried film.

Testing

The viscosity in millipoise is determined by the flow time in seconds through a standard pipette of a 12.5% solution of the glue at 60°C.

To determine the jelly value, the 12.5% solution is first chilled at 10°C for 16-18 hours. Then the gram strength is obtained by the use of a Bloom Geiometer or comparable instrumentation which measures the force necessary to move a 0.5 inch diameter plunger (resting on the surface of the jell) a distance of 4 mm at prefixed speed.

The solution pH is measured at 40°C. Moisture content, relative foam value, ash content, and grease content are also of concern.

Customer Preparation of Glue Solutions

The glue manufacturer often feels frustrated because some customers have inadequate mixing equipment and/or housekeeping problems. Although glues contain bacterial inhibitors the situation can get out of control if the equipment is not clean, and fresh glue solution is continually run in on the remains of older batches,

Glues are available in 10, 20 or 30 mesh granulation. The glue is dissolved in water preheated to 150-170°F, in an agitated stainless steel vessel which has been cleaned to avoid bacterial contamination from earlier batches. Concentration ranges from 5% to 50%. Large batches are usually processed in jacketed vessels either using electrically heated oil jackets or vented water jackets with low pressure steanf injection. Smaller vessels usually have electrically heated oil jackets or low wattage electrical elements placed directly on the vessel surface. Agitation is important for rapid and uniforms. Agitation of various types and speeds are used depending up the type of industry, the viscosity of the solution, and the need to keep foam levels within required limits.

Liquid Animal Glues

Liquid animal glues are glues modified by gel depressants so that they remain fluid somewhat below room temperature. Urea, thiourea, and ammonium thiocyan ate are the usual gel depressants, incorporated at approximately 8-20% by weight of the total formula. The ability of this product to stay fluid with normal temperature reduction allows for very slow assembly time, an important characteristic in the furniture industry. The final bond is achieved as the water is slowly removed from the glue, increasing its concentration and tack, thus overcoming the gel depressan effect, then setting and finally drying. The resulting film has high tensile strength Further modifications can be obtained by the addition of materials such as day calcium carbonate, plasticizers, wetting agents, etc. Formulations may range be tween 35% and 65% solids with viscosities of 3000—5000 cps at room temperature

Flexible and Non Warp Glues

Flexible and non-warp glues are compounded animal glues containing modifiers such as sucrose, corn syrup, dextrin, clay, acid, salt, magnesium sulfate, glycerine, glycols, sorbitol, water soluble organic solvents, surfactants, perfume, and preservatives; in the case of cake glue, water is added.

Because of differences in equipment, application, and end product, the cake glue is tailored for each user, and further alternations to the formula may even be made to compensate for seasonal changes in temperature and humidity. Properties of importance include viscosity at a particular running temperature (e.g., 135-155°F), speed and degree of tack, and bonding characteristics. Glues supplied as cakes have the advantage of easy meltdown and may be added directly to the applicator pans.

Flexible glues are used primarily in book binding, including telephone directories, also in soft luggage and other products where a permanently flexible, strong, resilient adhesive film is desired. A good flex product contains approximately two parts glue to one part plasticizer. The higher test glues employ more plasticizer to maintain a desired flexibility. Glue test can vary from 135 to 450 gram strength.

Non-warp glues do not have good flexibility, but can possess fairly good "lay flat" characteristics through the addition of sugars. They can be compounded to yield very strong dry films. The major areas of use are in the paper box trade in hand fed, semiautomatic and automatic covering machines, in the application of cover stock in the book manufacturing industry, in hard notebook binders, phonograph record covers, hard luggage, etc.

Dry non-warp glues are very similar to non-warp cake glue except that the manufacturer supplies this product as a dry fine mesh material which the customer must dissolve in hot water prior to use. Advantages are indefinite shelf life and lower shipping cost because of the absence of water.

A dry, moderately flexible glue, patented by M. Konigsberg, contains 8-20% glycerine but remains free-flowing indefinitely. The method utilizes the absorptive properties of synthetic alkaline earth metal silicates such as hydrous calcium silicates (e.g., Micro-eel, Johns-Manville) and other specially prepared synthetic silicas. It has met with considerable success in the bookbinding industry.

Viscosity measurements are made by Brook-field viscosimeter or Zahn cup. Readings of solids content, as a means of monitoring viscosity and water loss, can be made by refractometer. Manufacturers of glues and compounds can supply customers with viscosity/solids and viscosity/temperature graphs.

Glue Application

Cake glue, compounded dry glue, and straight dry glue are utilized at temperatures between 135 and 155°F (57 and 68°C). Too low a temperature does not allow for good wetting and filling of the pores of the substrate before the glue sets, resulting in bond failure. Temperatures that are too high create prolonged open time, with resultant slower productivity. Elevated temperatures also result in high moisture loss in the reservoir and heat hydrolysis, resulting in weaker glue strength. Dry glues are usually prepared at 25-55% solids, depending upon the test glue used, the speed of production necessary and the type of material to be bonded. It is bad practice to dilute high test glue in order to retard gelation. This practice can result in a "starved" glue bond or insufficient dry glue to perform the job. Instead, gel depressants can neither too hot nor too cold. Additional heat to the system can slow adhesion, while a cold substrate can cause premature gelling with poor bonding.

The woodworking industry observes four time-honored steps:

1. Deposit a thin continuous glue film on the surface to be bonded.
2. Permit the glue film to become slightly tacky before mating surfaces and applying pressure.
3. Apply uniform pressure.
4. Continue pressure to ensure initial bond strength.

Since it is applied from aqueous solutions, animal glue is not a filler, and only performs well as an intimate thin film in combining. The relationship of viscosity to concentration and test value is shown in Table 4.

Mating porous surfaces requires a heavier bodied (higher solids) glue, while thinner bodied glue is indicated for dense, nonporous surfaces.

Coated Abrasives

At the present time the largest consumer of animal hide glue is the abrasives industry. Abrasives are involved in the enormous production of wood products and the fine finishes essential to machinery, automobiles, household equipment, and appliances.

There are two principal classifications of coated abrasives:

1. Sandpapers and sand cloths in rolls, sheets, bolts, disks, cones, and other specialties.
2. Set up abrasive wheels, belts, disks, cones, and bobs, generally prepared in the user's own plant for grinding and buffing of metal, plastic, and wooden items.

In the production of coated abrasives there are five basic steps:

1. The backing material is presized, if necessary, with low test glue or glue/ starch blends. This loading at approximately 35-40% solids imparts body and strength.
2. The presized cloth or paper is fed through a glue applicator which deposits the making coat in the film thickness dictated by grit size. The larger the grit size, the thicker the glue laid down. The making coat takes full advantage of the jelling characteristic of glue. The glue concentration can be 25-45% and may be loaded with extenders such as calcium carbonate. The glue grades vary with the application and the type of grit. The higher grade glues are used for silicon carbide and aluminum oxide, the medium grades for emery and garnet, the lower grades for flint.
3. The grit is uniformly dispersed upon the unjelled glue film through a gravity feed hopper. The grit can be electrostatically oriented in the vertical position until the glue is jelled, by which time the product is partially dried.
4. A thin film of animal glue, and in some cases a resin, is laid down over the grit, further locking it into the adhesive matrix.
5. The abrasive cloth or paper is fed to a carefully controlled hot air drier. It is then wound into jumbo rolls for storage and later cut into various shapes.

Set-up Wheels

Under the heading of set-up polishing wheels are abrasive wheels, belts, disks, and bobs. The user prepares these on site by laying down a making coat and applying a particular grit. In some instances the grit is top coated with a more dilute glue and then carefully dried. Glues of various test values are utilized as dicated by the severity of the end use. Applications include metal finishing, glass grinding, granite finishing, and grinding in the leather industry.

Table 5.4. Viscosity in Centipoises at 140°F for Dry Glues of Given Grade Test and Millipoise Value.

Glue Concentration	*High Test (155 m.p.)*	*Medium High Test (102 m.p.)*	*Medium Test (63 m.p.)*	*Low Test (32. m.p.)*
5	3.0	2.4	2.0	1.6
10	8.8	5.6	3.6	2.6
12.5	15.5	10.2	6.3	3.2
15	28.0	17.2	8.4	5.0
20	79.2	46.0	22.4	10.0
25	196	112	49.6	19.6
30	524	264	108	37.6
35	1360	612	224	72.0
40	3216	1320	476	133
50	16320	7240	2400	566

Greaseless Buffing Compounds

Greaseless abrasive compositions are manufactured as sticks, finding a considerable market as abrasive compounds for recoating cloth buffing wheels used for metal finishing. The stick is held against a revolving wheel where the heat of friction melts the compound, transferring it to the wheel. A layer of grit compound is deposited which contains approximately 6-8% high test glue, 24% water, and the remainder, abrasive grains.

Of particular importance in these sticks is shelf life. Considerable attention must be paid to chemical preservation, guarding against bacterial breakdown which would lead to soft, non-performing sticks.

Gummed Tape

Both low test hide glue and bone glue have played an important role in the manufacture of gummed tape. Glue has to a certain extent been replaced by dextrin or combined with dextrin to lower cost. Glue is ideal for gummed tape because of its fast, aggressive tack, rapid set, permanent bond and excellent machinability. The open time, tack, set time, wetability, and strength of bond are often altered, depending upon the end use, by varying the glue test or adding modifies such as dextrin, wetting agents, jell depressants, and plasticizers.

Formulations usually have around 50% solids. The adhesive weight per square foot varies over a wide range, but typically the dry glue solids amount to 25% of the weight of the paper.

In the manufacture of gummed tape, large rolls of paper are fed through a glue applicator, where the adhesive at a temperature of 140-145°F is applied by the use of pick-up rolls. The tape is passed under tension over drying rolls or through a drying tunnel, then stored as jumbo rolls until slit and cut into standard sizes for the trade.

Glass Chipping

A unique application of glue has been perfected in the process of glass chipping. This procedure involves pouring warm glue solutions onto clean glass and allowing the glue to dry. As the film dries it shrinks and has a predisposition to curl. Since the dry glue is stronger than the glass and the bond formed with the glass is tenacious, the glass chips, leaving a rather uniform, floral like design. Lower, test glue leads to a finer, more evenly chipped texture. Patterns and lettering can be formed by appropriately covering areas of the glass with metal foil prior to introducing the glue.

Sizing and Coating

Glue as a size has been used to advantage for many years in the textile industry, particularly on cotton, rayon, acetate and viscose. The newer man-made fibers such as nylon, orlon, and Dynel have in some instances been successfully warpsized with animal glue. Compositions containing 2.5-8% glue solids are suitable. Various test grades of glue are utilized depending upon the application. For maximum stiffness, unmodified glues are used. Usually, however, the glue is modified with plasticizers and softening agents such as glycerine, sorbitol, sugars, sulfonated oils, and wax emulsions. The size composition usually contains 20-45% lubricants and softening agents.

In the process of weaving crepe the yarns used are held in a tight twist by glue while being woven into fabric. Later the glue is washed out during boil-off, thus releasing the twist and creating a creping or pebbled effect.

Paper

Animal glue has played an important role in the manufacture of papers and paper products. The important attributes of glue, including film formation, colloidal properties, and amphoteric nature, have led to its being used as a sizing agent, protective colloid, colloidal reagent, and adhesive.

Glue is a protective colloid for rosin particles during beater sizing, particularly when hard water is encountered. In practice the glue is added near the end of the beater operation. The paper fiber, with a pH of 4.5 or less, is positively charged in relation to the glue, whose charge is negative. The glue/rosin is therefore attracted to and held by the paper fiber. The addition of small quantities of glue improves the internal sizing, toughness, density, formation erasability, and resistance to scuffing of the final product.

Glue improves the wet strength of paper and can later be insolubilized, or it may be incorporated with resins that are aldehyde donors under certain conditions, rendering the glue water resistant. Glue as a surface size on papers such as fine writing paper, currently, and blue-print stock imparts strength, tear resistance, folding qualities, moisture resistance, and soil resistance and prevents feathering of inks.

For tissue paper made with a Yankee drier, glue or a combination of glue and polyvinyl alcohol is well established as an aid. Small amounts of glue or glue combinations are incorporated into the wet paper stock, creating a very slightly tacky film at the drier surface which prevents blowing or lifting to the doctor blade as it is peeled off the drum.

The process of making paper with the four-drinier machine or paper board with cylinder machines involves the use of modified animal glue as a colloidal flocculant. Incorporated with the fine cellulose fibers may be fillers, pigments, colors, and rosin. By adjustment of the pH of the system with acids, alkalies or salts, the amphoteric nature of the glue may be changed to a highly charged negative or positive colloid. The effective reaction of 0.5-1.0% glue solution on the system is that of flocculation, resulting in enhanced water drainage and paper formation. Normal usage rates are approximately two pounds of glue per ton of paper.

The same type of glue solutions are also employed in the Saveall process for recovery of solids by agglomeration in the effluent white waters of paper mills.

Compounded Rubber

Relatively large amounts of glue form the basis for the successful use of compounded synthetic rubber in textile mills. The accepted practice of maintaining heat and humidity in textile mills creates problems of fiber lapping, i.e., winding around the drafting roll during operation. The addition of approximately 25-50% glue by weight to compounded synthetic rubber produces cots and aprons with a very significantly diminished tendency to lap as long as humidity is present. This reaction is explained by the reduction of the electrokinetic or zeta potential between the rubber and moisture to near zero by the incorporation of an electrolyte such as glue. The zeta potential of approximately zero at the rubber-moisture interface of the system (fiber-moisture-moisture-rubber) effectively prevents lapping.

Gasket Manufacturing

askets have long been made from selected paper products of various thickness and density impregnated with animal glue. The object is to produce a gasket that is water and solvent resistant, flexible, compressible,resistant to distortion, and easily cut, one that provides a tight seal and will not fuse to the body.

The process involves the saturation of the paper stock by floating it across a tank j containing a glue/plasticizer solution, then passing through squeeze-rolls to remove excess liquid. In a second pass, the wet impregnated paper is moved through a bath of curing agent and (optional) plasticizer. The paper is then dried and later cut into shapes. The final product is flexible, waterproof, etc. Variables include paper type and thickness, glue test, and formula modifiers.

Matches

The match industry consumes animal glue in the manufacturing of "strike-anywhere," book matches, and wooden safety matches. Glues of various tests and foam characteristics are specially formulated. The glue acts as a binder for the ignition chemicals, combustible fillers, and inert materials and is also an important contributing factor in the formation of a head of correct density, form, and strength.

Match glues possess rigidly controlled grease content, usually below 0.3% on dry weight of glue. By careful blending, specific foam characteristics can be obtained. These are described as foam height, in mm, and foam half-life, or the time in minutes for half the foam to dissipate. The foam creates a uniform porous head which contains oxygen to promote the ignition and combustion.

Metal Refining

Electrolytic metal refining for gold, silver, copper, antimony, and lead is improved with animal glue. Without glue as a modifier in the electrolytic bath, the disposition of the metal at the cathode becomes coarse, with the formation of nodules. These can be eliminated by inclusion of 0.03-0.15% glue in the bath, resulting in a finer particle disposition with the absence of nodules. Some refiners request that the glue not be defoamed so that it can create a blanket of foam on the bath suppressing the evolution of fumes.

Other Applications for Animal Glue

Technical gelatin (high quality animal glue) of relatively iow test is being used successfully in microencapsulation. The gelatin can be used to encapsulate many materials as long as the latter do not react with or invade the thin film of gelatin surrounding them.

Carbonless paper uses the technique of gelatin encapsulation of ink, whereby the application of pressure ruptures the gelatin microspheres, releasing ink to a copy.

In the manufacture of printer's rollers, glue is compounded with glycerine/sorbitol, water, and a curing agent such as hexamine to produce a tough, flexible, resilient, water resistant, smooth roller with a long life. The roller is used in the printing industry to transfer ink to the impression plate. Glues for this purpose are in the 350-450 gram range.

Medium-to-low test undefoamed glue is utilized in the production of strong, cellular, light-weight concrete.

Technical gelatins are also employed in the manufacture of protein hydrolysates, an ingredient in personal care items such as skin creams, hair shampoos, and cosmetics. Generally the gelatin is reduced to a molecular weight under 2000 by the use of enzymes or caustic and further combined chemically at reactive sites to form modified proteins of interest to the industry.

6.

Casein and Mixed Protein Adhesives

The casein, soy protein, and blood adhesives are often considered as a family of adhesives because they have some properties in common. Although similar, the chemical structures of these three proteins are different enough to give unique properties to the adhesive which are made frcm each. This chapter will primarily cover the casein adhesives, but will touch also on some of the properties common to the three protein sources and the use of combinations of casein-soy, casein-blood, and casein-soy-blood in the same adhesive. In the matter of terminology, casein adhesive will be used as broad term embracing all the adhesives based on casein; but for the casein-lime,-sodium salt wood glue, the colloquial term casein glue will be used.

Manufacture of Casein

Commercial casein is obtained from cow's milk, in which it is the main protein at about 3% concentration. Most of the casein for adhesives is obtained by acid precipitation; however, some is preparation from milk by rennet, a preparation made from the stomach of young calves. Only the use of acid casein is covered here, since a very limited amount of rennet casein is used for adhesives.

Acid casein is manufactured by a selective precipitation process. Skim milk is prewarmed to 42-45°C and acidified with dilute acid. The acid may be hydrochloric or sulfuric, or it may be provided by the addition to the milk of a bacterial culture which produces lactic acid from the lactose. According to Spellacy, in some parts of the world sour whey which has been permitted to obtain an acidity of approximately 1-2% lactic acid by natural fermentation is used as the precipitating agent. After precipitation, the steps followed in the manufacturing process are: draining off the whey, washing and pressing the curd, and finally, drying and grinding the casein. Historically, lactic casein has been the type used for adhesives. However, the purity and quality of the product depend more on the structure of the curd and the thoroughness with which it is washed than on the type of acid used. In the last decade all three types of casein—lactic, sulfuric, and hydrochloric—have been available for adhesives.

Specifications and Typical Analyses for Casein

There are no universal specifications for casein as a raw material. Each manufacturing country has its own way of grading its product, usually based on purity, cleanliness, and solubility. A high quality casein is one which has a high protein and a low free acidity, total acidity, ash, fat, and lactose, indicating a product prepared under closely controlled conditions. It is low in insoluble material such as overdried casein particles or other protein fractions of the milk. It is clean and free of dirt or other extraneous material which can contaminate the casein during the manufacturing, grinding, or packaging process. It has a creamy white appearance, the clean odor of fresh milk, and a low bacterial and fungal count.

Table 6.1
Typical Analyses, Industrial Casein Used in the United States.

	High Grade	*Medium Grade*	*Low Grade*
Moisture, %	9-13	8-12	8-12
Ash (unfixed), %	0.75-1.8	1.2-2.0	2.0-2.7
Protein (N x 6.38), %	83-88	83-86	82-84
Free acidity, (as % lactic acid)	0.1, max.	0.2-0.7	0.9-1.8
*p*H value	4.0-5.5	4.0-5.0	4.0-5.0
Dirt content (mg per 100 grams)	0.5-3.0	2.7	8-14
Insolubles (ml per 100 grams)	0.1-0.6	1-2	2-20
Viscosity (15% solids, NH_4OH solution),cp	900-1200	800-1200	700-1000

The high quality casein described above is not necessary for all industrial adhesives. The important features for many adhesives. The important features for many adhesives are minimal viscosity variations and predictable performance in a formula. For some applications the particle size is important, and either the normal 30 mesh casein is pecified, or for many processes not using heat for solubility, a 60 or an 80 mesh.

Table 6.2
Typical Sieve Analyses on Casein, Percent (Cumulative)

	30M (a ll in)	*30M*	*60M*	*80M*
On 20 Mesh	0.1	0	—	—
On 30 Mesh	0.5	6.0	0	—
On 50 Mesh	60.0	72.0	10.0	0
On 70 Mesh		1.5		
On 80 Mesh	86.0	92.0	73.2	8.9
On 100 Mesh	91.0	95.0	87.2	30.9
On 200 Mesh	97.0	98.0	98.0	80.4
Passing 200 Mesh	3.0	2.0	2.0	19.6

Chemistry and Physical Properties of Glovularproteins

Casein, soy, and blood are globular proteins, soluble in water or agueous acids, bases, or salts. The molecules are spherical in shape and made up of heavily coiled (folded) chains of amino acids, whose side chains are crosslinked.

Because of hydrogen bonding with each other, the highly polar reactive groups of the amino acids are not available until after a dispersion process, which is usually an alkaline treatment. The usefulness of this group of proteins as adhesives is based on their high degree of polarity in the dispersed state.

Proteins are amphoteric. In neutral solution both the basic and carboxyl groups are generally charged, corresponding to the dipolar ions of the amino acids. At the isoelectric point dissociation as an acid is equal to that as a base, so that solubility and rate of migration in an electric filed is at a minimum.

Soy protein differs from casein in structure, as shown by Coco and Scacciaferro. In the soy molecule, much of the hydrophobic region is enclosed within the hydro-philic region, so that many of the polar groups are unavailable. In casein, the hydro-phobic and the hydrophilic regions are at opposite ends of the coiled chain, and the polar groups are more accessible. Coco and Scacciaferro have been able to restructure the soy molecule by thermochemical means to make more polar groups available. They showed that casein can be 90% solubilized at a pH of 6.5 but this solubility remains unchanged even if they *p*H is increased to 12. With the unmodified soy protein, on the other hand, the solubility shows a gradual climb, from 60% at *p*H6to88% *p*H 11.5.

The dried blood product which is used for the protein blend adhesives is the soluble blood type, which is 80-95% soluble in water. This product becomes strongly adhesive in alkaline dispersed from at a lower *p*H than the soy product.

Chemical Properties of casein

Casein exists in milk as the calcium salt, and is classified as a *phosphoprotein.* It is thought that the phosphoric acid is esterified with the hydroxyl groups of the lysine chains of the protein. Precipitation of casein by the enzyme *rennet* leaves organically bound phosphate, while *acid precipitation* causes the casein to split off the calcium phosphate. The ash content of rennet casein is high, about 7%, reflecting the presence of the calcium salt, while that of acid casein is relatively low, about 2%, with a small amount of calcium phosphate as an impurity.

The protein structure of the casein et al. to consist of chainlike compounds united through the peptide linkage where R may be —H, —CH_3, —C_6H_5, —$(CH_2)_4NH_2$, —CH_2COOH, etc. :

```
          |                   |
RCO — | — NH — CHCO — | — NH — CH — COOH
          |                   |     |            |
                              R                  R
```

Casein will dissolve in basic solutions. These solutions can be dried down yielding a soluble slat, e.g., sodium, potassium, or ammonium caseinate. The caseinate in solution will chelate heavy metal ions, such as calcium, aluminum, or zinc. The chelating mechanism is *p*H dependent—the higher the *p*H, the greater the chelating capacity. Reaction with metals whose salts are relatively insoluble gives water resistance to the casein.

The amino acid composition of casein is shown in Table 6.3. This breakdown was reported in 1949 and 1950 by Gordon and co workers. The classification of the amino acids into the hydrophilic and hydrophobic groups and sub groups was taken from a visual representation of the amino acids and side groups of the casein molecule by N. King.

Table 6.3. Amino Acid Composition of Casein, Wt. %

Hydrophilic, ionizable, acidic	
glutamic acid	22.4
aspartic acid	7.1
tyrosine	6.3
Hydrophilic, ionizable, basic	
lysine	8.2
arginine	4.1
histidine	3.1
Hydrophilic, non-ionizable	
proline	10.6
serine	6.3
threonine	4.9
methionine	2.8
tryptophan	1.2
Hydrophobic	
leucine	9.2
valine	7.2
isoleucine	6.1
phenylalanine	5.0
alanine	3.2
Sulfur bridge	
cystine	0.34
Unclassfied	
glycine	2.0

Physical Properties of Casein

Casein is a granular solid, varying in colour from cream to light yellow, typically having a sweet and milky odor. Poorly prepared casein may have a deeper yellow colour and at times a rancid or musty odor. The moisture content of casein usually falls between 8 and 11%, but it is not unusual to see ranges from 7 to 13%. Casein is insoluble in water and most non-aqueous media, but it forms colloidal dispersions in aqueous solutions of acids, bases, and some salts. Some organic substances can also disperse casein. The ones having practical applications are urea and the thiocyanates. (Although the term *dispersion* is technically the correct one when referring to casein treated in a manner to break the internal hydrogen bonding, uncoiling the molecule, the term *solution* is more frequently used. The two terms will be employed interchangeably in this discussion.) Casein is insoluble at its isoelectric point, *p*H

4.6. Although it has minimal solubility around this point, any success preparing solutions at *pH's* close to the isoelectric point require very careful control of conditions. There is a marked increase in solubility below pH3 and above pH 6. There is little application for acidic casein solutions (those prepared at *pH's* below 3.0) and they are seldom used for industrial purposes. Basic solutions are typically prepared in the 7-9 *pH* range at concentrations of from 10 to 20%, and show Newtonian properties. At concentrations greater than 18% most solutions are too viscous to be handled conveniently at 20°C. Casein solutions at 25% solids, prepared with most bases, are jellies at 25°C.

Urea can be used to disperse casein at a pH of 5.5 to 6.0. It can also be used to obtain a higher solids content, since it has thinning effect. Basic solutions are highly receptive to additional water, while urea-cut solutions have minimal water acceptance. Dried films of basic solutions are soluble in water, but the dried films of urea solutions will not dissolve easily unless the *pH* is raised by addition of a base. Addition of aldehydes and heavy metal ions increase the viscosity and water resistance of casein solutions. Dicyandiamide, used in a basic solutions, is a very effective viscosity reducer, and generally reduces the water resistance. The viscosity-temperature and viscosity-concentration relationship are exponential. Salzberg reported this relationship between viscosity and concentration, showing values in centipoises of 1080, 26,000, and 160,000 for 15, 20, and 25% concentrations, respectively. At 25°C a 20% concentration solution may hardly flow, but it will be free-flowing at 60°C. The variables which affect the apparent viscosity of casein solutions are: concentration, temperature, pH, type of cation, age, and method of preparation—especially the time, temperature, and order-of-addition factors. The complex relationship of the viscosity, type of cation, and *pH* factors was reported by Salzberg et al. and is shown in Table 6.4.

Table 6.4 Viscosity of Casein Solutions Prepared with Different Alkalies at Varying pH's.

Alkali Added	pH 6	7	8	9	10	11	12
Sodium hydroxide (NaOH)	300	700	900	100	900	300	100
Ammonuim hydroxide (26.6% NH4OH)	—	900	1000	1300	1000	1000	—
Sodium carbonate (Na_2CO_3)	—	1400	1700	2400	3600	—	—
Trisodium phosphate ($Na_3PO_4 . 12H_2O$)	800	1200	3200	5700	8000	10300	—
Borax ($Na_2B_4O_7 . 10H_2O$)	700	800	1300	3700	—	—	—

Other Viscosity Factors

The viscosity of the raw casein and its reactive potential upon exposure to metal ions directly affect the viscosity of casein adhesives and solutions. The inherent viscosity depends on several factors: the season of the year as it relates to the lactational cycle of the herd, the genetic makeup of the herd, and the protein content and the purity of the casein. The casein produced from milk obtained early season, shortly after the calving, will be twice as high in viscosity as that produced in late season. Creamer determined that in a controlled test, high pH and high calcium content of the casein will result in a higher viscosity product. Countries which have poor manufacturing facilities frequently lack control over the temperature and pH of precipitation, and have inadequate washing cycles. This results in a high ash, high acidity, low protein casein, containing a higher percentage of milk by-products. These caseins are lower in viscosity and less reactive in formulations which use metal ions for added water resistance. The viscosity difference between these poorer quality caseins and those manufactured under modern and controlled conditions shows up more sharply when they are tested in a higher solids urea solution at a *p*H below 7. It is essential, when testing a casein lot for suitability, that the viscosity be determined by running the test within the structure of the formula which is to be used, and with the intended dispersant and crosslinking chemicals.

Lime Free Casein Adhesive

Casein is utilized in diverse ways, as an adhesive, as a binder, and as protective colloid and stabilizer for emulsified adhesive systems. Casein in sold as a raw material, and casein adhesives are sold in both the dry and liquid forms. The useful wood adhesive known as casein glue, which is formulated with lime and sodium salts, will be addressed later. This section will cover other uses of casein, for which the solubilization of the casein is generally accomplished with the use of heat, and at lower *pH's* than for the lime-containing glues.

Preparation of Casein Solutions, General

When given sufficient time, casein can be solubilized cold with most alkalies and alkaline salts, but cold solubilization usually results in a lower viscosity product with very little stability. Most of the lime-free casein adhesives are prepared with heat because of many advantages, the most important of these being the ability to speed up and control the process, and to result in a uniform and stable product.Urea has widespread use as a dispersant for casein and is discussed in the section on label paste adhesives. Selection of one or a combination of two or more dispersants, is determined by many factors relating to the intended use of the solution, pH range desired, and other agents used in the system. Table 5 shows the percent of various alkalies needed to solubilize casein.

Ammonium hydroxide is the most commonly used alkali. It is generally added in excess of the amount necessary for solubilization, because frequently some of the ammonia volatilizes in the cooking process; also, excess ammonia has a preserving effect. Frequently ammonia is used in combination with borax, improving the preserving proprieties of each. Studies have shown that although a casein solution made with borax has good biocidal properties, at a *pH* of 6.9 it does not equal the adhesive and viscosity properties in storage of a solution made with 5% borax plus 10% ammonium hydroxide, which has *a pH of* 9-10. Ammonium hydroxide has also proven useful for *p*H adjustment at the end of the cooking period. Except for sodium hydroxide, ammonia-cut casein solutions are lower in viscosity than those cut with other alkalies. Borax imparts a very high viscosity to a casein solution, and when it is used alone at 12% on the casein weight, most of the caseins on today's market will dissolve at a *pH* of about 7.0.

Sodium hydroxide is a strong base and should be used in small amounts, just enough to achieve solubility, the amount needed varying with different caseins. Generally 2.0-2.5% will be sufficient to solubilize the casein and will result in a *pH of* 7. The amount of alkali needed varies with different caseins, so should be worked out in each instance. Table 6.4 shows the effect of *p*H on the viscosity of casein solutions prepared with several alkalies. Note that at pH 9, sodium hydroxide and ammonium hydroxide cut solutions are at their peak viscosity, but when alkaline salts are used, the viscosity increases continuously as the percent salt increase. The sharp drop-off in viscosity of the solutions cut with sodium hydroxide at *pH's above* 10 is also of special interest. Potassium hydroxide behaves in a similar manner, with the sharp drop in viscosity coming between *pH* 10.8 and 11.

Table 6.5. Typical Alkalies Needed to Dissolve Casein, and *p*H Values of Casein Solutions.

	Alkali, Parts per 100 parts of casein, by Wt.							
Alkali Added	2.5	5.0	7.5	10	12.5	15	17.5	20
N_aO_H	7.0	11.0	12.6	—	—	—	—	—
NH_4OH (26°Be)	7.7	9.2	10.0	10.3	10.6	10.7	10.8	—
Na_2CO_3	—	6.7	7.4	8.3	9.1	9.7	10.0	10.2
Na_3PO_4 $12H_3O$	—	—	—	6.8	7.2	7.4	7.7	7.9
$Na_2B_4O_2$ $10H_2O$	—	—	—	6.8	7.3	7.7	7.9	8.1

Preservatives

Casein, as a milk product, is susceptible to microbial attack, and requires protection with an appropriate biocide when the product containing it is to be kept in the liquid from more than a day. The level of biocide should not be based only on the casein present, but should be calculated to be effective in the total system of which the casein is a part. Sodium orthophenylphenate and sodium pentachlorophenate have a long history as effective preservatives for casein products. Less harsh preservatives are the esters of p-hydroxybenzoic acid. Other useful ones are chlorinated methylisothiazolin, tributyltin oxide, and chlorinated xylenols. Formaldehyde is effective, but its use is a concern for OSHA, and it also causes viscosity increases because of its strong crosslinking tendency with casein. It must be handled very carefully when used with casein. Many new biocides are now available due to recent advances in biological protection. An appropriate one should be selected after considering the use of the end product, the environmental impact of disposal of waste, and applicable governmental regulations.

Preparation of an Alkaline Casein Solution

A formula and the steps in the preparation of a 15% alkaline dispersed casein solution is given below:

(1) Using continuous agitation during the preparation, charge the water into a jacketed kettle. Add the casein and allow to soak for 10 minutes to wet the grains of casein thoroughly. (2) Warm the casein-water slurry to approximately

43-49°C. (3) Add the NH_4OH and continue heating until reaching 60°C, holding at this temperature for 20 minutes or until solubilization is achieved. (4) Cool to 49°C. Most bio-cides are added at this point. If the aim is to prepare a solution with long term stability, extend the solubilization period from 20 minutes to 30, and increase the temperature during solubilization to 71°C. (The extra time and temperature is necessary to destroy the proteoiytic enzymes, which could cause viscosity to drift down, or sometimes up, during the storage life of a casein solution. Enzymatic breakdown of casein can occur in solutions which are adequately protected with biocide, so this is an additional problem to be addressed.)

	Parts by weight
Casein	100
H_2O	555
NH_4OH (26°Be)	9
Biocide	*

*Follow the manufacturer's recommendation for level of selected biocide and guidelines on point and method of introduction.

Additives for Casein Solutions

For many purposes the formula and procedure would be modified. A casein solution quite often is high in viscosity and foamy. A casein film is brittle and adsorbs water easily. A number of additives have been used. *Antifoams and defoamers* include amyl alcohol, silicone oils and emulsions, octyl alcohol, tributyl citrate, pine oil, and tributyl phosphate. Frequently used *viscosity reducers* are urea, dicyandiamide, and ammonium thiocyanate. The *plasticizers* may be divided into true plasticizers, which dissolve in the polymer, and flexibilizing agents, such as the resins and latexes which do not dissolve, but merely form a blend of the two components, acting as a softening agent. Plasticizers used for casein are glycerol, sor-bitol, latex glycols, urea, sulfonated oils, water, and resin emulsions. The *hardeners to increase moisture resistance are* formaldehyde, urea-formaldehyde resin, aluminum formate, hexamethylenetetramine, melamine-formaldehyde resin, lime, glyoxal, zinc salts and oxides, and alum.

Application Using Casein Solutions and Adhesive

Casein as a Protective Colloid

Casein is also suitable as a stabilizer in resin emulsions, and as a thickener for anionic emulsions. On occasion, the resin emulsions are used as tackifiers for the latex systems. The amount of casein needed for stabilizing a resin emulsion must be balanced against the undesired loss in water resistance and tack when too much casein is used. The applications are covered in further detail elsewhere in this volume, particularly in the chapter on tackifying resins and natural and synthetic rubbers.

'Success in stabilizing a resin with casein is dependent on following the proper procedure when combining the materials. Levels of various components are given in parts by weight. The resin (40-43) is dissolved in toluene (10-14) in the presence of oleic acid (0.25-0.75). Resins can be blended, or toluene may be increased to achieve the desired viscosity of 25-30 poises and an optimum particle size. The potassium oleate plus the caseinate provide a versatile emulsifier system which delays the break of the emulsion. Then, potassium hydroxide (0.15-0.2) in a 2.0-2.5% solution is added slowly to form potassium oleate in situ, followed by ammonium caseinate (1.3.-1.5), added as a 10-15% caseinate solution. When an ester type resin is used, the caseinate is prepared with a low level of ammonium hydroxide. To this point there is a high viscosity *water-in-oil emulsion.* Then, there is a second addition of potassium hydroxide (a diluted KOH/ water premix) equal to the first, triggering an inversion to a low viscosity *oil-in-water emulsion,* which has a small particle size and is very stable. The resin emulsion may then be compounded with a latex to produce an emulsion adhesive. When the resin is a hydrocarbon type, the total solids are generally 45.7-50.0%, and the *p*H is 10.3-10.7.

Paper Coatings

Casein and isolated soy protein are the two protein binders used by the paper coating industry. They are normally used in combination with one of the latexes, styrene-butadiene, butadiene-acrylonitrile, or acrylic emulsions. Casein and isolated soy dispersions are usually compatible with each other; however, in practice, they are not generally combined in the same formula. The casein coatings show a better gloss and strength than the soy coatings. A soy protein coating is thixotropic, and a casein coating Newtonian, although these properties may be affected by the use of latex and the preparation process. The thixotropy of the soy coatings gives them the advantage of running better on high speed coaters. Because of difficulties in completely dispersing the isolated soy protein at a low pH necessary for dispersion, frequently, the soy protein cooks must be acidified after solubilization to bring the pH down. For prevention of flocculation of the pigment when the casein or protein solution is added, the pigment is generally alkalized first, and the first portion of the solution is added slowly. Sometimes casein is combined with starch as a binder for coatings for paper board and carton stock. When starch is cooked with casein, the temperature of the cook must be high enough to cook the starch. Generally 71°C is adequate, and this temperature is acceptable for casein.

The amount of binder (casein, soy protein, or latex) for a paper coating is given in dry parts of binder is used, and the ratio of casein (or soy protein to) latex is varied to give desired properties to the coating. Since excessive shear on the latex results in foam and possible physical breakdown, the latex should be added after the casein. When the latex is styrene-butadiene (SBR), an increase in casein and a decrease in SBR results in a higher viscosity at a lower solids. The reverse effect is used to advantage in preparing coatings: the latex-to-casein ratio is increased in order to accommodate a higher percent solids. At higher solids, heavier coating weights may be applied. The use of different latexes and different latex/casein ratios will result in different viscosities, rheology, and tack. SBR latex adds desirable erties to pigmented coatings bound with casein, improving the gloss, the varnish holdout, and the water resistance.

A comprehensive discussion of the use of casein and isolated soy protein in paper coatings may be found in Tappi Monograph Series No. 22.

Table 6.6 shows typical paper *coating formulations with* a 50 : 50 SBR-to-casein ratio, for use on two types of coaters. For a multiple roll coater, water would be] added to adjust to a percent total solids of 50-55, giving a coating weight of 3-4 lb) per 1000 sq ft. For an air knife coater, solids would be adjusted to 40-45%, yielding a coating weight of 2-3 lb per sq ft.

Table 6.6 Casein / Latex Paper Coating.

	Parts by Wt	
	Dry	*Wet*
Pigment		
Coating grade clay	94.0	134.2
Ti02 (rutile type)	6.0	8.6
Binder		
SBR latex	8.0	16.7
Casein	8-0	53.3
Water	(Sufficient to yield desired % solids)	

A typical formula for a casein cook is shown in Table 7, with choices of alkalies given. Due to the volatility of ammonia and in order to assure complete solubilization of the casein when ammonia is used, researchess. recommended dissolving casein to a predetermined *pH* value. The preparation steps are the same as given earlier for an alkaline casein solution, except that the 60°C temperature is recommended for solubilization. The practice of dropping the casein solution into a clean storage tank and rinsing out the kettle between batches or at least once a day should be followed.

Foil-to-Paper Laminating Adhesive

One of the better known uses of casein is the manufacture of foil-to-paper laminating adhesives. Because of its listing as GRAS by the FDA, casein is used for much of the packaging in the food and cigarette industries.

A typical foil adhesive is made by first preparing an ammonium caseinate solution with a low level of ammonium hydroxide, and then combining it with a styrene-butadiene (SBR) later with a *p*H of about 7.0. The *p*H of the resulting adhesive should be close to neutral because of the tendency of high pH adhesive should be dose to neutral because of the tendency of high pH adhesives to slowly eat through the foil. Some proprietary formulations at *p*H's below 7 contain additives to increase water resistance. To make a simple casein-latex foil laminating adhesive: (1) Dissolve 20 parts of casein in 78.75 parts of water, using 1.25 parts of NH_4OH (26°Be) as the dispersant. (2) Combine 16 parts of this 20% ammonium caseinate solution with 52 parts of SBR latex. (3) Add two parts of defoamer as needed, one of a sulfonated wetting agent, and 0.5 of preservative. (4) Add water to a total formula weight of 100. The SBR should be non-carboxylated with 25-50% styrene, with rosin acid as the protective colloid.

Ice Water Table Paste Adhesives

Ice water lable paste is a very specialized water-based casein adhesive which is used primarily to adhere paper labels to beer bottles. The labels must remain attached if the bottles are chilled in ice or otherwise subjected to wet conditions, but they must wash off reusable bottles easily with hot water. Casein is dispersed with urea at an approximate 50 : 50 ratio in the presence of ammonium hydroxide as an additional dispersant. The high percent casein solids in this type formulation is possible because of the urea, sometimes, along with ammonium thiocyanate, functions also as a gel depressant. Zinc oxide and zinc acetate are used to crosslink and provide water resistance. A defoamer and a preservative are always included. Starch is one of several agents incorporated to shorten the thread of the adhesive to improve its performance on high speed labelling machines.

Table 6.7. Typical Mill Formula, Low Solids Casein Solution.

Water	365 gal in clean jacketed kettle
Casein	500 lb
N_aOH	16.25 lb, or
NH_4OH(26°Be)	5 gal, or
Na_2CO_3	60 lb, or
Borax	75 lb
Yield	414.25 gal
Casein solids	14%, air dry basis
Casein solids	1.2 lb.
Viscosity at 800F	1000-3000cp
*p*H	8.0-8.4

Because the formulas in commercial use are proprietary, the one given in Table 8 gives typical ranges, not specific percentages. The compounding of the components is of equal importance to the formula. A successful order of addition must be established, along with a time-temperature log which relates to both the points of introduction of the various raw materials and the heat-up, cook, and cool-down periods. A recommended order of addition for the formula given is: H_2O, zinc oxide, zinc acetate, preservative, defoamer, starch, urea, casein and ammonium hydroxide. It has been established that for the primary components, use of the order: ammonium hydroxide, urea, and casein, gives a very unstable product, which tends to increase in viscosity sharply for several days, and then to drop off just as sharply. The typical cook temperature is 77-80°C. This temperature is held for 15-20 minutes before initiating the cool-down period.

A small formula change can make a large change in properties. Increased zinc oxide will give faster drying, but will shorten shelf life. Usually, to get a faster drying time, the gel depressant is decreased and the casein is increased, but a shift in this direction will shorten the shelf life. A very short shelf life is known in the industry as *setback*, and is a major problem when it occurs. The experienced formulator balances the formula to gain the best compromise in properties. A successful lable paste must also meet the special running conditions of the machines which apply the labels at a fast speed. Various grades of casein, and even different lots within a grade, may perform differently. It is helpful to use a test for the selection of casein which relates to the formula in which it is to be used.

Table 6.8. Typical Lable Paste Formula.

	Parts by weight
Water	47—50
Preservative	0.3—0.5
Defoamer	0.5
Starch	1.5—3
Zinc acetate	0.3—0.5
Zinc oxide[a]	0.5—0.75
Urea (microprilled)	21—23
Casein	20—25
Ammonium hydroxide 26°Be)	1.0—1.6

[a]Zinc oxide is usually added as a 50% dispersion

Specifications for viscosity, speed of set, and water resistance vary with the consumer. Table 6.9 gives the typical ranges for the properties desired in a lable paste.

Table 6.9. Typical Specifications for Ice Water Lable Paste.

Viscosity	45,000-75,000 cp @ 80°F (27°C)
Solids	48-50%
*p*H	7.5-8.5
Setting time	Fiber tear in 30 seconds
Water resistance	Pass 24 hr soak in water @ 35°F (2°C)[a]
Shelf life	3-6 months[b]

a) Label is adhered to bottle and is dried for 24 hours before soaking.Lable must not flag off the bottle following 24 hr. soak.
b) The shelf life must hold at a stable viscosity with no sharp climb or drop for this period of time.

Miscellaneous Uses for Casein Adhesives

A casein-lime adhesive and other casein based adhesive are involved in a cone winding process bonding paper to paper. The cones are used by the textile mills as yarn carriers. There are some specially manufacturers of stable casein solutions who sell their products for varied applications.

A casein coating on steel is one step in the manufacture of aperture masks for colour TV tubes. Casein is also used as a partial binder in some types of chalking adhesives.

Casein and Protein Blend Glues as Wood Adhesive

The wood adhesives discussed here will be the casein-lime-sodium salt glues and similar glues formulated with combinations of casein with soy flour, blood, or both. The *p*H of these adhesives is 11-12, due to the lime, sodium hydroxide, and sodium salts used for dispersion.

Casein can be dispersed with a number of alkalies at pH's of 7 and above, and with urea, an amide, at about , pH 6. Isolated soy protein can be dispersed at a slightly higher *p*H. However, soy bean flour, the product used in the protein blend glues, requires a highly alkaline treatment in the pH range of 11-12. Animal blood can be dispersed in water to a certain degree, but for complete dispersion, alkaline treatment is also required. The use of the high *p*H alkalies has proven to be the successful route with this group of wood adhesives, because in addition to the dispersion factor, the lime provides water resistance.

Chemistry of Protein Blend Glues

The key to formulating protein adhesives is understanding what happens to the protein under the influence of alkaline dispersion and in the presence of denaturing chemicals and conditions. Lambuth discusses the complex chemical process. At a pH of 11-12 the protein molecules are almost completely and irreversibly uncoiled, freeing their reactive and polar groups for adhesive bonding. Hydrolysis into peptones, peptides, and amino acids further enhances the adhesive potential, but with loss of water resistance and bond strength, unless the formulator intervenes. Alkaline dispersion proceeds rapidly, hydrolysis more gradually. Thus, viscosity rises quickly from a low to value again over several hours. It is up to the formulator to build into the formula a few hours of relatively level viscosity. This is much easier with casein than with soy flour and blood, because the casein glues do not demonstrate a rise in viscosity as rapid as that shown by the other two protein sources. With proper formulation, it is possible to obtain several hours of fairly level viscosity with casein, before hydrolysis takes over, or before certain formulations carry the casein glue to a gel. Casein makes an excellent contribution to the water resistance. Addition of blood increases the water resistance even more, but soya flour causes a decrease.

Proteins are extremely prone to undergo a form of alteration described as *denaturation.* The elements which cause denaturation may be chemical or physical. The chemical agents of importance are: (1) the agents used for adding water resistance—lime, metal salts and oxides, formaldehyde and formaldehyde donors—and (2) organic chemicals such as alcohols and ketones which block the action of the crosslinkers by reducing the polarity of the solvent. The physical agent which is of importance is heat or any mechanical situation such as grinding or friction which develops heat.

Formulation and Chemistry of Casein-Lime Glues

The simplest formula for casein glue includes casein, light mineral oil, lime, and sodium salts. The choice of sodium salts is restricted to salts of acids whose calcium salts are relatively insoluble. The sodium salts also cannot be hygroscopic and must not be capable of reacting with the casein, lime, or other chemicals in the dry state. The addition of oil retards the interaction of the casein particles with the chemicals until they can be completely wet out and also reduces the dustiness of the powdered casein glue. Upon addition of the dry glue powder to water, the lime (calcium hydroxide) and the sodium salts dissolve, yielding a highly basic solution. The sodium hydroxide, which is more reactive than the calcium hydroxide, disperses the casein, yielding essentially an ionized sodium caseinate. Thee is a slow reaction between the sodium caseinate and the excess lime, and the sodium caseinate slowly converts to the insoluble calcium caseinate. A simultaneous reaction is the hydrolysis of the casein molecule, a process which continues at an even slower rate.

The typical sodium salts include sodium fluoride, trisodium phosphate, soda ash, sodium bicarbonate, sodium sulfite, and others. The lime and sodium fluoride are essential for ready liquefaction of the glue. Casein may be dissolved with only lime, but this type of adhesive remains fluid only a short time before gelling. Additives, including defoamers and zinc compounds, and extenders, such as clays, wood flour, and shell flour, are frequently used.

The experienced formulator can customize a glue to perform specific jobs. At times a fast setting glue is important, but under other conditions, the glue must allow longer assembly time under warm conditions. The most successful formulas are closely guarded proprietary information. By finding the optimum balanced levels of sodium salts and lime, it is possible to control the viscosity of the wet glue in a manner which will provide a reasonable working life at a fairly level viscosity, and at the same time provide a glue with good dry and wet strength over the usable life of the wet mix.

The formulation of casein glues was described by Brown and Brouse. Using 100 parts of casein as a constant, when the gram equivalents of lime and sodium salts are equal, the casein glue will have no water resistance. As the excess equivalents of lime over the sodium salts increases, the level of water resistance will increase. Formula 1 in Table 10 has water resistance, while Formula 2 has none.

It is the balance between the equivalents of sodium salts and lime that controls whether or not a glue gels. Within a given formula, when using the same glue powder-to-water ratio and the same casein content, incremental increases in sodium salts, lime, or both, can carry the glue from a gel to a nongelling glue. The viscosity of a gel glue increases rapidly, so most casein glues that gel have limited pot lives, an undesirable feature. Formerly some casein glue specifications required a gel glue to assure that the glue had water resistance, and to prevent use of the glue after hydrolysis set in. The gelling carried the glue through an unusable stage before the glue hydro-lyzed.

In the earlier classification of casein glues by water resistance, a gel glue was the only example given for a glue which had water resistance. A glue which gelled only by the loss of water was described as non-water-resistant. However, very water resistant casein glues which do not progress to a gel are available today. With these glues the excess lime is the primary key to the water resistance. Also, the mix ratio of water to dry powder influences whether the mixed glue demonstrates the gel tendency.

Some of the older literature speaks of a casein glue going through a very heavy stage before breaking down to a usable glue. Current formulations may be slightly heavier during the first 10 to 20 minutes after mixing with water, but the bodying up described for earlier formulations is not evident. This might be due to the better quality of the casein available today or to advances in formulating.

These highly alkaline glues are not as susceptible to microbial attack as are the lower *p*H casein adhesives; however, addition of a fungal inhibitor is recommended for a glue to be used for a structural application. Salzberg warns that it should be clearly understood that fungal inhibitors protect only the glue line and the adjacent wood, not the bulk of the glued structure, which can support fungal growth unless separately, protected. Because of leaching, a graduals loss of fungal protection may be expected when water soluble biocides are used. *Sodium pentachlorophenate* is the fungicide with the longest history of successful use with casein glue, typically at 3% on the dry powder. In recent years only the glues that had to meet government specifications requiring a fungal inhibitor have been protected, because of increased concern about environmental impact of this type biocide in waste. Since recent Environmental Protection Agency (ERA) regulations, no biocide is being used in casein glue. See the Adhesive Specifications section of this chapter. Use of other, safer fungicides is being investigated. In addition, other means, such as paint and epoxy coatings, plus protection from humid conditions, are being used to protect most casein-glued laminations from biological attack.

Mixing Casein Glue

The formulas given in Table 10 are for the dry mix type of casein and protein blend glues which are currently in use in the United States. Several decades ago, the practice of formulating these glues as wet mixes was widespread, an approach which made a wider range of additives available. Frequently a phenolic resin or sodium silicate solution was added, liquids which could not be incorporated into the dry mixes. Also, the components could be added in the most advantageous sequence. The dry mixes, however, had the strong advantage of convenience, and replaced the wet mixes over the years.

The usual mix ratio for casein glue is 2 parts of water to one of dry glue powder; however, some casein-soy glues need a mix ratio as high as 2.5:1. Two kinds of mixers are used: a high speed double propeller type and a slower paddle type. With the preferred high speed type, the water is charged and the powder is added as fast as the mixer can introduce the material. With he low speed mixer, frequently a portion of the water is withheld, the lumps are rubbed out by agitation of the heavy mix, the remainder of the water is added, and the glue is mixed to uniformity. For both types of mixers, the glue is allowed to stand 10 to 15 minutes to allow time for the casein to dissolve, and is mixed again for several minutes before using. Casein glue develops an exothermic reaction when added to water, so the temperature of the water used should be about 5-6°C cooler than the desired temperature of the wet mix. Typically, 18°C water is used to give 24°C glue. Hot water should not be used.

Additives for Casein and Protein Blend Glues

Latex—The bonds achieved with these glues may be improved with two classes of additives. Latex is used widely to improve the bonding of difficult-to-glue skins. The problems with these skins are manifold, usually cased by high density wood, by extractive heartwood, by resin which has been brought to the surface when the plywood has been manufactured in hot press, or by glazed surfaces caused by dull knives used to cut the veneer. Latex is frequently added tot he casein-soy blend glues to improve the bond. It gives a plasticity to the glue line, a feature which reduces the brittleness of the cured casein or protein glue line, helping, as the lamination ages, to retain the normally high early (green) strength of the glueline.

Table 6.10. Formulas for Casein and Casein-Blend Glues (Dry Mix Type).

Materials	Formula No.1 Casein	Formula No.2 Casein	Formula No.3 Casein-Soy Blood	Formula No.4 Casein-Soy
Casein	59.1	70.8	36.0	15.0
Light mineral oil	3.6	3.6	2.6	3.00
Lime, hydrated	17.7	9.4	18.0	12.0
Sodium fluoride	2.5	2.8	2.5	3.0
Trisodium phosphate	11.2	9.0	7.6	—
Sodium carbonate	—	—	3.8	5.0
Sodium sulfite	3.7	4.4	—	—
Soluble Blood	—	—	2.0	—
Soy flour	—	—	24.0	57.0
Wood flour	1.0	—	—	5.0
Bentonite	1.2	—	3.5	—
Total Dry Parts by Weight	100.0	100.0	100.0	
Water	165.0	200.0	200.0	250.0

The recommended latex for use with both casein and protein blend glues is a *carboxylated styrene-butadiene,* with a styrene content of 60 to 65%. When this latex has a pH of 7.5-9.6, the effect on viscosity will be minimal. The latex must be added to the mixed casein or protein blend glue, not to the water. The typical addition is one gallon of latex for one 50 lb bag of glue.

Furfuryl Alcohol—The use of furfuryl alcohol is recommended to counter the effect of certain acid-treated fire retardant woods and is covered by U.S.A. and Canadian patents. This type additive extends the allowable assembly time by delaying thegelling action of the acid salts on the alkaline casein glue. The alcohol retards the reaction of the acid salts in the fire-retardant-treated lumber with the alkaline casein glue, and at the same time slows down the formation of calcium caseinate, which has a viscosity-building effect. Use of furfuryl alcohol is recommended for use with casein glues or with casein-soy flour blend glues where soy flour is only a minor fraction of the protein. It is not recommended for the high soy content gloues. A level of 30% furfuryl alcohol, based on the dry casein glue, has been found to be efective, although lower levels will also extend the assembly time of the glue to a lesser degree. There is some use of diacetone alcohol for this perpose, but it is less effective then furfuryl alcohol. These additives are sold under the trade names assigned by the adhisive companies prom promothing them.

Uses of Casein Glues

The casein wood glues have a long history of use as interior structural adhesives, assembly adhesives, and panel-to-frame adhesives. A limited but important use is as a non conductive adhesive in the construction of spacers for the large transformer boards for the electrical industry. The most popular use of casein and protein blend glues is in the production of hollow and solid core flush doors, an operation for which these glues are ideally suited. Most of the doors in this country are made with this type of glue.

Flush doors are produced by bonding "skins" of plywood,hardboard, or particle board to the vertical and horizontal frames (the stiles and rails), which are usually either a soft wood such as fir or a man-made hardboard, this frame having been fastened around a fire-resistant mineral core. Casein and casein-soy blend glues with and without the furfuryl alcohol additive are the primary adhesives currently selected for use in these operations.

Specifications Applying to Casein Glue

The specifications most frequently used for casein glue are of two types: those specifically written to apply to the generic adhesive, and industry specifications which control the end products for which casein glue is normally used.

Adhesive Specifications. There are two ASTM specifications covering casein glues:

(1) ASTM D 3024-84, 'Standard Specification for Protein-Base Adhesives for Structural Laminated Wood Products for Use Under Interior (Dry Use) Exposure Conditions." A request to drop this specification is currently in the balloting process. No conforming glue is currently being manufactured commercially for several reasons: a decreased demand for casein glue for structural purposes, availability of sodium pentachlorophenate only in the dusty powdered form (beads no longer available), and a recent EPA withdrawal of the registration of sodium pentachlorophenate for this application and others.

(2) ASTM D 4689-87, "Standard Specification for Adhesive, Casein-Type"—This specification is a replacement for Federal Specification MMM-A-125-D, "Adhesive, Casein Type, Water and Mold Resistant." Upon acceptance by the government, ASTM D 46-89-87 will be the designated specification regulating the testing of casein glues for purchase by the Federal government contracts. The new specification covers three categories: Class A, Water and Fungal Resistant; Class *B,* Water Resistant; and Class C, Dry Use (a new classification which will not require a test for water resistance). No conforming glue is currently being manufactured to meet Class A, but ASTM D 4300-88, "Standard Test Methods for Ability of Adhesive Films to Support or Resist the Growth of Fungi', may be used to test new biocides for compliance with the fungal resistance requirements. To meet the ASTM strength specifications. To meet the ASTM strength specifications, casein glue is tested with laboratory prepared birch plywood (ASTM D 906) and maple block (ASTM D 905) specimens.

Industry Specifications. The manufacture of doors in the United States is controlled by NWWDA Industry Standard, IS 1-86., written by the National Wood Window and Door Association. The glue lines of a finished door are tested for compliances with either: Type I, "Exterior Use," a two-cycle boil test, or Type II, "Interior Use," a three-cycle soak test. Casein glue is used to bond the skin (frequently plywood) and the frame, while other adhesives are used between the plies of the plywood, so if delamination occurs, it is important to pinpoint the Type II specification.

Casein-soy blend glues pass Type II if the percentage of soy flour is not too high. There are some highly water resistant casein glues that pass the Type I specification. Some of these glues are currently being used for exterior doors, although it is recognized that the doors must be painted or coated with a material which is impervious to water or humidity. It is important not to equate the NWWDA Type I bond with other much more highly water resistant Type I adhesives, such as the crosslinked polyvinyls, resorcinols and melamines.

Canadian Specifications. In Canada, CSA Standard for Wood Adhesives No. 0112.3-M 1977 covers the specifications for casein glue. Glue line requirements for wood doors are covered in CSA Standard 0132.2-M 1977. (Copies may be obtained from Canadian Standards Association, 178 Rexdale Blvd., Rexdale, Ontario, Canada, M9W 1R3.

Viscosity and Pot Life

In addition to the bonding properties, casein glue manufacturers pay close attention to the viscosity and pot life of their products, when mixed using the recommended ratio of water to dry powder. A glue with a four hour pot life when tested under laboratory conditions will last approximately two hours in a plant situation, when subjected to the agitation of a spreader. Because the glues containing soy flour are more thixotropic, they are made in a slightly higher viscosity range;

Certification of Fire Doors

Adhesives for uses in making fire doors must be tested and certified within a licensed construction system, currently available from four companies: Weyerhaueser, Georgia Pacific, Cal-Wood, and Masonite. The two certifying agencies for fire doors in the United States, Warnock Mersey (W-H) and Underwriter's Laboratories (U.L.), have lists of approved adhesives for each licensee's fire door construction, for 20, 45,60, and 90 minute fire doors. The 20 minute fire doors are solid core doors, and do not require the special frames and mineral cores of the other fire doors; but they still require W-H or U.L. approval.

Table 6.11. Viscosity Pattern of Casein and Casein-Soy Glues.

		Viscosity.cp @ 250CO	
Hours	*Minutes*[b]	*Casein Glue*	*Casein-Soy Glue*
1	20	4500	6500
2		3800	5000
3		3600	4800
4		4000	5500
20		6000	8000

*Test with a Brookfield rotational viscometer.

[b]Timed from the introduction of the glue powder to the water.

Properties of Casein Glues

Casein glue is known as a very forgiving glue. It can be used under warm conditions at ambient temperatures as high as 100°F and under cold conditions, at temperatures in the range of 40°F. Because improved water resistance is related to a faster curing cycle, bonds developed at lower temperatures will show less water resistance than bonds developed at the optimum 60-80°F. It has also been demonstrated that with even warmer ambient temperatures, in the 90-100°F range, the water resistance will increase as the speed of more rapid loss of moisture in the glue line under warm conditions, allowable assembly time is shorter. Casein glue works well with an assembly time which can vary from less than 10 minutes to over 30 minutes, a feature which is used to advantage in the door industry, where *a* stack of 40 to 50 doors is built before applying pressure. At temperatures of 65-80°F, sufficient strength will develop so that the stack may be removed from pressure after only 25 minutes, and *may be* trimmed only a few hours later. Low temperature bonding requires a longer press time because of slower curing time.

Some of the earlier work of Browne and Brouse was reported in Ref. 1 by Salzberg. Joints bonded with casein glue will average better than 90% wood failure when the following softer wood species are used: redwood, western red cedar, white fir, Sitka spruce, southern cypress, western hemlock, eastern red cedar, chestnut, red alder, and northern white pine. With the harder woods—red oak, maple, white ash, yellow birch, and persimmon-the joints will show 30-50% wood failure.

The highly alkaline casein-lime-sodium salt glues have a tendency to stain oak, maple, and some other species, a problem especially conspicuous in thin veneer. Discolored wood may be treated with sodium perborate and stained glue lines may be bleached with a dilute solution of oxalic acid. It is better, however, to avoid staining by preventing *bleed-through.* This may be accomplished by using drier stock, thicker glue, by releasing pressure sooner, and by drying the assembly immediately after pressing.

Durability of Casein Glues

In studies be Selbo and Johnson for Forest Products Laboratory, six types of joint designs, prepared with ten different adhesives, were subjected to three different humidity cycles over a period of three years. In maple wood joints bonded with casein glue containing preservative, the side grain-to-side grain joints retained the highest strength.

Although the dried casein glue line is hard and brittle, high frequency vibration of lap joints for 40 hours did not affect their strength. Glue lines 0.002 in. thick held up better than glue lines 0.002 in. thick, although initial shear strength was higher for the thinner glue lines.

Casein glue has a history of use as an adhesive for interior structural laminated products, beams, trusses, girders, and columns. As evidence of the durability of the bond, there are structures laminated with casein glue which have been standing since the 1930s. The durability of the casein bond on wood increases when the preservative sodium pentachloro-phenate is used to protect the glue line from the growth of fungi, a problem in the presence of conditions of heat and moisture. Selbo found that Douglas fir beams far outlasted Southern pine beams, both bonded with casein glue without preservative, perhaps because of the lower moisture content of the fir at the time of gluing.

At the Department of Forestry in Canada, it was determined that when a lamination bonded with casein glue is stored at an equilibrium moisture content of 15% or less there is an equal rate of loss of the strength of the glue line and the wood substance. At higher moisture contents the glue line failed sooner than the wood. This study resulted in the requirement by the Canadian Specifications Administration that structural laminates bonded with casein glue shall not be used for installations where atmospheric conditions produce a wood moisture content of more than 15%. Bergin has shown that for a casein glue line in yellow birch, the dry strength is not affected by a wide variation in temperature, but the ultimate wet strength is higher as the storage temperature is increased.

7.

Starch Based Adhesives

Starch is natural polymer, available in very large quantities and at relatively low and stable prices. It consists of glucose units chemically bound together so as to form a nonreducing polyhydroxy material. Because of the many hydroxyl groups, starch has a high affinity for polar substances such as water or cellulose. Starch can be reduced to low molecular weight sugars by enzymes called *amylases,* or by acid hydrolysis.

Some major changes in starch usage in adhesives and related fields are the large increase of cationic and amphoteric starches in paper manufacture and the increased use of high amylose starches in the corrugating industry.

The increased emphasis on recycling makes the use of starch desirable because amylases are able to degrade the starch with essentially no effect on the major part of the adherent matrix. There is a patent on the use of amylase as a release agent in starch glued materials recycling.

Most of the starch used in adhesives in the United States is produced from corn or maize. There are four commercially available starch types that are used in adhesives. These are *waxy corn starch, regular corn starch, high amylose type Vcorn starch,* and *high amylose type VII corn starch.* The major difference between these starches is in the amount of amylose contained in them-approximately 0, 28, 55, and 70%, respectively, by iodine titration. Other starches usable in adhesives include sorghum starch, potato starch, tapioca starch, wheat starch, rice starch, and sago starch. The term *sago* was originally applied to starch from the stem of *Metroxylon-type* palm trees, but is often used to describe starches from other palm trees, or even applied to some varieties of tapioca starch. Some characteristics of several commercially available starches are shown in Table 1.Regular corn starch consists of two major fractions that can be separated by precipitation with butanol under appropriate conditions. The fraction that precipitates out is called *amylose.* Amylose is essentially linear in form, stains blue with iodine solutions, tends to form a rigid gel from concentrated solutions or to precipitate from dilute solutions, and is about 95% digested by beta amylase (a test for strict linearity or lack of branching) when very carefully isolated. Amylose forms strong, water-resistant films when a solution is evaporated.

The other main fraction is called *amylopectin.* Amylopectin is highly branched (one branch every 14 to 27 glucose units), stains brown to purplish with iodine solutions, tends to remain in solution at room temperature, and is digested to about 55% by beta amylase. Amylopectin forms weak, water sensitive films.

Regular corn starch (when carefully fractionated) contains an additional *intermediate fraction.* This fraction is precipitated out of the original corn starch solution by butanol, but is not reprecipitated when water and butanol are added to the amylose fraction dissolved in dimethylsulfoxide. The intermediate fraction is precipitated by iodine from the various solutions, and is 5-7% of the starch in regular corn starch. The full analysis for regular corn starch is 25-27% fractionated amylose, 68% amylopectin, and 5-7% intermediate fraction.

Table 7.1. Commercial starches. Approximate Data and Ranges.

Starch	Corn	Wheat	Rice	Tapioca	Potato	Sago
Source	Seed	Seed	Seed	Root	Root	Pith
Granule size in diameter microns	5-26	3-35	3-8	5-35	15-100	10-70
Gelatinization Temp. (°C)	62-72	58-64	68-78	49-70	59-68	60-67
Amylose (%)	28	25	19	20	25	26
Amylose (DP)	480	-	-	1050	850	-
Amylopictin (DP)	1450	-	-	1300	2000	-

When *waxy corn starch* is carefully fractionated, 2% intermediate fraction is found. The remainder is amylopectin.

High amylose corn starches differ from regular corn starch in that the high amylose corn starches contain more amylose, much more intermediate fraction and much less amylopectin than regular corn starch. For example, a high amylose type VII starch having 70% amylose by iodine titration contained 63% recrystallized butanol complex (standard amylose), 31% intermediate fraction, and only 5% amylopectin. About half of the intermediate fraction is probably low molecular weight amylose (19,000) daltons. This low molecular weight amylose fraction may be responsible for some of the rapid bond formation noted in corrugating adhesives using high amylose starches. The standard amylose determination (70%) is not fully indicative of possible performance. A better analysis would be normal amylopectin 5%; low molecular weight, less branched amylopectin about 16%; high molecular weight amylose 63%. Total amylose is about 79%, and total amylopectin is about 21%.

Some of the true solution properties of starch appear to be related to the molecular weight of the amylose or amylopectin fractions. For example, the viscosity of jelly gums probably depends on the amylopectin molecular weight. The literature has tended to show increased molecular weights as the methods of isolating the fractions of starch and the methods of determining molecular weight have improved. Most literature indicates that amylose has a molecular weight of about 1,000,000 to 2,000,000 depending on its source, and amylopectin has a molecular weight of about 400,000,000. These are weight average molecular weights determined by light scattering experiments of the fractions with the starch dissolved in dimethylsufoxide. Commercially used starches probably have much lower molecular weights. For example, the amylopectin of one cultivarof potato starch was consistently determined to be 65,000,000, while the amylopectin from a second cultivar was just as consistently determined to be 440,000,000. A sample of waxy maize starch had a molecular weight of 400,000,000 but after shearing a 15% solution in ; boiling water the amylopectin molecular weight was determined to be 10,000,000. At high molecular weights the error of measurement becomes ; quite large. The error at 100,000,000 is ±10%, and at 500,000,000 the error is ±20%. The amylopectin from pea starch appears to be the highest recorded, being 1,5000,000,000 in one case.

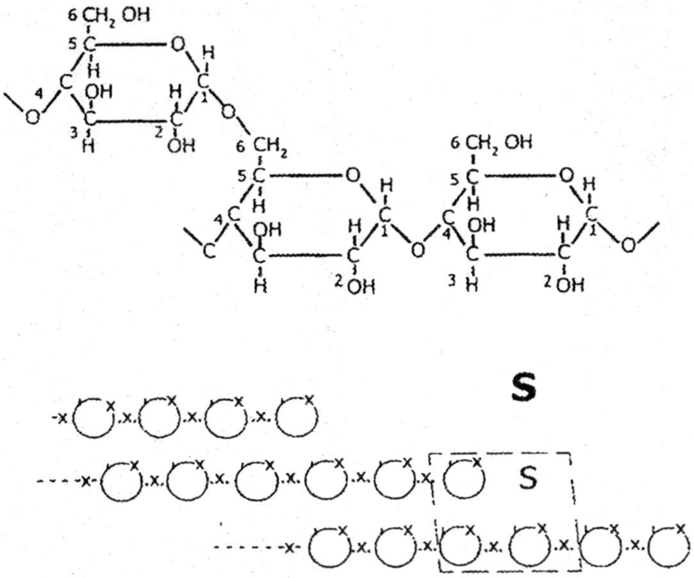

Fig. 7.1. Schematic representation of a segment of amylopectin molecule.

The terms *linear and branched were* used in the preceding discussion in describing amylose and amylopectin. Fig. 7.1 illustrates the way in which glucose units are linked together to form starch. Most of the glucose units in starch are linked in a (1-4) alpha-D-linkage. All of the linkages are of this type in amylose (theoretically at least). This is called the *linear polymer.* Amylopectin contains, in addition to the above linkage, a (l-6)-alpha-D-linkage once in about 25 glucose units. The 1-6 linkage is called a *branch point and* the linear extension of this branch point is called a *branch.* Amylopectin is therefore called a *branched polymer.* Many amyloses are able to hydrolyze at both the 1-4 and the 1-6 linkages, but beta amylose hydrolyzes only at the 1-4 linkage. Further, beta amylose is able to attack only at the no reducing end of the starch molecule, and hydrolyzes off one two-glucose unit at a time only if that units is linked 1-4 *(maltose).* Hence, the low digestion by beta amylase (65% in some commercial amylose) suggests an occasional short branch in all except the most highly purified samples.

When starch is suspended in water it tends to increase in volume and to absorb about its weight of water. If the temperature is slowly increased there is a point at which water absorption increase dramatically. The starch granule expands 10-100 times in volume depending on the type of starch. If the amount of starch present is greater than required to absorb all of the water available, then the viscosity of the starch dispersion becomes very heavy. The swollen granules can be partially destroyed by mechanical agitation, and the viscosity will decrease, depending on the type of starch. The temperature at which the starch suddenly swells when heated in water is called the *gelatinization temperature.*

The *unswollen starch* granule is in a crystalline stated and as such is anisotropic. Most of the starch granules are *birefringent* under the polarizing microscope, showing a "polatrization cross." These,disappear at or near the gelatinization temperature when heated in water, indicating a loss of crystal-linity. With further heating the granules tend to swell a little further, collapse to a degree, and fragment if sheared to any extent. Although some starches such as waxy starch, potato starch, tapioca starch, and sago starch cook to an almost clear suspension, the starch is not in solution. This can be seen by examining the starch cook with a phase contrast or interference contrast microscope, where the swollen granules or granule fragments are evident. Most starches start to swell at about 140-170°F (60-70°C), and appear to be reasonably dispersed at 203°F (95°C). In order to completely solubilize the starch a much higher temperature of 300-320°F(150-160°C) is required. Some granules in the high amylose starches tend to retain their polarization crosses above 212°F (100°C), but at the 300-320°F range these granules are also completely dissolved.

The cook texture of many starches can be explained by their composition. Waxy corn starch, which is all amylopectin, when heated at 8% starch solids in water becomes very heavy and cohesive as the granules swell. With continued heating, the viscosity decreases as the granules are broken up. On cooling, the viscosity increases. The texture remains cohesive, and the solution retains its clarity. This behaviour is typical when the amylopectin fraction dominates the cook characteristics. Regular corn starch, at the same solids, is much thinner, behaves like a short paste, and is quite cloudy when hot. On cooling, the cook becomes on opaque, rigid gel. In this case the amylose has modified the hot cook characteristics of the cooled cooked suspension. If the amylose has too high a molecular weight, then the gelling on cooling may not take place. Tapioca, potato, and sago starches behave more like waxy corn than corn, even though these are amylose containing starches. These amylose containing starches will set to firm gels if the starch is degraded with acid (see *fluidity starches}*. Many of the characteristics of common starches after cooking are given in Table 7.2.

Table 7.2. Cook Characteristics of Native Starches (cooked 1 part in 15 parts water at neutral pH).

Starch	Hot Cook Body	Hot Cook Visicodity	Viscisity on Prolonged Cooking	Gel Fornation on Cooking	Clarify (cold)
Corn	Short	Medium	Stable	Very high	Opaque
Wheat	Short	Relatively low	Stable	Very high	Opaque
Amioca	Stringy-cohesive	Moderately high	Thinning	Note	Fairly dear
Tapioca	Stringy-cohesive	High	Thinning	Very low	Quite clear
Sago	Stringy-cohesive	Moderately high	Thinning	Moderate	Fairly clear
Potato	Gummy, Very cohesive	Very high	Thinning	very low	Very clear

Likewise, many of the adhesive properties can be explained by reference to the amylose and amylopectin properties of the starch used. *Jelly gumsare* usually made from waxy starches (100% amylopectin) and are stable at room temperature for many months, as would be expected from the slow retrogradation rate of this starch. A corrugating formulation must set to form a bond and become water resistant in a short period of time. The low molecular weight portion of the amylose would be expected to come out of solution fairly rapidly to make a temporary bond, and the high molecular weight portion would more slowly tend to create water resistance.

Modification of Starches

The previous discussion was concerned almost exclusively with the use of native starches dispersed in water. The properties of the dispersions can be changed considerably by additives, or by modifying the starch. The principal modification in the adhesive industry is to decrease the molecular weight of the starch components so as to permit a higher solids content in the formulation. The starch is usually treated in granular form.

Fluidity Starches

Fluidity starches are made by hydrolyzing the starch in *dilute acid* below the gelatinization temperature of the starch. The range of fluidities is 20-90, with a 90 fluidity starch being very much thinner than a 20 fluidity. Fig. 2 gives an indication of the concentrations required to produce a given hot viscosity.

Oxidized Starches

A second modification to reduce viscosity is to treat the starch with *chlorine* under alkaline conditions. Lightly chlorinated starches use the water fluidity method of viscosity designation, but more heavily chlorinated products use a borax fluidity procedure. Chlorinated starches are generally called *oxidized starches.* They are *anionic,* in that they contain negative charges. This can be verified by staining with cationic dyes. *Methylene Blue* is a typical cationic dye.

Dextrinization

A third method of reducing viscosity is by the use of *dry heat,* usually in the presence of *acids.* This process produces *dextrins.* Their viscosity is also measured by using the *BF or borax fluidity method.* Dextrin viscosities are illustrated in Figs. 7.2,7. 3,7. 4. Other dextrin properties are given in Table 7.3.

Hydroxyethylation

Starch is treated with *ethylene oxide* under alkaline conditions. The major purpose is to *slow down retrogradation,* or precipitation of amylose from solutions of starch. This is effective because the amylose tends to be uniformly substituted, whereas amylopectin is substituted mainly near branch points.

Cationic Starches

Starch is reacted with *tertiary* or *quaternary amine halides* or *epoxides* under alkaline conditions. The cationic starches improve sheet strength, possibly through ionic bonding with slightly anionic paper. The cationic starches are also used in the bottle-labeling adhesives and in paperboard.

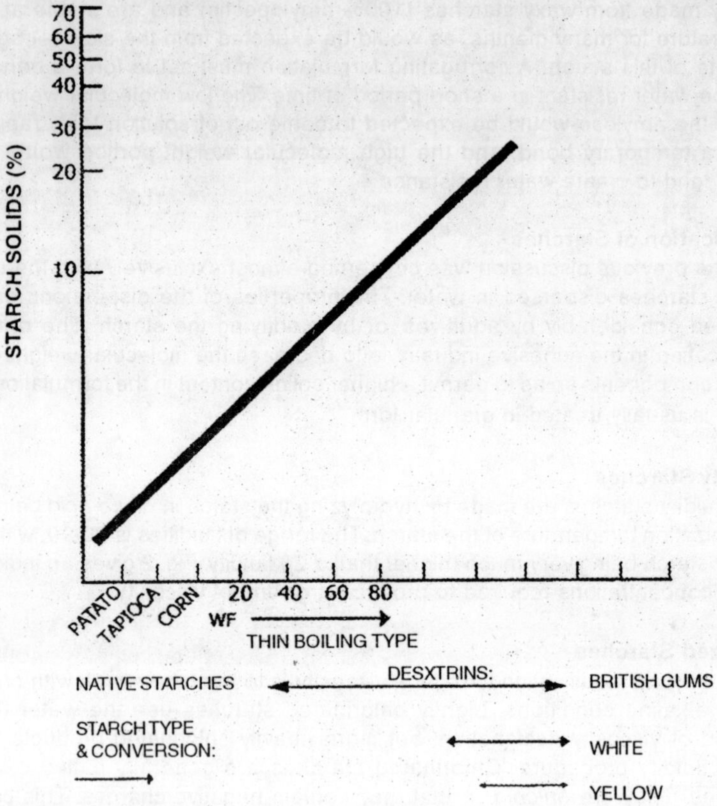

Fig. 7.2. Approximate concentrations of starch in thin flowing cooks (140°F)

Amphoteric Starches

Cationic starches are phosphated by heating with *orthophos-phateto* produce a starch with amphoteric (both cationic and anionic) properties. These starches offer improved pigment retention and dry strength over a wide pH range.

Miscellaneous Derivatives

These include *cross linked* or *inhibited* starches, *hydroxypropylated* starches, *phosphorylated* starches, starch succinates, grafted starches, and *carboxymethyl* starch.

Most of the formulations using starch adhesives appear to be obtained by Atrialth and error. The preceding listing of modifications and references is intended to enlarge the scope of possibilities for adhesive development. The discussion of the effects of amylose and amylopectin on starch dispersions serves a similar purpose.

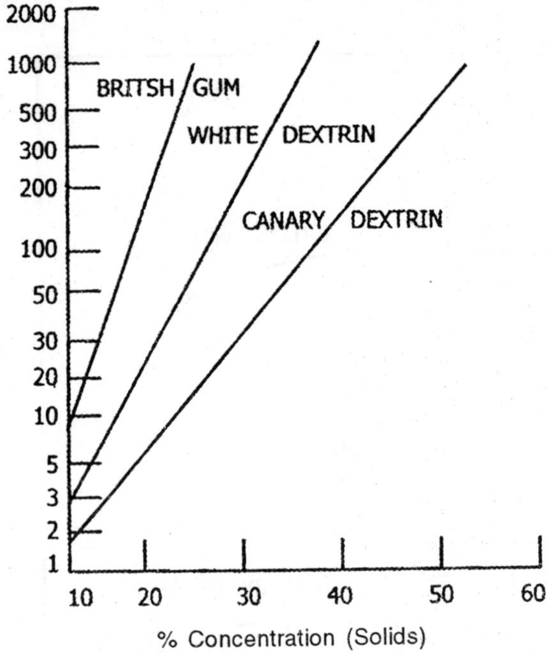

Fig. 7.3 Viscosity-concentration relationship of corm dextrins at 80⁰F

Table 7.3. Comparison of Dextrins.

Dry-roasting Process				Degree of Polymerization	Dextrin Properties	Cold water	
Dextrin	Acidity	Moisture	Temperature	(DPn)	Color	Swelling	Stability
White	high	high	low	20	white	Partial	Limited
Yellow or Canary	low	Low	Moderately high	20-500	Light	High	Good
British gums	Verylow -none	Very low	Moderately high to high	very wide range	Yellow to dark brown	Partial to complete	Good

Effect of Additives

Sodium Hydroxide

Sodium hydroxide (also called caustic soda) will increase tack, tend to solubilize the starch to a greater degree, increase viscosity, increase cohesiveness, and also increase colour. It is usually added after cooking in water, usually to the extent of about 0.5% based on total solids. The increase in *p*H tends to place negative charges on the starch, which tends to explain dispersion and higher viscosity.

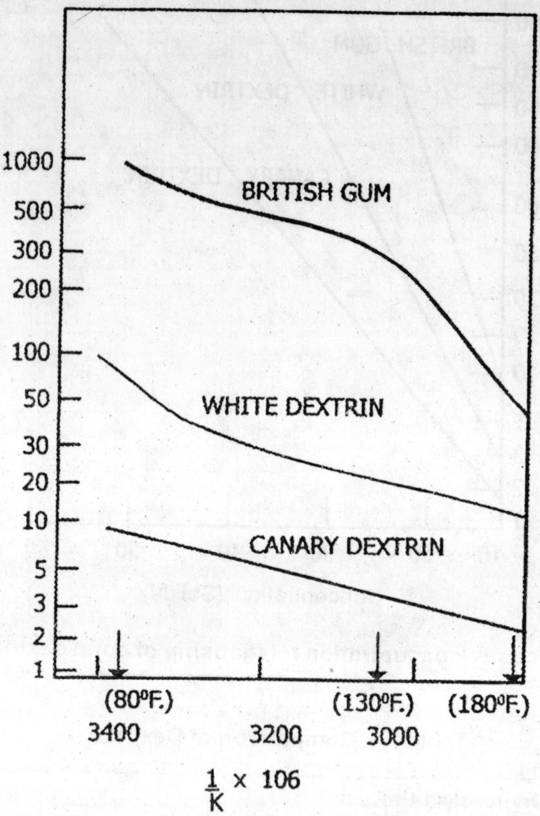

Fig. 7.4. Viscosity-temperature relationship of corn dextrins at 335% solids.

Borax

Borax (sodium tetraborate decahydrate) and sodium metaborate (essentially a mixture of borax and sodium hydroxide) change the properties of cooked starch dramatically. There is a large viscosity increase with increasing borax addition to about 15% (based on starch present); tack and cohesiveness are also increased greatly. Borax is used up to 10% based on starch and is usually added before cooking the starch. It acts by complexing with the starch to produce negative charges, and in addition tends to crosslink the starch. It is the *crosslinking* that causes the large increases in solution viscosity.

Urea

Urea is a *plasticizer* acts by forming solid solutions with starch and dextrins. The urea tends to prevent crystalization of the starch or dextrin when a film is dried. It is used at 1-10% based on starch present. Other chemicals with similar effects are *sodium nitrate, dicyanamide, salicyclic acid, thiocyanates, iodides, gunaidinium salts,* and *formaldehyde.* (Formaldehyde can also crosslink under acid conditions or be used as a preservative).

Glycerol

Glycerol acts as a *plasticizer by* slowing drying time, preventing excessive drying of a film. In this capacity it is a *humectant.* Other humectants are *ethylene-glycol, invert sugars, d-glucose,* and *sorbitol.*

Soluble Soaps

These are used as *lubricants to* impart flexibility regardless of atmospheric conditions. Too much lubricant will weaken adhesive bonds. Other lubricants are *sulfonated castor oil and sulfated alcohols.*

Urea-Formaldehyde Resin

This resin is added to give *water resistance. Resorcinol-formaldehyde, poly (vinylacetate), acrylics,* and *poly (vinyl alcohol) are* also used to increase water resistance.

Miscellaneous Additives

Clays and *bentonites are* used as *fillers' in* adhesives. *Sodium bisulfite, hydrogen peroxide, sodium perborate serve as bleaches. Solvents* are added to help wet water-repellent surfaces. *Preservatives* prevent foam during cooking. *Colloid stabilizers such* as soaps and *sodium chloride are* often added.

STARCH ADHESIVES

To be useful as an adhesive, starch must be dispersed in water, usually hot water, and a number of chemicals are added to modify the properties of the starch dispersion. The dispersion and formulation can be done by the user from the different types of starches of modifications of starches previously described. Or the user may purchase formulated adhesives from adhesives manufacturers.

Jelly Gums

These are used for *bottle labeling.* They are prepared by treating waxy starch or waxy fluidity starch with caustic under high shear. The starch swells in the caustic, and most of the caustic is neutralized with nitric acid. One formulation yields a final composition of 39% starch (40 fluidity waxy), 3% urea (an additive), 3% sodium nitrate (from the sodium hydroxide and nitric acid used), and 56% water (Ref. 10, p. 605). The viscosity as used is about 100,000 cP. The labels are cold water resistant.

Other Liquid Formulations

Alkaline starch formulations (prepared by adding enough caustic to gelatinize the starch) are used as carriers in *corrugating,* in *foil-to-paper* adhesives, and in *carton or case sealing* adhesives. If the caustic used to gelatinize the starch is neutralized, the adhesives at 18-25% starch solids are usable for *wall paper printing* or *foil-to-paper lamination.* Combinations of starches and water with added salts are the simplest adhesives, and can be used in *bill posting, bag making,* and *tobacco seam gluing.*

Pastes

Short, soft, nonstringy adhesives formulated from heavy bodied starches or dextrins are called *pastes.* A typical formulation for *library paste* is to cook a mixture of 45% low-soluble white dextrin, 5% corn starch, 5% glycerol, and 45% water.

Borated Dextrins

Dextrins are frequently formulated with borax, sodium metaborate, boric acid, or caustic in different proportions to give good tack and higher stable viscosities at moderate concentrations. The *ph* of the formulations is about 9.0 in most cases. Borated dextrins find use in case sealing, carton sealing, tube winding, and laminating.

White Dextrins

White dextrins are prepared by heating dry starch containing relatively large amounts of *add at low temperatures* (258°F, 120°C) for rather short times (3-7 hours). Their colour is white to cream, and their solubility and viscosity varies from low to high. They are used in *bag-seam, tube winding, case and carton sealing, laminating, gummed sheets, label,* and *envelope back seam* adhesives.

Canary Dextrins

Canary dextrins are prepared by heating dry starch containing a moderate amount of acid at moderate temperatures (300°F, 149°C) for a moderate time (11 hours). They are very light to dark tan in color, have a high cold water solubility, a low stable viscosity, and excellent remoistening ability. They are used in *gummed tape, envelope front seals, stamps, case and carton sealing, laminating and tube winding.*

British Gums

British gums are prepared by heating dry starch with a low amount of acid at high temperature (330°F, 166°C) for a long time (17 hours). They have low to high solubilities and low to high stable viscosities, dark color, and fast tack. They are used in *solid fiber laminating, bag-seam pastes,* and *winding* adhesives.

Waxy Starch Dextrins

Waxy starch dextrins are similar to dextrins made from non-waxy starch, but have a greater viscosity stability than the corresponding regular dextrin. *Envelope front seals, stamps,* and *gummed sheets are* some uses.

Dextrin/Silicate Blends

Fast tack, rigid films, low viscosity, and very good adhesion are obtained from this combination. *High speed case sealing and fiber foil cans are* some uses.

Pregelatinized Starches

Pregelatinized starches are prepared by heat swelling a starch water slurry, drying, and grinding the dry powder. The starch at 40% solids is fed to a steam-heated drum where it is gelatinized and dried, and finally scraped off the drum with a blade. These starches are used in some one-tank *corrugating applications, multiwall paper bags, wallpaper,* and *bill posting.*

Application Areas

Papermaking

Cationic, anionic, and *amphoteric* starch derivatives are cooked and added at the wet end of the papermaking machine at 5-20 pounds perton of paper. The starch flocculates pigments and fine pulp particles, improves retention of fines, helps drainage, and increases internal (Scott bond) and burst (Mullen) strengths. The starches are retained by the pulp because the pulp has a slight negative charge, which holds the positively charged starch. The positive charge is present directly in the cationic and amphoteric starches, and is formed by complexing with alum in the case of anionic starches.

Unmodified starch is also used at 20-40 pounds per ton of pulp. It is retained mainly by entrapment.

Although starch is largely added at the wet end of the paper machine, it can be placed directly on the formed sheet. The starch can be sprayed onto the fibers, applied as foam directly on the wet web. These alternative methods have certain advantages, but they lose the flocculating ability of cationic or amphoteric starches.

Paper Coating

In addition to adding starch at the wet end to hold the fibers together, starch can be added at the *size press,* at the size press with a pigment, at the *calender stack,* or as a pigmented coating as a separate operation. In all of the above applications, starch acts to bind the paper fibers together or to bind the pigment particles together or to bind the pigment to the fiber. The paper has been partially dried at the size press. The viscosity of the starch solution must be relatively low (50 cP) at the size press. The 2-12% solids used in coatings would have too high a viscosity. Therefore a viscosity reduction is usually necessary. This can be accomplished by enzymes or heat treatment in the case of regular starches, or oxidized, hydroxyethylated, acid fluidity, or acetylated acid fluidity starches can be used.

Oxidized starches are anionic, and if recycled may cause pigment and fines retention problems in the wet end. *Cationic starch* which has been preconverted to a low viscosity appears to have advantages in physical properties of the paper and in retention of the surface sized broke.

Starch is added at the calender stack for curl control, surface strength, laying of surface fuzz, clay coating holdout, printing characteristics, and grease or oil resistance. Solids vary from 2 to 24%, depending on the starch type used and on the paper requirements. Low viscosity starches, hydroxyethylated converted starches, and oxidized starches are used in this application.

Similar starches to those used on the size press can be used in *pigment binding* applications, but the viscosity of the starch should be lower. A possible formulation for a 59% solids coating is 0.2% sodium hexametaphosphate, 10.1%

calcium carbonate, 40.5% clay, 8.1% low viscosity starch, 0.05% pine oil, and 0.21% soap. Thin boiling cationic starch has also been recommended for this application.[12] The same starches as are used above can be used when starch is added with pigmental the size press. Solids are generally 30-40%, and the starch to pigment ratio can be as high as 1 to 1. The viscosity is usually below 300 cP.

Corrugating

Most of the corrugated board is made using the Stein Hall system, which consists of a mixture of gelatinized starch (called the carrier starch) and ungelatinized starch. Flat corrugating medium is fluted, starch is applied to the fluted tips, and a heated finer is brought in contact with the fluted tips under heat and pressure to produce a single facer. Adhesive is applied to the fluted tips on the other side of the corrugating medium and a flat liner called a double backer liner is applied. When the facers are brought in contact with the flutes containing the adhesive, the ungelatinized starch gelatinizes. This creates an extremely high viscosity at the flute-liner interface. The applied heat also evaporates water and further increases the flute-liner bond, so that the corrugated board can be cut without delaminating. The formulation includes sodium hydroxide and borax to decrease the gelatinization temperature of the raw starch and to increase viscosity at the flute after gelatinization.

A typical old formulation is: put 13 parts water, 3.2 parts starch, 0.54 parts caustic dissolved in 0.8 parts water into a tank (called tank 1, or the upper tank), heat with steam to 160°F, agitate 15 minutes, and then add 16 parts cold water. This gelatinizes the starch present and makes the carrier starch portion of the adhesive. In another tank (called tank 2, or the lower tank) 49 parts cold water is mixed with 0.54 parts borsx and 18 parts starch is added. The contents of tank 1 are slowly added to tank 2 with efficient mixing. It is possible to carry the entire operation out in tank 2, but control is more difficult.

So called *no-carrier*-or single-component systems depend on careful control to gelatinize the correct proportion of the granules present. One formulation, which increases water resistance by adding urea-formaldehyde, is: mix 20 parts starch, 77 parts water, 0.8 parts 50% caustic, and stir at 101°F until the viscosity reaches 25 Stein Hall seconds. Then add 0.04 parts alum, 0.4 parts boric acid, and 3 parts 60% urea-formaldehyde resin. Other ways to make "no-carrier" systems are to add exactly the correct amount of caustic and stop the swelling by carefully injecting steam into the mixture; or partially swell the granules by milling a 10-40% moisture starch to damage granules before suspending in water. A chemical-mechanical method of producing the carrier starch is to introduce a mixture of 12% starch and 30% caustic into a centrifugal pump. Final alkalinity was 14.4% and the viscosity was 4200 cP. at 76°F. The use of starches having different gelatinization temperatures is given in Ref. 14. Here 350 parts tapioca starch and 3000 parts corn starch are suspended in 9000 parts water and treated with 500 parts of borax are added. The Stein Hall viscosity is 52 seconds, and the gel point is 63°C (145°F). The tapioca starch swells before the corn starch, and essentially produces the two-component system.

High amylose starches improve water resistance and increase speed of corrugation. A formula for the carrier starch is: 1192 parts water, 424 parts high amylose starch, 6 parts borax: bring to 130°F (54°C) and add with stirring a mixture of 36.6 parts caustic in 47.5 parts water. The raw starch portion is made by mixing 3480 parts water, 1600 parts corn starch, 28 parts borax and 91.2 parts thermosetting resin. Mix the carrier into the raw starch.

It appears, at least in the case of high amylose carrier starch, that the carrier starch is the principal adhesive. The raw starch, when gelatinized, absorbs water to concentrate the dispersed high amylose starch on the flutes. Older ideas of the mechanism were that the carrier starch was simply a suspending agent for the raw starch, which was the principal adhesive. One suggestion was that amylose migrating out of the granules caused at least the initial tack.

There are many publications on the use of high amylose starches. High amylose starch is esterified with *acetic anhydride or sucdnic anhydride*to improve stability. Another patent concerns the addition of *dihydroxyethyleneurea* together with *acetone-formaldehyde to* improve water resistance.

The use of high amylose starches in the production of *cold corrugating* adhe-sives (not requiring extensive heating) has been published. A mixture of oxidized and hydrolyzed 70% amylose containing starches is dispersed as a 35% starch suspension, gelatinized at 140°C, and used in corrugating without steam. The high amylose starch was treated with 4% sodium hypochlorite at an initial *p*H 11 to make part A of the degraded mixture. Part B was made by hydrolyzing high amylose starch for 12 hours at 50°C (122°F) with 6% of 35% hydrochloric acid. Both A and B were neutralized to pH 5, washed, filtered, and dried Then 70% A and 30% B were mixed to a 35% suspension and cooked at 140°C. The use of the B portion is claimed to improve speed from 90 m/min to 230 m/min.

Mixtures of waxy, regular, and high amylose starches are degraded with a mixture of sodium persulfate, sodium sulfate, boric acid, and caustic, and cooked at 90°C (194°F) and about 33% solids to form a starch adhesive that hardens on cooling. The cold corrugating process is described in other references.

Other claims for improving corrugating formulations include increasing the carrier starch solids, addition of urea, using crosslinked starch in the carrier, and using cationic starch as the carrier starch.

Bag Adhesives

Three adhesives are used in paper bag manufacture: side seam adhesives, bottom paste adhesives, and cross pastes. The *side seam adhesive* is used to form a cylinder form a flat sheet of paper. This adhesive must develop a strong bond quickly, so the tube can be cut for further operation. The viscosity should be about 3,000 cP. and solids about 25%. One formulation is: water 68%; heat to 160°F(71°C), add 3% preservative.[4] A *water-resistant* formulation is: water 1700 pounds, white dextrin 700, soap 2, urea-formaldehyde 70, heat at 200°F (93°C), dilute with cold water to 260 gal volume, and add 14 pounds ammonium chloride. The formulation should be used immediately. Its *p*H is about 6.

Bottom paste adhesives are applied to one end of the tube formed above to close that end to form a bag bottom. These pastes are usually made from unconverted starches. Soap and/or salt may be added to produce a *thixotropic* paste (flows under shear but sets up if left undisturbed). A water resistance formulation is corn starch 13%, poly (vinylalcohol) 4.5%, poly (vinylacetate) 1%, soap 0.1%, water 81%, heat to 90°C (194°F), cool to room temperature.

Cross pastels used for multiwall bags to glue the plies together before forming a tube. This is similar to seam paste, but should not penetrate the ply. Clay or poly (vinylacetate) is added to prevent penetration. The seam *adhesive for* multiwall bags can be somewhat heavier than given above, and higher molecular weight white dextrins can be employed. The *bottom adhesive* is usually a fluidity starch. A mechanical way of converting potato starch for use in paper bags is also described.

Laminating Adhesives

The requirements of the particular equipment must be met for bonding paper to paper or to paperboard, for making poster displays, bonding paperboard to paper-board, or rotary lamination. *Lay-flat,* or *noncurling,* is an important attribute of these adhesives. High tack and low penetration are also required. One formulation is water 43%, high soluble white dextrin 21%, corn starch 4%, sodium nitrate 32%; heat to 200°F (93°C), hold 20 minutes, add preservative. Another formulation is high soluble white dextrin 20%, clay 13.5%, urea 6.7%, borax 5%, water 55%.

Foil laminations usually call for resins, but even here a small amount of starch is often added for its smoothing properties. One example is: poly (vinyl - alcohol) 3, starch 3, water 49, potassium persulfate 0.1; add dropwise a mixture of 5 dibutyl phthalate and 39 vinyl acetate at 70°C (158°F), dilute to 25% solids. Starch at 3-15% is claimed to prevent coarse particle formation in the following formulation: 45% aqueous emulsion containing 1:99 acrylic acid: vinyl acetate copolymer 100, corn starch 4, poly (vinylalcohol) 5, dibutyl phthalate 1.5 Aluminum foil was coated on paper at 300 m/min (meters per minute) without coarse particle formation, while a similar formulation omitting the starch formed coarse particles at 90 m/min.

Tube Winding

Tube winding is either *spiral* (a continuous winding where adhesive is applied to outer plies as they are wrapped on a cylindrical mandrel), or *convolute* (where the sheet is as wide as the mandrel is long, and the mandrel wraps the sheet over itself). The tube is removed from the mandrel by a pusher arm. Convolute adhesives are usually used cold, while spiral adhesives may be used at 131°F (55°C). Many starch products may be used, but 50% solids borated dextrins are common, as seen in Table 7.4.

Corrugated Boxes

The tops and bottoms of corrugated boxes are closed with *case sealing adhesive.* Although liquid glues and hot melts are preferred, carton adhesives are used, sometimes with added caustic. Carton sealing involves bonding the bottom and top flaps of folded paper boxes. A top bottom carton sealing adhesive is water 51%, white dextrin 37%, preservative 1%, borax 6%, antifoam 0.06%; cook to 185°F (85°C) for 20 minutes, cool to 120°F (49°C), add 5 water and 0.6 of 50% caustic.

Gummed Tapes

The types of remoistenable tapes are regular sealing tapes, reinforced sealing tapes, and box tapes. A regular sealing tape formulation is: thin boiling waxy sealing tape formulation is: thin boiling waxy starch 39.5, canary dextrin 17, poly-acrylamide 2, dispersing agent 0.4, water 41.1 is suggested. *Box tape* is usually made from animal glue, but one patent claims performance superior to animal glue from a starch acrylamide graft copolymer prepared as follows: water 51%, sodium nitrate 7%, waxy corn starch 33%, copper sulfate 0.03%, acrylamide 10%; mix, then add 0.05% ammonium persulfate and 0.03% sodium metabisulfate; heat rapidly to 200°F (93°C) and maintain for 15 minutes. Add sodium tartrate to adjust pH to 5.5.

The use of an oxidized starch acetate 180, urea 20, and water 200 as a gummed tape adhesive has been patented. The formulation of an acrylamide starch graft polymer is also claimed: hydrolyzed low viscosity acrylamide-starch graft copolymer 67, canary dextrin 20, animal glue 10, urea 10, petrolatum 0.25, and sodium hexametaphosphate 0.1, are heated for 3 minutes at 185-205°F (85-96°C).

Label and Envelope Adhesives

The general adhesives for these uses can be found in Table 4. Dextrins, enzyme-converted starches, or mechanically degraded starches are suitable, with white or canary dextrins made from tapioca, waxy corn, and regular corn starches the most used. The *envelope front seam* is *remoistenable and* can have 55-65% solids with a viscosity of 2,000-10,000 cP. After drying the adhesive should be non-blocking at high humidity. This requires a *nonhygroscopic plasticizer.* One formulation containing poly (ethylene glycol) is high soluble waxy corn dextrin 63, sodium bisulfite 1, Carbowax 4,000 (Union Carbide) 0.5, water 35.5. Backseam adhesives can be a little thinner with viscosities close to 1000 cP, and 40-50% solids.

Discrete particle, flat gumming, solvent-based adhesives are another method of making remoistenable adhesives. The cold-water-soluble material (usually a dextrin) is suspended in a solvent and applied to the paper and dried. Since the dextrin is not soluble in the solvent, it is deposited in discrete particles. On contact with water, the dextrin swells and will glue two pieces of paper together. The dextrin is usually used at 40% solids and a viscosity of 1000 cP.

Paper Box

Paper box manufacture involves the operations of *ending* (box body formation), *stripping* (coating the box walls with precut wrap and smoothing), *tight wrap* (machine wrapping a box with glue on most of the wrap), and *loose wrapping (adhesive* only on border of the wrap). Borated dextrins containing 10-15% borax and cooked at 30-50% solids are usually used. See Table 4 for more information.

Textiles

Starch is used predominantly in *warp sizing* in the textile field. The purpose is to strengthen the yarns for weaving operations. A typical formulation is corn starch 8.5%, softener (tallow or sulfonated oil) 1.5%, kerosene 0.2%, rook to 190°F (88°C), and homogenize at 2000 psi. Oxidized starches are used in finishing and printing, and low treatment starch acetates, starch monophosphate blended with poly (vinyl alcohol), cationic and amphoteric starches, as well as fluidity starches are used in finishing and warp sizing.

Table 7.4. Adhesive in Packaging Application.

Use, Fuction Type of Adhesive	Major Reqiurements	Acceptable Adhesives Sase	Approximate Solids (%)	Viscosity Requirement (cps) (Brookfield Spindle/RPM/°F)
Bag Adhesive :				
Cross pasting	Tacky and quick setting	Srarch-dextrin mineral filler	25-30	
Seam adhesive	well machining slower	Starch or borated dextrin	5-39	2800 (RV 44/20/80)
Bag bottom pastes	Heavy, short	Raw starches or comverted borax	15-300	
Laminating :				
Mounting	Rapid tack, good open time, nonwarp	Dextrin and low viscosity starches	50	3800(RV 4/20/75)
Rotary laminating	High tack	While dextrin with urea or sodium nitrate	55	4000 (VR 4/20/80)
Foil laminating	Adhesion to foil	Alkaline flues resoms (PVAC)[a]	60	2700 (RV 4/20/75)
Tube winding	Tough fast bond	Borated dextrin	48	2500 (RV 4/20/80)
Corrugated Box :				
Manufacture's Joint adhesive	Rapid tack, good open	PVC,[a] Hot-melt time PVOH[b]	60	2000 (RV 4/200/75)
Built-up pad adhesives	Nonwarp	Dextrin borated dextrin	35-36	1000 (RV 3/20/75))
Case seal adhesive	Very fast, nonwarp	Canary dextrin Borated white dextrin resin	40-50	
Tray maker adhesive	Rapid setting	PVAC[a] Hot-melt	59	800/1000 (RV 4/20/80)
Set-up Box :				
Machine laminating	Quick setting, nonwarping	Animal glue and suger, canary dextrin	70	
Hand laminating	Lay flat	Borated whote dextrin	48	
Ender pastes	Good flow and tack	borated dextrin	50	400 (RV 4/70/80)
Lable Adhesive :				
Porous substrate adhesive	Thin white	Borated dextrin		30 350 (RV 4/70/80)
Plastic container	Adhesion and high tack	PVC[a] (High modified starch)	52	4000 (RV 4/20/80)
Can labeling	Tack and adhesion	Converted starch	33	4000 (RV 6/20/72)
Glass bottle	High tack	Jelly gums dextrin	40-50	

Note : [a]PVAC = polyvinylacetate
[b]PVOH = polyvinyl alcohol

Wall Covering Adhesives

These require good wet tack and good slip. Plasticizers give slip (the ability to move the paper around to obtain a good fit), borax gives tack, and clay allows easier removal of the paper later. A formulation consists of acid modified pregelled starch 25, clay 20, urea 3.75, sodium metaborate 1.25, and water 50. A repolymers is: dry blend carboxymethyl cellulose 25, hydroxyethyl cellulose 8.5, sodium algi-nate 0.5, anionic polyacrylamide 0.3, urea 30, potato starch 27, colloidal silica 1, sodium stearate 2.5, sodium soap 3.5, sodium fluoride 0.5, and 4-chloro-meta-cresol 1. The mixture is suspended in 3 parts water, coated on paper and dried. A second formulation is: starch 375, carboxymethyl cellulose 400, urea 200, polyacrylamide 5, colloidal silica 5, parachloro-meta-cresol 10, sodium fluoride 5. An *inverted emulsion* formulation containing a starch graft copolymer has also been suggested for wallpaper adhesives.

Miscellaneous Uses

Gelatinized starch 100, dextrin 100 is used to make fish good stable in water. A 1:1 mixture of starch and polyacrylamide was used to make and adhesive for *high voltage transformers.* A mixture of poly (vinyl acetate) emulsion 100, plasticizer 20, and starch 20 has been used in *bookbinding.*

Governmental Regulations: Additives

The food and Drug Administration (PDA) of the U.S. Department of Health, Education and Welfare (HEW) has issued a series of regulations concerning the use of potentially toxic substances in packaging materials contacting food. Most of the regulations may be found in the Code of Federal Regulations, Title 21, revised annually (21 CFR 121.2520, “Adhesive”).

8.

Neoprene (Polychloroprene) Based Solvent and Latex Adhesives

Neoprene, or *polychloroprene,* was the first synthetic elastomer used by the adhesives in dusty, and is one of the most versatile materials ever developed as a backbone for elastomeric adhesives. Neoprene combines rapid bond strength development with good tack or auto-adhesion, and resistance to degradation by oils, chemicals water, heat, sunlight, and ozone. It is popular in numerous areas such as shoe sole attachment, furniture construction, automobile assembly, and a variety of construction applications.

History

Neoprene was the first synthetic elastomer developed which had many of the properties of natural rubber. Its development began when Dr. Nieuwland of Notre Dame synthesized divinyl acetylene from acetylene using CuCl as a catalyst. DuPont scientists, learning of his research, joined Dr. Nieuwland in pursuing the possibility of producing a synthetic elastomer from acetylene chemistry. In the late 1902s, they found that by varying the reaction conditions, monovinylacetylene could be readily prepared, with divinylacetylene present only as an impurity. They also discovered that monovinylacetylene could be reacted with hydrochloric acid to form *chloroprene,* 2-chloro- 1,3-butadiene, which formed a rubberlike polymer upon polymerization.

The first public announcement of this polymer was made in 1931; commercialization began in April 1932. At first known as "DuPrene," the polymer was designated "Neoprene" by DuPont in 1936.

Prior to the second World War, natural rubber was the only elastomer widely used in adhesives. It was used for such applications as tire building, adhering of sponge weatherstirps to automobile doors, and the temporary attachment of shoe soles. However, rubber cements were limited by their low cohesive strength and poor aging of the uncured film.

Following its development in 1931, DuPont Neoprene was slow in displacing natural rubber in the adhesive industry for the following reasons:

1. It was high in price, selling for two or three times the price of natural rubber.
2. It had to be dissolved in aromatic solvents, which were several times as costly as the petroleum naphtha used to dissolve natural rubber.
3. It was necessary to use about five times as much Neoprene as natural rubber to obtain equivalent viscosities.

The situation did not change until 1942, soon after the start of World War II.

At that time, a critical shortage of natural rubber developed because it was allocated! chiefly for the war effort. Neoprene was chosen as a replacement for natural rubber in adhesives because it was the only other synthetic rubber available. Animal glue and other water-soluble materials available at the time were unsatisfactory because of their slow drying rates, poor adhesion to many surfaces, inflexible films, and rusting of metals. The two Neoprene GN, a general purpose type, and Neoprene CG, a fast-crystallizing type. Both are copolymers of chloroprene and sulfur which contain a thiuram disulfide modifier.

One of the first applications in which Neoprene proved satisfactory was in the shoe industry, for both temporary and permanent sole attachment. However, early Neoprene cements were plagued by two problems: a decrease in viscosity on ageing and a black discoloration during storage in steel drums.

The Effect of Polymer Structure

Neoprene is produced from the chloroprene monomer, 2-chloro-l,3-butadiene in an emulsion process. During polymerization, the monomer can add in a number of ways as shown in Table 1. The proportion of each configuration determines the amount of *crystallinity* in the polymer and its reactivity.

Table 8.1. Molecular Structure of Neoprene

Chloroprene Monomer

C1
I
CH2 = C - CH = CH2

Type of Addition	Formula
trans-1,4	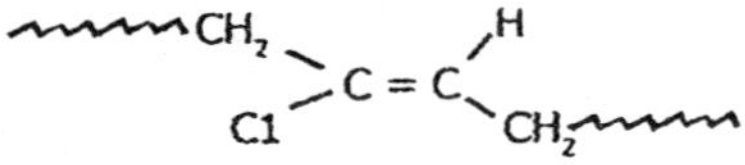
cis-1,4	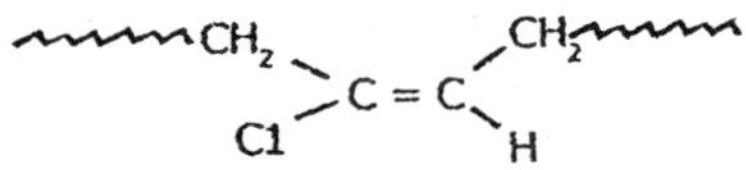
1.2	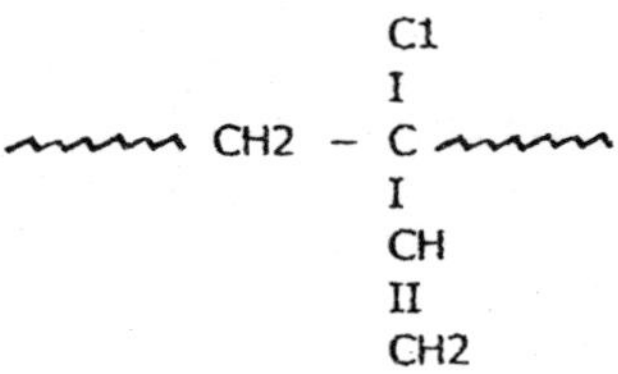
3,4	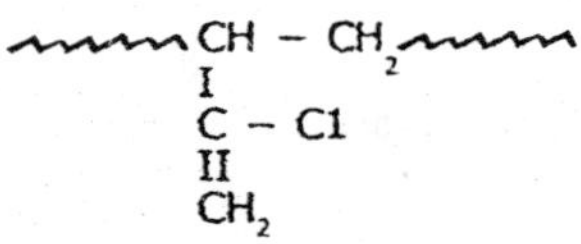

The *trans-1,4* addition is the most common. Very high percentages of this structure give high crystallinity and rapid bond strength development in contact adhe-sives. Neoprene AC and AD, both fast crystallizing grades, contain about 90% *trans*-1,4 structures; whereas Neoprene W, a slow-crystallizing type, contains only 85% *trans-1,4*. The other three types of monomer addition shown decrease bond strength development and lengthen open time by disrupting polymer crystallinity. In addition, the 1,2 structure provides active sites for polymer vulcanization.

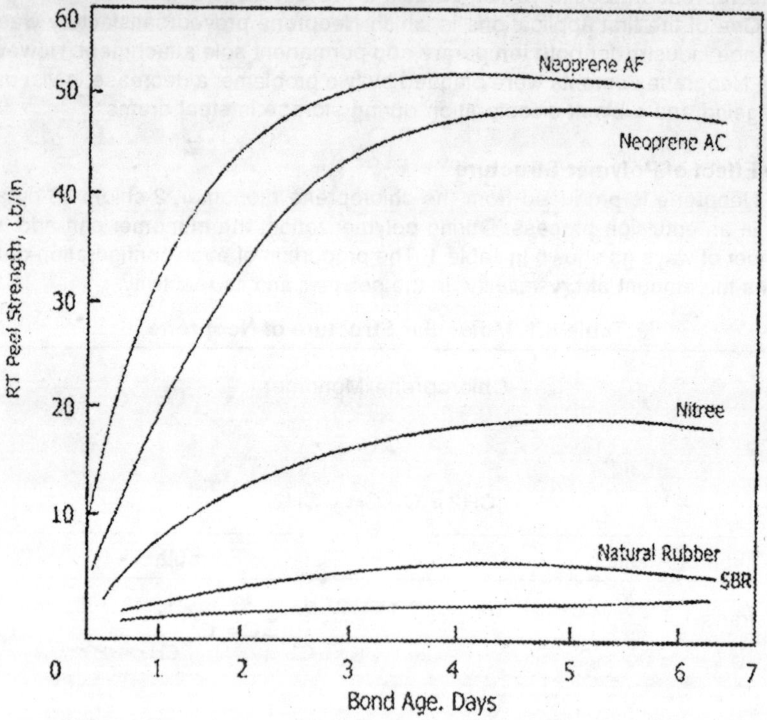

Fig. 8.1. Canvas/ Canvas bond strength development: neoprene vs. other elastomer

The ability of Neoprene adhesives to crystallize sets them apart from other elas-tomeric binders. As a result of crystallization, their cohesive film strength is much greater than that of amorphous polymers. Crystallization is a reversible phenomenon, and at temperatures over 52°C (126°F) uncured adhesives lose their high cohesive strength. Upon cooling, the film recrystallizes and cohesive strength is regained. A comparison of Neoprene AD, a fast-crystallizing type, and Neoprene AF, a reactive polymer, with several other elastomers is shown in Fig. 8.1. In addition to high film strength, crystallization is responsible for the *quick grab* for which Neoprene adhesives are noted. This rapid bond strength development allows the formation of immediate dry bonds without the need for further clamping, pressing or airing. Since Neoprene polymers are produced which crystallize at various rates, the adhesive compounder can use polymer blends to get the balance of properties he requires. The effect of crystallanity on polymer properties is summarized in Fig. 8.2.

The Neoprene polymers also vary in the amount of branching present in the polymer. Those which have little or no branching are referred to as *sol polymers,* while those with considerable branching are referred to as *gel polymers.* All of the solvent grade polymers, with the exception of Neoprene AG, are sol polymers. They are highly linear and soluble in aromatic solvents. The Neoprene latexes, on the other hand, vary widely in the percentage of polymer gel. As shown in Fig. 8.3, properties which are affected by the amount of gel in the polymer include cohesive strength, resilience, resistance to permanent set, elongation, open tack time and oil swell. Thus, particularly in latex systems, varying the gel content of the system through polymer choice offers another means of adjusting adhesive properties.

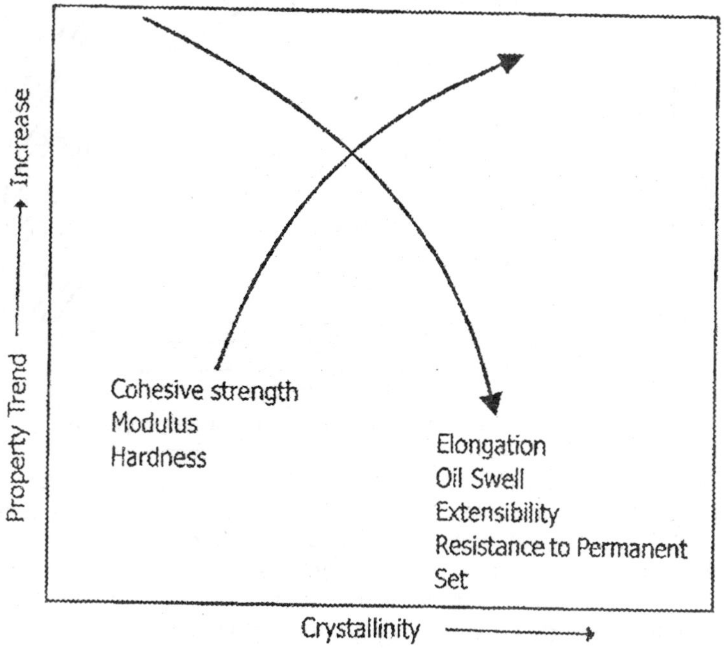

Fig. 8.2. Effect of crystalling on polymer properties

Neoprene Solvent Based Adhesive Cement

Neoprene provides a versatile elastomeric base in the formulation of solvent based adhesives. Properly compounded adhesives are resistant to degradation from exposure to heat, sunlight, ozone, water, oils, and chemicals. Neoprene can be dissolved in may solvent blends to give adhesive solutions which are stable for extended periods of time. Solvent selection, therefore, allows a great deal of variation in adhesive viscosity and drying rate. Other compounding ingredients, particularly resins, are used to achieve good specific adhesion to many porous and nonporous substrates. The compounding versatility associated with Neoprene adhesives allows the formulation of one-part contact cements, two-part curable adhesive, pressure-sensitive adhesives, and mastics and caulks.

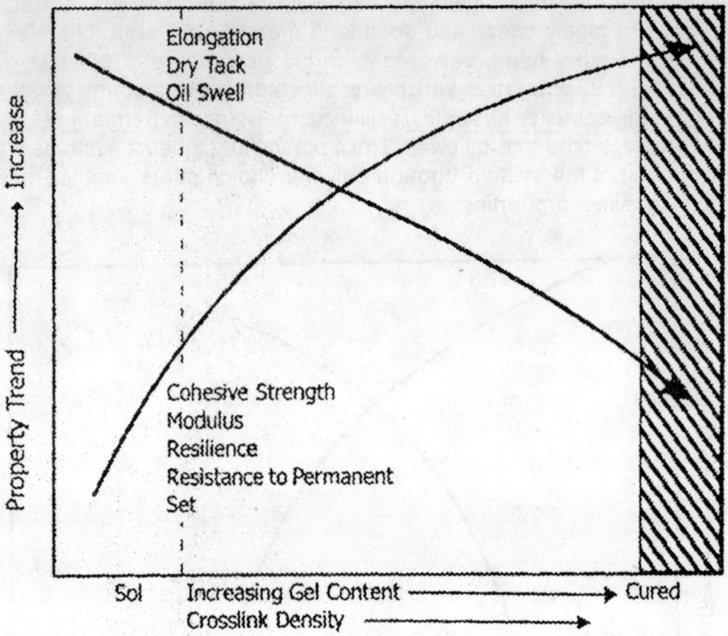

Fig. 8.3. Effect of sol, gel and curing on polymer properties.

Types of Neoprene

The principal types of Neoprene used in solvent adhesives are summarized in Table 3, along with their physical properties. Neoprene AC and AD are considered the general purpose adhesive types. Because they crystallize rapidly, both give, quick grab and high uncured strength. When properly formulated, they also give good application properties and resistance to heat and phasing. Most adhesive manufacturers prefer Neoprene AD over Neoprene AC because it offers superior viscosity stability in both raw polymer and adhesive form.

The fast crystallizing types are widely used in shoe sole attachment, adhering decorative high pressure laminates and automotive trim and in many other industrial applications. A general purpose adhesive formulation is presented in Table 8.2.

Neoprene AD-G is a Neoprene AD variant designed especially for use in grafting applications, although it is suitable for use in standard contact bond formulations as well. In the shoe industry, Neoprene AD-G is generally grafted with methyl methacrylate using a compound and procedure similar to that shown in Table 4. The resulting graft polymer has very good adhesion to plasticized PVC. EVA sponge, thermoplastic rubber, and other difficult-to-bond substrates. The principal use of graft adhesives is in isocyanate-crosslinked cements for shoe sole attachment. Neoprene AD-G differs from standard Neoprene AD in that it provides better brushability at equal viscosity and solids content and a longer pot life in two-part systems.

Table 8.2. Neoprene Contact Bond Adhesive

General	Parts	Typical Formula	Parts
Neoprene	100	Mill Mix	
Magnesium oxide	4-8	Neoprene Ad	100
Zinc oxide	5	Magnesium oxide	8
Antioxidant	2	Zinc oxide	5
Resins	as reqiured	Antioxidant	
Solvents	as reqiured		
		Chrun Mix	
		Milled stock	115
T-Butyl phenolic resin	45		
		water	1
		Tuluene / Hexane / Actone (2/4/4 by volume)	640

Table 8.3.
Peoperties of Dupont Neoprene Type Used in Solvent Adhesive.

Type of Neoprene	Characteristics	Specific Gravity	Rate of Crystallization	Grade	ML 1 + 4 at 100°C (2120F)	5% Solids in toluene, cps
AC	General purpose elastomer with fast bond strength development, good stability and cohesive strength	1.23	Very Fast	Soft	*	331-45
				Medium	*	46-63
				Hard	*	64-100
AD	General purpose elastomer with fast bond strength development and good cohesive strenth, Provides better viscosity stability than Neoprene AC.	1.23	Very fast	AD10	*	25-34
			AD20	*	35-53	
				AD30	*	54-75
				AD40	*	76-115
AD-G	Similar to Neoprene AD but gives smoother less stringy solutions and longer pot-life in isocyanate cured systems.	1.23	very fast			28-46
AF	Very slow-crystallinzing, curing elastomer, Bond strength and longer pot	1.23	very fast			145-275[a]

	life in isocyanate cured system.					
AG	High gel elastomer which give thixotropic solution with good application propeties even at high solids content.	1.23	Does not crystallize		>80	*
AH	Acrylic copolymer of chloroprene which forms colloidal dispersions in hydrocarbon solvents good application properties at high solids	1.23	Does not crystallize		*	<175⁰
FB	High viscosity, fluid elastomer.	1.23	slow		*	5000.000-1,300,000⁰
GN	Sulfer-modified elastomer with low cohesive strength and fast cure rate at room temperature.	1.23	Slow		44-65	*
GNA	Silimer to Neopreme GN but contains astaining antioxidant.	1.23	Slow		41-65	*
GRT	Similar to Neoprene GN but with a very slow crystallinzation rate	1.23	very slow		36-55	*
W	General purpose elastomer with good tack. Lower cohesive strength than Neoprene AC or AD.	1.23	slow		42-51	*
WHV	Similar to Neoprene W.	1.23	Slow	WHV-1000 WHV	90-105 1006-125	* *
WHV-A	Similar to Neoprene WHV but designed specifically for adhesives. Gives betterresistance to phasting and more reproducible solution viscosity.	1.23	Slow	*	52-85	
WRT	Similar to Neoprene W vut with very slow rate of crystallinzation.	1.23	very slow		41-51	*

*Not sold to this specification.
*Viscosity at 200% solids in a milled adhesive formulation.
*Viscodity of fluid polymer at 500C (1220F).

Adhesives based on Neoprene AF, a reactive copolymer of chloroprene and methacrylic acid, are characterized by faster bond strength development increased heat resistance, and better resistance to phasing than the fast crystalliz- ing types. However, because of its reactivity, the use of Neoprene AF requires special attention to processing, compounding, and raw polymer inventory control. If it is substituted directly into a formulation based on Neoprene AC or AD, the results may be disappointing.

The improved bond strength development and hot strength of Neoprene AF results from the interaction of its polymer carboxyl functionality with metal oxides. Its crystallization rate is very slow and plays no significant role in cohesive strength development.

Table 8.4. Adhesives Based on Graft Polymers of Neopreneand Methyl Methacrylate.

Formulation	*Parts*
Neoprene AD-G	100
Methyl methacrylate	100
Benzoyl peroxide (50% dispersion)	1
Antioxidant	2
Toluene	472
Methyl ethyl ketone	118

Procedure:

1. Slowly heat solution of Neoprene AD-G, methyl methacrylate, toluene, and MEK in a closed reactor vessel to 60°C (140°F).
2. Add benzoyl peroxide to initiate polymerization.
3. Continue heating to 80°C (176°F). React at 80°C (176°F) for 2-8 hours.
4. Add antioxidant to terminate the polymerization.

In compounding Neoprene AF adhesives the polymer interaction with metal oxides must be considered. Variables which are important include resin, type, solvent system, water content, polymer heat history and the order of addition of compounding ingredients. A typical Neoprene AF formulation is shown in Table 5. A comparison of the bond properties of Neoprene AF and Neoprene AD is shown in Table 8.6.

Brief milling of Neoprene AF, on a cool mill, is suggested to break down a light, gel-like association which builds up as the polymer ages and prevents preparation of a smooth solution under low shear conditions. Overmilling (past five minutes) will lead to Increased solution viscosity and poor solution stability.

Neoprene AG is a gel polymer which exhibits a high degree of thixotropy and provides improved application properties in both low viscosity sprayable adhesives and in high solids, high viscosity mastics. Mastics based on Neoprene AG have a nonstringy, buttery consistency and can be easily applied by troweling or extruding. Because they are highly thixotropic, they resist slump after application.

Table 8.5. Neoprene AF Formulation

Formulation	*Parts*
Mill Mix	100
Neoprene AF (5 min break down) Antioxidant	2
Magnesium oxide	8
Zinc oxide	5
Churn Mix[3]	
Milled stock	115
t-Butyl phenolic resin	40
Water	1
Solvent	610[b]

[a]Gelation can be minimized if the milled stock is added to a predissolved resin and solvent solution.
[b]A blend of aromatic/aliphatic/oxygenated solvents is used. Aproximately 20% of an oxygenated solvent is required for god solution stability.

Neoprene AG is often blended with Neoprene WHV-A or Neoprene AC or AD to adjust mastic properties. Blends with Neoprene AC or AD give increased shear strength but extrude less easily and provide less slump resistance. Blends with Neoprene WHV-A decrease cost and increase tack at the expense of both application properties and shear strength. A comparison of Neoprene AG and AC in a mastic formulation is presented in Table 8.7.

Mastics based on Neoprene AG can be prepared in a sigma blade mixer from polymer which has first been preswollen in solvent. Milling is not required to produce smooth, non-stringy products.

In low solids formulations, the gel structure of Neoprene AG provides improved spray performance compared to products based on other Neoprene types. Properly formulated compositions can be sprayed in uniform patterns with no cobwebbing at low atomization pressures (<70 psi). Preferred solvent systems for sprayable compositions fall in the range of 3.5-5.5 hydrogen bonding index and 7.5-9.8 solubility parameter. A low atomixation pressure, sprayable adhesive formulation is presented in Table 8. To obtain the best application properties, either milling or high shear processing is required to break up loose gel agglomerates in the polymer.

Neoprene AG is compounded like Neoprene AC and AD. However, formulations based on Neoprene AG give lower ultimate cohesive strength, specific adhesion, and open tack time than the fast crystallizing types. For this reason, Neoprene AG is often blended with Neoprene AC or AD to lengthen tack time and to obtain better substrate wetting and subsequently higher peel strength.

Neoprene AH is an acrylic copolymer of chloroprene which forms a colloidal dispersion when peptized in aliphatic solvents. The use of aliphatic solvents alone, without toluene or ketones, offers the advantages of low cost, acceptability under Rule 66, and the capability to bond substrates such as polystyrene which are sensitive to aromatic or ketone solvents.

Table 8. 6. Adhesive Properties: Neoprene AF vs. Neoprene AD.[a]

	Neoprene AF Pulled at R.T.	Neoprene AD Pulled at R.T.	Neoprene AF Pulled at 100°C (212°F)	Neoprene AD Pulled at 100°C (212°F)
Adhesive Properties				
Bond Strength Development,				
Canvas/canvas peel,pli				
After 1 hr at R.T.	16	1		
After 2 hr at R.T.	20	2		
After 4 hr at R.T.	24	4		
After 6 hr at R.T.	26	8		
After 1 day at R.T.	32	32		
After 7 days at R.T.			13	3
Adhesion to Various Substrates After 14 days at R.T, pli				
Canvas	39	38	18	1
Aluminum	30	26	16	0.5
Maple	30	21	15	0.5
Decorative laminate	38	37	13	1
Composition soling	40	37	7	0.5
Stainless steel	28	25	15	1

The stability of the dispersion is due to steric stabilization of the acrylic portion of the polymer in the solvent. The dispersion nature of Neoprene AH systems allows the formulation of high solids, low viscosity adhesives with excellent application properties. The separability of formulations with solids contents as high as 50% (2500 cps) is good, exhibiting none of the cobwebbing normally seen in Neoprene systems. The open tack time of Neoprene AH is shorter than that of the other types, generally around fifteen minutes.

Table 8.7. Neoprene Mastic Compound.

Formulation	*Parts*
Neoprene	100
Antioxidant	2
Magnesiumoxide	4
Zinc oxide	5
Treatred calcium carbonate	100
Ethylene glycol	2
t-Butyl phenolic resin	20
Terpene phenolic resin	15
Hexane/MEK/Toluene to 60% solids (5/3/2 by weight)	

Polymer Type	Neoprene AG	Neoprene AC
Slumpc after 20 min, inches	0.0	2.9
Extrusion Rate, b g / 5 sec		
At R.T.	70	19
Shear strength at R.T.,		
Plywood / plywood, psi		
After 3 says at R.T.	150*	140
After 7 days at R.T.	240*	250*
After 14 days at R.T.	240*	320*
shear strength at R.T.,		
Maple / maple, psi		
After 3 days at R.T.	40	38
After 7 days at R.T.	140	156
After 14 days at R.T.	160	250

*Indicates wood failure. All other failures were adhesive
cFlow measured on 1.5 in. drain; 3/8- in. -thick adhesive sample on a vertical surface.
dExtruded at 50 psi, 1/8-in. orifice
e1/16-in. glueline tested at ½ in./ min.

The preparation of a stable dispersion is the key requirement to obtaining dispersion is the key requirement to obtaining a stable adhesive system. Neoprene AH should be peptized in a low-napthenic, aliphatic hydrocarbon solvent. The suggested peptization system consists of the peptizing agent tetraethylthiuram disul-fide activated by Vanax 552 as is shown in the adhesive formulation presented in Table 8.9. The dispersion should be prepared under, shear the degree of which affects the time to disperse and the final viscosity. The time to make a 40% dispersion varies from about 30 minutes in a high-shear Silverson Mixer to a few hours in a Struthers-Wells churn.

Other Neoprene polymers which find use in solvent adhesives are Neoprene WHV-A, Neoprene GN and Neoprene FB. Both Neoprene FB and Neoprene GN are suflur-modified types which can be mechanically or chemically peptized to reduce molecular weight if desired. Both exhibit a faster cure rate than the fast crystallizing types and can be used in formulations which are intended as either two-part adhesives or curable compositions. Neoprene FB differs from the other solvent types in that it is a viscous, pourable fluid at 50°C (122°F) which can be used in the formulation of 100% solids caulks and sealants. Neoprene WHV-A, *a* member of the W-family of polymers, is a slow-crystallizing, high molecular weight polymer which is generally used in blends with lower molecular weight crystallizing types to increase solution viscosity. As a minor component in such blends, it will not have too adverse an effect on bond strength development.

Table 8.8. Sprayable Formulation Based on Neoprene AG.

Formulation	Parts
Mill Mix	
Neoprene AG	100
Antioxidant	2
Magnesium oxide	8
Zinc oxide	5
Churn Mix	
Milled stock	115
t-Butyl phenolic resin	40
Water	1
MEK/ Cyclihexane	620

Table 8.9. Neoprene AH Formulation.

Furmulation	Parts
Disperse by churn mixing:	
Neoprene AH	100
Heptane	150
Tetraethylthiuram disulfide	0.5
Vanax 552[a]	0.5
Add the following to the above dispersion::	
t-Butyl phenolic resin	20-40
Tackifier	0-20
Magnesium oxide	2
Zinc coxide	4
Antioxidant	2
Water	1

[a]Piperidinium pentamethlene disthiocarbamate.

Antioxidants

The presence of a good antioxidant is essential in all adhesive formulations for adequate protection against oxidative breakdown and acid tendering os substrates. Octylated diphenylamine antioxidants, such as Agerite Stalite S, afford the best protection but can be used only in applications where staining is of no concern. If discoloration can not be tolerated, a non staining hindered bisphenol such as Wingstay L (Goodyear) or Antioxidant 2246 (American Cyanamid) should be used. Two parts of an antioxidant is generally sufficient. For very demanding applications higher amounts may be advisable.The hindered bisphenol antioxidants, while useful for minimizing staining, can present problems in some formulations. For example, milled stocks containing some hindered bisphenols such as Santowhite Crystals (Monsanto) have relatively short bin stability. On aging, for as little as one week at 38°C (100°F), the stock may not make a smooth solution. If the stocks are dissolved within two or three days of million, no problems are normally encountered. Antioxidant 2246 (American Cyanamid) has been known to create color problems: a pink discoloration in latexes, a bluish or blue-green discoloration in some solvent systems, particularly those based on chlorinated solvents.

Metal Oxides

Metal oxides serve several functions in Neoprene adhesives as shown below:

Role of Metal Oxides

Acid acceptor	ZnO, MgO
Scorch retarder	MgO
Curing agent	ZnO, MgO
f-Butyl phenolic resin reactant	MgO

The prime function is that of an acid acceptor. Small amounts of HCl are released as Neoprene films age. The HCl must be absorbed by the adhesive to prevent substrate degradation. This is particularly important when the adhesive is applied to acid-sensitive materials such as rayon or cotton. Both magnesium oxide and zinc oxide function as acid acceptors. A combination of the two is more effective than either alone.

Magnesium oxide serves a second function as processing stabilizer. It is mill mixed with Neoprene before adding zinc oxide to retard scorch during processing.

Metal oxides also act as curing agents in adhesive films. Zinc oxide is the most effective, leading to increased strength as the bond line ages. At higher levels (20-40 phr) magnesium oxide also is effective, particularly if the bond is briefly exposed to elevated temperatures.

As will be discussed in the section on resins, metal oxides also react in solution with f-butyl phenolic resins. The reaction product, an infusible metal resinate, increases the heat resisaance of adhesive films. Although oxides of calcium, lead, and lithium also exhibit reactivity, magnesium oxide is the most useful and widely used reactant.

Generally about five parts of zinc oxide and four to eight parts of magnesium oxide are used in adhesives with 40 phr resin. Four parts of the magnesium oxide are included to act as an acid acceptor and to retard scorch. An additional four parts are included as resin reactant if the adhesive system contains a f-butyl phenolic resin.

There has been some interest in reducing or eliminating metal oxides in adhesive films in order to produce clear adhesives. The amount of magnesium oxide should not be reduced below that required to react fully with the f-butyl phenolic resin. Epoxy resins and zinc resinate have been used in place of zinc oxide as add acceptors, but are not as efficient. Some sacrifice in tendering resistance must be acceptable, therefore, if a clear adhesive is desired. At least

2 phr of an antioxidant is essential to obtain the best possible tendering resistance.

Resins

The choice of which resin to use in a given solvent adhesive application is of great importance. Resins serve to improve specific adhesion and autohesion, obtain longer tack retention and increase hot cohesive strength. The most widely used family of resins are the *paratertiary butylphenolics.* These resins give much higher heat resistance than other types of resins with similar melting points. This high heat resistance is due to their reactivity with the magnesium oxide present in Neoprene adhesive systems. The magnesium oxide resinate or resin salt is infusible. It has no melting point, and decomposes above 200°C (392°F). It therefore reduces the ther-moplasticity of the system, providing good bond strength up to 8°C (176°F) or higher in properly formulated adhesives. The resinate also increases adhesive bond strength development by accelerating solvent release. A comparison of f-butyl phenolics with other resins in Neoprene AD and AH adhesives is shown in Tables 8.10 and 8.11.

The f-butyl phenolic resins are generally used at levels between 35 and 50 phr. The optimum level for most adhesive applications is 40-45 phr, which provides a good balance of take can heat resistance. Lower levels are useful when the required level of adhesion is relatively low and a soft glueline is desirable. Higher levels of resin are used when the demand for good adhesion is high, such as in metal-to-metal bonding. The variation in open tack time and hot bond strength with increasing f-butyl phenolic resin content is shown in Fig. 8.4. at R.T.

Approximately 10 parts of magnesium oxide are required to react completely with 100 parts of resin. This is equivalent to 4 parts of magnesium oxide in a solution containing 100 parts Neoprene and 40 of resin. The reaction takes place at room temperature and requires the presence of water as a catalyst. Although there is generally enough water in the solvent system to ensure reactivity, it is common practice to add 1-2 parts of water by weight of resin to the formulation.

The solvent system used has a strong effect on the rate of the magnesium oxide and resin reaction. In toluene the reaction is very fast, reaching completion in one hour. In polar solvents the reaction proceeds more slowly, as shown in Table 12. In cases where the solvent system contains a high percentage of polar solvents, it may be advisable to prereact the resin in the nonoxygen-containing component of the blend to ensure the reaction reaches completion.

The use of f-butyl phenolic resins is essential in compounding Neoprene AF for maximum viscosity stability and the best balance of adhesion properties. This class of resins helps stabilize the carboxyl functionality of Neoprene AF in solution. The magnesia-tertiary butyl phenolic resin complex reacts with the polymer carboxyl groups as shown in Fig. 18.5, preventing gelation of the polymer with the metal oxide alone. Increased resin level are particularly effective in stabilizing compounds which are formulated for maximum heat resistance and contain high level of magnesium oxide.

Neoprene adhesives containing metal oxides and f-butyl phenolic resins may separate on standing into a clear upper layer and a lower layer of flocculated metal oxides. This separation, called *phasing,* may occur in days or months. Once an adhesive has phased, it must be agitated before use to obtain full utility of the metal oxides.

Table 8.10. Effect of Resin Type on Heat Resistance.

Based Compound	Parts
Neoprene AD-20 (10 min breakdown)	100
magnesium	4
Zinc oxide	5
Antioxidant	2
Resin	As shown
Water	1
Hexane	100
Toluene	400

Resin selection	A	B	C	D	E	F	G	H
t-butyl phenolic resin	46	-	33	33	-	33	-	33
Hydrocarbon resin	-	25	22	-	-	-	-	-
Rosin ester	-	-	-	22	-	-	-	
Terpene	-	-	-	-	65	22	-	-
Solids content, %	24	21	25	25	26	25	26	26
Canvas / canvas bond strength at R.T., pli[b]								
After 1 day at R.T.	31A	10C	12C	14C	10C	18C	16C	32C
After 7 days at R.T.	46A	25A	36A	42A	4F	23A	30A	40A
Canvas / canvas blood strength at 80°C (176°F), pli								
After 7 days at R.T.	5.5	0.5	0.5	0.5	0.5	0.5	0.5	00.2

aMagnesium oxide reacted.

bA = adhesive failure, C = cohesive failure, F = failure between films.

It is theorized that phasing is due to insufficient dispersion stability of the metal oxides, resulting from low molecular weight portions in commercial resins which are not large enough to prevent particle attraction and agglomeration when adsorbed on the metal oxide surface. Commercial f-butyl phenolic resins with a number average weight of 900-1200 can contain as much as 10-15% by weight of material having a molecular weight less than 500. By increasing the average molecular weight of commercial f-butyl phenolic resins from 900 to 1600 and fractionating out the low molecular weight portion, DuPont workers were able to produce cements that did not phase. A series of experiments conducts by a team of workers at Hitachi Chemical Co4. confirmed this and demonstrated further that phasing was caused primarily by various dialcohols such as *p-tert-buty* phenol dialcohol (BPDA). The DuPont and Hitachi work led to the development of so-called *nonphasing resins* (i.e., Schenectady's SP-154, and Union Carbide's CK-1636). In addition to resin choice, the formulator interested in minimizing phasing must also consider the type of Neoprene, solvent system, solids content, milling , time, etc.

Table 8.11. Effect of Resin Type of Neoprene AH Hot Bond Strength.[a]

Adhesive Properties	Resin Ester	Terpene Phenolic	t-Butyl Phenolic Resin Low Reactivity	t-Butyl Phenolic Resin High Reactivity
Bond strength after 1 day at R.T. pli				
Tested at R.T.	8C	21C	34C	42A
Tested at 600C (1400F)	-	--	18C	28C
Tested at 800C (1760F)	-	-	6C	16C
Tested at 1000C (2120F)	0.3C	0.8C	2.5C	7C
Open tack time, paper to steel, min	60	16	10-14	4-8

[a]Based on formulation Table 9 with 40 phr of resin.
C = cohesive failure, A = adhesive failure.

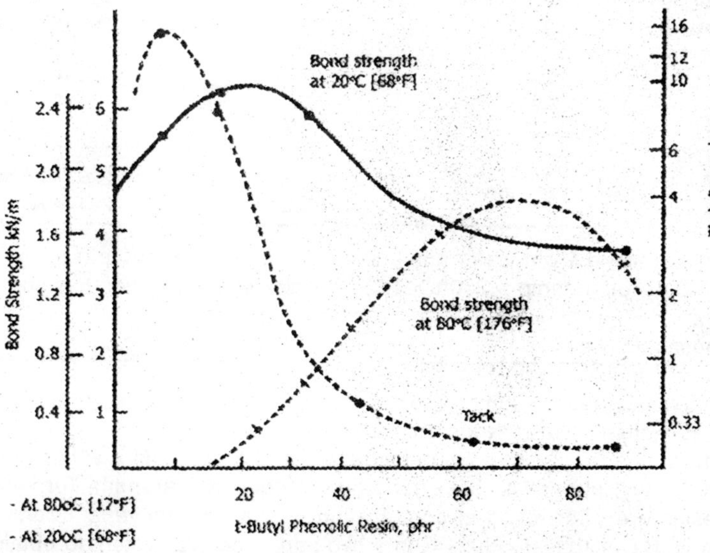

Fig. 8.4. Effect of t-butyl phenolic resin level on open tack time and heat resistance

Table 8.12. Effect of Solvent Blend on the Rate of the Magnesium Oxide/Resin Reaction.[3]

Solvent	*Reaction Time, hr*	*Ash Content of Reacted Resin, %b*	*Melt ofDecomp. Temp,of Reacted Resin, °C(°F)*
Toluene	1	6.5	250 (482)Dc
	24	6.8	258 (496) D
	96	6.7	252 (486) D
Tol/ ethyl acetate / hexane	24	6.9	255 (491) D
(1/ 1/ 1 by weight)	96	7.1	255 (491) D
Toluene / hexane	24	6.9	264 (507) D
(1/ 2 by weight)			
Hexane	24	7.0	252 (486) D
Acetone	24	0.4	181 (358) M
Hexane / MEK	24	0.4	125 (257) M
(1 / 1 by weight)	48	2.9	130 (255) M
	72	6.1	226 (439) M
	96	6.2	224 (435) M

[a]Formulation contained 1 phr water and about 10 phr MgO per 100 phr resin.
[b]> 6% ash and decomp. temp > 2500C (4820F) indicates the reaction has gone to completion
[c]D = decomosed, M = melted

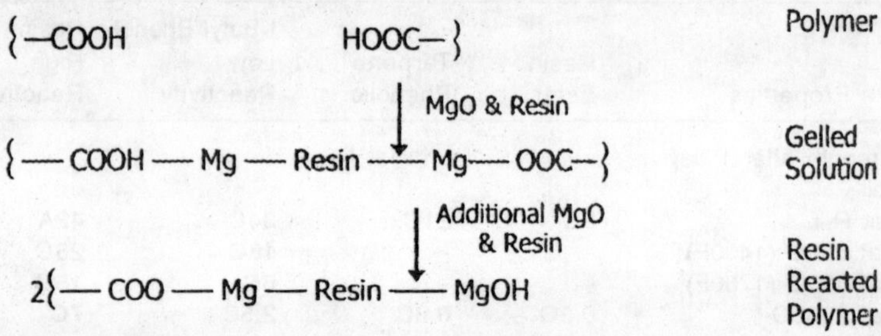

Fig. 5. Magnesia and tertiary butyl phenolic interaction with polymer acid. (The resin should be added before or at the same time as the MgO to prevent gelation during mixing.)

Terpene phenolic resin, such as Schenectady's SP-560 or Occidental's Durez 12603, are also often used in Neoprene adhesives. They are non reactive and thermoplastic in nature and so provide longer open tack time and a softer glue line than the f-butyl phenolics, but offer less hot cohesive strength. Terpene phenolic resins are often used in combination with a *polyisocyanate* curing agent, such as Bayer's Desmodur RF, in a two-part adhesive system to obtain better hot bond strength.

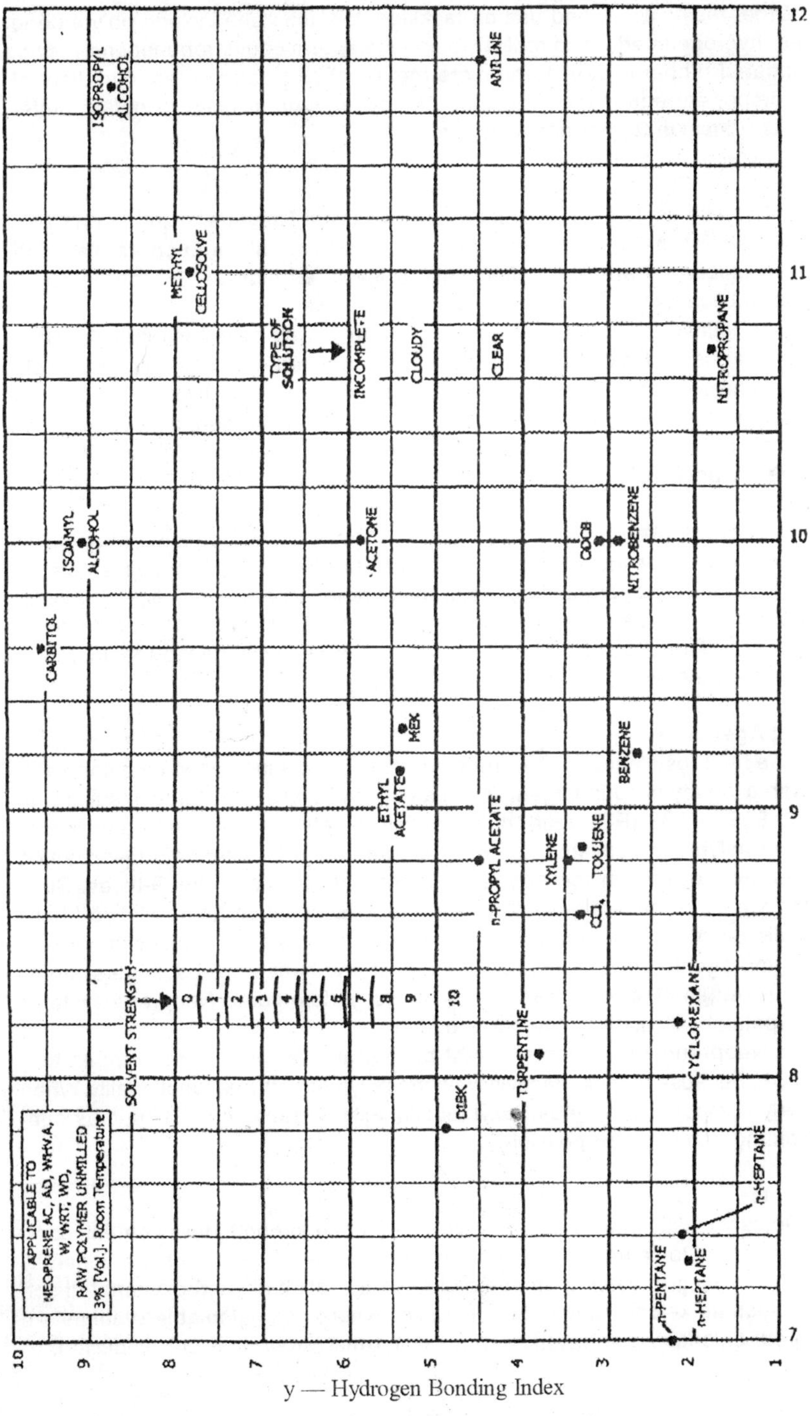

Fig. 8.6. Solvent strength chart

Other resins which find use as tackifiers for Neoprene include polyterpene resins, hydrogenated wood rosins, rosin esters, and coumarone-indene resins. Chlorinated rubber is use[H] to promote metal adhesion and as an ingredient of two-component adhesives. Poly-alphamethyl styrene is used to obtain better specific adhesion to thermoplastic rubber.

Fillers

Fillers find limited use in Neoprene adhesives. They are included primarily to reduce cost in high solids mastics. Conventional fillers such as clay and calcium carbonate are used effectively at levels as high as 250 phr in some mastic applications.

The optimum filler concentration in Neoprene AG based mastics depends on the filler used. Maximum bond strength is obtained with fillers of low particle size (~ 5 micron) and intermediate oil absorption (30 g/100 g filler); mastic extrusion rate and slump increase with decreasing filler absorption, almost independently of filler particle size.[6] Increasing the level of the treated calcium carbonate in Table 7 above 100 phr causes the mastic to slump and the impact resistance to decrease.

In general, fillers reduce the specific adhesion and cohesive strength of adhesive films. For these reasons, they are rarely used in low solids contact adhesives. In some formulations, e.g., Neoprene-terpene phenolics, the inclusion of a fine particle size reinforcing silica such as HiSil 233 (PPG Industries) will increase film strength. This effect is lost in formulations using reacted magnesium resinate systems.

Curing Agents

The heat resistance of Neoprene cements can be increased by compounding with a variety of curing agents such as thiocarbanilide, mixtures of sulfur with Vanax 808 or 833 (R.T. Vanderbilt), triethyl trimethylene triamine, and monomeric or polymeric isocyanates. Room temperature cure rates with these curing agents are slower with the A-types of Neoprene than with the G-types. Such systems are not generally employed in the U.S. because heat-reactive f-butyl phenolic resins provide equivalent or better heat resistance. Solutions containing curing agents are also relatively unstable and hence two-package systems are required. In other countries, however, isocyanate-cured Neoprene systems are popular, particularly in the shoe industry.

In Neoprene AF systems, metal oxides act as rapid room temperature curatives because of their reactivity with the polymer carboxyl functionality. When properly compounded, the carboxyl functionality is stable in solution; thus one-part curing cements are possible.

Solvents

Solvent choice affects adhesive viscosity, bond strength development, open time, cost, and to some degree ultimate strength. Trisolvent blends are generally used, consisting of varying amounts of aromatic, aliphatic and oxygenated solvents such as ketones and esters. In cases where non flammable systems are required, chlorinated solvents such as 1, 1,1-trichloroethane are employed.

Table 8.13. Properties of Commonly uses Neoprene Solvents.

Solvent	*Molecular Wt*	*Solubility Parameter*	*Hydrogen Bonding Index (HB)*	*Relative Evapora-tion Rate*[a]	*Flash Point °F*[b]	*Max. Allowable Concentration ppm*[c]	*Viscosity, cps at 20°C (68°F)*
Acetone	58.08	10.0	5.9	1160	15	1000	0.35
Cyclohexane	84.16	8.2	2.2	720	40	300	1.06
Ethyl acetate	88.10	9.1	5.2	615	45	400	0.44
Heptane	100.20	7.4	2.2	386	25	500	0.42
Hexane	86.17	7.3	2.1	1000	–25	500	0.29
Isopropyl alcohol	60.09	11.5	8.7	300	70	400	2.41
Methyl ethyl ketone	72.10	9.3	5.4	572	35	200	0.42
Pentane	72.15	7.0	2.2	2860	<–50	500	0.24
Toluene	92.13	8.9	3.3	240	44	100	0.59
Xylene	106.16	8.8	3.5	63	80	100	0.69
V.M. & P Naphtha	*	7.6	2.5	275	48	500	*

[a]n-Butyl acetate = 100.
[b]Cleveland Open Cup Method.
[c]Maximum allowable concentration in air where men work 8 hr/day "Dangerous

A graphical method can he used to predict the utility of solvent blends in adhesives based on Neoprene. It is based on using the solubility parameter (Š) and the hydrogen bonding index (y) of each constituent solvent to predict that of the blend. The Š and y of blends are additive according to their volume proportions.

Once the solubility parameter and hydrogen bonding index of the blend has been determined, the blend can be positioned on the chart shown in Fig. 8.6. Solvents or blends which fall within the kidney shaped area will yield smooth, free-flowing solutions with all solvent grade types except Neoprene AH. Those which fall outside the kidney shape will not dissolve Neoprene. If a particular solvent blend fall in the shady area it may or may not be suitable depending on the amount of true solvent (e.g., toluene) in the blend.

The evaporation rates of common solvents are also shown in Table 8.13. Because the open tack time of an adhesive is partially dependent on the evaporation rate of the solvent system, this property can be controlled to some degree through solvent selection. Small percentages of xylene (< 5%) are often added to increase open time, particularly in consumer products. In addition, the evaporation rates of the various components of a blend must be taken into account. If the better solvent is the slowest to evaporate, the adhesive will retain tack longer.

If, on the other hand, it evaporates the most quickly, cohesive strength will develop more rapidly.

Solvent choice also affects application properties. True solvents, such as toluene or 1,1,1-trichloroethane, give stronger solutions which tend to be more stringy and cobweb when sprayed. Improved application properties are obtained by using a bled which falls closer to the shady area of the kidney shaped solvent diagram. For example, sprayable adhesives are generally based on fast-evaporating solvent blends which fall in the upper left quadrant of Fig. 8.7.

A small amount of water, about 1 phr, is often added to catalyze formation of the magnesium oxide/resin reaction product and to improve the viscosity stability of Neoprene AF adhesives. However, excess water reduces the hot cohesive strength of the adhesive. Therefore, levels less than 3 phr are generally used.

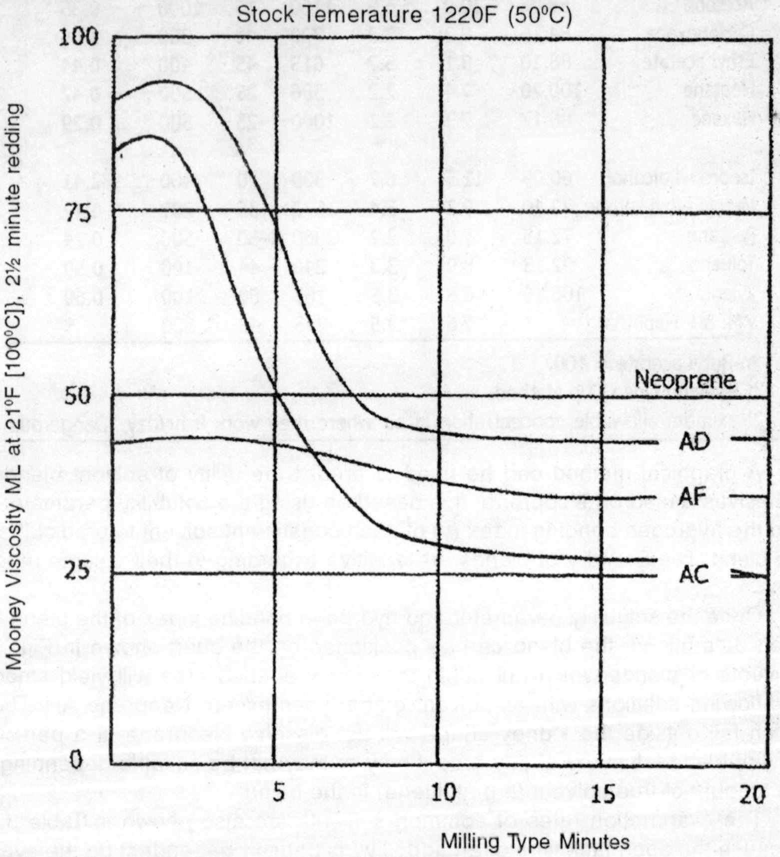

Fig. 8.7. Effect of milling on Mooney viscosity

Properties of Industisal Materials,
*Mixture of various hydrocarbons—no definable molecular weight or viscosity.

Adhesive Processing

The procedures used to prepare Neoprene adhesive cements can affect end use properties such as hot cohesive strength and separability. Techniques used to prepare cements include milling, direct dissolving, and direct dissolving plus high shear refining. A brief description of each follows.

Milling. The polymer is broken down on a two-roll rubber mill prior to dissolution. To be effective, milling should be carried out on a tight, cool for the greatest degree of chain scission. Neoprene can go through three phases on a mill depending upon its temperature: elastic phase <71 °C (160°F), grangular phase 71-93°C (160-200°F), plastic phase >90°C (200°F). Optimum breakdown and dispersion occur in the elastic phase.

The metal oxides and antioxidant may be added to the polymer as it is being broken down on a mill. The masterbatch is then dissolved with any other compounding ingredients. This procedure provides better dispersion of the metal oxides, which improves resistance to phasing in the final adhesive. The antioxidant and magnesium oxide should be incorporated before the zinc oxide to retard scorch during processing.

Milling aids in producing smooth, non stringly cements by selectively breaking down the high molecular weight fraction of the polymer. In applications requiring sprayable adhesives, milling is recommended in order to obtain the best application properties. Milling also increases penetration into porous substrates and decreases solution viscosity and early hot bond strength.

For example, milling Neoprene AC for 5 min [stock temperature ~ 50°C (122°F)] reduces initial 100°C (212°F) peel strength from 7 lb/in. to less than 1 lb/in. After a bond aging period of one month, both have 12 lb/in. peel strength at 100°C (212°F) as a result of partial curing with zinc oxide.

The effect of milling on the Mooney viscosity of Neoprene AC, NeopreneAD and Neoprene AF is shown in Fig. 7. Neoprene AF does not break down to the same extent as the fast crystallizing types. Milling, therefore, does not have as large an effect on the solution viscosity of Neoprene AF cements. Because the bond strength development of Neoprene AF is largely due to reaction with zinc oxide, it is not significantly affected by milling.

The granulators, dicers, and shedders used in the rubber industry are also employed in the preparation of mill-mixed adhesive stocks. They are used to precut mill stock prior to charging it to the chrun to increase the rate of solution.

Direct Dissolving. The polymer chips are dissolved with the other compounding ingredients in either high or low shear mixing equipment. This method is more economical than the previous one because milling equipment and the manpower required to operate it are not required. Direct addition of dry ingredients to solvent or to a solution of Neoprene is not recommended, however, unless the blending equipment is capable of creating a smooth dispersion of these materials. With a slow-speed churn, it may be necessary to make a separate dispersion of dry ingredients in solvent by ball milling before adding them to the Neoprene solution—hence this technique is often referred to as the *slurry method.*

Dissolvers can be classified as slow-speed churns, high-speed churns, or heavy-duty mixers, depending on their relative rates of solution of stock or their energy input. Slow-speed churns may be mounted either vertically or horizontally. Typical solution time ranges from 24 to 48 hours. Those mounted horizontally may contain an agitator or they may be agitated through rotation of the churn. Horizontal churns are well suited for the production of low viscosity adhesives. Vertical churns are jacketed vessels which are agitated by paddles on a vertical shaft. Vertical churns can be used for all types of cements but are especially suited for high viscosity cements.

High-speed churns are designed to speed up the preparation of smooth cements. Because of their shearing action, they provide some polymer breakdown and resultant viscosity reduction. They generate considerable heat, so a jacketed vessel is preferred to control heat history. The heat build-up increases the rate of solution, particularly with the crystalline types because in addition to the simple temperature effect on solubility, heating decrystallizes the polymer.

High-speed churns may be shearing disk type or propeller type. The latter, typified by the Struthers Wells churn, consists of two opposed propellers positioned in the sides of a closed cylindrical vessel, slightly off horizontal, one on top of the churn, the other at the bottom. Shearing disk churns usually have variable speed control and differ from one another in the design of the flat disk at the end of the shaft. Examples of such dissolvers include the Hockemery Disperser and the Cowles Dissolver. Solution time of high-speed churns ranges from 3 to 12 hours.

Heavy duty mixer or kneaders are adapted to the manufacture of heavy doughs or troweling compounds which have viscosities too high for practical processing in the equipment discussed above. These are high-energy internal mixers utilizing counter-rotating rotors like Banbury, with sigma-or Z-shaped blades. By careful addition of solvent, a smooth cement can be prepared in two hours or less. Too rapid addition of solvent will cause the compound to "liver" and an abnormally long period of time will be required for solution.

Direct Dissolving plus High Shear Refining. This procedure combines many of the attractive features of milling and nonmilling. It involves subjecting a previously dissolved adhesive to high shear for several minutes in equipment such as a Ross mixer emulsifier. The high shear refining step breaks down the high molecular weight fraction of the polymer, yielding non stringly adhesives and better metal oxide dispersion without the sacrifice in hot strength associated with milling. The adhesive viscosity obtained using this procedure is inter-mediate between that of milled and unmilled adhesives.

End Uses

Areas where Neoprene solvent cement is popular include adhesives for bonding high pressure plastic lamivates, automotive adhesives, ashesives for the construction industry and shoe adhesive.

Shoe adhesives have traditionally been a large market for Neoprene , particularly for the permanent attachment of shoe soles. However traditional Neoprene contact cements do not give adequate adhesion to plasticized PVC, a synthetic material of shoe uppers which has grown in significance in recent years, vecause of plasticizer migration into the vond line. In response to a need for vetter adhesion Neoprene AD-G was developed. As was dixcussed earlier, it is designed for grafting with methyl methacrylate at the adhesive manufacturer's facilities. The resulting graft polymer solution gives good adhesion to PVC without further compounding. For sole attachment it is used as a two-part adhesive in conbination with a polyisocyanate. The graft system also gives good adhesion to other hard to bond substrates such as EVA sponge thermoplastic rubbet and SBR. In some of these cases, small anounts of resins are used to increase specific adhesion.

Table 8.14. Effect of Adhesive Processing on Viscosity and Creep Resistance of Neoprene AD Adhesive.[b]

Processing	5 min Mill Breakdown	Churn Mix	Churn Mix Plush High Shear
Brookfield Viscosity, cps	220	1220	1050
Creep at 500C (122°F) after 120 min with 5 lb weight, Canvas / canvas Bonds, Inches separation[d]			
1 day bond again	1.7 C	00.8 C	0.7 C
5 days bond again	0.5 C	0.3 C	0.3 C
open time, chipboard to formica Bonds Assembled After			
30 min	4	5	5
60 min	2	5	3
90 min	0	5	0
120 min	0	5	0
180 min	0	0	0

[b]Neoprene AD - 30 adhesive with 40 phr t-butyl phenolicresin.
[c]3 min in homogenizer.
[d]C = Cohesive failure.
[e]Values 1 through 5 correspond to increasing bond strength.

Automotive uses for Neoprene adhesives also go back many years and include such things as adhering sponge insulation strips to doors and trunk and hood lids. Other applications include attachment of vinyl trim in panels and adhering vinyl landau tops to roofs. Traditional Neoprene/resin contact cements are used to bond plasticized PVC in these applications because the required adhesion level is not as great as in the shoe industry and/or a barrier film is employed.

Another large market for Neoprene adhesives is the bonding of high-pressure plastic laminates to substrates such as wood, metal stone, etc. The contact cement enables construction personnel to make kitchen cabinets in place. Neoprene's rapid bond strength make it feasible to install rolled edges for splash panels at the back of counters, etc. Greater and greater use of contact adhesives is also being found in factory manufactured plastic laminated panels.

In the construction industry, Neoprene finds use in a variety of jobs. Some of the larger volume applications include: adhering gypsum dry walls (walboard) to itself in double dry wall construction, adhering faces to paper and wood core materials in flush doors and curtain wall panels, and mastics for bonding plywood flooring to joists.

Application Methods

Neoprene adhesives are conventionally applied by spraying, curtain coating, roller coating, brushing, or extrusion (i.e., by a caulking gun). Spraying is by far the most important industrial technique, as it permits rapid laydown of adhesive and minimize drying time. The basic physical characteristics required of

Neoprene adhesives for these application techniques are summarized below.

1. *Spraying*— A low Mooney, low nerve Neoprene is preferred. Milling is required for the best spray characteristics. The viscosity should be below 250 cps. The solvent blend should contain predominantly fast-evaporating solvents which individually could not dissolve Neoprene.

2. *Curtain coating*— A low Mooney, low nerve Neoprene is preferred. Milling or high shear refining improves curtain coating characteristics by reducing nerve. Viscosity should be 200-300 cps utilizing relatively slow evaporating solvents.

3. *Roller coating*— Milling or h high shear refining is recommended to reduce stringiness. The viscosity should be 500-1000 cps using relatively slow evaporating solvents. The slowest evaporating solvents should be true solvents, either individually or as a" blend, in order to reduce "snap-back."

4. *Brushing*— The viscosity should be around 1000 cps. Solvent system, beneficial effect of milling, etc., depends on individual application requirements.

5. *Extrusion*— A high gel, low viscosity thixotropic Neoprene is best. The ideal candidate is Neoprene AG, by itself or in blends with AC, AD or WHV-A. The solvent blend should contain predominantly fast-evaporating solvents which individually could not dissolve Neoprene.

Neoprene Latex-Based Adhesives

Neoprene latexes can be categorized as anionic or nonionic. The one non-ionic latex available, Latex 115, is stabilized with polyvinyl alcohol and sold at a pH of about 7.0. Ten other latexes are available which are stabilized with anionic emulsi-fier systems. Seven of these are commonly used in adhesives. The properties of the Neoprene latexes used in adhesive applications are summarized in Table 8.15 and in the following text

Anionic Types

Latex 400 contains a fast-crystallizng polymer which yields the highest uncured strength of all the Neoprene latexes, but the shortest dry open tack time. Successful use requires that substrates either be bonded wet, heat reactivated or bonded under high pressure. Adhesives based on Latex 400 have good resistance to weather, water, heat, and ozone. The polymer in Latex 400 also possesses the highest chlorine content of the Neoprene latexes and is often used in applications which require good resistance to degradation by flame.

Latex 571 contains a very high gel polymer which offers high strength films with low permanent set. Latex 571 is primarily used in combination with other latexes and resorcinol-formaldehde resins for bonding elastomers to fibers and fabrics.

Latex 654 is a high solids, low viscosity latex containing a very low gel polymer which offers good tack and flexibility. It is generally used in wet laminating applications, for example, to adhere various facing materials to variety of fiberglass batts and boards.

Latex 671A is a high solids, low viscosity latex containing *a* medium-high gel polymer which offers high uncured cohesive strength combined with good open tack time. It is used in both contact bond and wet laminating applications. It offers better hot strength than Latex 654 with a sacrifice in contactability.

Latex 750 a contains medium gel, slow crystallizing polymer which gives an

Table 8.15. Properties of Neoprene latex Polymers

Latex Type	*400*	*571*	*654*	*671A*	*735A*	*750*	*842A*	*115*
Primary monomer	chloroprene	chloroprene	chloroprene	chloroprene	chloroprene	chloroprene	chloroprene	chloroprene
Comonomer	2,3-dichloro-1,3-butadiene	sulfur	–	–	–	2, 3 dichloro-1, 3-butadiene	–	methacrylic acid
Emulsifier type	potassium salt of disproportion-ated resin acids	principally sodium salts of resin acids	potassium salt of disproportion-ated resin acids	potassium salt of disproportion-ated resin acids	sodium salt of disproportion-ated resins acids	potassium salt of disproportion-ated resin acids	principally sodium salts of resin acids	polyvinyl alcohol
Class	anionic	anionic	anionic	anionic	anionic	anionic	anionic	nonionic
Latex characteristics:								
Percent solids	50	50	59	59	45	50	50	47
Initial pH at 25°C (77°F), minimum	12.5	12.0	12.0	12.5	12.0	12.5	12.0	7.0
Viscosity, cps								
Spindle 1 at 6 rpm	9	15	75	60	5	10	15	–
Spindle 1 at 30 rpm	9	15	55	45	5	10	15	–
Spindle 2 at 6 rpm	–	–	–	–	–	–	–	500
Spindle 2 at 30 rpm	–	–	–	–	–	–	–	350
Gel content	medium	high	low	medium	very low	medium	high	low
Film properties:								
Modulus at 100% elongation, MPa	1.8	0.6	0.2	0.6	0.2	0.4	0.4	0.2
Modulus at 300% elongation, MPa	3.8	0.8	0.2	0.6	0.2	0.4	0.4	0.4
Crystallization rate	very fast	med. to fast	medium	slow to med.	fast	very slow	slow	does not crystalize
Main features	high chlorine con-tend and fast crystallization	high tensile strength	good tack and extensibility	good balance of tack and hot strength	best open tack time and good adhesion	excellent extensibility and carboxyl	low cost, fast curing	mechanical, electrolyic stability, functionality

excellent combination of flexibility, dry tack, heat-reactivity and cohesive strength. It is used primarily in contact bond adhesives.

Latex 735A contains a sol polymer which gives the longest dry open tack time of all the latexes. Its films are also the most readily heat reactivated. Latex 735A is generally used in adhesives for wet laminating.

Latex 842A contains a very high gel polymer which crystallizers more slowly than the polymer in Latex 571. It is used primarily in foil laminating applications.

Nonionic Type

Latex 115 contains a copolymer of chloroprene and methacrylic acid, stabilized with polyvinyl alcohol. For many adhesive applications, Latex 115 offers two major advantages over the other Neoprene latexes:

1. Excellent colloidal stability.
2. Carboxyl functionality.

The excellent colloidal stability of Latex 115 gives it exceptional resistance to shear and a broad tolerance to a variety of materials that would destabilize the anionic Neoprene latexes.

The carboxyl functionality of Latex 115 gives it much better specific adhesion to a variety of nonporous substrates. In addition, it offers a means of room temperature cure through crosslinking with metal oxides. Zinc oxide is generally used at two to five parts, although other metal oxides are effective. Crosslinking agents such as methylol ureas, methylol melamines, and epoxies.

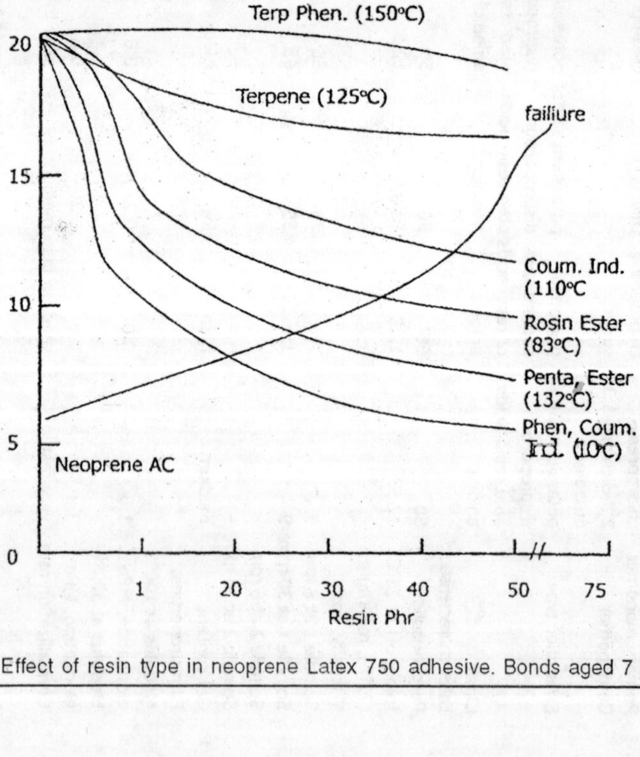

fig. 8.8. Effect of resin type in neoprene Latex 750 adhesive. Bonds aged 7 days at R.T.

Latex 115 is used primarily in industrial contact bond applications. Formulations based on Latex 115, such as the one shown in Table 17, come the closest to matching the performance of Neoprene solvent-based contact cements.

Neoprene Latex 115 reacts slowly with zinc oxide in adhesive from, causing a gradual increase in the adhesive gel content. In contact bonding, where gel content directly affects the contactability of dry films, it is suggested that adhesives be used within six months.

Compounding

Antioxidants— The presence of a good antioxidant in Neoprene compounds is essential for adequate protection against oxidation. Hindered *bis-phenols,* such as Wingstay L or Antioxidant 2246, are usually used where minimum discoloration and/or minimum staining is desired. Where discoloration is unimportant, amine type antioxidants are used.

Metal Oxides— Zinc oxide is the most effective metal oxide. French-process-type zinc oxide, which is low in lend content, is incorporated into the latex as a dispersion. Zinc oxide serves three main function: (1) promotes cure; (2) improves aging, heat, and weather resistance; and (3) serves as an acid acceptor.

For most adhesive applications, 2 phr of antioxidant, and from 2 to 5 phr of zinc oxide are adequate to provide the desired performance. In some more demanding applications, it may be beneficial to increase the amount of antioxidant and/or zinc oxide. Accelerated aging tests, simulating as close as possible the anticipated exposure the adhesive will encounter, should be conducted to be sure the amounts and types of ingredients added to the Neoprene will yield the performance required.

Resins—Because of colloidal incompatibility, the metal oxide t-butyl phenolic resin complex which in solvent adhesives provides improved adhesion largely and hot strength is ineffective in latex systems. Of the types of resins which are commonly used in Neoprene latex adhesives, only the *terpene phenolics* such as Durez 12603 (Occidental) and SP-560 (Schenectady) do not cause an appreciable loss in hot strength as the resin content is increased. Others such as coumarone indene resins, liquid terpene resins and rosin esters are valuable from a standpoint of increasing adhesion and open time, but decrease cohesive strength at elevated temperatures. This is illustrated in Fig. 8, where canvas-to-canvas peel strength at 70°C (158°F) is plotted against resin level with several different classes of resins in Neoprene Latex 750. Only the terpene phenolic systems provided adhesive failure, even at the 50 phr level. However, terpene phenolic resins are less tacky than many of the softer synthetic resins. They are frequently used in blends with other resins to achieve a better balance of hot strength and open time.

Resins are incorporated in Neoprene latex as solvent-cut emulsions, solventless pebblemilled dispersions, or sometimes as solvent-free emulsions prepared using *invert emulsification* techniques. In the latter case a resin with a melting point of 80°C (176°F) or lower is melted. Water and surfactants are added to the molten resin and he temperature of the mixture is decreased. Upon reaching a certain temperature, the water in molten resin emulsion spontaneously inverts to form a resin in water emulsion suitable for use in latex adhesives. A manner is shown inTable 8.16. This particular resin dispersion can be used to produce adhesives with moderate hot strength and good open time using the following recipe:

	% Solids	Dry Parts
Neoprene latex 671A	60	100
Antioxidant	33	2
Zinc oxide	50	5
Resin dispersion	50	30

Table 8.16. Resin Dispersion Made from Invert Emulsification Process.

Resin Suspemnsion	*Parts*
Arizona Zonester 65 Resin	100
Witcomul 4089	3
IgepalCO-970	3
Deionized water	94

Procedure:

1. Melt the resin and emulsifier in a 100°C (212°F) circulating air oven.
2. Add resin mixture to temperature controlled vessel 85-90°C (185-194°F), and stir until mixture cools to 90-95°C (194-203°F)
3. Add 6 g of 85°C (185°F) water.
4. Cool mixture to 85°C (185°F). Slowly add 6 g of 85°C (185°F)water.Mixture will become thick as it inverts.
5. Add remaining water with thorough mixing. Cool to room temperature without stirring. Particle size should be 1-3 μm.

The solvent-free systems offer several advantages over emulsions which utilize solvent to dissolve the resin:

1. Ability to produce lower viscosity adhesives, as one avoids the thickening action of the solvent;
2. Higher resin content;
3. Addition of flammable solvents is averted; and
4. Greater latitude in controlling rheology with synthetic thickeners is gained by omission or reduction of the amounts of solvent, soap, and casein usually present in the emulsions.

Fillers—The Neoprene latexes are not significantly reinforced by the addition of fillers. Fillers are used to reduce cost and control rheology, solids content, and modulus. Both tend to reduce cohesion and adhesion. Hydrated alumina is often used when resistance to degradation by flame is important. In other cases, calcium carbonate, clay, silica, and feldspar are commonly used.

Typical Formulations

Typical adhesives based on Neoprene latex are presented in Table 17. The first is a general-purpose contact adhesive. Either Latex 671A or Latex 750 provide a good starting starting point in this formulation. The latter provides better contactability at the expense of hot cohesive strength.

The second formulation is a contact bond adhesive based on Neoprene Latex 115. It provides good cohesive strength development because of the reactivity of Latex 115. For best results, it should be used within six months after formulation.

The third and fourth formulations are designed for high-speed lamination of aluminum foil to kraft and other papers. Neoprene Latex 654 is a suitable choice in the anionic recipe because it can tolerate high filler loadings while retaining adequate "wet grab" performance. Neoprene Latex 115 is also a good choice for this application because of its excellent shear stability and adhesion. The fourth formulation provides a suitable starting point for evaluation.

Table 8.17.
Neoprene Latex Starting-Point Adhesive Formulations.

	Dry Parts			
Ingredient	*Contact Bond*	*Contact Bond*[a]	*Foil to Paper Laminating*	*Foil to Paper Laminating*
Anionic Neoprene latex polymer	100	–	100	–
Neoprene Latex 115	–	100	–	100
Antifoam as required	–	–	X	X
Surfactants as required	X	X	X	X
Zinc oxide	5	2	5	5
Antioxidant	2	2	2	2
Terpene phenolic resin	50	–	–	–
Liquid polyterpene resin (low melting point)	25	–	–	–
Hydrogenated wood rosin or rosin ester	–	30	20	–
Filler	–	–	100	100
Resimene 717[c]	–	–	–	5
Ammonium chloride	–	–	–	0.2
Thickener as required	X	X	X	X

[a]Adhesive should be used within 6 months.
[c]Melanine formaldehyde resin, monsanto.

9.

Acrylic Adhesives

In 1901, at Tuebingen, Germany, a doctoral candidate named Otto Rohm published a thesis describing liquid condensation products obtained from the action of sodium alkyoxides on methyl and ethyl acrylate. He also discussed the chemical nature of the polymer materials formed simultaneously in these reactions. With this work, Dr. Rohm put in motion a chapter of chemical history which blossomed in the ensuing half century into a significant commercial factor in the adhesives, plastics, coatings, and other industries. During this half century, a number of processes have reached commercial utilization for the manufacture of the acrylate monomers and for the variety of polymer materials which are derived from those monomers.

Polymeric products used in the design of solvent and waterborne acrylic adhesives as well as 100% solids reactive adhesives all have a number of characteristics in common. The most noteworthy of these features are:

- Low Temperature performance
- Board adhesion spectrum
- Water resistance
- Easily formulated
- Excellent optical properties
- Durability
- Low toxicity

Acrylic adhesive polymers, both in aqueous emulsion from and solvent solution form, are widely used as the basis for adhesives for pressure sensitive tapes, labels, and other decorative and functional pressure sensitive products. These applications capitalize on the versatile adhesion and the excellent aging characteristics of this class of polymer.

Acrylic materials are also widely used as elastomers and thickener components in a variety of waterborne construction adhesives, laminating adhesives, and packaging adhesives. Sometimes, the polyacrylate portion of these adhesives is minor, contributing a thickening function to such other elastomers as styrene-butadiene latex and polyvinyl acetate compounds. A variety of specially laminating adhesives, in both filled and unfilled form, utilize acrylic elastomers to bond dissimilar surfaces in operations which are performed via wet laminating, pressure sensitive laminating, contact bonding, and heat sealing operations.

Finally, acrylic chemistry is the basis for a number of 100% solids reactive engineering adhesives used in structural bonding applications, generally involving metal or plastic nonporous surfaces.

Technology

Chemistry

Acrylic adhesive polymers are synthesized from a wide selection of acrylic and methacrylic ester monomers and almost always with low levels of monomers having pendant functional groups (for post crosslinking and/or special adhesion needs). More specifically, acrylic adhesives are based mainly on ethyl, butyl and 2-ethyl hexyl acrylate monomers, plus small quantities of methyl methacrylate, and acrylic and/or methacrylic acids, and other specialty acrylic monomers. Frequently, the acrylic monomers are copolymerized with ether vinyl monomers such as vinyl acetate, vinyl chloride, styrene, etc. The high reactivity of vinyl groups permits the synthesis of linear polymers of very high molecular weight.

Most commercial processes are free-radicaltype addition reactions conducted at elevated temperature in the presence of an initiator. Acrylic adhesives are made in a variety of physical forms, such as organic solutions, aqueous emulsions, suspensions, and carrier-free solid materials that are melt applied. Acrylics are available as thermoplastics, which melt and flow at high temperatures, and as semireactive or thermosetting crosslinkable systems which yield solvent-and heat-resistant polymers. In contrast, water soluble polymers can be made through proper monomer selection and functional group cappings. Chemically, these products are long chain polymers of methacrylate and acrylate esters. The physical properties of the acrylic polymers are influenced by the alpha position entity of the acid (hydrogen atom or methyl group) and by the length of the alcohol side chain modification. See Fig. 9.1.

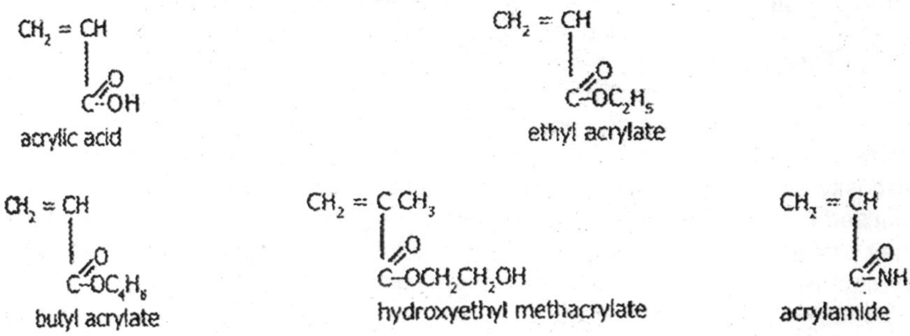

Fig. 9.1.

The acrylate polymers have an alpha hydrogen adjacent to the carbonyl group and, therefore, have more rotational freedom than the methacrylates. The substitution of *a* methyl group for the hydrogen atom (producing a methacrylate polymer) restricts the freedom of rotation of the polymer (steric hindrance) and thus produces harder, higher tensile strength and lower elongation polymers than their acrylate counterparts.

The ester side chain group also affects properties significantly. As the ester side chain becomes larger, the tensile strength of the polymer is decreased and its elongation increases.

Various monomers impart characteristic film properties to the acrylic polymer (see Table 9.1). These monomer modifications also affect polymer polarity and solubility, as well as the glass transition temperature of the polymer.

The characteristic properties of a polymer are greatly influenced by the conditions of polymerization. Variations in catalyst level, reaction time, temperature, and monomer concentration make it possible to adjust the polymer's molecular weight and ultimately its physical properties.

Solution thermoplastic acrylics from coherent films simply by solvent evaporation without post-filming reactions taking place. Therefore, the properties of thermoplastic resins depend primarily on the necessity of physical entanglements between long chain molecules and secondary bonding forces (<5 kcal/mole). Thus,it is possible to obtain with the same monomer esters, by molecular weight variation, polymers with broad variation in viscoelastic mechanical properties.

Table 9.1. Mechanical Properties.

	Tensile Strength (psi)	*Elongation (%)*
Polymethacrylate		
Methyl	9,000	4
Ethyl	5,000	7
Butyl	1,000	230
Polyacrylates		
Methyl	1,000	750
Ethyl	33	1,800
Butyl	3	2,000

The viscosity of solution polymers increases directly with molecular weight. Performance properties begin to plateau as molecular weight increases, but viscosity continues to increase. Thermosetting solution acrylic resins are polymerized to lower molecular weight than thermoplastic acrylics, since they attain their property performance by conversion to infinite three-dimensional networks by chemical reaction (forming primary chemical bonds).

Glass Transition Temperature (T_g)

The glass transition temperature of acrylic polymers is one of the most important characteristics governing many of the properties that are important in adhesives.

All polymers exhibit a second order transition temperature range at which the polymer changes from a hard, glasslike solid to a rubbery or liquid state, depending on the molecular weight and/or chemical bonding. This transition is a reflection of the entropy (freedom of motion) characteristics of the polymer. At a certain temperature range, polymer molecules receive sufficient thermal energy to break out of their "frozen" configurations into a state of rapid segmental motion. In this highly agitated state, the physical entanglements between the long-chain molecules have more freedom of motion and thus impart the rubbery or tacky semi-solid properties. The brittle point of the homopolymer drops to its lowest value with 8 and 12 carbon atoms in the alkyl group and thereafter increase with increasing chain length of the alcohols, the polymers attaining a wax-like consistency.

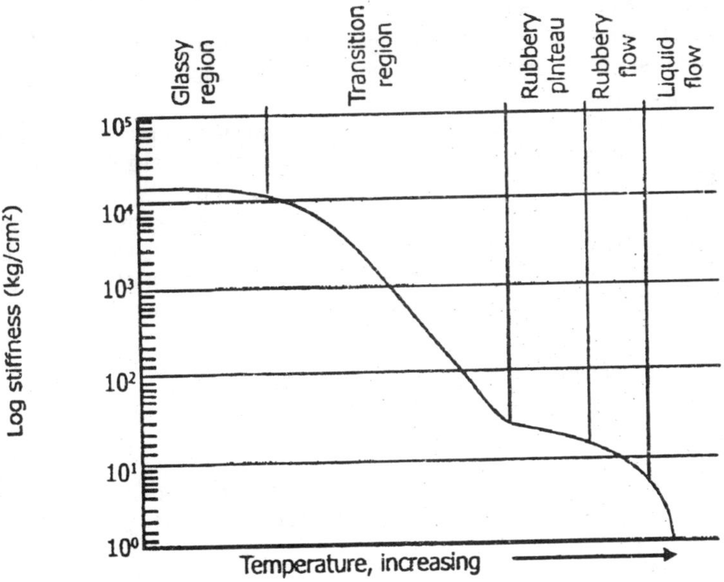

Fig. 9.2

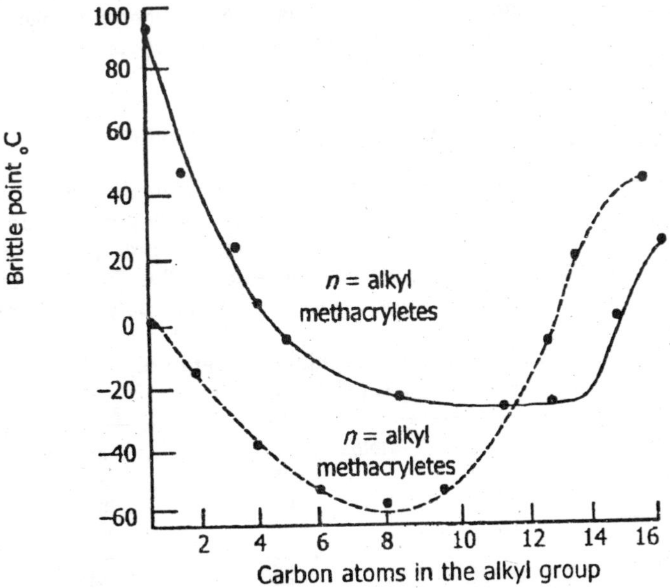

Fig. 9.3. Brittle points of polymeric n-alkyl acrylates and methacrylates.

Numerous investigations have been made into the factors influencing T_g. Most of' these are related to the effect of molecular structure and chemical composition.

1. Side Chain Effects. The further apart the chains in the polymer, the greater the segmental mobility.
2. Chain Stiffness. The extra CH_3 group in a methacrylate causes additional steric hindrance to movement which, in turn, raises the glass temperature.
3. Branching. A branched group on the side chain also raises the t-butyl has a much higher *Tg* than t-butyl. These trends are illustrated in Table 9.2.
4. Copolymers, Internal Plasticization. By copolymerizing more than one typeof acrylic monomer, polymers with intermediate T_g values can be prepared. Fox' has proposed the following equation for calculating the T_g of copolymer from known values of the homopolymers:

$$\frac{1}{T_g}\text{ (copolymer)} = \frac{W_1}{Tg_1} + \frac{W_2}{Tg_2} + \frac{W_n}{Tg_n}$$

5. Crosslinking. Crosslinking prevents the onset of rubbery flow by the formation of chemical bonds which impede segmental motion.

Crosslinked Thermosets

Thermosetting acrylic resins are charácterized as vinyl addition polymers having pendant chemical groups capable of further reaction. The most important commercial materials used or epoxy functionality. As in other interpolymer systems, the film properties may be altered in several, use of curing catalyst, and variation in the amount of Crosslinking agent.

Catalysts, either internal or external, have the effect of accelerating cure response at a lower bake temperature. Curing temperatures are normally reduced by 50-100°F by the addition of catalyst.

The level of Crosslinking agent added should be determined for the various ther mosetting types to determine optimization of property performance. If the degree of Crosslinking is too high, brittle products are produced, and, conversely, too lowa level results in poor resistance properties. Table 9.3 outlines the typical catalysts and crosslinkers for the thermosetting acrylic systems.

Table 9. 2. Glass Transition Temperature, T_0 (°C).

Ester	*Methacrylate*	*Aery/ate*
Methyl	105	9
Ethyl	65	-22
f-Butyl	107	41
5- Butyl	48	*-A3*
n-Butyl	20	-54
2-Ethylhexyl	-10	-82

Bonding Processes

We can classify acrylic adhesive bond formation into four different processes.

- Pressure sensitive bonding
- Wet laminating
- Contact bonding
- Heat and pressure bonding

These approaches are dictated by coating and drying requirements, substrate porosity, water and solvent sensitivity, open time requirements, and urgency of bond strength development. Acrylic polymers are being used in all the above bonding processes. A comprehensive review of each follows.

Pressure Sensitive

Pressure sensitive adhesives from a permanent tacky film after the evaporation of the liquid phase or after cooling of a hot melt. Bonding is effected by slightly pressing the adhesive surface onto the adherend. Pressure sensitives can demonstrate a wide range of adhesive properties, from permanent bondings to removable tapes and films.

A number of polymeric raw materials are used in the pressure sensitive adhesive market. They include: natural rubber, polyisobutylene, polyvinyl ether, various types of synthetic rubber such as styrene-butadiene and -ethylene copolymers, polyure-thane, and acrylics.

The most important properties of any pressure sensitive adhesive are a balanced relationship of tack, cohesion, and adhesion. To these properties, acrylic pressure sensitives add the valuable qualities of heat resistance and resistance to aging and UV radiation. Another desirable characteristic of acrylics is that, in general, tackifiers are not required because tack can be designed into the polymer through the proper choice of acrylic monomers. These and other properties of acrylic pressure sensitive adhesives have gained them a significant share of the pressure sensitive market.

Principal applications for pressure sensitive acrylics are a broad assortment of tapes and labels, decals, and other decorative films. Acrylics also have some uses in laminating adnesives, primarily for film-to-film laminates. In addition, acrylics have been used in sound-deadening pads for automobiles and appliances.

To be suitable as a pressure sensitive adhesive, acrylic adhesives are based on acrylic esters with four or more carbon atoms, the most common of which are *n*-butyl acrylate and 2-ethylhexyl acrylate. These acrylates are copolymerized with other monomers such as acrylonitrile, methyl methacrlate, other acrylates, styrene, vinyl acetate, and d, β unsaturated carboxylic acids, depending on the adhesive properties required. This versatility inherent in the acrylics has led to the design of products requiring widely different adhesive properties, from those of permanent labels and high performance tapes to removable labels and films.

Pressure sensitive acrylic adhesives are available in the form of solutions in organic solvents, aqueous emulsions, and 100% solid (hot melt). Traditionally, acrylic adhesives have been provided in organic solvents, but recently aqueous emulsion acrylic polymers have been developed that in many cases match the performance of the solvent based acrylic adhesives. The ability to coat water based systems on high speed film coating machines, along with the obvious advantages in lower cost, safety, and environmental protection has led to a rapid growth in the use of water based adhesives. While the acrylic hot melts have offered the same advantages, there have been technical difficulties in obtaining adequate cohesive strength without an excessively high melt viscosity which have limited their commercial use.

Table 9.3. Catalysts and Crosslinkers for Thermosetting Acrylic Systems.

Pendant Group on Acrylic or Methacry/ic Polymer	Reactive Monomer Containing Pendant Group	Resin Co-reacted to Effect Cure	Catalyst
$-COHCH_2OH$	Acrylamide or methacrylamide converted with CH_2O + alcihol to an ether	Epoxy, alkoxy aminoplasts, carboxyl containing	Acidic-AA or MAA (internal); H_3PO_4 PTSA
-COOH	Acrylic or methacrylic acid	Epoxy	Basic—benzyl, dimeth Ylamine, triethanolamime
$-CH_2OH$	Hydroxyethyl or hydroxylPropyl methacriate	Alkoxy aminoplasts	Acids
-CH-CH- O	Glycidyl metharcylate	Carboxylic polymers	Acidic-MAA or AA (internal), NH_4Cl. PTSA; Basic—DMAEM (internal) quat-ammonium compounds

AA: acrylic acid. MAA: methacrylic acid. PTSA: *p*-toluenesulfonic acid. DMAEMA: dimethylaminoethyl methacrylate.

Formulation—Unlike the natural rubber pressure sensitive adhesives, acrylic adhesives are often supplied in a ready-to-use from. Natural rubber adhesives require time-consuming and costly mastication of the rubber followed by dissolving in solvent. In addition, they must be formulated with a tackifier resin and antioxidants, neither of which is required with an acrylic adhesive. The acrylic adhesives are known for their good UV and oxidative stability while the rubber-based adhesives, because of their chemical unsaturation, are poor in these properties. In general, tackifiers are not required with acrylic adhesives as tack can be designed into the polymer by the proper choice of acrylic monomers. However, if very high tack is required, some of the tackifiers used with natural rubbers, e.g., rosin ester and low molecular weight polyaromatics, can be added to the acrylic adhesive.

Two critical parameters of an aqueous adhesive formulation are its viscosity and Theological properties.[11] Different types of conventional coating equipment will require different viscosities, and the rheological properties will determine the flow and leveling characteristics of the formulation.

In solution-based adhesives, the viscosity is controlled by the type of solvents used and the solids content of the adhesive. The rheology of solution acrylic adhesives is generally Newtonian. In aqueous emulsions, the viscosity of the unformu-lated adhesive is low—around 100 cps—and, if needed, a thickener is added to raise viscosity. Aqueous emulsion-based adhesives generally have non-Newtonian rheology; that is, they experience significant viscosity changes as a function of shear rate. Usually emulsions are thixotropic, i.e., shear thinning, but in rare cases a dilatant rheology can occur, i.e., an upward viscosity progression with increasing shear rate. A shear rate/viscosity profile should be obtained for all new aqueous adhesives.

Thickeners that are commonly used in acrylic emulsion adhesives include alkali-soluble acrylic emulsions, polyvinyl alcohols, and cellulosics. By proper choice of thickener the theology properties can be optimized for specific coating head configurations.

This flexibility has proven invaluable in the design of "coater-ready" aqueous adhesives which are specifically designed for a wide range of application techniques. These techniques include reverse roll coating, curtain coating, gravure coating, and spray application. Key characteristics built into the aqueous adhesives to permit such a wide variety of application techniques include:

Good flow and leveling (rheology)
Low foam generation
God substrate wet-out
Mechanical stability
Uniform, efficient drying

The aqueous-based adhesives may require the addition of a surfactant to help stabilize the dispersion against shear-induced coagulation and to achieve good wetting on low energy surfaces, such as a silicone release liner. However, the presence of excess surfactant can lead to excessive foam generation during coating, which can affect the coating properties. Excess foam can be controlled with a defoamer, but certain defoamers can cause poor wetting of the surface, as evidenced by fisheyes and cratering. Thus a careful balance between surfactant and defoamer is required to get a good coating.

Properties and Testing—The adhesive requirements for a pressure sensitive adhesive will vary greatly with end use. While each application will have certain specific tests, the three most common adhesive tests are peel adhesion, shear (creep) resistance, and tack. There are standard test procedures developed for these tests by PSTC, ASTM, and the Tag and Lable Manufacturers Institute.

Peel adhesion is the force required to break the adhesive bond between two substrates. Usually this is measured by peeling back the adhesive backing at 180° or sometimes 90° from the surface at a standard rate and under carefully controlled environmental conditions. In some cases the bond is broken within the adhesive layer, not at the surface. This Is called *cohesive failure,* and is generally acceptable for permanent applications but not for removable applications.

Shear adhesion is the ability of a tape to resist the static forces applied in the same plane as the backing. It is a measure of the cohesive strength of an adhesive. Usually it is expressed in the time required for a given weight to cause a given area of adhesive to come loose from a vertical panel.

Tack is the measurement of the quick grab or stickiness of an adhesive. Tack is a surface phenomenon that is not always indicative of an adhesive's performance. There are several methods of measuring tack. One test is called the *quick stick.* It is a measure of the force required to remove a tape at a 900 angle from a surface to which it has been applied under no other pressure than the weight of the tape itself. Another version of this test is called *loop tack,* in which the pressure sensitive tape is applied in a loop form using only the pressure of the tape as the applied force. Another common test is the *tack rolling ball test.* A steel ball is rolled down an inclined trough onto an adhesive. The length of adhesive required to stop the ball is measured and used to quantify the tack of an adhesive. The higher the number, the poorer the rolling ball tack. It should be noted that the correlation between quick stick (loop tack) and rolling ball tack is sometimes poor. Formulations containing high concentrations of tackifiers can have excellent quick grab properties as measured by quick stick and loop tack, but high rolling ball tack. One other tack measurement is the Polyken Probe. This is an instrument that measures tackiness by bringing the tips of a flat probe into contact with an adhesive under known conditions and then measuring the force necessary to break the bond. The force is measured in grams and reported as *grams of tack.*

Contact Bonding

Contact adhesives are used where immediate and high bond strength is required. The adhesive is applied to both surfaces to be joined, and allowed to dry completely. Then the substrates are bonded, generally with hand pressure for consumer applications and nip rollers and presses for industrial bonding operations. Open time can vary from several minutes to several hours.

Contact adhesives are used to manufacture furniture and countertops of high pressure plastic and particle board, movable and permanent office partitions, assemblies of cold rolled steel to honeycomb cardboard, and foamed substrates for both steel doors and prefabricated curtain wall. Other applications for contact adhesives include small product assembly such as toys, sporting goods (with substrates such as leather), aluminum foil, plastic films, rigid plastic and foams.

Use of contact adhesives is a good solution for a variety of miscellaneous bonding problems in the home where non porous surfaces are involved and immediate high bond strength is a requirement. The adhesive is applied via paint brush or paint roller, with normal application recommending two coats to be applied to the non porous surface, chipboard in this case. Aqueous acrylic contact adhesives contain no solvents which could represent inhalation or flammability hazards. In addition to eliminating these hazards, some aqueous acrylics provide other benefits:

- Heart resistance
- Clarity
- Adhesion to a broad spectrum of substrates, including plastic and metals
- Ease of formulation
- Ease of handling—can be applied by brush, spray, or roller.

- Ease of cleanup

While some of the earlier acrylics had a short open time (bonding window), the more recent entries permit the homeowner more flexibility in bonding time. Thus, good bonding may be achieved for hours after the clear point is reached.

Heat and Pressure Bonding

With heat-activated bonding techniques, a non-blocking (tack-free) film is applied to one substrate and later reactivated by the application of heat, which produces adhesive flow onto the second substrates during a nipping operation, thereby effecting a bond on cooling. Open time is very short, in the several-second range. It should be noted that, generally, acrylics may require longer dwell time than crystalline polymers since, as is typical of amorphous polymers, they do not show the sharp melting or freezing points characteristics of crystalline polymers. This bonding technique provides immediate bond strength, as do contact adhesive bonding and pressure sensitive adhesive bonding. Obviously, this method is not suitable for heat sensitive substrates. Some typical examples can be found in heat-seal food packaging and a variety of vacuum forming operations such as automotive door panels.

Applications where acrylics see use include the heat sealing of cellophane to metal foil and metallized polyester film or polypropylene film. These films are used primarily in the food packaging area. Other applications are in the overlay area, where clear or photoembossed vinyl films are bonded to wood substrates to produce a simulated expensive wood grain finish.

Vacuum Bonding

Vacuum bonding is practiced in the manufacture of various automotive interior PVC trim items such as door panels, instrument panels, and van side panels. The process consists of spraying adhesive on the rigid fiberboard or plastic (usually and ABS substrate), drying the substrate, then inserting in into a vacuum forming unit where the preheated vinyl is mated to the rigid ABS or chipboard and maintained under vacuum and the residual heat for several seconds. Immediate high bond strength is required, since the vinyl in some cases has been elongated several hundred percent to conform to contoured areas

The rigid substrate, usually containing contoured and deep-draw areas, is mounted to a mated metal mold which has predrilled holes to allow sufficient vacuum draw on the surface of the rigid fiberboard or plastic. Substrates like ABS that are vacuum barriers themselves also require holes to allow vacuum forming.

Wet Laminating Adhesives

The wet laminating approach allows for immediate but relatively low strength bonding of two surfaces. A short open time dictates that the substrates be mated while the adhesive is still wet. In addition, at least one of the substrates must be porous to allow water or solvent to escape through the laminate. Drying occurs subsequent to substrate combination. Examples of the wet laminating technique include bonding of printed vinyl film to fabric for wallpaper and vinyl to foam for soft goods or furniture covering.

Waterborne adhesives, used almost exclusively in wet laminating operations, offer nonflammability and the low toxicity of acrylic-based products. These two characteristics are especially significant, since the volatile carrier migrates into the porous substrate and subsequently dissipates into the environment after bond formation has been completed.

Wet laminating allows for adhesive polymer selection from permanently tacky pressure-sensitive-type products in the T_g = -40°C range to fairly stiff polymers that require some coalescence for adequate film formation. Generally, the lower T_g polymers are used to manufacture flexible laminates, while the stiffer analogs find more use in the product assembly areas.

Typically aqueous acrylic emulsion polymers of 5,000-10,000 cps viscosity are coated onto the plastic film using roll coat techniques set to yield coating weights of 15-35 pounds per ream. Within a few feet after the coating station the second substrate (i.e., cotton/polyester fabric, polyurethane foam, etc.) is married to the wet plastic and then nip bonded. The laminate may then pass through a series of heated rolls, lamp station, and finally cooling rolls prior to being wound onto the take-up-roll. Line speeds are relatively slow, generally being in the 30-90 feet per minute range. Initial adhesion testing is usually a subjective hand peel test, with fabric or foam failure being the ideal target. More sophisticated tests may be done after the laminate has aged at least 24 hours. These may include standard T-peel tests on conventional testing machines. If water sensitivity is a criterion, the T-peels may be performed after an overnight water soak of the preconditioned laminate (Preconditioning usually consists of a 3-7 day aging at 50% relative humidity and 75°F.)

Typical wet bonding applications involve bonding of films, paper, or plastic sheet to such nonporous surfaces as fiberglass, fabric, thin gauge open cell foams, and plywood or chipboard. The diversity in substrate surface energy, porosity, combining and drying techniques, and in-service end use performance requirements demands careful adhesive selection.

Bonding of vinyl film, paper, or foil to fiberglass for a variety of insulation products (e.g., acoustical tile, roll insulation, fiberglass/fiberglass for increased thickness, rigid fiberglass scirp/foil board fire retardant modified) is normally accomplished by overcoat or spray application of the adhesive to the paper, film, or foil.

Various gauge PVC and styrene films are bonded to a variety of fabrics and foams for miscellaneous soft goods applications such as luggage, sporting equipment, lamp shades, and wearing apparel. The bonding technique normally employs roller coat application with a gravure cylinder of the adhesive to the film, and at times a partial dry before nipping to the fabric or foam. Wet tack or wet grab is an important criterion, since upon cooling there can be differential expansion of the two substrates. This can result in a variety of surface imperfections in the final product—especially when thin films are used.

Vinyl film, saturated paper, and fabric are bonded to plywood, chipboard, and steel to produce a variety of decorative panels, from simulated wood paneling to fabric-covered modular office sections. Generally, the adhesive is coated onto the rigid substrate via roll coater or spray application. Roll coater adhesive application to plywood and chipboard generally requires more than one pass for sufficient adhesive deposition, since the surfaces tend to absorb the adhesive. The primer or sealer coat is generally dried completely before a second coat is applied. Then, this second coat is subjected to a partial dry before nipping—sometimes under heat—to the decorative surface film. When the flexible laminate is bonded to a metal surface such as office partition sections, the adhesive usually is deposited via spray application onto the metal.

The wet bonding of rigid plastic sheet (high pressure plastic) to chipboard requires that the laminated section be maintained in a rigid position until the adhesive has completely dried and crosslinking, if applicable, has commenced. The adhesive is roll coated or spray applied to the chipboard.

Filled Adhesives

The broad spectrum of adhesion displayed by acrylic adhesives make filled acrylics excellent candidates for bonding substrates made of cellulosics, leather, fabric, ceramic, foil, plastic, metal, and various foams. Typical examples include panel and subflooring adhesives, decorative brick mastics, ceramic tile adhesives, carpet adhesives, floor tiie adhesives, and contact adhesives.

Acrylics permit high pigment loading. The oustandig pigment-binding capability, adhesion, and durability of acrylic polymers allow formulation at high pigment-to-binder ratios. This permits production of cost-efficient formulation that still retain acrylic permanence properties.

With their wide range of high specific adhesion, acrylic emulsions may be used in a variety of formulations for different end uses. This permits the compounder to reduce inventory and storage costs.

Filled adhesives typically are designed for the construction and do-it-yourself trade. Filled adhesives consist primarily of the base polymer, fillers such as calcium carbonate or day, solvents, surfactants, dispersants, preservatives, and thickeners. Formulations are specifically tailored for numerous end uses including brick mastics, carpet tile and continuous carpet adhesives, floor tile adhesives, ceramic tile, subflooring, and panel adhesives.

Brick Mastics—Brick mastics are the most highly filled adhesive formulations and are used to attach decorative brick and stone for both interior and exterior applications. The benefits of acrylic resins for brick mastics are specific adhesion, water resistance, weatherability, excellent flexibility retention, and formulating versatility.

The formulation provided in Table 9.4 is a starting point recommendation. Further adjustments to obtain desirable color texture and handling properties can be made.

Carpet Tile Adhesive—Carpet tiles and continuous carpeting can be adhered to the floor with a variety of adhesives products. These range from essentially nonfilled pressure sensitive adhesives modified to allow application by brush, paint roller, or notched towel, to very highly filled adhesives similar to those used for applying vinyl and vinyl asbestos tile.

Features of aqueous acrylic resins for carpet tile adhesive sare:

- Water resistance
- Durability
- Specific adhesion to a variety of surfaces
- No solvent toxicity

Formulations for removable and permanent carpet tile adhesives are shown in Table 9.5.

Table 9.4. Brick Mastic Adhesive—Moderately Extended.

Components	*Parts by Weight*
Rhoplex AC-64 (60% solids)	100.0
Triton X-405	1.4
Tamol 850	0.7
Foamaster	0.4
Biocide	0.2
Propylene glyco	5.0
Varsol	2.0
Camel Carb	50.0
#60 Sand	25.0
#45 Sand	25.0
Sno Cal Clay	25.0
Cellufloc	6.0
Hi Sil 422	5.0
Acrysol ASE-60/Water (1/1)	1.5
Water	1.5

Table 9.5.

	Removable	*Permanent*
Components, parts by weight		
Rhoplex N-619 (high tack PAS)	-	100
Emulsion E-1791 (low tack PSA)	100	-
Acrysol ASE-60 (thickener)	0.75	0.8
Triton X-155 (surfactant)	-	0.3
Physical Properties *p*H	9.2	6.7
Viscosity (#4/20 rpm), cps	2000	5000
Solids, %	55	55

Floor Tile Adhesives—Mastic floor tile adhesives are highly filled adhesive formulations designed for use in adhering vinyl and vinyl asbestos tile, wood parquet, carpet, and other flooring materials. The formulations in Table 9.6 can be used to join two nonporous substrates, provided the substrates are joined after the adhesive mastic has dried. If at least one porous substrate is involved, optimum bond strength can be obtained by joining the two surfaces in a wet laminating operation—that is, before the adhesive has dried. The viscosities of the three systems can, of course, be adjusted to meet specific needs. Lower RMC (raw material cost) formulations can be achieved, at some compromise in performance, by extending the pigment/ binder ratio.

Ceramic Tile—Ceramic tile adhesives are highly filled adhesive mastics designed for adhering tile to walls and floors. Even though these adhesives are highly filled, they still must exhibit a high degree of bond strength and water resistance along with desirable handling characteristics like ease of trowelability, sufficient open time, and long term storage characteristics. Ceramic tile adhesives based on Emulsion E-1997 posses such desirable properties as smooth trowelability, wet adhesion, low odor, adhesion to a variety of substrates and permanence of properties.

Table 9.6. Wet Mastic Floor Tile Adhesive—Permanently Pressure Sensitive.

Components[a]	*Parts by Weight*
Rhoplex N-580 (55 % solids)	100.0
Water	1.8
Propylene glycol	3.0
Nopco NXZ	0.09
Triton X-405	2.5
Stabilite® ester #10/xylene (70/30)	76.7
Ammonium hydroxide (10%)	2.0
Gold Bond R Silica(300 mesh)	80.55
Acrysol ASE-60/water (1/1)	5.0
Constants	
Pigment/binder ratio	6/1
osin/binder ratio	1.5/1
Percent solids	71.7
Viscosity, Brookfield #4/0.3 rpm, cps	2,000.000
pH	8.0
Freeze/thaw stability, cycles	5

[a]A suitable biocide is recommended for in-can preservation.

The ceramic tile adhesive shown in Table 9.7 is suitable for formulating an adhesive to meet ANSI Type I and II specifications. One can significantly reduce cost while still meeting ANSI requirements by modifying the ratios of the same ingredients to achieve a pigment/ binder ratio of 6 to 1. Likewise, repositionability and open time may be extended by incorporating a plasticizer, such as Paraplex WP-1, at a rate of 5 parts per 100 of polymer emulsion.

Engineering Adhesives

Engineering adhesives are solventless, liquid, reactive, durable adhesives for bonding durable substrates. There are six recognized chemical types of engineering adhesives: acrylic, anaerobic, cyanoacrylate, epoxy, silicone, and urethane. Strictly speaking, the first three in this list are varieties of acrylic, but only the first will be discussed here. There is, however, considerable overlap in the chemistry and properties of acrylic and anaerobic adhesives. Since considerable progress has been made in acrylic adhesives over the last two decades, those used in engineering applications are now referred to as "modified" acrylic adhesives.

Chemistry and Technology

Early acrylic engineering adhesives were quite simple in composition and thus service well to illustrate their basic technology. An example of such an adhesive is as follows:

Component	Part by Weight
1. Methyl methacrylate	85.0
Polymethyl methacrylate	15.0
N, N-Dimethyl aniline	0.5
2. Benzoyl peroxide	0.5

Table 9. 7. Ceramic Tile Adhesive—High Bond Strength.

Components[3]	*Parts by Weight*
Emulsion E-1997 (49% solids)	210.0
Propylene Glycol	10.0
Water	70.0
Tamol 731	5.0
Urea	30.0
Defoamer	1.0
Duramite Calcium Carbonate	500.0
Acramine Clear Concentrate NS2R	14.0
Constants	
Pigment/binder ratio	5/1
Percent solids	76.0
Approximate open time	15-30 min.
Storage stability, 1 month @ 50°C	Pass
Freeze/thaw stability	5 + cycles
ANSI #1, wet type	80 psi
Viscosity, TE/4, poise	600,00-

[a]A suitable biocide is recommended for in-can preservation.

When its components are mixed the adhesive has a pot life of about one-half hour. The mixture is placed between adherends and allowed to polymerize via a free-radical mechanism. The free radicals are supplied from the decomposition of peroxide activated by dimethyl aniline. I effect, the adherends serve as the reaction vessel for the polymerization of methyl methacrylate to a plastic with adhesion to the adherends.

Modified or second generation acrylic engineering adhesives are more complicated than those described above. In modified acrylic adhesives, polymerization between adherends leads to *impact resistant* plastics with adhesion to the adherends. The following formulation of Brigs and Muschiatti illustrates an early modified acrylic engineering adhesive:

Component	Part by Weight
Methyl methartylate	85
Metnacrylic acid	15
Ethylene glycol dimethacrylate	2
Chlorosulfonated polyethylene	100
Cumene hydroperoxide	6
N, N-Dimethyl aniline	2

The Chlorosulfonated polyethylene separates into small rubber domains during polymerization of methyl methacrylate. These domains absorb fracture energy generated in the glassy poly (methyl methacrylate) under loading. Grafting between the rubbery and the glassy phases appears to be necessary to effect transfer of energy to the rubber.

Component	Part by Weight
Methyl methartylate	85
Metnacrylic acid	15
Ethylene glycol dimethacrylate	2
Chlorosulfonated polyethylene	100
Cumene hydroperoxide	0.4

In this example the aniline activator is replaced by a condensate of butyraldehyde and aniline which is applied to one or both adherends in a thin film prior to application of the adhesive. The activator generates a free-radical flux on contact with the adhesive. This flux spreads across the adhesive layer to polymerize it. This phenomenon is unique to acrylic adhesives. A difficulty with this process is that the radical flux tends to die out with distance from the activator. Practical bond thickness is thus limited.

The following two formulations illustrate the effect of the impact improver. Both were polymerized between aluminum adherends which have been primed with 3 thin film of butyraldehyde and butylamine condensate.

Component	Parts by Weight A	Parts by Weight B
Butadiene-styrene/methyl methacrylate core/shell polymer	30	-
Hydroxypropyl methacrylate	60	77
Acryloxypropionic acid	10	14
Cab-0-Sil® (thickener)	-	9
Cumene hydroperoxide	2	3

Impact-modified formulation A gave 2,200 psi (15 MPa) lap tensile shear strength when tested by ASTM Method D-1002 and greater than 80 in.-lb (9 N m) of impact resistance as tested by ASTM G-17 falling weight method. The comparative formulation B gave 960 psi (6 MPa) shear and 20 in.-lb (2.3 N m) impact.

Radiation Curing

The polymerization of the monomer is acrylic engineering adhesives can be initiated by electron beam or ultraviolet (UV) radiation, provided that the adherends or the fillers in the adhesives are not barriers to radiation. Acrylic monomers are generally more reactive to radiation than methacrylate. Electron beams generate free radicals directly in the adhesives, whereas UV curing requires a photosensitizer or photoinitiator to provide free radicals.

Application Processes

Because of their reactivity, acrylic engineering adhesives are necessarily two-part adhesives. No special application equipment is required for the two-part surface activated type, which is also called the no-mix type. As mentioned earlier, it is only necessary to wipe the activator on to the surfaces before spreading the adhesive and mating the surfaces.

Two-part mixed-type acrylic adhesives are applied like two-part mixed epoxy adhesives with meter or meter-and-mix equipment. The two parts may be metered into *a* container for immediate mixing and application, or metered into a static mixer and immediately dispensed to the adherends to be joined. A simple illustration of meter-and-mix equipment is the double-barrel syringe, which delivers the two parts of the adhesive to a nozzle containing static mixing elements. These elements are alternating right and left hand helices connected off centre to each other. At the other end of the complexity spectrum is the equipment for automated assembly lines.

Current Uses

Modified or toughened acrylic adhesives have been used since the early 1980s to bund metal stiffening strips to the glass fiber-reinforced plastic window panels of rail cars. There is a similar use in truck cab construction. In another transportation use, an acrylic adhesive is used to bond the components of bodyside doors of freight locomotives. These components are made of steel with a zinc coating. Adhesive bonding eliminates the surface blemishes of spot-weld bonding. A two-part premix acrylic adhesives was the only one that met all of the requirements of manufacturing and use, namely, minimum surface preparation, fast cure, and resistance to impact, high humidity, water, and oil coolant.

General sheet steel bonding is done with acrylic adhesives. Wood/aluminum sails of wind-powered electric generators are bonded with an acrylic engineering adhesive. Other uses are aircraft windshields, satellite antenna dishes, solar energy modules, outdoor signs, computer housings, and filtration screens.

The use of a second generation two-part acrylic adhesive has allowed a sports car manufacturer to assemble a bumper which passes a five mile per hour impact.

10.

Gum Arabic

Introduction

Gum arabic was used at least 4,000 years ago when it was shipped as an article of commerce be Egyptian fleets. Ancient Egyptian inscriptions make frequent mention of gum arabic, called kami, which was used largely in painting as an adhesive for mineral pigments. Eventually the gum found its way into Rurope through various Arabian ports and acquired the name gum arabic after its place of origin or port of export. During the Middle Ages the trade was carried on through ports controlled by the Turkish Empire, and the name Turkey gum was given to this material. At one time a re-export trade also developed in India, cheifly around Bombay. Here the gum acquired the name East Indian gum or Indian gum, but it was not of Indian origin since it was imported from Africa and Arabia and then re-exported to Europe and America. Indian gum should not be confused with Indian gum which is an entirely different product more commonly knwon *as* gum which is an entirely different product more commonly known as gum ghatti. Gum arabic is alos known by various names 'pertaining to the local area' where it is collected. In addition, other names relating to the colour and grade have been given to it so that there is a great deal of confusion concerning the relationship between the name, the actual gum and the species of *Acacia* from which it is derived. In Table 10.1 the various names, localities, and species of gum arabic that are known to exist in the industry are tabulated and correlated.

Table 10.1. Varieties of Gum Arabic

NameGeographical Origin		Botanical Source
Australian	Abyssinia	AcaciaAbyssinia
Acacia	Africa, Near East	*Acacia species*
Adad	British Somaliland	*Acacia senegal*
Aden	East Africa	*Acacia senegal (Acacia verek)*
Amrad	India	*Acacia arabica*
Amrawati	India	*Acacia arabica*
Angra pequena	South Africa	*Acacia karroo (Acacia horrida)*
Australian Black Wattle	New South Wales	*Acacia pycnantha, decurrens, dealbata, sentis or homalophylla*
Babool	India	*Acacia arabica*
Babul	India	*Acacia arabica*
Berbera	French West Africa	*Acacia sengal*
Black wattle	Australia, New South Wales	*Acacia pycnantha, decurrens,*

		dealbata, sentis or homolophylla
Blanche gomme	French West Africa	*Acacia senegal*
Blonde gomme	French West Africa	*Acacia senegal*
Brown barbary	Morocco	*Acacia gummifera, spirocarpa or arabica*
Cape	South Africa	*Acacia karroo (Acacia horrida)*
Catechu	Indian, Burma, Ceylon	*Acacia catechu*
Cutch	Indian, Burma, Ceylon	*Acacia catechu*
East India	India (domestic)	*Acacia species*
East Indian	India (from Africa)	*Acacia sengeal*
Falli	Nigeria	*Acacia senegal*
Gedda	Africa	*Acacia species*
Geddaref	Sudan, Egypt	*Acacia senegal*
Gehzirah	Africa	*Acacia senegal*
Gomme blanche	French West Africa	*Acacia senegal*
Gomme blonde	French West Africa	*Acacia senegal*
Gomme de galam	French West Africa	*Acacia senegal*
Gomme de podor	French West Africa	*Acacia senegal*
Gomme de Tombuctou	French West Africa	*Acacia senegal*
Gomme du bas du fleuve	French West Africa	*Acacia senegal*
Gomme du haut du fleuvo	French West Africa	*Acacia senegal*
Gomme fabrique	French West Africa	*Acacia senegal*
Gomme friable	French West Africa	*Acacia senegal*
Hashab	Sudan	*Acacia senegal*
Hashab geneina	Sudan	*Acacia senegal*
Hashab wady	Sudan	*Acacia senegal*
Hobloho	East Africa	*Acacia species*
Jalefan	British Somaliland	*Acacia species*
Jeddah	Morocco	*Acacia senegal*
Khair	India	*Acacia catechu*
Khartoun	Sudan	Acacia Senegal
Khor	India	*Acacia senegal*
Kolkol	Nigeria	*Acacia senegal*
Kordofan	Sudan	*Acacia senegal*
Kumta	India	*Acacia senegal*
Mamrah	India	*Acacia modesta* and *Acacia arabica* mixed.
Marrons et bois	Africa	*Acacia species*
Marrua	Nigeria	*Acacia seyal* and *Acacia xanthophloea*
Mimosa	South Africa	*Acacia species*
Mogador	Morocco	*Acacia gummifera, spirocarpa, or arbica*
Morocco	Morocco	Acacia gummifera, spirocarpa

Nujal	East Africa	*Acacia species*
Ondurman	Egypat	*Acacia species*
Sadra Beida	French West Africa	*Acacia senegal*
Salabreda	French West Africa	*Acacia senegal*
Savakin	East African near Red Sea	*Acacia verek, seyal, fistula, stenocarpa, or procera*
Sudan	Sudan	Acacia *senegal*
Sunt	Sudan	*Acacia arabica*
Tahl	Sudan	*Acacia seyal*
Talba	Sudan	*Acacia seyal*
Talea	Sudan	*Acacia seyal*
Talha	Sudan	*Acacia seyal*
Talki	Sudan	*Acacia seyal*
Tripoli	North Africa	*Acacia* species
Tunis	North Africa	*Acacia* species
Turic	Africa	*Acacia* species
Turkey	Near East	*Acacia* species
Verek	Sudan	*Acacia senegal*
Wattle	India, South Africa, Australia, New South Wales	*Acacia* species
White	French West Africa	*Acacia sengeal*
	Gum Arabic Substitutes	
Angico	South America	*Piptadenia* species
Cashew	India	*Anacardium* species
Goma de guanaeaste	Central America, West Indies	*Enterolobium* species
Mesquite	U.S., Mexico, South America	*Prospis* species
Mumuye	Nigeria	*Combretum* species
Siris	India	*Albizzia* species
Sonora	U.S., North and South America	*Prosopis* species

True gum arabic is a dried, gummy exudation obtained usually from the trees belonging to the various species of the genus *Acacia*, subfamily *Mimosodeae* and family *Leguminosae*. There are about 500 species of *Acacia* distributed over tropical and subtropical areas of Africa, India, Australia, Central America, and southwest North America. The gum is produced in many hot, dry, elevated locations, but only a few of the known *Acacia* species are commercially important. The effect of climatic conditions can be illustrated by the behaviour of *Acacia decurrens* Willds., which produces a sparingly soluble gum in its native Australia, but when transplanted to Java, yields a completely soluble gum.

Gum arabic is unique in that its is produced by tress only when they are in an unhealthy condition. Healthy trees have never been observed to yield gum. Most authorities believe that the formation of the gum is a pathological condition resulting from a bacterial or fungoidal infection of the injured tree. Natural factors that tend to lessen the vitality of the trees, such as poorly nutritioned soil, lack of moisture, and hot weather, improve gum yields. However, some observers suggest that the production of gum is a normal metabolic process in the plant and that the quantity and quality produced is a function of environmental conditions. To date there has been no consclusive evidence to substantiate either theory.

The most important gum-yielding area is the Republic of the Sudan (formerly Anglo-Egyptian Sudan) in Africa followed by French West Africa, comprising Sengal, Mauretania, and French Sudan. Nigeria, Tanganyika, Morocco, Abyssinia, and Somoliland also produce sizable quantities of gum, but of an inferior quality. In addition, lesser amounts of *Acacia* gums are collected in South Africa, India, and Australia.

Production

1. Republic of the Sudan

More than two dozen distinct species of *Acacia* are found in the Sudan, but the great majoirty of the commercial gum collected comes from a single species, *Acacia senegal(Ncada* verek). This species of tree is about 15-20 ft. tall and has a life span of 25-30 yrs. It grows in poor, sandy, reddish soil, the color of which is due to the presence of substantial amounts of iron. These orchards of *Acacia senegal are* found throughout the province of Kordofan in a large uninterrupted belt stretching westward through the province of Darfur and eastward to the Nile River. In some areas these trees are cultivated and tended in small gardens. The gum collected from these cultivated tress is colloquially known as Hashab geneina (garden gum) as opposed to Hashab wady (wild gum) which is collected from untended, wilds trees.

The best grade of gum comes from *Acacia Senegal and* is commonly known as Hashab in the Sudan and as Kordofan gum in this country. One of the reasons for its excellent quality is the limitation of botanical sources which results in a very uniform product. About 90% of the Sudan's production of gum arabic comes from these trees.

Less then 10% of the Sudanese gum production comes from *Acacia seyal* which is prevalent in the southwestern part of the country and in the Nile region. These trees are not tapped and only the natural exudates are collected and sold astahl gum and also as talca, talha, talki, or suakim gum. This gum is markedly inferior to the regular Hashab and does not find a very ready market in the United States.

Several other species of *Acacia* occur in the Sudan and are known to exude gums. Few of these are collected, but some find their way to the market mixed with the other gum. These *Acacia* species are *abyssinica, albIda, arabica, compylacantha, drepanolobium, farnesiana, flava, kirikii, laeta, mellifera, orfota, sieberiana, spirocarpa, stenocarpa,* and *thunbergiana.* The gum from *Acacia arabica* is sold under the name Sunt gum.

Gum-producing infections star in breaks or wounds in the trees which are sometimes caused by nature but more commonly by the natives. Originally all gum arabic marketed was the result of natural exudations, but about 50 years ago tapping was introduced. For the tapping operation, a small axe is used to break the outer bark horizontally by making a shallow cut about 1.5 in. wide. The bark is then peeled one strip up and one strip down to from 2-3 ft. wounds. The gum then forms in the wound area in 3-8 weeks depending on weather conditions. As the gum exudes slowly from the exposed area, it forms tears or droplets which gradually dry and harden on exposure to the atmosphere. These tears are 0.75-3 in. in diameter.

Each season the bark is torn from the tree in a different place, gradually working around the trunk. If this is done carefully, the tree is not harmed and the wounds eventually heal completely. A single tapper can tap about 100 tress a day. Usually the trees are not tapped until young tree is tapped, an early death might be caused. As the trees reach the latter part of their life, they yield less and less gum. Annual yields from young tress have been reported to range from 188 to 2,856 g.; older trees give 379 to 6,754 g. The average yield from young trees is about 90 g. and from old trees about 2,000 g. In order to collect the gum the dry tears are simply pulled off with the fingers or dislodged with a stick or spear if they are cut of reach. Collections are is *a* fairly recent process employed only in certain districts, Brakna district in Mauretania and North Ferlo district in Senegal.

After collection, most of the gum is brought to various ports and trading posts on the Senegal river and is transported down the river and then exported, mainly to France.Since a control service was established at the ports of call on the river, the quality of the gums was definitely improved as reflected by the prices paid to producers. At present there are two main gum qualities varying in colouring: gum bas du fleuve and gum Ferlo. There are also some smaller amounts of inferior gums known as gomme du haut du fleuve, gomme friable, Salabreda, and Sandra beida.

Upon arrival in Bordeaux, most of the gum is sorted by hand into whole and broken tears. Whole tears are then again sorted into the following color grades of decreasing quality: gomme blanche (almost colorless), gomme petit blanche (same, but smaller), gomme blonde (darker colour), gomme petit blonde (same, but smaller), gomme vermicelle (almost white to pale yellow), gomme fabrique (unusual shape or dark colour). Broken tears are also further sorted by sifting, giving material of uniform size but with colours varying from pale yellow to deep bronw: Gomme possiere grabeaux, Gomme menus grabeaux, Gomme moyens grabeauxd, and Gomme gros grabeaux.

In comparison with the Sudan or Kordofan gum, gum Senegal from French West Africa is more yellow or reddish. It is not as clean and is in larger but more brittle tears than Sudan gum. Reported to be more viscous but much less adhesive, it is not used much in the U.S. but has an extensive European market.

3. Nigeria

The Nigerian gum trade is of fairly recent origin, having come into prominence only during the past 40 years. With the active interest and encouragement of thegovernment, the industry in now the third largest producer of gum arabic in the wold, although still very small compared to the Sudan and French West Africa.

The best and most important grade of Nigerian gum comes from *Acacia Senegal* which is found in heavy concentrations in Bornu province. Before 1930 only natural exudates were collected, but with the development of the Sudanese tapping method, tapping has been extensively adopted and is in common use at the present time. The collection season usually lasts from January or February untill the beginning of the rains in the late spring.

Three general classes of gums are recognized:

a. Falli or Kolkol gum which is white or colourless and derived from *Acacia Senegal.* This is the best grade and compares favorably with Kordofan or Sudan gum but produces slightly darker mucilage.

b. Marrua gum, which is yellowish or reddish and is derived from *Acacia seya/or Acacia xanthopholea,* is equivalent to the Tahl gum of the Sudan Nile region and is poorer material than the Kordofan gum.

c. Mumuye gum is dark and found in lumps or masses. This is an inferior gum and is not derived from an *Acacia* species but from the *Combretum* genera of plants.

Several other species, of which the following are the most promising, are known to give commercial quality gums: *Acacia sieberiana, Acacia campylacantha, Acacia lata, Acacia albida.* The gum from *Acacia laeta* is extremely interesting in that it has a tendency to from gelatinous mucilages in comparatively weak solutions.

4. Tanganyika

The fourth largest producer of gum arabic is Tanganyika which had an established export industry before World War II. Before the war the average of the exports for the preceding five years was 662 tons per year, most of which went to India.

At least 18 species of *Acacia* in Tanganyika are known to yield gum, but the bulk of the gum is derived from *Acacia drepanolobium.* This is one of the smaller *Acacia* species; the tree usually reaches a height of about 10-12 ft. and the trunk diameter is only a few inches.

A substantial amount of gum is also obtained from *Acacia sengal which* is found in the low-rainfall areas of central Tanganyika. This gum was compared to the Kordofan gum from *Acacia senega/* and was found to be similar in all respects except in viscosity. A 10% solution of Tanganyika gum at 20° gives a viscosity of 5.21 cps. are compared to 13.50 cps. for the Kordofan gum. It is thought that the difference in season is responsible.

Minor quantities of gum are collected from the following species of *Acacia: fistula, fischeri, stenocarpa, spriocarpa, stuhlmanii, kirikii, seyal, malacocephala, seberiana benthami, orfota, usambarensis, me/lifers, arabica, albida, exanthopholea.*

The collection season begins after the rains cease in May or June and ends in November. Tapping is not practiced at all, and the natives collect only natural exudates, usually by picking off the tears of gum with a forked stick or spear.

No grading or bleaching of the gum is carried out in Tanganyika. The gum is sold by the natives to itinerant traders, and eventually most of it is exported to Bombay, In Bombay it is hand-picked graded, and possibly mixed with other gums before being re-exported to Europe or America as East Indian gum arabic.

5. Morocco

At one time Morocco exported a substantial amount of gun arabic, but at present the trade is negligible. Gum arabic from Morocco was known as Morocco gum, Mogador gum, or Brown Barbary gum. This gum is dark and inferior to Kordofam gum. It is derived from *Acacia gummifera, Acacia spirocarpa*, or *Acacia arabica.*

6. British Somaliland and Abyssinia

Gum arabic has been produced in these countries for hundreds of years and exported for re-export to Aden where it becomes Aden gum or to Bombay where it becomes East Indian gum. In Somaliland tapping is not practiced, but sometimes the bark of the trees is bruised so as to encourage production. In general, four classes of gum are recognized. Adad gum is the best quality and is derived from *Acacia Senegal.* Jaflean gum is not as good as Adan but is sometimes mixed with it. It is derived from an *Acacia* but the species is unknown. Hobloho and Nujal gums are inferior materials. Other local *Acacias from* which gum is collected *are Acacia abyssinica, Acacia glaucophylla,* and *Acacia mellifica.*

7. South Africa

Thirty-eight species of *Acacia* are known to exist in South Africa. These species are fairly widespread, but few attempts have been made to collect gum systematically on a large scale. All collections are from natural exudates without tapping. Before the growth of the Sudan trade or in times of shortages, gum was exported as Cape gum or Angra Pequena gum. However, is normal times these gums cannot compete with Kordofan gum because of their poor colour and inferior adhesive properties. They are believed to have originated from *Acacia karroo (Acacia horrida).*

8. India

About two dozen species of *Acacia* are indigenous to India. Most of the gum from these species is utilized locally as a foodstufll, but some is sent to Bombay, the hub of the gum trade. Native gatherers usually mix *Acacia* gum with any other non-acacian gum that might be available. Since native Indian gums are notorious for their mixed character, pure *Acacia gums* are seldom seen in the markets.

As previously mentioned, Bombay has long been an important export center for gum arabic, but it must be emphasized that very little of the native Indian gum enters this export trade. Gum arabic is imported from Aden, Red Sea ports, and East Africa. In Bombay, it is cleaned, sorted, and garded before being exported as East Indian gum arabic. Indian gum arabic is the name for gum actually produced in India.

Kohr or kumta gum is derived from *Acacia sengea/ which* is prevalent in the dry, rocky, hill country of India. It is the best gum found in India, but its limited distribution restricts the amount available.

Babul or babool gum is collected from *Acacia arabica* which is the source of most of the native gum. This tree can be cultivated but it is not tapped. The gum exudes naturally in March and April in the from of irrgeular and broken tears that are agglutinated in masses. It is which reddish-brown or straw-coloured and has poor adhesive properties which make it makredly inferior to Kordofan gum. It also forms the bulk of amrad or amrawatti gum.

Khair gum is the exudate of the *Acacia catechu tree* which is common in small tears or angular fragments having a translucent yellowish colour. It gives a good plae-coloured mucilage. Sometimes itis mixed with the gum from *Acacia arabiaca,* and then it is called gum mamrah.

Other fair quality gums are yilded by *Acacia farnesiana Acacia jacquemcntii, Acacia leucophloea,* And *Acacia ferruginea.*

9 Australia

Over 300 species of *Acacia* are found in Australia and are known locally as wattles. The gums from these wattle trees vary greatly even from the same species in different areas. They are usually poor-grade materials having poor solubility, a dark reddish-brown colour, a strong taste due to the presence of tannins, and a remarkable tendency to form a gel rather than a mucilage with water.

There are a few species that yield pale-coloured gums of good solubility that are comparable to Kordofan gum. These best quality gums, which are completely soluble in cold water, are yielded by *Acacia homalophylla, Acacia sentis,* and *Acaciapendu/a.* Lower grade gums are exuded by *Acacia binervata, Acacia dealbata, Acadaelata, Acacia glaucescens,* and *Acaciapenninervis while* still poorer quality comes from *Acacia decurrens, Acacia dealbata, Acacia eata, Acacia glaucescens,* and *Acacia penniervis while* still prooer quality comes from *Acacia decurrens.* Other Australian gum-yielding speices of *Acacia are bakeri, cunninghamii, harpophylla, leiophylla, maideni, oswoldi, pycnantha, retinoides, salicina, and verniciflua.*

10. Miscellaneous

Some gum is collected in Central and South America, probably from *Acacia famesiana,,* and sold as Sennar gum.

Several gum arabic substitutes are found in the western hemisphere. Sonora gum, mesquite gum, and cactus gum are found in the United Sates, Mexico, and South America. They are derived from the *Prospopis* genera of plants. Coma de Guanacasta from an *Enterlobium* species is produced in the West Indies and in Central America.

Type of Gum in the United States

Almost all the gum arabic used in the United States is Kordofan or Sudan gum and is imported from the Sudan Republic. It is usually handsorted before exporting and is commonly shipped in burlap sacks having a net weight of 220 lbs. The sorting is done on the basis of colour, size of tears, and freedom from gross impurities. One of the largest importers of this material, Morningstar, Paisley, Inc., of New York, lists four grades of material that are commonly imported.

1. Selected Sorts.—These are the cleanest and largest pieces having the lightest colour. This grade commands a permium price.
2. Cleaned and Sifted Sorts.—The colour varies from pale amber to dark amber, and the gum contains a minimum of material smaller than 0.25 in., four mesh size.
3. Clean Amber Sorts.—The color vaires from light to dark amber, and the gum contains various amounts of fines, chips finer than four mesh.
4. Siftings.—This, the cheapest grade of gum, is the residue formed by sorting the abve choicer grades. Siftings are fine chips containing

considerable sand, dirt, and bark.

Upon its arrival in this country, most importers reprocess and regrade the gun into the from and quality most suited for their customers' needs. The most popular grade is the #1 U.S.P. Powder which sells for 25-27 lb. There are several other grades varying from #2 Technical Grade Powder at 15 lb. to Refined U.S.P. Powder (spray-dried grade) at 50 lb. The price of the curde gum before processing is about 16-18 lb. The gum is also processed into various physical sizes: coarse, granular, powder of varying mesh sizes.

Structure

Gum arabic, as found in nature, exists as a neutral or slightly acidic salt of a complex polysaccharide containing calcium, magnesium, and potassium cations. In spite of its antiquity, very little was known about the structure of gum arabic until relatively modern times. Even today its complexity has opposed attempts to elucidate its final structure although several interesting hypotheses have been proposed. Hirst and Jones described methods used to determine the structure of gum arabic and other acidic gums. The steps are outlined below.

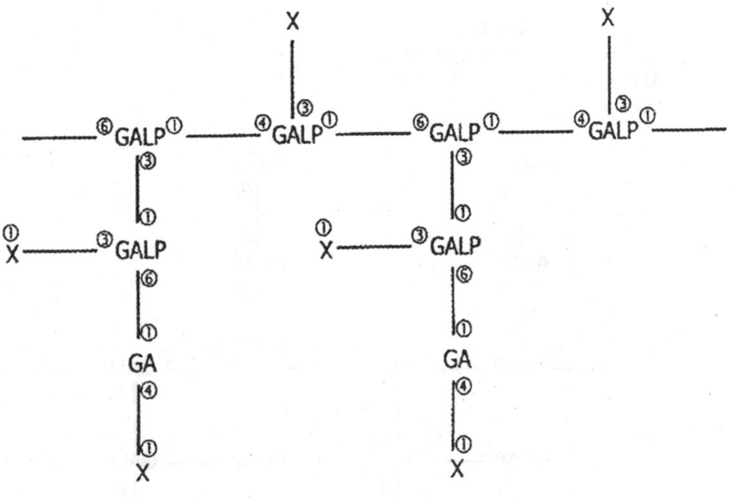

X=L-Rhamnopyranose or L-araboi-Uranose
Galp=Galactorpranose
GA=Glucuronic Acid

1. The homogeneity of the gum is determined.
2. The gum is converted to the free acid, and the equivalent weight of the acid is then ascertained.
3. A portion of the acid is boiled with 12% hydrochloric acid to liberat furfural and carbon dioxide which give estimates of pen tose and uronic acid contents.
4. Another protion of the acid is hydrolyzed with dilute acid, and the liberated sugars are quantitatively identified.

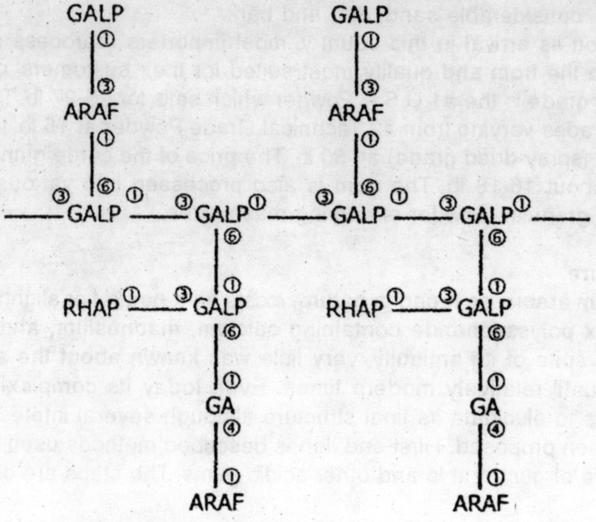

ARAF = L - ARABOFURANOSE
RAHP = L - RHAMNOPYRANOSE
GALP = D - GALACTOPYRANOSE
GA = D - GLUCURONIC ACID

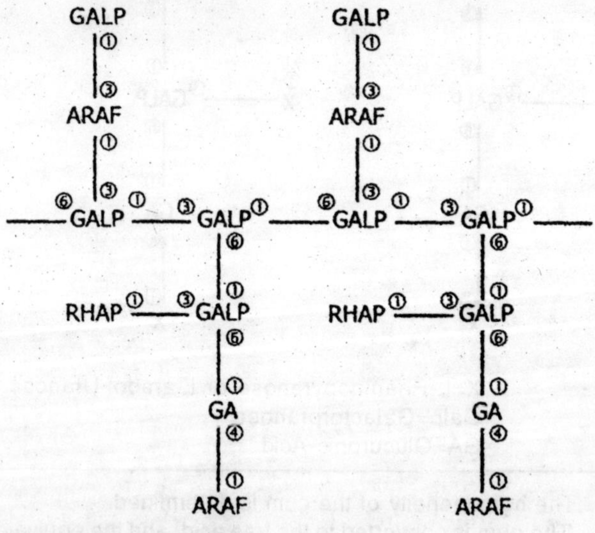

ARAF = L - ARABOFURANOSE
RAHP = L - RHMNOPYRANOSE
GALP = D - GALACTOPYRANOSE
GA = D - GLUCURONIC ACID

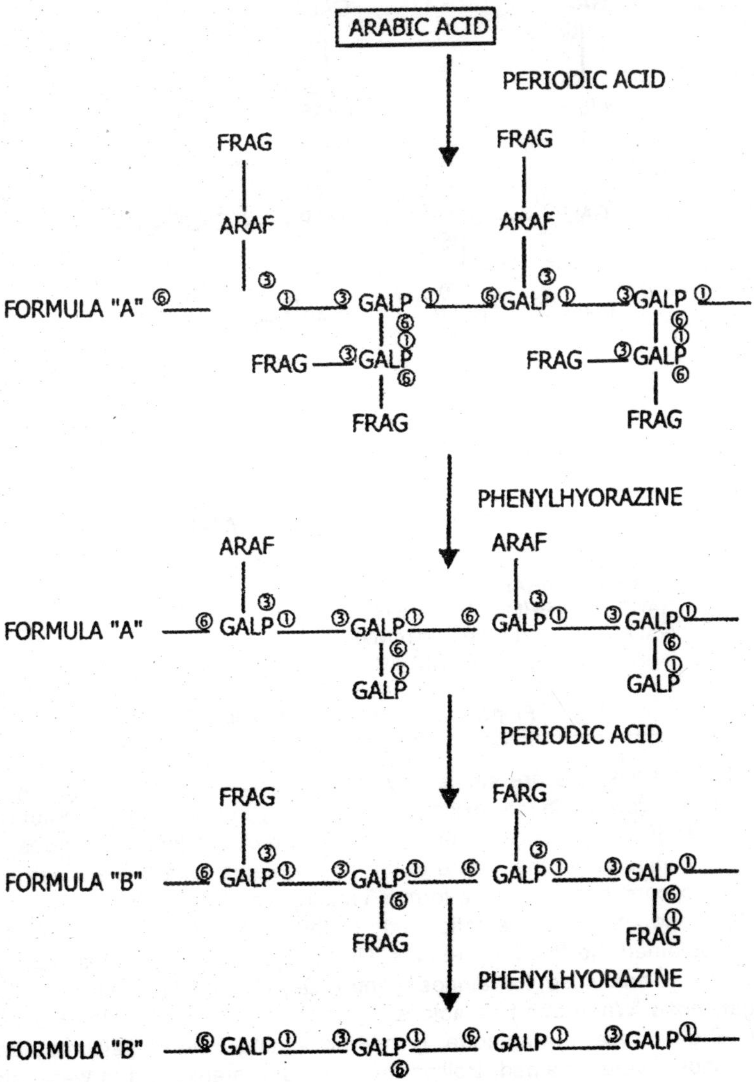

ARAF = L - ARABOFURANOSE
GALP = D - GALACTOPYRANOSE
FRAG = RESIDUE (S) OF A PARTLY OXIDIZED SUGAR MOLESCUE

Degradation of arabic acid

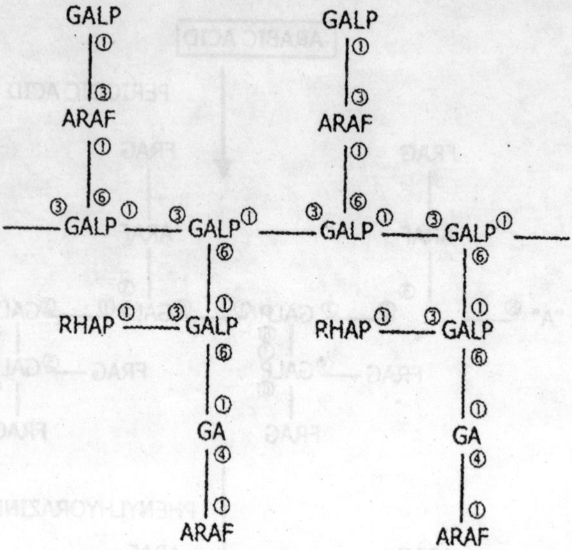

ARAF = L - ARABOFURANOSE
RAHP = L - RHMNOPYRANOSE
GALP = D - GALACTOPYRANOSE
GA = D - GLUCURONIC ACID

Proposed structure for gum arabic.

5. The linkages are studied by three principal procedures, methylation analysis, periodate oxidation, and autohydrolysis or room temperature hydrolysis to oligosaccharides. The rate of autohydrolysis gives information about the nature of the ring systems since L-arabinose which occurs in the furanose form is usually hydrolyzed first.

By conducting a systematic study of this kind on gum arabic, Hirst and Jones obtained the following results. Hydrolysis gave D-galactose, D-glucuronic acid, L-arabinose, L-rhamnose, and *6-O-* β- D-glucopyranosyluronic acid) -D-galactose. When ash-free acid was heated in water, a deguraded arabic acid, D-galactose, L-arabinose, L-rhamnose, and 3-0-β-D-galactopyransyl-L-arabinose were obtained. Boiling the degraded arabic acid in water slowly released D-galactose, 6-0-β-Q-glucopyranosyluronic acid)-D-galactose, and a small quantity of 3-O-β-D-galactopyranosyl-D-galactose.

Methylation and hydrolysis of degraded gum arabic gave 1 mole of 2,3,4,6-tetra-O-methyl-D-galactose, 5 moles of 2,3,4-tri-O-methyl-D-galactese, 3 moles of 2.4-di-O-methyl-D-galactose and 3 moires of 2,3,4-tri-Omethyl-D-glucuronic acid. Methylation and hydrolysis of arabic acid gave the same reaction products as above except for the 2,3,4-tri-O-methyl-D-galactose, which was not obtained. In addition, there was produced 2,3,4-tri-O-methyl-L-rhamnose, 2,3,5-tri-Omethyl-L-arabinose, 2.5-di-Omethyl-L-arabinose, and 2,3-di-O-methyl-D-glucuronic acid.

It is now apparent that the methylation evidence is not sufficient to decide whether the main chain is (l—>6)-linked, (l—>3)-linked, or some combination of these. Spriestersbach's work was directed at establishing the structure of the main chain. His general procedure was to eliminate the aldobiouronic acid side chains and study the residue. Degraded gum arabic was oxidized with sodium periodate and periodic acid to convert the aldobiouronic acid side chains to dialdehydes. The dialdehydes were reduced to dialcohols with sodium borohydride or with hydrogen and Raney nickel. The oxidation, the reduction to the dialochol and the subsequent hydrolysis of the fragments proceeded readily without affecting the main chain. Methylation and hydrolysis of the product gave only 2,3,4,5-tetra-O-methyl-D-galactose. Thus,evidence was obtained that the main chain was (l—>3) linked.

However, Hirst and Jones found that methylation and hydrolysis of degraded arabic acid gave 2,3,4,6-tetra-O-methyl-D-galactose, 2,3,4-tri-O-methyl-Dgalactose, 2,4-di-O-methyl-D-galactose, and 2,3,4-tri-O-methyl-D-glucuronic acid. Inasmuch as 2,4,6-tri-O-methyl-D-galactose was not obtained, the evidence would indicate that the main chain is (1—>6)-linked. If Hirst and Jones' evidence is tentatively accepted as a working hypothesis and combined with other methylation studies, a formula for gum arabic can be proposed which reasonably agrees with their information. If Spriestersbach's (l—>3) main chain linkage should porve to be correct, minor modifications must be made in the strucutre another polysaccharide with very little degradation; if the Smith-Percival formula were correct, the compound would have been completely degraded at this point. This resistance to oxidation is favorable evidence for proponents of the (l—>3) linkage of the main chain. The extra oxidation step needed to rid the gum of L-arabinose seems to indicate that there are two L-arabinoses linked together. A solution of 200 mg. of commercial gum arabic per ml. of 0.9% sodium cholride solution was neutralized and centri-fuged to remove insoluble matter. The gum recovered from solution by its specific precipitant, type II antipneumococcus serum, contained only 1/3-1/5 as much L-rhamnose as the starting material. This result appears to demonstrate that gum arabic is a mixture and that no single over-all formula has significance. When the gum was precipitated from solution with ethanol or glacial acetic acid, the precipitate differed only slightly or not at all from starting material. It would be interesting to repeat the work of Heidelberger and his colleagues under the conditions that the gum arabic used was known to be obtained from a single tree or at least one variety of tree and that no hydrolysis could have taken place.

It is known that hydrolysis of gum arabic yields four sugars which make up the basic gum arabic molecule: L-arabinose, L-rhamnose, D-galactose, D-glucuronic acid. The glycosidic bonds vary in lability. Thus, autohydrolysis of arabic acid in water (pH about 2) gives 34.4% of L-arabinose, 14.2% of L-rhamnose, *3-O-α-D*-galactopyranosyl-L-arabinose, and degraded gum arabic. When mineral acid is used for further hydrolysis, there is obtained 42.1% of D-galactose, 15.5% of D-glucuronic acid, and some *6-O-* (β-D-glucopyransoyluronic acid)-D-galactose.

Although molecular weight studies were important in clarifying the structure of gujm arabic, the various molecular weight determined were highly dependent upon the method used. Osmotic pressure measurements using concentrations down to 0.3% gave a molecular weight of 240,000 for gum arabic, and 200,000-245,000 for a series of gum arabic salts. Svedberg's sedimentation method gave molecular weight of 280,000-300,000 for the free acid and 250,000-270,000 for the sodium salt. Lamm's method, based on sedimentation equilibrium, was in close agreement, giving a value of 300,000. However, more recent determinations based on light scattering studies give much higher molecular weight values of 1.00 ± 0.05 X10. These results were supported by viscosity measurements.

Table 10.2 . Molar Ratio of Carbohydrate Components in Various Acacia Gums

Gum Source	Approximate Molar Ratio			
	D-Galactose	L-Arabinose	L-Rhamnose	D-Glucuronic Acid
Gum Arabic[31]	3	3	1	1
Acacia mollissima[22]	5	6	1	1
Acacia cyanophylla[33]	11	2	5	5
Acacia karrocf[33]	25	22	1	6
Acacia veretf[29]	4	2	1	1
Acacia pycnantha[31]	65	27	2	4

These same light-scattering studies have also led to the conclusion that the gum arabic molecule is in the shape of a stiff coil with many side chains. The length of the coil is 1050A° at maximum charge. Uncharged arabic acid has an equivalent radius of 555 A° and an effective volume of 7.2 X 10^{-16} cc./mole. This picture of gum arabic as flexible chain polyelectrolyte with an unusually high degree of banching is supported by the viscometric studies of Basu, Dasgupta, and Sircar which can only be explained by the existence of gum arabic as flexible chain molecules. Overbeek also found that the calculated change in the dissociation constant for gum arabic was samller than that found experimentally. This would further indicate the existence of branched chains in the gum arabic molecule.

Arabic Acid

1. Preparation

Until recently there was only one general method of the preparation of arabic acid. This was the method used by Thomas and Murray or a variation thereof. Commerical gum arabic was dissloved in about 0.1 *N* hydrochloric acid. Ethanol was added with stirring, and the precipitate was allowed to settle and then filtered out. This procedure was repeated four times to give a very pure product. The purified gum was redissolved in water and electrodialyzed for 50 hr. at which time a 1% solution showed a *pH* of 2.70. Thomas and Murray kept the final arabic acid in solution, since drying with ethanol or distilling under reduced pressure yielded an insoluble product.

Moorjani and Narwani prepared arabic acid in a similar manner by electrodialysis through cellophane, drying on a water-bath, powdering, and sieving through a fine mesh screen. They reported that drying arabic acid at 100° yield an insoluble material.

Table 10.3. Comparison of Commercial Gum Arabic and Purified Gum Arabic

	Commercial Gum	Purified Gum
[α]D (cl.O, water)	-24.30	-24.30
Ash, %	2.78	0.08
Dextrin	None	None
Reducing Sugar, mg. Cu20/g. gum	6.5	None
Nitrogen, %	0.36	0.33
Phosphorus	Trace (<0.1%)	Trace (<0.1%)
Chloride ion	None	None
Sulfur	None	None

Recently Schleif and co-workers prepared arabic acid by ionexchange methods and successfully dried it by spray-drying at 205° to yield a fluffy, white finely subdivided powder. This procedure was also used by Swintosky and co-workers for the preparation of arabic acid and several other polysaccharidic acids, and a similar ion-exchange process for this purpose was patented by Wood.

2. Properties

Arabic acid is a moderately strong acid having a *p*H of 2.2-2.7 in aqueous solution. For a moderately concentrated solution, Ka = 2.0 X 10^{-4} at 22°, ranking it about the same as lactic, stronger than acetic but weaker than the chloroacetic acids. However, the Ka varies considerably with concentration and K_a = 1 X Id^{-3} for a 5% solution and 2 X 10^{-4} at infinite dilution. Potentiometric titration of arabic acid with strong alkali and alkaline earth bases gives titration curves typical of strong monobasic acids. Conductometric titration curves show two inflection points indicative of dibasic acids. However, the first inflection point does not occur at exactly one-half of the amount of the base required for the second inflection, and probably indicates the neutralization of the free acidity or the hydrogen ion activity of the solution. This would further suggest that the acid is not dibasic. The second inflection point is quite sharp and represents the total neturalization of the acid. Total acidities by both potentiometric and conductometric methods agree and confirm the monobasicity of arabicacid.

Arabic acid has an equivalent weight that has been consistently shown to be about 1,200 by various workers. In contrast, the equivalent weight of black wattle gum from *Acacia mollissima* has been reported to be 1,880.

Upon addition of acid, arable acid shows very little change in *p*H suggesting the operation of a buffer mechanism even in the presence of considerable amounts of hydrochloric acid. The addition of netural salts lowers the *p*H of arable acid solutions. Barium chloride shows a greater depression of *p*H than sodium chloride at corresponding concentrations.

Arabic acid has lower viscosity than any of its salts or gum arable itself. Its viscosity can be lowered further by the addition of sodium cholride and lowered to an even greater degree by the addition of calcium chloride or similar divalent salts. Emulsions prepared with arable acid will cream rapidly and are not as stable as those made with its salts. Also, the presence of any salts decreases the efficiency of the emulsifying agent; divalent salts produce a greater decrease than monovalent salts.

Table 10.4. Reported Equiralent Weights of Arabic Acid

	Equivalent Weight
Tiebackx	1,210
Amy	1,600
Thomas and Murray	1,000-1,200
Briggs	1,175
Oakley	1,000-1,200
Saverborn	1,000-1,300
Moorjani and Narwani	1,162
Mukherjee and Ghosh	1,190
Basu,Dasgupta and Sircar	1,208

Pure arable acid is nonreducing towards Fehling's solution and has a specific optical rotation of —27° to -30° in water.

3. Degraded Gum Arabic

When solutions of arable acid are warmed in water, a unique polysaccharide gum called degraded gum arable is produced. The arable acid undergoes autohydrolysis and spiits off L-arabinose, L-rhamnose, 3-0-α-D-galactopyranosy-L-arabinose, and 3-Oβ-D-galactopyranosyl- D-galactose from a core which contains only D-glucouronic acid and D-galactose.

A less satisfactory preparation of degraded gum arable is by hydrolysis of gum arable with dilute sulfuric acid. The product is isolated by neutralization with calcium carbonate, filtration, evaporation to a small volume, and precipitation. The calcium salt is then dissolved in a small amount of water and reprecipitated with methanol. Alternatively, the calcium salt of the degraded gum arable is treated with oxalic acid, giving degraded arable acid, a free-flowing, white powder soluble in water and methanol.

The molecular weight of this core of degraded gum arable is less than 10,000. The chain of degraded gum arable was shown to consist of D-galactose and to have present the same linkage as those of the main chain of gum arabic, damson gum and cherry gum. Degraded gum arabic is very soluble in water. It reduced Fehling's solution, and gives a strong 1,3-naphthalenediol (naphthoresorcinol) test. It is optically active [α]D + 1.8°. Hydrolysis of degraded gum arabic yields D-glucuronic acid, D-galactose, and 6-0-(β-D-glucopyranosyluronic acid)-D-galactose.

4. Derivatives of Arabic Acid

Several procedures have been reported for preparing soidum arabate from gum arabic which is normally a mixture of potassium, magnesium, and calcium salts. Krantz and Gordon precipitated the calcium ions in a gum arabic solution by the addition of sodium carbonate. The solution is then filtered and evaporated to dryness to yield sodium arabate. Briggs used direct neutralization of an arabic acid solution with sodium hydroxide followed by evaporation to dryness under reduced pressure at 70°. Similar methods have been used for preparing calcium arabate and other salts.

Schleif, Higuchi and Busse prepared sodium arabate using ionexchange methods. Arabic acid solution prepared by ion exchanging wasy treated with 0.5 *N*sodium hydroxide until a pH of 8 was reached. The solution was then spray-dried at 205° to give a fluffy, fine, white powder. This method was extended to prepare spary-dried arabic acid salts of potassium, calcium, magnesium zinc, iron (ferric), and aluminum. Wood also prepared arabic acid salts was patented by Adams. Upon passage of gum arabic solution through a cation-exchange resin in the salt form, a high-purity arabic acid salt is formed. Potassium, sodium, lithium, and ammonium salts were prepared.

Organics salts and esters of arabic acid were prepared by Schleif and co-workers by reacting a solution of arabic acid with the appropriate amine or alcohol and spray-drying the neutral mixture. In this way, tri methyl benzyl arabate and salts formed by neutralization of arabic acid with butylamine, ethylenediamine, diethylenetriamine, and triethylenetetraamine were prepared.

The gum arabic esters of acetic and propionic acids can be prepared by treating a gum arabic dispersion in formamide with the appropriate anhydride.

Moe prepared the sodium carboxymethyl ether of gum arabic. This material is very readily dispersible in cold water and yields stable, low viscosity solutions of very good clarity. Two percent solutions are capable of forming clear films of good strength. The sodium carboxymethyl ether of gum arabic is useful as a sizing and finishing agent.

Gaver and co-workers described the preparation of a new series of compounds from the reaction of gum arabic with primary, secondary, tertiary or quaternary-substituted ammonium hydroxides.

Factors With Affect Viscosity

Of all the physical characteristics of gum arabic, the most important one and the one studied most extensively is viscosity. Viscosity is not only important in the utilization of gum arabic but also in the understanding of its molecular structure. The importance of intrinsic viscosity is that it is directly related to the molecular weight of the polymer by a modification of Staudinger's equation, and from its determination a great deal can be learned about the material being investigated. However, when the molecular weight is known from osmotic pressure determinations or other measurements, valuable information regarding the length and shape of the polymer can be obtained from determinations of intrinsic viscosity. Thus, it can be seen that the viscosity measurements of a polymeric colloid, such as gum arabic, are of great importance, both from a practical and a theoretical viewpoint.

Whereas most gums from very viscous solutions at low concentrations, 1-5%, gum arabic is unusual in that it is extremely soluble and can form solutions of high viscosities over a much wider range of concentrations. It is easy to prepare solutions containing up to 37% of gum arabic at 25°, and this ease of preparing high-solids solutions is responsible for its excellent stabilizing and emulsifying properties when it is incorporated with large amounts of insoluble materials.

The properties of the raw gum exudate are affected by the age of the parent, tree, the amount of rainfall, the time of exudation, and the type of storage conditions. Viscosities of solutions of commercial gum arabics of supposedly similar grades can vary as much as 50% and are affected by pH, addition of salts or other electrolytes, and temperature.

In addition, the techniques and apparatus used in measuring viscosities play an important part. Different viscometers will give varying results. The method of preparation of the test solutions will also affect the viscosity. If the gum is dissolved in the total volume of water desired, a higher viscosity will result than if the gum is dissolved in a small amount of water and then diluted to the desired concentration. Higher viscosities are also obtained when powdered gums are used instead of whole gums. However, when carefully standardized techniques are used on pure gum arabic, its solutions have an intrinsic viscosity of 0.20.

Table 10.5. Effect of Concentration 66 on the Viscosities (cps.) of Gumsa

%	Gum Gum Arabic	Traga-canth	Carra-geenan	Sodium Alginate	Methyl-cellulose ,500 cps.	Locust Bean Gum	Guaran
0.5	—	—	23.5	86	16.75	20.0	1,380
1.0	—	54	57	214	38.9	58.5	3,025
1.5	—	—	—	1,102	—	—	—
.0	—	906	397	3,760	512	1,114.3	25,060
2.5	—	—	—	8,300	—	—	—
3.0	—	10,605	4,411	29,400	3,850	8,260	11,150
3.5	—	—	—	—	—	—	—
4.0	—	44,275	25,356	—	12,750	39,660	302,500
5.0	7.25	111,000	51,425	—	67,575	121,000	510,000
6.0	—	183,500	—	—	—	—	—
10.0	16.50	—	—	—	—	—	—
20	40,50	—	—	—	—	—	—
30	200.00	—	—	—	—	—	—
35	423.75	—	—	—	—	—	—
40	936.25	—	—	—	—	—	—
50	4,162.5	—	—	—	—	—	—

1. Concentration

Taft Malm determined the effect of concentration on the viscosity and denistyof purified gum arabic solutions. The viscosities were measured with Ostwald pipettes at 300 ($pH = 7.14 \pm 0.02$), giving results shown in Table 10.8.

Similar results were obtained by Osborne and Lee with *Acacia* mucilages found in pharmaceutical preparations. The viscosities were determined with a Brookfield Synchrolectric Viscometer at room temperature (25.5 ± 05°) on *Acacia* mucilage prepared from powdered gum. The viscosity of the mucilages increased considerably with slight increases in concentration.

Kruyt and Tendeloo found that the viscosity of gum arabic solutions at very low concentrations follows Poiseuille's law governing the flow of liquids through capillary tubes. Their results at 25° showing viscosity as a function of concentration are given in Table 10.10.

Table 10.6 . Effect of Gum Arabic Concentration on Density of Viscosity

Concentration, by weight	% Density, g./cc.	Absolute Viscosity, poise	Relative Viscosity
1.22	1.000	0.0132	1.65
2.10	1.003	0.0160	2.00
2.70	1.006	0.0184	2.30
3.85	1.010	0.0234	2.92
3.95	1.011	0.0235	2.93
4.77	1.014	0.0250	3.23
5.54	1.017	0.0287	3.95
7.33	1.024	0.0390	4.87
8.55	1.029	0.0440	5.50
11.73	1.042	0.0707	8.84
15.68	1.050	0.0959	11.90
16.48	1.062	0.1400	17.50
18.69	1.071	0.190	23.70
34.92	1.141	2.410	300.00

Table 10.7. Effect of Concentration on Viscosity of Acacia Mucilage

Concentration, %	Viscosity, cps.
5	7.25
10	16.50
20	40.50
30	200.00
35	423.75
40	936.25
50	4.162.5

Table 10.8. Relative Viscosity of Gum Arabic at Low Concentrations

Concentration, %	Relative Viscosity
0.0311	1.060
0.0622	1.104
0.1244	1.185
0.2490	1.321
0.4983	1.564
1.0000	2.015

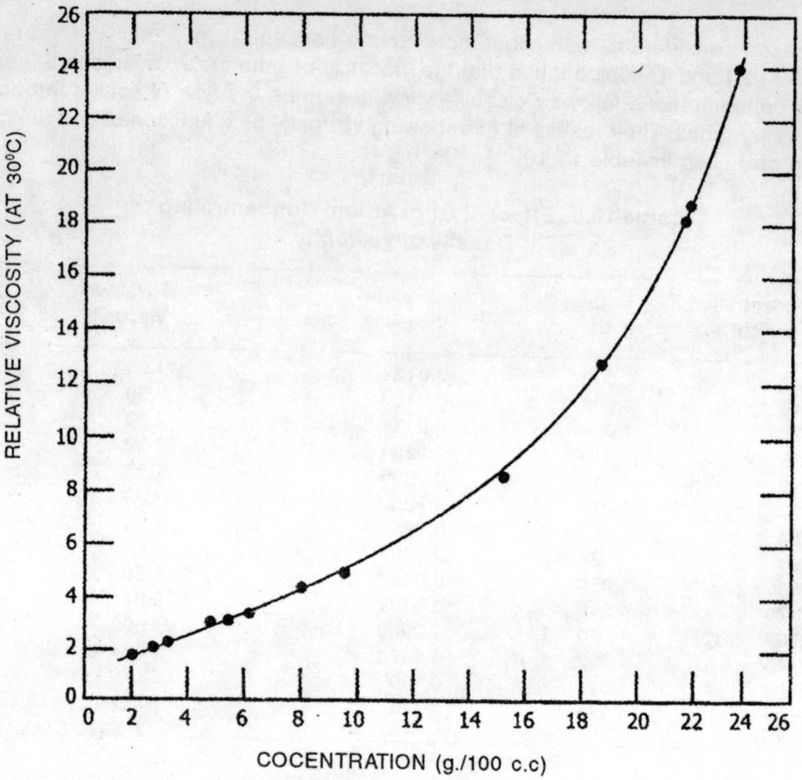

Fig. 10.7. Relative viscosity as a fuction of concentration (redrwn from Taft and Main)

2. Temperature

Taft and Malm also investigated the effect of temperature and showed that as the temperature increased the relative vicosity and density of gum arabic solutions decreased (Table 10.11). Using higher concentrations (a 35% solutions *of Acaciam*-cilage, U.S.P. XV), Osborne and Lee confirmed the fact that the viscosity is inversity proportional to temperature but varies to a smaller degree as the temperature is increased. Their results are given in Table 10.12.

Table 10.9. Effect of Temperature on Viscosity and Density of Gum Arabic Solutions

Concentration, %	Temperature	Density, g./cc.	Absolute Viscosity, Poise	Relative Viscosity
3.84	0°	1.019	0.0605	3.38
	15°	1.018	0.0357	3.13
30°	1.101		0.0234	2.93

	45°	1.009	0.0170	2.74
9.09	0°	1.197	0.1280	7.17
	15°	1.034	0.7049	6.57
	30°	1.031	0.0478	5.97
	45°	1.025	0.0327	5.48

Table 10.10. Effect of Temeprature on Viscosity of Acacia Mucilage (35%)

Temperature	Viscosity, cps.
10°	344.5
20°	219.8
30°	136
40°	107.6
50°	79.9
60°	62.75
70°	52,75
80°	42.8
90°	39

The viscosity of gum arabic solutions can be increased by drying the gum over sulfuric acid or by heating the dry gum. An untreated control solution of 35 g. of gum arabic in 100 ml. of water had an average relative viscosity of 12. Heating the dry gum at 40° for 48 hr. gave a product whose 35% solution had a viscosity of14.5; heating at 100° for 72 hr. gave a product with a 35% solution viscosity of 61.4. This unusual effect is totally unexpected and does not seem to be in accordance with the general behaviour of other polysaccharidic gums. However, Moorjani and Narwani repeated and confirmed Gabel's results and attempted to explain this unusual phenomenon. They studied the changes in gum arabic that had been subjected in a dry state to various temperatures above 100°. The viscosity of the gum solutions increased as the gum was heated from 100° to 160°. This was explained as being due to an increase of imbibed water in gum micelles. The water appears to be oriented in a sheel surrounding the micelles, and thus the disperse phase becomes highly solvated, resulting in the increase of viscosity. When heated to 170" and then put into water, gum arabic does not dissolve, but swells to form a nonstick; gel. However, there is practically no change in the chemical composition. This insolubility is explained as being due to complete dehydration and the consequent removal of protective aqueous films from the micelles. The loss of moisture on heating is shown in Table 10.13.

Moorjani and Narwani also examined the effect of sodium hydroxide on gum arabic that was heated to temperatures of 100°-170°. These effects were studied by potenticmetric titrations, and it was found that the quantity of sodium hydroxide required for neutralization increased with the rise in temperature. This was explained as being due to the difference between the extent of ionization of calcium and sodium arabates and the difference in hydration rates of calcium and sodium ions.

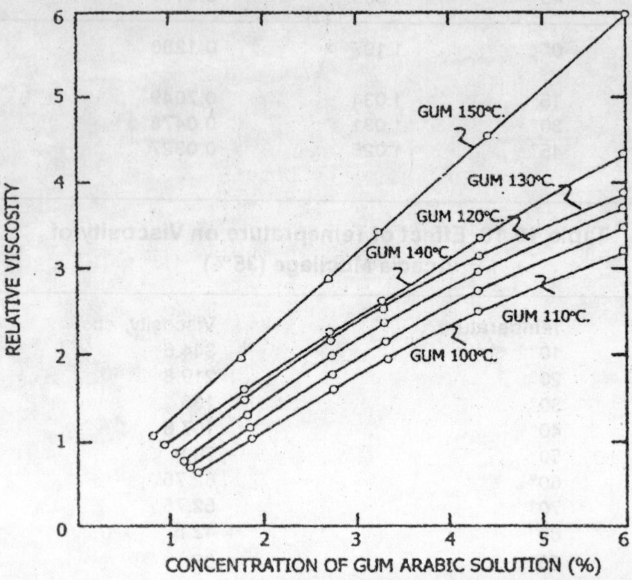

Effect of heating dry gum arabic on the relative viscosity of its soulutions.

Table 10.11. Loss of Moisture When Gum Arabic is Heated

Temperature to Which Gum was Heated	Loss of Moisture, %
110°	10.38
120°	11.47
130°	11.94
140°	13.32
150°	13.65
160°	13.65
170°	13.73

Table 10.12. Neutralization of Heat-Treated Gum Arabic

Temperature of Which Gum Was Heated	Milliliters of 0.02 N Sodium Hydroxide Required to Neutralize 2g. of Gum Arabic
100°	4.55
120°	5.9
130°	7.55
140°	8.05
150°	10.7
160°	12.2
170°	14.3

3. *Electrolytes*

The effect of electrolytes upon gum arabic solutions has been investigated by many authorities. The additon of electrolytes to 1% gum arabic solutions decreased the viscosity. This decrease in viscosity is proportional to the increase in the valence of the cation or the increase in the concentration of electrolyte. The addition of more than one electrolyte gives an additive effect.

All electrolytes, even in dilute solutions, lowered the viscosity of gum arabic. This lowering was much more pronounced in the more concentrated solutions as can be seen in Table 10.15. In preparation of emulsions, the lowering of viscosity and interfa-cial tension produces favorable emulsifying conditions. Thus, while a very good benzene-water or kerosene-water emulsion can be produced with a 10% gum arabic solution, equally good emulsions can be obtained with 0.5% gum arabic solutions in the presence of sodium hydroxide or sodium iodide for benzene and sodium sulfate or sodium bicarbonate for kerosene. However, the over-all effect of salt additions varies and depends upon the particular salt used. Taft and Malm studied this effect by adding various sodium salts to a solution of 5 g. of gum arabic in 100 g. of water at 30°; the concentration of the salt was 0.1 molal. The results are shown in Table 10.16.

Table 10.13. Effect of Elecrtrolytes on Relative Viscosity of Gum Arabic Solutions

Cone, of gum arabic, % by weight	No electrolyte	HCl	NaI	NaOH	$NaHCO_3$	$Na2SO_4$
0.5	1.380	1.114	1.107	1.190	1.208	1.343
5.0	3.170	2.101	2.479	2.624	2.604	2.887

Table 10.14. Effect of Various Sodium Salts on Viscosity of Gum Arabic69

Salt	Density g./cc	Relative Viscosity of Salt Solution	Relative Viscosity as a Function of Salt	Relative Viscosity as Compared to Water
Original Solution	1.014		3.23	
NaF	1.016	1.014	2.18	2.21
$Na2SO_4$	1.026	1.041	2.18	2.27
NaCl	1.017	1.000	2.19	2.21
NaBr	1.023	1.005	2.22	2.23
$NaNO_3$	1.018	1.005	2.22	2.23
NaI	1.024	0.999	2.22	2.22
NaSCN	1.017	0.997	2.23	2.22

Taft and Malm also investigated the effect of a single electroylte, calcium chloride, over a wide range of concentrations. They found that the addition of calcium chloride lowered the viscosity of gum arabic solutions, but as the concentration of I calcium chloride increased, the relative viscosity increased. The natural content of calcium in the gum itself did not have any effect on the viscosity. Borkowski and Olszak showed that there was no interdependence between the calcium content of the gum and the viscosity of gum solutions. The calcium content of the gums investigated ranged from 0.6345 to 0.9511%.

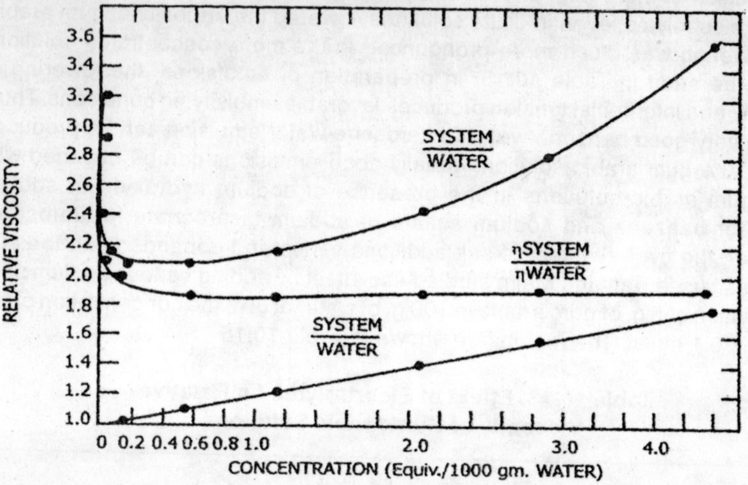

Effect pf calcium chloride concetration on relative siscosity of a 5% gum arbic solution; tempreature, 300, pH of all soultion 7.33-7.36.

Basu, Dasgupta, and Sircar, working with dilute solutions of purifed sodium arabate, showed that the reduced viscosity, $n)_{sp}/C$, increases as the concentration of the gum decreases and when sodium chloride is added, the viscosity decreases. However, when very concentrated solutions of gum arabic (about 35%) are mixed with aqueous solutions of salts, the effect is identical to that caused by dulution with distilled water, that is, the effect of the solute is negligible as compared with that of the solvent.

At low concentrations, there is another phenomenon known as the electroviscous effect which must be taken into consideration when dealing with gum arabic. This effect is graphically shown when the reduced viscosity is plotted against concentration. As the concentration of the gum decreases, the reduced viscosity decreases to a minimum; then at low concentrations a rapid rise occurs. This rapid rise at low concentrations is believed to be due to the charge on the molecule which has a greater effect on the viscosity at low concentrations. The addition of electrolytes will suppress this charge and give a lineal plot. The charge of a negatively charged colloid is more greatly suppressed by the addtion of a divalent cation than a mono-valent cation, and the additon of a trivalent cation depresses it sitll further, resulting in less hydration and a lower viscosity.

Gum arabic as negatively charged colloid is affected in this way and Bungenberg de Jong, Kruyt, and Lens have investigated this effect on very dilute gum arabic solutions (0.028-2.558%), both without added salt and in the presence of potassium chloride. With the gradual addition of potassium chloride, the curve straightens out and becomes linear as the electoviscous effect is neutralized. The comparative effect of monovalent and divalent salts can be seen by the addition of potassium chloride and barium chloride to gum arabic solutions. Bungenberg de Jong, Kruyt, and Lens have also shown the effectiveness of calcium chloride in neturalizing the electroviscous effect of gum arabic solutions of increasing concentrations.

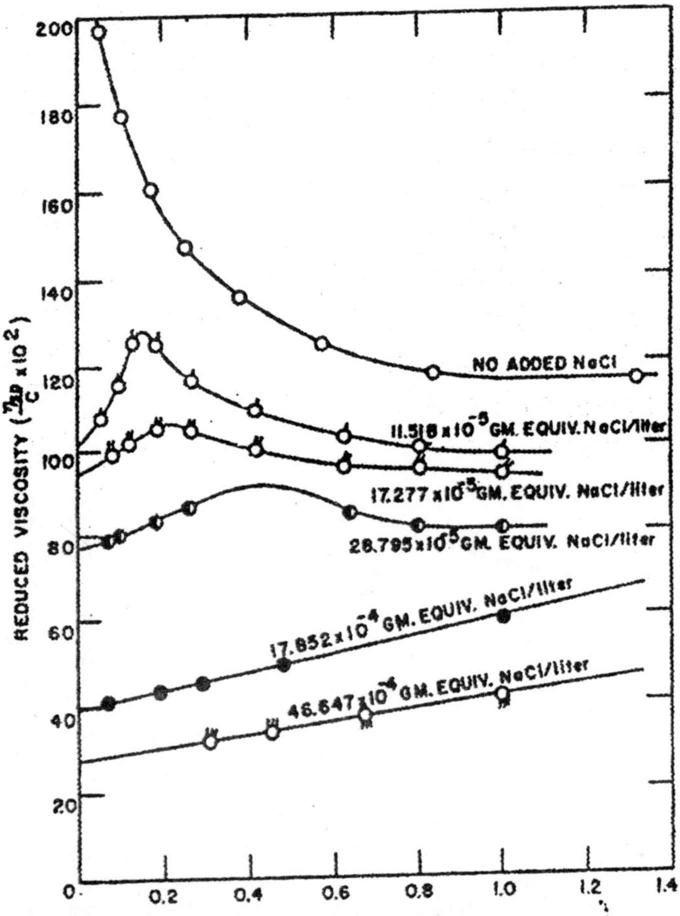

Reduced viscosity of sodium arbate as a function of sodium choride concentration.

At higher concentrations and in gum arabic solutions it will only be found in the 0-10% concentration range. The explanation for this is that the macromolecular electrolyte itself acts as an indifferent electrolyte and diminishes the interaction between its own charged areas, thus leading to a denser coil and a smaller, nonevident electroviscous effect.

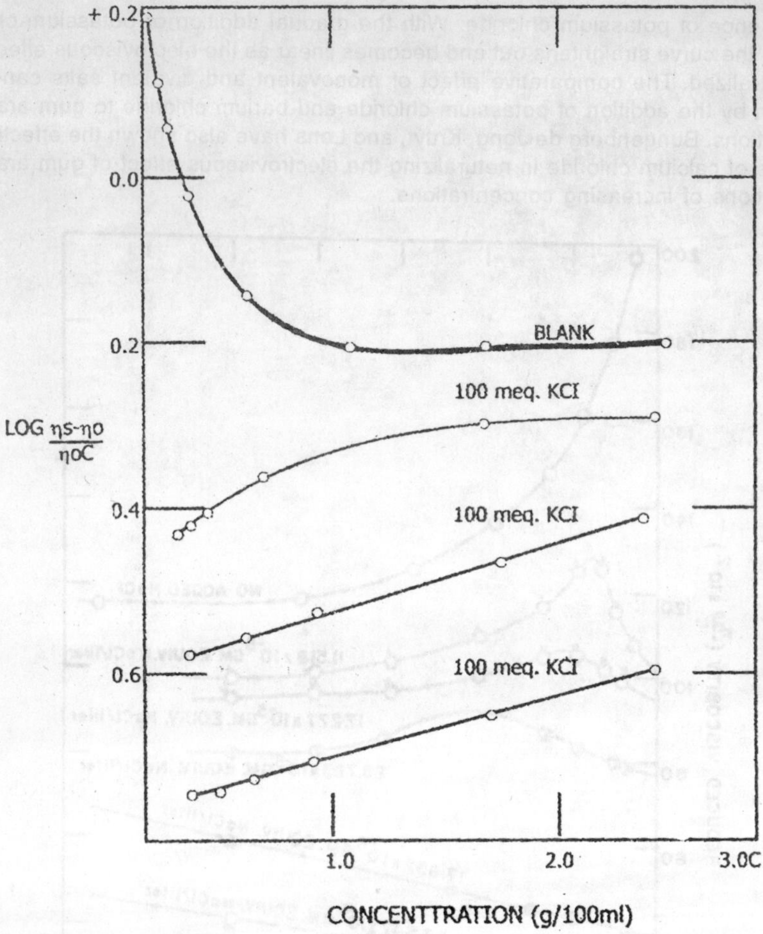

Neutralization of electroviscous effect with potassium chloride

4. *pH*

Thomas and Murray studied the effect of pH on gum arabic as shown in Fig. The data lie on a smooth curve, the maximum point of whichis pH 4.58-6.30. In the pH range from 5 to 10, there is a gradual change in viscosity with a marked change in pH. They also showed that arabic acid is a strong monobasic acid. Taft and Malm, who showed that the viscosity of gum arabic changes with pH (the maximum being in the range of pH 6-7), confirmed that arabic acid is a strong monobasic acid.

The relative viscosity of dilute sodium arabate solutions with respect to increasing pH at constant gum concentration (1.05%) was measured. The pH change was obtained by the addition of a few drops of alkali to a large volume of the gum arabic solution. (pH 6.8) so that there was virtually no change in concentration. Initially, the viscosity fall with increasing pH was small, while above pH 9 the fall was much more rapid. When the pH was reversed by the addition of acid, the viscosity remained practically constant from pH 11 to 6.8. Upon dialyzing the final solution the viscosity gradually increased with time until the original value was almost regained after 8-10 hr.

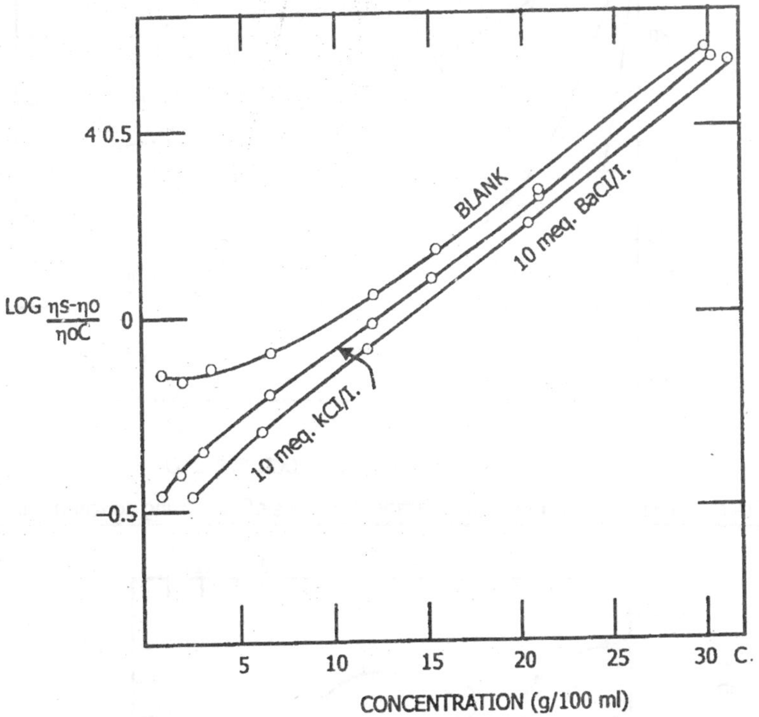

Comparative effect of monovalent and divalent salts on electroviscous phenomenon

Since a similar fall in viscosity is obtained by addition of sodium chloride, this effect has been attributed to the presence of the sodijm ion in the alkali, rather than to the effect of the specific *p*H value. This behaviour is due to the shape of the gum arabic molecule. The constitutent units of the gum arable molecule are arranged in an irregular flexible chain with the carboxyl groups of the uronic acids distributed along the chain. By changing the degree of ionization and the pH with the addition of an electrolyte, such as sodium hydroxide, the average distance between the charge centers in the polymer chain increases; the coulombic repulsion between the charge centers decreases, and the polymer chain coils up, causing a decrease in viscosity. With reversal of pH by the addition of hydrochloric acid, the excess hydroxide is simply neutralized to sodium chloride. There is no change in sodium ion cencentration, and therefore the viscosity of the solution remains unchanged because the coiling of the chain remains constant. But upon dialysis, the sodium salt in the system passes out, resulting in an increased viscosity due to an increased extension of the polymer chain.

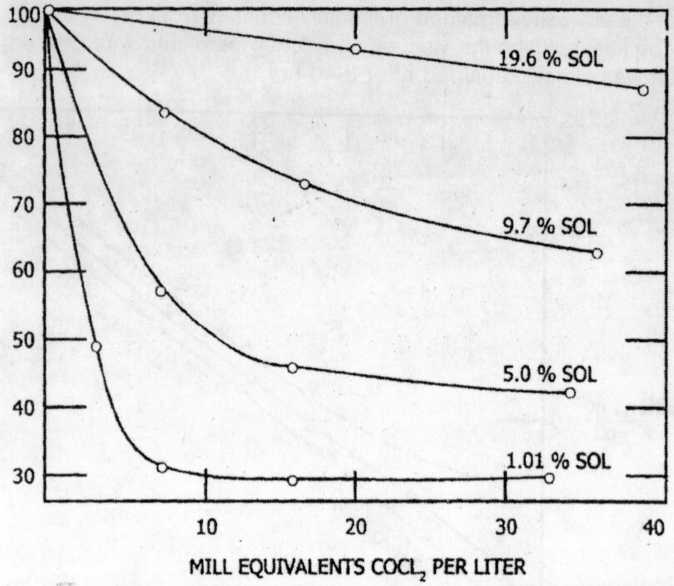

Effect of calcium chloride on gum arabic solutions of increasing concentration

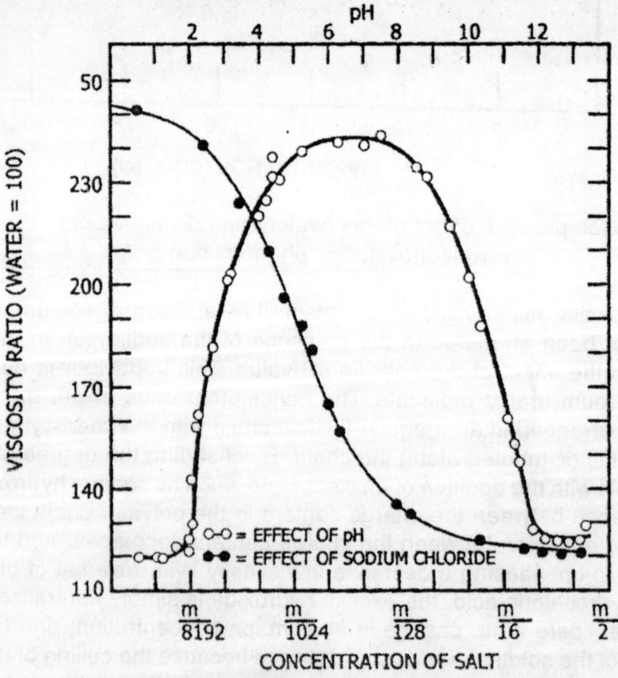

Siscosity of gum arabic solutions as a function of *p*H and salts.

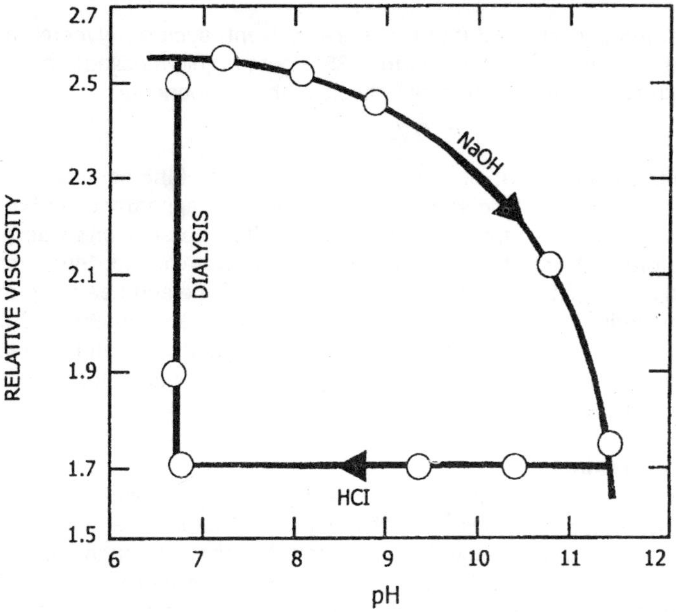

Effect of pH and sodium ions on viscosity of gum arabic solutions.

A detailed study of the effect of electrolytes that produce pH changes in gum arabic sirup was made by Woo and Huyck. They prepared a gum arabic sirup containing sodium benzoate, tincture of vanillin, and soluble saccharin for use as a vehicle for the following salts: potassium bromide, ammonium chloride, sodium citrate, ferric ammonium citrate. The base sirup was stable for 2.5 months at room temperatures and for two months at 37.5° at which time a precipitate formed. There was little change in pH, and the viscosity increased, reaching a maximum in 4 weeks and then decreasing. The *Acacia* sirups with the added neutral and acidic salts appeared to be stable for 6 months, but the sirup made with sodium citrate was stable for only 2 months.

In another series of experiments, *Accacia* sirup was prepared with glycerol as a preservative and evaluated under acidic (0.1% hydrochloric acid), neutral, and alkaline (0.1% dibasic sodium phosphate) conditions at 25° and 37.5°. All electrolytes lowered the viscosity of the solutions upon standing except sodium citrate, which increased the viscosity. Neutral and acidic preparations stored at room temperature were stable at the end of 1 month, but alkaline sirups developed sediment after 3 weeks of storage.

5. *Solvents Others Than Water*

Beutaric and Roy showed that the relative viscosity of gum arabic solutions decreased slowly with the addtion of ethanol; this decrease gradually became more rapid as the concentration of ethanol increased. The absorbance began to change tat about 50% ethanol and changed rapidly with the increase in alcohol concentration. At about 60% ethanol, gum arabic precipitated.

Osborne and Lee showed that a miscible solvent, such as glycerol, acts essentially as a diluent, when added to a 35% gum arabic mucilage, and the viscosity is a resultant of the combined effects of the components.

6. *Aging*

Taft and Malm found that dilute gum arabic solutions of the same temperature and concentration had the same viscosities until the appearance of bacterial growth, which usually appeared in 36-48 hr. after the solutions was prepared. Therefore, the time for measuring viscosities was limited. Since more concentrated solutions take longer to be attacked, Osborne and Lee performed a series of experiments to establish the effect of aging upon preserved and unpreserved *Acacia* mucilage, U.S.P. There was a substantially greater decrease of viscosity in an unpreserved 17.5% mucilage than there was in the mucilage preserved with 0.2% of benzoic acid.

7. *Mechanical Treatment*

Mechanical treatment of gum arable selutions does not affect their viscosities. A gum arable solution drawn through a Viscometer capillary about 20 times was found to be unchanged. However, mechanical passage through capillaries can be used to prepare emulsions using gum arable as the stabilizer. Emulsions of benzene or mixtures of benzene and liquid paraffin in water were prepared by passing the components, together with gum arabic, through capillaries under pressure.

8. *Ultrasonic Vibrations and Ultravilent Irradiation*

The maximum frequency of ultrasonic waves used for commercial applications is of the order of 10^a cycles per second, and the energy input for colloidal studies is somewhat greater than 10 watts/cm^2. Industrially, ultrasonic irradiation has been used for production of colloidal dispersions, but the structure of colloidal systems is easily broken down by these means; for example, irradiation lowers the viscosity of gum solutions. The gum arabic solutions are depolymerized by ultrasonic waves. Troger suggested the use of piezoelectric vibrations for the conditioning of varnish and dispersing of paint pigments, but these vibrations diminished the viscosity of gum arabic solutions by reducing the molecular weight rapidly to 150,000 and more slowly to 30,000. Continued capsoure of gum arabic solutions to ultrasonic vibration to release monosaccharides.

Ultraviolet radiation also markedly reduced the viscosity of gum arabic mucilage irradiated for 2 hr. in opendishes, gum arabic has an absorption maximum at *265μ*.

This lack of gum arabic stability to vibrational energy resulted in other emulsifiers being perferred for certain pharmaceutical preparations made by ultrasonic means. Hard soap, polyethylene glycol 400 monostearate, and polysorbate 80 were shown to be more stable emulsifiers than gum arabic, while sodium dodecyl suflate and gum tragacanth were inferior.

Other Physical Properties

1. *Surface Tension*

The addition of gum arabic to water results in a lowering of the surface tension as shown in Table 10.17. The temperature had a very important effect on the surface tension of a gum arabic soluton is also shown. Using a 4.066% solution of purified gum arabic at temperatures of 30°, 40°, and 50°, the values for surface tension were 61.80, 60.46, and 59.03 dynes/cm., respectively. The surface tension measurements were made with a modified Traube stalagmometer. Since it was observed that the surface tention changed significantly with age, each complete series of measurements was made within one day. There is first a slight increase and then a gradual decrease in surface tension with an increase in gum arabic concentration. The addition of electrolytes usually gives lower values, with hydrochloric acid being extremely effective. Sodium hydroxide is found to have the greatest depressing effect in solutions containing up to 0.5% of gum arabic, after which the acid is most effective. This lowering of surface tension (or intefacial tension in mixtures) simultaneously with the lowering of viscosity by the addition of electrolytes produces ravorable emulsivying conditons. The comparative effect of electrolytes on surface tension is shown in Table 10.18. Surface tension is lowered more by monvalent ions than by divalent ions. The power of the different ions in lowering surface tension is in the order of Li^{+}> Na^{+}> K^{+}> Ca^{++}> Ba^{++}.

Table 10.15. Effect of Gum arabic Concentration on the Surface Tension of Water

Gum Arabic Concentration,%	Surface Tension at 30", dynes/cm.
0.000	71.18
1.016	69.93
2.033	67.09
4.066	63.16

Table 10.16. Effect of Electrolytes on Surface Tension of Gum Arabic Solutions

Concentration of gum arable, % by weight	No electrolytes	Surface tension, dynes/cm. HCl	Nal	NaOH	$NaoH_2$	NA_2SO_4
0.01	72.26	—	—	—	—	—
0.1	72.30	—	—	—	—	—
0.5	72.18	68.75	72.24	70.88	72.08	73.18
1.0	72.04	—	—	—	—	—
5.0	69.69	61.98	63.28	65.41'	65.56	66.29
10.0	61.49	—	—	—	—	—

2. *Freezing Point*

The freezing point of gum arable solutions decreases as the concentration of gum arable increases. These freezing point data should be taken as evidence that gum arabic dispersions should not be frozen. Thawing of a frozen gum arabic soultion that has had a separation of ice crystals might not bring it back to the original condition, and it might be impossible to repreduce the original viscosity.

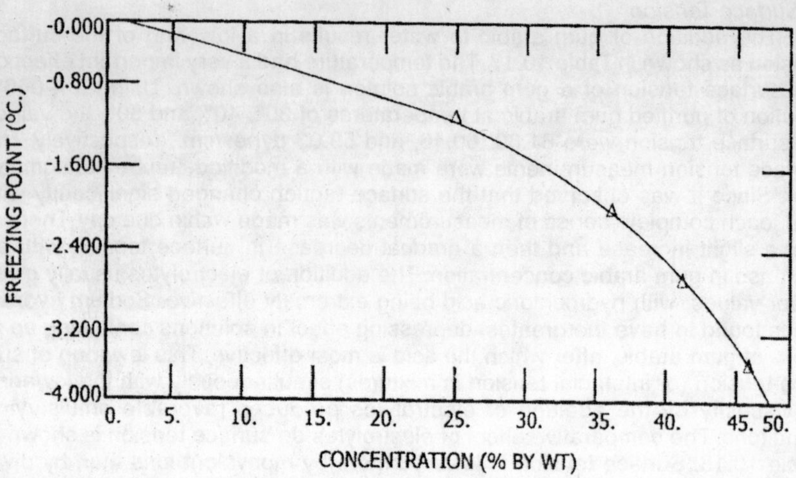

Freezing point of gum arbic soultions as a function of concentration.

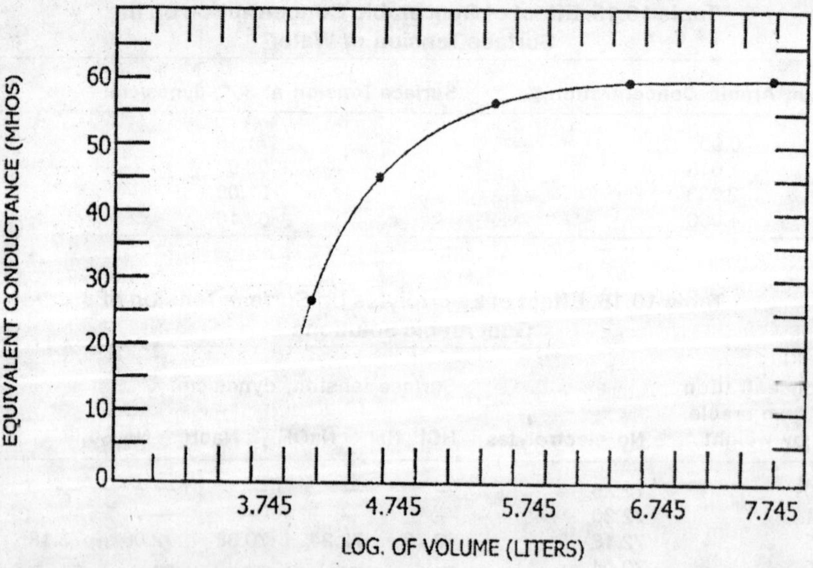

Equivalent conductance of a gum arabic solution as a function of volume

Since the equivalent conductance of the gums is of the same order of magnitude as that of their positive ions, it is assumed that the positive ions are the chief carriers of the current in these solutions. The slight difference is believed to be due to the effect of the presence of the very large arabate ion and possibly also to the method of extrapolation used to obtain these values.

COACERVATION

1. *Introduction*

The separation of colloid, solutions into two phases is a phenomenon knwon as coacervation which can be manifested by turbidity, droplet formation or actual separation of a liquid layer. The usual coacervate encountered is the single colloid type, as exemplified by the coacervate formed by addition of sodium suflate or ethanol to a gelatin solution. However, many coacervates are known which contain two or more colloids.

Coacervates fall into two main classes, simple and complex. While coacervates of different classes might appear similar, they are actually quite different in their properties. The number of colloids present has no direct bearing on whether the coacervate is simple or complex. A simple coacervate is caused by a partial miscibil-ity effect. Thus, it is formed with the two colloids, gelatin and gum arabic, at pH's above the isoelectric point of gelatin. In this region, both colloids are negatively charged. If the solutions are sufficiently concentrated, there will be separation caused by mutual salting out. Simple coacervates occur only in concentrated solutions since the main requisite is water deficiency. Addition of non reacting salts to the coacervate might have no effect but often enhances simple coacervate formation. The effectiveness of a particular salt is largely dependent upon its position in the ; lyotropic series. No disintegration of a simple coacervate occurs in a direct current electric field in as much as charged particles are not responsible for the phenomenon. Both layers of a simple coacervate are found to be rich in colloid, but each layer contains mainly one of them.

By way of contrast, complex coacervates can occur only with two or more colloids having opposite charges. In the case of gelatin and gum arabic, a complex coacervate is formed with the negative gum arabic when the gelatin is positive (at pH's below its isoelectric point). Complex coacervates cannot occur in concentrated solutions, but only in dilute solutions, even as low as 0.001%. Nonreacting sate suppers complex coacervates with effectiveness depending upon valency. Position in the lyotropic series in important. Direct current electric fields cause disnitegration of complex coacervates. Both layers in a complex coacervate contain colloid; one is fairly concentrated and the other relatively dilute. However, both layers contain the same proportion of the two colloids which are held together by their charges.

It is not the purpose of this chapter to discuss coacervates in general, since an excellent discussion already exists. However, the complex coacervate between gum arabic and gelatin has many interesting features, and the main portion of this section will be devoted to that coacervate. Some mention will be made of other coacervates of gum arabic.

2. *Gum Arabic-Gelatin Coacervates*

Typical coacervates are formed with gum arabic and gelatin at certain optimum concentrations. The phenomenon is manifested by the formation of clear stable emulsions of concentrated solutions as microdroplets suspended in comparatively dilute solutions. Many factors affect coacervate formation, such as pH, salts and other variables. It is the combination of these factors that determines the properties of the coacervates formed.

The nature of the materials forming the coacervate is exceedingly important. Thus, an amphoteric substance, such as geltain, can form complex coacervates with basic colloids at pH's above its isoelectric point and also with acidic substances at yoH's below its isoelectric point. Nonamphoteric, acidic substances, such as gum arabic, can form complex coacervates only with basic materials.

Proof that a loose compound is formed in coacervation was offered by Dervichian and Magnant, who observed that a gelatin solution was capable of forming a film of a certain strength, while gum arabic formed no film. Mixtures of gum arabic and gelatin, however, formed a double-strength film when mixed at pH 3.5 and 40° and allowed to set. The increase in strength was observed in the same pH region, 2-4.8 knwon to be optimum for coacervate formation. The flow birefringence of gelatin is known to change in the presence of arabate ions. This is accepted as additional evidence of complex formation.

A recent paper discussed coacervation phenomena from the standpoint of modern polymer theory. Coacervates were considered to be immense aggregates containing large amounts of trapped, immobilized solvent. The coils are contained in a medium of poor solvent. Consequently, no coacervation is expected in systems where the coils are extended. This theory was confirmed by precipitation of gelatin and gum arabic from aqueous solution with ethanol at both high and low pH's. High *fl* caused the gum arabic to be extended due to the repulsive effect of the negative carboxyl groups, while low pH had a similar effect on the basic centers of gelatin. As expected, extended chains resulted in pressing effect and led to precipitation of viscous liquids or gels at all *p*H values. This effect was attributed to common ion effect of the salt.

Bungenberg de Jong and co-workers consider the complex coacervate of geltain and gum arabic to be a structure of gelatin cations to which portions of anion centers of gum arabic are randomly attached. Gum arabic does not contribute at all to the gel structure but is merely held by electrostatic.

3. *Preparation of Coacervates*

Coacervates of gelatin-gum arabic are easy to prepare. One merely mixes 3% solutions of gelatin and gum arabic in the desired proportions and makes the solutions weakly acidic with acetic acid. The optimum proportion of gum arabic is 59%. Coacervation does not occur below 19% nor above 81% of gum arabic.

A very stable coacervate can be prepared by mixing solutions of 6 g. of gum arabic in 10 ml. of water and 5 g. of gelatin in 190 ml. of water and then adding a solution of 2 g. of resorcinol in 10 ml. of 0.03 *N*hydrochloric acid. The purpose of the resorcinol is to prevent gelation of the gelatin at room temperature, thus giving a coacervate that is stable at room temperature for long periods. Hydrochloric acid is, perhaps, too strong an acid for coacervate formation; some workers prefer acetic acid or dilute acetate buffers. Buffers are more desirable than acids when *p*H is an important factor in the investigation.

When gelatin is partially heat-degraded by heating to 60° and the resulting product is reacted with gum arabic to form a coacervate, it can be observed that significantly less coacervate forms. Enzyme degradation has a similar effect. The reason for the lower volume of coacervate is that the gelatin has been sufficiently destroyed by hydrolysis so that the resulting coacervate is more soluble in the medium than when undergraded gelatin is used.

Coacervates in the form of hollow spheres with skinlike walls can be readily formed. The art of preparing these spheres invovles mixing gelatin and gum arabic solutions of the same pH, heating to 40°, allowing to cool, warming again to 40° and removing the supernantant solution by decantation. The coacervate is then added to a dilute hydrochloric acid solutions, at the same OH, and the mixture is thoroughly shaken. Slowly settling hollow spheres are thus formed. The wall material of the spheres contains both components, gum arabic and gelatin, but it has significantly less water than the original coacervate.

4. *General Properties, Physical Appearance, and Composition*

They physical`apperance of a geltain-gum arabic complex is directly related to its history and mode of preparation. Thus, coacervates made by mixing and acidifying 3% solutions of gum arabic and gelatin may be homogeneous with interposed large vacuoles, network-like, or foamy and filled with many hollow spaces. If the material gels, it is auctally a gelatin gel in which the gum arabic is ionically bound to the gelatin molecules.

5. *Effect of Temperature*

It was found that, as long as the material is not permitted to gel by keeping it above 30°, the optimum ratio of ingredients (59% of gum arabic) did not change. However, higher temperatures gave lower volumes of coacervate, probably due to increased solubility of the coacervate in the medium. Coacervates prepared at higher temperatures contained somewhat less water than rose made at lower temperatures. This might be due to the overpowering effect of the repulsion factor together with the hydration of the two colloid ions since hydration is less at increased temperatures. Vacuole formation does not seem to be directly related to temperatures, but is caused by gel formation. The avoid vacuoles at 33-40° special techniques can be used. However, in spite of these, upon cooling to 28°, vacuoles are again formed.

6. *Effect of pH*

Complex coacervate formation depends strongly upon pH. Optimum pH is that at which one partner of the coacervate is strongly negative and the other strongly positive. The same consideration holds true if one member is amphoteric, for example, gelatin, Thus, at *p*H 4.7 acidic gelatin is only weakly positive while gum arabic is strongly negative. As the *p*\\ is lowered, the situation is reversed, with the gelatin becoming strongly positive and the gum arabic weakly negative. In the absence of salts, the optimum acidity for gelatin-gum arabic coacervate formation is about pH 3.7. Measurements showed that coacervate droplets of about 50μ in diameter reached their equilibrium size within 10 min. The minimum diameter and hence the greatest mutual bonding was at pH 3.7. At pH 1.2, the electric charge on both gelatin and gum arabic is so low that coacervate formation does not occur.

7. Reactions of Salts

The effect of salts was studied by sealing a mixture of 6 g. gum arabic and 5 g. of gelatin in a colloidal membrane and causing coacervate formation by flowing dilute acetic acid down the membrance.[110] Low salt concentration had little or no effect, but increasing salt concentration caused first uniform vacuolization, then local vacuolization, and finally complete solution of the coacervate. Potency of a salt to react with a coacervate is as follows: $M^{+}_{3}A$— < $M^{+}{}_{2}A$-< $M^{+}A$ < $M^{++}A$-2 < M^{+++} $A_{.3}$. Suppression of separation was favored by polyvalent anions and cations.

In another series of experiments, the optimum acid concentration for maximum coacervate formation was meacured with respect to salts added while the gelatin and gum arabic concentrations were held constants. Multivalent cation salts interact more strongly with the negative partner of the coacervate than do monovalent cation salts. Hence, poly cationic salts require a more alkaline medium to produce the additional negative charge needed to match the existing positive charge on the other member of the coacervate, for example gelatin. The polyvalent cation salt has he effect of reducing the negative charge on the gum arabic, while the higher *p*H tends to increase the negative charge, thus achieving balance. In a similar manner, a divalent anion tends to lower the optimum pH of coacervate formation by reacting primarily with the positive partner of the coacervate. Trivalent anionic salts do not readily ionize completely in the acid region *p*H 3-4, and hence it is difficult to, see why these salts should have any different effect on complex coacervates than monovalent anionic salts. Therefore, with the omission of the incompletely ionized $M^{+}_{3}A$— salts, the effect of a series of salts of different valencies should be as follows: $M^{+++}A_{3}$, highest optimumu *p*H*;* $M^{++}A'_{2}$, $M^{+}A''$, no effect on optimum pH; $M^{+}_{2}A$—, lowest optimum *pH.*

When *p*H was held constant, addition of salts required variation of the gum arabic: gelatin ratio for optimum coacervate formation as follows: (high gum arabic: gelatin ratio) $M^{+++}A'_{3}$, $M^{++}A_{2}$, $M^{+}A$~, $M^{+}_{2}A$—, $M^{+}_{3}A$— (low gum arabic: gelatin ratio).

Swelling of coacervate droplets is lowest at pH 3.7 where water content is least. Reversible swelling at this *fH* due to salt addition is, in general, least for monovalent salts and increases for divalent and trivalent salts. The concentration of the salt is also important. In an experiment, coacervate droplets were suspended in a series of pH 3.7 dilute acetate buffer solutions until equilibrium diameter was reached. The droplets were then cuspended in the same buffer with increasing amounts of potassium chloride which caused them to swell. They were then resupended in dilute buffer identical to the original buffer and observed. It was found that when the potassium chloride concentration was 0.08 *M* or less, the droplets returned to the original diameter. In 0.01 *M* potassium chloride they did not quite return to their original size. When 0.12 M or greater concentrations were used, an increase of swelling was obtained by resuspension in the original buffer.

Normally, minimum swelling occurs at pH 3.7 However, the minimum swelling point could be raised as high as pH 4.81 merely by treatment of the coacervate with potassium chloride solution. Further experiments showed that reaction time of the salts was critical. Only with 0.04 *M* potassium chloride was the *fM* for minimum swelling constant for as long as 5 hr. For concentrations of potassium chloride of 0.1-0.5 M the pH for minimum swelling rose rapidly the first hour, then tapered off to equilibrium values.

8. *Physical Phenomena*

It was found early in the study of gelatin-gum arabic coacervates that droplets could be obtained that would move toward either the catchode or the anode or would remain stationary in an electric field. Additional studies indicated that the component in excess was critical in deciding how the particle would migrate in an electric field. It was also found that in an individual geltain-gum arabic coacervate droplet, the gum arabic accumulated at the anode side while the geltain accumulated at the cathode side. In general, complex coacervates tend to disintegrate in a direct current electric field.

Lower intefacial tensions were obtained were obtained when potassium chloride was added. The change in interfacial tension observed in electric fields was ascribed not to *p*H changes, since the systems were adequately buffered, but to migration of the components within a single droplet.

Coacervate droplets exhibit a phenomenon of motion in a diffusion field due to local concentration changes.

9. *Uses of Gum Arabic-Gelatin Coacervates*

Coacervates of gum arabic and gelatin have interesting properties which suggest many potential uses. By pouring some coacervates into water, immediate gels are formed containing fine vacuoles. There are many potential uses for these rapid-gelling systems. Coacervates also very readily develop edible hollow spheres that have many potential uses in the food industry, such as in fixing flavors and colours.

By addition of a little salt to a gelatin-gum arabic coacervate, a viscous liquid or gel is formed that is stable over a wide (pH range. Since the system is edible, uses in the food industry are obvious.

10. *Coexisting Coacervates*

Still more complicated coacervates can be prepared by combining three substances that can mutually react to form them. Thus, one can form a coexisting complex coacervate by mixing solutions of gelatin, gum arabic, and sodium nucleinate at the proper *pH.* Best coacervate formation is obtained with three parts of gelatin and one part each of gum arabic and sodium nucleinate at *p*H 3.6. At a higher *p*H (3.77), an electric field indicates a negative complex coacervate, while at *p*H 3.43, the coacervate is positive.

It is apparent that two types of complex coacervation can exist within a three-colloid system. In the above example, the gelatin was positively charged while the other two components were negatively charged. In such coexisting complex coacervates, each layer contains all three colloids, but one is rich in arabate and poor in nucleinate and the other is rich in nucleinate and poor in arabate. In this system, the two coacervates, gelatin-arabate and gelatin-nucleinate, are only partly miscible in each other. Difference of properties, for example, equivalent weight, of arabate and nucleinate are at least partly responsible for this effect.

Another type of three-colloid system with two positive colloids can be formed from gelatin, arabate, and ichthyocol. Here, both proteins are postive and the arabate is negative. The coacervates, gelatin-arabate and ichthyocol-arabate, are mutually miscible in all proportions so that only two layers are formed. The similarity in' properties of gelatin and ichthyocol is the determining factor that permits complete miscibility.

11. *Other Coacervates*

Gum arabic forms its best-known and most important coacervate with gelatin but it is known to form coacervates with many other substances. It forms an interesting coacervate with toluidine blue. The coacervate is normal in that coacervation is more rapid with increasing toluidine concentration and is inhibited by neutral salts. A coacervate of gum arabic and lecithin which was added to the surface of catechol solution buffered at pH 5.35. Another interesting coacervate is formed with trypaflavin.

Gum arabic forms coacervates readily with many proteins. A coacervate is formed between gum arabic and hemoglobin at pH 2.2^{-4}, but not at pH 4.2. These coacervates are stable up to 50°. Addition of myristylcholine forms a 3-component coacervate. Other proteins known to complex with gum arabic are serum albumin, egg albumin, and casein.

Micheel and Heuer formed compounds of gum arabic with gelatin and other substances. These compounds should not be considered coacervates as there is a true covalent (amide) bond between the gelatin and gum arabic instead of the electrostatic linkage of the complex coacervate. Arabicyl proteins are soluble in water at pH 7.5-8, contain considerable amounts of polysaccharide, and are precipitated at pH 6-6.5. The general procedue for preparation of these compounds is to esterify the gum arabic and couple it to the protein by the azide method.

Gum arabic forms an important coacervate with carrageenam which is useful as a stabilizer for milk products. The material has been recomended as a stabilizer for icecream when 6-9 oz. are included in each 100-gal. batch of ice cream mix.

Chemical Properties

1. *Chemical Reactivity*

Gum arabic as the calcium, magnesium, and potassium salt of arabic acid reacts with many reagents in a manner similar to that of other polysaccharidic acid salts. Solutions of gum arabic will produce precipitates or heavy gels on addition of any of the following reagents: borax, ferric chloride, basic lead acetate, mercuric nitrate, gelatin, potassium silicate, sodium silicate, Millon's reagent, Stake's acid mercuric nitrate reagent. In general, trivalent metallic salts will cause precipitation of gum arabic. Dilute (1%) gum arabic solutions can be coagulated by the addition of Ruthenium red, Hexol nitrate, or Desogen Geigy.

However, in many applications the flocculation or thickening of gum arabic can be prevented or retarded by the addition of soluble alkali polyphosphates in a concentration of 0.1-1.0% of the total solution.

Upon treatment with dilute acids, gum arabic is hydrolyzed to yield a mixture of L-arabinose, L-rhamnose, D-galactose. With nitric acid treatment, gum arabic yields mucic, saccharic, and oxalic acids.

Five ml. of *Acacia* mucilage, U.S.P., (35%) was treated with 5 ml. ov various reagents and observed. Under these conditions, it was soluble with concentrated and dilute hydrochloric acid, concentrated and dilute acetic acid, concentrated and the ammonium hydroxide, and dilute sodium hydroxide. It was soluble in 10% solutions of sodium chloride, mercuric chloride, bismuth chloride, and silver nitrate, but insoluble with 10% ferric chloride and concentrated sodium hydroxide. *Acaca* mucilage showed complete, compatibility with 1:1,000 dilutions of morphine sulfate, ephedrine hydrochloride, quinine sulfate, strychnine, and caffeine. The U.S. Dispensatory reports the following as being incompatiable with gum arabic: aminopyrine, pyrogallol, morphine, vanillin, phenol, thymol, carvol, a- and p-naphthol, pyrocatechol, guaiacol, cresols, eugenol, acetyleugenol, apromorphine, eserine, epinephrine, isobarbaloin, caffeotannic acid, gallic acid, tannin.

In its reactivity with plastic films, gum arabic has been reported to be generally compatible with methycellulose derivatives. Tests run with Methocel 65 HG (high-' gel-point Methocel) showed that the upper limit of compatibility is a solution of 6% of Methocel 65 HG, 50 cps., and 4% of gum arabic, which is stable after standing for 3 days at room temperature. Carboxymethylcellulose (Hercules CMC-70 Medium)is compatible with gum arabic in both solutions and films. A 2% CMC-70 Medium solution and a 2% gum arabic solution are compatible when mixed in ratios of 3:1, 1:1, and 1:3.

2. *Solubility*

Gum arabic is insoluble in oils and in most organic solvents but is one of the most water-soluble of all gums. It dissolves completely in hot or cold water, forming a clear, mucilaginous solution. Solutions containing up to 50% of gum arabic can be prepared, and, as previously shown, the solubility in water increases as the temperature increases. Certain samples of gum arabic, usually the exudates collected at the beginning of the dry season, are not completely soluble. They form a stringy, mucus-like fluid which separates into two phases upon standing. After storage for 2-3 months, enzymatic changes occur and the gum becomes completely soluble.

Gum arabic is soluble in aqueous ethanol up to a limit of about 60% of alcohol. Arabic acid behaves similarly.

The solubility of gum arabic in organic solvents was studied by Taft and Malm, Solubility was tested in aliphatic and aromatic alcohols, ketones, ethers, esters, halogen derivatives, glycols, pyridine, hydrocarbons, and liquid ammonia. Onlyeth-ylene glycol and glycerol were effective solvents with low-viscosity gum arabic when the temperature was raised. Very slight solubility was shown with some acetate esters and acetate-alcohol mixtures. Gum arabic was completely insoluble in most of the organic solvents.

The gum arabic mucilage (35%) can ge mixed with glycerol in all proportions to given a compatible solution with a viscosity equal to the resultant of the viscosities of both components. Evaporation forms a thick gel.

Although gum arabic is very soluble in water, finely divided colloid particles tend to clump when dispersed in water and do not dissolve readily unless vigorous agitation is used. This is due to the fact that when the material is added to water, a quantity of it becomes coated with a gel-like layer on the outside as a result of the rapid hydration of the outside, particles which prevents the penetration of moisture to the inside. Many techniques have been developed for preparing gum arabic and other hydrophilic gum solutions. Two of the simpler methods are to mix the gum intimately with the other powdered ingredients before adding them to the water or to wet it thoroughly with ethanol or glycerol before dispersing in water.

3. *Enzymes*

Gum arabic contains both oxidases and peroxidases which can be inactivated by heating the gum solution to 80° or higher for 1 hr. The peroxidase content varies with different gum arabic preparations, but these enzymes can be inactivated without affecting the viscosity by heating to 100° for 30 min.

Separation and Identification of Gum Arabic

Gum arabic occurs in such a wide variety of complex substances and mixtures that it is often difficult to detect. However, by following the procedures given in this section, little trouble should be encountered in isolating and identifying it. It is recommended that the analyst proceed according to the following steps: (1) isolation (if required); (2) analysis by a systematic scheme; (3) physical confirmatory tests; (4) chemical confirmatory tests; (5) direct tests for gums in some commercial products (optional). The rest of this section will discuss each of the above steps with special emphasis on gum arabic.

It should be brone in mind that standards of purity have been established for the various gums. Frequently, a knowledge of these standards can be helpful in gum analysis. For gum arabic, the following standards have been set up for a good quality gum.

Total ash. - Not over 4%

Acid-insoluble ash.— Not over 0.5%.

Water. — Not over 15%.

Insoluble residue. — Boiling a mixture of 5 g. gum arabic, 100 ml. of distilled water and 10 ml. of dilute hydrochloric acid for 15 min. should not yield a residue exceeding 50 mg.

Starch.— A boiled and cooled 2% solution of gum arabic should not give a bluish or reddish color with iodine.

Tannins. — The addition of ferric chloride to a 2% gum arabic solution should not give a blackish discoloration or precipitate.

Heavy metals— The heavy metal content should not exceed the following arsenic, 0.5 p.p.m.; lead, 1.7 p.p.m.; zinc, 10 p.p.m.; copper, 10 p.p.m.

1. *Isolation of Gum Arabic from Commercial Products*

Gum arabic occurs in a great many commercial products. In simple cases, the gum mixture is heated with dilute acetic acid, filtered, cooled, and treated with ethanol or acetone to precipitate the gum. The isolation and identification of gum arabic in a complex product is usually a problem that has a be solved for each specific product on an individual basis, depending on the properties and complexities of the material under consideration.

2. *Systematic Analytical Scheme*

When the gum has been isolated, a systematic analytical scheme, can be used. This method is based on precipitation reactions with calcium chloride, sodium hydroxide, barium hydroxide, and lead acetate. In addition, reactions are given for the gums using a cationic soap, ammonium sulfate, mercuric nitrate, papain, and gelatin. The scheme is designed for identification of common gums and illustrates'how gum arabic can readily be distinguished from a vast groups of other gums. A confirmatory test must always be used when a positive test for a gum is obtained.

The sodium hydroxide test as given is often indefinite. It could be improved by carefully distilling a portion of the strongly alkaline gum solution and cehmically examining the distillate for methanol. A positive test for methanol indicates pectin; a negative test indicates pectic acid or algin. Gum arabic and most other *gums* would also give a negative test.

It should be emphasized that confirmatory tests must always be used since gums of different sources or histories might not act as expected. Also, the presence of foreign materials can give a result that is false or misleading. However, the scheme is sound and workable and is a valuable tool for the practicing gum chemist.

3. *Physical Confirmatory Tests*

After the gum is identified, physical and chemical confirmatory tests must be made. These tests utilize the basic knowledge of the properties and reactions of the gum being analyzed. The standards and specifications of the common grades of gum being used should be kept in mind, and it should be noted with respect to gum arabic that the U.S.P. grade is utilized extensively in this country.

a. Physical appearance—The spheroidal tears (unground gum) of gum arabic are yellowish, white or translucent, almost odorless, and mucilaginous when wetted. Tears can be as large as 32 mm. in diameter or can be broken into angular fragments. The material is very brittle. 137 Gum arabic powder is nearly white. Microscopically, it is seen to consist of minute angular fragments.

b. Infrared spectra.— Gum arabic can be identified by its infrared spectra. Neuberger and co-workers determined the infrared spectra of gum arabic and many other common gums. The process can be used to identify gums isolated from foods, drugs, and cosmetics.

c. Solubility tests— Gum arabic is practically unique among gums because of its very high water solubility. A good confirmatory test consists in mixing the gum with twice its weight of water at room temperature. Gum arabic will dissolve almost completely and usually gives a weekly acidic solution. Although it is insoluble in ethanol and other organic solvents, its aqueous solutions will dissolve in glycerol.

d. Optical activitiy— A 10% aqueous gum arabic solution has almost no optical activity but might be slightly levorotatory.

4. *Chemical Confirmatory Tests*

Additional chemical tests which can aid in distinguishing gum arabic from other gums are listed below. For a rapid test to distinguish gum arabic from gum traga-canth, iodine solution is added. Since gum arabic contains no starch, no colour will be developed. Solutions of tragacanth, which is almost always accompanied by starch, turn blue. Similarly, addition of 0.02 *N* iodine solution to powdered gum arabic causes no colour change, while other gums, such as agar and tragacanth acquire a crimson or olive-green colour.

Gum arabic can be readily distinguished from quince or pectin gums by the procedure of Bryant. To 10 ml. of a 1% gum solution, 1 ml. of 10% thorium nitrate is added. The solution is stirred and allowed to stand for 2 min. A gel indicates pectin or quince gums; gum arabic gives a negative test. Arabic can be distinguished from tragacanth, agar, karaya, carrageenan, quince, and locust bean gums by reacting 3 ml. of gum solution with 0.5 ml. of Millon's reagent. A gel indicates carrageenan, agar, or locust bean gum. A flocculent, nonsettling precipitate indicates quince or tragacanth. A fine, powdery, or curdy precipitate shows gum arabic or karaya. If this precipitate dissolves in excess reagent, gum arabic is indicated.

In as much as gum arabic contains enzymes, a drop of hydrogen peroxide added to a mixture of gum arabic solution and tincture of guaiacum produces a blue colour. This serves as a useful identity test. A deep blue colour is also produced when 0.5 ml. of hydrogen peroxide solution and 0.5 ml. of a 1% benzidine solution (in 90% ethanol) are added to a solution of 0.25 g. of gum arabic in 5 ml. of water and allowed to stand. Particles of gum arabic can be distinguished from agar and karaya be mounting the gums in solutions of ruthernium red and examining them under a microscope. Gum arabic particles will not be stained red.

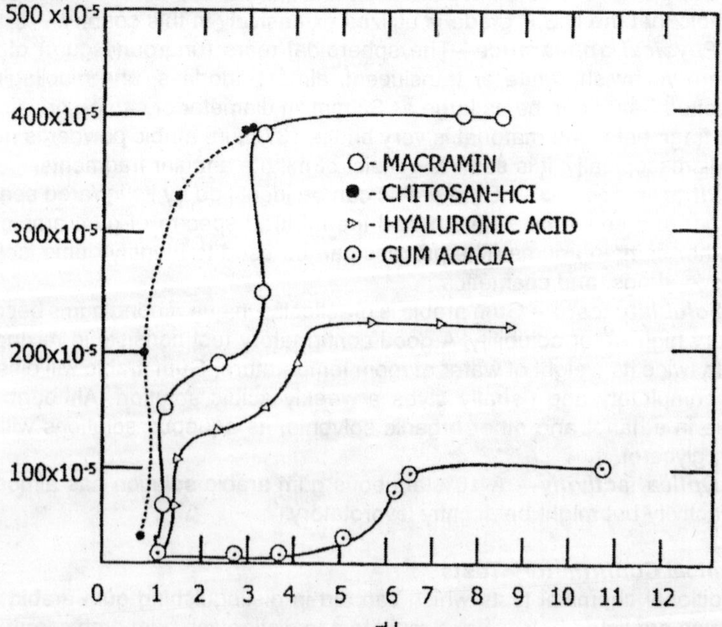

Colloid titration curves

Since an ionic combination between positive and negative polymer ions takes place stoichiometrically and rapidly even in dilute solutions, it is possible to perform general titrations of hydrocolloids. Terayama has developed a novel method of colloid titration based on the stoichiometric combination of positive and negative colloid ions. Metachromatic dyes such as toluidine blue are used as indicators. The standard colloid reagents are the potassium salt of polyvinyl alcohol sulfate and Macramin (/V-polymethylated chitosan derviatives). The colloid titration curves are somewhat different from the acid-base titration curve obtained potentiometrically, but they are characteristic and reproducible under definite conditions and so are useful in qualitative and quantitative conditions. Extremely dilute conditions (5 X 10^{14} *N)* can be used and the precision is about ± 5%. The colloid titrations are influenced by the presence of organic or inorganic salts and by temperature. High temperature hinders the metachromasy, and so the end-point at higher temperatures is indicated by the abrupt precipitation of the colloid complex. The method can be used for the measurement of the degradation of various kinds of high molecular electrolytes with acids, alkalies, or enzymes and for the measurement of the polymerization of ionic monomers like potassium methacrylate.

The colloid titration curves of gum arabic and other charged polysaccharides are shown in Fig. Other indicators that can be used for this type of titration are birlliant cresyl blue and new methylene blue G.

5. *Direct Tests for Gum Arabic in Some Commercial Products*

Frequently it is convenient to analyze for a single gum in a commercial product without first isolating it. A number of useful schemes for gum arabic and other gums are known, and many workable tests for spot checking for gum arabic have been developed.

Methods are available for the detection of gum arabic in dairy product and in catsup. Gum arabic is detected in blood by spectrophotometric examination and in drugs by reaction with oxalic acid. , ɩn excellent process by Redfern has been found effective for detection of the presence of gums in starehy foods.

USES

1. *Foods*

Although gum arabic has a multitude of uses, its largest use seems to be in the food industry in which about 55% of the total imports of gum arabic into the United States are consumed. The main purpose of gum arabic in the food industry is to impart desirable qualities through its influence over the viscosity, body, and texture of foods. Gum arabic imparts certain properties to foods that cannot be obtained from other materials. It is non toxic, odorless, colourless, tastless, and completely water-soluble, and does not affect the flavor, odor, or colour of other food ingredients. In addition, since it has been used for so many years, it is readily accepted by many governmental regulatory bodies, such as the Food and Drug Administration.

a. Confectionery— Gum arabic is used extensively in the confectionery industry primarily because of its ability to prevent crystallization of sugar and also because of its thickening power. It is used as a glaze in candy products and as a component of chewing gum, cough drops, and candy lozenges. Originally, gum drops were produced from gum arabic, but they are now made with thin-boiling starches or pectins.

When used in the manufacture of most confectionery products, gum arabic has to important functions. The most important is to retard or prevent crystallization of sugar, and thus it finds its greatest application in canfections where the sugar content is high and the moisture content comparatively low, as in jujubes and pastilles. Its second function is to act as an emulsifier I keeping the fat uniformly distributed throughtout the product so as to prevent it from seeping to the surface and forming an easily oxidizable, greasy film.

In the preparation of jujubes, pastilles, or gum drops, the technique of incorporation of flavors is very important. Usually the gum arabic is dissolved in water and the solution is filtered, mixed with sugar and boiled. The desirable flavor is added with a minimum of stirring to prevent formation of bubbles or opaque spots.

Lozenges are also prepared from gum arabic by mixing finely ground or powedered sugar with a thick mucilage of gum arabic. The flavors, usually peppermint or fruit, are added, and the entire mass is thoroughly mixed to from aa stiff dough which is rolled into sheets and stamped out.

b. Dairy products—Gum arabic has been used as a stabilizer in forzen products, such as ice creams, ices, and sherbets, because of its water-absorbing *properties,* The function of the gum in these products is to produce a finer texture by inhibiting the formation and growth of ice crystals. Ice cream is prepared from a mixture of milk (skimmed, condensed, or powdered), butter, sugar, honey, eggs, flavoring agents, and a stabilizing colloid. Since ice cream is whipped during freezing, it contains numerous small ice crystals which tend to coalesce and form larger crystals, giving an inferior, coarse and gritty product. Alternate melting and freezing due to changes of temperature during storage and transportation enable the water crystals to grow. The addition of gum arabic as a stabilizer prevents the formation of ice crystals be combining with large quantities of water and holding it as water of hydration, thus producing a finer texture in the ice cream. The chief obejction to this use of gum arabic is that the ice cream does not melt readily.

A very good stabilizer for ice cream and other milk products is a coacervate of gum arabic and carrageenan. Gum arabic and carrageenan are converted to their sodium salts and interacted in the presence of ethanol to form a creamy white powder. This material is compatible with milk and very satisfactory as a stabilizer in the proportion of 6-9 *03.* per 100 gal. of ice cream mix.

The proper amount of milk or cream is mixed with gum arabic; the mixture is heated mildly, poured into molds, cooled, and packaged. The product dissolves easily in hot beverages and keeps better under refrigeration than plain milk or cream. It is used as a protective colloid in the preparation of processed baby food.

c. Baking Industry— Gum arabic is widely used in the baking industry for its comparatively low water-absorption. The gum is cold-water soluble, forming clear solutions with viscosities roughly twice that of sugar. In addition, the favorable adhesive properties of gum arabic are valuable for its use in glazes and toppings. It also bestows smoothness when used as an emulsion stabilizer.

When used in a bun glaze, gum arabic imparts stability in conjunction with free-flowing and adhesive characteristics. The glaze is applied while still warm and will adhere firmly to the bun upon cooling.

d. Flavor fixative— With the introduction of spray-dried flavors into foods, an extensive use was found for gum arabic as a fixative for flavors. Spray-drying is a fairly simple production operation, with the economic advantage of inexpensive, easy drying resulting in desirable particle size, density and solubility. In spray-drying, a solution or suspension is dispersed into a current of hot air in the form of minute droplets which are dried instantly. The temperature of the dried particle is therefore immediately lowered far below that of the surrounding air. By proper selection of spray-dryer nozzles and inlet pressures, droplets of various sizes can be formed and different drying times obtained. The extremely rapid drying at comparatively low temperatures is particaularly advantageous for flavoring materials which are volatile or easily oxidized.

When utilized as a fixative gum arabic forms a thin and impenetrable film around the flavor particle, protecting it from oxidation, evaporation, and absorption of mositure from the air.This is very advantageous when hygroscopic materials are spray-dried. In all cases, it was found that flavors spray-dried with protective colloids lasted 10-20 times lnger than the same flavors air-dried on a solid. Tests made on spray-dried emulsions of hydroxycitronellla, benzaldehyde and other very easily oxidized aldehydes showed that the colloid film was effective in protecting them from oxidation for years, while the unprotected materials oxidized in seconds.

Citrus oils and imitation flavors are prepared by emulsifying them in a gum arabic solution before spray-drying. The resulting particle size can range from 1 to 50 microns (in general, the better the emulsion, the better the protection for the dried particle). Other colloids, such as gelatin, gum tragacanth, and carboxymethylcellulose, are also used for tghese purposes, but gum arabic is the most important and most widely used due to its easy solubility and low cost.

The comparative effectiveness of gum arabic as a flavor fixative in a series of tests in which dispersions of the volatile flavoring compound diacety! (b. p. 88°) plus various gums were heated for 15 min. in an oven at 14°- and analyzed for retention of diacetyl. Without gum, all diacetyl was lost. Most gums retained about 12,4-20.5%, with gum arabic retaining 18.3% of the diacetyl.

e. Flavor emulsifier— Many flavor emulsions, such as orange, lemon, lime, cherry, root beer, and cola, are also prepared with gum arabic as the emulsifier. Some flavor emulsions make use of the additive properties of a blend of gum arabic and gum tragacanth. In these cases gum tragacanth is the true emulsion stabilizer, while gum arabic provides a smoother, better type of emulsion.

In the preparation of bakers' citrus oil emulsions consisting of citric acid, lemon oil, glycerol, water, and colouring matter, the best emulsions were prepared with gum arabic-gum karaya mixtures rather than with gum arabic-gum tragacanth mixtures or gum arabic alone.

f. Miscellaneous.— In the manufacture of beet sugar the settling rates of the carbonated raw juice can be accelerated, and the juice quality improved, by the addition of 2 p.p.m. of gum arabic based on the amount of juice.

The foam-stabilizing ability of gum arabic is utilized in the manufacture of beer and soft drinks. About 2.5-3 lb. of gum arabic can stabilize 50 barrels of beer. The addition of gum arabic solutions to beverages has a tendency to precipitate pectin due to the action of its enzyme, pectinase. However, pectinase can be destroyed and the precipitation of pectin prevented by heating the gum solution before addition. Gum arabic is also an ingredient in some preparations used for wine clarification.

Among the more recent uses of gum arabic has been its utilization in the preparation of diabetic foods in which non-caloric bulking or bodying properties are desired. A good syrup substitute for diabetics can be made from saccharin, methyl-phydroxybenzoate, water, and a water-soluble gum, such as gum arabic.

2. *Adhesives*

The industrial applications of gum arabic adhesives are quite limited. It is generally used in water solution and is dissolved in 2-3 times its weight of water. Gum arabic sold in powdered form is considered a safe, simple adhesive for miscellaneous paper products.[211] A simple 40% solution will make an excellent mucilage for home and office use. Wolfe employed gum arabic together with sodium hydroxide as an adhesive agent for paper products. in the *preparation of animal glues, gum* arabic can sometimes be blended to bring out various desirable qualities.

Adhesives for envelopes, labels, and stamps have special problems peculiar to their usage. The adhesives necessary for thse applications must be of the water remoistenable type; the adhesive, which is applied to the surface of the paper and dried, remains inactive until moisture is reapplied. A desirable gum for use in these applications should have a good affinity for water or saliva and should not cause discoloration of the paper or become brittle on aging. Dextrins or starches are commonly used for this purpose, but gum arabic finds some usage, particularly in the manufacture of adhesive for postage stamps. A typical formula contains 100 parts of gum arabic, 2.5 parts of sodium chloride, 2.0 parts of glycerol, 2.0 parts of starch, and 130 parts of water.

Gum arabic glues have certain qualities that make them desirable. They are easy to prepare, light in colour, odorless, and very stable. In addition, the adhesive strength of the gum can be improved by the addition of certin metal salts, such as calcium nitrate and aluminum sulfate. However, these glues also have shortcomings. When heated in water or subjected to too high a temperature for too long a time, gum arable is degraded, resulting in a decrease in viscosity and loss of adhesive strength. This degraded gum arabic will discolor bronze and colored papers. Gum arable gives a very brittle film which is usually plasticized by the addition of 8-10% of glycerd, based upon the weight of dry gum. Other plasticizing agents, such as diethylene glycol, ethylene glycol, or sorbitol, can be used.

In the preparation of adhesives it is preferable to disslove the gum in 2-3 parts of cold, soft water. Hot water has a tendency to degrade gum arabic. More dilute solutions can be used, and these can *be* made more viscous by the addition of compatible thickening agents, such as gelatin, gum tragacanth, or methylcellulose. Spoilage can be prevented by the addition of a little calcium hydroxide or glycerol. Gum arable-based adhesives are frequently used for smooth, hard-surfaced glassine papers and as glue for cellophane.

A good transparent cement can be made with gum *arabic. In* order to reduce costs, small amounts of gum arabic can be used, and the lower viscosity can be corrected by the addition of a thickening agent such as gum tragacanth. A strongly caustic glue has been patented for use on greasy or waxed paper. Caution should be used with this formula because its strong alkalinity can weaken paper or cloth. Wallpaper paste has been based on a mixture of gum arabic, bentonite, and starch. Gum arabic is compatible with flour, starch, and dextrins, and is used in conjunction with them in postage-stamp adhesives, mounting pastes, an extremely adhesive paste, and Lunel's paste for artificial flowers. Gum arabic is sometimes uses as a binder for water cements in foundry applications, such as gray[214] and iron cement for castings. In the preparation of laminated papers, gum arabic has found specialized applications. The bonding of regenerated cellulose film to itself can be accomplished by use of a special gum arabic paste. In the past, adhesives for bonding aluminum foil to paper have been prepared from gum arabic solutions modified with small amounts of tartaric or similar acids. These had to be used with discretion since they were capable of corroding the aluminum foil.

3. *Paints*

The incorporation of protective colloids into a pigment-vehicle system, such as paint, is and old, established art. This is usually done to obtain improved properties by controlling particle size during precipitation of pigments, pigment aggregates and wetting qualities, consistency and settling. Gum arabic was used in this connection as early as 1870. Johnson treated pigments for use as distemper colours by grinding the pigment in an aqueous suspension of gum arabic. Gum arabic was added to all solutions used to precipitate the pigment, thus acting as a protective colloid. Acheson prepared graphite dispersions in water by use of tannic acid, and as a protective colloid he used infusions of vegetable matter, such as gum arabic.

In paints and similar formulations flocculation prevents hard settling of pigments. Water has been used for many years to prevent hard settling of the pigment in paint. Frequent reference has been made to the effect of water on increasing the plasticity of paints. Such controlled floatation has frequently been achieved by means of additives which presumably affect the coherence of particles in an immiscible liquid. Gamble and Grady treated pigments with water-soluble hydrophilic colloids, such as gum arabic, to give controllable thioxtropic properties to paints. Less than 1%, based on the weight of the pigment, was recommended, but by varying the quantity, the thixotropic properties of the paint could be adjusted to any desired degree. Pigments that are readily wetted by water, such as titanium dioxide, zinc oxide, clays, and silica, require very small quantities. The amount of water required to produce suitable thixotropic properties in a paint is usually less than 1%. In recently developed water-emulsion paints, the use of gum arabic is limited due to its unfavorable effect on the water resistance of the final paints film, but it has found some use in the preparation fo vinyl resin emulsions.

4. *Inks*

Gum arabic is an important constituent of many inks. While the majority of record inks or fountain pen inks today do not use gum arabic, most special purpose inks do make use of its excellent protective colloid action.

A measure of the effectiveness of the protective colloid action of gum arabic in inks or similar products is given by the gold number. The god number is a standardized measurement which is defined as the number of milligrams of gum that, when added to a standard gold dispersion, are just sufficient to prevent a change in colour from red to blue when 1 ml. of 10% sodium cholride solution is added. The comparative effectiveness of several common colloidal materials can be seen from the following gold numbers:

Gum arabic	0.1-0.5
Gelatin	0.005-0.1
Casein	0.1
Gum tragacanth	0.5-2.0
Wheat starch	4-6
Potato starch	25

This use of gum arabic can best be illustrated by the following examples which are representative of the variety of ink products that can be prepared using gum arabic. For a more detailed discussion many excellent books on inks are available.

Early inks were simply dispersions of lampblack in water.When it became appar-entthata suspending agent or a protective colloid was needed, experimenters used gum arabic. Sometimes, the lampblack and gum were mixed into a thick paste and allowed to harden in molds. These ink sticks have been in continuous use with little or no change in processing for over 3,000 years. To use an ink stick, the operator moistens a small brush with water or saliva and then rubs the brush on the end of the stick. To make liquid ink, he rubs the end of the stick in a little water in a shallow dish until the ink solution develops the proper colour.

a. Record ink— Government record ink had long used gum arabic in the formula as a protective colloid. Some years ago, due to a clerical error, gum arabic was omitted from the formula when proposals for bids were being typewritten. This error was not discovered until too late. However, tests made by the Department of Agriculture, Bureau of Chemistry, showed that the omission of gum arabic was a slight improvement, and it has been left out of the formula for standard record ink ever since.

b. Soluble ink—An easily soluble ink is used by textile workers to mark the doth for cutting or sewing operations. The operator marks the position of buttonholes, hems, pleats, lapels, and pockets. When the garment is finished, a hot-water wash is used to remove the ink. A typical ink used is a mixture of dilute acetic add, albumin, a basic dye, gum arabic, molasses, and triethanolamine.

c. Water-colour ink— An ink suitable for water-colour work must remain in suspension without settling. Gum arabic is an excellent binder for this type of ink since it has excellent suspending properties. A typical formula is illustrated by Hoefflers patent: I part of gum arabic is dissolved in 1 part of water and 9 parts of glycerolare added. The mix ture is warmed in a good current of air to encourage evaporation until the specific gravity has reached about 1.28. The pigment is then ground in, preferably using a colloid mill.

d. Quick-drying inks— Inks designed to dry faster than ordinary writing inks are usually based on solvents other than water. Ethanol is commonly used in conjunction with gum arabic as a thickener and suspending agent. However, some fast-drying formulas using water as the solvent are known, such as one consisting of water, Lysol (as a preservative), sodium nitrate, gum arabic, and a water-soluble dye.

e. Fabric and laundry marking inks— Many formulas for cloth marking ink are known. Some of the more interesting ones are the following.

For ink used for marking cotton cloht before it is bleached, one liter of water containing 200 g. of tartaric acid is heated; 100 g. of aniline are added, and the mixture is stirred until homogeneous. Solid potassium chlorate (100 g.) is added, and the mixture is stirred until dissolution is complete. (It might be necessary to add additional water.) The solution is cooled and allowed to stand 24 hr. Crystals of potassium acid tartrate which form are removed by filtration. This solution of aniline chlorate should be clear and about 7° Bé. Gum arabic is added to bring the ink to the desired viscosity for smooth writting on cloth. Immediately before use, 20 g. of copper sulfate are added, and the ink is ready for application. About 24 hr. are required for drying. The bleach solution, acting on the ink, develops and makes permanent the black colour.

Another similar formula is composed of two solutions which are mixed just before use. *Solution A:* 85 parts of cupric chloride, 106 parts of sodium chlorate, 53 parts of ammonium chloride, 600 parts of water.

Solution B: 67 parts of gum arabic, 200 parts af aniline hydrochloride, 335 parts of water. When needed, mix 1 volume of solution A with 4 volumes of solution B.

Other indelible inks make use of metallic pigments and contain gum arabic as a thickener and protective colloid. Sometimes the formulas call for a reducing agent, frequently an organic acid or salt. Some of the metallic pigments used are silver, gold, platinum, manganese, chromium, and lead.

Another good laundry ink is based on a fine silver suspension. It is made as follows: *Solution A:* 5 parts of silver nitrate, 5 parts of water, enough ammonium hydroxide to cause the precipitate to redisslove, *Solution B:* 3 parts of sodium carbonate dissolved in 15 parts of water. *Solution C:* 5 parts of gum arabic in 10 parts of warm water. For use, mix solutions A, B, and C, and heat until the mixture starts to darken.

A platinum ink is made by rnixing 1 part of chloroplatinic acid, 2 parts of gum arabic, and 10 parts of water. The fabric is treated with a solution of 3 parts of oxalic acid, 3 parts of gum arabic, and 10 parts of water. After the fabric is dry, the cloth is washed thoroughly.

Gold ink can be made by mixing 1 part of sodium chloroaurate, 1 part of gum arabic, and 10 parts of water. The fabric is initially treated with a solution of 1 part of stannous chloride, 10 parts of gum arable, and 100 parts of water. When the fabric is dry, the chloroaurate solution is used as an ink and allowed to dry. The cloth is then washed.

f. Pigmented inks (white bronze)— The suspensions of a pigment in a gum arabic solution makes a satisfactory ink that can be applied with a brush or pen. Pigments, such as titanium dioxide, or bronze powder of ethanol or acetone before mixing with the gum solution.

A white ink, typical of this class of inks, is made in the following manner. To a filtered solution of 20 parts of gum arabic in 160 parts of water, titanium dioxide paint pigment (30 parts) and 0.5 part of sodium salicylate (a preservative) are added, and the ink is ready for immediate use.

g. Emulsion or typographic inks— Some inks consist of emulsions instead of suspensions and gum arabic is then used as a binding agent to help keep the ink from separating. Usually, emulsion inks are oil-in-water type emulsions with the pigment dissolved in the oil phase.

A typical ink of this class consists of lampblack, mineral oil, rosin, catechu, formalin, sodium silicateth, sodium *carbonate, gum 3rabic,* aluminum resonate,, *colouring* agent, and water.

h. Hectograph ink— An ink that has been used for many years in Hectograph duplicating equipment is prepared by mixing methyl violet dye with water or ethanol. Some formulas using hydrochloric acid, oxalic acid, lactic acid, tannic acid, or pyrocatechol, employ gum arabic to obtain the proper viscosity. The ink must be strained before use.

i. Gloss-finish inks— Decorative inks with a glossy finish for showcard work or other display purposes can be prepared by incorporating a day into the following formula: 25 lb. of D-glucose, 0.5 pint of Lysol or other preserving agent, 10 gal. of water.

j. Electrically conductive ink— Inks which conduct electricity are becoming increasingly important because of their potential use in the manufacture or repair of printed circuits in electronic applications. Activating electronic calculators by electrically conductive areas on a card rather than by punched holes is also becoming of increased interest. One reason for this is the relative ease of putting a conductive ink mark on a card as compared to the work involved in punching a hole.

Most conductive inks are made of carbon black, powedered graphite, finely divided silver, or powdered copper. The suspending agent can be a lacquer, but water-based inks function well when gum arabic, sodium chloride, and citric (or tartaric) acid are used.

k. Wood-grain ink— This ink was devised to imitate expensive grains by printing a pattern of the costly wood on metal, paper, stone, or inexpensive woods. Thus, pine or maple can be made to simulate a more expensive material, such as mahogany or oak. Similarly, wall-paper or metallic objects are frequently decorated with a wood-grain pattern. A typical formula is 60% of ethylene glycol, 7.5% of water, 30% of pigment, and 2.5.% of gum arabic.

5. *Lithography*

Gums are extremely important in lithorgaphy. Generally, gums are used as sensitizers for lithographic plates, elements in the light-sensitive composition, ingredients of the fountain solution which is used to moisten the plate during printing, and protectors during storage of the plate. Gums, such as gum arabic, find wide application in this field, in spite of recent discoveries of the lithographic uses of cellulose and starch ethers.

The desensitizing use of gum arabic takes advantage of the good wettability imparted to the solution by the gum and also of the viscosity control which allows the wash solution to cling to the plate without running off or forming isolated droplets or pools on the plate. The role of gum arabic in the desensitization process is not completely understood. On metal plates, the effect might be due to the formation of an insoluble film (for example, aluminum or zinc arabate). A more plausible explanation is that a film of gum is absorbed by the plate. Studies have shown that such films occur on plates of zinc, aluminum, copper, silver, iron, tin, lead, glass, and fused silica. These films are not monomolecular but are actually composed of many molecular layers. Measurement of the wettability of desensitizing solutions is conveniently evaluated by measurement and study of the contact angles. In this process, a section of a plate is partially immersed in water or in a solution of the gum to be tested. The plate is then turned at an angle to the surface of the liquid until the meniscus appears to be eliminated. The resutling angle of the plate to the surface of the liquid is known as the contact angle and is a measure of the wettability of that particular plate with the solution being tested

Mixtures of gum arabic and idchromates are tanned by the action of light to form water-insolube susbstances. Certain other gums and proteins are reported to be superior to gum arabic and might be used in place of it, but gum arabic continues to be used to some extent as a constituent of the light-sensitive coating. Thus, a wettable, plastic-impregnated paper sheet, a metallic sheet, or even a stone surface can be made light-sensitive by application of a gum and a dichromate solution whichis allowed to dry. Exposure of a pattern through a negative will cause tanning or hardening of all areas which are struck by light, and the unexposed material can be removed by a water or dilute acid wash. The surface can be used either for planographic printing or for an etching process if the plate is used for direct printing. A related use is in the preparation of etched circuits and in the manufacture of small metallic parts. In the latter process, the part is sketched or photographed onto a transparent sheet, exposed onto a metallic sheet made light-sensitive with gum arabic and a dichromate, washed in water, and etched to remove unwanted parts of the sheet. In this manner, very intricate and delicate parts are readily produced.

Gum arabic used in lithography should be of the best quality and, prefereably, should undergo an in-exchange purification process. This is done by preparing the gum in a 20-22% concentration, filtering the solution, treating it with a cation-exchange resin and decanting. The resulting product has increased stability, better viscosity characteristics, and greater immunity to bacterial and mold attack when compared to the starting material.

The purified gum solution can now be used directly for deepetch sensitive coatings..To each 3.65 parts of gum solution, I part of ammonium dichromate is added, and the solution is made slightly alkaline (*p*H 8.8-10.0) with ammonium hydroxide. The final viscosity is preferably 26-29 cps. Coating, drying and exposure follow conventional procedures.

High viscosity grades of gum arabic are not recommended for deepetch coatings since they will not flow uniformly over the plate surface and can therefore produce streaks. The strength of the solutions can be controlled by specific gravity readings with a Baume hydrometer, and the viscosity can be adjusted by thinning with water.

Substitutes for gum arabic in offset copying have been used for many years. They include dextrin, fish glue, methylcellulose, yeast protein, and others. However, it is difficult to find a product as inexpensive and as satisfactory as gum arabic for this process.

6. *Textiles*

Gums are widely used in the textile industry as sizing and finishing agents and in printing formulations for imparting designs or decorations to fabrics. Gum arabic thus finds limited use in finishing silk and rayon by giving body to the fabric without interfering with the transparency. Although very desirable effects can be created on cotton, the cost is usually too high for use with this materials. However, sizings are sometimes added to cotton fabrics to give them a fuller finish and to make them feel more firm and compact. This treatment has been used to disguise poorly made cloth. Gum arabic is an efficient size for cloth, although other gums (for example starch, wax, and clay) are all used. Usually, most cloth sizings are lost in washing. Usual low-cost sizes are made of starch from rye flour. A typical composition would be 90 kg. of starch heated in 700 1. of water and cooled.

A considerable improvement in properties can be obtained by using the following formula, which substitutes gum arabic for some of the rye starch: 45 kg. of rye flour starch, 24 kg. of gum arabic, and 700 1. of water heated to boiling. A spearate solution of 16.5 kg. of castor oil, 2.5 kg. of oleic acid, 7.5 kg. of 15% sodium hydroxide, and 23.5 kg. of water is added to the starch-gum arabic solution. After mixing 1 1. of oleic acid is added; the mixture is stirred and boiled for 20 min., and acetic acid is added until the mixture is netural.

A typical vat gum using British gum as the principal thickener and binder contains 7% of starch, 21% of British gum, 5% of glycerol, 12% of potassium carbonate, 8% of Ronagalite C, and 47% of water. For discharge prints, an extra addition of Rongalite C is made.

Recently, it has been shewn that black *Acacia* gum from *Acacia decurrens is* an excellenta substitute for British gum as a thickener in formulas, such as the one above. The gum is light yellow to reddish in colour and is free from tannins. It has excellent adhesive properties and will not interfere with the colors or dyes used in printing.

7. *Miscellaneous*

In addition to those already mentioned, gum arabic has a multitude of varied and unusual applications, some of which will be described here.

A coating of gum arabic on typing paper allows erasures to be made much more easily. A double coating is preferred, with a short drying period between applications.

When gum arabic is used in the formulation of transfer inks, these inks can also be used for the preparation of good-grade carbon papers. Twelve parts of dextrin and 2 parts of starch are boiled in water and then mixed with a composite of 400 parts of sodium sodium carbonate and 400 parts of Colophony in water. To this is added 200 parts of egg albumin in water, 200 parts of sulfur, 400 parts of gum arabic, and 2,000 parts of glycerol.

Eichron described a novel photographic method for making templates utilizing gum arabic. A woven glass sheet is impregnated with a polyester of alkyl resin and an opaque drawing is made upon the surface which has excellent heat and light dimensional stability. Conventional blue-print salts containing gum arabic (or other gums) and a tanning agent are poured over the work, which, for example, might be a sheet of metal being formed into an airplane wing. When the pattern has been printed photographically upon the metal sheet, the sheet can be cut, drilled or otherwise mechanically manipulated, according to the pattern printed on its surfaces.

Photographic use is also made of the dicarboxylic acid esters of gum arabic. Gum arabic phthalateand gum arabic succinate are used as overcoating and backing layers for photographic material.

Gum arabic is used to inhibit metal corrosion in many applications. The addition of the gum, in the amount of approximatley 2% of the weight of the negative plate of a storage battery, increases the life of a storage battery by reducing the growth of surface projections on the negative electrode. The gum arabic is intimately mixedwith the active negative plate material, such as zinc oxide, producing an increase in electrical resistance and reducing the rate of corrosion.

The corrosion of iron is considerably accelerated by light and the presence of salts, but it is inhibited by the presence of gum arabic. It has also been tested for controlling the corrosion of aluminum.

The gum is useful in the immersion plating of copper on aluminum. A bright dense, strongly adhering copper coating is formed on aluminum by dipping the aluminum with an electrically connected piece of iron into a copper sulfate bath containing 0.75-1.25% by weight of gum arabic.

Gum arabic has been used in the preparation of drilling fluids and oil-well cement. It has been used as a glaze binder in ceramics where it has had to meet rigid specifications pertaining to bonding power, absence of slip and stability for long periods at elevated temperatures. A recent Japanese patent utilizes gum arabic as a binder for termite insecticides. Horn and Samko[262] have developed a nonglare coating for automobile windshields based on a water-soluble dye dissloved in a gum arabic solution. A typical formulation contains 0.25% of brilliant green dye, 0.25% of the dioctyl ester of sodium sulfosuccinic acid, 5.00% of gum arabic, and 94.50% of water.

11.

Guar Gum

Introduction

The consumption of guar gum has grown rapidly since its commercial introduction in 1953. This rapid growth is largely due to the fact that guaran functions not only in the traditional role of a viscosity builder for water systems, but also as a hydrogen-bonding, reagent-type chemical for such industries as mining and paper making. The gum, a nonionic, neutral polysaccharide, is a galactomannan.

Productoin

1. Source and Producing Areas

Gaur gum is derived from the seed of the guar plant, *Cyamopsis tetragonolobus,* family Leguminosa. The guar plant is a pod-bearing, nitrogen-fixing legume. It has been grown for centuries in India and Pakistan, where it is one of the principal crops and is used as a good for both humans and animals. Guar was introduced into this country in the early 1900's. However, not until 1946 did its potential as a cash crop and its value in contributing to soil fertility arouse interest here. Guar has been steadily increasing in popularity as both a rotation and a strip cropt in the Vernon and Kenedy areas of Texas.

2. Agronomics

The guar plant needs very little surface water during its growing season' and is, therefore, adaptable for growth in these semiarid regions in which less hardy crops perish. In India, the crop is harvested with hand labor, while in Texas grain combines have proved satisfactory for this purpose. It is essential that the crop be harvested before the first rain following the first frost. If it is not, many of the seeds wither and turn black. This results in a lower yield of gum and also causes the gum manufactured from such seeds to be contaminated with black specks.

3. Purification

The guar seed is dicotyledonous, having a diameter of approximately 1/8 of an inch. Table 1 summarizes the average composition of the various seed components. It is apparent from an examination of the data in Table 1 that, in order to obtain relatively pure gaiactomannan, the endosperm must be separated from the hull and germ. In practice there are several methods for accomplishing this; these are enumerated below.

a. Hull removal— (1) The seed is treated with 55% sulfuric acid and is ashed free of acid when the hull is completely charred and loose. (2) The hull is loosened and charred by water soaking and subsequent flame treatment. (3) The difference in hardness of the various seed components is utilized and a purification is accomplished by multi-stage grinding and sifting.

Tablel. 11.1 Composition of the Components of Guar Seed

Seed Part	Protein (NX6.25), %	Ether extract, %	Ash, %	Moisture, %	Crude fiber,	Type of carbohydrate
Hull (14-17%)	5	0.3	4	10	36.0	D-Glucose
Endosperm (35-42%)	5	0.6	0.6	10	1.5	Galactomannan
Germ(43-47%)	55.3	5.2	4.6	10	18.0	D-Glucose

b. Germ Removal— Differential grinding is used for germ removal. There are many types of grinders, such an attrition mills and special types of hammer and roller mills, which can be employed because of the difference in hardness of the endosperm and germ.

c. Endosperm grinding— After the endosperm is separated from the hull and germ, it is ground to a fine particle size and marketed as guar gum.

4. Grades

There are no standards for grade identification of guar gum. However, the available grades can be differentiated on the bases of purity and viscosity.

a. Food grades— Food-grade guar gum is substantially pure endosperm. It is usually slightly contaminated with hull and germ owing to imperfect purification. However, because the entire seed is edible, this contamination only dilutes the amount of available galactomannan. Guar gum is included in the Food and Drug Administration's standards of identity for cheeses and cheese products, frozen desserts, and salad dressings.

A typical analysis of the impurities in food-grade guar gum is as follows: crude fiber, 2.5%; moisture, 10-15%; protein (nitrogen X 6.25), 5-6%; ash, 0.5-0.7%; ether extract, 0.5-0.8%. A comparision of this analysis with that of pure endosperm (as shown in Table I) shows the effectiveness of the separation as done by usual commercial processing techniques.

Cold water viscosity is important in the selection of grades of guar gum to be offered for food uses since the food industry's use of it is principally dependent on the viscosity of its solutions and its water absorption. However, the water-binding properties and solution viscosity are only slightly related to purity and are more dependent on the processing techniques. It is important that a specific viscosity-measuring techniques be used for establishing specifications since guar gum does not form a true solution. Also, its solution has thixotropic characteristics, and, therefore, the method of measurement is particularly important. One viscosity-measuring techniques follows: 4.00g. of guar gum are dispersed in 400 ml. of water at 25° with rapid hand stirring. The solution is then stirred occasionally, and after 2 hr., its viscosity is measured with a Brookfield viscometer at 20 r.p.m. and 25°. According to this method, most guar gums used in the food industry have viscosities ranging from 2,000 to 3,500 cps. (1% dispersions).

Mesh size is also a criterion for grade definition. Since guar gum retains some of its particular characteristics when it hydrates in water, the mesh size of the powdered gum affects the appearance of the gum solution. The coarser the particle size, the more grainy will be the solution, and, conversely, the finer the particle size, the smoother and more homogeneous the solution. The three mesh size distribution most commonly used in the food industry are:

{80% between 100 and 200 mesh
20% minus 200 mesh

{15% between 150 and 200 mesh
85% minus 200 mesh

{40% between 80 and 200 meshl
60% minus 200 mesh

b. Technical grades— Technical-grade guar gum usually is a less purified gum in which the amount of hum and germ contamination is appreciably higher than that in food grade gums. Typical analyses of technical grades are as follows: crude fiber, 2.5-8.0%; moisture, 8-14%; protein, 6-12%; ash, 0.6-1.3%; ether extract, 0.6-1.5%.

c. Industrial grades— Industrial grades of guar gum can have the purity of either food or technical grades, but in industrial grades, the gum is compounded with chemicals which aid in dispersion, control viscosity, cause gelling, act as preservatives or which in any other way aid in achieving specific results for a particular industrial use. In addition, such properties as rate of hydration, controled gelation and viscosity breakdown can be varied. These properties can be controlled by processing techniques, and, therefore, specific grades of guar gum can be tailormae for special applications. Many grades and modifications are commercially available; one company today is regularly marketing over 20 grades of guar gum.

USES

1. HISTORY

In this country guar was first investigated as a source of gum in 1945. General Mills undertook agricultural production of the plant in the Southwest, and, by 1949, 1,700 acres had been planted in Texas. At the same time the Institute of paper chemistry in Appleton, Wisconsin, was comparing the use of guar gum with that of locust bean gum and other beater and size press additives in paper manufacturing.

However it was not until 1953 that the gum was produced in commercial quantities. During this intervening period, the demand for locust bean gum grew rapidly because of the requirements of the food, paper and textile industries. By 1951, the demand for locust bean gum had exceeded its limited supply, forcing its price to new highs. (Locust bean gum is harvested from perennial trees.) Two Amercian companies, Stein, Hall & Co., Inc., and General Mills, Inc., built plants in the United States and began commercial production of guar gum in the middle of 1953. Some time later, the European processors of locust bean gum also began to produce guar gum.

Guar gum was originally developed as a replacement for locust bean gum. However, it soon became obvious that, although both gums are galactomannans, there are significant differences in their chemical composition and behaviour. Locust bean gum requires cooking at elevated temperatures to achieve its maximum viscosity, while guar gum will hydrate in cold water. Locust bean gum has an average of only one D-galactopyranose unit branch on every fourth D-mannopyranose unit. Guar gum has a D-galactopyranose branch on every other D-mannopyranose unit. The greater number of branches in guar gum is believed to be responsible for both its easier hydration and its greater hydrogen-bonding activity as compared to that of locust bean gum. Some industrial applications will be described in order to indicate both the conventional uses of this hydrophilic colloid *as a* viscosity builder and water binder and also its specialized uses, which depend on chemical composition and molecular configuation.

2. Mining Industry

a. Depressant and auxiliary reagent -In the froth flotation process for concentrating ores, frothing and collector reagents, such as fatty acid soaps or fatty amines, are used to produce a froth which collects in a flotation cell. The froth carries the collector reagent and the values of the ore to the top of the flotation cell, at which point they are floated off as an ore concentrate. Slimes impair the efficiency of the collection system. As an auxiliary reagent, guar gum depresses the gangue minerals, which might be clay, talc and/or shale. This increase the recovery of the purified ore value by reducing the loss of values to the tailings. A further saving is effected by reducing the amount of collector reagent absorbed by the gandue. Figure 1 is a diagrammatic representation of the action of guar gum as an auxiliary reagent. This action of guar gum results, from the hydrogen-bonding activity of the gum molecule with the hydrated mineral surfaces of the clays. The over-all straight chain configuration of the molecule with its regularly occurring D-glactopyranose branches makes it will suited to this type of reaction. The fact that both the D-mannopyracose and D-galactopyranose components of guaran have *cis* hydroxyl groups is also thought to promote more efficient hydrogen bonding.

Dilute guar gum solutions (0.1-0.5%) are added to the ore system to allow complete distribution of the gum throughout the pulp. Contact times of 1-5 min. are recommended for flocculation. The amount of guar gum added varies; however, ranges of 0.1-0.5 lb. per ton of ore are most commonly used. A detailed description of the use of guar as an auxiliary reagent in potash refining can be found in the literature.

b. Settling agent— Guar gum is also used as a flocculant or settling agent to concentrate ores and tailings in the mining industry. In practice, slimes and tailings from ore benefication processes must be concentrated so that the water can be reused and the solids, easily disposed of or reprocessed. Normally, large tanks or thickeners are used to effect this settling. By adding guar gum to the thickener, faster settling of the suspending solids can be achieved. This reduces the amount of thickener required to settle a given amount of pulp solids. The solids thus concentrated can still be pumped, thereby facilitating subsequent handling. Here again, 0.1-0.5 lb. of guar gum per ton of dry solids is normally used. The solution is metered into the thickener close to the pulp intake so that there is agitation which is sufficient for good mixing but which is not violent enough to break up the floes that form.

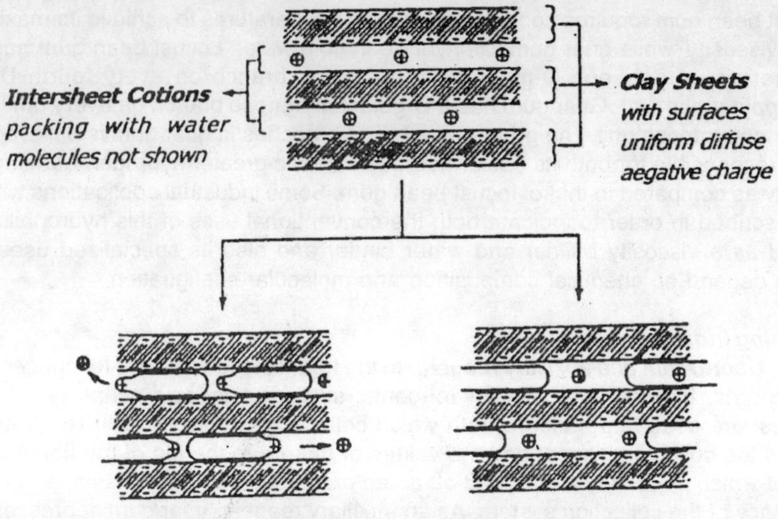

Fig 11.1. Diagram of hydrated mortmorillonite.

c. Filter aid— In mining, filtration operations are designed to remove suspended slimes or clay particles. These small particles have a tendency to form a very compact filter cake which traps water within itself and plugs the filter surface. The addition of guar gum to a pulp, by methods similar to those described above, results in the flocculation of these small particles. Twice as much guar gum is used in this connection as is required for settling operations. These large floes no longer have a tendency to blind the filter screen and, at the same time, they allow a quicker channeling of liquid through the filter cake. This action increases filtration efficiency and results in a drier cake.

d. Industrial water treatment— Guar gum is used in water treatment systems after the addition of ferric sulfate and calcium hydroxide. The inorganic reagents are used to remove dissolved silica from water which is to be used for boiler feed. Guar gum enlarges the size of the floe and thereby increases filtration efficiency. It is non toxic and can also be used in potable water treatment plants.

3. Foods

Guar gum is often used in foods as a thickener and a binder of free water. For example, when used as a thickener in salad dressing, it raises the viscosity of the emulsion and decreases the separation rate. In addition to its viscosity-increasing role, guar gum acts as a protective colloid for emulsion stablization. It is ordinarily used in amounts of 0.2-0.8%, based on the total emulsion. Its advantages here are its cold water hydration properties, its compatibility with highly acidic emulsions, and its economy which is due to the high viscosity of its water solution.

Guar gum is also used as a binder of free water or as a stabilizer in foods such as ice cream. Free water in an ice cream mix causes a grainy texture, is crystals, poor melt-down properties, and poor heat-shock resistance in the finished ice cream. The incorporation of a stabilizer containing guar gum in quantities of about 0.3% of the ice cream mix yields a smooth-textured, chewy product with slow melt-down properties and good heat-shock resistance. Guar gum binds the free water without disturbing the viscosity characteristics of the mix. It is also particularly suitable for use in flash pasteurization because of its rapid hydration properties. It is included in the ice cream standards.

This gum is used in the stabilization of ice pops and sherbets. The principle of use here is the same as that which applies to ice cream. The retention of maximum hydration properties in acidic media is an important factor in this use of guar gum. Other foods which can be stabilized with guar gum because of its ability to bind water are frozen foods, cheeses, pie fillings, icings and dog foods.

4. Cosmetics and Pharmaceuticals

Guar gum is also used to thicken various cosmetics and pharmaceuticals. In products such as toothpaste, it can be used alone or in combination with other gums, such as carrageenan or sodium alginate, to bind the free water and impart a smooth appearance. Other applications involve the use of guar gum as a binder and disintegrator for compressed tablets. Coarse granulations are ordinarily used for this purpose. Guar gum in coarse granulations is also being investigated as a bulk laxative.

5. *Paper Industry*

The paper industry has become one of the largest users of galactomannans. It is estimated that about 14 million lb. of galactomannans (locust bean gum and guar gum) are used annually by this industry, with guar gum accounting for about one-half of that amount.

a. Wet end additive— Most of this amount of galactomannan is used in the wet end of the paper-making process. This means that the gum is added to the pulp suspension before the sheet is formed on either a Fourdrinier machine (an endless wire) or a cylinder machine. The pulping process, which is designed to remove lignin and thereby produce a fibrous cellulose pulp, also removes a large part of the hemicellulose normally present in the tree. These hemicelluloses, which are mostly mannans and xylans, contribute greatly to the hydration properties of the pulp and the strength of the paper which can be formed from the pulp. Galactomannans replace or supplement the natural hemicellulose in paper. Listed below are some of the advantages gained by their addition: (1) improved formation with a more regular distribution of pulp fibers throughout the sheet (less fiber bundles); (2) increased Mullen bursting strength; (3) increased fold; (4) increased tensile strength; (5) increased pick (In printing grades, pick is a measure of the force required to pull a fiber from the surface of a sheet)! (6) easier pulp hydration (The pulp is normally passed through jordans or wet mills which increase the surface of the fiber, thereby allowing it to bind more water. Galactomannans added to a pulp aid in the binding of water and decrease the amount of jordaning necessary, consequently lowering power consumption.)!

(7) improved finish (as measured by the smoothness and a count of protruding fibers); (8) decreased porosity; (9) increased flat crush of corrugating medium (This refers to the pressure required to crush a corrugated flute; (10) increased machine speed with maintenance of test results; (11) increased retention of fines.

It is generally agreed that the hydrogen-bonding effect is one of the major factors affecting fiber-fiber bonding. An examination of the molecular structure of galactomannans reveals a rigid molecule with primary and secondary hydroxyl groups at all available positions and no nonpolar groups. In addition, the single-membered branches do not shield the avilable reactive hydroxyl groups, resulting in maximum utilization of hydrogen-bonding area per weight of material. At the same time, the regular branching is sufficient to prevent the retrogradition that results with straight chain molecules, such as amylose, that also contain no nonpolar groups. It is difficult to comare the efficiency of locust bean gum and guar gum in paper products, for too many variables exist, such as type of gum product formulation, pulp type, beating time and machine conditions. However, it has been our experience that, under controlled conditions, the guar gum products will perform the more efficiently. This could be expected because guar generally behaves as a more reactive gum than does locust bean gum in other uses which depend on hydrogen-bonding efficiency; for example, as measured by flocculation and settling rates, guar gum shows a much higher reactivity with hydrated mineral surfaces than does locust bean gum. In addition to its efficiency, there is one other consideration which makes guar gum the more suitable in paper production. Since both gums are extracted from seeds containing hulls, there is always a small amount of hull present as a contaminant. Locust bean hulls are red-brown, and in white sheets these particles often appear as small but visible specks. However, in guar products the hull contamination is almost white and is industinguishable from the bleached pulp in a formed sheet.

For some uses, it has been found that smaller additions of gums will give equivalent results if cooked with starch. This apparently synergistic behaviour between starch and the galactomannans is not always evidence and seems to be largely dependent on individual pulp and mill conditions. One possible explanation is that the highly branched amylopectin fraction of starch allows better distribution of the more reactive gum molecules throughout the pulp suspension. The mill might buy blended products or add the starch itself to the pulp if it wishes to achieve greater economy.

There are two general methods of preparing the gum solution, a batch system and a continuous cooking system. After preparation, the solution is usually pumped to the suction side of the fan pump. For mills that do not wish to install cooking equipment, there are specially processed guar gum products that can be added dry to the beater.

b. Filler retention— Galactomannan products are also used to improve retention of fillers, such as calcium carbonate, titanium dioxide, and clays, in almost all paper grades. The techniques of use within the mill are extremely important for the achievement of maximum retention. In addition, the product must be formulated to function efficiently in the particular methods employed. Some of the procedures used are as follows: addition of the gum product to the tray water, addition of the gum solution to the filler slurry which is then added at the fan pump, addition of the gum solution to the discharge side of the fan pump.

c. Size press and calender applications. - Guar gum is used as an additive in size press or calender operations in many mills. In these operations, either enzyme converted, oxidized, or etherified starches are ordinarily employed. Guar gum increases the viscosity of the starch paste, thereby controlling the amount of pick up. This is often desirable because it allows an increase in viscosity without increasing the risk of gelation, which might occur with an underconverted starch. When used as a viscosity-controlling agent, guar gum can replaces as much as one third of the starch solids; normally 2-3% is replaced with about 0.5% of guar gum (based on the total solution).

6. Explosives

In the production of a water-resistant, ammonium nitrate type of explosive, guar gum is blended with the ingredients. Then, when the explosive stick is immersed in water, the gum that first touches the water swells rapidly, and a gel forms which prevents the water from penetrating further into the mixture and leaching the salts (a major cause of misfires). The ability of guar gum to hydrate fully in concentrated salt solutions is responsible for its efficient behaviour in this application. The quantity of guar gum used is about 1% of the toal misture.

7. Derivatives

Many derivatives of guaran have been prepared and reported in the literature. These include oxidized guaran, carboxymethylated guaran and methylated guaran. At the present time, none of these has found commercial use.

Stucture

Guaran, a D-galacto-D-mannoglycan (1:2), is a straight chain mannan with sin-gle-membered galactose branches. The D-mannopyranose units are joined by β-(l->4) linkages, and single D-galactopyranose units are joined to this chain by α-(l->6) linkages. On the average, the gaiactose branches occur on every other mannose unit. A representation of this molecule is shown in Fig. 11.2. The molecular weight has been reported as 220.000.

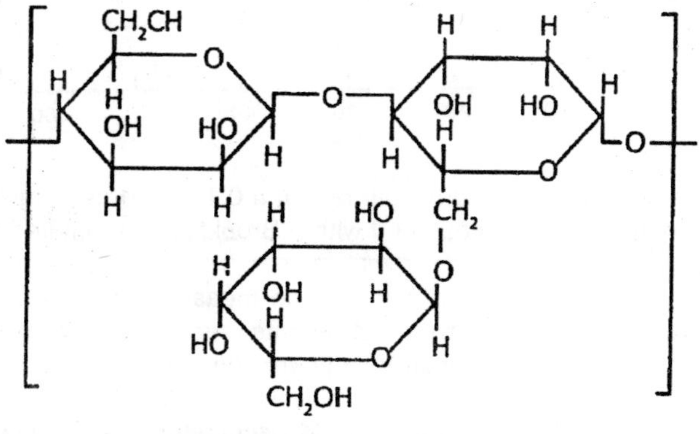

Fig 11.2. Structure proposed for guaran.

Properties

1. Viscosity

Guar gum forms viscous, colloidal dispersions (solutions) when hydrated in cold water; viscosities can be measured with a rational, shear-type viscometer, such as the Brookfield Syncro-Lectric. Its solutions exhibit the variance of viscosity with shear-type viscometer, such as the Brookfield Syncro-Lectric. Its solutions exhibit the variance of viscosity with shear rate which is typical of non-Newtonian fluids.

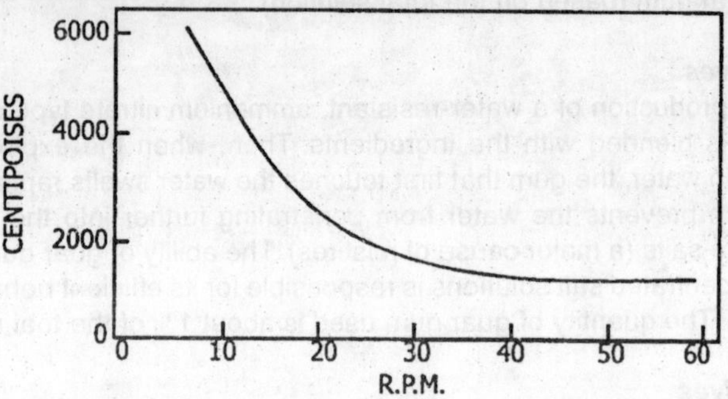

fig. 11.3. Viscosity versus shear rate in a 1% food-grade guar gum solution at 25° with Brookfield spindle No. 3.

Figure 11.3 illustrates the change in viscosity of a 1% food-grade guar gum solution with shear rate at 5°. Dilute solutions of guar gum show less thixotropy than do high concentration (1%). Viscosities of 0.3% solutions change only slightly with increasing shear up to 60 r.p.m.

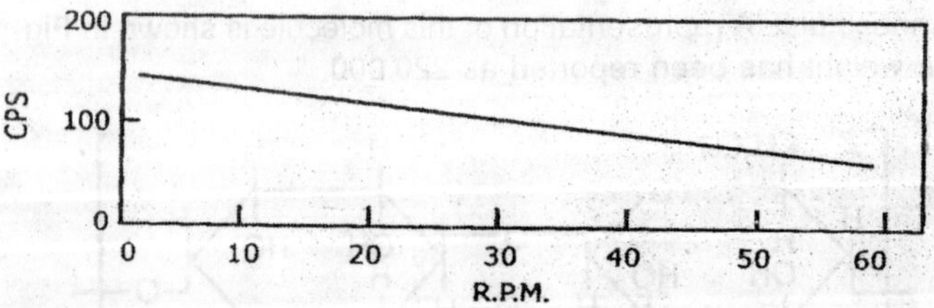

Fig. 11.4. - Viscosity versus shear rate in a 0.1% food-grade guar gum solution at 25° (measured with a Brookfield viscometer).

scosity of guar gum solutions can also be measured by determining the capillary flow rates from pipette-type instruments, such as the Dudley, Engler, and Ostwald viscometers. These instruments are standardized for size of orifice and volume of fluid contained. Their use, however, is limited to guar gum concentrations of less than 1%. Calibrated ostald viscometers meausre concentrations as low as 10-100 p.p.m. of guar gum, whereas the lower limit of the Brookfield instrument is about 1,000 p.p.m. Guar gum viscosities (in centipoises), determined with Nos. 100 and 400 Ostwald tubes at 27° after 24hr. hydration, are shown in Table III. When this method of determination is used, the outflow time in seconds is sufficient to express the behavior of guar in most applications.

Table 11.2. Viscosity of Guar Gum Solitions[a]

Gum (p.p.m.)	Centipoises
0	0.900
1X10	0.906
$1X10^2$	0.995
$5X10^2$	1.557
$1X10^3$	2.567
$1X10^4$	4.280

[a] Measurements were made with Ostwald tubes, Nos. 100 and 400, at 27° after 24 hr. hydration at this temperature.

To prepare guar gum solutions, the dry gum is rapidly sifted into a vigorously agitated tank of water. When the material is dispersed, the agitation is reduced, but stirring is continued until the solution become viscous. The guar gum is permitted to hydrate and thicken for at least 0.5 hr. and preferably, for 2 hr. (The gum will continue to hydrate for 24 hr.) Viscosity dependent on time, termperature, concentration, pH, ionic strength, and type of agitation.

a. Time —The viscosity in centipoises, measured as a function of time on a 1% guar gum solution at 25°, is shown in Fig. 5. A hydration time of 2 hr. is preferred,

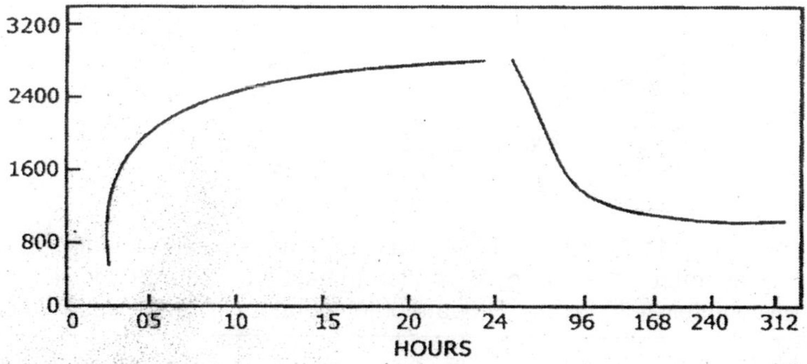

Fig.11.5. - Change in viscosity with time of a 1% food-grade guar gum dispersion at 25° (measured with a Brookfield viscometer at 20 r.p.m.)

for it produces nearly maximum viscosity. The gradual decrease in viscosity which occurs after 24 hr. is usually accompanied by a drop in pH. Two factors responsible for this viscosity decrease are fermentation and enzymatic hydrolysis. However, bacteriostatic and bacteriocidal preservatives in sufficient concentrations provide ample protection for guar gum solutions. Among the more effective are formaldehyde, chlorinated phenolics, and phdenylmercuric acetate, which, in a concentration of 0.1% based on the guar gum weight, preserves solutions for at least 8-9 months. Also used are food preservatives, such as benzoic and sorbic acids.

b. Temperature—The effect of temperature on the rate of viscosity development is illustrated in Fig. 11.6 in which the time (in min.) required to reach maximum viscosity at different temperatures is shown. Higher temperatures require shorter hydration times and result in higher viscosities.

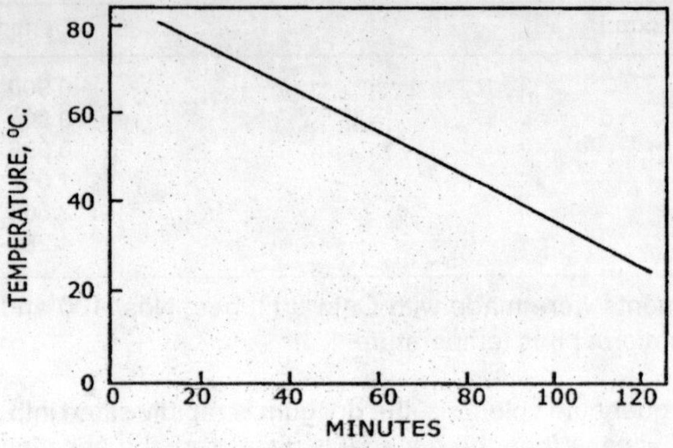

Fig. 11.6. - Effect of temperature on the rate of viscosity development of guar gum dispersions.

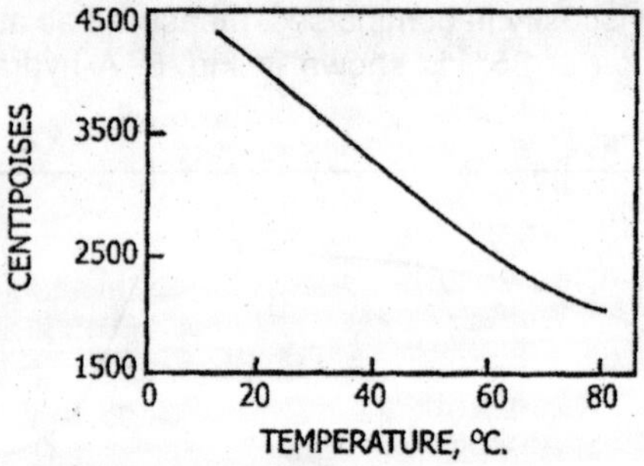

Fig. 11.7. - Effect of temperature on the viscosity of a fully hydrated, 1% guar gum solution (measured with a Brookfield viscometer at 20 r.p.m.). The rate of temperature increase was 2°/min.

The viscosity of a fully hydrated 1% guar gum solution varies almost directly with changes in temperature over the range 20-80°. Fig. 8 shows the maximum viscosities which can be obtained when dry guar gum is dispersed in water at various temperatures for periods up to 2 hr. The factors influencing the rate of viscosity development are the increase in viscosity due to time and short-term heating and the decrease in viscosity due to the degradative effect of prolonged heat.

After maintaining the desired temperatures for 2 hr., the solutions are immediately brought to 25°. Viscosities are again measured at the latter temperature after 24 hr. Guar gum exhibits good stability toward prolonged heat for periods up to 2 hr. at 80'. Maximum viscosity of the guar gum dispersion is achieved with temperatures of 25-40°. The lower is the temperature, the lower the rate at which the viscosity increases.

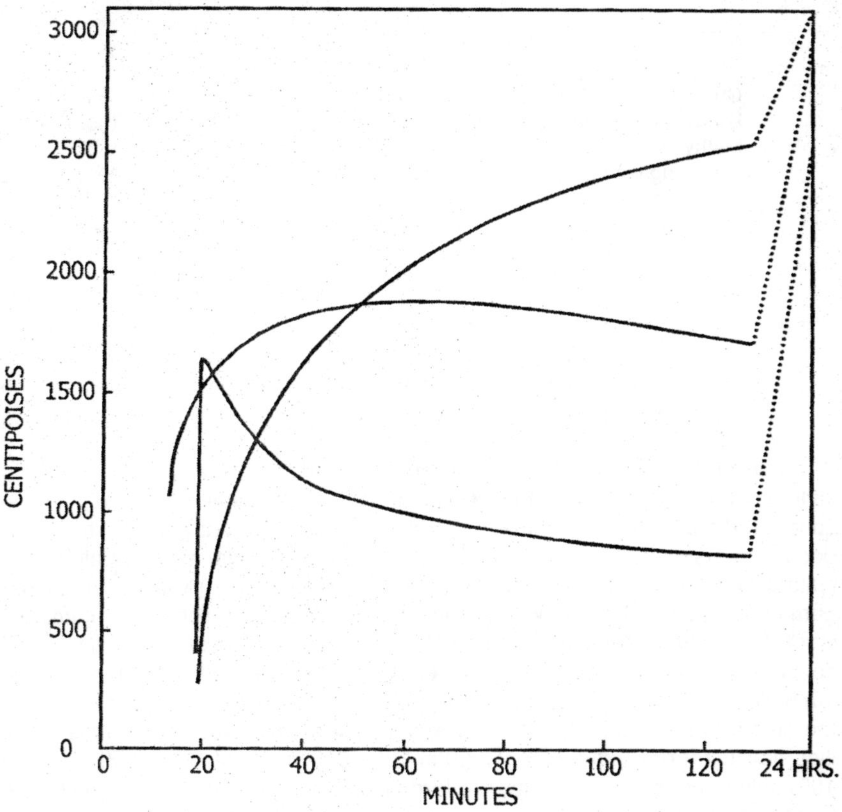

Fig. 11.8. - Viscosity variation with time of a 1% food-grade guar gum dispersion maintained at constant temperature (measured with a Brookfield viscometer at 20 r.p.m.). After 2 hr. the temperature of all dispersions were reduced to 25°.

C. Concentration— In dilute solutions, the viscosity of guar gum increases, lineally with concentrations up to about 0.5%. Thereafter, guar gum solutions behave as non-Newtonian solutions, mainly as a result of the complex surface attractions at higher concentrations. The relationship between viscosity and concentration at 25°, as measured

with a Brookfield viscometer, is illustrated in Fig. 11.9. Table IV compares the viscosity imparting ability of various colloids which were measured in a similar manner.

d. pM— Guar gum is stable over a wide pH range. The nomionic nature of the molecule is responsible for the almost constant viscosity of solutions with pH's of 1-10.5. At *pH's* above 11, hydration is depressed and low viscosity results. However, previously hydrated guar gum is compatible with high alkalinity. The optimum rate of hydration occurs

TABLE 11.3. Comparative Viscosities of 1% Gum Solutions[a]

Gum	Cps.
Gum arabic (20% by wt.)	50
Locust bean gum	100
Methylecellulose	150
Gum tragaeanth	200
Carrageenan	300
High-viscosity sodium carboxymethylcellulose	1200
Gum karaya	1500
Sodium alginate	2000
Guar gum	3300

[a] Measurements were made at 25° after 24 hr. hydration at this temperature, between pH 7.5 and 9. Yet the maximum viscosities are the same in both acidic and alkaline media, despite the rate differences.

e. Ionic strength— Since guar gum is nonionic, it is not susceptible to salting out. Comapatibility with salts is exhibited over a wide range of electrolyte concentrations. For salts containing mono-, di-, or trivalent cations stability is good and viscosity increases. Even with polyvalent salts, such as aluminum sulfate, viscosity is maintained until a salt concentration of 10% is reached. Guar gum hydrated in solutions of 10% sodium chloride, calcium chloride, aluminum chloride, or aluminum sulfate reats differently to change in pH. The viscosity of solutions of guar gum hydrated in 10% sodium chloride is constant at *pH's* up to 10-10.5; above this point it begins to drop, at a *p*H of 7.3 in 10% calcium chloride, the gum forms a strong gel which is very similar to the borax gel. It forms large, wet, flocculant precipitates at pH 7.0 in 10% aluminum chloride. At *p*H 6.2 in a 10% solution of aluminum sulfate, a large increase in viscosity is caused by the formation of a loose, stringly gel.

2. *Gels*

The transformation of a colloidal solution into a coherent, liquid-rich system is gelation. This type of system solififies or sets when the temperature is lowered or a cross-linking agent is added. At low concentrations, guar gum forms aqueous colloidal solutions, at 2-3% concentrations, it loses fluidity and becomes a gel, although it does not set into a typical structural gel, like those of gelatin or pectin, until higher concentrations are reached. The nature of the linkage involved is not wholly understood. No incompatibilities with proteins or other polysaccharides have been reported.

The borate ion acts as a cross-linking agent with hydrated guar gum to form cohesive structural gels. The formation and strength of these gels are dependent on the *p*H, temperature, and concentrations of reactants. The optimum pH range for gel formation is 7.5-10.5. A viscosity of 6,000 cps. is obtained at *p*H 9-

10 with a 0.25% solution of guar gum containing 20% of sodium tefeborate, based, on the weight of the gum. The solution-gel transformation is reversible; the gel can be liquefied by dropping the pH below 7 or by heating. By the former method, a normal solution is obtained; by the latter, a stringy solution results. Polysaccharides with numerous adjacent hydroxyl groups in the *as* position can form these 3-di-mensional borated gels. In an alkaline medium, the borate ion can react at C2 and C3 of the mannose units and C3 and C4 of the galactose side branches. Lowering the *p*H below 7 decreases the concentration of borate ion and the amount of crosslinking, increases the concentration of undissociated boric acid and liquefies the gel.

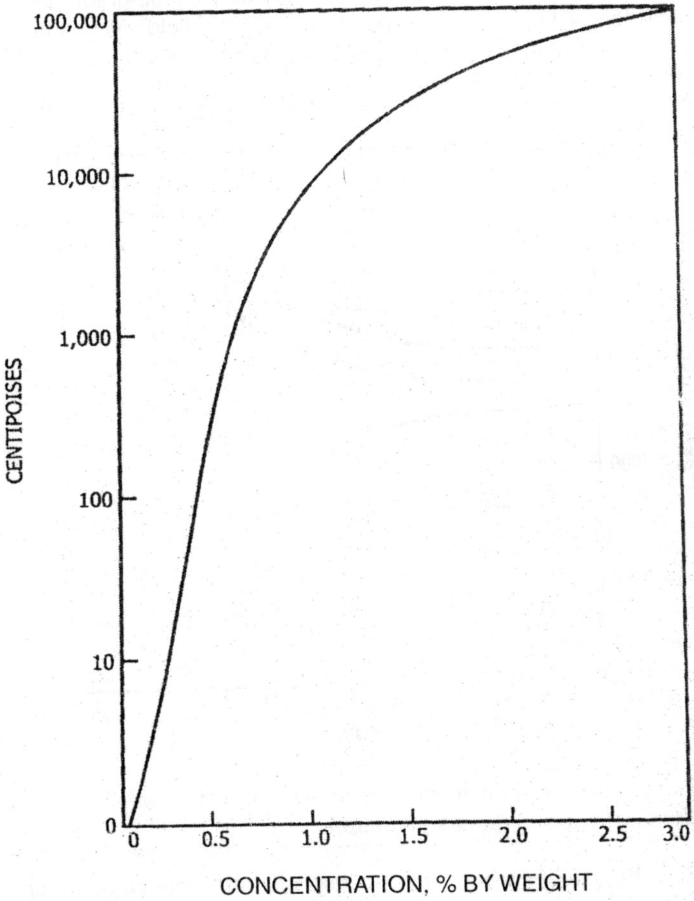

Fig. 11.9. - Viscosity as a function of concentration of food-grade guar gum hydrated for 24 hr. at 25° (measured with a Brookfield viscometer at 20 r.p.m.).

Borated gels can also be liquefied by the addition of a low molecular weight polyol, such as glycerol or manitol. The mechanism in the former case appears to be the formation of a compex, glyceryl-borate, which is a strong acid and serves as the basis for the analytical titration of boric acid.

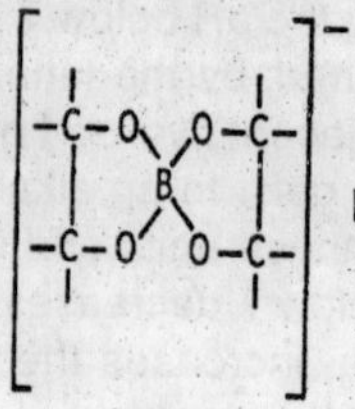

Fig., 11.10. - Effect of salts on the viscosity of 1% food-grade guar gum solutions held for 24 hr. at 25° (measured with a Brookfield viscometer at 20 r.p.m.).Curve 1, aluminum chloride (*p*H 3); 2, calcium chloride (*pH* 5); 3, sodium chloride (pH 6); 4, aluminum sulfate (*pH* 3-4).

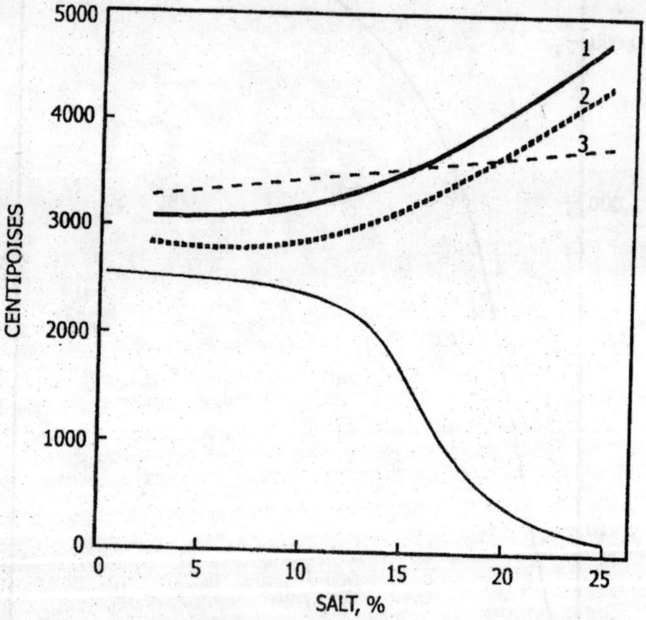

Fig. 11.11. - Representation of the complex formed between pentavalent boron and the cis hydroxyl groups of guaran.

However, the use of sodium tetraboration with non hydrated guar gum depresses the hydration of the gum and results in the formation of a precipitate. The minimum concentrations which are necessary to inhibit precipitate. The minimum concentrations which are necessary to inhibit hydration are dependent on *p*H. For example, with 1% of guar gum, 0.125-0.5% of borax (based on the guar gum weight) is needed at pH 10-10.5; at pH 7.5-8.0 1.5-2.0% of borax is required. The complexing reaction is reversible since decreasing the *p*H below 7 permits the gum to hydrate normally. Advantage of this type of reaction are : (1)

better mixing and easier dispersion; (2) added viscosity due to gelation on the alkaline side in the cold; (3) facilitation of sol-gel reversibility.

In the food industry, guar gum-starch combinations prevent frozen pie fillings from dehydrating, shrinking, and cracking.

In the manufacture of paper, it has been suggested that guar gum-starch combinations as wet-end additives are superior to either used separately.

Starch containing guar gum has improved sizing qualities in textiles.

3. Films

Guar gum forms tough, pliable films which are sensitive to water. Palmer and Ballantune described a method for producing highly oriented films which are elongated 150%. Smart and Whistler examined the triacetate derivative. The films produced from the triacetate are colourless, transparent, and have a tensile strength which is slightly lower than that of films of cellulose triacetate or potato amylose triacetate. Its films can be plasticized to make them soft and pliable.

4. Adhesiveness

The fact that guar gum shows very little adhesiveness in solution is consistent with its long straight chain, singly branched structure. This contracts with the adhesiveness displayed by a highly branched structure, such as amylopectin. The adhesiveness of guar gum solutions can be increased to some extent by conversion with acid. However, the viscosity will be reduced by this technique.

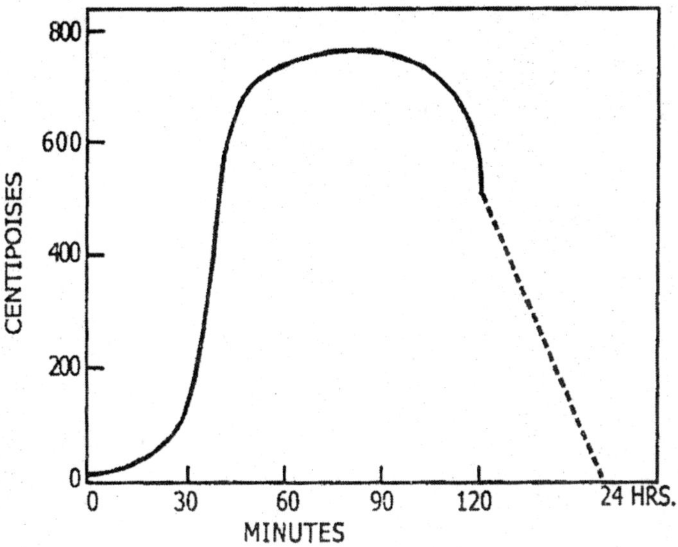

Fig. 11.12 . Viscosity versus time for a 1% dispersion of a spedial grade of guar gum which has a temporarily inhibited hydration and whose solutiion has a complete loss of viscosity after 24 hr. (Measurenemnts were made with a Brookfield viscometer at 250 and 20 r.p..m.).

5. Miscellaneous

Guar gum can be insolubilized or gelled by low concentration of polyvalent cations. The reactions are not as sensitive as are those with sodium tetraborate, and, in general, these gels do not have the rigidity and strenght of borated gels. If 10% of aluminum chloride (based on the weight of guar gum) is added to a 0.5% solution of the prehydrated gum, a gel is formed when the pH is raised to 11. Addition of the aluminum chloride to a *pH* 11-hydrated guar gum solution produces insoluble masses. Aluminum sulfate reacts similarly, but the gum precipitates directly without passing through a gel stage. Instead, an insoluble precipitate forms at the higher pH's.

Divalent cations exhibit similar pH-sensitive reactions. Copper ions afford a very choppy, weak gel with guar gum at a pH of 5.5 As the pH is increased above 5.5, complete precipitation occurs.

Some industrial grades of guar gum under current investigation are prepared so that they have a temporarily inhibited hydration in acidic media. Viscosity of the dispersion begins to develop after 10-15 min. This time lag enables the gum to disperse uniformly. The viscosity then increases, approaching a maximum after 1 hr. Thereafter, the viscosity gradually decreases until it reaches water thinness at the end of 24 hr. Useful variations of these properties include: (1) initially inhibited hydration with subsequent building of viscosity for 24 hr., (2) rapid initial hydration followed by a reduction in viscosity.

12.

Aerobic Acrylic Adhesive

Introduction

A new type of non-volatile reactive acrylic adhesives, bringing the gap between an aerobic acrylic and volatile reactive acrylic adhesives, has recently been developed. The term "aerobic" acrylic adhesives has been coined solely to identify and to set apart these adhesives from other acrylics; it does not necessarily describe their cure mechanism. The term "aerobic" will be used to refer to a diminished sensitivity to air inhibition of thick layer curing properties and the ability to cure between two surfaces regardless of the presence or the absence of air.

Aerobic acrylics will not cure by themselves due to the absence of air. They require the use of pre-applied activators to initiate the cure mechanism. This property is distinct from an aerobic adhesives which are intrinsically single component products. Even when accelerators or primers are used to increase their cure rates to meet the demands of rapid assembly techniques, an aerobic adhesives require the absence of air as a necessary condition of cure.

Second Generation Limitations

Reactive acrylic adhesives have been called "second generator acrylic," toughened acrylics," modified acrylics," and in Europe, "honeymoon adhesives." They offer advantages, shown in Table -12.1, over other adhesive systems.

Inspite of this impressive list of characteristics, the use of reactive acrylic adhesives has been limited to selected high performance adhesive markets. Their growth, otherwise, has been less rapid than expected. One of the principal reasons is due to the toxicity characteristics associated with methyl methacrylate and methacrylic acid monomers, major formulation constituents of "second generation" acrylic adhesives, with regard to inhalation,, ingestion and skin contact. Compositions containing large quantities of these monomers have been rejected on certain production lines such as automotive assembly. The low flash point and resultant flammability hazard have also been important contributors to the restricted use of modified acrylic adhesives.

Moreover, preferred activators for some reactive acrylics, dimethyl aniline and generically similar materials, are suspected carcinogens. Other reactive adhesives use schiff base activators, which are considered to be less toxic.

Recently, techniques or "use" problems have been cited as inhibitions to the growth of reactive acrylic adhesives. The main problems are described as a high sensitivity to the concentration of activator and movement in the substance prior to fixturing both of which cause less than optimal bond strength. Of course, disturbance of parts during fixturing will have the effect of reducing bond strength of any adhesive.

This chapter examines a new reactive acrylic adhesive that overcomes most of these disadvantages. This new family of adhesives, called aerobic acrylic, maintains, in some cases improves upon the performance advantages of second generation acrylics. The products are low in odor, essentially non flammable, and lower in toxicity. Their higher speed of cure and fixture rate of 10 to 60 seconds and their solvent diluted activators have minimized other problems associated with acrylic adhesives, namely, sensitivity to high concentrations of activator and movements in the substrates prior to fixture

Cure Mechanisms

The type of adhesives considered to be in the acrylic class are an aerobic, cyanoacrylate, and reactive acrylics. The differences in the types of acrylic adhesives that lead to their suitability for different end uses lie in the initiation and the mechanism of polymerization. All but the cyanoacrylates polymerize by a free-radical mechanism.

The growing polymer chain can be terminated by a number of mechanisms including two radicals joining to form a molecular species, abstraction of hydrogen, or radical transfer. Oxygen is particularly effective in terminating free radical polymerization and is responsible for the familiar air inhibition property (wet or tacky surface) noted by users of acrylic adhesives. The absence of oxygen or air is, therefore, required in order to obtain the most complete cure (polymerization) and hence, the best properties of acrylic adhesives.

Cyanoacrylates: Cyanoacrylates polymerize by an ionic mechanism initiated by moisture and basic ions. The polymers formed tend to be more brittle than those formed from other acrylics, and the bond lines are usually not resistant to degradation by moisture. Adhesive formulation are single component, fast curing product, however, and suited to many hard-to-bond surfaces such as rubber and many thermoplastics.

Anaerobics:

Anaerobic adhesives take extreme advantage of the air inhibition of acrylic polymerization. They are catalyzed in such a manner that they depend upon the presence of oxygen to remain an unpolymerized liquid. Cure is effected only in the absence of oxygen.

Anaerobic adhesives cure as single component product only on certain "active" metal surfaces when ions from the surface act as accelerators for the rate of adhesive cure. Single component, anaerobic direadlocking adhesives are examples, deriving their speed of cure from both the anaerobic catalysts and the accelerating effect of transition metal ions derived from copper, iron, or steel surfaces.

Aerobic Acrylic Adhesives

For most other surfaces, however, accelerators of various kinds similar to the activators of two-component acrylics are often required to achieve cure rates of practical lengths. Structural anaerobic adhesives cured without the use of pre-applied accelerators of primers frequently cure too slowly for rapid assembly techniques.

Reactive acrylics:

Reactive acrylics differ significantly from anaerobics in that they depend upon the presence of a chemical initiator, not the absence of oxygen, for their cure. These adhesives exhibit a high solvent action allowing the bonding of many unprepared surfaces, even oil contaminated metals. Less surface preparation is required for bonding plastics with reactive acrylics than with most other adhesives. In part, this is due to the presence of monomers in the reactive acrylic formulations that may dissolve contaminants and may also attack the polymer substrate.

Compositions are suggested in the patent literature. The concept is, essentially, that an elastomer is colloidally dispersed in a monomer or in a monomer/oligomer/polymer solution. The resultant polymer is toughened by "elastomeric domains" resulting from the dispersed elastomer.

A reactive adhesive is used by applying the adhesive (polymer solution) to one of the surfaces to be bonded; and activator, frequently in solution, is applied in a thin film to the opposing surface. In some types of reactive adhesives the two films may be left open and unbonded for many hours without adverse effects on the resulting bond.

Aerobic acrylic adhesives are composed of proprietary catalysts, "elastomeric domain" fillers, and low vapor pressure monomers. Formulations derived from this technology do not exhibit the same sensitivity towards air inhibition drawn by other acrylic adhesives. The result is that aerobic acrylics are usable on more porous surfaces and in wider gaps than previously considered practical.

Some of the physical properties that are recognized as being affected by air inhibition mechanisms are compared in Table- II. Cure through a gap is considered a function of air inhibition, as well as diffusion of accelerators and the nature of monomer used in the adhesive formulation.

Air beaten into several adhesives formulations and cured for only part of the recommended optimum time shows the effect of this type of inhibition. The aerobic acrylic appears to be only marginally affected.

An adhesive fillet, or the amount of excess adhesive squeezed outside of a lap shear joint on assembly, can also be used as a measure of air inhibition,. The less the fillet cure, the greater the inhibition. A porous material, pine wood, was chosen as a substrate that would allow air to remain in intimate contact with the Industrial Gums & Adhesives Technology Hand Book curing adhesive. The ability to lock the threads of an iron nut and bolt without use of an activator is a recognized test for determining whether or not a formulation is capable of anaerobic cure.

Properties and Performance

Today's increasingly severe regulatory constraints on industries' use of chemicals make the properties of uncured adhesive systems of paramount concern to the end-user. The methyl methacrylate base of most of die second generation acrylic adhesives introduces significant plant handling problems dial are not present in aerobic acrylic adhesives. Table III also presents a summary of curing information of second generation and aerobic acrylic adhesives, important factors to be considered in the selection of adhesives for assembly. While bodi second generation and aerobic acrylic adhesives are classified as 100% solids non-solvent systems, the volatile base of the former can also cause loss of strength due to evaporation during die open time. A slowing of the fixture rate, but not loss of the ultimate strength, is noted after long open times with aerobic acrylics.

Although, acrylics are slightly less versatile with respect to bondable substrates than are modified acrylics, they are more versatile than anaerobic adhesives, which are usually limited to the assembly of cleaned or prepared,, closely mating metal, glass, and ceramic parts.

Bondable substrates for aerobic and second generation acrylic include clean as well as oily or "as received" metal polyurethanes, filled polycarbonates, filled nylon, phenolics, thermoset plastics, wood, concrete, ceramics, glass, and other common materials of manufacture. Some thermoplastic materials are bonded better by using a second generation acrylic adhesive. Examples are unfilled nylon, ABS, and rubber.

Table 12.3 adjusts a comparison of cured properties of aerobic with second generation acrylic adhesives. The data shows diat, while tensile strengths are similar, the toughness and durability parameters are superior for the aerobics.

A torsional impact test, is used to compare the relative toughness and impact resistance of structural adhesives. In this test, a 3.6 kg weight falls in a 20 inch, 90 arc to impact a one-half inch overlap bonded lap shear positioned at a right angle to the bond. The impact scale reads directly in inch 1 kg of force needed to break the bond. Sixty inch pounds is the limit of the test. Steel and aluminium lap shears severely deform above this limit. Table-12.4 illustrates the typical values obtained.

In cured and curing properties, aerobic acrylic adhesives have a clear advantage for use as a structural adhesive.

The cost per kg of adhesives is an important, though not a limiting consideration on the choice of an acrylic adhesive. The cost of assembly usually far outweighs adhesive cost per kg. Generally, cyanoacrylates cost the most per kg, followed by anaerobics, aerobics, and then second generation acrylics.

Bonding Methods: *The* bonding techniques for aerobic acrylic adhesives are similar to other acrylics. First, the activator is applied to one of the surfaces to be joined as a thin film (quasi monomolecular layer). Roller, brush, and spray methods work equally well as long as the activator layer is kept very thin. While the permissible ratio activator to adhesive is quite wide, too much activator will lower bond strength. Activators are available in solvent to help assure thin film applications. Second, the adhesive is applied to the mating surface, and the two are brought together and held until handling time is reached. This is the preferred technique for bonding motor magnets, metal cladding and wood veneers, stepping motors, golf clubs, and other objects of similar geometries.

Application of activator to both substrates is recommended where one substrate is porous or where gaps more than 20 mils are to be filled. Activator and adhesive may be applied to the same surface, but this initiates the bonding action so that the parts must be joined immediately. For example, in automobile hem bonding, adhesive is applied in "chocolate drops" and activator is sprayed over the drops. The hem is formed immediately, squeezing activator and adhesive into intimate contact.

Aerobic Applications

Aerobic adhesives have a wider latitude in formulating for specific end-use requirements than do second generation acrylic adhesives. Flexibility, opacity, cure speed, and surface compatibility may be controlled over a wide range to produce adhesives for metal, glass, many plastics, ceramics, and hard woods. The cured properties of specific aerobic formulations are scarcely affected by efficient thickening agents such as fumed silica. As a consequence, it is possible for an end-user to pick a set of cured properties and then have the adhesive's viscosity modified to specific requirements. The properties of three representative cured formulations are outlined in Table-12.5.

Formulation "A" is frequently used when a substantial amount of time is required for alignment and adjustments during assembly operation. A typical end-use is the production of precision optical gauges. The parts are in the forms of concentric circles of glass and stainless steel. They must be carefully rotated and adjusted to exact tolerances before the adhesive fixture to the parts.

A manufacturer of high speed printers also requires five minutes of assembly time before fixture occurs in a 10 mil shimmed bond line gap. In this application, a number of ferrite magnets are bonded to metal frames and assembled in the proper geometrical arrangement in one step. This adhesive process replaces a combination of mechanical clamps, spacers, and holding screws.

High level of noxious odours and concerns over worker safety have resulted in acrylic adhesives being removed from consideration in automotive hem bonding plant. They were rejected despite a five-year development programme that showed that replacing spot welding with a rapidly fixturing adhesive would substantially lower hood and lid assembly costs. However, an aerobic acrylic similar to the "B" formulation shown in Table-V has been approved for trial production because of its low odor and non flammable properties.

Aerobic acrylics also show enhanced cure speed, tensile strength, moisture resistance, and the ability to resist automotive bake cycles, which can be as high as 232°C. The operation also requires fixturing through a variable 10 to 20 mil gap in less than 30 seconds. Thixotropic adhesive is applied to the area to be bonded and activator sprayed directly on top of the adhesive. The metal is immediately folded to form a "hem" joint.

A photocopier manufacturer uses an aerobic adhesive to attach large glass lenses to metal frames. The application requires an adhesive that can absorb the forces generated from the large differences; in expansion characteristics between glass and metal. Type "B" formulated adhesive were shown to provide adequate bonds with tensile strength exceeding the deformation strength of the metal frames. However, when subjected to a 148°C temperature range, the glass lenses frequently broke. Increasing the bond line thickness to 10 mils and using a flexible type "C" formulation produced shock absorbing bonds and the lenses now pass the thermal cycle requirements.

An aerobic acrylic adhesive has also been used to increase both product performance and reliability while reducing assembly costs in the manufacture of motorcycle alternators. A major manufacturer of high performance motorcycles had been holding ceramic magnets in place with a plastic retaining ring. The manufacturer had to increase the alternator's output from 17 to 22.5 amps at

3600 rpm without increasing the size of the alternator. It was known that replacing the retaining ring with a bonding process would permit more magnet mass in the same space.

A number of attempts with anaerobic adhesives, epoxies, urethanes, and second generation acrylic adhesives had proved unsuccessful. The bonded alternator had to withstand a -50°C to +182°C operating temperature range and the rigors of constant vibration. The nature of the production process required rapid fixture times and could not tolerate noxious or toxic vapors. A type "B" formulation aerobic acrylic adhesive is now used because it meets necessary production and performance criteria.

Medallions and handles are mechanically attached to metal knife frames by combination \of welding, riveting, and staking. Several years ago, reactive acrylic adhesives were used to replace riveting in medallions with a resulting 65% savings on assembly costs. Controlling vapors in the labour intensive assembly plant and 15-minute fixture times limited this use to a small part of the total assembly. Ease of handling and lack of noxous vapors have led to additional savings.

A fuse manufacturer replaced a 30-minute epoxy used in a heat cure process to assemble stainless steel inserts into phenolic holders. By utilizing an aerobic adhesive bonding process, the assembly was complete in 30 seconds at room temperature. The resulting increase in productivity was more than offset the higher adhesive cost. A cyanoacrylate bonding process was even faster but did not resist aging in a moist atmospheric environment or pass a drop test for impact resistance.

Many kinds of adhesives are utilized in the bonding of loudspeaker magnets, DC motor assemblies, and other types of magnet bonding. Some manufacturers still prefer to use mechanical clamps. The factors that contribute to the choice of a joining process include the cost of the adhesive, labour rates, speed of adhesived fixture, acceptability of odour level and energy costs. Aerobic acrylic adhesives have been used primarily for their rapid fixture (as little as 10 seconds) resulting in faster assembly rates.

A manufacturer of restaurant appliances fastens a stainless steel top to a combined counter/refrigerator/stove unit. The standard attachment technique included both welding and the use of self-tapping screws. An aerobic acrylic adhesive has replaced these techniques resulting in a lower cost assembly requiring less skilled labour. The same adhesive is used to tack refrigerator coils in place.

A similar application involves the use of an aerobic adhesive to assemble large insulated aluminum doors for storage rooms. The replacing of a difficult aluminum welding process led to more efficient techniques.

Conclusion

Acrylic structural adhesives have been specified in a number of applications due to their ability to increase productivity through rapid cure while providing equal or better performance than mechanical means of fastening. Second generation reactive acrylics overcome the limitations imposed by scrupulous cleaning or preparation of surface prior to bonding and the tendency towards requiring small, thin bond lines. Their use has been limited, however, by concerns arising from the use of potentially toxic, flammable noxious monomers.

Aerobic acrylic adhesives have most of the advantages of other acrylic adhesives while offering improvements in cure time, toughness, ease of use, and gap curing ability. The lack of obnoxious odours are a benefit to adhesive users.

TABLE-12.1 Advantages of Reactive Acrylics

* Simple no - mix application
• Rapid bonding at room temperature
• Tolerance for oil contaminated surfaces
• Bond flexibility
* Peel strength and impact resistance
• Low shrinkage during polymerization
• Excellent reproducibility
* Good heat resistance
* Excellent solvent resistance
• Good low and high temperature properties
• Wide latitude in cure rates
• Long open time
• Broad applicability to a wide variety of substrates with little or no surface preparation
• Formulating flexibility for specific end-use requirements.

Table - 12.2 Effect of Air Inhibition on the Phygical Properties of Aerobic Acrylic Adhesive

Tensile shear - steel , psi	an aerobic structural Acrylic	2nd generation	Aerobic Acrylic
(astm d- 1000)			
24 hour cure			
2 mils	4,500	5,00	4,000
20 mils	2,500	3,200	3.500
60 mils	0	1,000	2,500
20 mils (air beaten into adhesive)	1,000	2,000	3,000
Length of fillet cure from the edge of the joint, steel, inches	.05	.15	.25
Cure on pine wood, 40 mil gap	500psi	partial substrate failure	substrate failure
Time to fixture iron nut and bolt at 25*C. No accelerator used	2-6 hr	4-24 hr	no fixture after 30 days; test discontinued

TABLE-12.3 - Typical Peoperties of Acrylic Adhesive

Properties	2nd Generation	Aerobic
Toxicity of monomers	moderate to high	low
Odor	substantial	faint
Flash time	7-1 5°C	over 95°C
Fixture tune		
2 mil gap	5-1 2 min	10-60 sec
20 mil gap	10-20 min	5 min
50% strength	4-8hr	15-90 min
100% strength	24 hr	4-24 hr
Effect of "open time"		
30 sec	Up to 2 5% strength loss	no effect
5 min	Upto 50% strength loss	no effect
4hr	no bond	1 0% slower fixture rate
Maximum gap tolerance, mils	30-40	60-80
Tensile shear		
Degreased, sandblasted steel	to 5,000 psi	to 4,500 psi
Oily steel (as received)	to 4,000 psi	to 3,500 psi
Torsional impact		
Automotive steel, aluminium	to 20 in lb	to 60 in lb (limit of test)
Heat resistance	to 121°C	to232°C
Solvent resistance	good	excellent
Creep resistance	feir	excellent

* Properties vary depending upon grade of adhesive chosen and ambient temperature.

Table -12.4- Typical Torsional Impact

Adhesive	Values
Polyamide epoxy	7 ± 5 in lb
Cyanoacrylate	2 ± 2 in lb
Anaerobic	12 ±5 in lb
"2nd Generation" acrylic	20 ± 7 in lb
General purpose	40 ±10 in lb
Acerobic acrylic	(Metal deformation)
High impact aerobic acrylic	60 ± in the lb

* On degreased, sandblasted steel. 1/2 inch overlap.

TABLE- 12.5- Effect of Aerobic Formulation Variation

Properties	A	B	C
Fixture rate on glass*	5 min	15 sec	7 sec
Complete room temeprature cure	24-72 hr	4-24 hr	2-8 hr
Bond line appearance	opaque, white	hazy	transparent

Gap filling	70 mils	50 mils	30 mils
Shore D	50	75	10
Hardness Texture	tough, resilient	rigid	very flexible
Typical end-use	ferrite bonding shim bonding fibreglass assembly graphite	steel metal galvanized steel, Kevlar mounts composites	lenses bonding "plexiglass" window glass
Tensile, cold rolled steel	2,000 psi	3,500 psi	1,000 psi

* Fixture rates are defined as the time required for two microscope slides, bonded in 1 / 2 inch overlap, to resist movement from light finger pressure gaps estimated at 1-3 mils. Varies with ambient temperature and condition of the substance.

Utraviolet Light Curing "Aerobic" Acrylic Adhesive

The concept of cross-linking polymers with ultraviolet (UV) light attained full commercial acceptance in the coatings and ink industry in the late 1970s. The extension of UV curable technology to smooth, non-porous substrates, however, created problem in adhesion. Surfaces that had poor adhesion qualities included metals, which have smooth, non-porous surfaces and are frequently coated with lubricants during manufacture; plastics, which have low energy surfaces or are heavily plasticized; and glass, another smooth, non-porous surface. Early attempts at formulating structural adhesive reflected those limitations. Consequently, the use of UV technology with adhesives gained little acceptance.

Utraviolet light curing grades of "aerobic" acrylic adhesives ever, have been developed to provide structural bonds within seconds at room temperature on a wide variety of substrates. Parts may be precisely positioned and then structurally joined "on demand," at a time convenient to the assembly process.

Tough, impact resistant structural adhesives with tensile strengths up to 3,000 psi or more may join metal, plastic, glass, ceramics, and other substrates. Adhesive potting to 1/4 inch can be produced in a single exposure to high intensity UV light Transparent stability and resistance to mechanical and thermal shock are also derived from this technology.

Aerobic Acrylic Advantages

The advantages of "aerobic" acrylic adhesives are retained, and in a few cases improved upon in their ultraviolet light curing analogues. The term "aerobic" acrylic adhesives has been adopted solely to identify and set apart these adhesives from other acrylics; it does not describe their cure mechanism. "Aerobic" refers to a diminished sensitivity to air inhibition of which layer curing properties and the ability to cure between surfaces regardless of the presence or absence of air.

UV aerobic acrylics will not cure by themselves due to the absence of air. They require the presence of long wave ultraviolet light for cure. Some grades will also cure by the pre application of activator to the substrate that is to be bonded.

UV curing aerobic acrylic adhesives have structural properties that appear to be significantly different from other UV curing product. For example, poor adhesion to substrates exacerbated by high shrinkage on cure has been cited as a prime deficiency of UV cured adhesives and coatings. This could have been a greater factor for limiting the acceptance of adhesives than of UV cured coating because of the higher performance generally expected of adhesives. Shrinkage on cure of coatings type UV products can be 10% to 25%. One UV aerobic acrylic formulation has a shrinkage on cure of 1.5%, although 3 to 5% shrinkage is a more typical rate (Table-12.6).

The cured properties of UV aerobic acrylics include high tensile strengdis, temperature resistance, impact strength, and other properties expected of aerobic acrylics. Formulations have been developed with properties ranging from hard, tough adhesives with a shore D hardness of 80 to soft, elastomeric materials with a shore A of 10, similar to silicone rubber,

Surface dryness and depth of cure are dependent on both the lamp used and the individual formulation. High intensities are required for the most rapid and deepest cures. A potting grade UV aerobic will cure to 1/4 inch in 30 seconds under a 100,000 microwatt/cm^2 mercury vapor lamp. Table-12.2 shovw curing times with various lights.

Curing Lights and Mechanisms

Some studies have indicated that UV lights represent a significant capital expanse. While this is still the case for high speed UV ink and coatings "dryers." Many low and modest cost lights will cure UV aerobic acrylic adhesives (Table-12.7). Significant advances have also been made in fibre optics which will transmit UV light, and small "Penlight" lamps have become available too. These light sources are ideal for hand assembly of small parts such as electronic components.

Ultraviolet light consisting of electromagnetic radiation in the 200-400 nanometer range has proven useful for producing free radicals from sensitive molecules such as ketones. The radicals can then initiate free radical polymer reactions. It follows that cure with UV light depends on the specific wavelength absorption of the catalyst, the ease of radical formation, the intensity of the light, and the ability of the formulation to cure after being initiated.

Only initiators sensitive to long wave ultraviolet light over 325 nanometers are used in UV aerobic acrylic adhesives. Long wave UV light is sometimes referred to as "black light" and is generally considered harmless. Short wave radiation, on the other hand, can produce burns. (Sunburn from over exposure is a familiar example). The high intensity lamps shown in Table-VII all require shielding to protect workers from the short wavelengths that they emit in addition to long wave UV light.

Bonding Categories

The ways in which UV aerobic acrylic adhesives are used have been divided into categories (Table-12.8). One category is the bonding and lamination of clear materials such as glass and plastics.

Because UV aerobics exhibit high strength, toughness, and good structural properties, the second category has been designated "light welding" a process of joining parts by bridging the joint with cured adhesive replacing long cure times or mechanical fasteners.

A third category is that of adhesive potting and speciality coatings on smooth surfaces like metal.

"Light Welding"

The ability to bridge bond many surfaces while retaining structural properties has led to a new concept for the joining of abutting surfaces. "Welding with Light" is the process of laying a bead of liquid adhesive across as the joint formed by abutting metal, glass, ceramic.thermoplastic, paper, and other surfaces and joining them by polymerising (curing) the adhesive in a few seconds with exposure to long wave UV light.

A laboratory example will serve to illustrate the process of "Welding with light". Cold rolled steel joints were prepared using the same aerobic acrylic adhesive. A l-in bonded overlapped joint was measured at 1,750 kg tensile pull. The "welded" joint showed 200 kg tensile pull, since the same adhesive was used, the difference in adsolute tensile strength can be ascribed to the differences in surface areas. Depending upon design strength requirements, therefore, "light welding" can rapidly join a large number of diverse parts. Properties can range from hard, thermoset structural "welds", which can exceed the strength of some substrates, to soft, pliable elastomeric adhesives, potting and tacking systems (Table 12.6 and 12.8).

Industrial Applications

Part to be joined can be positioned to exacting tolerances. The adhesive may be applied either before or after positioning and then fixtured or "welded" on demand by exposure to UV light. The low shrinkage of UV aerobics helps assure non-movement of parts due to the curing cycle. Small parts can be joined in 1-10 sec at room temperature. Thick bond lines require longer times or more pwerful light sources.

Some ferrite parts require bridge bonding because adhesive between the surfaces interferes with electrical properties. The common technique of using a paste epoxy requiring long time cycles or heat cures can be replaced by a fast curing "light welding" technique. The parts are held in position, a bead of thixotropic UV aerobic adhesive is applied across the joint and cured with UV light A 200 watt per inch industrial light required 2 sec, while a low power "black light" effected cures in 300 sec.

A fabricated plastic holder for an electronic pickup head is assembled and the concentric parts are adjusted to a fine tolerance. An adhesive is applied across gaps that may very to gain wide and cured. A filled UV curing aerobic adhesive has been chosen due to its rapid cure "on demand" and low shrinkage on cure, keeping the parts within the required alignment of six seconds of arc.

A common method of wiretaking today is to use cyanoacrylate adhesive and primer. In this process, a drop of cyanoacrylate is placed on top of the wire to be tacked followed by a drop of primer. The resulting wiretack is usually serviceable in 5-15 sec although several hours can be required for full cure. The usage of the wire tack, although limited by a lack of moisture, temperature, and impact resistance, has been finding increasing application in the electrical industry.

UV curving aerobic acrylic adhesive, while less expensive on a per kg basis than cyanoacrylates, provide a structural wire tack that resists environmental conditions. A useful property is that the aerobic acrylics fluoresce to optimum brightness only upon completion of cure, providing a visual means of end point determination. An elastomeric formulation is recommended for permanent wire tacking in a high vibration environment. Removing wire tacking formulations are also available.

Loudspeaker software is frequendy assembled and bonded with solvent based and epoxy adhesives requiring long drying times or heat assisted cures, UV aerobic adhesives have been used to increase the speed of some assembly operations.

Many different materials are used in loudspeakers. Several kinds of paper or fabric are bonded to each other, to coated foil, to aluminium, and to other metal surfaces. Some speakers use engineering plastics instead of paper for a sound generating surface. The bond lines must be rigid enough to transmit vibrations from the speaker coil to the sound generation surfaces, tough enough to withstand long-term vibration, and in some cases, able to withstand temperatures of 150°C or more.

In one assembly process, a plastic cone is placed over a metal coil. A UV acrylic adhesive is applied to the mating surfaces and cured in 4 min using a low powered "black light". A higher volume producer uses a similar procedure, however four, 3-sec passes under a high intensity light is required due to the nature of the substrate and the design of the mating coated paper surfaces. Adhesive that was absorbed by the black paper surfaces could not be completely cured because of the blocking effects of the paper. To assure cure in this and other "shadow" situations, a pre-application of activator was required.

An electronic manufacturer attaches a plastic base to a 1-in square ceramic circuit holder with a UV adhesive. Cure time is 10-sec, which is about the same as the previously used cyanoacrylate. The lower cost, higher performance, and worker safety features justified the change in adhesive.

Beryllium copper bellows have typically been joined by applying a two part epoxy and accelerating the cure with heat A single component structural UV aerobic acrylic performs the same operation in 30 sec with the added advantage of having eliminated surface preparation.

Electronic chips are temporarily bonded with a 1-sec UV curing adhesive. The bonds hold the chip to a PC board prior to wave soldering. The adhesive must continue to bond during the soldering process, which could reach up to 32°C for 2-5 sec. A special adhesive was developed that would stand up to these conditions, as well as bond even under the chips where light rays could not penetrate.

UV Transparent Surfaces

Bonding UV transparent surfaces is easily accomplished depending on the surfaces chosen. Some grades of transparent plastics contain UV absorbers that prevent light induced curing, and therefore, require care in substrate selection.

Glass is efficiently bonded with UV aerobic acrylic and epoxies, anaerobics by heat fusion techniques. A manufacturer of pressed glass stoneware required an adhesive that would resist repeated exposures to detergent and water while providing a faster cure rate to an epoxy bonding process. A transparent UV acrylic was developed that cured a 2 mil gap completely in 2.5 sec under a 250 watt mercury lamp. It did not discolor on aging and was moisture resistant

A copier manufacturer assembles a glass lens system to an aluminium base. The parts must be aligned to close tolerances, a process which can take variable amounts of time, and then bonded. A UV aerobic acrylic accomplishes this task in 15 seconds using a low power"black light".

A non-UV absorbing grade of polycarbonate window is bonded to a cast aluminium case by a manufacturer of off-road vehicles. The 30 sec UV curing system replaces a process in which holes were drilled and tapped into the aluminium and in which the window was sealed with a rubber ring before screwing on a metal retaining ring.

Coloured polyacrylate windows are bonded over instrument gauges designed for an airplane instrument panel.

Automotive head lamp manufacturers usually heat fuse glass to join lenses to reflectors and to seal assembly holes. Heat curing epoxy adhesives provide some energy savings over the fusion process, but still require long heating times and substantial capital investment.

Manufacturers have begun using UV adhesives because of the very large differences in the cost of energy used for cure and the increase in productivity associated with faster cure cycles. Specially designed UV aerobic acrylics cure rapidly, adhere to borosilicate glass, and withstand the severe environmental and vibration resistance required for automotive parts.

Potting and Sealing

Adhesive potting is achieved through the proper choice of adhesive, UV light, and substrate section. Hard or elastomeric potting formulations can be used depending upon requirements. Depths of more than 1 /4 inch are obtained by using a step wise technique. In a structural adhesive potted plug 3/4-in deep three applications and curing cycles of adhesive (30 sec each) were faster than a two-component epoxy with its long curing.

Properties of the UV curing aerobic acrylics-good adhesion and environmental resistance-suggest their use as sealing and coating agent. Speed of sealing and energy savings over the cost associated with two-part or heat curing systems are two of the productivity increasing advantages. Use of these systems may be limited, however, by the thickness of the desired coating and the ability to deliver UV light to all surfaces involved.

Design Considerations

Glass and clear plastics must not contain UV light absorbers that will prevent the light from reaching the bond line. Cure of aerobic acrylic adhesives only proceeds when UV radiation is directly contacting the bond line. If the light is turned off or dimmed, or if shadows come between the light and the adhesives, cure may not occur. UV light must directly strike the total surface of the bond (adhesive) in order for polymerization to occur.

Surfaces can be activated to assure cure in applications where shadows are present or if the depth of the adhesive is such that UV light cannot penetrate completely.

TABLE-12.6 - COMPARATIVE CURED PROPERTIES OF SELECTED ADHESIVES

Particulars	Optical Adhesive (acrylic)	UVCuring Epoxy	V Curing Anaerobic	UV Curing' Rigid'	Aerobic Elastomeric	Adhesive flexible
Commercial availability	mid 1970s	late1970s	mid 1970s	1981	1982	1980
Apparent gap filling (in)	0.15	0.020	0.050	0.15	0.25	0.30
Tensile on cold rolled using optional activator of primer			2,500 psi	3,800 psi	3,000 psi	1,000 psi
Shore D hardness	85	80	80	80	50	10
Thermal shock *time to failure	15 sec	15 sec	5 min	2hr	4hr	4hr
Impact resistance glass	poor	poor	good	excellent	excellent	excellent
Adhesion to oily cold rolled Steel	poor	poor	poor	excellent	good	fair
Relative cost index (Epoxy=100)	2,000	100	1,000	500	400	400
Shrinkage on cure	10-25%	10-15%	8-15%	1-5%	1-5%	1-5%
Temperature resistanoo	NA	121°C	121°C	204°C	148°C	148°C

* 1/4" x 1" square soft glass wasixmded over a 1/2" area. The glass was not treated with adhesion promoters or cleaned. Each specimen was then cured for 5 min under a 275 watt mercury arc lamp and cooled to 0°C. After 30 min specimens were dropped into boiling water and tested to failure with tongs for 4 hrs. Typical values taken from published technical data sheets.

TABLE - 12.7 - SOME SOURCES OF UV LIGHT

Sources	Wavelength	Intensity at 350400 nanometers (watts/cra2)	Approximates price range Rs.	Seconds to cure (2 mil gap between glassslides)	Seconds to cure(18inch deep wire tack)
Sunlight	full spectrum	very low		10-30	not recommended
Mineral light, "black light"	350400 nanometers	100-7,000	75-500	5-20	15-100 (higher intensities only)
275 watt consumer style sunlamp	full spectrum + heat	5,000+7,000	40-75	1-10	5-30

Industrial grade mercury are lamp Type I	300-400 nanometers + visible light	5,000-10,000	200-500	1-15	5-30
Industrial grade mercury are lamp Type II	full spectrum + heat	1,500,000	800-5,000	0.54	2-10
Pulsed xenon arc lamps; solar simulators	full spectrum + heat	very high intensities	50,000 +	fast	1-5

* Shielding recommended.
Shielding required.
Speed of cure varies according to formulation.

TABLE-12.8 - BONDING CATEGORIES USING UV AEROBIC ACRYLIC ADHESIVES

Bonding	'Welding'	Potting/coating (other)
Glass window assembly lens bonding polycarbonate shield assembly plastic film lamination costume jewellry glass/plastic stemware lamp assembly	Chip bonding speaker softwere assembly wire tacking temporary bonding ferrite magnet assembly electrical leads to lamp housing sealing motor parts tamper proofing of mechanical fasteners costume Jewellery	Potting to 1/4 deep abrasion resistant coatings solder mask encapsulating

13.

Acrylic Adhesive and Sealants

Introduction

Acrylics for adhesives are polymers and copolymers which are mainly based on acrylic and methacrylic acids and their derivatives, especially the acrylic acid esters:

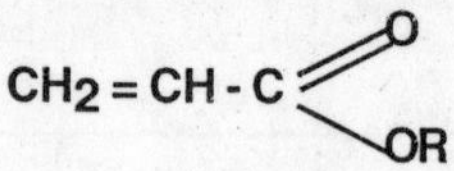

Other acrylic compounds, e.g. acrylic acid and methyl methacrylate, are normally used only as auxiliary monomers for adhesive raw materials. By judicious selection of the monomers and polymerization condition it is possible to develop a great variety of acrylics eminently suitable for adhesives. They are available in the form of solutions, dispersions, and liquids containing 100% polymer.

Polymerization

All industrial polymerization processes are carried out at an elevated temperature in the presence of an initiator. Polymerization can be carried out in bulk, solution, suspension, or emulsion. The most important processes for producing acrylics for adhesives-solution, emulsion and polymerization-are dealt here.

Solution Polymerization

In solution polymerization, the monomer or monomer mixture is dissolved in a solvent which is relatively inert to free radicals, e.g., ethyl or butyl acetate, benzene, toluene, petroleum solvent or ketones; then polymerization is effected at elevated temperatures in the presence of an initiator such as an organic peroxide or an azo compound which is soluble in the solvent .

A typical solution polymerization formulation for producing a pressure-sensitive adhesive is given below:

Formulation

Ingredients	Parts by Weight
n-Butyl acrylate	500
Ethyl acetate	500
Benzoyl peroxide	0.55

Dissolve the destabilized acrylate in ethyl acetate in a mixing vessel and heat 150 parts of the solution in a flask with stirring to 75-80°C. After moderate reaction has set in, the residual solution is gradually added within 2 hrs at reflux temperature. After the incorporation has been completed, the compound is further polymerized for 1-2 hrs.

Properties of the Product	
K Value	50-60
solids content	50%
Film properties	very tacky

The type of solvent used has a great influence on the reaction speed and the molecular weight of the resulting polymer in solution, because of the different chain transfer activities of the various solvents. Thus, the viscosity of a polymethyl acrylate solution, and the molecular weight of the polymer, decreases in the following order: benezene, ethyl acetate, ethylene dichloride, butyl acetate, methyl isobutyl ketone, and toluene.The solvent with the highest chain transfer activity gives polymers of lowest molecular weight. The molecular weights of solution polymers are normally lower than those of emulsion polymers. In selecting the solvent to be used, consideration must also be given to the economic and safety aspects.

Emulsion Polymerization

The emulsion polymerization process for homo- and copolymerization of acrylic compounds is of greater significant than the solution polymerization process. It is effected in the presence of emulsifiers and initiators (e.g. alkali persulfates), normally in water as the external phase. Suitable emulsifiers are, for example, alkali salts of long chain aliphatic carboxylic or sulfonic acids, or sulfated ethylene oxide adducts.

A typical formulation for an acrylic emulsion for producing a multiple-purpose adhesive, e.g., for laminating:

Formulation

Ingredient	**Parts by weight**
n-Butyl acrylate	1375
Vinyl acetate	1375
Acrylic acid	50
Soap	25
Ethylene oxide condensate	25
Water	2500
Potassiumperoxide disulfate (Calculated on monomers)	0.05%

To an enamelled vessel with water-cooling jacket and stirrer, add the water , emulsifier, and acrylic acid. Neutralize with aqueous caustic to pH 7-8. Then add the other monomers and, finally, the catalyst. Keep the mixture cool; 15-20% of the mixture from the mixing vessel is introduced by pressure and heated to 70-80°C. When the reaction has set in after 1/2-3/4 hr. (this can be seen from the reflux), the residual amount from the mixing vessel is gradually incorporated within 2-3 hrs. The reaction is usually not yet completed after this procedure. The mix must be kept at 80-90°C for another 1-1/2 hr.The conclusion of the reaction can be recognized from the viscosity or solids content. Residual monomers are removed by passing a stream of nitrogen over the surface for 30 min at 80-90°C. The compound is then cooled down to 35°C.

This yields a dispersion having the following properties:

Properties of the dispersion:	
Solids content	0.50%
Average particle size	0.2 wm
Viscosity (250C)	0.20 cps

For meeting certain requirements, e.g., in the production of packaging materials, it is often necessary to remove even the smallest amounts of residual monomers from the dispersions. The unconverted monomers can be removed with the aid of water vapour or hot air or by incorporating substances with basic nitrogen atoms, certain peroxy esters, and/or peroxy ketals. The dispersions are atomized and the resultant droplets are mixed with water vapour, the liquid monomer being thus evaporated out of the droplets. In process water vapour is passed through a boiling polymer dispersion and the resultant foam-like steam dispersion mixture is broken at flow rates of about 100 m/sec by rapid pressure reduction.The steam is then separated from the collapsed foam, and the residual monomers are thus removed to a great extent. A lower content of residual monomers can generally be achieved by increasing the amount of catalyst and by carrying out the final phase of conversion over a period of several hours.

Aqueous acrylic dispersions have important advantages over acrylic solutions, e.g., lower costs, no solvent reclaiming necessary, no fire hazard, no toxic solvents, easier handling, higher solids content, and higher molecular weight at lower viscosity. In most applications, these advantages outweigh the disadvantages, such as lower resistance to freezing, lower storage stability, longer drying time of film, and higher water absorption of film.

Properties

At room temperature, the homopolymers of methacrylic and acrylic acid as well as those of the lower methacrylic acid esters are hard, non tacky products which are suitable only for special applications in the adhesives field. Homopolymers of acrylic acid esters from alcohols with at least 2 carbon atoms, which are elastic, soft, and partially highly tacky products, are used for a much larger range of adhesive applications.

Further physical properties of the most important acrylic homopolymers in comparison to those of polyvinyl acetate are given in Table 1 (properties' increasing in direction of arrow).

Formulations and Applications

Adhesives for Paper Converting

The requirements imposed on adhesives for bonding paper to paper are normally not too severe. Because the absorptivity and surface condition of paper, animal and vegetable adhesives can attain satisfactory wetting and anchorage and thus yield adequate bonding strength.

However, since the requirements imposed on the bonding speed have increased steadily, they can no longer be met with adhesives based on natural products. Thus, it was not possible to design and use modern automatic paper converting machines until it was discovered that polymer dispersions based on polyvinyl acetate are suitable for this application. By modifying these homopolymeric polyvinyl acetate dispersions by adding, for instance, plasticizers, solvents and resins, it was even possible to render these adhesives suitable for bonding coated and lacquered paper and to a certain extent also for bonding paper to polymer films. The range of applications for dispersions modified in this way is, however, limited by the fact that plasticizer migration may adversely affect the adhesion and/or bonded materials. The demand for raw materials and adhesives with improved specific adhesion therefore increased with the improvements of the materials used in the paper converting industry, such as printing, lacquering, application of water vapor impermeable coatings on paper and board, and the use of polymer films.

Because of their high specific adhesion to a great variety of surfaces, polyacrylic acid esters in the form of aqueous dispersions and organic solutions were found suitable for the production of adhesives for surfaces which are difficult to bond. The products in question are either copolymers of acrylic acid esters with one another, or, especially in the case of packaging adhesives, copolymers of acrylic acid esters with vinyl propionate or vinyl acetate.i.e. copolymers of vinyl acetate with acrylic acid esters. Terpolymers produced from acrylic acid, acrylic acid ester, and vinyl acetate have increased adhesion to metal foils and various plastics and are therefore used for producing adhesives for this field of application. Terypolymers of this type are also very resistant to plasticizer migration, e.g., from plasticized PVC films.

Laminating aluminium foil-to-paper:

Formulation

Ingredient	**Parts by Weight**
Acrylic copolymer (AGP)	95.5
Nitrosol 5% in water	4.5

Viscosity : 1900 cps (25°C).

The adhesive is applied on the aluminium foil by means of rolls. Lamination can be effected either while the adhesive is still wet or by sealing at 130-150°C after drying.

Laminating rigid or soft PVC film to paper:

Formulation Ingredients	**Parts by Weight**
Acrylic copolymer (ACP)	100
Ammonia 25%	2
Water	15

Viscosity : 670 cps (25°C).

The adhesion to printed surfaces can be increased by adding 10-20 parts by weight ACP (I) or ACP (II) to the above mentioned formulation. Moreover, the laminating temperature can be reduced in this way.

The required viscosity for application is obtained by thickening with ammonia and, if necessary, by adding, water. The adhesive is applied on the film. Lamination can be effected either while the adhesive is still wet or by pressing between rolls at 60-70°C after drying. The adhesive is usually applied at a rate of 10-12g/m^2 (calculated on solids).

Typical applications include lamination of pocket books, maps, posters, etc., with rigid or soft PVC film.

Laminating polyester film to paper:

Formulation Ingredients	Parts by Weight
Acrylic copolymer (ACP)	90
ACP (II)	10
Ammonia 25%	2
Water	10

The adhesive is applied as mentioned above but because of the addition of ACP (II) the lamination temperature is reduced to 50-55°C.

Laminating high-gloss films:

Formulation	Parts by Weight
ACP (s) 40% in ethyl acetate	100
Rosin modified acrylic acid (RAA)	90
40% solution in toluene	60
Toluene	55
Coat weight on acetate film: approximately	12 g/m^2 solids
Laminating temperature	40-50°C
Laminating pressure	8-10kg/Cm^2

In laminating acetate film it is advisable to use toluene as a solvent in order to prevent the film from being slightly dissolved by the ethyl acetate in the ACP (s) solution.In this case, too, the adhesive is applied onto the film.The coated film is laminated to the paper web or board sheets after the bulk of the solvent has evaporated. This is carried out with the aid of laminating rolls at moderate temperature in order to prevent the laminate from warping.

Laminates of aluminium fail and paper with good resistance to heat and water

Formulation	Parts by Weight
ACP (s) 40% in ethyl acetate	70
Vinyl chloride/vinyl propionate copolymer *(VC/VP)* 50% in ethyl acetate	30
Laminating temperature : approximately	60°C.

The heat resistance of the bond can be increased to above 100"C by adding 5 parts by weight an isocyanate, 75% in ethyl acetate, to the above mentioned formulation. The compound of this type has a pot life of approximately 8 hrs at room temperature.

Adhesive coating for heat-sealable protective polymer films:

Formulation Ingredients	**Parts by Weight**
ACP (iii)	90
Vinyl pyrolidone copolymer (thickening agent)(VPC)	1
Type of film	rigid PVC film, unstretched
Coat weight	6-10 g/m^s (solids)
Sealing temperature	approximately 100°C
Blocking temperature	approximately 40°C

Film coated in this way can be wound up without blocking.

For the production of heat-sealing papers it is advisable to reduce the tendency to blocking by adding VC/VP to ACP (III) .This slightly increases the sealing temperature.

To paper coated with PVDC:

In the application of adhesive to paper coated with PVDC or laminated with polymer film it is very difficult to produce adequate adhesion. Satisfactory results are normally not obtained by modifying homopolymeric polyvinyl acetate dispersions with plasticizers, solvents, and resins. For this reason, vinyl propionate or vinyl acetate copolymer dispersions are used for these applications. The required adhesion is obtained by mixing these dispersions with acrylic dispersions. Because of its excellent adhesion to most surfaces which are difficult to bond, ACP (I) has proved very suitable. A typical formulation is as follows:

Formulation Ingredients	**Parts by Weight**
ACP (II)	30
Vinyl propionate copolymer. (VPCP) Viscosity : 3800 cps (25°C)	70

Delayed Tack Adhesive

In the packaging field, acrylics are often used for delayed-tack adhesive coatings for labels. Copolymer dispersions of acrylic ester with vinyl acetate, vinyl chloride, or styrene are usually also employed for this application.The backing material, usually paper, is coated after the dispersions have been modified accordingly. The coated papers are tack-free under normal conditions so, that the sheets and cuttings can be rolled up or stacked.These types of delayed tack adhesives consist primarily of one or a mixture of a polymer film formers in dispersion form and one or several crystalline plasticizers.The plasticizer is usually employed in the form of a dispersion with very small particle size.

Resin solutions or resin dispersions are used as additives for obtaining certain adhesive effects.The adhesive coating must be dried at a temperature below the melting point of the plasticizer in order to obtain a tack-free surface.

A typical formulation for a delayed-tack adhesive based on acrylic copolymers is given below.

Formulation

Ingredients	**Parts by Weight**
ACP(III)	25
VPC	3
Plasticizer dispersion	75
Resin solution	20

Viscosity: 1300 cps (25°C)

The individual constituents of the mixture are incorporated in the order listed; but it is also possible to add the thickening agent, VCP to the plasticizer dispersion before hand.

The plasticizer dispersion in this example has the following composition :

Formulation

Ingredients	**Parts by Weigh**
Emulsifier	0.4
Water	9.4
Defoamer	0.2
DCHP (Dicyclohexyl phthalate)	40.0

Emulsifier and defoamer are added to the water before the plasticizer powder is dispersed by vigorous stirring. The stability, i.e., the resistance to settling, is largely dependent on the fineness of the plasticizer particles and the' viscosity, which may be increased by adding a thickening agent.

The resin solution has the following composition:

Formulation

Ingredients	**Parts by Weight**
RAA	50.0
Ethanol	26.5
Water	10.0
Ammonia 25%	13.5

Labels produced in this way are applied as follows:

The adhesive coat is heated directly by infrared radiation or hot air, or by hot plates from the reverse side to a temperature above the melting point of the plasticizer. The polymer is plasticized, i.e., the coating is tackified by the liquefied plasticizer, which is present in excess.In this condition, the label can be bonded to the substrate by applying slight pressure. The adhesion to glass, metals, PVC, wood, etc., remains durable even after the plasticizer has recrystallized.

Hot melt adhesives or heat-scalable coatings are made from copolymers of ethylene and acrylic acid and/or the acrylate esters. The properties of the polymers can be varied within wide limits by altering the molecular weight, content of acrylic acid, and type and proportion of the acrylic acid ester. The unmodified products are extruded onto baking materials, e.g., paper or aluminium foil, which are later combined with other surfaces by heat sealing.

By incorporating waxes and resins one can adapt the heat sealing properties to the requirements or produce melts for bonding paper and board.

Adhesives for Laminating

Because of their outstanding properties, acrylic adhesives play a dominant role in the two most important laminating processes in the textile industry — fabric-to-fabric lamination and fabric-to foam lamination.

Comparatively good durability to dry cleaning can be obtained even at low crosslinking temperatures, say at approximately 130°C, by adding suitable reactive urea-formaldehyde or melamine formaldehyde resins. However, these additives have a drawback because they reduce the shelf life and increase the stiffness and hardness of the resultant laminate. Reactive resins such at a modified methylol urea, or a low molecular weight etherified methylol melamine can be used for this purpose. A typical formulation is as follows:

Formulation

Ingredients	**Parts by Weight**
VCP	2
Defoamer	0.2
ACP (III)	100

Viscosity: 10,000 cps (25°C)
Crosslinking conditions : 3 min at 150°C

Laminating Ptasticized PVC film to textiles :

Formulation

Ingredients	**Parts by Weight**
ACP	70
Ammonia 25%	1.5
ACP (I)	30

Viscosity : 9000 cps (25°C)

Laminates with substantially higher resistance to water can be obtained with adhesives compounded according to the following typical formulation:

Formulation

Ingredients	**Parts by Weight**
ACP	75
Defoamer	0.3
Dibutyl phthalate	2.0
Silica	1.0
Percipitated chalk	20
Ammonia 25%	1.5

Viscosity : 10,000 cps (250C)
Resistance of bonding to low temperature :

approximately - 20°C
Heat resistance of bonding: approximately 75°C

The adhesive is usually applied to the wood by means of a roll or a spray gun, Lamination is effected while the adhesive is still wet, and the laminates are kept in a stack under pressure until adequate adhesion is attained.

Laminating PVC film to particle board :

More recent processes for lamination PVC film to particle board indicate that wet bonding is becoming obsolescent. In these processes the adhesive applied onto the wood is allowed to dry, then lamination is effected under pressure by exploiting the thermoplastic character of the adhesive film.The same method of hot bonding is also employed for laminating PVC film to wood by vacuum forming.The following typical formulation is suitable for producing adhesive: for dry/hot bonding:

Formulation

Ingredients	**Parts by Weight**
ACP (I)	80
ACP (III)	
Viscosity : 13,000 cps (25°C)	20

The film is laminated to the wood by vacuum forming at 30-150C.

The wettability of plasticized PVC film by adhesive can be improved by adding small proportions of a solvent, e.g., 5% of toluene.

Laminating plasticized PVC film to split leather:

Another application for acrylic adhesives, which is largely dependent on fashion trends, is the lamination of plasticized PVC film to split leather to produce patent leather.Although the highest bonding strength of PVC film split leather laminates is obtained with adhesives based on plasticizer containing vinyl chloride copolymers, the use of acrylic adhesives for this application has the advantage that adequate bonding strength for many applications can be obtained more readily and under milder pressing conditions. An excellent bond between split leather and plasticized PVC film can be obtained according to the following typical formulation:

Formulation

Ingredients	**Parts by Weight**
ACP	50
Ammonia 25%	1
ACP (I)	50
Viscosity : 8000 cps (25°C)	

High temperature and pressure lamination:

Normally the adhesive is applied to the film and lamination is effected while the adhesive is still wet. However, lamination can also be carried out at 80°C at a pressure of approximately 5 kg/cm^s after the adhesive coating has dried.A typical formulation is :

Formulation

Ingredients	**Parts by Weight**
ACP (s) 40% in ethyl acetate	80
VC / VP 50% in ethyl acetate	20
Isocyanate 75% in ethyl acetate	5-10
Ethyl acetate	30

Viscosity : 4500 cps (25°C)
Pot life at 25°C : approximately 10 hr.

The adhesive is applied either to the film only or preferably to both film and leather. After drying, lamination is effected at approx. 70°C and approx. 5 kg/cm^2.

Flocking Adhesives

The term flocking is taken to mean a special type of surface treatment in which fibre dust, ground fibre of different length, and diickness or cut fibres of defined lengdi and thickness are applied onto an adhesive-coated subst - rate.Velvet or pile-like surfaces of varying densities are thus obtained, depending on the type, lengdi, and amount of flocks, and the flocking mediod employed Either the whole surface (overall flocking) or part of it (print flocking) can be flocked; the adhesive is applied accordingly.

Typical materials which are flocked include woven and nonwoven fabrics, yarns, leather, paper, wood, rubber, and plastics. For overall flocking of sheet-like substrates, the adhesive is applied by means of a blade or rolls. Print flocking is carried out by conventional textile printing methods, i.e. the adhesive is applied by means of doctor blade, engraved roll, or a rotary screen. Mouldings are flocked by applying the adhesive by spraying or dipping.The rheological properties of the adhesives based on acrylic dispersions must be adapted to the application method in question through proper formulation.The flow and the open assembly time of the adhesives are also of great importance; premature skinning could prevent the flocks from penetrating into the adhesive coating.

The flocks can be applied to the various types of substrates by different methods.The following three techniques are most widely used.

1. Mechanical flocking
2. Electrostatic flocking
3. Electrostatic/mechanical flocking.

Flocks of all natural and synthetic fibres as well as leather dust, mica flakes, metal dust, etc., can be used for flocking. The type of flocks to be used must be selected according to the flocking method and the requirements imposed on the flocked article.In electrostatic flocking, specially treated textile flocks are used exclusively.

Because of the exacting requirements imposed on flocked textiles, e.g., durability to washing and dry cleaning, high dry and wet rub-resistance, and textile handle, crosslinkable or self crosslinking acrylic dispersion adhesives are being used on a large scale for this application in addition to PVC plastisols, polyurethane systems, and acrylic solutions.

The composition of adhesives based on aqueous acrylic dispersions for flocking textiles is very similar to that of the lamination adhesives. The details concerning formulation and crosslinkage indicated for these adhesives are therefore generally also valid in this application. A typical formulation for an adhesive for over-all flocking of textiles is given below :

Formulation

Ingredients	**Parts by Weight**
APC (IV)	93.0
Defoamer	0.2
Thickening agent	5.0
Ammonia 25%	2.0

Viscosity : 50 00 cps (25°C)

The viscosity of the adhesive paste can be controlled by varying the proportion of thickening agent. The pH of *the* ready-to-use mix must be adjusted with ammonia to 8-9. Durability to washing and dry cleaning can be improved by incorporating a reactive urea-formaldehyde or melamine formaldehyde resin. However, this may increase the hardness of the handle of the flocking.

By using ACP (III) instead of ACP (IV) according to the following typical formulation one can obtain better durability (the handle is, somewhat harder):

Formulation

Ingredients	**Parts by Weight**
VPC	3.0
Defoamer	0.2
ACP III	100.0

Viscosity :27 000 cps (25°C)

The material should be dried carefully in the initial stage in order to prevent the formation of blisters, which will not only affect the flocking but also impair the adhesion of the adhesive film. Crosslinkage subsequent to drying should be carried out at 130-150°C for 1-5 min. These processing conditions,e.g., the temperatures attained by *the* adhesive have a great influence on the durability properties of the flocking, of course.

The increasing popularity of flocked plastics for packaging and decorative purposes necessitated the development of new aqueous flocking adhesives with good adhesion to plastics even under the conditions involved in vacuum forming and adequate resistance to plasticizers. In this case, too, the various types of acrylics, particularly in the form of copolymers, were found very suitable. The typical formulations based on ACP (IV) and ACP (III) indicated above for flocking textiles can also be used for producing flocked polyurethane foam which is resistant to dry-cleaning.

Overall or print flocked decorative plasticized PVC films are often coated on the un-flocked side with a pressure sensitive adhesive.The following typical formulation can be used for this flocking process:

Formulation

Ingredients	Parts by Weight
ACP	100
Ammonia 25%	2
Water	5

Viscosity: 55 cps (25°C)

In this case, the amount of water indicated is used for adjusting the spraying consistency.

Flocked rigid PVC films and impact polystyrene suitable for thermoforming are being widely used in the packaging field. For this application, one can produce aqueous acrylic adhesives which do not only have good adhesion to the substrate and high abrasion resistance but also excellent flow properties necessary for the thermoforming process.

A typical formulation for rigid PVC film is as follows:

Formulation

Ingredients	Parts by Weight
VPC	2
VC/VP	50
ACP	50

Viscosity 700 cps (25°C)

A typical formulation for impact polystyrene film is as follows :

Formulation

Ingredients	Parts by Weight
ACP (W)	50
VP/PC	50

Viscosity:3500 cps

A typical formulation for flocking electrically or chemically pretreatel polyethylene:

Formulation

Ingredients	Parts by Weight
ACP	2
Polyethylene	40
ACP	60

Viscosity : 600 cps (25°C)

Building Adhesives

The classic adhesives used in the building industry for bonding floor coverings (linoleum) and wall paper were almost exclusively based on natural products or modified natural products, e.g., copal resins, bitumen, sulfite waste liquor, starch, and cellulose products. Because of the increasing demands on the materials to be bonded and the lying techniques, i.e. mainly as a result of the rapid advance of plastics in the building industry, these natural products were no longer capable of meeting the requirements. The increase in usage of PVC floor coverings, for instance, necessitated the development of new adhesives.

Adhesives based on bitumen or butadiene styrene lattices and polyvinyl acetate dispersions proved very satisfactory for bonding rigid tiles containing or only a very small proportion of plasticizer. However, in many countries, where ' plasticized PVC tiles or sheet goods are used, these was a trend to develop elastomeric solvent-based adhesives (polychlorobutadiene). These contact adhesives are particularly advantageous in application: the adhesive is applied onto both sides to be bonded and the floor covering is laid after the solvent has evaporated; high initial adhesion and bonding strength are thus obtained. In spite of their good adhesion to PVC and their high plasticizer resistance, the aqueous acrylic adhesives do not offer this advantage initially. Adhesives based on dispersions were used for a long time only for wet bonding floor covering.

It was not possible to produce aqueous acrylic adhesives which can be applied in the same way as solvent based adhesives and which have comparably high bonding strength properties and plasticizer resistance until new acrylic copolymers were developed which could be crosslinked by adding alkali at room temperature. In spite of their exceptionally high cohesion, the films of these dispersions are very tacky.

Adhesives for plasticized PVC floor tiles

The main advantages of the adhesives based on these dispersions are their non-inflammability and ease of application.Unlike solvent-based elastomeric adhesives, aqueous acrylic adhesives do not involve fire hazards so that they can be processed and applied without any special precautions. Moreover, aqueous acrylic adhesives are characterized by ease of application and good ageing resistance. The products have therefore obtained a considerable share of the floor covering adhesives market in India within a few years. A typical formulation of a adhesive for plasticized PVC floor tiles is given below:

Formulation

Ingredients	**Parts by Weight**
AGP (VI) 60%	100.0
Caustic soda solution 10%	6.0
Defoamer	0.3
Thickening Solution 12%	8.5
Balsam resin, 70% in toluene	27.0
Ground quartz, particle size <0.06 mm	42.0
Chalk	18.0

The water resistance of the bondings of this type of adhesive is good.The bonding strength is dependent on the type of floor covering bonded and the duration and intensity of the effect of the water. In contrast to bondings of solvent-containing elastomeric adhesives based on polychlorobutadiene, bondings of aqueous acrylic adhesives attain their original strength on re-drying.

Adhesives for ceramic tiles

Previously, ceramic tiles were fixed to walls or floors in India exclusively by means of cement mortar.In this process, which is also referred to as the "thick-bed-setting" method, the tiles are laid in a mortar bed of 10-20 mm thickness. This process is very expensive because it is very time consuming. For this reason, and because prefabricated building components are steadily gaining significance, aqueous acrylic adhesives are being used on an increasing scale in "thin-bed-setting" of ceramic tiles. The smooth and non-dusting substrate required in this process and the higher price of the adhesive are readily compensated by the considerably higher lying speed. Tiles bonded with aqueous dispersion adhesives, particularly those based on polyvinyl acetate dispersions or butadiene styrene latex, have much poorer water resistance than bondings produced with cement mortar. However, as a result of the development of new acrylic dispersions which form films with very low water absorption and very high alkali resistance, it became possible to use this type of adhesive also for installing ceramic tiles in high moisture areas, such as bathrooms and shower stalls.A typical adhesive of pastelike consistency for this application can be produced according to the following starting formulation:

Formulation

Ingredients	**Parts by Weight**
Petroleum solvent 145/200°C	5
Defoamer	0.5
Preservative	0.9
Polyacrylic acid ,	0.1
Sodium polyphosphate	0.1
4% Thickening agent solution	37.5
Chalk, particle size 1-100 μm	300
Methanol	5

Open assemble time : 30 min

Relative density 1.602

The resistance of this type of adhesive to frost is shown by the following cyclic freezing test:

(a) -10°C/+20°C 30 cycles OK

(b) - 20°C/+20°C 30 cycles OK

The following values were obtained in determining the bonding strength in relation to the drying condition by means of a Herion tensile strength testing apparatus:

Time	Bond strength kg/cm^2
24 hr	3.8
7 days	9.3
28 days	25.0
28 days drying plus 24 hr immersion in water	10.9

Pressure-Sensitive Adhesives

Pressure-sensitive adhesives form a permanently tacky film after evaporation of the liquid phase or after cooling of a hot-melt.Bonding is effected by slightly pressing the adhesive surface onto the adherend. This type of adhesive is used in those cases where a permanent bond is undesirable or unfeasible for technical reasons. Pressure-sensitive adhesive materials can be readily applied and need not be flashed off. Unlike wet bondings, there is no danger of exceeding the open assembly time. The significance of these adhesives has therefore increased for many applications; they did not only open up new applications but are also often used for those bondings for which contact of heat-sealing adhesives were employed previously. According to survey done by Tata consultancy, the volume of pressure-sensitive is 200,000 tons per year. For some applications it is advisable to use a mixture of different types of polymers. Instead of using ACP alone for pressure sensitive adhesive tapes one can, for instance, use a mixture of ACP (II) and ACP (IV) according to the following starting fomulation:

Formulation

Ingredients	**Parts by Weight**
ACP (II)	60-80
ACP (IV)	40-20
VPC	1

Coat weight approximately 25 g/m' (dry).

This mixture yields an adhesive film with high cohesion and tackACP (II) is used for increasing the tack. The adhesion to the above mentioned substrates is normally good.

It may be difficult to obtain adequate adhesion on some hydrophilic substrates, such as cellophane, rigid suspension PVC film, and polymer films containing a large proportion of plasticizers and lubricants. In such cases the backing material must be primed (approximately 2 g/m^2). Aqueous acrylic dispersions, such as are suitable primers for solvent-sensitive rigid and soft PVC films. In case of inadequate adhesion, the adhesion coat may be transferred to the reverse side of the baking material during unrolling.

Aquous emulsions, too, may require a wetting agent to improve their adhesion to various types of backing, if necessary, the viscosity of the dispersions and hence the flow on the processing and machines can be adjusted by means of thickening agents, such as VPC, hydroxyethyl Cellulose, or methyl cellulose as indicated in die above formulation. The proportion of both wetting agents and thickening agents should be kept as low as possible because these substances have a negative effect on the tack and water resistance of the resultant adhesive film. An addition of 0.5 to 2% of VPC has proved very suitable for adjusting acrylic copolymer dispersions to the required viscosity. The addition of VPC also increases the stability and compatibility with, for instance, resins and improves the wetting effect on, substrates which are difficult to wet.

Mixtures of ACP I, ACP II can also be used for pressure-sensitive antidrumming materials. The following is a typical formulation:

This pressure-sensitive adhesive film has high tack, good resistance to low temperatures, and adequate heat-resistancne. If a certain thixotropy is required for applying the adhesive by blade coating, satisfactory results can be obtained by adding for instance, 1% of Aerosil 200 impressed.

Formulation

Ingredients	**Parts by Weight**
ACP-I	80
ACP-II	20
VPC	1

Coat weight: 100-200 g/m² (dry)

Backing: biturninized board, bitumen sheer.

The following mixture of an acrylic copolymer dispersion and a plasticizer is suitable for producing pressure-sensitive adhesive advertising plaquettes:

Formulation

Ingredients	**Parts by Weight**
AGP	18
DBF	15

Coat weight :approximately 30 g/m² (dry)

Backing: plasticized PVC film.

DBF acts as a tackifier.In order to ensure that the plasticizer is taken up by the dispersion particles, the compound must be allowed to mature for 1-2 days before application. In some cases the tack can be increased by adding resins or polyvinyl ether. However, these additives also have a tendency to reduce the strength values. Generally speaking, the resins for natural rubber adhesives can also be used for acrylics, i.e. petroleum hydrocarbon resins, rosin ester, alkyl phenolic resins, terpene phenolic resin, B"-pinene resins, cumarone-indene resins, ketone resins, methyl styrene/vinyl toluene resins, and rosin. The effect of these resins on acrylics is, however, not comparable with their effect on natural rubber. These resins are preferably incorporated in the form of solutions in water-insoluble solvents into aqueous dispersions by emulsification. Since not all resins mentioned above are equally compatible with the various types of acrylics, and because their tackifying effect may vary to a great extent, the suitability of a resin must be tested in each individual case. In selecting the resins, due regard must also be given to the ageing resistance and solvent retention power. Dispersions containing resin additives dry at a lower rate than pure dispersions. When polyvinyl ether is used as a tackifier, it is advisable to add, say, 0.5% antioxidant in order to increase the aging resistance of the polyvinyl ether.

Low molecular weight soft acrylic resins are also suitable for use as tackifier.

The following formulation can, for instance, be used for producing pressure sensitive adhesive labels:

Formulation

Ingredients	**Parts by Weight**
ACP (s) 25% in acetone/gasoline	95
50% solution of hydrogenated resin ester in toluene	5

Coat weight: 20-25 g/m² (dry)

Baking : plasticized PVC film.

This adhesive meets the requirements imposed on tack, creep resistance, and resistance to yellowing. If a higher tack is required (e.g., for permanent labels) the amount of resin can be increased to 20-30 parts. Acrylics in combination with resins have also proved very satisfactory for the production of pressure-sensitive carpets. Adhesives of this type can be compounded according to the following starting formulation:

Formulation

Ingredients	**Parts by Weight**
ACP (III)	85
70% solution of balsam resin in toluene	15

Coat weight: 100-150 g/m² (dry)

High viscosity free-flowing acrylate/vinyl acetate dispersions which are very compatible with inexpensive petroleum hydrocarbon resins and which yield an adhesive film with excellent strength and high tack are also being used for this application. Acrylic dispersions where films are characterized by good resistance to plasticizer and low water absorption were developed by the inclusion of additional monomers. Such products are suitable for producing articles such as electrical insulation tapes with plasticized PVC as carrier. A typical formulation is as follows:

Formulation

Ingredients	**Parts by Weight**
ACP-I	80
ACP-II	20

Coat weight 80-100 g/m² per side (dry)
Backing: PVC, paper, cotton, celluar plastics.

Instead of a tackifying acrylic dispersion, such as ACP-II one can also use resins in this formulation for adjusting the tack.

Pressure-sensitive adhesive laminating films can be produced according to the following guiding formulation:

Formulation

Ingredients	**Parts by Weight**
ACP	80-90
ACP-II	20-10

Coat weight 40-45 g/m² (dry)
Backing: plasticized PVC film.

The proportion of the comparatively tacky ACP-II should be kept as small as possible so that any crease formed can still be smoothened immediately after lamination.

Acrylic solutions are also used for producing decorative films. Such adhesives can be compounded according to the following starting formulation:

Without being dissolved before hand the resin can be stirred into the acrylic copolymer solution direct Decorative films of this type exhibit good tack, adequate resistance to plasticizer migration, and good adhesion to, for instance, board, glass, and coated or uncoated wood.

Formulation

Ingredients	**Parts by Weight**
ACP-I 25% in acetone/gasoline	70
ACP-II 50% in ethyl acetate	20
Hydrogenated rosin ester	10

Coat weight approximately 25 g/m² (dry)
Backing: plasticized PVC film, printed.

An important application for acrylic solutions and dispersions is the production of surgical tapes. Since the polymers do not irritate the skin and are physiologically harmless, acrylics are particularly suitable for these types of tape. Typical backing materials used in this field are fabrics, nonwovens, and PVC film.

Flame Resistant & Pressure Sensitive Adhesive

For some applications it may be necessary to use a flame resistant pressure-sensitive adhesive. Acrylics can be rendered flame resistant.

Pressure-sensitive acrylic adhesives can normally be applied by the conventional methods, e.g., direct or reverse roll coating or by air-knife coating. The adhesive compound is applied either directly to the final substrate or a release paper, in the latter case the adhesive on the carrier is dried or crosslinked before it is transferred to the final substrate. This transfer method is necessary in those cases where the backing material would deteriorate during the drying or crosslinking process. The transfer method is, for instance, commonly used for producing decorative films.

For protecting the adhesive coat of pressure sensitive adhesive materials during transport and storage, the adhesive coat except in the case of adhesive tapes in rolls, is usually covered by a release paper or a release foil. Silicone treated paper, polyethylene or PVC films are, for instance, suiable for this purpose. Long-chained acrylates exhibit good release effects. The release material must not have any adverse effect on the pressure-sensitive adhesive coating. Undesirable effects can be obtained when unsuitable silicones are used or when the silicones are not properly processed.

Acrylic Sealants

Linseed oil and bitumen were for a long time the commonest base materials for building sealants. Further developments in building construction and the steadily increasing demands on quality resulted in the development of a number of synthetic polymers for sealants.The first work on acrylics for building sealants was carried out in response to the technical and economic success which was achieved by this product class in the last 10-15 years in the field of surface coatings, such as paints. The first serviceable acrylic compounds were placed on the market in about 1960. In tne meantime the acrylics, particularly the aqueous acrylic dispersions, gained considerable significance in the production of sealants because of their outstanding ageing resistance and adhesion properties as well as their favourable price.

It is expected that the increase of the consumption of aqueous acrylic sealants will be above average in the next few years.The total consumption of sealants will increase approximately 20% during the same period.

The acrylics used nowadays for sealants are tailor-made copolymers of acrylic and/or methacrylic acid esters and other monomers.

Usually several monomers are present in order to achieve the desired properties, such as elasticity, adhesion, resistance to UV radiation, resistance to chemicals, and hardness. Suitable polymers are linear polymers, most of which are thermoplastic, as well as polymers which can be rendered adequately elastic by cold vulcanization, oxidation, or by the effect of alkaline substance, such as caustic soda solution, cement, or lime. Acrylics which can be crosslinked with the aid of oxidative catalysts or epoxy resins are also well known. The dominating raw materials for acrylic sealants are based on aqueous acrylic dispersions.

Solvent-containing products and solvent-free products are also available on the market The solvent-free products have been on the market only for a short time and the experience gained with them is still inadequate. The solvent-containing products have been on the market for a long time but they gained considerably less significance than the acrylic dispersions.

Solvent-containing products are usually 80-90% solutions in xylene. In the initial stage, aqueous dispersions were available with solids content of only 50-55%. Dispersions with a higher solids content, were obtained by improving the polymerization technique. All acrylics must be modified with fillers and other aids in order to achieve optimum properties.

Aqueous Acrylic Sealants : Aqueous acrylic sealants are employed mainly for those applications for which compounds based on linseed oil, butyl rubber, or polyisobutylene have been used hitherto, i.e., the sealing of joints which are subject to little elongation, viz. joints between curtain walls and door and window frame joints.

In view of the experience gained hitherto, it appears that the aqueous acrylic sealants are also suitable for joints between prefabricated concrete building components with a practical elongation of approximately 10-15%.

Soft acrylic sealants with a high degree of elongation have already been successfully used for many years for joints between small building componentsand special applications, e.g., aerated concrete.

Even the results obtained hitherto in the trials for expansion joints, which , were commenced some time ago, have been positive until now.Practice will show whether aqueous acrylic sealants are in fact suitable for this application.

Harder compounds are mainly used for do-it-yourself application and for sanitary equipment, e.g., bath tubs and wash basins.

A typical aqueous acrylic sealant, which has proved satisfactory for many years, particularly for joints between concrete and window frames, can be compounded according to the following guiding formulation.

Formulation

Ingredients	**Parts by Weight**
Acrylic copolymer 60% pH 3	392.0
Pigment disperser	0.5
Antifoam	0.5
Polyisobutylene	82.0

Emulsifier (emulphor)	1.0
Hydrophobic chalk, particle size 2-20 m	440.0
Tack, very fine powder	89.0
Titanium dioxide	58.0

Pigment Disperser improves the stability and suitability of the compound for application by gun. Antifoam reduces the foaming tendency and thus the amount of air bubbles in the compound. Polyisobutylene is a plasticizing resin with a medium molecular weight of approximately 800. It increases the solids content and hence reduces the shrinkage of the compound. Because of its plasticizing effect, this resin also improves the elongation of the compound. Instead of polyisobutylene one can also use low molecular weight acrylic resins, or derivatives of polypropylene glycol. The formulation must then be modified accordingly. Emulphor acts as an emulsifying agent for the plasticizing resin. The fillers, i.e., chalk and talc, are used not only for the cost reduction and increasing the strength of the compound but also for imparting a decisive influence on the gun consistency and shore hardness of the compound.

The incorporation of titanium dioxide not only increases the strength properties of the sealant but also lightens its shade.

The properties of an aqueous acrylic sealant produced with acrylic copolymer according to the above mentioned formulation and the performance test results obtained with this compound are listed below :

Total solids content	86%	
Pigment volume concentration	42.5	
Density	1.3 g/cm^3	
Shrinkage in volume	20%	
Stability to creep test room temperature	50^0 C	
profile A	good/good	
profile B	2mm/5mm	
Resistant to heavy rain after	50 min	
Shore hardness at 20°C	30	
Elongation and tensile strength at break (test specimen) after 14 days at room temperature	400% 5kg/cm^2	
4 weeks at room temperature		
Adhesion-Elongation Test		
Test I: force required at	50%	0.5 kg/cm^2
	100%	0.6 kg/cm^2
	150%	0.6 kg/cm^2
Test II: break at	425% (joint failure)	

This type of aqueous acrylic sealant and even the harder grades have become very popular mainly because of their numerous advantages over oil - and/or solvent-based compounds.

The most important advantages include : (1) one-component site, (2) simple processing, (3) can be readily applied by gun, (4) no sagging in the joint, (5) surface of compound can be readily smoothened with water, (6) no undesireable odor, (7) no solvent vapours, (8) nontoxic, (9) can also be applied in moist joints, (10) sealant can be over painted with conventional outdoor coating compositions after a short time, (11) the tools can be readily cleaned with water, (12) repair work can be carried out simply applying the compound onto the old acrylic sealant by means of a gun or a trowel, (13) high solids content and therefore low degree of shrinkage, (14) low degree of residual tackiness and therefore only little tendency to soiling, (15) outstanding resistance to ageing, i.e., the compound does not harden or become brittle even under very severe conditions, (16) acrylic sealants can be produced in all shades, (17) nonstaining, (18) very economical.

Experience has shown that the good performance of aqueous acrylic sealants is mainly due to the fact that this material has a certain degree of both elasticity and plasticity.

In contrast to completely elastic compounds, aqueous acrylic sealants are, because of their partially plastic character, capable of reducing any stresses in building joints resulting from irreversible movements.

It must be taken into consideration that freshly applied aqueous acrylic sealant is sensitive to heavy rain. However, the sealants which are now available on the market form a skin within approximately one hour after application and thus become insensitive to rain. This drawback is compensated by the feet that the aqueous sealants can also be applied in moist of wet joints-an advantage which is not offered by any other system. At the present stage of development, aqueous sealants can probably not yet be used for underwater joints; their water resistance is, however, completely adequate for interior and exterior building joints.

Aqueous acrylic sealants have been subjected to a water resistance test In this test, a precoated joint (15 mm x 15 x 50 mm) is filled with the sealant, allowed to dry and then immersed in water for four days. The specimen is subsequently elongated by 100% and kept in this condition under water for 25 hours. No separation of the interfaces occurred in these tests.

Long-term open-weathering tests carried out with aqueous acrylic sealants under Indian climatic conditions showed that the moisture content does not exceed 100%.

The suitability of a sealant for interior and exterior application cannot yet be determined by laboratory tests. A reliable assessment can only be made on the basis of the behaviour of the material in practice. Due consideration should be given to this fact in working out standard test methods.

The adhesion of aqueous acrylic compounds to hydrophilic, absorbent substrates (plaster, concrete, wood, bricks, etc.) is excellent. In order to ensure optimum results, it may be advisable to moisten the gap with water or to coat it with diluted sealant (sealant/water =1:3 to 1:4). For substrates such as plastics and metal, it is necessary to use a special primer, e.g., a silane solution. The effect of a primer must be determined in each individual case.

In spite of the many advantages, acrylic sealants are also subject of certain limitations. The compounds which are available at present are not yet capable of meeting the ISI standard requirements for the more stringent architectural and expansion joint type applications. Elastomeric sealants are still being recommended for these applications.

Solvent-Based Acrylic Sealants : As already mentioned above, these types of acrylics are 80-90% solutions, preferably in xylene. In common with aqueous acrylic sealants, solvent-based acrylic sealants are characterized by the typical properties of acrylate, namely, outstanding resistance to ageing and good adhesion to many substrates. In addition, the solvent based acrylic sealants, are capable of adhering to wet, oily, and dusty surfaces, so that a careful and costly pretreatment of the surface can be dispensed with.

Unlike acrylic dispersions, acrylic solutions for sealants required a fairly long time for obtaining a foothold in the building industry. This was mainly due to the feet that the solvent-based acrylic sealants have to be heated to 50-60°C to obtain a consistency low enough for application. Sealants applied at room temperature have a tendency to sagging. Other disadvantages of solvent-based acrylic sealants include: content of combustible solvents, lower molecular weight than that of dispersion copolymers and hence lower elasticity, a certain residual tackiness, and a fairly strong odour.

Like aqueous acrylic sealants, solvent-based acrylic sealants are most appropriate for those areas where low joint movement is expected, e.g., joints between window frames and concrete, for which the butyl compounds are unsuitable because of their high shrinkage and inadequate elongation, and for which the elastomeric compounds are too expensive. Solvent based acrylic compounds are also used for sealing insulating glass panels.

TABLE 13.1. COMPARISON OF PHYSICAL PROPERTIES OF ACRYLIC HOMOPOLYMERS WITH THOSE OF POLYVINYL ACETATE

Homopolymer from Glass	Temperatur, Tg COW.	Hardness	Tackiness	Elongation	T ensile Strength	Solubility in a bcde
Methyl methacrylate	105	↑	↓	↓	↑	+++--
Vinyl acetate	28					+++-+
Methyl acrylate	3					+++--
Wthyl acrylate	-23					+++-+
n-Butyl acrylate	-70					++++-
2-Ethylhexyl acrylate	-75					++++-

(a=esters; b=aromatics; c=ketones; d=aliphatic hydrocarbons; e=alcohols; +=soluble;-=insoluble)

14.

Amino Resin Adhesive

Introduction

Amino resins are the condensation products of amino compound with aldehydes. The most common and widely used amino compounds are urea and melamine where as formaldehyde is almost always the aldehyde.

In a poly condensation reaction, a reactant of functionality greater than two leads to branching and crosslinking. The resultant three dimensional network can attain greater size indefnitely, becoming insoluble and infusible. The over all reaction of amino resin can be described in three stages. The first stage is the reaction of amino compound and formaldehyde to a form a methylol derivatives

$$RNH_2 + HCHO \qquad RNHCH_tOH$$

Urea is tetrafunctional and melamine is hexafunctional. Theoritically therefore, the initial reaction can lead to the formation of a tetramethylol derivatives of urea or a hexamethylol derivatives of melamine, of the ratio of formaldehyde to ammonia is high enough for urea, formation of a methyl group slows formation of another. These methylol derivatives are condensed with the evolution of water or formaldehyde.

$$RNHCH_2OH + HOCH_2NHR \longrightarrow RNHCH_2OCH_2NHR + H_2O$$

$$RNHCH_2OH + HNHR \longrightarrow RNHCH_2NHR + H_2O$$

$$RNHCH_2OCH_2NHR \longrightarrow RNHCH_2NHR + HCHO$$

$$2\ RNHCH_2OH \longrightarrow RNHCH_2NHR + H_2O + HCHO$$

$$RNHCH_2OH \longrightarrow RN = CH_2 + H_2O$$

Further condensation by similar reactions lead to the final stage, where a three dimensional net work is formed.

The properties of the adhesive intermediates are very much dependent on the reaction condition. Molecular weight may vary from a few hundred to a few thousand, with a wide distribution of molecular size. Characteristic of commercial products are solubility, viscosity, pH and concentration. The products are available either in dry form or in aqueous solutions. Urea resin adhesives are usually marketed in aqueous solution where as melamine resin adhesives are available in powder form.

Manufacturing Technology

Fig. 14.1 is a flow chart for the manufacture of amino resin adhesives. All the commerical processes are batch type. The unit operations are reflux and condensation, filtration and spray drying. Because of the corrosiveness of formaldehyde and its formic acid content, the reaction is usually carried out in a stainless steel vessel. The reaction vessel is equipped with a turbine agitator and reflux condenser, and jacketed for heating or cooling. Some typical methods are described below.

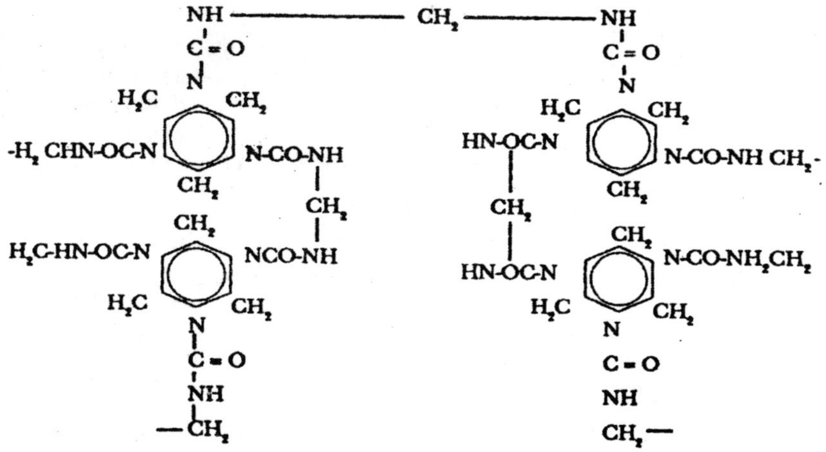

Urea Adhesive for Plywood

A typical charge of raw materials based on formaldehyde to urea mole ratio of 2 is as follows :

Formulation

Ingredients	**Parts by Weight**
Urea	100.0
Formaldehyde (37%)	333.3
Boric acid	16.6

The order of addition to the reactor is formaldehyde, boric acid and urea, When all the components are added to the reactor. pH is adjusted to 7.0-7.8 and die charge is heated to 120°C. Disappearance of urea causes die pH to drop to about 4.0 . The reaction mixture is refluxed at atmospheric pressure for 2 hr, Vacuum is applied and distillation is carried out under vacuum of 28-29 in. Of mercury, until approximately 33 parts by weight of water is removed. Then the system is shifted to total reflux and cooled to about 30°C. The pH is adjusted to 7.2-7.4 with sodium hydroxide. The molar ratio: formaldehyde, urea, is usually 1.75:1 to 2:1 for plywood adhesives.

Urea Adhesive for Particle Board

A lower ratio of formaldehyde to urea is used for particle board applications, to avoid the smell of formaldehyde in the final product General practice is about

1.3-1.5 moles of formaldehyde per mole of urea. The pH is adjusted to 8.5 to 9.0 and the mixture is heated to the boiling point under agitation. The solution is refluxed for 40 min and cooled. The pH is then adjusted to 7.0 -8.0 with a saturated solution of trisodium phosphate.

Advantages & Disadvantages of Urea Resin & Melamine Resin Adhesive

Advantages	
Urea	Low cost '
	Colourless glue line
	Room temperature curing
	Resistant to mold and fungus
	Gap filling and craze resistant
	Adaptable to electronic gluing
Melamine	Excellent boiling water resistance
	Colourless glue line
	Resistant to mold and fungus
	Gap filling and craze resistant
	Adaptable to electronic gluing
DisadvarUages	
Urea	Poor boiling water resistance
	Generally two component
Melamine	High cost
	High temperature curing

Spray Dried Melamine-fromaldehyde Resins

For laminating type resin a mole ratio of 2:1 formaladeyde : melamine is used. The charge to the reactor is as follows :

Formulation

Ingredients	**Parts by Weight**
Melamine	100
Formaldehyde (37%)	133

Melamine is added to the formaldehyde solution in the reactor, and pH is adjusted to 7.0 with sodium hydroxide.

The mixture is heated to reflux for about 30-40 min. Then the pH is adjusted to 3.0-9.0 with sodium hydroxide or formic acid. The reaction mixture is cooled to about 60°C and held at this temperature until the required viscosity. The pH is adjusted to about 9.5 with sodium hydroxide and the resin is filtered. The resin solution is then spray dried and packed.

oundry Resin

A typical method to prepare furfuryl alcohol-modified urea formaldehyde esin for a hot core box is as follows .

A reaction mixture containing 2.5 mole of formaldehyde per mole of urea is repared by adding 22 parts by weight of urea to 100 parts of UF concentrated, eated to 80°C under agitation and held at this temperture for about 20 min. Then 5 parts by weight of furfuryl alcohol are added and the pH is adjusted to 4.5-5 vith dilute acid. The reaction mixture is reheated to 80°C and maintained at this emperature for a minimum 30 min. The resin solution is cooled and neutralised.

niline- Formaldehyde Resin

Strictly speaking, the foregoing amino plastic are hot amines but are amides or amidines. True amine, such as aniline do react with formaldehyde under strongly acidic and alkaline conditions in the ratio 1:2. These reaction are summarized by the following chart.

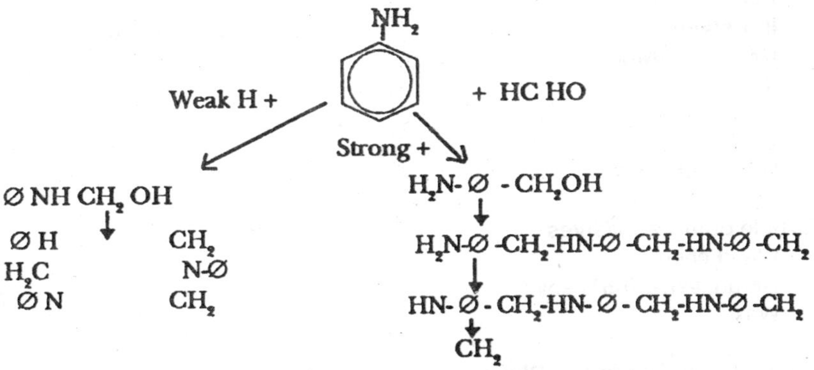

Represents benzene ring

Since the resin has good electrical properties, it is useful as an insulating adhesive medium in high frequency electrical field. Often used to replace mica, ceramics, phenolics or polystyrene because of its low power factor, high *dielectric* strength, mechanical strength inertness to moisture and ease of application.

Sulfonamide- Formaldehyde Resins

Saccharin has obtained widespread recognition as non caloric substitute of sugar. During the synthesis of this material from toluene via o-toluene sulfon amide, p-toulene sulfonamide accumulates as a by-product In order to decrease the cost of production of saccharin much research has been carried out to find technical uses for p-sulfonamide. One of the most promising field has been that of its use in adhesives. When equimolecular proportion of formaldehyde reacts with p-toulene sulfonamide, a semisolid viscous mass is obtained which sets to a hard, colourless resin. These resins are believed to form by the following general sequence :

Sulfonamide formaldehyde resins exhibit excellent adhesive properties and have been used in the manufacture of laminated safety glass where their stability to light is also an advantage. Combined with cellulose acetate, it increases the retentivity of plasticizer and production of heat sealing lacquers.

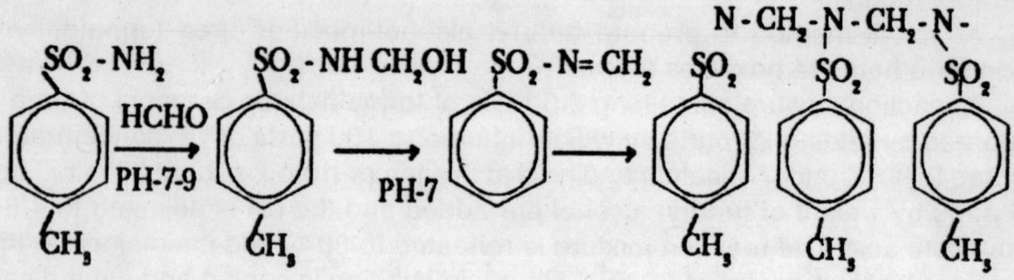

Applications

The largest application of amino resin adhesives is in the area of wood products, including particle board, hardwood, plywood, decorative laminates.

Adhesives for corrugated fibre board

Formulation

Ingredients	**Parts By Weight**
UF resin powder	100
Shell flour	75
Wheat flour	25
Water	110
Hardener	15

Particle board adhesives

Wood chips	100
UF adhesive (65% solids)	7-10
Wax	1

Adhesives for Hardwood Plywood

Plywood is an assembly of an odd number of layers of wood (Veneer) joined together by means of an adhesive. The difference between hard wood, plywood and soft wood plywood is that the former has a ply of wood from the broad-leaf tree, e.g. oak, walnut, maple etc. where as the veneers for softwood plywood comes from coniferous trees. Hardwood plywood is generally used for decorative purposes, softwood plywood for structural purposes. The adhesive is applied by means of rubber covered rollers in the glue spreaders. The coated veneers are alternated with the uncoated veneer in the final assembly. Then the assembled veneers are pressed in a hot press at approximately 90°C and 150-300 psi pressure. Press time is about 5-7 min. Some adhesives cure in the cold press. A typical formulation is shown below. Different steps of manufacture is also shown in fig-14.1.

Formulation

Ingredients	**Parts By Weight**
UF resin	100
hell flour	115
Water	120
Hardener	44

;and Core Binder

Cores are projections of sand in the mould cavity for the purpose of marking oles in the casting. After casting, *the* cores are surrounded by metal and should e removed without damaging the casting. Urea resins are capable for forming nechanically strong cores. A typical formulation is as follows which is oven baked t 100-150°C for 30-90 min. and is then ready for use.

JF resin Shell flour Water Hardener

Formulation

Ingredients	Parts By Weight
Sand	100
Corn flour	1
UF resin	1
Water	1
Paraffin wax emulsion (25%)	0.3

ire resistance adhesives

Formulation

Ingredients	Parts By Weight
UF resin	60
Dicyanadiamide	5
Phosphoric acid	2
Phenolic resin	16
Melamine resin	6
Hardener	1

Vater Proof Corrugated Board

Urea resin is used to fortify starch adhesive for use in corrugated board. ncorporation of urea resin improves water resistance. The conventional method of adding urea-resin to fortify starch works better in an acid medium than under alakline condition. A formula is shown below.

Carrier portion

Formulation

Ingredients	Parts by Weight
Unmodified corn starch	100
Water	325
Caustic soda	1

Secondary portion

Urea	100
Para formaldehyde	50
Unmodified corn starch	500
Water (50°C)	1585

The carrier portion is heated under agitation with live steam at 50°C for 15 min. About 310 parts of water are added and the mixture is cooled to 35°C and added to secondary portion.

Transparent adhesive

Formulation

Ingredients	**Parts By Weight**
Thio urea	52
Urea	200
Trioxymethylene	250
Sodium acetate	10
Formamide	20

The ingredients are mixed carefully and heated at 140°C for 20 min. to give a viscous mass. On curing it solidifies into a hard and white mass.

Compounding and Formulation

The basic differences in the curing of melamine resin and urea resin is that the urea resin can be cured at room temperature of about 60°C, the melamine resin can be hardened at much lower temperature by lowering the pH, but the cured product has poor cohesive and adhesive strength.

Unmodified melamine resins are used for the production of water proof plywood, as fortifiers of urea adhesives. For this the resin is dispersed in water Shell flour is added to obtain a spreadable consistency. Catalyst may be added to shorten the cure cycle, but normally the adhesive is hot pressed in the uncatalysed state. The following formula is suitable.

Formulation

Ingredients	**Catalysed**	**Uncatalyse**
M-F resin	100	80
Shell flour	12	20
Water	50	60
Catalyst	1	
Working life, 25°C	5hrs	15

Water Proof Melamine Adhesive

	Parts be Weight
MF resin	100
Starch	50
Dextrin	20
Ethyl alcohol	300

Melamine based plywood adhesive

Furmulation

Indication	**Part by weight**
MF resin	100
Urea	50
Thio urea	20
Water	200
Ammonium chloride	30
Saponin	20

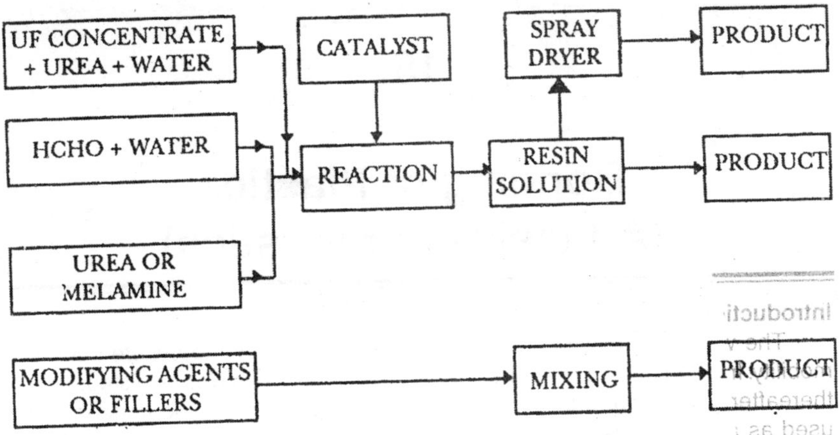

fig. 14. 1. Process Flowsheet Manufacture of Amino Resin Adhesive

In all these applications curing takes place due to comdensation polymerization with the elimination of water.

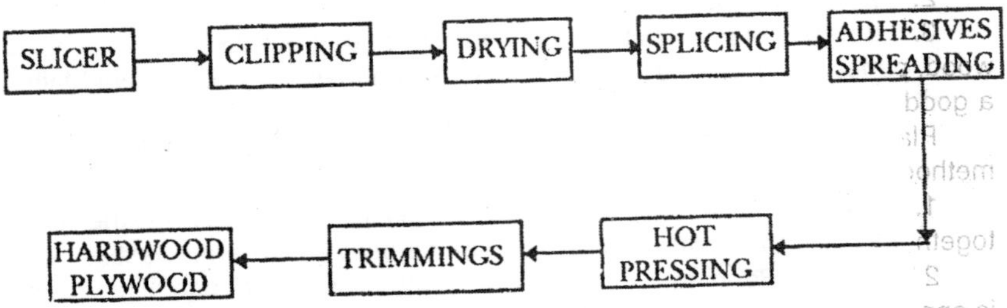

Fig. 14.2. Process Flow diagram manufacture of Amino Resin Adhesive

15.

Bonding of Plastics (Adhesive For Plastics)

Introduction

The word plastic was originally used as an adjective to denote degree of mobility. In 1909 edition of "Webster's Dictionary" the noun was not listed. Shortly thereafter, with the introduction of Bakelite by Dr. Baekeland, the work was often used as a noun. A list of basic commercial plastic is in Table-15.1. Bonding of plastic is an old art, attaining greater importance with increasing use of plastics in all fields of life with greater modernisation. Methods of bonding plastics differ very much from methods of bonding of other adherents. Bonding of plastics may be broadly divided in to following three categories :

1. Bonding of plastic to same plastic.
2. Bonding of dissimilar plastics.
3. Bonding of plastics to other nonplastics adherents like rubbers, metals, wood, paper etc. A general idea of what type of adhesives suitable for obtaining a good bond is given in Table-15.2.

Plastics may be bonded to die similar or other plastics by the following three methods :

1. *Heat welding* - In this method the two plastics are heated and then joined together to give the bond. This method can be used with thermoplastics only.
2. *Solvent Bonding* - A solvent which dissolves both or one of the plastics is applied at the two surfaces and when the solvent operates a bond is formed.
3. *Adhesive Bonding* - Adhesive which is normally a solution of a polymer is applied to the surfaces to be joined, and two surfaces are pressed together, when solvent evaporates a bond is created. The polymer used may be that of thermoplastic or thermosetting type. The former is useful when bonds are not subjected to high temperatures, or continuous load, but are less resistant to solvents and have low creep characteristics. Thermoplastics are usually cheaper.

Solubility Parameter

Where the surface is chemically similar to the bulk of plastic, solubility parameters is a helpful tool in formulating adhesives for plastics. Table-15.3 and Table-15.4 gives the solubility parameters of many plastics and solvents respectively.

While thermoplastics can be bonded by heat welding or solvent cementing also but the thermosetting plastics can be effectively bonded by adhesive bonding technique. Whatever be the method of bonding, the adherents must be cleaned by suitable solvents, abrasion or chemical treatments.

Heat Welding

Thermoplastics can be easily, cheaply and cleanly bonded by the process of heat welding. In this method the plastic is heated sufficiently to permit fusion and is joined under slight pressure. The temperatures at which thermoplastic materials may be heat welded are dependent upon a number of factors. Some materials require low temperature, while others require surface heat exceeding the decomposition range for the material. Polyvinyl acetate, rubber hydrochloride, polyvinyl acetals, plasticized ethyl cellulose and polyvinylidene chloride are some of the themoplastics possessing good heat-weldability. Rigid-type high polymers such as cellulose esters, polymethyl methacrylate, polystyrene and PVC-acetate etc. can also be heat-welded but at much higher temperatures. Usually the welding temperature varies between 160 to 200°C depending on the plastic. Overheating should be avoided otherwise bubbling and charring may take place due to decomposition.

Hot gas welding is used to join themoplastics to themselves. A heat gun with electrical or gas heat with an orifice temperature of 200°C to 400°C is used. A welding rod of the same plastic as the parts being joined is usually employed to butt join the two pieces of the plastics. As with other heat welding methods, PVC and olefin polymers e.g. low and-high-density polythene and polypropylene are specially suitable for hot gas welding. Heat sealing is commonly used to join plastic films. The two films are kept one above the other and a hot jaw or roller is passed on it where it is to be sealed. For thin films heating is done from one side while for thicker films heating from both the sides is required. Uncoated cellophane and uncoated polythene terephthalate (Mylar) cannot be heat sealed. Friction welding or spin welding is sometimes used to bond cylinders, rods and sics. The two plastic parts are rotated in contact; due to the factional heat the plastic melts and bonds under pressure on cooling. Nylon, acrylics, casein and others have been bonded in this manner.

Cellulose nitrate is not heat welded because of the fire hazard. Regenerated cellulose is not readily heat sealed, unless some cellulose ester has been applied to it. The cellulose acetate sheets do not readily heat weld until high temperatures are reached. Ethyl cellulose can be easily heat sealed making it suitable as an insulating foil to electrical equipments. Heat welding in general should give bonds approaching or equal to the strength of the parent plastic.

Heat Welding Dissimilar Thermoplastics

Heat welding of dissimilar thermoplastics is question of chemical compatibility. If the two materials may be hot blended together in all porportions they should be amenable to hot welding operations.

Solvent Bonding/Cementing

Solvent cementing means the application of solvent or solvent-polymer solutions for bonding of thermoplastics and sometimes thermosets. Solvent and polymers should be chosen which match closely to the solubility parameters of the plastics to be bonded.

Solvents

Solvents act as agents in cementing the thermoplastics. By themselves, solvents are generally volatile, possessing little or no pronounced adhesion to chemically incompatible substances. The solvents should be chosen, which evaporate neither too rapidly nor too slowly. Fast-evaporating solvents fend to give unbonded areas, stressed joints, crazing and blushing, while slow-evaporating solvents are more suitable from these angles but take much longer time to produce a satisfactory bond. Therefore, mixtures of slow and fast evaporating solvents are preferred. Toxicity of the solvents should also be kept in mind and good ventilation is, therefore, a must Chlorinated solvents, *benzene* and toluene etc. are toxic in nature. Indication of suitable solvents for some of the plastic bondings is given below :

Surfaces to be Bonded

1.	Cellulose acetate to itself	CJ.GK
2.	Polyvinyl butyral to itself	D.E.
3.	Polymethylmethacrylate to itself	F.G.H.I
4.	Cellulose nitrate to itself	C.J.L.M.
5.	Ethyl cellulose to itself	C,A(80%) + S(20%)
6.	Cellulose acetate butyrate to itself	C,G,L,M.
7.	Polyvinyl Chloride-acetate to itself	O.P.Q
8.	Polyvinyl acetate to itself	C.R.J
9.	Polyamide to itself	Difficult-Hot T or U
10.	Polyethylene to itself	Difficult-Hot N and D
11.	Polyvinylidene chloride to itself	Very difficult
12.	Polystyrene to itself	A.B.C.

Solvents Index

Benzene-A, Toluene-B, Acetone-C, Isopropyl alcohol-D, Furfural-E, Ethylene dichloride-F, Chloroform-G, Clacial acetic acid-H, Methyl-methacrylate monomer-I, Methylethyl ketone-J, Nitromethane-K, Ethylacetate-L, Butyl acetate-M, Xylene-N, Isophorane-O, Mesityl oxide-P, Cyclohexanone-Q, Methyl acetate-R, Alcohol-S, Formic acid-T, Phenol-U.

One common complaint about solvent cementing agents for thermoplastics is the tendency for crazing to occur. This defect is more apparent when transparent thermoplastics are joined, though it may also occur in opaque joints. Crazing occurs most often in the hard brittle plastics. It is most common in PMMA and unmodified polystyrene. Fast-evaporating solvlents are, therefore, not recommended when bonding these plastics. Highly stressed joints are much more subject to crazing than the lightly stressed joints.

Solvent Cement

Solvent plus thermoplastics possess much higher viscosity than pure solvent alone, it will deposit a thick film thereby retaining the solvent at the glue line for a longer period of time. Thus it is better to dissolve the chip of the same plastic in the solvent before applying to the plastic. Various plasticizers may also be included in such formulations. Following are some of the solvent cements for bonding some plastics to themselves.

Acrylics can be bonded to themselves by using an adhesive containing 60 parts methylene chloride, 40 per cent MMA monomer and 0.2 part benzoyl peroxide. Some polymer chips may be dissolved in this adhesive to get an adhesive of suitable consistency. Water with 10 to 20 per cent glycerin can be used to cemet polyvinyl alcohol. For polystyrene solvents as indicated in the above list may be used and as usual some polystyrene may be used in the solvent to get the requisite viscosity. Very slow-drying solvents like ethyl naptthtalene will give craze-free joints with good optical clarity for several years. Fast-drying solvents are MEK, ethyl acetate and methylene chloride, while medium drying solvents are perchloroethylene and trichloroethylene. Polycarbonate may be bonded to itself using a cement containing polycarbonate polymer (40 parts), methylene chloride (147 parts) and ethylene dichloride (80 parts); this plastic can be efficiently bonded using heat sealing and hot gas welding techniques.

Cellulose acetate can be easily solventemented and for this purpose a cement containing acetone (60 parts), methyl cellosolve (30 parts) and cellulose acetate (10 parts) is used. For bonding cellulose acetate butyrate, acetone (40 parts), ethyl acetate (40 parts) and cellulose acetate butyrate (20 parts) solution may be used. These three polymers can be bonded with similar solvents. PVC and its acetate copolymers can be cemented using solvent solutions containing ketones. Cyclohexanone and tetrahydrofuran are stronger solvents. Addition of 2 to 5 per cent of DOP improves the flexibility of the joint. The bite of the cement can be increased by adding some acetic acid. A solvent mixture containing 20 parts dioxane, 12 parts medianol, 60 parts MEK, 3 parts DOP, 2 parts glacial acetic acid and 3 parts isophorone with some dissolved polymer is a good cement for this purpose. The following adhesive has been found to be good for bonding unsupported PVC film or sheet or rigid PVC to itself.

Formulation

Ingredients	**Qty**
PVC	100 parts
Tetrahydrofuran	100 parts
M.E.K.	200 parts
Tin organic stabilizer	1.5 parts
DOP	20 parts
Methyl isobutyl ketone (MIBK)	25 parts

This cement should be handled with care as tetrahydrofuran is rather toxic.

Cementing of Dissimilar Thermoplastics

Cementing of two dissimilar thermoplastics is more difficult than the cementing of materials of same chemical nature. Thus acetone, which is a good solvent for both cellulose-acetate and cellulose-acetate-butyrate, when used as a cementing agent to bond these material compatibility between the polymers and their plasticizers is required; only then a common solvent can produce good results. The best method is to prepare a solution of both polymers in the common solvent and spread it on the surfaces to be joined.

Adhesives Bonding

Using adhesives is the best method of bonding plastics to plastics (similar or disimilar) and to non-plastic adherents. Adhesives based on thermoplastics are often cheap and satisfactory for bonding plastics, when the joints are not subjected to high temperatures of continuous loads. But these adhesives have poor resistance to creep and solvents.

Epoxies and modified epoxy based adhesives give good bonds with thermosets. Traces of mould release agents and other impurities on the adherent sufrace often result in poor bonds hence the plastic surfaces should be wiped with a clean cloth wetted with MEK, acetone toluene, petroleum naphtha, and trichloroethylene etc. This is particularly important with thermosets. When bonding a plastic to other adherents e.g. metals, cloth, glass etc. is to be considered the difference in the coefficients of thermal expansion should be kept in mind. Inorganic fillers may be used in the adhesive thicker glue line or a two coat adhesive system may be used. When an adhesive bonds well to one surface but poorly with other surface the second surface may be primed. For example R-F adhesive bonds well to nylon but not to steel; thus steel is primed with a nitrile-phenolic or epoxy primer resulting in a very good bond of both the adherents.

In some cases bond strength is increased by pretreating the surface of the plastic. This pretreatment usually means acid etching of the plastic surface. Reinforced plastics e.g. Plastics reinforced with glass fibres, asbestos fibres, cotton, nylon etc. can be equally well bonded with adhesives as parent plastics are bonded, but surface must be clean.

Epoxy adhesive can be used for bonding plastics especially the diermosets, though fluorocarbons require special surface treatment. To obtain the best result different hardeners, fillers and flexibilisers may be experimented with. A large amount of polyamide increases adhesion to nylon and PVC, epoxy-polyamide adhesives can be used as general adhesive for bonding plastics. This type of adhesive gives a very good bond when polyester glass cloth laminates are to be bonded.

Polyvinyl acetate is not only a good adhesive for a large number of porous and fibrous materials such as paper, wood and leather, but also for non-porous materials especially transparent plastic-films such as cellophane, cellulose esters, vinyl and polythene terephthalate.

Thermoplastics

Resorcinol-formaldehyde adhesives can be used to get good bonds with polymethyl methacrylate (PMMA). Polyurethane adhesives can also be used for this purpose but operating temperature should be below 70°C. For bonding PMMA to aluminium with a polyurethane adhesive the latter surface may be primed with a polysulphide-epoxy resin. Polymerizable acrylate adhesives give a good bond of cyclised rubber to PMMA. Cellulose nitrate solvent solution can be used for bonding cellulose nitrate, cellulose acetate and cellulose acetate-butyrate, Polyurethane adhesives provide good to excellent bonds to these polymers, but give poor bonds at above 70°C. Cyanoacrylate adhesives also give good bonds with these adhesives. Ethyl cellulose can be bonded with epoxy; nitrile-phenolic and neoprene solvent type adhesives.

R-F adhesives can be used to bond nylon. Nylon can be bonded to metak by priming the latter with epoxy adhesive and using a R-F adhesive. Epoxies, nitrile-phenolic and neoprene solvent type adhesives give bonds of low strength,

Polycarbonate plastic can be bonded with various adhesives. Unsaturated polyester styrene adhesives give a good bond of polycarbonate with steel; similarly polysulphide-epoxide, cyanoacrylate and urethane prepolymer adhesives give good bonds. For the bonding of polystyrene rubber with polystyrene solution in toluene with 2 to 3 per cent DOP may be used; this adhesive is suitable for bonding polystyrene with porous substrates like paper and wood etc. High strength bonds may be obtained using polyurediane or cyanoacrylate adhesives. Polyurethane can be bonded with urethane prepolymer adhesives. R-F adhesives and also unsaturated polyester-styrene adhesive may be used to obtain comparatively low strength bond.

Polyurethane adhesives may be used for bonding PVC. Unsaturated polyester-styrene adhesive also gives a high bond strength, but epoxies may also be used when too high bond strength is not required. An adhesive for bonding PVC has already been described before. Fair bonds of vinylidene chloride can be obtained with nitrile ruber-phenolic or specially compounded vinylchloride acetate resin solvent adhesives. Nitrile-phenolics adhesives resist migration of plasticizer hence are suitable for bonding supported PVC fabrics to itself or wood, metals, fibre bond and phenolics. Vinyl backed with uncoated fabrics can be bonded satisfactorily using nitrile rubber and neoprene rubber water emulsion based adhesives. The following process is for bonding vinyl films to rubber.

Formulation

Ingredients	**Parts by Wt.**
Synthetic rubber	5 gms
Sulphur	2 gms
Ethyl acetate	100 ml.
Ethyl acetoacetate	50 ml.
Butyl acetate	100 ml.

The above solution is coated over the surface to be bonded. Upon assembly the adhesive joint is heated at 120°C while subjecting it to 5 kg/cm^2 pressure.

Aqueous dispersions of polyacrylic esters and copolymers with acrylic or methacrylic acid are used primarily for coatings but are also useful for gluing of PVC sheet paper. The polymers of ethyl acrylate, vinyl acetate and sodium methacrylate in the ratio of 50:507 give bonds between wood and PVC. Similar copolymers, but with varied quantities of an acrylate salt will cause vinyl resins to bond to themselves, wood and leather.

Unreacted olefin plastics can be bonded with a silicate resin adhesive with xylene solvent Polythene and polypropylene require surface preteatment for good adhesion. The polymers of vinylacetate 30-40 parts, acrylic ester 20-35 parts, dialkyl ester of an unsaturated carboxylic acid, especially a maleate ester, make suitable adhesives for polyethylene and polypropylene, giving good tack and having a viscosity sufficiently high to avoid excessive absorption into porous substrates or being squeezed out by pressure. The following is a emulsion of a polythene adhesive.

Monomer Phase

Formulation

Ingredients	**Qty.**
Vinylacetate	33.33 parts
Di-2-methyl hexyl maleate	33.33 "
2-ethyl hexy acrylate	33.33 "

Aqueous Phase

Formulation

Ingredients	**Qty.**
Nonyl phenol-ethylene oxide condensate (86 percent ethylene oxide)	1.0 parts
Acid phosphate ester of alkylphenyl ethylene oxide condensate, free-acid	2.0 "
Alkyl substituted starch ether	1.5 "
Polyvinyl alcohol, 75-80 per cent hydrolysed	1.5 "
Ammonium hydroxide	0.14 "
Water	71.52

Initiator

Formulation

Ingredients	**Parts By Weight**	
	A	**B**
Potassium persulphate	0.42	4.00
Water	8.40	0.40
Neutralising slurry		
Sodium bicarbonate		0.25
Water		0.25

The water phase is first prepared, heated to 58°C, 5 per cent of the monomer is added over 5 min. followed by initiator A, and balance of monomer is added over about 3 hours, finally adding balance of initiator at 87-89°C, and heating further for half an hour. The product has a solids content of 54-56 per cent and viscosity 3000-5000 cps.

The adherence of polyvinylidene chloride film to a polythene object can be improved by using a composition, in paste form, based on 70-98 per cent of a SBR emulsion in which either component can vary between 20 and 80 per cent with the balance as a copolymer of vinyl acetate (30-50 per cent) with a monomer such as 2-ethylhexyl acrylate or dibutyl maleate. The final laminate is impervious to water, organic vapours and oxygen. Alkaline solutions of copolymers of vinyl acetate with 5 per cent crotonic acid are useful for the heat-sealing of polyolefines.

Thermosets

Thermosetting plastics can be readily bonded using thermosetting adhesives. Some of the more important thermosetting adhesives are phenol and resorcinol formaldehyde, urea and melamine formaldehyde, polyester resins furfuryl alcohol polymers. Some of the thermosets and adhesives suitable for bonding them are as follows :

Thermosets	Adhesives
1. Moulded phenolics to phenolics	Cold setting furane, resorcinol, and phenolic adhesives
2. Cast phenolics to cast phenolic	Furane and resorcinol adhesives
3. Laminated phenolics to laminated phenolics	Furane and resorcinol adhesives
4. Moulded and laminated ureas to molded and laminated ureas	Furane, urea, and melamine adhesives
5. Polyester resins to polyester resins.	Liquid polyester monomers and furane adhesives.

These adhesives set at room temperature except polyester monomers which require heating to 150°C. These adhesives have open assembly time of about 5-20 minutes. Pot life of polyester adhesives is several days, while for others it is about 2-3 hours; for furane adhesives it is 6-8 hours.

Phenolic laminates can be sufficiently bonded using R-F and U-F adhesives, the former being more water-resistant. Epoxies provide excellent bonds to phenolics as well as to furnaces and melamines. General purpose nitrile rubber-phenolic cements (solvent type) can be used to obtain bonds of a lower degree of strength to all these urea plastics. Polyurethane adhesives can be used to obtain fair to good bond strength. U-F/UF resin products can be bonded by adhesives compounded from unpolymerized phenol and urea resins dissolved in ketone, ester, alcohol or water from, shellac dissolved in alcohol, or from casein glue, but joints cannot withstand any load or pressure. Resin adhesives are prepared by dissolving unpolymerized resins in acetone to the required viscosity.

Epoxy laminates can be bonded with epoxy adhesives. The following formula is good for bonding of epoxy glass-laminates.

Epoxy Adhesives

Formulation

Ingredients	**Qty.**	**parts**
Epoxy resin	100	"
Aromatic, diamine	20	"
Aluminium silicate filler	100	"

The assembly is cured for 1-1 /2 hours at 85°C. and contact pressure followed by a post cure at 150°C for 2 hours. Relatively good adhesion can be obtained to epoxy laminates with unsaturated polyester-styrene adhesives, R-F, phenolics and furanes. For lower bond strength other adhesives like polyurethanes, nitrile rubber, phenolic and neoprene solvent adhesives and various thermoplastic resin solutions can be used; polyester laminates can be bonded with either unsaturated polyester, styrene adhesives or epoxies; the former is cheaper and easier to handle, but the latter shows less shrinkage.

Bonding of Foams

High strength adhesives are not usually required for bonding plastic foams, since these foams have rather low mechanical strengths. Mastic or rubber based adhesives may be used to bond elastomeric or flexible foams to themselves or other flexible materials. They may also be used to bond rigid foams, when high bond strengths are not required. Solvent type adhesives, such as rubber and mastic based adhesives should not be used to bond two non porous surface e.g. closed cell foam to metal. When using adhesives containing solvents, care should be exercised to avoid solvent that will attack the plastic since these solvent may cause the cellular structure to deform or collapse at the bond surface. When bonding rigid foams to themselves or other rigid materials to flexible materials, room temperature curing thermosetting adhesives are normally recommended for maximum adhesive properties. When bonding rigid foams which have a skin, sanding of the mating surface is sometimes desirable to remove trace of mould releasing agents.

Adhesive for Lamination of Vinyl & cloth

TABLE -15.1- CHARACTERISTICS OF THE VINYL OF CLOTH BONDING WITH VARIOUS ADHESIVES

Property	Prepolymer Emulsion	PVC Plastisol	PVC Solution	Synthetic RubberLatex
Bond	Highest	Low	High	Fair
Hand	Fair	Very flexible	Varies	Varies
Water resistance	Fair	Excellent	Excellent	Fair
Machining	Excellent	Excellent	Poor	Poor
Coverage	Excellent	Poor	Good	Good

A vinyl to metal adhesive that eliminates expensive metal pretreatment is given below. The material can be roller coated or sprayed on film or metal, when the two materials are laminated at speeds up to 60 M/min. at 3 to 5 kg/ cm^2 at 200°C.

Formulation

Ingredients	**Qty.**	**parts**
Epoxy resin	100	"
Nitrile rubber	3.810	"
Phenolic resin	0.954	"
PVA resin	14.300	"
MEK	37.610	"
Isobutyl ether	18.510	"
Toluene	20.000	"
MBT	0.066	"
Carbon disulphide	4.750	"

The distinctive factor between an adhesive and a cement is that whereas the former merely holds to the surface by reason of its adhesive nature, the cement will breakdown the surface thus fusing the two surfaces together.

15.2- ADHESIVE SELECTION FOR SPECIFIC PLASTIC

Plastic to be Bonded	Adhesive Useful - No:
Polymethyl methacrylate	15,14,17
Cellulose acetate	1,14,2
Cellulose acetate-butyrate	1,14,2
Cellulose nitrate	1,15,2
Ethyl cellulose	3,10,81
Polyethylene	16,13
Polyethylene (treated)	3,5,10
Polypropylene	16.
Polypropylene (treated)	3,5,10
PTFE	16.
TFE (treated)	3,5,12
Rigid PVC	14,17,3,5
Flexible PVC	10,11,7,9
Polystyrene	17,2,14,3,5
Polyurethane	14,15,5
Nylon	15,3,10,8
Polyethylene tetraphthalate (Mylar)	8,10,16,17
Epoxy	3,17,15,6,12
Polyester	10,19,4,3,17,14
Furane	6,3,4,14
Melamine	3,4,14
Phenolic	3,4,10,15,17,18,14

Adhesive Code

I. Cellulose nitrate
2. Cyanocrylate
3. Epoxy
4. Phenolic-epoxy
5. Polysulphide or polyamide epoxy
6. Furane
7. SBR solvent based
8. Neoprene solvent based
9. Neoprene-emulsion based
10. Nitrile-phenolic
II. Nitrile emulsion based
12. Phenol-formaldehyde
13. Polybutadiene
14. Polyurethane
15. Resorcinol formaldehyde
16. Silicon resin in xylene
17. Urisaturatcd polyester styrene
18. Urea-formaldehyde
19. Vinyl phenolic.

TABLE -15.3- SOLUBILITY PARAMETERS OF PLASTIC

	S. hide brands
Poly tetrafluroethylene	6.2
Polychlorotrifluorothylene	7.2
Polydimethyl siloxane	7.3-7.6
Ethylene propylene rubber	7.9
Polyethylene	7.9-8.1
Polystyrene	8.6-9.1
Poly (methyl methacrylate)	9.3
Poly (vinyl chloride)	9.5-9.7
Amino resins	9.6-10.1
Epoxy	9.7-10.9
Polyurethane	10.0
Ethyl cellulose	10.3

Poly (vinyl chloride-acetate)	10.4
Poly (ethylene terephthalate)	10.7
Cellulose acetate	10.4-11.3
Cellulose nitrate	9.7-11.5
Phenol formaldehyde	11.5
Poly (vinylidene chloride)	12.2
Nylon, 6, 6	13.6

TABLE -15.4 - SOLUBILITY PARAMETERS OF SOLVENT

	S.hide brands
n-Perfluorohexane	5.6
n-hexane	7.3
Cyclohexane	8.2
Amyl acetate	8.45
1,1,1 - Trichloro ethane	8.3
Carbon tetrachloride	8.6
Toluene	8.9
Ethyl acetate	9.1
Trichloro ethylene	9.2
Methyl ethyl ketone	9.3
Chloroform	9.3
Methyl acetate	9.6
Cyclohexanone	9.9
Dioxane	10.0
Acetone	10.0
Carbon disulfide	10.0
Nitrobenzene	10.0
Dimethyl formamide	12.1
Nitrom ethane	12.6
Ethanol	12.7
Dimethyl sulfoxide	13.4
Ethylene carbonate	14.5
Phenol	14.5
Mathanol	14.5
Water	23.2

Table 1. (Basid Commercial Plastics

Descriptive Name	Chemical Structure of Monomers	Outstanding and / or Typical Properties or Uses	Thermosetting, Rhermoplastic or Casting
ADDITION POLYMERS			
Polyethylene	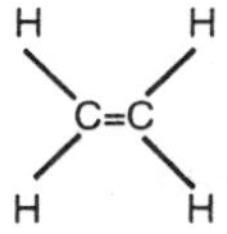	Excellent electrical properties Good impact strenth. Excellent colorability but translucent in thick sections. Good chemical resistance Used in film, mouldings, wire insulation, pipe, paper coating, and flexiblebottles. Available in flexible and semirigid forms only umless heavily filled. Film widely used in packaging.	Thermoplastic
Polypropulene	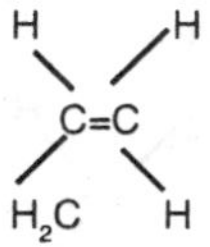	Lowest density of anuy plastic. Fair to good inpact. Fair rigidity and dimensional stability. Excellen colorability. Translucent in thick sections. Good chemical resistance Properties vary widely with degree of crystallinity.	Thermoplastic
Plyubinul chloride and copolymers with vinyl acetate and vinylidene chloride ("Vilylite")	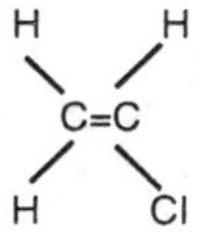	Good electrical properties and flame resistance with proper platicizers. Rigid as polymerized Good impact strength especially in polyblends with elastomers. Good chemical resistance. Require heat stabilizers. Many diverse uses.	Thermoplastic
Polyvinylidene chloride, always as a copolymer with vinyl chloride	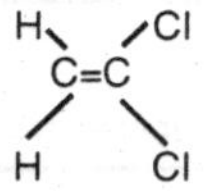	Very low moisture vapor transmission. Good chemical resistance. Self-extinguishing	Thermoplastic

Table I (Basic Commercial Plastics))

Descriptive Name	Chemical Structure of Momomers	Outstanding and / or Typical Properties or Uses	Thermositting, Thermoplastic or Casting
		Flame resustance, used in pipe linings, film.	
Polystyrene; also copolymerzed with a-methyl styrene and vinyl toluenes to improve heat resistance	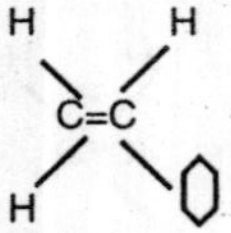	Excellent color, utansparently, rigidity, dimensional stabilyty, electrical properties, molding speeds. Used principally in molding; also in phonograph records and rigid foams.	Thermoplastic
Polystyrene-based graft and / or polyblend polymers with styrene/ buradiene copolymer synthetic rubbers	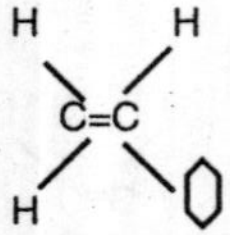 H2C==CH==CH2	Excellent rigidity, dimensional stability, molding speeds. Good colorability in opaqies. Used extensively in moldings and for extruded sheet which is them vacuum formed. Packaging is large market.	Thermoplastics
Styrene / acrylonitrile copolymer grafte or polyblended to butadience / crylonitrile rubber (ABS)	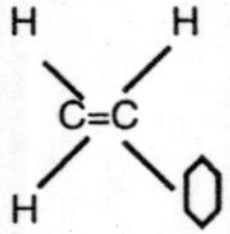 H2C==CH-CH==Ch2 CH2==CHCN	Outstanding impact, Good chemical resistance. Fair weatherability. Fair colorability in opaques. Used in pipe, mouldings, extruded sheet.	Thermoplastic
Styrene / acrylonitrile copolymer	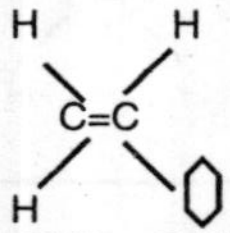 CH2==CHCN	Better chemical resistance, crazing resistance, weatherability, better impact strenth than polystyrene. Good colorability including transparents. Used in moldings, film.	Thermoplastic

Table I (Basic Commercial Plastics)

Descriptive	Chemical Structure of Monomers	Outstanding and / or Typical Properties or Uses	Thermosetting, Thermoplastics or Casting
Polymethylmethacylate ("Plexiglass")	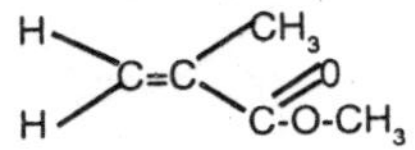	Excellent color, transparency, rigidity, dimensional stability, outdoor stability. Good impact strength. Used in mouldings and as heavy sheeting. High impact graft copolymers abailable.	Thermoplatics / casting
Polyesters (Combination of comdensation and addition polymers.	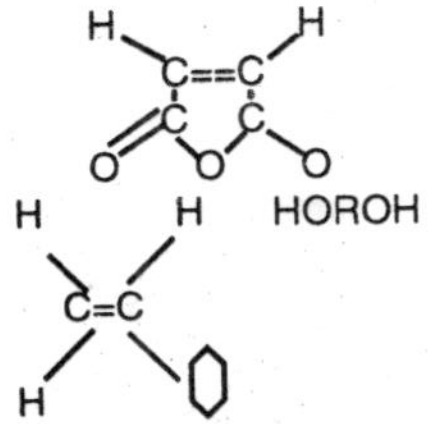	Used with glass clith or fibres to achieve very high tensile and flexural strengths approaching those of steel. Used to make laminates in aircraft, boats, furniture. Some potting of electrical compression and low-pressure moulding.	
Caprolactum (nylon 6)	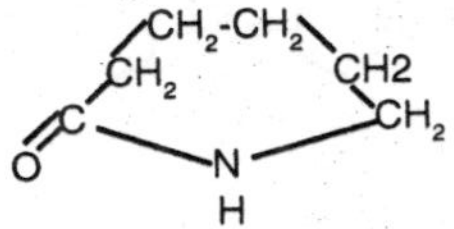	Properties very similar to nylon 66.	Thermoplatics
Melamine-formaldehyde	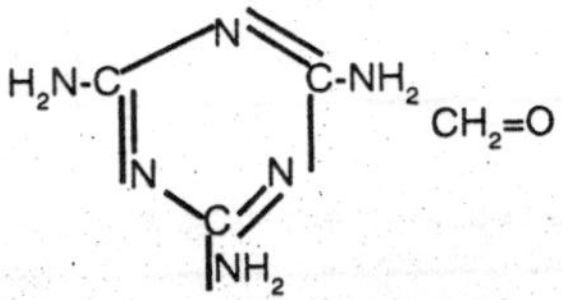	Excellent hardness abrasion resistance, flame resistance, heat resistance,Good colorability in opaques, stain resistance, electrical properties. Used in laminates. Used with alkyd surgace coatings and for adhesive.	Thermosetting

Table I (Basic commercial Plastics)

Descriptive Name	Chemical Structure of Monomers	Outstanding and / or Typical Properties of Uses	Thermosetting Thermoplastic or casting
Urea-formaldehyde	H2NC(=O)NH2 CH2=O	Similar to melamine but poorer aikali resistance, crazing, resistance heat resistan, dimensional stability. Also poorer wear and hardness.	Thermosetting Used in adhesive.
Epoxy	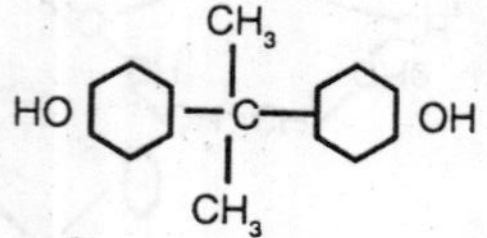 CH_2-$CHCH_2Cl$ (epoxide O bridge) animals, organic anhydrides	Outstanding adhesion to metals. Good chemical resistance. Fair to excellent inpact in flexible furmulations. Glass laminates have excellent tensile fand flexural strength plus good chemical and outdoor resistance if properly formulated. Widely used in sirface coatings and adhesive.	Thermosetting and casting
Ethylene glycolterephthalic acid.("Mylar")	$HOCH_2CH_2OH$ 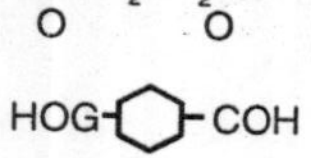	Outstanding toughness and tear strength in films. Also widely used in fibres.	Thermoplastic
Polyvinyl butyral (Chemically modified	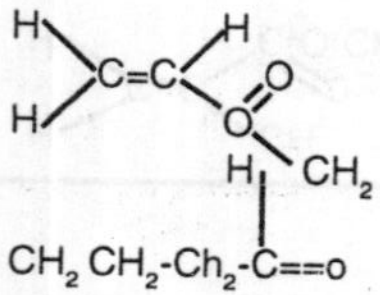	Primarily used for safety glass interlayer has excellent adhesive to glass. Excellent ultraviolet light resistance in absence of air.	Thermoplstic

Table I (Basic Commercial Plastics)

Descriptive Name	Chemical Srtucture of Monomers	Outstanding amd / or Typical Properties or Uses	Thermosetting, Thermoplastic or Casting
Polychlorotrifluoroethylene ("Kel-F")	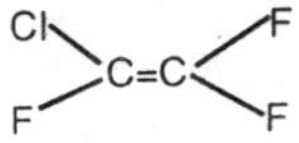	Excellent resistance to chemicals, Used as gasketing, paxking, and cirrisuib resistant coating.	Thermoplastic
Polytetrafluoroethylene ("Teflon")	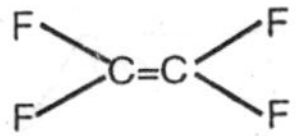	Excellent resistance to chemicals. Used as gasketing, paking, and corrosion resistant coating. Attaked only by alkali metals and hot strong bases.	Fuse alowly under high presure and 450-5000F
CONDENSATION POLYMERS Phenol-formaldehyde ("Bakalite")	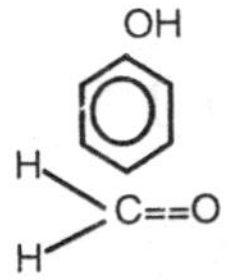	Good electrical properties with proper formulation. High heat resistance. Good to excellent impact and tensile strengths. Very slowto essentially no burning rate depending on filler. Acid resistant used for mouldings, particularly for industrial and electrical applications where its poor colorability is not important. Used extensively for decorative laminate backing.	Thermosetting and casting
Nylon 66	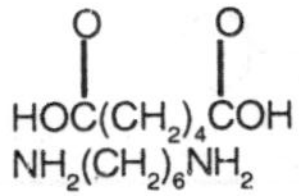	Excellent wear resistance, tensile and inpanct strengths. Low coefficient of friction. High heat distortion temperature. Selfextinguishing to fire. Used for gears. rolls and other moving parts.	Thermoplastic

Table I (Basic Commercial Plastics)

Descriptive Name	Chemical Structure of Monomers	Outstanding and / or typical Properties or Uses	Thermosetting, or casting
Polyphenylene	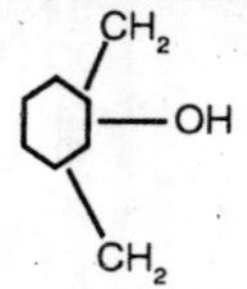	Very high heat distortion resistance for a thermoplastic; nondripping and selfextinguishing in flammability tests.	
Polysulfone	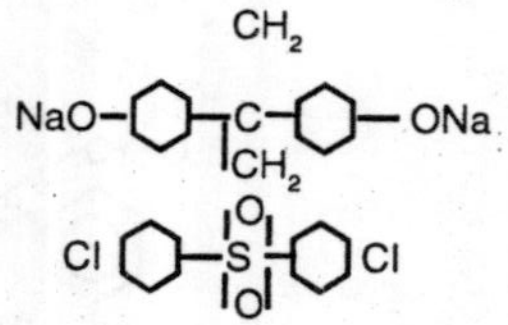	Very high heat distortion resistance for a thermoplastic; nondripping and selfextinguishing in flammability tests.	Thermoplastic
CELLULOSIC	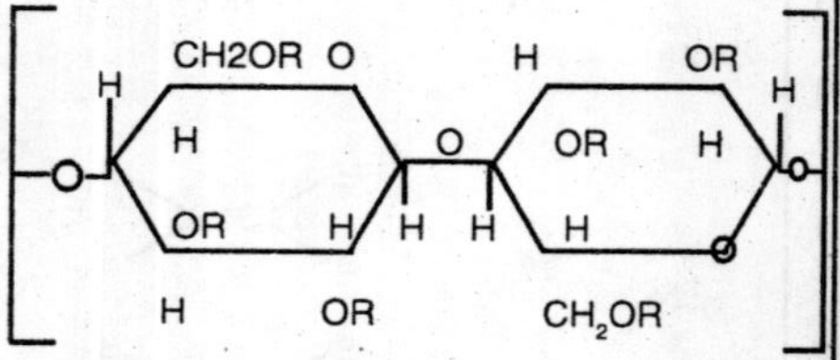		
Cellulose acetate	n= 50-100 R = - C(=O)-CH$_2$ (2.2-2.3 R's ring)	Good inpact strength. Good transparency. Excellent colorability. Fair outdoor stability. Slow to self-extinguishing burning rate. Reqiures plasticizers to form. Used for photo--graphic film and moulding.	Thermoplastic

Table I (Basic Commercial Plastics)

Descriptive Name	Chamical Structure of monomers	Outstanding and / or Typical Properties or Uses	Thermosetting, Thermoplastic or Casting
Cellulose nitrate	n = 250 R= NO2 (19-20 R's per ring)	Outstanding impact strength. Used as plastic declining.	See text
Cellulose acetate butyrate	R = - C(=O) - CH3 (1 per ring) R = - C(=O)CH2CH2CH3 (1.7 per ring)	Similar to cellulose acetate with better dimensional stability and weather-ability. Used for pipe, telephone housing, moulding.	Thermoplastic
Ethyl cellulose	n = 250 R = - CH2CH3	Outstanding impact of all cellulosics, otherwise similar.	Thermoplastic
Silicones	(CH2)2SiCl2 	Outstanding heat resistance. Unusual solubilities give anti-foam and water repellent properties. Used for insulating varnish on electric motors, for high temperature rubbers, greases and lubricants, for high temperature glass laminating to increase adhesion of polyesters to glass fibers and a multitude of other specialty uses most of which are not "plastic" applications in the strict sense.	Thermosetting in plastic applications
Polyurethanes	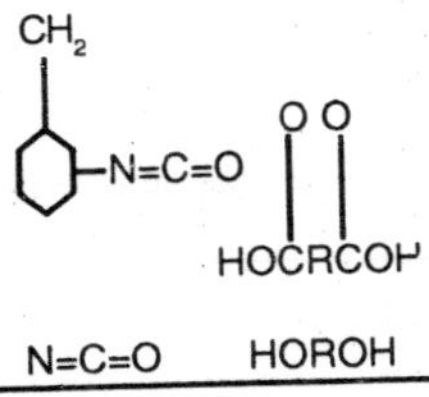	Best properties as rubber with excellent wear resistance. Widely all flexible foams; also for rigid foam and surface coating applications.	Thermo-setting

TABLE 1 (Basic Commercial Plastics)

Descriptive Name	Chemical Structure of Monomers	Outstanding and / or Typical Properties or Uses	Thermosetting, Thermoplastic or Casting.
Polyoxymethylene	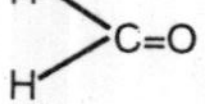 See text	Excellent abrasion resistance. Tough Excellent colorability in opaques only Good chemical resistance. Excellent Dimensional stability.	Thermoplastic
Polyoxetanes ("Penton")	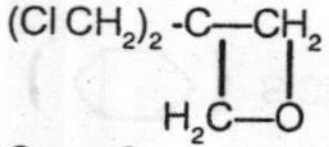	Best chemical resistance of easily moulded rigid polymers. Selfextinguishing to fire.	Thermoplastic
Polycerbonates	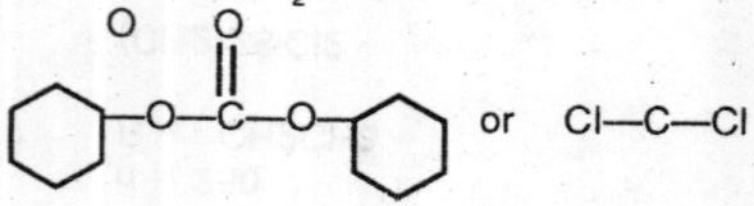 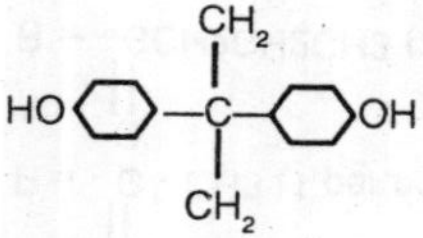	Excellent impact dimensional stability at high temperatures, colorability Good electrical properties. Selfextinguishing.	Thermoplastic

16.

Carboxylic Polymers in Adhesive

Introduction

Anhydride rubber, prepared by the treatment of rubber and other unsaturated elastomers with maleic anhydride, is readily converted by moisture and other hydrolyzing agent into carboxylic elastomers.

```
                                                              HO-C=O
                                                                 |
CH2 = CH2 + CH2 = CR = COOH  —  -CH2-CR-CH2-CH2-CH2-CR-CH2
                                      |
                                    O=C-OH
```

Use in Adhesives

The carboxylic elastomers may be employed as adhesives in solutions of suitable solvents, as latexes, or as aqueous solutions or dispersions in alkaline or ammonical media when the carboxyl content and molecular weight are suitably selected.

Carboxylic Elastomers as Metal to Rubber Adhesives

In the bonding of rubber-to-metal with unsaturated carboxylic elastomers in the presence of vulcanizing or other reagents not reactive with carboxyl groups, the bond to rubber is accomplished by cross linkages dependent on the unsaturation, while the bond to metal arises from interaction of polar groups with the metals. This requires fairly simultaneous cures of the cement, the rubber stock and the metal to cement interface. Cement prepared from carboxylic butadiene acrylonitrile copolymers blended with phenolic resins, like the analogous cements prepared with noncarboxylic butadiene acrylonitrile copolymers are adhesive agents for steel to rubber. Employed without curative agents the carboxylic copolymers give better steel to rubber adhesion than the analogous non carboxyl copolymers. Carboxyl nitrile rubber adhesive is used in rubber to metal adhesive containing chloride rubber and phenolic resin. The carboxylic copolymer cements generally show greater bond strength as well as a desired cohesive failure within the rubber, whereas the analogous non carboxylic copolymers show failure at the steel surface. Inclusion of carboxyl groups in butadiene acrylonitrile copolymers widens their range of compatibility with phenolic resins and increases the strength and hardness of the resultant adhesive,

Carboxylic Elastomers in Adhesive for Non Metallic Adherents

Dispersion of copolymers of butadiene with acrylic acid in aqueous potassium hydroxide as a dip for adhering rayon tyre cord to rubber. The effect is most evident when carboxyl groups are present in the adhesive, they tie cement and the cover stocks.The bonding of fibres of paper, fabric or similar material by rubber latexes may be enhanced by the inclusion of carboxyl groups in the adhesive or binder copolymer molecule. For example in the bonding of semi-bleached kraft crepe paper with polyethyl acrylate latex, the inclusion of 0.045 ephr of carboxyl gave approximately 50% further improvement in internal bond strength similarly, a butadiene-acrylonitrile copolymer improved the internal bond strength of semi bleached kraft paper by 15% with the addition of 0.09 ephr of carboxyl. The beneficial action of carboxyl group is probably due to improvement in copolymer adhesive penetration and subsequently greater hydrogen bonding with the paper cellulose.

In cotton lamination the use of carboxylic elastomer latexes double the bond strength and improved the solvent resistance over that normally found with conventional non carboxyl latexes.

Carboxylic Elastomers as Metals to Metal Adhesives

Carboxylic butadiene acrylonitrile copolymers have been employed in blends with selected phenolic resins as metal to metal adhesives.The inclusion of carboxyl in adhesive imparts elongation, elasticity and resilience.The inclusion of carboxyl groups in polyethyl acrylate improves the adhesion to steel.

Carboxyl Reactive Liquid Elastomers in Structural Adhesives

One of the new technologies developed is the use of carboxyl functional liquid nitrile copolymers for toughening structural plastics and adhesives such as those made from the crosslinked epoxy resins, the term toughening is used to denote a marked increase in impact resistance and an ability to absorb energy without catastrophic fracture. This phenomenon of toughening occurs without any appreciable loss of mechanical properties such as is normally encountered with the flexibilization of crosslinked resins. As applied to structural adhesives, it is observed that the area under the stress - strain curve is tremendously increased without loss of tensile strength or heat resistance. This alone makes this new technology of great interest to the adhesive industry.

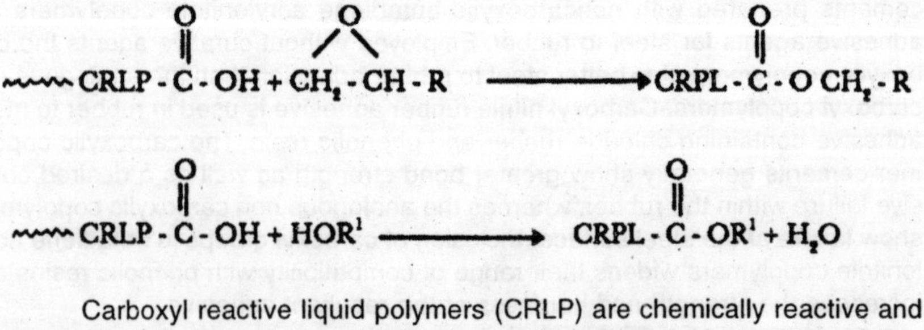

Carboxyl reactive liquid polymers (CRLP) are chemically reactive and capable of chain extension and crosslinking through typical reactions of carboxyl groups. The reactions most important in adhesive applications are those with epoxide groups and with aliphatic hydroxyl groups.

Formulations Ingredient	Parts by wt.		
	A	B	C
Epoxy resin	98.0	48.0	103.5
1,5 Naphthalene diol	12.4	-	-
Bisphenol - A	18.0	18.0	
2,2-bis (4-hydroxyphenyl) sulfone	-	-	18.0
CRLP	15.0	15.0	15.0
Triphenyl phosphine	0.2	0.2	0.2
A and C are reacted for 1 hr at 130-16CPC then added.			
Dicyandiamide	8.0	8.0	8.0
2-ethyl-4-methylimidazole	1.0	1.0	1
121°C lap shear (psi)	*3250.0*	*1450.0*	*3210.0*
Cured. I hr at 121°C			

Particulate structural adhesives using carboxylated rubbers:

Formulation Ingredients	Parts By Wt.
Epoxy resin (liquid)	89.00
Epoxy resin (solid)	11.00
CRLP	36.00
Dicyandiamide	3.50
Monuron	2.25
Properties	
T-peel at 24°C (kg/in)	24.0
82°C lap shear	2130.0
121°C lap shear	750.0
Cured 1 hr at 120°C	

The epoxy resins are milled in to the rubber and then the curatives are added.The stock is sheeted from the mill and ground in to powder.

Carboxyl Elastomers in PSA Sensitive Adhesive

The carboxylic polyacrylates are effective laminating adhesives for both flexible and rigid surfaces. The particular carboxylic acrylate used for a given laminating application is determined by the characteristics of the surfaces to be adhered, wheather adhesive or cohesive bond failure is desired, the bond strength required for the adhesive and many other factors. These may include stiffness, friability, extensibility, clarity, cold flow, moisture resistance, solvent or chemical resistance, heat and light insensitivity, radiation resistance, compatability with resins and vulcanizability. The peel strength enhancement using the corresponding carboxyl acrylates is most striking.Some times carboxylic butadiene acrylonitrile copolymer in conjunction with tackifying resins and a butylated melamine formaldehyde curing resin as PSA on a polyster film backing. One of the useful attributes of PSA tapes made with carboxylic polyacrylates is that essentially no compounding is required provided that proper balance of creep peel, shear and tack properties are build in to the elastomer. Some PSA tapes including surgical tapes have been reported to contain carboxylic acrylate copolymer.

Carboxylic Functional Neoprenes as Contact Adhesives

Single component adhesive systems based on carboxyl polychloroprenes exhibit properties of a cured adhesive even in a freshly prepared bond.The carboxyl functionality undergoes crosslinking reactions with divalent metal oxides such as magnesium oxide.

Adhesion with Non-elastomeric, Carboxyl function, Olefin Copolymers

Qualities of vinyl polymers were enhanced through the addition of carboxylated olefin copolymers. Copolymers of olefins are used in adhesives in wood metal.Waxy adhesive products have been prepared by grafting small amounts of maleic anhydride on polyolefine.Incorporation of the polar monomer improved adhesion to polar textiles, metals and plastic films and aluminium paper laminates.

Although acrylic acid is considerably more expensive, it has gained acceptance as a comonomer in specially applications.

Carboxylic Polymers in Hot-melt Adhesives

Hot melt adhesives for packaging applications have been formulated using carboxyl polymers with acrylic acid and polyethylene.These laminates which are useful in packaging have high strength, toughness and clarity, excellent sealability and firm bonding between the layers.

The development of high strength thermpolastic adhesive copolymers of the Ethylene Acrylic Acid type containing reactive carboxyl groups has made it practical to bond insulation such as polyethylene to metal conductors to provide adequate bonding and long term environmental resistance.

Carboxyl functional vinyl copolymers resin in adhesive

The incorporation of small amounts of maleic anhydride in to the copolymers of vinyl chloride and vinyl acetate substantially improves their adhesion. A 50% replacement of standard copolymers vinyl dispersion resin with carboxyl functional resin double the force required to pluck fibers loose. Such plastisols also show improved adhesion to glass and polyester fabrics.

17.

Cyanoacrylate Adhesives

Introduction

Cyanoacrylate adhesives first appeared in the industrial market more than 20 years ago. Since then, cyanoacrylates have become widely used in the product assemble applications. Ease of application, rapid cure at room temperature, and high bond strengths are qualities which make cyanoacrylates attractive.

Unlike most acrylic based adhesives, cyanoacrylates are essentially the same today as they were when they were first introduced. There are two reasons for this-first, any change in the structure of the cyanoacrylate molecule, other than in the ester group, results in a dramatic change in the cure rate and the adhesive properties of the monomer. Second, the industrial preparation of cyanoacrylate monomer is beset with problem, and a great deal of research has gone toward developing efficient industrial monomer processes. Only recently has more attention been directed towards improving the adhesives properties.

Cyanoacrylate adhesives are based upon esters of alpha cyanoacetic acid. The predominant ester are methyl, ethyl, but n-butyl and allyl are used occasionally. But in this case a modified ester has been developed.

The preparation of cyanoacrylate monomers is theoritically simple. An alkyl cyanoacrylate and formaldehyde are condensed in the presence of a basic catalyst. The resultant polymer is carefully dried and stripped of solvent. The dry polymer is pyrolysed to generate the monomer which is redistilled in an atmosphere of sulphur dioxide to give the final product. Major hurdles in this process have been the tendency of the monomer to polymerize spontaneously and the difficulty encountered in drying and handling the polymer prior to the cracking step. Today the problems of manufacuring have largely been overcome, and cyanocrylate of consistent, high quality are available.

The cyanoacrylate molecule has powerful electron with drawing groups, the cyano and ester moieties, attached to the same carbon. These groups strongly activate the beta-carbon towards nucleophilic attack and stabilize the resultant negative charge on the beta-carbon. Cyanoacrylate adhesive appear to polymerize rapidly when spread in a thin film between substrates because of facile attack by moisture adsorbed on the substrate surface.

Polymerization is initiated by nucleophilic attack on the beta carbon which generates anionic. This stable carbanion then propagates the polymerization by attacking more monomer. Both the chain transfer process and the chain termination step may be more complex than shown in depending upon the initiator species and the stabilizers present in the adhesive. The cyanoacrylate polymerization rate *is* high at room temperature and polymer with high molecular weight can be formed in a few seconds. The rate of cure, however, decreases marginally as the molecular weight of the monomer increases.

Because cyanoacrylate are susceptible to radical and anionic polymerization, two types of inhibitors are necessary to stabilise these adhesives. Radical inhibitors are used to prevent light induced or adventitious radical polymerization. Anionic polymerization suppressors such Lewis and Bronstead acids, for example, SO_2 and H_3PO_4, control spontaneous ionic polymerization.

Although the cyanoacrylates readily polymerize on most surfaces, a surface activator must be necessary for acidic or porous substrates. A typical activator consists of organic nucleophilic dissolved in a volatile solvent. Finally, the surface curing character of cyanoacrylates may necessitate the use of surface activators to improve through-cure of thick selection of adhesive.

Cyanoacrylate adhesives may be divided into three classes—General purpose adhesive which bond rubbers and plastics, adhesives for metals and specialty adhesives. Unlike most other adhesives, cyanoacrylates consist almost entirely of monomer. Because the monomers are low viscosity fluids, a typical formulation will include a thickener such as poly (methyl methacrylate). Other additives include stabilizers, plasticizers, adhesion promoter, heat resistance and moisture resistance promoters. An entire line of cyanoacrylates may be based upon a single ester. The components of a typical cyanoacrylate adhesive are listed in Table-17.1.

Bonding with Cyanoacrylates

Nearly all substrates can be bonded with cyanoacrylate. This versatility is one of the advantages cyanoacrylates have over others, competing adhesives. Few substrates exist which do not bond well with most cyanoacrylates. But after modification with gum rosin this drawback has been removed.

Generally the cleaner the surface the stronger the bond will be. This is particularly true for cyanoacrylate adhesives. An initial cleaning with a compatible solvent or cleaning agent followed by abrasion and a final solvent wipe will remove dirt, grease of milling oil and will provide a good bonding surface. Also the sooner the clean surfaces are bonded the better the bond will be. Because cyanoacrylates generally bridge gaps poorly, stroger bonds will occur between closely fitted substrates. Porous and acidic substrates often require priming with a surface activator to ensure the formation of a strong bond.

After the adherend surface have been prepared the adhesives should be applied to one surface and evenly distributed over the bonding area. This is best accomplished by mating the adherends only spreading the adhesive between them. Sufficient adhesives should be used to allow "squeeze out" from all edges of the bond. This ensures that the bonding surfaces are thoroughly wetted and that air bubbles are removed. Any delay in mating the adherends once the adhesive is applied will result in premature polymerization and a weakend bond.

Once the adhesive is spread, no further movement of adherends should be attempted; the rapidly curing adhesive will be distributed and a weaker bond will result. Contact pressure to closely mate the adherends is sufficient and should be maintained until handling strength is achieved, usually two seconds to five minutes. Because adsorbed moisture is an initiator, the temperature of the adhesives and the relative humidity have an effect upon the cure rate of adhesive.

Electromechanical and electroneumatic dispensing equipment is available which can precisely meter the quantity of cyanoacrylate applied. This equipment reduces bond strength variability and the waste associated with manual application.

Adhesive Properties

To properly evaluate whether an adhesive fits a particular application the user must consider the properties of the adhesives as well as the environment to which the finished product will be exposed. Among the adhesive properties which should be examined are the ease of handling and application; adhesion to the chosen substrate; the rate of cure; and the response of the cured adhesives to the stresses which the bond will encounter. The properties and behavior of cured cyanoacryiates are examined.

One Part

Cyanoacryiates are one part adhesives obviating the need for metering or mixing, but retaining long storage and pot lives. Occasionally a surface activator is needed, but this is the exception not *the* rule.

100 Percent Reactive

Cyanoacrylates contain no solvent, thus eliminating the need for costly solvent evaporating, recovery, or pollution control equipment.

Rapid Cure

Cyanoacryiates cure rapidly at room temperature; handling strength is achieved in seconds to minutes depending on the substrate. Complete cure is usually achieved in 24-28 hours, depending on substrate and cure condition.

High Strength

High bond strengdis are attainable with cyanoacrylate adhesives. Tensile strength in the range of 5,000 psi have been recorded. Overlap shear strength, too, are excellent.

Versatility

Cyanoacryiates are capable of bonding most substrates. Although the cost of cyanoacryiates appears high, the quantity of adhesive necessary for a strong bond is very low, the cost per bond is reduced to minimum.

Solvent Resistance

Cyanoacrylates generally resist most solvents. The exception are acetone, nitromethane, dimethyl sulfoxide and dimethyl formamide.

Pure cyanoacrylate adhesives are generally deficient in the following area.

Brittleness

Cyanyoacrylates are known for their poor peel and impact resistance. This fault is magnified with bonds between rigid substrates and is due to brittleness inert in polycyanoacrylates. The problem has been mitigated to some extent by the inclusion of plasticizers or adhesion promoter.

Moisture Resistance

Another problem with pure cyanoacrylate is poor moisture and humidity resistance. This is particularly apparent on exposure to moisture is partially because of degradation of the polymer. Loss of adhesion between the polymer and the adherend, caused by the exposure to moisture, also decreases the bond strength. This problem is overcome by the addition of gum rosin to pure cyanoacrylate resin.

Heat Resistance

Pure cyanoacrylates suffer from poor heat resistance. Because polycyanoacrylates are thermoplastic, these adhesives perform poorly at elevated temperature. At the same time, exposure of cyancoacrylate bond to heat causes weakning, even after a return to ambient temperature, because of polymer degradation at high temperatures. The normal operating limit for pure cyanoacrylates is about 70°C. This is improved to about 120°C by the addition of gum rosin and its derivatives.

Gap Filling

The surface curing nature of cyanoacrylates limits their ability to bridge gap. This problem can be overcome to some extent by the use of a rosin modified high viscosity adhesive and a surface activator.

Cyanoacrylates are sensitive to surface cleanliness and surface preparation methods. They cure rapidly and form strong bonds on contact with human skin. Careful handling is necessary at all times.

Applications

The cyanoacrylate adhesives have unusual characteristics, due to the fast setting adhesive. Care must be exercised to avoid (1) contact with skin and eyes, (2) prolonged breathing of vapour, (3) use near sparks, heat or open flames. In Table-17.2, the rapidity of bonding action and bond strength are qualitatively described for a wide variety of adherends. The bonds of the cyanoacrylate adhesives have high initial tensile strength and the bonded article can be handled within minutes after the bond formation. Shear strength of the adhesive between a variety of substrates are given in Table-17.3. Age and weather slowly deteriorate bonds, however modified adhesives overcome this problem and have withstood ageing for as long as 7 years and have maintained very useful bond strengths.

These adhesives generally do not possess good heat resistance. At about 70°C, they begin losing bond strength. But the modified adhesive was formulated for use in high temperature applications (Table-17.4). The effect of common solvents, chemicals and indusrial fluids and immersion time are shown in Table-17.5.

The properties which make this adhesive have been used to solve numerous problems such as trophies, fountain pens, rubber imprinting plates, optical lenses, tools, high fidelity, phonograph cartridges and rubber swimming marks.

TABLE -17.1- Formulation : Medium Viscosity General Purpose Cyanoagrylate Adhesive

Components	Parts By Weight
Rosin cyanoacrylate	90.000
Poly (methyl methacrylate)	4.000
Dimethyl sebacete	5.000
P-Methoxy phenol	0.1
Sulfur dioxide	0.005

TABLE - 17.2 - Effect of Adherent Combination onBonding , Action and Strength

Substrates	Bonding Action	Bond strength
Glass-glass	Rapid	Strong
Aluminium-Aluminium	Intermediate	Intermediate
Steel-Steel	Intermediate	Strong
Glass-Rubber	Rapid	Strong
Porcelain-Porcelain	Rapid	Strong
Polyethylene-Polyethylene	Intermediate	Intermediate
Polyester-Polyester	Rapid	Intermediate
Metal-Cork	Rapid	Strong
Metal-Felt	Rapid	Strong
Glass-Felt	Rapid	Strong
Wood-Wood	Slow	Strong
Metal-Leather	Intermediate	Strong
Metal-Rubber	Rapid	Strong
Rubber-Rubber	Rapid	Strong
Rubber-Cardboard	Rapid	Strong
Glass-Steel	Intermediate	Strong
Nylon-Nylon	Rapid	Intermediate
Steel-Neoprene	Rapid	Strong

TABLE -17.3 - Shear Strength of Bond Formation

Substrates	Age of bond	Shear strength (psi)
Steel-Steel	10 min	1920
	48 hr	3000
Aluminium-Aluminium	10 min	1480
	48 hr	
Butyl Rubber Butyl Rubber	10 min	150
SBR Rubber-Phenolic	10 min	110
Phenolic-Phenolic	10 min	
	48 hr	750
Phenolic -Aluminium	10 min	960
	48 hr	910
Aluminium - Nylon	10 min	720
	48 hr	1440
Nylon - Nylon	10 min	330

	48 hr	1400
Rubber-Polyester	10 min	110
Acrylic-Acrylic	1 0 min	810
	48 hr	790

TABLE - 17.4 - Effect of Temperature on Bond Formed by Pure Adhesive and Modified Adhesives

	Shear strength of adhesive bonds (psi)	
Sample aged 7 days ("C)	**Pure adhesive**	**Modified adhesive**
25	2900	3300
100	430	1450
150	0	970
200	0	1070
225	0	1130
250	0	430
275	0	225

TABLE - 17.5 - Chemical Resistance of Cyanoacrylate Adhesives

Chemical	Immersion time	Immersion Temp (°C)	Tensile strength after immersion (psi)
None (Control)	-	-	4000-6000
Water	24 hr	25	2225
Water	9 days	25	2455
Water	24 hr	75	3050
Water	24 hr	100	150
Ethyl alcohol	24 hr	25	3420
Ethyl alcohol	9 days	25	4165
Acetone	24 hr	25	4465
Benzene	24 hr	25	4355
10% Na OH	24 hr	25	1680
10% H°C1	24 hr	25	3135
Dioctyl phthalate	2 weeks	25	4200

18.

Epoxy Resin Adhesives

Introduction

Because of their strength, versatility and excellent adhesion to a variety of surfaces, epoxy resin adhesives have gained wide acceptance by diverse users. The popularity of expoxy adhesives is a consequence of the following important characteristics.

(A) Adhesion

Because of their epoxide, hydroxyl, amine and other polar groups the epoxies have high specific adhesion to metals, glass and ceramics. They can be formulated to give mixes of low viscosity with improved wetting, spreading and penetration action. Epoxies are also used for the bonding copper to phenolic laminate in printed circuits.

(B) Cohesion

When the resin is properly cured, the cohesive strength within the glue line is so great, and adhesion of the epoxy to other materials is so good, that failure under stress often occurs in one of the adherends rather than in the epoxy or at the interface. This happens with glass and aluminium as well as with weaker adhrends such as concrete and wood.

(C) 100% Solids

Unlike phenolic and some other resins resinous adhesives, the epoxies cure without releasing water or other condensation by products. This makes it possible to bond the epoxies at only contact pressure, or with no pressure at all. Also, since there is no water to remove and no volatile solvent, the epoxies are convenient for the assembly line bonding of imprevious surfaces such as metal and glass.

(D) Low Shrinkage

The epoxies cure with only a fraction of the shrinkage of vinyl type adhesives such as the polyesters and acrylics, consequently less strain is built in to the glue line, and the bond is stronger. Also, the epoxies do not pull away from glass fibres as polyesters do. The shrinkage can be reduced to a fraction of 1% by incorporation of silica, aluminium, and other inorganic fillers.

(E) Low Creep

The cured epoxies like other thermoset resins, maintain their shape under prolonged stress better than thermoplastics such as polyvinyl acetate, nitro cellulose and polyvinyl butyral.

(F) Resistance to Moisture and Solvents

Unlike proteins, starches, dextrin gums and polyvinyl alcohol the epoxies are insensitive to moisture. Their resistance to solvent is also outstanding and accounts for their rapid advance in the coating field. They are effective barriers to heat and electric current.

(G) Modification

The properties of epoxy adhesives can be changed by (a) selection of base resin and curing agent; (b) alloying the epoxy with another resin; (c) compounding with fillers.

(H) Curing

Adhesive curing within 5 min. at room or lower temperatures can be formulated by selection of special curing agents.

(I) Resistance to Temperature

Epoxies can be formulated for use in cryogenic applications or for continuous service in high temperature environments. The main disadvantages of pure epoxies are:

(a) Toxicity:

Some epoxies and diluents are known to cause dermatitis. Some amine diluting agents are toxic. Good housekeeping is the best preventive measure. The cured epoxies are not deleterious to health.

(b) Pot And Shelf Life:

Most two component adhesive formulation must be mixed shortly before use. Some film and tape adhesive must be stored at low temperature for extended life, partially offsetting their advantage of convenience and reliability.

(c) Cost

Epoxies are not cheap however their cost in a thin bond-like is hardly a factor in the overall cost of the assembled product in most industrial applications.

Chemistry

The epoxy group ia a three membered ring consisting of an oxygen atom atached to two connected carbon atoms.

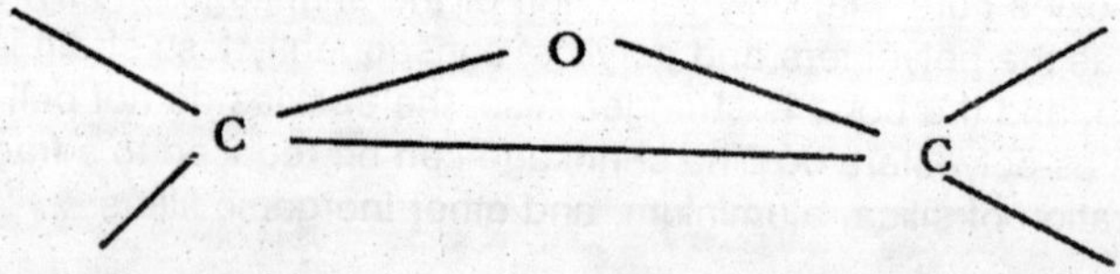

The term 'Epoxy Resin' usually refers to an intermediate molecule which contains at least two reactive epoxy groups. Such resins are categorised as thermosetting since they are capable of curing to form crosslinked net work.

The rings can be opened by either acidic or basic materials, functioning either as cataysts for homopolymerization or as reactive hardners.

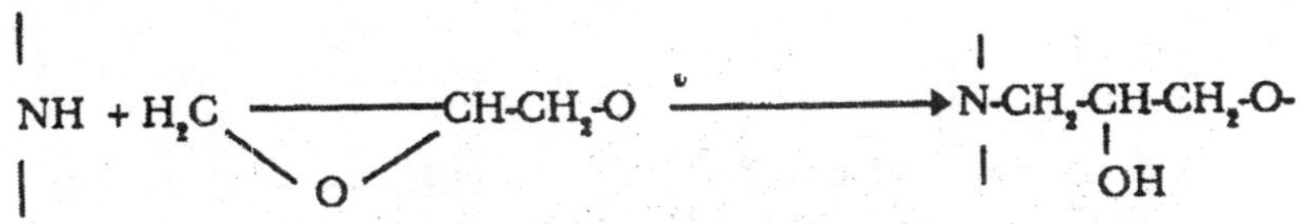

The most common epoxies used in adhesives are derived from bisphenol and epichlorohydrin and are usualy cured with reactive hardness containing primary and secondary amine groups.

Aliphatic primary and secondary amines react with epoxy groups rapidly at room temperature. Epoxy resins can also be homopolymerized by certain catalysts. Acid anhydrides also react with epoxides in the presence of hydroxyl groups to yield ester linkages. Mercaptans also react with epoxy groups to form thickeners. Other compounds which enter into reaction with epoxide groups but are less commonly used include isocynates, hydrazides, aminamides, aziridines boron containing compounds.

Epoxy Novolac Resins

The epoxy novolac resins combine the reactivity of epoxy group and thermal resistance of the phenolic backbone and can be represented by the following structural formula.

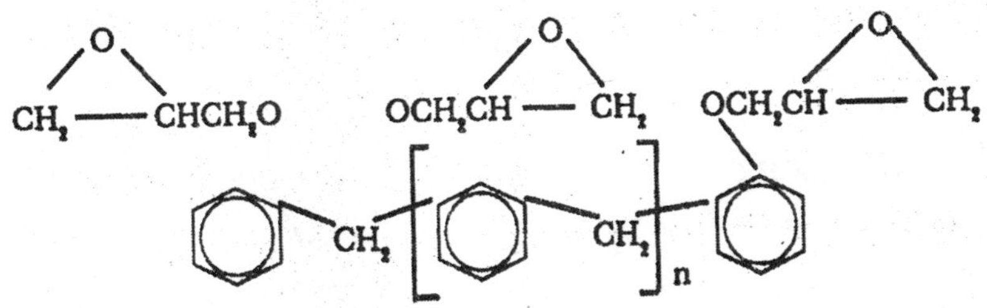

Flexible Epoxy Resins

Epoxy resins derived from polyols such as propylene glycol and glycerine have lower viscosity and yield flexible products. Another type of flexible epoxy resin is derived from dimerized unsaturated fatty acids. The structure of the diglycidyl ether of linoleic dimer acid is shown below.

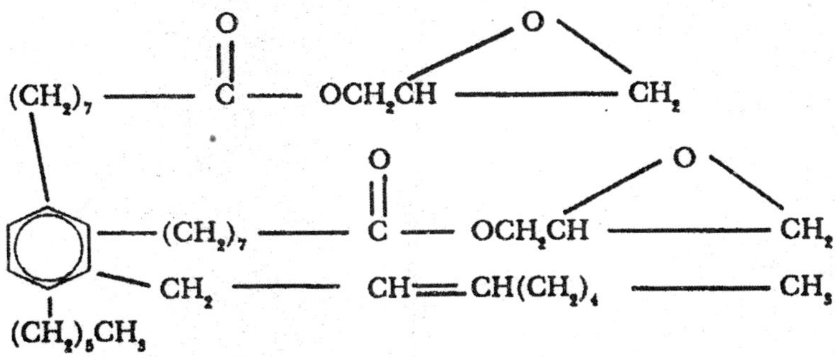

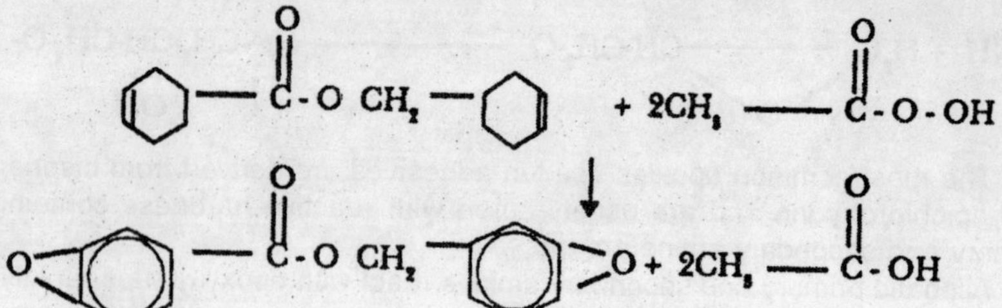

Epoxidized olefins

These are derived by a different route. Polyolefines are epoxidized by peracetic acid.

Speciality Epoxy Resins & Derivatives

Some of the specially epoxy resins useful for adhesives are described below :-

(a) A high functionality solid resin derived from tetrakisphenylethene. It is used in the preparation of high temperature adhesives. Its idealized structure shows four epoxides per molecule.

The highest epoxy content in an aromatic diepoxide is available in diglycidyl ether of resorcinol.

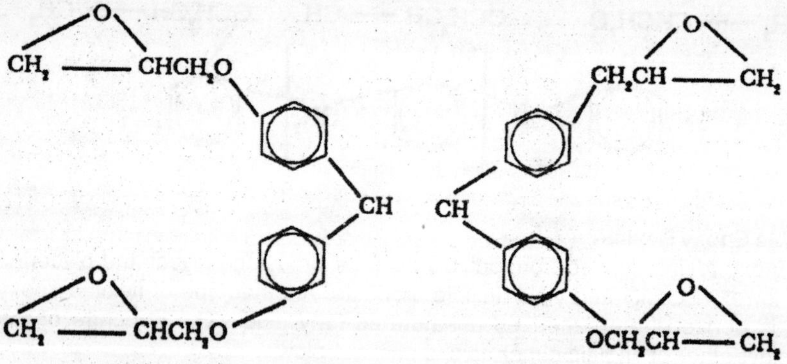

A methylolated version of the conventional epoxy resin has the following structure.

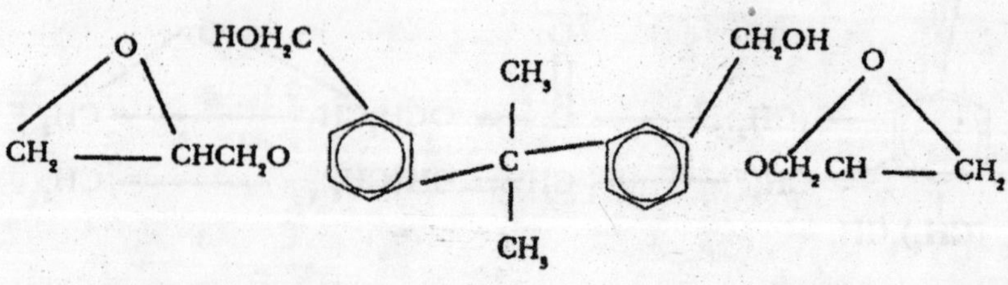

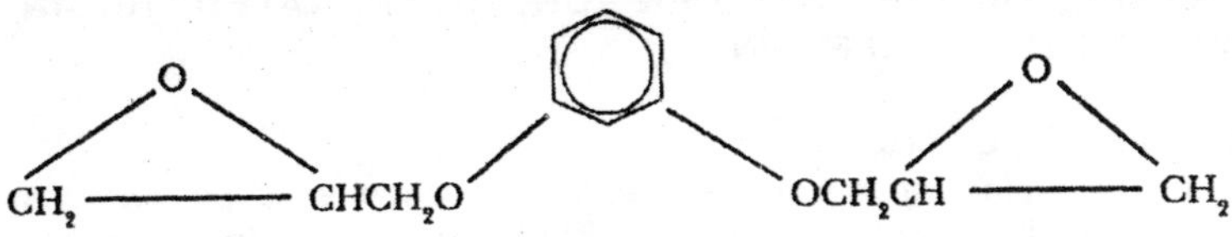

Vinyl esters are made by reacting epoxy resin with acrylic or methacrylic acid.

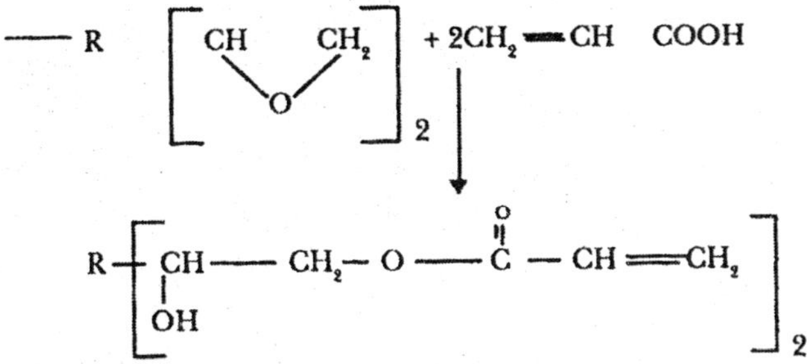

Epoxy Esters of Rosin

Epoxy esters of rosin are the products of reactio between the carboxylic group of rosin and both the epoxy group and hydroxyl group of the epoxy molecule having following strcuture.

Epoxy Esters of Styrenated Rosin

The rosin-styrene adduct when reacted with epoxy resins have epoxy esters of styrenated rosin, a new type of ester results in the adhesive field, which can be represented by the following formula.

Epoxy Esters of Disproportionated Rosin

Glycidyl ether based disproportionated rosin ester is prepared by the reaction between epoxy resin and disproportionated rosin, a modified from of rosin as shown:

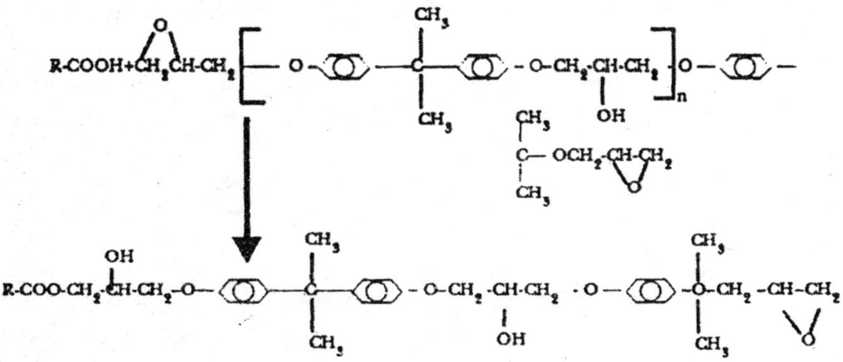

Where R-COOH = ROSIN OR, STYRENATED ROSIN OR, DISPROPORTIONATED ROSIN

Epoxy Novolac Esters

Epoxy novolac esters were synthesized by condensing epichlorohydrin with novolacs and then with rosin, By virtue of their properties, these esters can be used in high quality adhesives.

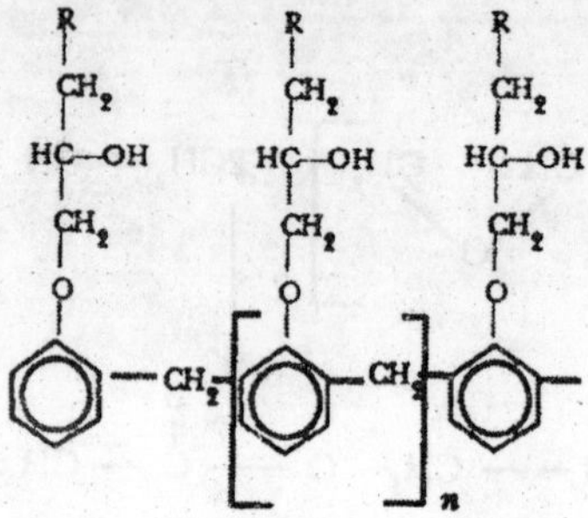

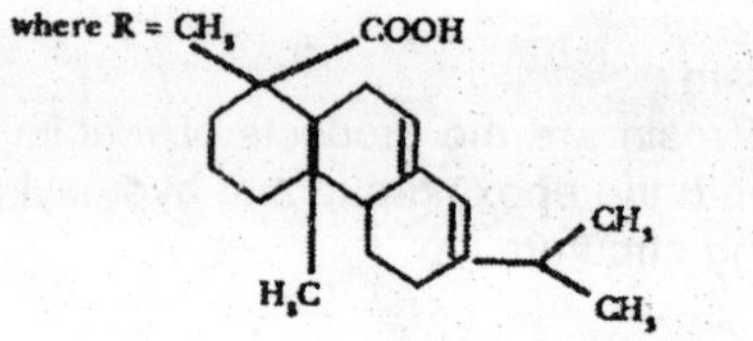

(ABIETIC ACID)

Epoxy Ester of Maleopimaric Acid

Maleopimaric acid is a polybasic acid esterified with epoxy resin to prepare epoxy ester of maleopimaric ester, the structure of which is as follows :-

These products are used in adhesives especially with the items used for baby i.e. sanitary napkins, baby suits, shoes. They are used with foams for toys. At present this particular material is imported for domestic consumption.

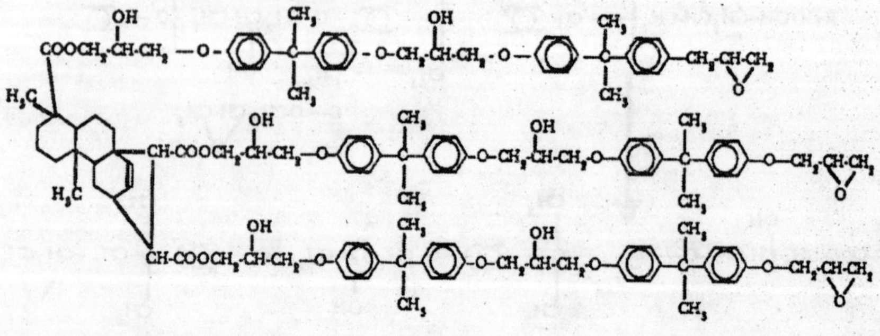

Compounding

The adhesive formulations have a wide choice of resins, hardners, modifiers, fillers, diluents, flexibilizer, reinforcement and miscellaneous additives.

Curing Agents

Epoxy resin can be cured catalytically by reactive curing agents. Three main classes of hardners are amines, anhydrides and low acids. Table 18.1, summarizes the characteristics of important curing agents.

Diluents

These are used primarily to reduce the viscosity of epoxy resin system, Diluents may be reactive or non reactive. About 1.2 part of butyl glycidyl ether reduce the viscosity of the standard resin from over 10,000 CPS down to 500-700 CPS at 25°C. Some of the commercial medium viscosity (2000 to 4000 CPS) epoxy resins contain dibutyl phthalate as a nonreactive diluents. Table 18.2 lists some of the diluents used. Before using only diluent, its compatibility with the total formulation should be checked.

Modifiers

Various types of modifiers are incorporated in adhesive formulation to impart flexibility, impart resistance, or other properties.

Flexibilizers

Flexibilizers is a nebulous term applied to epoxy adhesives. Slight flexibility that is needed for shock can be achieved by decreasing the crosslink density. This is done by adding a higher molecular weight resin, by increasing aliphatic amine concentration, or by decreasing anhydride concentration. For increased toughness and better overall mechanical properties, polyamide can be blended with an aromatic amine. The resultant system has higher heat stability, with about 6,000 psi tensile strength and 8,000 flexural fatty acids, epoxized oils, aliphatic, monomers, asphaltic compounds, polysulfides, styrene derivatives, hydrocarbon resins and glycols.

Various thermoplastics as well as thermosetting polymers including elastomers have been used to modify the properties of the cured epoxy resins. Combination of epoxies with nylons, phenolics and nitrile rubber is of major significance in case of film or tape adhesive. When a reinforcement or carrier is used, the adhesive is referred to as tape, whereas the self-supporting product is called film.

Fillers

Fillers are most common additives in epoxy resins. Their primary role is to reduce shrinkage, lower cost, lower coefficient of thermal expansion, greater heat resistance, better thermal conductivity, better electrical properties, fire retardance etc. Table 18.3 lists various fillers rienforcements and additives.

There are many exceptions. Talc fillers should not be used if the adhesive bond line will be exposed to acids; metalllic fillers should not be used if electrical insulation is necessary; Zinc dust contributes high adhesive shear strength under certain conditions.

Accelerators

Materials that accelerate any given epoxy resin/hardener cure do so by chemically leading the attack on the involved reaction groups in the resin or hardeners. In the case of amine cures this act is accomplished by proton donors, which facilitate opening the oxirange ring on the epoxy molecule. Such materials include phenols and alcohols and even water in minute traces. In the case of anhydride cures, materials that open the anhydride ring such as tertiary or cyclic amines and some metallic salts serve as accelerators.

Speciality Additives

Beyond the modification already discussed, speciality adhesives are used to impart particular properties to epoxy adhesives. For example, flame retardency is not inherent inconventional epoxy systems. Varying degrees of flame retardancy may be achieved by using halogen-containing epoxies, or epoxies curing with anhydride containing chlorine or bromine in their molecular structure. Halogen or phosphorous containing plasticizers, as well as small amounts of antimony trioxide are often used to improve fibre and flame retardancy.

Manufacture of Adhesives

A reaction vessel fitted with a heater, stirrer, thermometer and distilling head having a seperator providing return to the reactor of the lower layer is charged with a solution containing mole ratio of epichlorohydrin to bisphenol A of 10:1. The solution is heated to about 100°C and maintained at this temperature during addition of 1.90 moles of sodium hydroxide per mole of the bisphenol-A, caustic being introduced as a 40 per cent aqueous solution. Water and epichlorohydrin distilled from the reaction mixture are condensed in the head, and only epicholorohydrin layer returned to the reaction mixture. The rate of addition of caustic and rate of distilling keep the temperature at about 100°C so that the reaction mixture contains about 1.5 per cent water, the addition taking approximately two hours upon completing caustic addition. The bulk of the unreacted epicholorohydrin is distilled from the reaction mixture followed by application of vacuum at a pressure of 1mm llg and 160°C to remove residual epichlorohydrin. The resulting diglycidyl ether of bisphenol - A is a pale yellow liquid in which other components of adhesive are mixed one by one till homogenous mixture depending upon the type of adhesives is obtained.

Some important points to remember when selecting and using an epoxy adhesive are :

1. It is essential to inspect the materials to be joined and make sure they are clean and free from grease. Abrading or etching of the surface of the joint is recommended.
2. Choose an adhesive with a cure time and temperature that are practicable. For example, a hot setting adhesive that requires cure temperature of 140°C arid above cannot be used to bond wood, because wood carbonises at this temperature, and a cold or warm setting adhesive should therefore be used.
3. Cold setting adhesives give excellent bond strengths when cured at room temperature. A higher cure temperature, even a few degrees above room temperature, will, however, increase their bond strength

4. If the bonded assembly is designed to operate at temperatures above 100°C then choose less as its temperature is increased. Joints bonded with hot setting adhesives have the greatest resistance to heat.
5. Select an adhesive with a suitable viscosity. Adhesives of low viscosity are the simplest to apply and are recommended for large, closely fitting joint surfaces. Adhesives of high viscosity are more suitable when application is to vertical or overhead surfaces, or when the gap along the joint is of irregular width.
6. The thickness of the adhesive layer in the joint should be between 0.001 and 0.0008 in, but it may be greater if a paste adhesive is used.
7. When solvent containing adhesives are used, the solvent must be allowed to evaporate before the joint is assembled, this does not apply so strictly when one or both of the surfaces is porous, as the solvent is then absorbed.
8. Design the joint to take shear 01 tensile stress, not peel stress.
9. The relative coefficients of expansion of the material and the adhesive may be important if the adhesive is hot setting or the bonded assembly is designed to cooperate over a range of temperatures. Stresses in joints can be minimised by matching coefficients of expansionas as far as possible. The use of glass fabric carriers minimises the stresses set up in the joint during cure. Typical carriers, such as single layer of open scrim or plain-weave glass-cloth improve peel strength, give better strength retention above the HDT of the adhesive and tend to reduce the effect of stresses that result from the bonding of materials with dissimilar coefficients of expansion.
10. It is preferable to use an adhesive with a low modulus of elasticity if the bonded assembly is designed to withstand vibration or heavy impacts.
11. The strength of a composite joint will be that of its weakest part Fcr example, aluminium alloy bonded to steel will fail at 2000-3000 p.s.i. (14-21 MN/mm^2), whereas aluminium alloy bonded to polythene will fail at 100 p.s.i. (7 MN/mm^2) because the degree of adhesion even to treated polythene is less.

The strength of the adhesive bond is dependent on two factors, the adhesion of the adhesive to the materials being bonded and the cohesion of the adhesive itself. Bond strengdis are little influenced by glue line thickness (at least over the range 0.005-0.004 in) but are dependent upon :

1. The materials being bonded.
2. Surface preparation.
3. Formulation of the adhesive.
4. Cure schedule.
5. Temperature of the test.

Formulations

General Purpose Adhesives

Though, general purpose adhesives are obtained by formulating with amidoamines. Some typical adhesive formulations based on standard liquid repoxy resin (eq. wt. = 180-200) are as follows :

Formulation

Ingredients	Parts by Wt.
1. Epoxy resin	100
Polyamide resin	70
Filler or reinforcement	as desired

Formulation

Ingredients	Parts by Wt.
2. Epoxy	100
Polyamide resin	35
Tertiary amine	5
Filler or reinforcement	as desired

Formula 2 is faster curing adhesive than the formula 1 but is not as flexible.

Formulation

Ingredients	Parts by Wt.
3. Epoxy resin	100
Amido amine hardner	*175*
Filler or reinforcement	as desire

Flexible Adhesive

Formulation	Parts by Wt
4. Component I. Epoxy resin	100
Component II. polysulfide resin	175
Fumed silica	8
Tertiary amine	10

Cures overnight at room temperatue or 2 hr. at 71.1 °C

One Component Adhesive

Formulation

Ingredients	Parts by Wt.
5. Epoxy resin	100
Gellant	25
Alumina	25
Dicyandiamide	6

Cures 1 tol.5hratl76°C

Quick Cure Adhesive

Formulation

Ingredients	Parts by Wt.
6. Component I. Epoxy resin	100.0
Silica flour	60.0
Carbon black	0.1
Asbestos	3.0
Component II. Polymercaptan resin	75.0
Polyamide resin	12.0
Tertiary amine	8.0
Silica flour	50.0
Titanium dioxide	10.0
Asbestos	4.0

Gel time 8 min at 24°C

Metal-Metal Sealant

Formulation

Ingredients	**Parts by Wt.**
7. Epoxy Novolac resin (ENR)	12.0
Ethylene glycol esters of ENR	88.0
Phthalic anhydriede	43.0
Pyromellitic dianhydride	2.5
Silica	5.0
Aluminium powder	35.0
Asbestos	350.0
Pyridine	0.3
Curesl5minat205°C	

Room Temperature Curing

Formulation

Ingredients	**Parts by Wt.**
8. Component I. Epoxy novolac resin	40.0
Epoxy Novolac ester	40.0
Asbestos	20.0
Component II. Triethylene tetramine	12.0

Phenolic-eopxy Tape Adhesive

Formulation

Ingredients	**Parts by Wt.**
9 Phenolic resin (80% solids)	125.0
Phenolic resin (60% solids)	33.0
Epoxy resin	20.0
Ethyl acetate	20.0
I-Hydroxy-2-naphthoic acid	2.8
n-propyl gallate	1.4

Tape adhesive is prepared by impregenating the above liquid adhesive into glass mat and precuring at 132°C for 30 min. The adhesive can withstand temperature up to 237°C.

Tape Adhesive

Formulation

Ingredients	**Parts by Wt.**
10. Polyglycidyl ether of disproportionated rosin	80.0
Tetrahydrofuran	55.0
Epoxy resin	20.0
Polyvinyl formal	20.0
Aluminium dust	100.0
Diaminodiphenyl sulfone	24.0

The adhesive is deposited on glass cloth and dried at 93.3°C for 15 min. It takes 30 min. to cure at 240°C.

High Peel Strength Nylon-Epoxy Adhesive

Formulation

Ingredients	**Parts by Wt**
11. Epoxy resin	52
Nylon resin	75
Dicyandiamide	10

This is cured for 60 min at 162°C

Powder Adhesives

Formulation Ingredients	Parts by Wt
12. Epoxy rsin	100.0
Polymeric aromatic amine	11.0
Fumed silica	3.0
Red iron oxide	3.0

It takes 3 min to cure at 240°C

Concrete Adhesive

Formulation Ingredients	Parts by Wt.
13. Component I.	
Epoxy resin (Solid)	90
Epoxy resin (liquid)	60
Urea resin	20
Methyl Ethyl Ketone	95
Component II. olysulfide resin	100
Titanium dioxide	100
Carbon black	5
Methyl ethyl ketone	45
Tertiary amine	15

Glass Adhesive

Formulation Ingredients	Parts by Wt.
14. Epoxy resin	100.0
4-aminopropyl triethoxy silane	2.4
Modified aliphatic amine	20.0

Metal Glass Adhesive

Formulation Ingredients	Parts by Wt.
15. Epoxy resin	40
Polyamide	30
Titanium dioxide	22
Powdered quartz	8

Putty for Sealing

Formulation Ingredients	Parts by Wt.
16. Component I. Epoxy resin	100
Fumed silica	12
Alumina	200
Furfuryl alcohol	5
Polyethylene glycol	1
Component II. Polyamide resin	100
Modified aliphatic amine	12
Fumed silica	15
china clay	250

This is used together with an open-weave fabric which is wrapped around flame treated polyethylene that has been primed with epoxy-polyamide.

TABLE -18.1 - Characteristics Curing Agents

Curing Agent	Recommended Concentration range with Standard resin (Phr)	Curing temp (0"C) Range	Remarks
Diethylenetriamine	8-10	RT-150	Fast cure
Triethylenetriamine	10-13	RT-150	Fast cure
Diethylaminopropylamine	4-8	RT-150	Req. heat
Aminoethylpiperazine	20-23	RT-150	Req. heat
Adduct of epoxy resin + DETA	10-15	RT-150	Fast cure
M-phenylenediamine	13-14	60-200	Req. heat
Methylenedianiline	28-30	60-200	Req. heat
Diaminodiphenylsulfone	20-30	115-175	Req. heat
Dicyandiamide	4-6	150-175	Long RT
BF3-monoethylamine	2-4	150-175	Long RT
Polyamides	50-100	RT-100	Less Toxicity
Amidoamines	30-70	RT-100	Flexibility
Polysulfides	50-100	RT-100	Flexibilities
Polymercaptans	50-100	RT-75	Fast cure

TABLE 18.2- Diluent for Epoxy Rsin

Reactive	Non Reactive
Butyl glycidyl ether	Dibutyl phthalate
Allyl glycidyl ether	Dioctyl phthalate
Cresyl glycidyl ether	Pine Oil
Phenyl glycidyl ether	Coal tar
Styrene oxide	
1,4-Butanediol glycidyl ethe	Solvent type
Nonyl phenol	Ketones
Tri phenyl phosphite	Esters
	Glycol ethers
	Toluene
	Butyl Alcohols

TABLE -18.3- List of Various Fillers Reinforcement and Addtives

Property Improved	Fillers, Reinforcements & Additives
Mechanical strength	Asbestos, glass fibres, alumina, silica.
Specific strength or modulus (higher)	Graphite fibre, boron fibre.
Specific gravity (lower) shrinkage and coefficient of thermal expansion (lower)	Hollow microspheres Alumina, silica quartz, calcium carbonate.
Heat-resistance (higher)	Asbestos, mica, glass flakes, silica.
Thermal conductivity (higher)	Metal powder, quartz, alumina.
Electrical conductivity (higher)	Copper or silver powder, graphite.
Are resistant and dielectric strength.	Mica, hydrated alumina, silica.
Cost (lower)	Sand, calcium carbonate
Fire retardance	Antimony oxide
Thixotropy	Colloidal silica, modified clays
Adhesion	Silane coupling agents.

19.

Phenolic Resin Adhesive

Introduction

Phenolic resins are the reaction products of phenol or substituted phenols with formaldehyde. An unlimited variety of resins are possible depending on; (1) the choice of phenol; (2) The phenol: formaldehyde molar ratio; (3) the type and amount of catalyst used; (4) the time and temperature of the reaction.

Resole Resin

The active positions on the phenol molecule are the two ortho and one para positions.When there is more than one mole of phenol in the presence of an alkaline catalyst, resole is formed. The amount of heat determines the final form of product, e.g., whether the resin is of low viscosity, water soluble liquid or a grindable solid. If the reaction is carried too far, the resole can gel.Therefore the reaction is always conducted under carefully controlled conditions of time, terperature, pH and mole ratio of formaldehyde to phenol.

Novolac Resins

The reaction of one mole of phenol with less than one mole of formaldehyde, under acid conditions, results in a novolac resin. Novolac resin contains methylene links and are phenol terminated. Methylol and methylene ester groups that are present in resole resins are absent in a novolac.Therefore, this type of resin is incapable of further reaction without the addition of more formaldehyde. This is accomplished by the addition of hexamethylene tetramine, which is known as "hexa".Hexa makes the non-heat-reactive thermoplastic novolac capable of reacting under heat to a cross linked advantage that novolac resins have over resoles is that no water of reaction is evolved during cure with hexa, Molecular weight of phenolic novolacs are in the 500-900 range.

Manufacture

A typical phenolic resin is made by a batch process in a jacketed stainless steel reaction kettle, equipped with anchor type agitator and condenser.Molten phenol and formaldehyde (37-40%) are charged into the kettle and agitation begin. For a novolac, an acid catalyst is added and steam is introduced into the jacket to heat the batch with atmospheric reflux. The reaction is continued for 3-6 hrs at 100°C. The reaction time is dependent upon pH and phenol: formaldehyde mole ratio. Following the reaction period, the batch is dehydrated under atmospheric pressure and than vacuum. If the resin is to be solid in solution, the solvent is slowly added to the molten resin in the still, cooled by refluxing and discharged into drums. Most of the solid resins discharged into pans are pulverized and blended with hexa before packaging.

To make resole resin, an alkaline catalyst such as sodium hydroxide is added to the phenol and formaldehyde before heating the batch to 80-100°C. Reaction times are generally 1-3 hr. Since resole resin is capable of gelling in the still, dehydration temperature is kept below 105°C.By the application of vacuum solid resoles are discharged into resin coolers. The low molecular weight, water soluble resins are finished at as low a temperature as possible, usually about 50°C, whereas the less reactive para-substituted resoles can be finished at temperature as high as 120°C.

Applications and Formulations

Phenolic adhesives are used in bonded abrasives and coated abrasives in which they are used as binder adhesives as shown below.

1. Cold Pressed Coarse Abrasive Snagging Wheel Test Formulations:

Ingredients	Foundry	Steel-Billet
	Part by Weight	
Aluminium oxide	840.00	780.00
Powdered phenolic resin (two step)	60.00	120.00
Cryolite	70.00	97.00
Liquid phenolic resin (one step)	30.00	—
Furfural/cresylic acid	—	25.00
Calcium oxide	—	3.00
Creosote oil	5.00	5.00
Cold pressed density (g/cc)	2.64	2.93

2. Cold Pressed Medium Abrasive General Purpose Test Formulation:

Ingredients	Part by Weight	
Aluminium oxide	1050.00	1050.00
Powder phenolic resin (two step)	130.00	150.00
Liquid phenolic resin (one step)	20.00	—
Furfural/cresylic acid	—	18.00
Cold pressed density (g/cc)	2.64	2.64

3. Hot Pressed Coarse Abrasive Snagging Wheel Test Formulation :

Ingredients	Part by Weight	
Aluminium oxide	780.00	—
Powdered phenolic resin (two step)	120.00	—
Cryolit	97.00	—
Calcium oxide	3.00	—
Creosote oil	12.00	—
Hot-pressed density	3.03	—

Contact Adhesives

Phenolic resins are used in polychloroprene and nitrile contact adhesives as tackifiers and adhesion promoters. Phenolic resin contribute the following properties to polychloroprene adhesives.

(1) Improved adhesion to metals, glass and other rigid and nonporous substrates.
(2) Improved cohesive strength.
(3) Inhibition of HC1 formation in the ageing of polychloroprene.
(4) Improved viscosity stability.

In addition to above, phenolics contribute specific properties such as elevated temperature performance, flocculation resistance, and increased tack time. Following table lists typical performance properties of adhesives based on polycholoroprene adhesives.

Formulation: Typical Performance of Phenolic Resin as Contact Adhesive

Ingredient	Part by weight	
Polychloroprene Grade I	100	100
Antioxidant	22	2
Phenolic resin	45	45
MgO	48	8
ZnO	55	5
Water	11	1
Toluene	115	160
Hexane	115	160
Ethyl acetate	115	160
Tack time, min	16	25
Properties		
Peel strength,Kg/in		
Canvas/canvas at 30°C		
Bond aged 1 week	35	35
Bond aged 3 weeks	45	45
Canvas/steel at 30°C		
Bond aged 1 week	25	20
Bond aged 3 weeks	30	30

Adhesive Compounding

There are two methods in general used for compounding polychloroprene/phenolic adhesives.The first method involves masticating the rubber on a two roll mill to reduce crystallinity and improve solubility. The time of milling and degree of shear are frequently used to control adhesive viscosity. The magnesium oxide and zinc oxide are compounded into the rubber on an unheated mill.The magnesium oxide is always added before zinc oxide to preclude premature curing of the rubber.The antioxidant is also added.The compounded rubber is then dissolved with the resin in the solvent blend in a cement tub.

Compounders who do not have milling equipment use the slurry method for adhesive preparation.This method consists of simply adding of resin, pigments and antioxidants togedier with the unmilled rubber to the solvent blend in the cement tub. Adhesives made from unmilled rubber will be more viscous arid therefore, are usually produced at lower solid content.They will also have higher initial cohesive strength. Adhesives from milled polymer are however uniform and retain their uniformity upon ageing.

Some commercial applications (e.g. construction) require the use of non flammable solvent. When this is the case, 1,1,1 trichloroethane can be used successfully as the sole solvent.

Comparision of 1,1,1-Trichloro ethane and Toluene Solvent System

Particulars	1,1,1-trichloroethane System	Toluene System
Polychloroprene	100	100
Antioxidant	2	2
MgO	4	4
Phenolic resin	45	45
Phenolic resin	45	45
MgO	4	4
Water	1	1
1,1,1-trichloro ethane513	513	-
Toluene	-	513
Total solid = 23.8% by weight		
Adhesive properties:		
Tack time, min		
Peel strength, Kg / in	16	25
Canvas/canvas at 25°C		
Bond aged 1 week	38	40
Bond aged 3 week	50	45
Canvas/steel at 25°C		
Bond aged 1 week	15	16
Bond aged 3 week	36	25
Flocculation at 20% solids	none	none

Nitrile/Phenolic Contact Adhesives

Nitrile/phenolic contact adhesives are used in a variety of non structural applications. They show excellent oil resistance. A typical formulation is shown below:

Ingredients	Parts by Weight
Nitrile rubber	15
Novolac resin	15
Acetone	70
Total:	100

Peel strength Kg/in. Canvas/Canvas		
Bonding Conditions		
Room temperature	18	12
15 min at 75°C and 300 psi	35	17
15 min at 100°C and 300 psi	35	24
5 min at 120°C and 300 psi	35	24

Structural Adhesive

Phenolic resins are used in structural adhesives not as tackifiers, but for their strength, durability and heat resistance. They are used for bonding air craft structures, honey comb, brake lining to brake shoes, clutch facings, automatic transmission discs and curtain wall construction. Following table shows some typical examples.

Formulation Ingredients	Part By Weight		
	1	2	3
Nitrile rubber	15	15.0	15.0
Novolac hexa	15	15.0	15.0
Acetone	70	70.0	70.0
A1000 silane	—	0.3	—
A 189 silane	—	—	0.3
Lap shear strength (psi)			
30°C	1450	2350.0	3120.0
60°C	185	420.0	375.0
125°C	110	250.0	360.0

Vinyl/Phenolic

Vinyl formal, vinyl acetal, and vinyl butyral may be combined with phenolic resin to produce tough structural adhesives with good impact strength, resistance to oil and aromatic fuels and good salt spray and weathering resistance. The presence of hydroxyl groups on the vinyl chain makes it likely that crosslinking occurs between the phenolic resole resin and hydroxyl groups during elevated temperature cure. A typical formula is shown below :

Formulation Ingredients	Parts by Weight
Poly vinyl butyral	18
Phenolic resin	30
Toluene	16
Ethanol	36

Epoxy/Phenolic

Combination of epoxy and phenolic resins provide structural adhesives with superior high temperature resistance to the elastomer modified adhesives. Both novolac and resole formulation for this adhesive are as follows :

Formulation Ingredients	Parts by Weight
Phenolic resin	100.0
Epoxy resin	20.0
Ethyl acetate	20.0
Hexa	4.0
n-propyl gallate	8.8

Adhesive bonds prepared with this formulation exhibit good salt spray resistance. One drawback of the above formulation is its poor filleting action when used to prepare honeycomb cores in sandwich constructions. A formula that provides improves flow and filleting action is as follows:

Formulation

Ingredients	**Parts by Weight**
Phenolic resin (solid)	125.0
Phenolic resin (liquid)	33.0
Epoxy resin	20.0
Ethyl acetate	20.0
l-Hydroxy-2-napthoic acid	2.8
n-propyl gallate	1.4

Hot Melt Adhesives

Phenolic resins play a small but significant role in the formulation of hot-melt adhesives. Several starting formulations are shown below.

Hot Melt Vinyl Film to Wood Laminating Adhesives

Formulation

Ingredients	**Parts by Weight**
EVA copolymer	40.0
Phenolic resin	25.0
Hydrogenated resin ester	15.0
Wax	20.0
Antioxidant	0.1

Heat Resistant Hot-Melt Adhesives

Formulation

Ingredients	**Parts by Weight**
EVA copolymer	45.0
Phenolic resin	30.0
Polyterpene resin	10.0
Wax	15.0
Antioxidant	0.1

Hot - Melt Adhesives for Polystyrene

Formulation

Ingredients	**Parts by Weight**
EVA copolymer	40.0
Phenolic resin	15.0
Hydrogenated resin ester	25.0
Wax	20.0
Antioxidant	0.1

Melt Adhesives for Polyethylene

Ingredients	**Parts by Weight**
EVA copolymer	40.0
Phenolic resin	15.0
Polyterpene resins	12.0

Silica	12.0
Additive	20.0
Antioxidant	0.1

Pressure Sensitive Adhesives : (PSA)

Phenolic resins are one type among many that are useful as tackifiers for elastomers in the manufacture of PSA.The most familiar use of PSA is in the manufacture of flexible tape that has found innumerable uses in the home and in the industry. High molecular weight polyvinyl ethyl ether imparts basic cohesive strength whereas low molecular weight polyvinyl ethyl ether serves as a plasticizer for improving tack and low temperature flexibility. The type of phenolic resin found useful is para-tertiary butyl-formaldehyde resole. A recommended formulation is shown below.

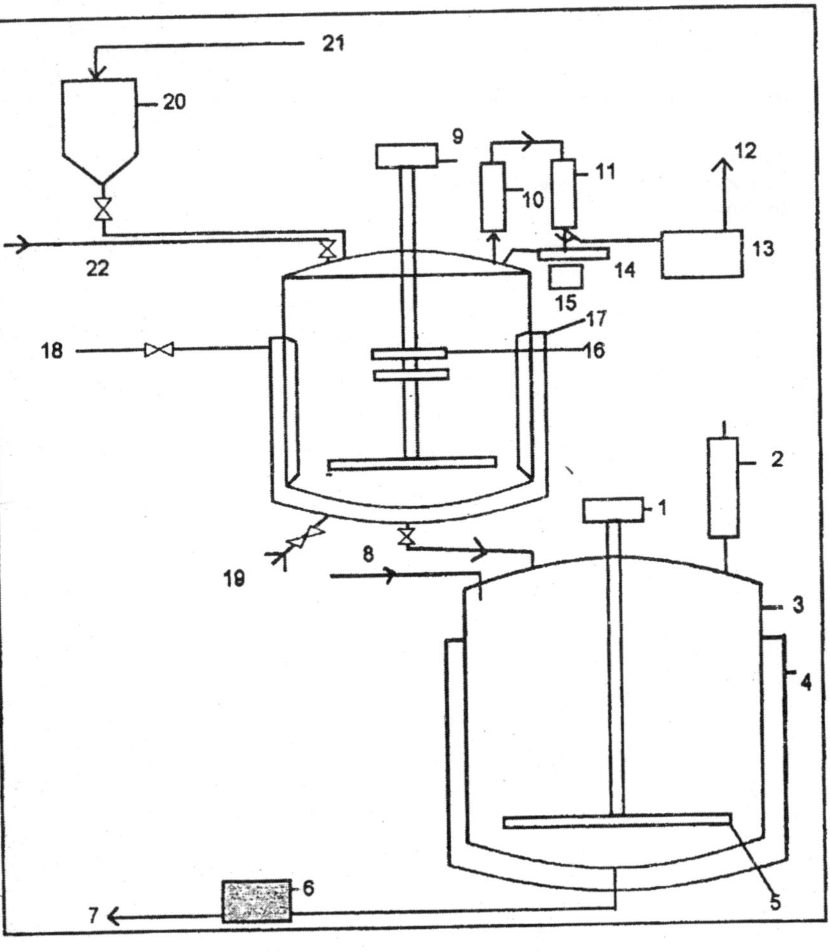

FIG : 19.1 - Systematic Diagram of Typical P/F Resin and Adhesive Processing Plant:

1. Motor
2. Condenser
3. Adhesive Kettle
4. Steam or Water Jacket
5. Agitator
6. Filter
7. To Storage
8. Inert Gas Line
9. Motor (Resin Kettle)
10. Partial Condenser
11. Total Condense
12 Vent
13 Scrubber
14 Decanter
15 Water Receiver
16 Foam Depresser
17 Baffle Plate
18 Dowtherm Vapour
19 Dowtherm Liquid
20 Weigh Tank
21 Raw Material Inventory
22 Raw Material Feeding

Clear Laminating PSA

Ingredients	**Parts by Weight**
Polyvinyl ethyl ether (high m^{2}ol.wt)	4.50
Polyvinyl ethyl ether (low mol.wt)	13.50
Phenolic resin	7.20
Plasticizer	0.01
Hydrogenated methyl ester of rosin	4.80
Toluene	27.50
MEK	27.50
Hexane	18.00

20.

Polychloroprene Adhesives: Solvent and Latex

Introduction

Polychloroprenes, is the basis for one of the largest and most important groups of rubber adhesives. Polychloroprene was at disadvantage for adhesives for several reasons namely; (1) High price;(2) aromatic solution required is costly; (3) it requires a higher solid level than natural rubber cements. During World War II, however, a critical shortage of natural rubber developed. At the start of the war polychloroprene is the only rubber available for adhesives.

Types of Polychloroprene

Polymer structure of commercial polychloroprene is determined by the manner in which the chloroprene monomer, 2 chloro-l,3-butadiene reacts with the growing polymer chain.Upon polymerization the chloroprene moiety may take any of four isomeric forms as shown in Table -1.Rapid bond strength development of contact adhesive is associated with crystallization resulting from a very high level of trans configuration in which there are no side groups bulkier than the chlorine atom.

Components	Parts By Weight						
	1	2	3	4	5	6	7
Polychloroprene	100	100	100	100	100	100	100
Phenolic resin	46	39	50	-	-	-	-
Pentaester gum	-	-	-	8	50	39	25
Hydrocarbon resin	-	-	-	-	-	7	25
Rosin	-	-	-	42	-	-	-
Chlorinated Rubber	-	-	17	-	-	-	-
Dioctyl phthalate	-	-	-	-	-	-	2
Antioxidant	2	2	2	2	2	2	2
Toluene	417	417	-	542	542	466	606
Benzene	-	-	374	-	-	-	-
Hexane	-	57	217	-	-	-	-
Methyl ethyl ketone	57	-	-	-	-	-	-

Applications and Formulations

Polychloroprene adhesives enjoy a pre-eminent position as an elastomeric binder at the expense of other less costly materials, e.g. natural rubber and SBR, primarily because of early bond strength development, bonding range, high ultimate strength and creep resistance, adhesion to many surfaces, durability, flexibility, chemical resistance and resistance to burning. A typical contact adhesive formulation is shown below :

The major uses of the fast crystallizing types are to adhere decorative laminates and laminated panels for curtain walls and partitions, automotive trim and a host of industrial applications. The examples of a typical fast crystallizing formulations as well a general purpose industrial adhesives are shown below:

Formulation	Decorative Laminates	General Purpose
Components		**Parts by Wt.**
Polychloroprene	100	100
Magnesium oxide	5	5
Zinc oxide	2	2
Antioxidant	1	1
Phenolic resin	45	45
Terpene phenolic rosin	-	20
Hexane	275	277
Acetone	215	138
Methyl ethyl ketone	-	138
Toluene	122	138
%Solids	20	20

Mastic Compounds	Parts by wt.
Polychloroprene	100
Antioxidant	2
Magnesium oxide	4
$CaCO_5$	100
Zinc oxide	5
Ethylene glycol	20
T-butyl phenolic resin	15
Hexane	
Toluene	by weight to 65%
MEK	

Sprayable Formulation

To achieve maximum sprayability characteristics, a high shear mixer is suggested.

Formulation

Ingredients		Parts by Wt.
Polychloroprene	100	100
Antioxidant	2	2
Magnesium oxide	8	8
Zinc oxide	5	5
Milled stock	115	115
t-butyl phenolic resin	40	40
Water	2	2
Ethyl acetate	-	300

n-propyl acetate	115	340
Di-isobutyl ketone	620	-

Sprayable Contact Adhesive

Formulation

Ingredients	Parts by Wt.
Polychloroprene	100
Heptane	150
Thiuram	0.5
Accelerator	0.5
To above dispersion add the following	
t-butyl phenolic resin	40
Tacldfier	0.20
MgO	2
ZnO	4
Antioxidant	2
Water	1

The effect of compounding and processing variables on polychloroprene adhesives are.

Tertiary butyl phenolic resins provide best balance of adhesive properties and solution viscosity stability. Increased resin levels are particularly effective in compounds containing high level of magnesium oxide and formulated for maximum heat resistance

Increasing magnesium oxide content markedly increases elevated cohesive strength. Polar solvents are required to reduce the stringiness of adhesive and to improve its viscosity and stability. Metal oxide serves as that of an acid acceptor, and with phenolic resin it forms resinous products which do not melt and give better heat resistance. Antioxidants help in order to achieve the excellent long term ageing propertiers. Fillers are used primarily to reduce cost. The heat resistance of polychloroprene cements can be increased by compounding with a variety of curing agents. Solvents effect the rate of strength development, open time, cost, adhesion, application properties, solution viscosity and to some degree ultimate strength.

Applications

Four important applications for polychloroprene contact adhesives are bonding of high pressure plastic laminates, automotive adhesives, shoe adhesives and adhesives for the construction of industry.

Shoes have long been a major consumer of these adhesives, particularly for the permanent attaching shoe soles. The original adhesives for the soles attaching were based on nitrocllulose, but polychloroprene's rapid development of bond strength has since allowed it to dominate this field.

Automotive uses for these adhesives also go back to many years and include such things as adhering sponge insulation strips to doors and trunk hood lids and tops to roofs.

About one half of high pressure plastic laminates are adherend to substrates such as wood, metal, stone etc. with polychloroprence contact adhesives.

Polychloroprene Latex Adhesive Formulation :

	Parts By Weight		
Ingredients	**Contact**	**Mastic**	**Foil**
Latex I	100	—	—
Latex II	—	100	—
Latex III	—	—	100
Zinc oxide	10	15	15
Antioxidant	2	2	2
Terpene-phenolic resin	85	—	—
Liquid terpene resin	50	—	—
Ester gum	—	75	—
Casein	—	—	50
Methyl cellulose	—	4	—
Defoaming agent	—	—	2
Stabilizer/surfactant	2	2	2

Latex Based Contact Adhesives : Foam to Wood

Ingredient	**Parts By Weight**		
Latex I	100.0	—	—
Latex II	—	100.0	—
Latex III	—	—	100.0
Zinc oxide	5.0	5.0	5.0
Antioxidant	2.0	2.0	2.0
Phenolic resin	87.5	87.5	—
Coumarone-indene resin	50.0	50.0	—

TABLE-I
MOLECULAR STRUCTURE OF CHLOROPRENE
(2 - CHLOROBUTADIENCE -1,3) $H_2C = CHCCL= CH_2$

Type of addition	Formula	Comments
Trans 1,4	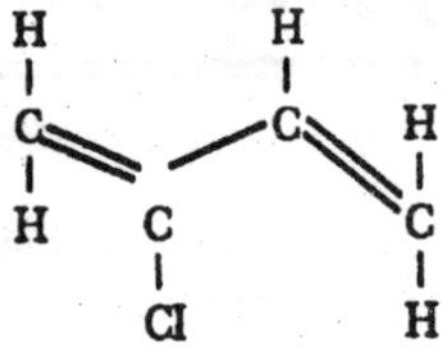	increase crystallization
Cis-1,4	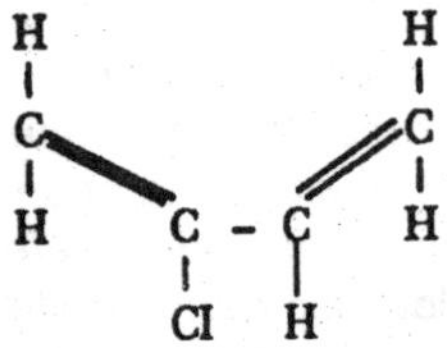	decrease crystallization
1,2	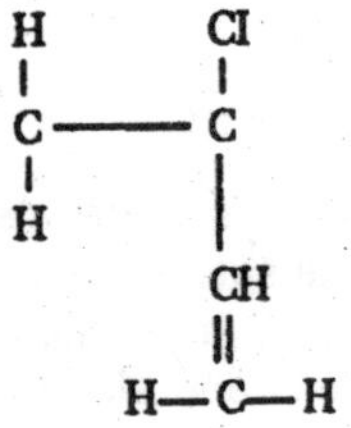	active sites for vulcanization. (decrease crystallization)
3,4	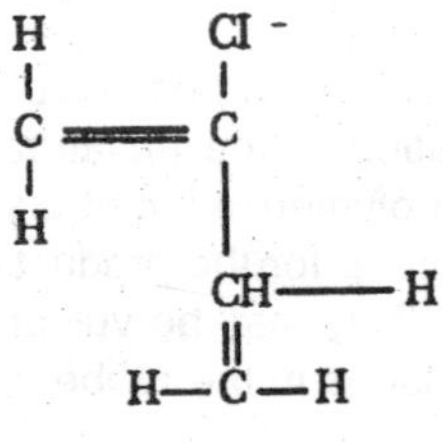	decrease crystallization

21.

Polyester Adhesives

Introduction

Polyesters are thermosetting and thermoplastic resins for various applications. They may be saturated or unsaturated. Due to high cost they are used with other resins for the application of adhesives.

Linear Polycarbonates

A very recent development in the field of condensation polymers has been the synthesis of organic polycarbonates when Bishphenol-A is reacted with phosgene in the presence of caustic soda or an organic base, a polycarbonate is formed. The polycarbonates made thus far are colourless, transparent solids. They are reported to have low gas permeabilities and good electrical and mechanical properties. Further, the impact strength is reported to be unusually high. Current interest is in producing adhesives, particularly for electrical insulating uses.

Polymerized Oils

Useful vulcanizable type poleyster materials are derived from polymerized drying oils. When three points of unsaturation are present in the molecule, three dimensional polymers are formed as insoluble, coherent masses. They occur in the drying of linseed and other oils and also in the preparation of factice. The term factice (often called "rubber substitute") is used for certain semielastic materials which are mixed with rubber during adhesive manufacture to lower the cost of production.

Thermal treatment of natural drying oils involves the creation of polybasic esters by addition polymerization of the unsaturated fatty acids radicals. The acids and esters obtained by polymerization of drying oils, may since then contain more than one carboxyl group for the production of unsaturated polyesters by condensation with glycols. They may be vulcanized by heating with sulphur and accelerators. Their main use is in the rubber base adhesives.

Alkyd Resins

Alkyd resin is an unsaturated polyester resin. They are the reaction products of glycerol and phthalic anhydride modified with drying, semidrying or nondrying oils. Alkyds form the non-drying oils combined with aminoplasts, silicone resins or cellulose nitrate lacquers as plasticizers which ultimately find its use in adhesives. Pure nondrying and semidrying oil modified alkyds are used in sealants, putties and caulking compounds because of its excellent adhesion, good resistance to heat, light and chemicals. Alkyds of drying oik are used in pressure senstitive adhesives which show excellent bonding with linoleum, leather, fabrics and rubber.

Unsaturated Polyester Adhesives

In recent years a number of unsaturated polyester resins have been produced industrially which possess a number of advantages compared with ususal types of thermosetting resins, such as alkyds, the phenoplasts and the aminoplasts. These advantages are all based on the feet that the curing of these unsaturated polyester resins is due to a polymerization reaction which causes cross linking among the individual linear polymer chains. No by-product is formed during the reaction. It is perhaps suitable to call the ester portion a linear, unsaturated polyster and the combination of the unsaturated ester and the unsaturated vinyl type monomer, i.e., the final product, an unsaturated polyester resin.

Unsaturated polyester resin are the reaction products of a dibasic unsaturated acid and a glycol. A highly reactive polyester resin may be produced by reactions of maleic anhydride and 1,2 propylene glycol, carbon dioxide is blown into solution to remove water of reaction and to drive out oxygen of the air. The substitution of phthalic anhydride for maleic anhydride reduces unsaturation and increases aromaticity and compatibility with styrene, 1 mole maleic anhydride, 1 mole phthalic anhydride and 2.2 moles of propylene glycol gives a polyester of medium unsaturation. At least 16% of styrene is necessary to get good results as crosslinking agent. Usually 0.015% by weight hydroquinone is added as inhibitor.

Cured unsaturated polyester adhesives have good durability and resistance to weather, and organic solvents, but have poor resistance to fire. Polyester resin is usually dissolved in an unsaturated solvent before use. A typical example is shown below.

Adhesives for Flexible Printed Circuit

In recent years, with the development of electronic and electric instrument industry, reduction in size and weight has been required and a printed circuit board having light and flexible plastic film as an insulation base board has been desired. However, these plastic films are poor in surface'activity, and accordingly, it is very difficult to obtain an adhesion to a metal foil strong enough to satisfy requirements for a printed circuit The following composition is excellent in flow property and rapid curability.

In MEK were dissolved 100 parts by weight polyester resin (ethylene glycol, terephthalic acid and sebacic acid in 1:0.5:03) 10 parts epoxy resin, 4 parts triphenyl methane triisocyanate, 1 part of copolymer (maleic anhydride : dimethyl styrene 1:1) 2 parts heptyl alcohol to prepare an adhesive.

Allyl Eater Adhesives

A number of allyl esters have been proved useful because of readiness with which they form fluid, soluble partial polymers. Among these compounds are diethylene glycol, bis (allyl carbonate), diallyl maleate, diallyl fuinarate and diallyl benzene phosphonate. Quite recendy, another allyl compound, triallyl cyanurate, has shown tremendous heat distortion temperature in combination with unsaturated polyesters. They are used mainly in adhesives for gluing metals and optical components.

22.

Polythyleneimine in Adhesives

Inroduction

Ethyleneimine monomer is synthesized by ethylene dichloride and ammonia.Polyethyleneimine (PEI) is a highly branched polymine produced by the acid catalyzed polymerization of the monomer. The polymer segments, with two carbons per nitrogen , are randomly distributed in the approximate ratio of one primary amino nitrogen to secondary amino nitrogens on tertiary amino nitrogen.

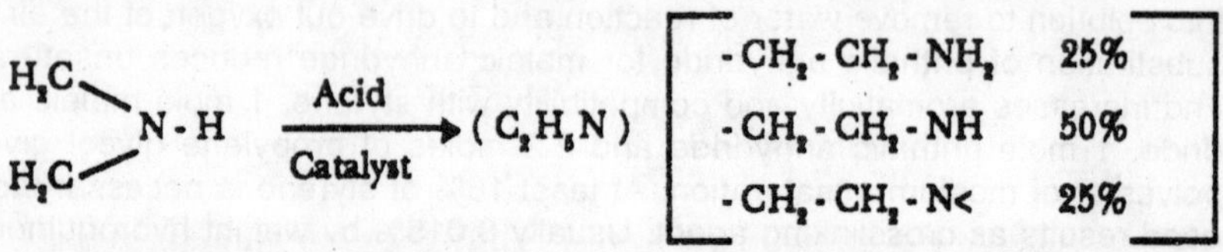

This distribution gives rise to what is believed to be a spheriod shaped molecule which is composed of many branched segments tertiary amino nitrogen as branching sites and primary amino nitrogens as terminal groups. The primary and secondary amino nitrogens comprise reaction sites whereby PET can be conveniently modified.

When PEI is contacted with water, the amino nitrogens react to form positively charged nitrogens in the same manner as simple amino. (hereby yielding alkaline solutions. Since PEI is composed of many nitrogens per molecule. The average number of charges per molecule, charge density, can be determined from the position of the equilibrium. The addition of acid will increase the charge density and addition of base will decrease it. Thus polyethyleheimine can function as a cationic polyelectrolyte and is strongly attracted to anionically charged colloids and surfaces. The PEI polymers very in molecular weight from 300 to 100,000.

The low molecular weight polymers are anhydrous whereas the high molecular PEI are produced with water as a solvent As a chemical polymeric intermediate, it can undergo reactions with ethylene oxide, chloroacetic acid, acrylic acid, urea, methyl chloride, epichlorohydrin, stearic acid etc.

Applications

PEI is an adhesive by virtue of its attractiveness for electronegative substances as well as its reactivity. It provides improved action through electrostatic bonds, improved bonding on nonpolar films, improved water resistants and chemical modification and introduction of new functional groups into the system. PEI often functions as a tie coat, used to bond together dissimilar substrates.

General Adhesives

Polyethyleneimine applied to high tenacity rayon improves the bonding of polyvinyl chloride coatings, rubber and other plastics. Pressure sensitive adhesives were prepared by adding a polyalkylene polyamine to a solution of either polyvinyl alcohol or polyvinyl pyrrolidone. PEI was cited as a component with polyvinyl lactom in a water or a water miscible solvent solution.

An epoxy adhesive containing butyl phthalate and PEI has been recently described. Another type of adhesive is prepared from a polyalkylene polyamine and a chlorinated natural or synthetic rubber elastomer. A varnish composition which inculdes PEI has been patented. A gypsum board and a magneside base cement particle board binder for foundry moulding compositions has been patented. A ceramic tile adhesive has been described in which an acrylated polyalkylene polyamine is an integral part of the formulation. An additive prepared from abony fat and a polyalkylene polyamine improves the adherene of bitumen compounds to damp or wet mineral aggregates. PEI has been used to precoat glass bottles and glass stands.

Tie Coat Adhesives

Regenerated cellulose was found to have improved adhesion to various plastic laminates if first treated with PEI. Such laminates and coatings include vinyl ; resins ; polyolefins, thermoplastics resins, and lacquers. PEI has been used commercially to bond polyester tyre cord to rubber. Adhesion of polyolefins to cellulose fibres and paper is basically poor which is improved greatly by pretreatment with PEI. PEI is now used as a primer for milk carton board stock which is subsequently laminated with polyethylene. PEI has been proven effective for improving the adhesion to polyethylene coatings to aluminium foil, polyester film, uncoated cellophane, nitrocellulose coated cellophane and saran film.

PEI has been found effective for a variety of paper and board stocks , both sized and plain, including glassine and smooth pouch papers.

23.

Polysulfide Sealants and Adhesives

Introduction

Polysulfide Sealants

Sealants based on polysulfide liquid polymers have found wide acceptance in a number of applications requiring a flexible, adhering, chemically resistant composition of matter.

Chemistry

The general preparation of polysulfide liquid polymers involves first the reaction of bischloroethyl formal with a sodium polysulfide solution containing specific emulsifying and nucleating agent as shown below :

$$nClC_s\,H_4\,OCH_2\,OC_8\,H_4\,Cl + nNa_2S\,2.25$$
$$(-\,C_sH_4OCH_8OC_2H_4S2.25)n + 2n\,NaCl.$$

The sulfur is present as a mixture of disulfide and trisulfide. In the first step, the high molecular weight polymer is split into segments which are simultaneously terminated by mercaptan groups as shown below:

$$RSSR + NaSH + NaHSO_3 \longrightarrow 2\,RSH + Na_2\,S_2O_2$$

The mercaptan terminated liquid polymers are readily polymerized to elastomeric solids by the use of active oxidizing agents. Lead dioxide has been the most widely used in sealant applications.The general reactions are as follows:

$$2\,RSH + PbO_2\,2 \qquad -RSSR- + PbO + H_2O$$
$$2\,RSH + PbO \qquad -RSPbRS + H_2O$$
$$RSPbSr + S \qquad -RSSR\_- + PbS$$

$$RSPbR \xrightarrow{\text{heat}} RSR + PbS$$

$$RSPbSR \xrightarrow{[O]} RSSR + PbO$$

Compounding

In order to obtain the optimum properties, a polysulfide sealant has to be specifically formulated to best meet the requirements at hand. Working life has to be adjusted to fall within the desired range.

Curing Agent

Although a number of curing agents have been found for the polysulfide liquid polymers, lead dioxide has been the most widely used for sealants due to its high reactivity, availability and reasonable cost Formulation for lead oxide pastes is shown in the following :

Lead dioxide accelerator paste

Formulation

Ingredients	Parts By Weight
Lead dioxide	55
Stearic acid	7
Accelerator	20
Toluene	20

Retarder

The oxidation and reaction of thiol groups is accelerated in an alkaline environment and retarded in an acidic environment; consequently, pH plays a major part in cure rate.A number of acidic retarders have been evaluated for lead peroxides, the two most effective being stearic acid and lead stearate.

Reinforcement

Most uses for liquid polymers require reinforcing fillers which both strengthen the physical properties and reduce the cost of the compound; further more fillers are used to impart thixotropy and colour to the sealant compound.

Adhesion Additives

A number of adhesion additives have been evaluated for the adhesion to glass, aluminium and steel in the presence of water, cold and heat. They are mainly phenolic resins and liquid epoxy resins.

Primers

The use of primers may be necessary on occasion when certain curing agent are too sensitive. Few primer formulations are shown below :

Formulation

Ingredients	Parts By Weight
(1) Silicone tetrahydrate	3.35
Tetrabutyl titanate	1.15
Isopropanol	45.00
(2) Chlorinated rubber	20.00
Toluene	30.00
Silicone tetrahydrate	2.50

Improved Heat Resistance

When maximum retention of physical properties after heat ageing is desired, selection of curing agent becomes a prime factor after selection of the proper reinforcing agent.

Manganese oxide and ammonium dichromate as well as specifically formulated compound based on cumene hydroperoxide give cured sealants having improved heat resistance.The resultant by-products of the oxidizing agents used also have a considerable effect on heat ageing properties.Typical formulations, which exhibit improved heat resistance are givien in the following :-

Formulations

Component	Part	Part	Part
Polysulfide polymer	100.0	100.0	100.0
TiO_2—	50.0	—	—
Sulfur	0.1	—	—
$(NH_4)_2Cr_20_7$	6.0	—	—
DMF	14.0	—	—
Carbon	40.0	—	—
Stearic acid	1.0	—	—
Phenolic resin	5.0	—	—
Manganese dioxide	—	2.0	—
Dinitrobenzene	—	0.5	—
Silica	—	—	20.0
Ethyl hydroxy ethyl cellulose	—	—	1.2
MgO	—	—	4.0
Cumen hydroperoxide-	—	6.5	—
Maleic anhydride	—	—	0.5

The use of non black reinforcing agents gives composition having very satisfactory electrical resistant properties.

One Part Sealant

The principal advantage of one part sealant is the elimination of mixing before application of sealant. However, since the sealant is dependent on moisture and temperature for cure, it may require 4 to 6 weeks before complete cure, during the cold season.This may present a problem where excessive movement can occur.The prefered curing agents used for one part sealants are zinc peroxide or calcium peroxide.

Applications

Sealants for Air Craft Industry

Polysulfide sealants are used for sealing and repairing of integral fuel tanks and fuel cell cavities.The sealant is further required to prevent leakage in spite of temperature variation from 200°C to 600°C.

Sealants for Electrical Potting

Polysulfide sealants formulated with proper reinforcing fillers have good electrically resistant properties over wide temperature ranges. These sealants are used to pot electrical connectors and assemblies where they absorb considerable mechanical vibrations. Their low water absorption properties prevent any possible shorting, which is another advantage.

House Repair Compounds

This sealant covers the requirements in sealing methyl methacrylate sheets into aluminium window assemblies.The requirements are adhesion of sealant to the acrylate sheet and aluminium frame under various exposure environments and the property of non crazing.The sealant must be flexible over a wide temperature range and perform over a pressure gradient It also finds its use for repairing large oil suction and discharge lose covers. Some of the formulations are shown below:

Recommened Strating Formulations

Ingredient	Parts By Weight				
	A	B	C	D	E
Part (A)					
Polysulfide polymer	100.0	100.0	100.0	100.0	100.0
Stearic acid	1.0	1.0	1.0	1.0	1.0
Phenolic resin	5.0	—	—	—	—
Calcium carbonate	—	25.0	—	—	—
TiO_2	—	10.0	10.0	—	—
Lithopone	—	30.0	90.0	50	—
Kenflex	—	—	—	15.0	—
Sterling	—	—	—	—	10.0
Sulphur	—	—	—	—	0.15
Butylphthyl butyl glucolate	—	25.0	40	—	—
Part (B)					
Accelerator	15.0	15.0	15.0	15.0	15.0
PbO_2	—	—	—	—	13.8
Dibutyl phthalate	—	—	—	—	—
Recommended use	Aircraft Sealants	Building Sealants	Casting Sealants	Potting Seal	Deck

Adhesives from Polysulfide Liquid Polymer Epoxy Resin Reactions

In formulations developed for adhesives, the epoxy resin is the major component. However, modification of the epoxy resin with polysulfide liquid polymers gives compositions which in many cases have unique physical and chemical properties.This reaction between polysulfide liquid polymers and epoxy resin is catalyzed or promoted by organic amine compounds.

Applications

One very practical application for these modified polysulfide adhesives is in bonding old to old concrete and new to old concrete. These adhesives have definite applications in the construction and maintenance of concrete structures such as highways, bridges, buildings, dams, airport runways, sidewalks, driveways, commercial and industrial floors for patching, overlaying, surface sealing and skid proofing. In the following table a comparision is made between these modified adhesives with pure epoxy adhesives.

Stranight Epoxy Poly Sulfide / Control Adhesive

Ingredients	Parts By Weight	
Polysulfide	100	
Liquid epoxy	100	100
Calcium corbonate	179	71
Ethyl hydroxy cellulose	30	15

Tensile shear bond strength (psi)

Ingredients	Parts By Weight	
Room temp.	1700	4500
Tested at 75°C	2000	1500
Tested at 25°C	1400	2500
Peel strengdl	8	18
Bond strength	100	140

Shear bond Strength after 30 days drop immersion

Ingredients	Parts	By Weight
Water	1000	1700
Sea water	0	1100
Isopropyl alcohol	2000	3200
Ethylene glycol	1600	3700
Methyl ethyl ketone	1600	500
Dibutyl phthalate	1800	3400

24.

Polyurethane Adhesives

Introduction

The fundamentals of polyurethane chemistry were established by Otto Bayer and his co-workers not by accident but by design. There are many ways of classifying polyurethane adhesives. Most frequently this classification is made by the job they perform or the process in which they are used. While this method of classification is useful and practical for the final consumption of the adhesives, it more often does not, cause confusion to many adhesive compounders. There is no industry guide to answer these questions. This has led many users of polyurethane adhesives to hire their own polyurethane chemical experts and to produce their own multitude of proprietary variants

A polyurethane is a polymeric product that has been formed by the reaction of a di-or polyisocyanate and a di-or poly hydroxyl bearing molecule (Fig-35.I). The growing markets for polyurethanes have helped encourage the chemical manufacture of a wide range of intermediates. All polyurethanes can be subdivided into two broad categories by using the reacting isocyanate functional groups to distinguish them. Those that have available NCO (For further reaction) can be called coreactives, and those that have essentially no pendant NCO can be called prereacted. All the commercial adhesives are prepared with some particular application system in mind. The system design is a highly important factor; and when a user ignores this, he will not obtain satisfying results from the polyurethane adhesives, this is not molecular behaviour but processing behaviour.

Types of Urethane Adhesives

There are three types of polyurethane adhesives available namely reaction adhesives solvent free or low solvent content, hydroxyl polyurethane solvent adhesives, and aqueous dispersions (Polyurethane ionomers).

(a) Reaction Adhesives

Two component reaction adhesives are of particular interest in the formulation of low solvent and solvent free adhesives. They utilise either a polyol/polyisocyanate combination or an isocyanate terminated prepolymer with a polyol or polyamine curative. The most widely used polyols are of the ester or ether type in a molecular weight range between 500-3,000. Best adhesive properties are imparted by polyesters whereas polyethers offer, aside from lower cost, hydrolysis resistance, excellent low temperature properties, and lower viscosity, which provides more latitude in compounding. Branched polyols are employed for rigid high strength bonds while linear polyols offer good flexibility and can be used to adjust any intermediate hardness by blending.

All the compounding ingredients, such as fillers, must be dry otherwise foaming will occur as a result of reaction with moisture after the polyisocyanate addition. Polyols are inherently hygroscopic. It is a good practice, therefore, to add substances that either react with water such as triethyl orthoformate, or absorb moisture such as molecular sieves.

The polyisocyanate ratio necessary to react with polyol part can be calculated by the formula.

$$\text{Weight of polyisocyanate for 100 parts of polyol} = \frac{247 \times \%\,OH}{\%NCO \text{ (in polyisocyanate)}}$$

(b) Hydroxyl Polyurethane Solvents

They are used as solvent adhesives, either as one or two component system.Hydroxyl polyurethanes are produced by the polyaddition of diisocyanates, usually TDI or MDI, and polyester diols. The molecular weight is controlled over the NCO/OH ratio and must be in the neighborhood of 100,000 for useful polymer properties. The various grades of hydroxyl polyuretyhane differs widely in viscosity, thermoplasticity, crystallization and solubility. The most common solvent used is the methyl ediyl ketone. The largest single user of this type adhesive is the shoe industry for attaching soles and binding lining into slush moulded PVC boots.

(c) Polyurethane Dispersions

Polyurethane dispersions are becoming more important, at least for environmental reasons. In some cases they exhibit properties superior to hydroxyl solvent adhesives, the procedure that currently yields the higher quality products involves the reaction of an isocyanate terminated pre-polymer in a water miscible solvent, such as acetone, with a diamine carboxylate or sulfone (Fig. 24.2). The resultant polyurethane ionomer solution is mixed with water, which forms the dispersion and further extends the polymer over the remaining isocyanate groups. Finally, the organic solvent is removed by distillation. Just as with hydroxyl polyurethane dispersions can also be manufactured to offer different degrees of crystallinity and exhibit excellent stability and yield water resistant films since they do not contain protective colloides or emulsifiers. They offer excellent adhesion performance in the unmodified foam. Polyurethane dispersions open up fascinating possibilities for the compounder. They permit polymer blends that normally cannot be blended with polyvinyl acetate, ethylene copolymers, polyacrylics and nitrile rubber can be made with dispersions. Suitable fillers are whiting, barytes, hydrated alumina, and clays, provided they are added as a preslurry in water. Viscosities can be adjusted with acrylic thickner or partially hydrolized polyvinyl alcohol and high viscosity levels with alginates or cellulosic thickners.

Judging from their properties, polyurethane dispersions could be good candidate to partially replace solvent system. Potential applications include wash and dry clean resistant textile laminations, plastic film laminations, flocking, sole attaching, and additives to other aqueous systems to improve their adhesion performance.

FORMULATIONS

(1) A polyurethane elastomer dissolves in 20% by weight in a mixture of dry ethyl acetate and acetone and 8.3 parts of triphenyl methane triisocyanate in 20% methylene cholride (for natural and synthetic rubber adhesion) or 5 parts of TDI - trimethylol propane adduct in 75% ethyl acetate (for non rubber adhesion) is added. These combinations are versatile adhesives for bonding vulcanised rubber to itself, scather, urethan, PVC, cork, wood etc. Cure occurs at room temperature and fester at elevated temperature.

(2) Cyanabond textiie adhesives

Formulations

Ingredients	**Qty.**
Aliphatic olyester - urethane resin MEK(40%)	1 00 parts
Acrylic dispersion	45 "
" Vinyl copolymer	15 "

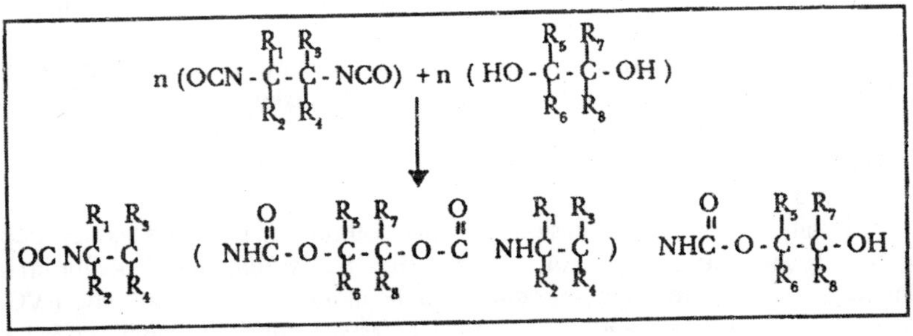

fig.24.1 Polyurethane Adhesives

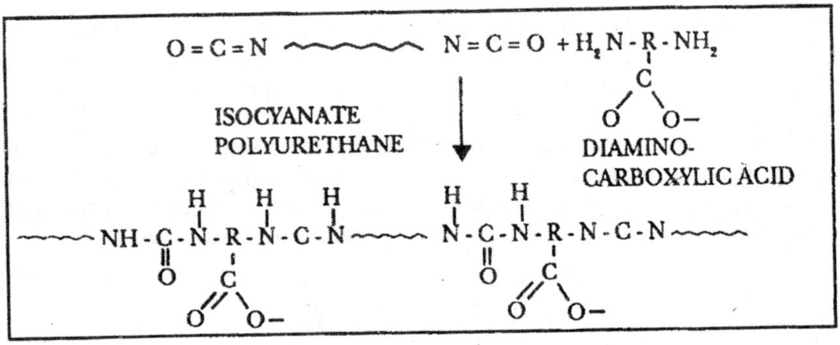

Fig. 24.2 Polyurethane Dispersion

25.

Polyurethane Dispersions

Introduction

Water based polyurethane adhesives are easier to work with 100% solid system and are an environmentally attractive alternative to the volatile organic compund (VOC) emission compliance required with solvent based polyurethane. This system also offers other advantages including.

(1) lack of emulsifying agent, providing improved adhesive
(2) functional groups, yielding better anchoring to low energy surfaces
(3) ease for use (no additional catalyst of reactants are needed to improve adhesive properties.
(4) adhesive properties and film forming achieved at lower temperatures
(5) ability to go from wet to dry without being tacky
(6) low temperature flexibility
(7) small particle size, and
(8) high cohesive strength.

In addition, thermoset versions of polyurethane dispersions exhibit superior heat resistance. As a result of these benefits, water based polyurethane adhesives are used for many speciality applications, including bonding PVC to polyurethane foam, ABS PVC and metalilized Mylar, paper to aluminium foil, PE film, HDPE, LDPE and BOPP, plant to metal, PE to PP, polyurethane film to rubber and fabric; PVC plastisol to glass and metal and fabric; CDPP and MDPP to themselves.

The trend from solvent to aqueous system in both wetting and adhesvies industries has intensified over the past decade due to environmental and safety restrictions, as well as the cost of solvents, including the costs of any solvent recovery system.

Although PU dispersions for adhesives use have been produced commercially using extraneous surfactants, most PU dispersions are made[1] from PU ionomers, for example, polyurethane containing either negative to the introduction of a tertiary nitrogen atom. A typical reaction scheme is shown below:

CH$_3$
|
CN-(U)~(U)-NCO + HOCH$_2$ CH$_2$-N CH.CH$_2$OH

CH$_3$
|
(U)-(U>~- (U)-(U) N-(U)-(U)~ (U)-(U)

This reaction is follwed by either quaternization with an alkylating agent and/or protonation with an acid to form ammonium salt as shown below:

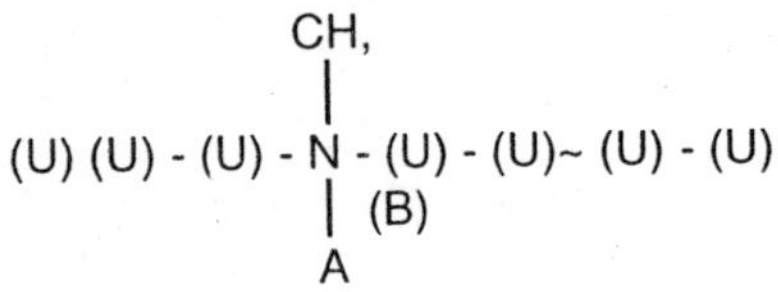

Where,
A = alkylating agent or acid
B = counter ion

Because most PU ionomer dispersions are thermoplastic, various methods can be used to crosslink these emulsions in order to increase their water and solvent resistance as well as their thermal resistance.

Both internal and external crosslinking techniques can be employed. External crosslinking can be carried out in a number of ways prior to application. These mediods include the reaction of pendant carboxylic acid groups present in the urethane anionomers with trifunctional aziridines, medioxymediylol derivatives of melamine or urea resins, polyisocynates or blocked isocyanates and polycarbodimides.

Internal crosslinking of water borne PU is carried out by invorporating reactive groups in to the urethane polymer. This can be done by producting PU dispersions containing usaturation by either using a water born alkyd or combining saturated and unsaturated polyester polyols in the formation of PU and subsequendy crosslinking them via free radical polymerization. Another approach for crosslinking is the use of hydrophobic crosslinkers which can be codispersed (after emulsification with a surfactant) with the hydrophilically modified PU dispersion. This can be done for instance, by using aqueous dispersions of blocked polyisocyanates. Several other modifications employing other aqueous polymers as codispersants have been reported.

Applications

Water based polyurethane adhesives can come in a broad range of physical properties (Table 25.1). Following are various applications using polyurethane dispersion.

Foil to Kraft Paper Laminate

A manufacturer of building product for the construction industry required secure long term adhesion of an aluminium foil to kraft paper laminate that would be part of a composite exposed to inclement weather. The firm was using an Ethylene acrylic acid dispersions (EAA), however, due to bond failure with time between the two substrates, it was looking for better adhesive. The company's success with water based polyurethane dispersions prompted it to change all the adhesives used to make these products.

The performance of the new polyurethane dispersion vs the ethylene acrylic acid (EA) was tested in all but one case, all polyurethane dispersions were judged superior to EAA dispersions. Based on average peel strength for each resin, aromatic and aliphatic thermoset polyurethane are the preferred resins. The thermosets generally yielded results two or three times higher than unmodified urethane disperions. The EAA system is not preferable for application where water may reach the resin.

Glass-Plastisol

A manufacturer of glass bottles for the cosmetic and medical industries was encountering problems with poor adhesion and solvent emissions. The bottles are generally put under pressure for spray purposes in use. The pressurized bottles are plastisol coated to prevent them from exploding on impact, but a tie coat was needed because of poor adhesion between glass and plastisol. The coating not only functions as an adhesion promoter, it also helps prevent the glass from shattering when crushed.

The tie coat previously used was a solvent, based acrylic. Faced with Govts. regulation, the manufacturers were searching for an alternative system to lower VOC emissions. The company tried PU dispersions. The dispersion was cut 3:1 with water to obtain a 13% NV polyurtethane dispresion dried in a 10 ft forced air dryer at 250°C then dipped in the plastisol bath and dried, while it was not possible to conveniently measure peel strength between the glass and plastisol, a qualitative method using a scotch tape peel test was used. Results indicated that the adhesvie strength of plastisol to glass was improved significantly.

Vinyl Applications

A manufacturer of decorative trim for the appliance and automotive markets wanted to change from organic solvent based adhesives to reduce emissions and comply Govt's regulations. The firms processing included the lamination of composites of vinyl/mylar and vinyl/metallized mylar, the solvent based adhesives being used were acrylates, ethylene vinly acetate and polyurethane. After a series of laboratory evaluations, it was discovered that the aqueous PU dispersions out performed the solvent based adhesives in peel strength tests (Table 25.2).

Adhesion to Steel

A manufacturer was producing a component part that consists of a laminated clear mylar film to thin gauge painted steel. He was not satisfied with the processing consistency of the three component solvent based system in use. Additionally, VOC compliance regulations mandated a switch to lower VOC products within a year. Aqueous PU dispersion was tried, and found to be simpler to use, as it has only one component and is less labour intensive, there was no trade off in the performance of the laminating adhesive. The swtich was made, and mandated emissions requirement were met.

Using aqueous polyurethane dispersion helps manufacturer cut down on VOC emissions and regulatory paper work. The adhesive also offers numerous performance benefits that make them suitable for use in a variety of laminating applications.

TABLE - 25.1 - Property Range of Water Based Polyurethane

Property	Low	High
% Solids (NV)	35.00	60.0
Volatile organic content (VOC) (Kg/Lit)	0	1.5
Viscosity (CPS,, 25% C)	50.00	1000.0
pH	7.20	9.20
Particle size (microns)	0.15	0.7
Flash point (°C)	6200.00	6200.0
Shelf life	6.00	12.0
Film Property :		
Tensile strength (psi)	1000.00	7000.0
Modulus (100%)	380.00	4000.0
Ultimate elongation *(%)*	550.00	870.0
% Stick temperature (0°C)	340.00	500.0
Tg (0°C)	-33.00	59.0
% recovery at 100% elongation	30.00	35.0

NV = Non Volatiles

TABLE - 25.2 - Peel Strengyh Comparison (psi)

Bond Type	Aqueous Polyurethane	EVA	Acrylate
Vinyl to vinyl	5-6	1-2	1
Vinyl to metallized mylar	4-5	1	1
Vinyl to aluminium	3-4	1	1

26.

Polyvinyl Acetal Adhesives

Introduction

Polyvinyl acetal resins depends for most applications on their excellent adhesive characteristics to a variety of surfaces. They are used in many structural adhesives applications involving metal, glass, paper and plastic films. There is excellent adhesion to glass making polyvinyl butyral an almost universal interlayer for safety glass. As coating they provide unusual performances. Excellent pigment binding capacity has led to their use in printing inks, electrographic toners and electronic ceramic tapes. In each application, their outstanding adhesive characteristics are a prime consideration.

Acetals are formed by the well known reaction of one molecule of aldehyde and two molecules of polyvinyl alcohol.

R—CHO + 2 ROH R—CH -OR + H_2O

Acetal

Aldehyde Alcohol.

Properties

Tensile strength varies from 6000 to 11,000 psi, increasing with molecular weight and hydroxyl content and as we go from butyral to formal. Glass transition temperature ranges from about 60°C to l50°C. In general, polyvinyl butyrals are soluble in alcohol, glycol ethers. For a given type of polyvinyl acetal, the solution viscosity increases sharply with molecular weight Low temperature flexibility of adhesive of polyvinyl acetal resin may be improved and brittleness reduced by incorporation of plasticizers which may also be employed to reduce the viscosity of hot melt formulation. Polyvinyl acetals are compatible with a variety of natural gums and resins.

Structural Adhesives

Structural adhesives based on polyvinyl acetal resins can be applied as a solution, on unsupported film, supported film, paper, cloth or mixture of liquid and solid.

Formulations

Wide variations in performance are possible by varying the formulations of polyvinyl acetal phenolic adhesives. Acetal phenolic ratio from 10 : 1 to 10 :20 have been used; polyvinyl butyral and polyvinyl formal resins are compatible with many epoxy resins and can confer such improvements to epoxy based systems as increased impact resistance, peel strength and room temperature shear strength.

(1) A one package solution system is:

Formulation

Ingredients	**Parts By Weight**
Polyvinyl butyral	100
Phenolic resin	150
Epoxy resin	100
Aluminium powder	200
Isopropyl acetate	200
95 % isopropyl alcohol	100

A two package polyvinyl acetal epoxy phenolic system involves coating the substrate with an epoxy phenolic solution, sprinkling polyvinyl formal powder on to the wet surface, and shaking off the excess powder. The solution used is.

(2) Two package palyvinylacetal epoxy phenolic system:

Formulation

Ingredients	**Parts By Weight**
Epoxy resin	100
Phenolic resin	100
Methyl ethyl ketone	200

The addition of small amount of plasticizers to an adhesive system combining a polyvinyl acetal resin with a thermosetting resin increases the flexibility and impact resistance of the bond.

Hot Melt Adhesives

Polyvinyl butyral resins, when properly compounded, form excellent hot melt adhesives providing a tough, clear film with good adhesive strength. The preparation of hot melt is simple. The ingredients other than polyvinyl butyral are added and melted to a homogenous state. Thp resin is gradually added and the temperature raised until the melt is uniform. A typical starting formulation is shown herein :

Formulation

Ingredients	**Parts By Weight**
Low hydroxyl polyvinyl butyral	75
Plasticizer	15
Modified rosin	150
Modified wax	3
Additives	150

By varying the preceding proportions, this formulation can be used for adhering numerous surfaces. More specific formulations are shown in Table-26.1.

Applications

The original and largest use of polyvinyl butyral is as the interlayer in laminated automotive safety glass. In this application the excellent adhesive properties of the plasticized film prevent fragments of glass from flying off from a suddenly cracked or broken pane of safety glass. By means of careful control of the level adhesion between the glass and polyvinyl butyl interlayer, a significant increase in the penetration resistance of laminated safety glass has been achieved in recent years.

Wire Enamels

The high degree of adhesion toughness and abrasion resistance of wire enamel containing polyvinyl formal resins enables the magnet wire to maintain its coating integrity during high speed motor winding and service.

Surface Coatings

In protective coatings for metal the best known polyvinyl acetal application is in 'wash primers' also referred to as metal conditioners. Wash primers are more effective than other corrosion inhibiting materials, because they adhere better and dry faster.

Metal Coatings

This particular combination provides excellent abrasion resistance, adhesion and chemical resistance :

Formulation Ingredients	Parts By Weight(%)
Diacetone alcohol	17.4
n-Butanol	17.4
Ethanol, 95 %	7.7
Xylol	34.7
Hydrocarbon	5.1
Epoxy resin	13.0
Polyvinyl butyral	2.0
10 % pliosphoric acid	2.7
Total	100

Wood Sealer

The following starting formulation is representative of the kind of wood sealer:

Formulation Ingredients By Weight	Parts
Polyvinyl butyral	6.1
Nitrocellulose	9.2
Butyl acetate	32.9
Ethanol, anhydrous	5.5
Isoproapanol, 99 %	10.9
Methyl isobutyl ketone	3.3
Xylol	13.3
Toluene	13.3

Textile Coatings

In textile coatings, polyvinyl butyral can be compounded to make fabrics water proof and stain resistant.:

A typical formulation is :

Formulation Ingredients	Parts By Weight
Polyvinyl butyral	48.0
Tricresyl phosphate	48.0
Ethanol 95 %	84.2
Toluene	64.8
Water	8.0

Melamine resin	3.5
Catalyst	0.7
p-Nonyl phenol	0.2

Miscellaneous Applications

In ink formulation for gravure, letter press and flexographic printing polyvinyl butyral resin imparts toughness and adhesion. This resin also finds its use in toner for xerographic images, binder for organic photo conductors in the electro-photographic process and in the direct electrostatic recording process due to its high adhesive power. When polyvinyl butyral is mixed with polyvinyl formal and dibutyl phthalate, a good adhesive for leather and cloth in the manufacture of shoes can be prepared.

TABLE -26.1- Polyvinyl buyal Hot Melt Adhesive Formulation

Ingredients	Aluminium to steel	Lable adhesive	Low melting coating	Label adhesive in tin	Wax *paper Adhesive*	Frozen food container adhesive	Frozen food container adhesive	Leather to wood adhesive
Low hydroxy polyvinyl butyral	-	-	-	10	15	18	-	20
High hydroxy polyviny-1 butyral	40	10	15	-	-	-	10	-
Plasticizer I	-	6	-	-	-	-	-	2.5
"II	—	—	3	10	9	-	-	-
"HI	30	-	-	-	-	-	-	-
Dibutyl sebacate	-	2	-	-	-	-	-	-
Modified rosin	-	24	43	90	43	25	45	-
Rosin	-	-	-	-	-	-	-	60
Modified wax	-	24	36	10	36	44	35	25
Synthetic wax	-	-	-	-	2	-	-	-
Additives	—	2.4	3.6	1	3.6	4.4	3.5	2.5
TiO_2	-	-	-	-	-	1.9	-	-
Aluminium silicate	-	-	-	-	-	10.4	-	-
Cellulose ether	-	-	-	-	-	3	-	-
Polyvinyl methyl ether	0.5	-	-	-	-	-	-	-

27.

Polyvinyl Acetate Emulsions and Polyvinyl Alcohol for Adhesives

Introduction

Polyvinyl acetate came into widespread use in adhesives in the 1940's as a synthetic resin substitute for hide glue. Superior properties of the synthetic resin offset their higher price. Polyvinyl acetate adhesives were adaptable to new highspeed machinery in the paper converting and packaging fields and were enthusiastically received. They found a place in wood adhesives and later were introduced in the familiar household "white glue". Significant advances in polyvinyl acetate technology occurred in the 1050 and 1060s. A large number of sophisticated polymer and copolymer products were commercialized to meet the needs of changing technology.

The property of excellent adhesion of polyvinyl acetate emulsions to cellulosic materials gave rise to a variety of applications. Some examples of the range of products and uses for polyvinyl acetate emulsion follow: book binding, paper bags, milk cartons, drinking straws, envelopes, gummed tapes, convolute tubes, folding boxes, multiwall shipping bags, labels, foils, films and paper board decals, cigarette tips, lagging compounds, wood assembly, padding, automobile upholstery, pencils, leather binding, and tile cements.

Because of their relatively low cost, ready availability, wide compatibility, and excellent adhesive characteristics, many polyvinyl acetate resins, solution, and emulsion are treated as commodity items by the adhesives industry. Among the 40 to 50 manufacturers of polyvinyl acetate based resins "fevicol" brand enjoys the best market position. The resulting competition has benefited adhesives manufacturers with low prices, good quality, new improved products, and greater technical service from the resin manufacturers. Price variation is common experience in this competitive market. Grade of resin and volume are important factors in selling price.

Emphasis on the use of polyvinyl acetate in the adhesives industry alone gives a rather confining picture of the resin. Its use in other industries actually depends on its adhesive, binding and film properties as much as it does in the adhesives industry. Emulsion of vinyl acetate and polyvinyl acetate/acrylate coploymer are used as binders for nonwoven or bonded fabrics. The paper industry uses small particle size ployvinyl acetate emulsions as pigment binders for clays in paper and paper board coatings.

Monomer

Vinyl acetate is the most available and widely used member of the vinyl ester family. This colourless flammable liquid was first prepared in India by Vam organics. The more recent technical development is the production of vinyl acetate monomer from ethylene and acedc acid. Palladium catalyst is used for both liquid and vapor phase processes.

The following have found speciality uses, principally as co-monomers with vinyl acetate: vinyl propionate, vinyl laurate, and vinyl versatate.

Figure 27..1 shows the derivation of vinyl acetate-based adhesive products from natural products, and figure-27.2 shows vinyl acetate flow sheet.

The discussion that follows covers (1) aqueous dispersions and (2) solid resins derived from aqueous dispersions.

Polymerization

Vinyl acetate polymerizes by the free-radical addition reaction. Free radicals generated by the decomposition of organic peroxides such as benzoyl or hydrogen peroxide or of inorganic "per" salts such as potassium or ammonium persulfate are commonly used to initiate polymerization. Reactions ordinarily are accomplished at above room temperature. Other techniques of ploymerization have been used to make novel products: low temperature redox polymerizadon, irradiation, and ionic catalysis.

Vinyl acetate copolymerizes with various vinyl monomers. Acrylate esters, vinyl chloride, vinylidene chloride, dibutyl and other dialkyl maleates and fumarates, crotonic, acrylic, methacrylic and itaconic acids, vinyl pyrrolidone, and ethylene are commercially important comonomers. A monomer that does not combine wida vinyl acetate alone can be combined by use of a third monomer. "Grafting" can be used with monomers such as styrene that do not copolymerize with vinyl acetate.

Emulsion

Polyvinyl acetate is most widely used in the form of a dispersion of solid resin in water. These dispersions are produced by emulsion polymerization and are more commonly termed "emulsions". Most products for adhesives are sold at 55% solids at a sufficiently high viscosity level to facilitate use. These products are manufactured by one of several techniques-batch, continuous or delay feed, dependent on properties desired. The large volume usage depends not only on the outstanding adhesive properties of the resin but also on the excellent compatibility of the emulsions with many modifying agents.

Most manufacturers specify properties of their emulsions in terms of percent solids, emulsion viscocity, pH, acid content, percent unreacted monomer, and density. Other properties generally described are particle size, molecular weight, film properties such as clarity, water and grease resistance, and tolerance of the emulsions to various organic and inorganic chemicals.

Other tests may be necessary to characterize an emulsion polymer more thoroughly. In Table 1 a variety of properties studied by the polymer chemist and the adhesion chemist in a complete characterization is shown,

Adhesive Formulations

One way of classifying polyvinyl acetate adhesives is by the type of the formulation: emulsion and aqueous solution, dry-mix, hot-melt, and solution in organic solvent. The tables in this section present "starting" formulations that illustrate a few of the many adhesive uses of polyvinyl acetate. Thousands of actual "working" formulations exist in the laboratories of adhesives manufacturers. Formulating principles are thoroughly reviewed in the literature of the resin manufactures.

Adhesives for paper or paper composition substrates is one of the largest uses for polyvinyl acetate emulsions. Often the emulsion can be used with little, if any, modification. Usually, however, it is necessary to alter physical properties such as viscosity, solid, and water resistance; to vary application characteristics such as tack and machinability and to reduce cost.

Starches, ployvinyl alcohol solution and clays are examples of cost-reducing agents. Starches provide high viscosity and "body". Polyvinyl alcohol builds viscosity, improves machinability, and water resistance. Clays improve setting properties by controlling penetration into porous substrates.

Improved fast-setting and tack characteristics are achieved by addition of plasticizers, solvents and film coalescing agents. Thin boiling starches and clays also facilitate the speed of set by raising the solids content. Examples of formulations of several paper adhesives are shown in Table 27.3.

Fast-setting packing or case sealing adhesives require high wet tack, machinability, low cost, and often, water resistance in addition to fast set. Addition of rosin derivatives in the solvent or plasticizer improves wet tack. Machinability can often be improved by addition of ployvinyl alcohol solution. Most emulsions have sufficient machinability to prevent "cottoning" and "throwing" at high speed operation and coagulation under shear. They also have good "clean up" properties. Fast-setting packaging and case sealing adhesives are illustrated in Table 27.4.

Ployvinyl acetate emulsion and polyvinyl alcohol, or combinations, are well suited for remoistenable adhesives for envelopes, stamps, sealing tapes, and ribbons. Major requirments of remoistenable adhesives for paper are rapid reactivation with water after ageing, glossy film with low coeffecient of friction, and resistance to blocking (temperature and humidity) and to curing. "All-synthetic" remoistenable adhesives can be obtained by adding polyvinyl alcohol (20 to 40% acetate content). The polyvinyl alcohol improves remoistenability, gloss and block resistance. Addition of humectant-type plasticizers controls curling and improves remoistenability. Addition of special plasticizers such as butyl ricinoleate improves blocking resistance. "Resin-dextrin" remoistenable adhesives have such advantages as lower cost and gloss, when a large proportion of dexrin is used with the emulsion. However, they present problems such as curing and possible loss of remoistenability with age, even "All-dextrin" systems can be improved by the addition of polyvinyl acetate emulsions. In tape, ribbon and paper applications, high quality remoistenably adhesives can be obtained with polyvinyl alcohol systems. Table-5 contains several remoistenable adhesive formulations.

Polyvinyl acetate and polyvinyl alcohol are important raw materials for wood adhesive applications. High bond strength, fast set, controllable open and closed assemble times, colourless glue lines, and ease of application at room temperature are some of the many advantages of polyvinyl acetate emulsion adhesives over natural and thermosetting resin adhesives. Water and heat-resistance are improved by the addition of alkyd resins.

Polyvinyl acetate emulsions, specifically plasticized or copolymer emulsions, are bases for successful adhesives for difficult-to-adhere surfaces to a variety of porous substrates. Heatsealing or wet-bond methods are applicable. Some of the formulations in Table-6 are capable of bonding such difficult surfaces as polyvinyl chloride, pyroxlin, aluminum foil, polystyrene film and cellulose acetate to paper, chipboard, wood and cloth.

Where improved water, heat, arid abrasion resistance are required, polyvinyl acetate emulsions can be compounded with water-soluble thermosetting resins. Plywood lamination, metal-to-wood, metal-to-metal, plastic to metal and particle board are possible applications. General limitations are those of thermosetting systems: reduced storage stability, short pot life, coloured glue lines, and use of heat or catalyst for curing.

Dry-mix adhesive formulation containing redispersible polyvinyl acetate powder, polyvinyl alcohol, starches, clays and thermosetting resins are shown in Table-7. Particular advantages of dry-mix adhesives not mentioned previously are found in "on-the-job" preparation of adhesives and in the stability of components mixed dry which would interact or gel in paste or liquid form. Wall board joint adhesives and concrete additives are special applications of dry-mix adhesives in the building products industry.

Polyvinyl acetate resin is considered as the basic film forming and adhesives component "Fluxing" resin are added to lower viscosity, melt temperature, and cost, plasticizers improve film flexibility and adhesion and affect flow and tack, waxes improve flow, spreading, slip and nonblocking. Fillers, pigments, dyes and antioxidants are also added depending on the end use.

Adhesives are formulated with polyvinyl acetate in organic solvent using plasticizers and other materials similar to those mentioned with emulsions and hot melts-with the limitation of solubility or dispersibility in the solvent system. Such solvent system adhesives are specifically tailored to particular uses.

The final table contains a few miscellaneous "starting" formulations to illustrate further uses for polyvinyl acetate/alcohol adhesives.

Polyvinyl Alcohol

Polyvinyl alcohol is one of a group of synthetic polymers which competes in the multimillion pound market for water-soluble resins. Over 90% of the market is served by natural products sues as starch, dextrin, and casein; however, sales of synthetic water-soluble polymers have grown substantially in recent years. The synthetics, though higher priced, compete in a variety of applications by virtue of uniform quality and unique properties.

The major markets for polyvinyl alcohol are adhesive, textile, emulsifier, and protective colloid in polymerization, paper, and plastic film. There is an amazing number of smaller speciality uses for polyvinyl alcohol including synthetic sponges, cosmetics, pharmaceuticals, photosensitive coatings, ceramics, mouldings, extrusions, release agents, and many others.

Applications

The largest use of polyvinyl alcohol is in adhesive formulations, usually in combination with polyvinyl acetate emulsions of other resin dispersions. Polyvinyl alcohol got its start in the adhesives industry in the United States during

World War II in the packaging industry. It was widely used at that time as an adhesive in waterproof v-board packing cases that could be floated ashore from cargo carriers. Since that time, polyvinyl alcohol has become firmly established in the burgeioning markets for synthetic adhesives in packaging, paper-converting, furniture, book binding, envelopes, etc. The polyvinyl alcohol functions as a protective colloid, emulsifier, thickener, and film former in adhesive formulations. It promotes incorpoiation of water immiscible solvents, plasticizers, waxes, and oils. It contributes improved adhesions and tensile strength Fully-hydrolyzed grades are particularly important in promoting increased water resistance. High molecular weight grades facilitate lower adhesive solids by maintaining high solution viscosity; they also impart excellent mechanical stability properties. Medium, hydrolyzed grades give the best combination of adhesion, viscosity control, and emulsifier protective colloid action. Polyvinyl alcohols are used universally in the polymerization of polyvinyl acetate emulsions, Low hydrolyzed grades have excellent cold-water solubility, and their films exhibit remoistenability, gloss, and noncurling properties on paper. Such grades are widely used as binders and additives. Low-cost paper laminating adhesives are obtained by combining polyvinyl alcohol with starches, dextrins, and clays. Ployvinyl alcohol is generally considered safe for food packaging adhesives.

For paper application, the use of dilute solutions of fully hydrolyzed grades applied by coventional equipment can impart improved wet strength, flexibility, grease-resistance, and better appearance and printing qualities. Plasticizer is usually incorporated in these paper coatings formulations.

In textile warp sizing and finishing applications, excellent adhesion to natural and synthetic fibers, high tensile strength and abrasion resistance, good filming, ease of preparation and uniformity of solutions, ease of removal of size, and low BOD requirements make polyvinyl alcohol desirable.

Polyvinyl alcohol, an effective binder, is used in the preparation of ceramics,' sand moulds, and metal slip castings. It is also used as a binder for non-woven fabrics and is gaining importance as a concrete additive in the building products industry.

Polyvinyl alcohol film is tough, resistant to organic solvents, and impermeable to most gases. It has been used in a variety of moulding techniques for reinforced plastics, as a polarizer in optical instruments, protective packaging, and water-soluble packaging for detergents, dyes, bleaches, etc. Mention of fibres and photosensitive coatings completes the list of current major or interesting applications.

TABLE -27.1-Characterization of Emulsion Polymers

Properties of the emulsion	Surface tension foaming tendency stability (dilution mechanical shear freeze/thaw heat bacterial) compatibility (plasticizers thickeners pigments extenders coalescing agents)
Properties of the polymer	Solubility Tg Molecular weight distribution Rheological behaviour infra red spectra
Adhesive properties,	Heat seal temperature Bond strength (miscellaneous Sub strate Tack Peel Creep
Properties of a Film	Blocking Flex Tensile/elongation Hardness

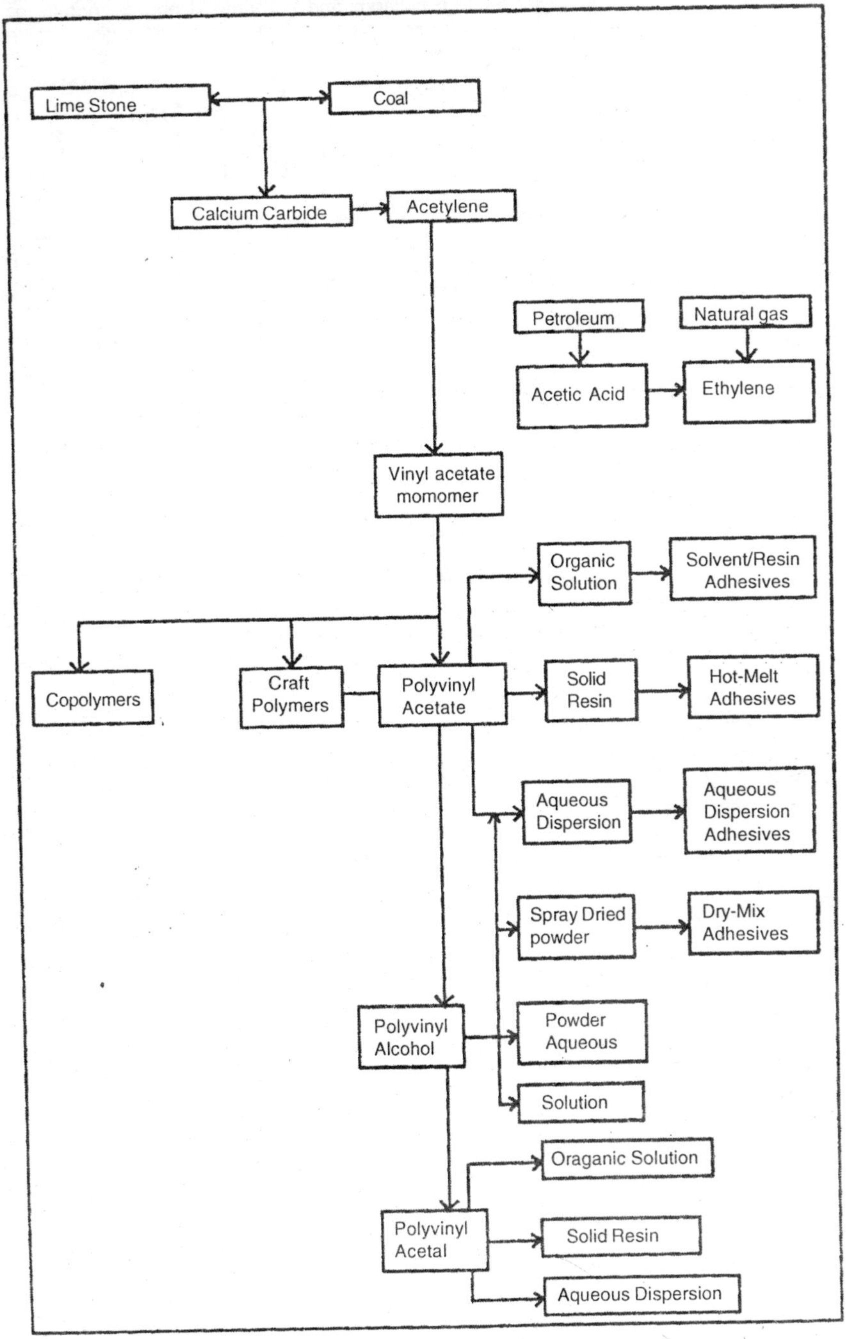

fig. 27.1. Adhesives derived from vinyl acetate monomer product

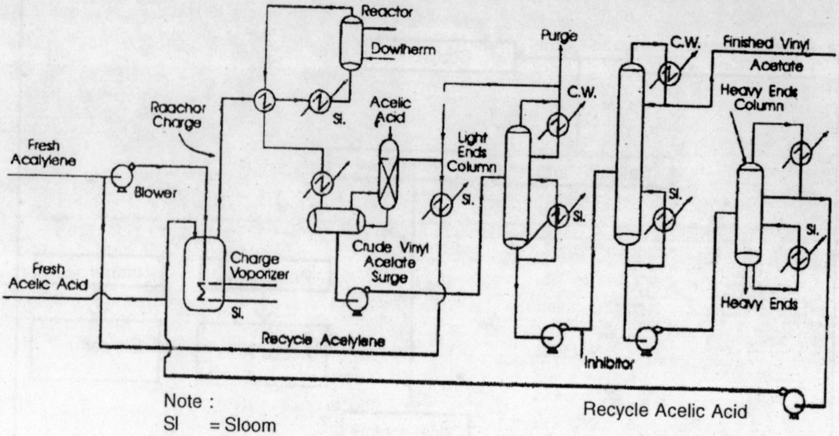

Note :
Sl = Sloom
C.W. = Cold Water

Fig: 27.2 - Flow Diagram for Manufacture of Vinyl Acetate

TABLE - 27.2 - Redispersible Polyvinyl Acetate Powders

Manufacturer		Fevicol	Flexicol	Apicol
Particle size of Powder		20 microns	15 microns	99% through 100 mesh
Volatile content		1.5%	3.0%	2%
Bulk density		32-38 lb/cu ft	32-38 lb/cu ft	33 lb/cu ft
Viscosity (cps)		1660	200	5000-7000 (50% solids)
At 55% solids in water				
At 60% solids in water	7800	700	-	
At 70% solids in water	-	11,000	-	
Borax stable		No	Yes	No

TABLE - 27.3 - General Adhesives for Paper Surfaces

	Parts by Weight					
Materials	**Bag Bottom paste**	**Bag Bottom paste**	**Kraft Surfaces**	**Seam Adhesive**	**Tube Winding**	**Quilon Paster**
Vinyl acetate latex emulsion (55% solid) VALE,	20-30	10-20	X	39-41	X	
VALE (High molecular weight)	X	X	10-20	X	X	
VALE (50% solid)	X	X			38-40	
Dibutyl phthalatc					2	
Butyl benzyl phthalate					X	
Dipropylene glycol dibenzoate					X	
Polyester plasticizer				7-9		
Pearl starch	10-20		10-15	1-2		8-10
Polyvinyl alcohol 125		2-5	2-5	2-4	25-7	
Polyvinyl alcohol 225		X	X	X	X	
Polyvinyl alcohol 250		X	X	X	X	
Aluminium silicate (I)			10-20	5	24-26	3-4
Aluminium silicate (II)			X		X	X
Clay				7-9		
Hydrogenated methyl ester of rosin				X		
Methyl ester of rosin				2-4	1-2	
Trichloroethylene						4-6
Ethanol						0-2
Preservative	0-2	0-2	0-2			
Water	70-50	78-60	77-58	38-28	33-28	80-73
Remarks :	Low cost high viscosity	Low cost, resistant	Low cost fast setting water resistant	Medium cost, rapid setting	Low cost, water resistant	High viscosity water resistant

x = other suitable components.

TABLE - 27.4 - Fast Tack and Packaging Adhesives Paper

Materials	Parts by Weight					
Materials	General Packing	General Packing	Carton Scaling	Cup Adhesive	Box Board	Glassine Paper
Vinyl acetate latex emulsion (VALE) 55% solid	X	X	95		30	
VALE (50% solid)	90	25		75		X
VALE (52% solid)					90	
Dibutyl phthalate	10		1.5	5		
Butyl benzyl phthalate	X	5				
Dipropylene glycol dibenzoate	X					
Clay						10
Hexylene glycol					3	
Trichloro ethylene			3.5	6		10
Benzene		25				
Vinsol resin		25				
Phosphoric acid				1		
Polyvinyl alcohol		10		19	40	
Water		10			1	10
Remarks :	Fast tack	High wet tack, dark colour	Fast set, high wet tack	Water and heat resistance	Very fast tack	Low cost colourless

x = Other suitable components.

TABLE -27.5- Remoistenables Adhesives

Materials	Parts by Weight				
	All Synthetic	Anti Block	Resin Dextrin Combination	Lay-flat Dextrin	Resin High Dextrin
Vinyl acetate latex emulsion (VALE) 55% solid	50	50			
VALE (52% solid)			35	35	10
VALE (50% solid)	15	10			
VALE (45% solid)				3	
VALE (40% solid)				X	
Dibutyl phthalate			3		1
Butyl ricinoleate		3			
Polypropylene glycol		3	3	3	8
"Arlex" 1				3	X
70% sorbitol				X	X

Dextrin			35	30	40
Water	35	34	24	26	41
Remarks :	Colorless Film, good aging, fair glpss	Fair Gloss, good aging	Good gloss tan color	Non curling, good gloss, tan color	Low cost, improved aging

x = Other suitable components.

TABLE - 27.6 - Adhesive forDifficult to Bond Surfaces

Materials	Parts by Weight									
	General porous to Non-porous surfaces um Foil	Porous surfaces toPVCl and Alumin-surface	doth Backed PVCl to porous	Porous Surfaces to polyet-hylene and Mylar	Porous Surfaces to polyes-ter Film	PVCl Film to wall board	Alumin-ium Foil to Paper and chip	Book binding cover stock	Alumin-ium Foil to chip board	Polythy-lene to porous surface
VALE (55%)	X									
VALE (30%)			60							
VALE (70%)	73							90		
VALE (71%)								X	85	
VALE (50%)	X	85		76	90	90	65			65
Butyl benzyl phthalate	7	10				5				
Dibutyl phthalate			5					6	10	10
Polyester plasticizer				19						
Toluene sulfonamide sensitizer							10		5	
Ethyl acetate	8									
Butyl acetate	12									
Methyl isobutyl ketone		5								
Toluene			10							
Butyl lactate					10					
cydohexanone						5				
Clay								4		
Polyvinyl alcohol										25
NH_4OH (3% aq.)			25							
casein (15% aq.)							5			0.1
santomerse							20			
water					6					

TABLE - 27.7 - Dry Mix Adhesives

Materials	bag bottom paste	wood adhesive	wood adhesive	wood adhesive	remoist enable	wood laminating	Kraft bag seams paper board	bag side seams
				Parts by Weight				
Potyvinyl acetate powder (PVAP)		20	20	39		15	2	
PVAP					49			
VALE (55%)	6		3.3					4.4
VALE (52%)							2	
VALE (50%)					7			
Lauxein		40						
U/F reiin					13			
VALE/Acrylic						100		
Gay 100							12	
Clay 400								11
Walnut shell flour						10		
Pearl starch	9						5	
Tapioca starch						8.6		
Dibutylin dilaurate			7					
Ammonium sulfate				1.5				
Ammonium chlordie				1.5				
Preservative	1						1	
Reconstitute to	16% solid	60% solid	80% solid	55% solid	56% solid	desired	22% solid	24% High
Remark	High Viscos-ity. water resistant	High bond strength short life	High viscosi-ty Low cost	Thermo-setting	Add3 parts DBF	Heat curable 100'C	Water resistant	Visco-sity, water resist-ant

TABLE - 27.8 - Miscellaneous Polyvinyl Acetate Adhesives

Product Formula	1	2	3	4	5	6	7	8
				Parts by Weight				
PVA/Acrylic (50%)	41							
PVA/VP		90						
PVA/Alkyd (52%)						24	51	
PVA / VA			40	80				
PVA / Acrylic (58%)								60
VALE (55% solid)			55				11.5	
VALE (50% solid)					9			
Ethyl en e glycol	3							
Dibutyl phthalate		10	5	1			3.5	
Resoflex					10			
Toluene				6				7
Glycerin						4		
Glycerol salt						4		
Tapioca starch						8		
Clay 100	29						34	30
Clay 400						16		
Titanium dioxide	5							
Antimony oxide	5							
TKPP	0.1							
Epoxy resin	5			13				
water	16.5				81	44		

Fire retardant lagging compound padding Concrete bond coat. Quick cure Solvent & oil resistance For PVCl backed wall paper Parquet wood flooring Mastic composition.

28.

Resorcinolic Adhesives

Introduction

Adhesives resistant to water and to all kinds of exterior exposure became an urgent necessity for mankind. For these, and many other purposes, the resorcinolic adhesives were found to be outstanding, not only for their excellent durability, but also for their unique property of curing rapidly without heat, giving high strength bonds to such a large variety of adherends.

Joints made with resorcinolic adhesives are of high structural strength, usually greater than the wood, itself. They are resistant to almost any of the condition to which wood may be exposed and will retain their original load bearing strength during exposure to all kinds of climatic changes. They provide excellent endurance when subjected to such conditions as : fatigue, boiling water, extreme temperature humidity cycling, freezing and thawing; and most types of solvent except highly caustic solution. They are capable of bearing heavy loads indefinitely, without evidence of creep.

Resorcinolic adhesives are useful in the bonding of many materials such as wood, paper, textiles, plastics, rubbers, metals, glass,ceramics and concrete. Textile like cotton, rayons and nylon are easily bonded. Plastic materials like phenol-melamine and urea-formaldehyde thermosets, the epoxies, polyurethanes, poly amides, rubbers, acrylates and polyesters may be effectively bonded to each other. However, most of the thermoplastics such as polystyrene, polyolefins, poly vinyl chloride, polyfluroethylene, ethyl cellulose and polycarbonates are not easily bonded with these adhesives because of low surface polarity.

Metals are bonded after being primed with epoxides, polyurethanes or with casein- elastomeric primers. By means of this, metal facings may be applied to wood at room temperature. This provides a method for eliminating the thermally induced stresses. The resorcinolic adhesives have the disadvantages of dark colour so that the glue lines appear as dark steaks which cause dark, spotchy areas on the surface which are very difficult to remove.

Resorcinol is similar to phenol in that it readily combines with formaldehyde to form methylol derivatives, with the methylol groups occupying the position to both hydroxyl groups. The meta position is not ordinarily reacted. The reactivity of methylol derivatives is so high that they cannot easily be isolated in pure stable form. They continue to react under ambient, uncatalyzed conditions with formaldehyde or other methylol containing molecules to form polymer chains of higher molecular size, with branched as well as linear, configurations of great complexity as shown below:

Thus, resorcinolic resins, do not exist as resoles, as phenolics do, but are similar to the novlacs. The greater reactivity of resorcinol compared to phenol is due to the presence of two hydroxyl groups, meta to each other.

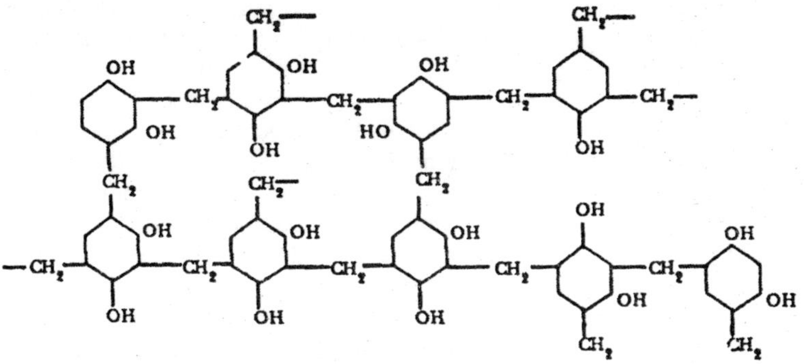

Resorcinol Phenol Formaldehyde Resins

In order to produce resorcinol phenol-formaldehyde resins, the phenol is combined with the formaldehyde before the resorcinol is introduced. If resorcinol was added to the initial charge, it would attempt to react with all formldehyde and form a gel, because it is many times as reactive as phenol. As a result, most of the phenol would remain unreacted. So first phenol was reacted with excess formaldehyde to form a low condensed resole. Resorcinol would then be added in sufficient properties to combine with all the methylol groups, thus forming a resinous copolymer.

Modified Resorcinol Resins

Resorcinol resin may be modified in order to obtain characteristics which make them useful for purposes where the straight resorcinol or resorcinol phenol resins are not as suitable. Thus alkyl resorcinol resins may be made from alkyl substituted resorcinol to confer special solubility or compatability properties. In such cases the alkylated resorcinol is directly reacted with higher formaldehyde to obtain a modified polymer. Such resins have been found to be useful because of better compatibility in elastomers such as butyl or ethylene propylene rubber. Resorcinol resin may also be modified by formation of ether, acrylation or by combination with isocyanates to alter their solubility and reactivity characteristics. They are used to aid in penetration of the crystalline fibrils, and thus obtain good adhesion to the fibre surface. Resorcinol resins have also been converted to oil soluble resins, suitable for the preparation of flexible binders, coating or for compounding rubber composites.

Aspects of Adhesion Mechanism

The adhesion of resorcinolic adhesives is strongly dependent on the kind of surface which must be joined. A properly formulated resorcinolic adhesive has sufficiently low viscosity, in aqueous alcoholic solution, to flow easily in to all of the interstices of the surface. Good wettability and penetration is prompted by alcohol. As formaldehyde from the hardener reacts with the resin, excessive amounts of methylol groups are temporarily formed. At the same time, the molecules interact with each other forming high molecular weight polymers.

There is a high degree of intermolecular attraction between these growing resorcinol polymers and the hemicellulosic (non- crystalline) and lignocellulosic molecules. The phenolic hydroxyl groups and the methylol groups on the resin are both highly polar in nature and easily attract the hydroxyl groups on the cellulose, or the phenolic groups of the lignin. Resorcinol resins, because of the presence of two hydroxyl groups in each resorcinol nucleus have a high degree of hydrogen bonding capacity. This is advantageous in several ways. It permits the resin to compete with the water molecules on the fibre surface and thus displace them to some extent. Secondly, it facilitates adsorption on the crystalline cellulosic surfaces to improve bonding of the summer wood areas of the wood. Lastly, it serves to draw the molecules of resin and cellulose or lignin closer together, thus increasing the forces of intermolecular attraction and facilitating the formation of covalent bonds with the lignin molecules.

The rapidly growing polymers in the bulk of the glue spread continue to interact with each other to form colloidal particles and finally coalesce to a soft gelatinous film. One advantage of room temperature curing is that the resulting glue film sets to a hard, strong binder with a minimum of residual stresses. Another is that moisture escapes so gradually dial a molecularly porous solid is formed. This minimizer checking or crazing permits the joints bonded with resorcinol glues to survive exposures to extremes of humidity cycles.

Formulation of Glue Mixtures

Commercially, the resorcinolic adhesives are available in two part systems. The liquid portion, part, A is the resinous constituent. It is generally a solution of the performed formaldehyde deficient resin in a mixture of alcohol and water, having a solid content of about 50 %. The reactivity of the glue is controlled by the pH at which the liquid is buffered.

The solid portion, 'B' part is a solid, powdered mixture of para formaldehyde and fillers. The para is selected for control of glue mix working life and curing efficiency. Fillers are used to provide suitable consistency to the mix, to form a fibrous reinforcement for the adhesive film and to control thixotrnpic behaviour. Wood flours are often used to obtain better 'gap- filling'. Once the liquid and solid portions are mixed the life of the mixture is limited.

Laminating

The glue components must be thoroughly mixed with good agitation to ensure smooth flowing, uniform dispersions. Non uniform mixes give localised gelation and poor spreading characteristics. The amount of glue spread is an important consideration. Inadequate amounts may result in gaps between the plies with no adhesion. In other places the presene of porous elements in wood surface will induce over penetration and hence starvation of the glue line with resultant poor bonds.

In order to speed up laminating processes the beams may be moved into large ovens or heated areas under 'intermediate, temperature conditions. It has the advantage of fast production throughout.

29.

Thermoplastic Resin Adhesives

Introduction

Various types of adhesives based on thermoplastic resins have already been given. Here some of the less important synthetic and natural thermoplastic resin based adhesives are being given. These adhesives find applications for particular purposes. Coumarone indene resins, shellac, and asphalt etc. come under this category. Coumarone-indene resins are synthetic in nature; shellac has animal (insect) origin; CNSL vegetable origin, while asphalt or bitumen has a mineral origin adhesives based on them have only low stress application and coumarone-indene resins are used as adhesive constituents particularly as tackifiers. Individual adhesives are given below.

Cashew Nut Shell Liquid (CNSL) Adhesives

CNSL is obtained from cashew nuts by solvent extraction or by heating of shells. It is made up of phenolic compounds with heating of shells. It is made up of phenolic compounds with unsaturated aliphatic side chains. The main constituents of the liquid are anacardic acid and cardol in the ratio of approx. 9:1. On heating the anacardic acid is decarboxylated to a product known as anacardol or cardanol.

Commercially available CNSL contains mostly cardanol and cardol as it is supplied mosdy after heat treatment either during the extraction of oil. In addition CNSL contains trace quantities of gallic acid, glucosides and certain metal salts and sulphur compounds.

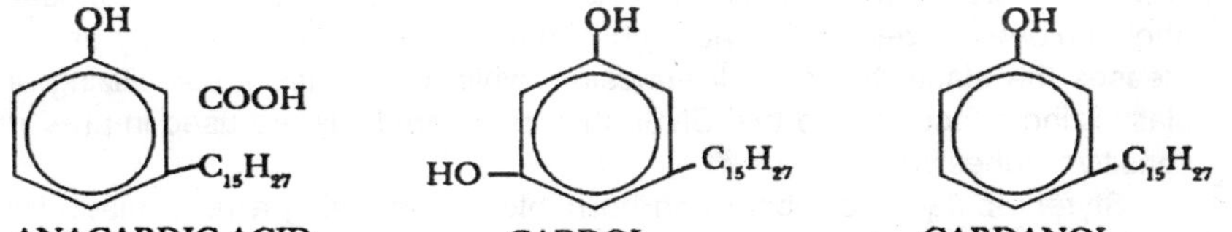

ANACARDIC ACID ($C_{22}H_{32}O_3$)   CARDOL   CARDANOL ($C_6H_4OH\,C_{15}H_{27}$)

Adhesives for Plywood

CNSL- aldehyde resins mixed with tannin aldehyde resins have been used tamarind seed powder as filler to control the flow properties. Cold setting wood adhesives are made from CNSL- phenol-HCHO resins with NaOH as a catalyst. The same resin with 12-20% p-toulene sulphonic acid is used as hardener. Polymerized CNSL can also be used with aldehydes to make plywood adhesives.

Plywood adhesives prepared from CNSL- HCHO or their mixtures with phenol-HCHO, urea- HCHO or CNSL-tannin-HCHO can be made fire proof by incorporation with ammonium phosphate, ammonium dihydrogen phosphate or dialuminium hydrogen phosphate. These adhesives made from CNSL-HCHO and urea can also be used with cuprous chloride or cuprous carbonate for hardness.These adhesives have also been modified by using a polyhydric alcohols along with CNSL and HCHO.

Epoxy resins have also been modified to get solventless adhesives which would cure to room temperature and give greater impact strength and shear resistance by preparing liquid resins from bisphenol-A, epichlorohydrin and a diglycedyl ether of CNSL as plasticizer.

Combination of CNSL and gluten have been used as plywood adhesives. The CNSL adhesives generally appear to cure and increase strength after pressing over prolonged periods. Addition of 2-3% $KMnO_4$ as accelerator was found useful in decreasing the pressing time. Condensation products prepared from CNSL, salicylic acid and aldehydes and then mixed with asphalt, rubber and petroleum resin at -20°C give rust proof tacky adhesive compositions with good impact strength at 20°C and resistant to salt water.

Adhesives can also be prepared from CNSL with gelatinous materials like animal glues, gelatine, blood and eggs, albumin e.g., raw blood, defiberinated haemoglobin white blood albumin, casein, skins as untanned leather, hide powder and gelation. Mixture of CNSL with aqueous solution of casein in the presence of setting agent gives emulsions with high degree of adhesives. Adhesives from CNSL and casein can also be cured by using copper salts as hardners. Reaction of CNSL and shellac under steam pressure gives an adhesive.

CNSL added to rubber adhesives to help the process of incorporation of sulphur and other ingredients. Chloroprene can also be reacted with CNSL to get products from resilient rubber like materials are used to plasticize polychloroprene. They reduce the shore hardness and improve aging characteristics.

Adhesives used for binding nylon, rayon and other fibrous materials, plastics and metal to elastomers or to bond different elastomers are made from rubber (Natural, SBR or nitrile), maleic anhydride adduct and CNSL modified phenol-aldehyde resins. Phenol and naphthol increases the rigidity and decreases the elasticity and self adhesion, while CNSL has a solubilizing and plasticizing effect. Due to this CNSL the above products are used in pressure sensitive adhesive.

Styrene-butadiene rubber can be reinforced by using a resin made from cardanol, cresol and HCHO with hexamine. Compounding is done with ZnO, stearic acid, carbon black and santacure and the vulcanizates have better modulus and hardness. CNSL- aldehyde products can also be melted with styrene-butadiene rubber to improve their tear strength and hot tensile strength. Compoundings of less than 10% cardanol with natural rubber reduces viscosity, increases tackiness and improve tensile strength abrasion resistance and ageing.

Reaction product of cyclopentadiene with CNSL, are useful in adhesive especially in electric insulation tapes.

Asphalt or Bitumen Adhesives

Asphalt or bitumen is a dark, thermoplastic highly viscous or solid substance obtained from petroleum sources. Coaltar pitch is also a related material of almost similar nature. Asphalt or bitumen is obtained as residue of petroleum distillation. It is completely soluble in carbon disulphide. Asphaltic or bitumen adhesives are made in the form of water emulsions, hot melts or solvent solutions.

Properties

These dark materials have poor strength. Their adhesives may be soft, sticky or hard and brittle, depending on the formulations. The adhesive layer is resistant to water, acids and alkalies, but not to oils and many solvents. Their resistance to temperature above 45°C and low temperatures is limited. They are suitable for low stress applications, where durability is important. They have tendency to cold flow even at room temperature. Some of the emulsions resist flow up to even 105°C. It may be compounded with epoxy resins to improve strength properties.

Water may be absorbed in bitumen if the latter contains small amounts of water-soluble components. This water absorption becomes an important factor only with permeable or porous adherends, in continuous contact with pure water at high temperatures.

Applications

Asphaltic adhesives are used for bonding of concrete, glass, metals, felt, paper, and for bonding of tiles to %alls, paper to metal foil. These adhesives are also used for water proofing of walls, road binding, cordboard insulation, lamination and a hot melt component. Their applications may be divided into three broad categories namely lamination, binding and intermediate of the two. Examples of lamination applications are :

(i) Manufacture of laminated paper (duplex or multiples). This paper is then used for packing of tea etc. which is impervious to water and moisture.

(ii) Manufacture of laminates of paper with hessian, metal foil etc. of their combination for packaging.

(iii) Application of tiles to walls and floors, and cork sheets etc. for insulation and other purposes.

Examples of binding applications are :

(i) construction of roads and floors etc.

(ii) Manufacture of coal briquettes

(iii) Manufacture of tiles, pipes and cork sheets etc.

Examples of application of intermediates between laminating and binding are:

(i) Surface treatment of roads,

(ii) Manufacture of coherent slabs of glass wool etc.

Formulation

Bitumen based adhesives are formulated in the following three main categories :

(1) Those containing a bituminous base, volatile solvent together with modi-

fying resins with or without drying oils.

(2) A bituminous base with a large percentage of drying oils.

(3) Emulsified asphalt base plus resin or rubber compounds in water or a latex form.

An example of the first type adhesive for rubber belts is given below :

Ingredients	**Qty. by weight Part**
Asphalt	1
Rosin	1
Gutta pare ha	1
Gasoline	1
Carbon disulphide	15

These materials are allowed to stand; when gutta parcha has swelled, it is stirred and kept covered to prevent loss of solvent. The glue is applied to the surfaces which are then joined, passed between two hot plates.

Gas Tight Joints Cement.

The following formula is of hot melt type containing rosin, rubber small percentage of drying oils.

Asphalt	1 parts
Rosin	6 "
Rubber	3 "
Turpentine	1 "

Rosin and asphalt are melted and then rubber is incorporated. It is kept melted until the rubber also melts : this requires 2-3 hours. Turpentine is tlien added : the mixture is heated and stirred to make it uniform. The molten material is cast into sticks and when required it is applied directly to the objects to be cemented, in the same way as sealing wax. A harder and less cement may be made by increasing the amount of rosin.

Photographic & Optical Lenses Adhesive

The following adhesives are also used as hot-melts.

Formulation

Ingredients		**Qty By Weight**
Black pitch	85 Parts	10 parts
Tallow	10 "	10"
Powdered charcoal	5 "	10 "

Bituminous emulsions may be classified into 3 categories according to the nature of emulsifier used viz. anionics e.g. sodium soaps, cationic e.g. amine hydrochloride or quarternary ammonium salts and finely divided solids e.g bentonite clay etc. The first two types of emulsions show purely viscous behaviour up to about 60% vol. of bituminous phase. When clay is used as emulsifier the emulsion has a marked yield stress and thixotrophy.

Following formulation as suitable as adhesive for paper or wood veneers:

Formulation

Ingredients	**Qty. By Weight**
Refined asphalt	80 parts
Oxidised mineral oil	16 "
Rubber	3 "

The mixture is swilled and dissolved in a suitable solvent.

The following formulation is for an inexpensive adhesives, which may set at high temperatures, suitable for bonding felt pads to metal panels.

Formulation

Ingredients	Qty. By Weight
Emulsified asphalt	12 parts
Sodium silicate 40° Be'	60 "
Clay, 325 mesh	28 "

The following formula is for similar purpose i.e. for bonding felt pads to car bodies. It may set from 100 to 165°C.

Formulation

Ingredients	Qty. By Weight
Asphalt	40-45
Soap emulsifier	0.8-1.2
Clay	1.3
Rubber latex	6-9

The asphalt chosen is low in asphalteus and instead equal parts of asphalt and coumarone-indene resin may also *be* taken. Clay inhibits flow under heat and rubber latex increases bonding strength. The adhesive may be sprayed or brushed.

The following formula is for hot-melt adhesive for making paper containers:

Formulation

Ingredients	Qty. By Weight
Bitumen	30 part
Linseed oil	4"
Petrolatum	15"

Coumarone-indene Resin Adhesives

Coumarone indene resins are mainly used as a modifier in adhesive formulations, rather than as main adhesives. Coumarone and indene are present in coal tar naphtha. They are resinified with sulphuric acid, to give coumarone indene resins, below 20°C.

Properties

Coumarone-indene resins are stable, inert resins having low acidity, varying from pale yellow to dark amber colour. These resins are available in various grades, with various ranges of softening points, varying from heavy viscous liquids to brittle solids. Their m.p. range from 110-127°C for adhesive formulations. These resins have m.wt. of 480 to 700; sp. gr. 1.13 and flash point of 270°C. These resins are usually compatible with various waxes. They are soluble in oils, thinners, solvents, esters, aldehydes ketones and chlorinated hydrocarbons.

Coumarone indene resins give rigid tough films which soften at high temperatures. Due to their non-saponsifiable nature they are attractive for coatings for resisting alkalies. The glue line is thus resistant to water and alkalies, but not oils and greases. They give bonds of low strength.

Applications

As mentioned earlier coumarone resins are predominantly an adhesive constituent rather than an adhesive. They are used for bonding of wood, fabrics, felt; component of hot-melt adhesive formulations and for flooring applications. In conjunction with shellac they are used in the manufacture of grinding wheels. C-I resin solutions are used as surface coatings for making concrete and fabric water proof. C-I. resin and portland cement mixture are strongly adhering surfacing agents for floors or roads.

The following formulation is a very good adhesive :

Formulation

Ingredients	**Qty. By Weight**
Karaya gum	2-5 Parts
Coumarone-indene resin	25
Machine oil	1'
Rubber latex 33 % solids	100

Chlorinated rubber and rubber hydrochloride together with C-I resins give good adhesive formulation. The following formulation is very good for crack and woodwork filling:

Formulation

Ingredients	**Qty. By Weight**
Paracoumarone resin	2-5 parts
Chlorinated rubber	1-4 parts
Toluene	3-15 "
Wood flour	to give a doughy consistency

Pressure-Sensitive Tapes

1 part chlorinated rubber (65-70% chlorine content) is added to 5-10 parts of coumarone resin. This is melted at 150°C and applied to cloth backing without any solvent Chlorinated diphenyl is used as plasticizer for C-I adhesives. One example for such an adhesive is :

Formulation

Ingredients	**Qty. By Weight**
Chlorinated diphenyl viscous liquid	25 parts
Chlorinated diphenyl solid	50 "
Coumarone-in Jene resin	25 "

A coating of coumarone-indene solution in xylene greatly improves adhesions of rubber to the metal after vulcanization. This is particularly used for the preparation of ferrous type breading wires:

Linoleum Cement

Formulation

Ingredients	**Qty. By Weight**
Coumarone resin	283 parts
Benzene	140 "
Denatured alcohol	71 "
Whiting	412 "
Crepe rubber solution in benzene	(5.5%) 55 "

All the ingredients, except whiting, are mixed together and then whiting, is ball-milled with it to get a uniform dispersion.

Phenol-modified indene resins are produced by polymerising coumarone-indene in the presence of phenols or cresols and activated clay at 100°C or lower temperatures in the presence of sulphuric acid. These resins are compatible with alcohols and polyvinyl acetals and give good adhesives particularly the hot melt type e.g.

Formulation

Ingredients	Qty. By Weight
Phenol modified coumarone indene	20.0
partsCoumarone-indene resin, medium soft	66.7
"Polyvinyl acetate	8.3"

The phenol modifed resin is melted at 150-170°C and to it polyvinyl acetate is added; when it shears the C-I resin is introduced. This melt is prepared in an inert atmosphere.

Coumarone-indene Resin Adhesives

Caulking Formulation

Ingredients	Qty. By Weight
Coumarone-indene resin.(60°C)	60 parts
Asbestos filler	20 "
Iron oxide	5 "
Xylene	15 "
Pigment	5 "

Adhesives for linoleum

Formulation

Ingredients	Qty. By Weight
Coumarone-indene resin (115°C)	28.0 parts
Coumarone indene resin (30°C)	2.8 "
Portland-cement	57.2 "
Asbestos	4.6 "
Acetone	2.1 "
Methyl ethyl ketone	8.3 "

Surgical Dressing Adhesives

Formulation

Ingredients	Qty. By Weight
Film scrap	100 parts
Benzene	550 "
Butyl alcohol	8 parts
Castor oil	12 "
Ester gum	20 "
Coumarone-inden resin	10 "
Denatured alcohol	250 "

Moisture Vapour Resistant Film

Formulation

Ingredients	Qty. By Weight
SBR	9 "
Coumarone-indene resin	37 "
Microcrystalline & paraffin	37 "
Wax mixture solvent	as required

Vinyl to Fabric Adhesives

Formulation

Ingredients	**Qty. By Weight**
Nitrile rubber	100 parts
Calcium silicate	40 "
Titanium dioxide	10 "
Coaltar, refined	25 "
Coumarone-indene resin	25 "
Chlorinated rubber	100 "

Solution for Joining Cycle Tubes

Formulation

Ingredients	**Qty. By Weight**
Smoked sheets	100 parts
Calcium silicate	20 "
Coumarone-indene resin	5 "
Zinc oxide	20 "
Stearic acid	1 "
PEN	0.5 "
HPN	0.5 "
Solution	Required for 10 % solution

Shoe Adhesive

Formulation

Ingredients	**Qty. By Weight**
Smoked sheets	110 parts
Calcium carbonate	50 "
Stearic acid	1 "
Zinc oxide	5 "
Antioxidant	1 "
Soft clay	25 "
Coumarone-inden resin	5 "
Solvent	As required

It may be made curable by adding.

MBTS	0.5 "
MBT	0.5 "
Sulphur	1.5 "

Shellac Adhesives

It is a natural resin exuded by insects that infest certain fig trees of India. There are various grades with various degrees of purity and colour for surface coating industry bleached varieties are preferred.

Properties

Shellac gives rigid, tough film, which soften at high temperatures. It is readily soluble in ethyl or methyl alcohol, forming a solution from which it may readily be applied. It has good electrical insulating properties. It lacks flexibility unless compounded with other materials and is resistant to water grease and oils. The bond strengths are moderate.

Applications

Shellac find applications for bonding of porous materials, metals, ceramics, cork and mica flakes. It is used as primer for metals and mica intended for adhesive bonding. Shellac is used for insulating and sealing waxes and as a component of holt-melt adhesives and in electrical industry applications.

The well known use of shellac is as sealing wax; it is sosftened with heat applied and then embossed with a seal. It may be blended with resins to give it the required degree of hardness. The following formula is based on shellac for sealing purposes :

Formulation

Ingredients	**Qty. By Weight**
Shellac	9 parts
Rosin	3 "
Turpentine	1 "
Red vermillion pigment	7 "

Metal to Metal Adhesive

Formulation

Ingredients	**Qty. By Weight**
Bleached shellac	100 parts
Sandrac gum	40 "
Castor oil	15 "
Denatured alcohol	430 "

ILRI has suggested the preparation of laminated board, adhesive board, using modified shellac. 50 parts of formalin and 100 parts of shellace are refluxed at 120°C; to this 200 parts of alcohol is added followed by further refluxing with 15 parts of urea. Addition of 10 parts of p-toluene ethyl sulphonamide, as plasticizer, improves the elasticity of the adhesive film.

Cement For Porecelain Sc China

Formulation

Ingredients	**Qty. By Weight**
Bleached shellac	50 parts
Mastic gum	35 "
Venetian turpentine	10 "
Zinc oxide	5 "

The formulation of adhesives for bonding of mica flakes to get larger, more usable sheets, shellac solution and zinc oxide is used. After removal of solvent they are pressed at 15kg/cm^2 at 125-250°C forming an insoluble reaction product. Small quantity of ethyl cellulose (5 to 20% based on shellac) assists in the bonding offtakes .

Gum Arabic etc. Adhesives

Gum arabic and gum tragacanth come under the category of natural gums and are obtained as exudations of certain trees. These gums differ from rosin, as they are soluble while the rosin is insoluble in water, Cum arabic is obtained from acacia tree. It is sold in powder form or in the form of small lumps, which are quite brittle and range in colour from dark to light according to purity. It is a safe and simple adhesive for miscellaneous paper products. Gum tragacanth is generally employed as a thickening or sizing agent for other adhesive products.

Gum arabic has limited use as an adhesive due to its high cost and also due to brittle nature of the film. Its important speciality applications are use in pill coatings and as a postage stamp glue. Humectants are incorporated to slow down the drying of the film and prevent cracking and crazing. Gum tragacanth is used in bonding cigar wrappings and in temporary bonding of hides to stretching boards in the tanning process. It further promotes creaming of latex emulsions in very low concentrations i.e. 001 to 0.01 %.

Although gum arabic is a good adhesive its properties can be enhanced by the addition of certain salts such as calcium nitrate and aluminium sulphate etc. Gum arabic modified with a small amount of tartaric or similar acids is used to bond aluminium foil to paper. Its other uses are wall paste formulations, adhesive for glassine papers and bonding of regenerated cellulose or cellophane.

Following are some of the adhesive formulation using gum arabic:

Formulation

Ingredients	Qty. By Weight
Gum arabic	100.0 parts
Glycerin	8.0 "
Water	250.0 "
Calcium hydroxide	0.2 "

All are mixed in cold water with stirring and then filtered. Excess glycerin is avoided.

Postage Stamp Adhesive

Formulation

Ingredients	Qty. By Weight
Gum arabic	100.0 parts
Sodium chloride	2.5 "
Glycerin	2.0 "
Water	100.0 "
Starch paste in water 6.2%	32.0 "

Tapioca starch paste is heated to get a clear solution and after cooling it is added to the filtered solution of the other components. The mixture is then stirred till homogenous.

Water Resistant Glue

Formulation

Ingredients	Qty. By Weight
Gum arabic	20 parts
Aluminium sulphate	2 "
Gum tragacanth (20% solution)	15 "
Water	63 "

Gum arabic and aluminium sulphate are dissolved in water and the solution is filtered followed by the incorporation of gum tragacanth.

Cellophane Adhesive

Formulation

Ingredients	Qty. By Weight
Gum arabic	16.5 parts
Glycerin	29.5 "

Water	49.5 "
Formaldehyde, 40 %	4.5 "

Waxed Paper Glue

Formulation

Ingredients	**Qty. By Weight**
Gum arabic	40 parts
Potassium hydroxide	34 "
Water	75 "

Potassium hydroxide is dissolved in water, the solution is cooled and then gum arabic is incorporated in it This glue is very caustic.

Gum arabic should be dissolved in water with wanning and in any case the solution should not beocome very hot, otherwise the gum will lose its tacky nature. One-night soaking in water is preferred.

30.

Vinyl Acetate - Ethylene Copolymer Emulsion Adhesives

Introduction

Polyvinyl acetate and its uses in adhesive application is well known. Unmodified PVA is a horny, hard, brittle resin. The PVA homopolymers were used because of their rapid setting speed, their strength and their ability to adhere to difficulty to bond surface. Good adhesion to these difficult surfaces, however, could be obtained when plasticizers were added in the compounded adhesive mixture. Subsequently when plasticizer migrated to the interface the adhesive joint becomes brittle and could occur on ageing when used in contact with some plastic films, staining occurred presumably due to plasticizer and contaminant migration. To overcome these drawbacks, polyvinyl acetate copolymers, originally developed for paint, came into prominent use. These products were described as internally plasticized PVA. With such experience, the entry of a vinyl acetate ethylene copolymer emulsion on to the commercial scene specifically designed for adhesives use, met with immediate acceptance. These VAE copolymers were not new, but their availability in high solids aqueous dispersions with the rheological properties was novel and responsible for their rapid adoption in the market place.

Today commercially available VAE polymers can be divided into three groups:

(1) Those with low vinyl acetate content (10-40%) polymers are used for hot melt and plastic moulding applications.

(2) Those with nearly equal vinyl acetate and ethylene (45-55%) used for specially rubber application and as a graft base for PVC polymerization for impact modifications.

(3) Those with high vinyl acetate content(60-95%). In this chapter we shall deal with VAE copolymers in which the ethylene content is less than 40 %.

The copolymerization of vinyl acetate with ehtylene provides the opportunity to produce an emulsion in which the dispersed resin may have any flexibility, which a given application requires in the Tg range from 28 to 30°C. Tg is glass transition temperature microscopically, the glass transition is marked by a noticeable increase in the mechanical rigidity as the polymer system changes from a viscous or rubbery state above the Tg to a hard and brittle glass below Tg. In order to visualize this matter, it is helpful to consider that PVA is in effect a modified linear polyethylene. Visualizing polyethylene by the following diagram is instructive.

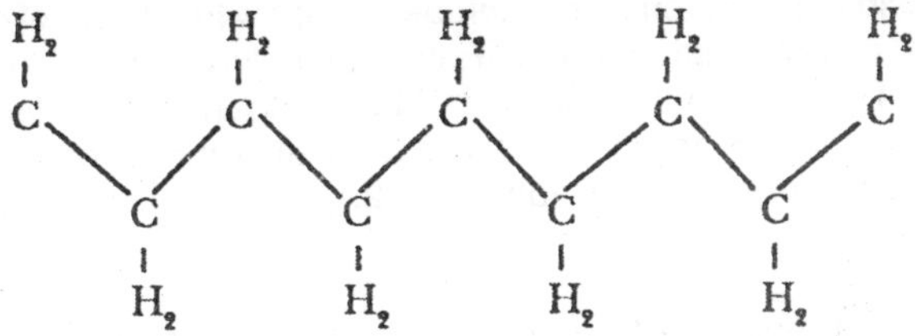

PVA may be represented by a similar diagram with pendent acetate groups on every second C atom. These acetate groups confer polarity to the polymer and specific adhesion to polar substrates.

It is interesting to note that in the range of useful adhesive polymers, the flexibility of a VAE copolymer emulsion is directly dependent upon the % of ethylene in the copolymer and conversely of course the % of acetate groups will decrease as the flexibility goes up. This flexibility increases and of itself will promote adhesion to a wider variety of surface and take advantage of the lowered frequency of acetate groups along the chain which still retains sufficient polarity to adhere to specific surfaces where they are needed. Properties can be varied by changing the emulsion protective system. For example, high viscosity and good machinability are conferred by a polyvinyl alcohol protective system.. Such additives do not interfere significantly with the specific adhesion properties of the resin in suspension. Molecular weight of the resin can be controlled as well as the distribution profile of molecular weight in a given product It is possible to obtain a varying degree of dry tack or to control the tackiness of a given resin by virtue of the % of low molecular weight fraction in the resin body itself. Products can be designed which will be relatively tack free at room temperature but have a high degree of tack at elevated temperature. Table 30.1 demonstrates some of the working properties which are affected by the emulsion protection system and gives a rough idea of some of the methods by which emulsion polymerization chemists can design products for specific uses. In general it is possible to obtain high molecular weight at high solids and with useful viscosities by the use of protective colloids. The type and amount of protection used in polymerization has a great bearing on the physical properties of the resin and the working characteristics of emulsion. It is common to use mixtures of protective colloids and surfactants to obtain the required properties.

Properties

The value of adhesive composition rests upon two basic considerations:

(1) The physical characteristics of the total composition prior to its application to the substrate and its adaptability to the machinery or process that will carry it to the site where it will function as an adhesive.

(2) The properties of the dried or cured adhesive solids with respect to their intended function between spicific substrates.

VAE copolymer is unique in its value as an adhesive resin. As a flexible polymer, the increased elongation at break relative to PVA is not accompanied by the expected loss of tensile strength as occurs in conventional copolymers. To the formulator, this means that VAE affords a means to obtain flexibility in an adhesive resin with minimum loss of tensile strength. Thus the greater adhesion of a flexible resin to nonporous films can be utilized without loss of creep resistance. The addition of plasticizer to VAE emulsion gives" rise to an increase in peel strength of PVC to cloth lamination. This is in striking contrast to the response of conventional copolymer emulsion to plasticizer additions. Typical properties of the emulsion is shown in Table - 30.2.

Applications

The VAE emulsions have found their greatest use in industrial applications. Lasted below are some of those areas : There are two categories.

1. **PVC and other film laminating:**
   - interior wood panelling
   - exterior curtain wall
   - fabrics laminate in upholstery,
   - automotive, luggage, footwear
2. **Packaging adhesive**
   - carton forming and sealing
   - cup manufacture
   - window cartons
   - heat sealing coatings
   - film to film laminating
   - pencil adhesives

TABLE -30.1- Emulsion Properties Controlled by Protective System

polyviny alcohol	Surfactant colloid	Surfactant
Fair water resistance	good water resistance	excellent water resistance
Excellent wet tack Rapid setting Best setting adhesion good polystyrene adhesion	poor wet tack slower good PVC setting fair PVC adhesion Best polystyrene adhesion	poor wet tack slower good PVC adhesion PVC adhesion Fair polystyrene adhesion

TABLE -30.2-TYPICAL PROPERTIES OF VAE EMULSION

Properties	Value
% Viscosity	55
Viscosity	1100-1700 Cps
PH	5.0-6.5
Residual monomer	0.5% max.
Protective colloid	partically acetylated polyvinyl alcohol
Average particle size	0.2 to 1
Density	4.3 kg/let
Benzene insoluble	30-40 % Tg 0°C - 2° C
100 % modulus	280 psi
Ultimate tensile strength	280 psi
Ultimate elongation	1800%
Reaction to borax	Coagulate's

31.

Butyl Rubber and Polyisobutylene Adhesives

Introduction

Butyl rubber and polyisobutylene are elastomeric polymer which are used quite widely in the adhesive and sealants area both as primary binders and as tackifiers and modifiers. The principle difference between them is that butyl is a copolymer of isobutylene with a minor amount of isoprene, while polyisobutylene is a homopolymer. As shown in the following figure, the carbon-hydrogen back bone of butyl rubber is relatively long and straight, containing between 47,000 and 60,000 units. This regular structure, with few double bonds or reactive sites, renders butyl very stable and quite inert to the effects of weathering, age and heat. It has good resistance to vegetable and animal oils to attack by chemicals. Being an all hydrocarbon material, the butyl polymer has a very low water absorption and they do not interfere with the orientation of the rubber molecule.

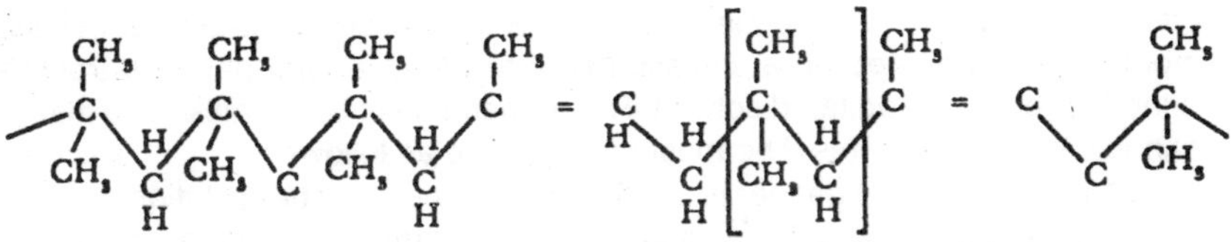

Polymers of isobutylene have little tendency to crystallize and depend upon molecular entanglement The completely amorphous character of these polymers give an internal mobility which imparts flexibility, permanent tack and resistance to shock. Since these polymers are hydrocarbons with no or very little polarity, even though their tack is high, their chemical attraction to many surfaces is weak and therefore they are often mixed with resins which impart some polar character to the blend.

The polyisobutylenes have the same chemical backbone as butyl rubber, but they are essentially free of double bonds in the polymer chain.

Chlorobutyl rubber' is prepared by chlorinating the regular butyl polymer under controlled conditions so that reaction is primarily by substitution and little of unsaturation originally present in the macromolecule is lost. Chlorobutyl can be readily blended and cured with other more highly unsaturated elastomers.

Butyl rubber latex is a water dispersion of a polymer grade. It has a solid content of 63% weight and a pH of 55. Butyl latex has excellent mechanical, chemical, and freeze thaw stability which allows for a wide latitude in compounding and blending with other ingredients. A number of partially crosslinked butyl rubber and other modified forms are available. These products are used in adhesives and sealants where equipment limitation prohibits the use of tougher, regularable forms of butyl rubber.

General Compounding

This wide selection of completely compatible polymers allow the knowledgeable compounder to achieve a wide of properties. Cohesive strength of adhesive can be increased while maintaining other valuable characteristics such as tack. Very fine pigment increases cohesive strength and stiffness, reduces cold flow and also reduces tack. Coarser pigments increase tack. Platy pigments such as mica, graphite and talc are preferred for acid and chemical resistance and gas impermeability. Zinc oxide increases tack and cohesive strength. A wide range of tackifiers and plasticizers are used to extend the viscosity range. The most common plasticizer is polybutene. Resins like polyterpenes, modified rosins, blocked phenolics are added to develop the desired level of tack. Butyl rubber and polyisobutylene are soluble in hydrocarbon and chlorinated solvents which give solutions of much higher viscosity on an equal weight percentage basis. There are four curing systems (1) quinoid cure (2) cure with sulfur (3) resin cure (4) zinc oxide cure.

Processing for Butyl Polymers

Butyl latex is normally compounded with quite simple equipment, commonly a propeller mixer and an open tank. When maximum filler dispersion is required, ball mill may be necessary for part of the mix. Butyl and PIB are often shredded before solvation to greatly increase surface area and thereby decrease solvation time. One clever and quite inexpensive unit uses a modified meat grinder mounted on a solvation tank to feed polymer particles from the grinder directly into agitated solvent. The preparation of butyl caulks and mastics can follow several routes. The most common are as follows :-

(1) A heavy duty kneader is used to make a butyl rubber solution, normally in a mineral spirit. Normally this solution is transferred into another less expensive, lower powered mixer for further compounding with pigments, resins, plasticizers and other ingredients.

(2) A master batch of polymer and filler can be prepared on a mill and the master batch can be solvated in another mixer.

Applications and Formulations

All the formulations are in parts by weight.

(1) Miscellaneous cements

Formulation

(a) Paper cement:

Ingredients	**Parts by Weight**
Isobutylene polymer	100
Hydrocarbon solvent	900

This cement is similar to that sold for home and office use.

(b) Laminating cement for polyethylene film :

Ingredients	**Parts by Weight**
Butyler rubber	100
Terpene phenolic resin	5

Hydrocarbon solvent to appropriate viscosity.

This cement is solvent coated on one substrate and dried. The second substrate is then laminated to the adhesive with moderate roll pressure. In this way the natural lack of the formulation allows impervious materials to be laminated without solvent entrapment.

(c) Flocking adheisve:

Formulation

Ingredients	Parts by Weight
Isobutylene polymer	100.0
Terpene phenolic resin	20.0
Butyl zimate	0.5

Hydrocarbon solvent to appropriate viscosity.

2. Self curing cement

(a) Butyl self curing cement:

The dry ingredients are milled in to the rubber and the resultant mill base is dissolved as indicated. The two parts are mixed just before use.

(b) Chlorobutyl high strength cement: Ingredients

Formulation

Ingredients	Parts by Wt
Chlorobutyl rubber	100
Ditridecyl phthalatek	5

Formulation

Ingredients	Parts by Wt Part A	PartB
Butyl rubber	50.0	50.0
Zinc oxide	2.5	2.5
Stearic acid	1.5	1.5
SRF black	—	40.0
Hydrogenated rosin	20.0	—
Sulfur	0.7	0.7
P-quinone dioxime	2.0	-
PbO_s	—	4.0
Sovent : heptane	400.0	400.0
92% isopropanol	5.0	5.0

Toluene	360
Isopropyl Alcohol	40

3. Pressure Sensitive Adhesives

(a) PIB based PSA for removal Lable stock :

Ingredients	Parts by Weight
Polyisobmylene rubber	100.0
Hydrogenated methyl ester	35.0
Hydrocarbon resin	45.0
Polybutene	70.0
Antioxidant	0.5

Solvent to coatable viscosity

(b) Chlorobutyl blend PSA for general purpose Tape

Ingredients	Parts by Weight
Chlorobutyl rubber	50.0
Styrene - butadiene rubber	50.0
Polymerized rosin	30.0
Polyisobutylene	30.0
Ethyl antioxidant	0.5
Solvent to coatable viscosity	

(c) Simple butyl PSAfor transparent tape

Ingredients	Parts by Weight
Butyl rubber	100
Polyisobutylene	75
Solvent to coatable viscosity	

(d) PSA far vinyl floor Tile:

Ingredients	Parts by Weight
Butyl rubber	100
Polyisobutylene	20
Terpene phenolic resin	70
Solvent to coatable viscosity.	

(e) Solvent adhesive for surgical tape

Ingredients	Parts by Weight
Polyisobutylene	100
Zinc oxide	50
Hydrated alumina	50
White oil	50
Phenolic resin	70
Hydrocarbon solvent to coatable viscosity.	

4. Pipe Wrap and Electrical Tape

Ingredients	Parts by Weight
(a) Pipe Wrap:	
Butyl rubber	100
Carbon black	90
Whiting	20
Polymerized rosin	3
Phenolic resin	7
Copper oxide	2
Process oil	5

(b) Electrical Insulation tape,

Ingredients	Parts by Weight
Butyl rubber	100
Polyisobutylene	10
Resin D	1.0
Zinc oxide	5.0
Vapour talc	60.0

Clay	60.0
Carbon black	10.0
Polytethylene	5.0
Hydrocarbon resin	5.0
Polyac	0.5
P-quinone dioxime	0.2

5. Solvent release sealing compound:

Ingredients	Parts by Weight
Butyl rubber, 50% mineral spirit	200.0
Polyisobutylene	20.0
Isostearic acid	5.0
Fiber talc	300.0
Whiting	200.0
TiO2	25.0
Phenolic resin	35.0
Polybutene	100.0
Blown soya oil	15.0
Cobalt naphthenate, 6%	0.5.0
Silica	20.0
Mineral spirit	55.0

6. Architectural sealing tapes:

Ingredients	Parts by Weight
Butyl rubber	100
Silica	50
Ti02	50
Whiting	300
Talc	150
Polybutene	200
White antioxidant	2

7. Automotive Sealants:

Ingredients	Type A	Type B
Butyl rubber	100	60.0
Chlorobutyl	- -	40.0
Silica 50	-	
$CaCO_5$	-	50.0
Carbon black	140	100.0
Polybutene	140	115.0
Hydrogenated rosin	30	-
Zinc oxide	-	2.0
Magnesium Oxide	-	0.4
Stearic acid	-	0.4

8. Insulated Window Sealant

Ingredient	Parts by Weight
Polyisobutylene	100
Talc	48
Carbon black	2

9. Chemically curing insulated window sealant

Ingredients	Type A	Type B
Butyl rubber	60.0	40.0
$CaCO_3$	75.0	-
Epoxy silane	4.0	-
Polybutene	10.0	-
White antioxidant	1.5	–
P-quinone dioxime	3.5	-
Thixseal	6.0	-
PbO_s	,	7.5
Fumed silica	-	10.0
Toluene	46.0	30.5

10. Wax blends and hat mdt adhesive

Ingredients	Parts by Weight
Ethylene-vinyl Acetate compolymer	25.0
Microcrystalline wax	30.0
Petroleum hydrocarbon resin	35.0
Polyisobutylene	10.0
Antioxidant	0.5.0

11. Rope form of hot mett adhesive

Ingredients	Parts by Weight
Butyl rubber	20
Beta-pinene resin (m.p.)15°C	20
EVA copolymer	20
Lowmol. wt polyethylene (12,000)	20
Low mol. wt polyethylene (20,000)	19
Antioxidan	1

12. Latex Adhesives Dry

Ingredients	Parts by weight
Butyl latex	100.0
Piccovar	65.0
$CaCO_3$	90.0
Polybutene	40.0
Piccopale	45.0
Dispersant	1.0
Thickener	0.9

13. Latex general purpose adhesives

Ingredients	Parts by Weight
Butyl latex	100
Casein (ammoniated)	25
Piccopale	50
Silica	25

32.

Natural Rubber and Reclaimed Rubber Adhesives

Introduction

Latex

Latex is tapped from the tree Hevea brasiliensis and contains about 35 % solids. It is immediately ammoniated to prevent bacterial attack and coagulation. It is to be marketed as latex rather than solid rubber, it is concentrated to a total solid content of 62-72 % by one of three processes-centrifuging, evaporating or creaming.

Natural Rubber

These are prepared directly from latex by deliberate coagulation and treated with hydroxylamine to eliminate aldehydic groups responsible for changes in the viscosity and gel content of the rubber. Some rubbers have their viscosity lowered as well as stabilized. Obviously it is advantageous to the adhesives manufacturer to use a viscosity stabilized rubber of low viscosity because a minimum of mastication is required to obtain solution in the usual solvent and moreover, smoother solutions are obtained due to the virtual absence of gel.

Reclaimed Rubber

In general, a reaction with a high proportion of natural rubber is preferable for adhesive use than one with a high proportion of SBR.

A typical analysis for a whole reclaim is as follows :-

Component	% by wt.
Rubber hydrocarbon	42
Carbon black	26
Acetone extract	21
Ash	11

Natural Rubber Grafted with Methyl Methacrvlate

The very modem introduction of synthetic block copolymers in to adhesion technology may serve as a reminder that a grafted copolymer based on natural rubber has been available and is probably insufficiently utilized. The thermoplastic rubbers are block copolymers of the A-B-A type. The latex is run into the reaction kettle followed by the ammonia solution and then slowly one third of the monomer with additives is run in and stirring is continued for 15 min. One third of the tetraethylene pentamine solution is next added slowly with stirring continued 5 min after the addition. Stirring is then stopped and the reaction allowed to proceed for at least one hr until the reaction temperature is fallen below 30°C. During the whole of this time cooling should be used as necessary to keep the reaction temperature below 40°C. After this initial period of reaction, stirring is restarted and a further one third of the reagents are added exactly as before. This is repeated for remaining one third of the reagents and the reactor is then allowed to stand for 8 hr after which it is discharged through a stainless steel strainer.

The latex form of natural rubber is compounded in the usual way by the addition of additives. Solution polymerized natural rubber is made from masticated pale crepe rubber. A laboratory scale preparation is as follows. About 10 g are dissolved in 170 ml of toluene and 20 g of inhibitor free methyl methacrylate monomer is added with stirring for 30 min. Then 10 ml of a 2% solution in toluene or benzoyl peroxide is added. The mixture is refluxed for 10 hrs at 80°C in inert atmosphere. The mixture has a conversion of original 60 % monomer to 55 % grafted polymer. Following table shows the recipe for preparation of latex.

Manufacturing Recipe for Latex Formulation :

Ingredients	Parts **by Wt.**
Natural rubber latex concentrate (high ammonia, 60 % total solids)	1000.00
Ammonia solution (2% by wt)	738.00
Methyl methacrylate monomer (stabilizer less than 0.02% hydroquinone)	610.00
T-butyl hydroperoxide	1.80
Oleicacid	3.00
Tetra ethylene pentamine aqueous solution (10%by wt.)	7.00

Depolymerized Rubber

This is of minor interest only, and this is because of its use as an adhesive for fixing bristless in brushes, is depolymerized rubber. This material is a liquid rubber prepared by heating raw natural rubber in air at 250°C. This material is soluble in most organic solvents except alcohols and ketones and is compatible with many drying oils.

All the formulations are based on parts by weight and normally dry weight unless otherwise stated.

1. Self Adhesive Envelopes

Formulation

Ingredients	**Parts by Wt.**
60 % Natural latex	100.00
10 % potassium hydroxide	0.20
50 % aqueous dispersion of zinc ethyl dithiocarbamate	0.50

2. Ceramic Tile Adhesive (A)

Formulation

Ingredients	**Parts by Wt.**
60 % Natural latex	100

(sodium pentachlorophenate preserved)	
Methyl cellulose (added as 5% sols.)	5
Gypsum	130-200
Bentonite	10
Surfactant 10 % soln.	10
Tackifying resin dispersion	20

3. Ceramic Tile Adhesive (B)

Formulation

Ingredients	**Parts by Wt.**
60 % Natural latex	100
(sodium penta chlorop henate preserved	
50 % polyvinyl acetate	120
Surfactant (10% solu.)	10
Gypsum	200-250
Bentonite	20
Tackifying resin dispersion	20

4. Floor Tile Adhesive (C)

Formulation

Ingredients	**Parts by Wt.**
60 % Natural latex1	00
Methyl cellulose (added as 5% sol.)	5
Clay	150
Black reclaim dispersion	50
Tackifying resin dispersion	
High boiling point naphtha	30-80
(added as emulsion)	10

5. Leather Adhesive :

Formulation

Ingredients	**Parts by Wt.**
60 % Natural latex	100.0
Sodium ethylene diamine tetraacetate, 20 % soln.	2.5
Antioxidant (Polymerized trimethyl hydroquinine as 50 % dispersion)	0.5

6. Automobile Internal Trim

Formulation

Ingredients	**Parts by Wt.**
60 % Natural latex	100.0
Methyl cellulose (added as 5 % soln.)	2.0
Antioxidant (as 50% dispersion)	2.0
Clay as 50 % dispersion	50.0
Coumarone-Indene dispersion	20.0

7. Food Jar Sealing Compound

Formulation

Ingredients	**Parts by Wt.**
60 % Natural latex (ammonia preserved)	100
Clay (as 50 % dispersion stabilized with food grade Surfactant)	200

8. Crown Cork Adhesive

Formulation

Ingredients	**Parts by Wt.**
60% Natural latex	100.0
Fungicide	0.2
Ethylene glycol	0.8
Ammonium caseinate. 20% soln in water	11.2
Sodium hydroxide	0.1
Added with water	0.3
Formalin	5.1
Ester gum	3.7
Mineral oil	0.4
Water	6.2

Fungicide is dissolved in ethylene glycol. Ester gum and mineral oil are mixed and then dispersed in the given quantity of water.

9. General Purpose Pure Gum Adhesive

Formulation

Ingredients	**Parts by Wt.**
60 % Natural latex	100
Zinc dibutyl thiocarbamate 50 % dispersion)	.2
Ammonium caseinate 10- % solution	10

10. Tufted Carpet Adhesive and Backing

Formulation

Ingredients		**Parts by Wt.**
Natural latex (high ammonia)	100.0	100.0
Stabilizer/wetting agent	1.0	1.0
Thio urea (added as 10% solution)	1.0	1.0
Antioxidant to give 75 % solids	1.0	1.0
Water Whiting (added as slurry)	400.0	250.0
Polyacrylate thickener (added as 5 % solution)	0.2	0.3

11. Adhesive Binder far non-woven Fabrics

Formulation

Ingredients	**Parts by Wt.**
Concentrated natural latex	100.0

Anionic stabilizer	0.5
Sulfur	2.0
ZDC	1.5
Zinc mercaptabenzthiozole	1.5
Antioxidant	5.0
Zinc oxide	5.0

12. Tufted Carpet Vulcanizing Composition

Formulation

Ingredients	**Parts by Wt.**	
Natural latex	25	25
SBR latex	75	75
Whiting	200	225
Barytes	10	-
Clay	10	
Sulfur, zinc oxide, and accelerators	10	10
Dispersing agents, alkali and karaya gum	as required	

13. Surgical Tape Adhesive

Formulation

Ingredients	**Parts by Wt.**
Natural rubber	100
Ester gum	100
Lanolin	20
Zinc oxide	50

14. Industrial Pressure Sensitive Tape

Formulation

Ingredients	**Parts by Wt.**
Natural rubber (pale crepe)	100
Poly (B-pinene) resin,m.p.700C	75
Colourless petroleum oil	5
Polymerized trimethyldihydro	2

15. Industrial Pressure Sensitive Tape

Formulation

Ingredients	**Parts by Wt.**
Natural Rubber	100.0
Coumarone Indene resin(30)	30.0-150.0
Antioxidant	1.5
Calcium carbonate or zinc oxide	30.0-15

16. General Purpose Transparent Adhesive

Formulation

Ingredients	**Parts by Wt.**
Natural rubber	100
Rosin	10
Antioxidant	1

17. General Purpose Black Adhesive

Formulation

Ingredients	**Parts by Wt.**
Natural rubber	100.0
Whole tyre reclaim	100.0
Coumarone resin	50.0
Whiting	50.0
Antioxidant	1.5
Parts by Wt.	

18. General Purpose Black Adhesive with better heat resistance:

Formulation

Ingredients	**Parts by Wt.**
Natural rubber	100.0
Whole tyre reclaim	100.0
Zinc resinate	50-80.0
Clay	50.0
Antioxidant	1.5
Polyisocyanate	10.0

19. Vulcanizing Cement

Formulation

Ingreients	**Parts by Wt.**	
	Type A	**Type B**
Natural rubber	100.0	100.0
Sulfur	2.0	-
Butyl zimate	-	7.0
Zinc oxide	20.0	-
Antioxidant	5.0	

20. Fabric Combining for Double Texture Water Proof

Formulation

Ingredients	**Parts by Wt.**	
	Part A	**Part B**
Natural rubber	100	100
Zinc oxide	10	-
Sulfur	8	-
Zinc isopropyl xanthate	4	-

21. Fabric Combining For Coated Fabrics

Formulation

Ingredients	Parts by Wt.		
	Part A	Part B	Part C
Robac gamma (ultra accelerator)	15.0	-	-
Waxolene red	0.12	-	-
Coal tar naphtha	84.88	-	-
Natural rubber	-	21.60	7.90
Zinc oxide	-	1.10	-
Antioxidant	-	0.30	-
Rubber petroleum solvent	-	77.0	73.20
Sulfur	-	-	17.40
Waxolin yellow	-	-	1.50

The above types are mixed by volume in the proportion of 1 : 20:1

22. Reclaim Rubber Dispersion with Asphalt

Formulation

Ingredients	Parts by Wt.
Whole tyre reclaim	100
Surfectant	2-5
Caustic potash	1-2
Ester gum	0-30
Clay	30-40
Asphalt emulsion	175-185
Water	70-80

23. Road Repair Compound

Formulation

Ingredients	Parts by Wt.
Natural rubber (powder)	1
Asphalt	60
Sharp sand with fine aggregate broken stone	54

24. Great Copolymer Primer far Pvc

Formulation

Ingredients	Parts by Wt.
Copolymer	5.0
Titanium dioxide	0.1
Solvent	100.0

33.

Nitrile Rubber Adhesives

Introduction

Nitrile rubbers are rubber-like copolymers of unsaturated nitriles with dienes. The commerical nitrile rubbers are predominantly copolymers of butadiene and acrylonitrile. The oil resistance and adhesive properties of these copolymers increases with an increase in nitrile content. The nitrile rubbers are compatible with phenol-formaldehyhde resins, resorcinol-formaldehyde resins, hydrogenated rosins, epoxies and coal tar resins which can be cured and which can provide excellent adhesives of high strength. They are superior to chloroprene in compatibility with resins. The nitrile rubber adhesives are applied in the form of latexes, cements, mastics and tapes. They have outstanding shelf stability and high temperature properties. They have been used for coating fabrics to provide oil resistance and wear resistance. Blended with phenolic resins, they have been used to:

1. laminate aluminium to stainless steel
2. fabricate many airplane structures
3. bond abrasives to metal
4. bond break lining to brake shoes
5. fabricate panels for curtain-wall construction.
6. bond metal to nitrile rubber stocks
7. laminate leather
8. attach soles in shoe manufacturing
9. bond cork, card board, leather board, paper, nitrocellulose, nylon and other polymeric films.

The nitrile rubbers have excellent compatibility as adhesives with polar adherends such as protein fibres, textiles paper and wood.

(1) Recipe for Spraying Applications

Ingredients	Parts by Wt. Type A	Parts by Wt. TypeB
Nitrile rubber	10.0	10.0
Methyl ethyl ketone	79.0	79.0
Water	11.0	11.0
Carboxylic vinyl polymer		0.5
Di-(2-ethyl hexyl) amine		0.5

(2) Compounding Nitrile Rubber Cements

Nitrile rubbers may be compounded for many cement applications and are preferable where oil resistance is of .prime importance for self/adhesion of nitrile rubber stocks. The use of a cement solution of the rubber stock itself is an excellent and usually preferred adhesive. Additional tackifier and accelerator are often added. Cholorinated rubber has been used to improve tack stability and adhesion. Curing agents are used with nitrile rubbers when high strength and especially strength at elevated temperatures is a requisite of the adhesive. Softeners are sometimes employed to improve tack and adhesive properties. Pigments are included for the improvement of heat resistance and reduction of cost Carbon blacks enhance the strength of cured nitrile films. The best black for cement is channel black, usually used in amounts of 40 to 60 parts of the nitrile rubber. Softer blacks give lower tensile properties but provide longer shelf life and some where lower costs. Among the non black pigments, iron oxide zinc oxide, hydrated silica, titanium dioxide and clays are the most commonly employed. Iron oxide yields smooth cement of relatively high tensile strength, improved tack and storage life but lacking good abrasion resistance. Zinc oxide improves tack but not film strength. Hydrated silica is used to improve tensile strength. Titanium dioxide is used to impart whiteness, promote Jack and extend storage life. Clays are employed to reduce cement cost Antioxidants are added to improve heat resistance. They may also contribute stability and tack. A typical black curing cement recipe for nitrile rubber is the following.

(1) Black Curing Cement

Formulation

Ingredients	**Parts by Wt.**
Nitrile rubber	100
Zinc oxide	5
Sulfur	3
EPC black	50
Resin D	5
Coumarone-Indene resin	25
Refined coal tar	25

(2) Non Black Curing Cement

Formulation

Ingredients	**Parts by Wt.**
Nitrile rubber	100.0
Stearic acid	0.5
Zinc oxide	10.0
Sulfur .	2.0
Calcium silicate	100.0
TiO_2	25.0
Coumarone Indene resin	10.0
Dibutyl Phthalate	10.0
Accelerator	1.5

(3) Laminating Adhesive

Ingredients

(A) High activated adhesives

Adhesive for leather to leather	Parts by Wt.			
Recipe No.	1	2	3	4
Nitrile rubber	20.0	10.0	20.0	10.0
VMCH	-	10.0	-	5.0
Phenolic resin	10..0	5.0	10.0	5.0
Triphenyl phosphate	-	-	-	2.0
Monochloro benezene	-	-	90.0	40.0
Methyl ethyl ketone	100	75.0	30.0	40.0

Adhesives for Leather to Vinyl

	1	2	3	4
Nitrile rubber	9.0	9.0	9.0	9.0
VMCH	18.0	18.0	18.0	18.0
Triphenyl phosphate	2.0	2.0	2.0	-
Phenolic resin	-	-	-	2.0
Terahydrofuran		-	58.0	-
Methyl ethyl ketone	73.0	-	20.0	73.0
Toluene	-	-	48.0	-
Cyclohexanol	-	25.0	25.0	-

B. Low Temperature Curing Adhesives

Formulation

Ingredients	Parts by Wt.
Nitrile rubber	10-50
Epoxy resin	90-50
Methyl ethyl ketone	80
Triethylete tramine	2-20

Such cement will cure in 4 to 24 hr. at room temperature or in less than 30 min. at 60°C.

C. Miscellaneous Lamination

Polyvinyl chloride, polyvinyl acetate and other polymeric films have been laminated to aluminium, brass and other metals by coating the polymeric film and the metal with an adhesive consists of:

Formulation

Ingredients	Parts by Wt.
Nitrile rubber	150
Vinyl chloride-vinylidene	50
Chloride copolymer	20
Plasticizer	10
A barium stabilizer	6
Sulfur	1
Benzothiazolvl disulfide	1

Cellulose acetate flock has been adhered to textile material to make a pile surface using following cement:

Formulation

Ingredients	**Parts by Wt.**
Nitrile rubber	100.0
Sulfur	3.0
Mercaptobenzothiazole	2.4
Phenyl guanidine	0.6
Zinc oxide	7.5
Coumarone resin	37.5
Dimethyl phthalate	300.0
bis (2-ethyl hexyl)phthalate	45.0
Methyl ethyl ketone	378.0
Methyl isobutyl ketone	256.0

(4) General Purpose Cements

Formulation

Ingredients	**Parts by Wt.**
(A) Heat Activated:	
Nitrile rubber	100
Phenolic resin	50
Methyl ethyl ketone	100

(B) Self Curing Cements:

Formulation

Ingredients	**Parts by Wt.**
Master Batch	
Nitrile rubber	100
Zinc oxide	5
Carbon black	100

Component A

Formulation

Ingredients	**Parts by Wt.**	
Base Master batch	**205**	**205**
DBA	4	-
MBT	-	4
Sulfur	4	4
MEK	40	40

Components B

Ingredients	**Parts by Wt.**	
Base Master batch	**205**	**205**
ZBX	4	-
Ethazate	4	-
Butene	-	4
CPB	-	4
MEK	40	40

(C) Low Temperature Curing Cements

Formumation

Ingredients	**Parts by Wt.**	
	Part A	**Part B**
Nitrile rubber	100.0	100.0
Zinc oxide	5.0	5.0
Sulfur	6.0	
Channel black	50.0	50.0
Coumarone indene resin	5.0	25.0
Aldol-c-nepthyl amine	5.0	5.0
Aromatic oil	25.0	25.0
Mercaptobenzothiazol		6.0

(D) Splice Adhesive

An adhesive designed for splicing cured or uncured nitrile compounds to themselves with heat is shown below :

Formulation

Ingredients	**Parts by Wt.**
Nitrile rubber	100
Zinc oxide	15
Aminox	2
Carbon black	50
Coumarone- Indene resin	25
Phenolic resin	20
MBT	2
Sulfur	2

(E) Cement of High Tack

Formumation

Ingredients	**Parts by Wt.**	
	Part A	**Part B**
Nitrile rubber	100.0	100.0
Carbon black	10.0	10.0
Zinc oxide	150.0	150.0
Resin D	5.0	5.0
Refined coal tar	35.0	35.0
Benzyl alcohol	18.0	18.0
Dibutyl metacresol	35.0	35.0
Sulfur	5.0	-
Butyraldehyde aniline	-	8.0

An extra tacky cement may be prepared as follows : Dissolve 1400 gms of A in 1/2 it chlorotoluene and make up 1 it with chlorobenzene. Dissolve 1400 gms of B in 1/2 lt of chlorotoluene and make up to 1 lt with chlorobenzene. Mix equal proportion of A and B volume just before using.

(F) Spreading Compounds

The following spreading compounds is recommended for maximum resistance to petrol and oil and for low temperature flexibility.

Formulation

Ingredients	Parts by Wt.	
Nitrile rubber	100.0	100.0
Zinc oxide	5.0	5.0
Sulfur	2.0	2.0
Carbon black	75.0	60.0
Triacetin	35.0	-
Benzothiazolyl disulfide	1.5	-
Litharge	-	10.0
Resin D	-	2.0
Dioctyl phthalate	-	25.0

(G) General Purpose Spreading Compound

Formulation

Ingredients	Parts by Wt.
Nitrile rubber	100.0
Zinc oxide	5.0
Sulfur	2.5
Carbon black	75.0
Castor oil	10.0
Synthetic resin extender	20.0
Benzothiazolyl disulfide	1.5
Stearic acid	1.0

The above spreading compounds are dissolved in nitroethane before use .

(H) Coating Cement for Paper Resistant to Oils :

The recipe below is for a fast curing cement for paper coating that retains good adhesion after hot oil aging at 70°C.

Formulation

Ingredients	Parts by Wt.
Nitrile rubber	100.0
Zinc oxide	5.0
Sulfur	1.5
Carbon black	20.0
Clay	75.0
Whiting	75.0
Phenolic resin	40.0
Plasticizer	10.0
Resin D	1.0
Benzothiazolyl disulfide	1.0

Add 3 % hexamethylene tetramine, 5 % is propyl alcohol and 95 % methyl ethyl ketone to make up as a 35 % solids before use. The cement can be cured at 70°C and can be refrigerated to prolong working life if it cannot be used immediately.

(I) White Cement Formulation

Methyl ethyl ketone is used to make 15 % total solids.

Formulation

Ingredients	**Parts by Wt.**
Nitrile rubber	100.0
Zinc oxide	5.0
Sulfur	1.5
TiO_2	15.0
Hydrated silica	25.0
Chlorinated paraffin wax	10.0
Tetramethylthiuram Monosulfide	0.4
Stearic acid	1.0

(J) Non Black Cement Formulation :

A similar non black cement suggested for the adhesion of cotton , wood paper, leather nuclear shoe lining is given below :

Formulation

Ingredients	**Parts by Wt.**
Nitrile rubber	100
Stearic acid	1
Zinc oxide	5
Calcium silicate	10
Sulfur	2
Dibenzylamine	2
Methyl ethyl ketone	600

(K) Leather Adhesives Have been Formulated from Nitrile Rubber Using the Following Composition:

Formulation

Ingredients	**Parts by Wt.**
Nitrile rubber	100.0
Vinyl chloride-vinyl acetate copolymer	100.0
Zinc oxide	5.0
Stearic acid	1.5
Calcium silicate	2.0
Solvent	600:800

(L) Vinyl to Fabric Adhesive

Formulation

Ingredients	**Parts by Wt.**
Nitrile rubber	100
Calcium silicate	40
$Ti0_2$	10
Refined coal tar	25
Coumarone-indene resin	25
Chlorinated rubber	100

(M) Nitrile Rubber Phenolic Resin Tape Formulation :

Formulation

Ingredients	**Parts by Wt**
Nitrile rubber	100
Phenolic resin	75
Zinc oxide	5
Sulfur	3
Accelerator	1
Stearic acid	1
Carbon black	20
Filler	100
Plasticizer	10

(N) Pressure Sensitive Adhesive

This adhesive especially useful as a gum coating for plastic, paper, fabric tapes and labels :

Formulation

Ingredients	**Parts by Wt.**
Nitrile rubber	100
Coumarone-Indene resin (m.p. 45-55°C)	100

Solvent- Mathyl ethyl and toluene Solid concentration 20 % by wt.

Blend rubber and resin in a shaker and add solvent until a smooth, free flowing cement is obtained.

(O) Structural Adhesives

Nitrile rubbers blended with phenolic resin may be used to bond a wide variety of construction material including iron, wood, glass, masonite, fibre board, card board, cork, phenolic resin, vinyl chloride and many porous materials.

Part A

Ingredients	**Parts by Wt.**
Phenolic Resins	45.00
MEK/M Chlorobenzene 70/30 by rol	90.00

Part B

Formulation

Ingredients	**Parts by Wt.**
Nitrile rubber	100.0
Carbon black	50.0
Zinc oxide	5.0
Stearic acid	0.5
Sulfur	3.0
Benzothiazyl disulfide	1.5
MEX/M-chlorobenzene	165.0

Nitrile Rubber Latex Adhesives

The principal advantages in employing nitrile rubber latex adhesives, rather than solvent cement adhesives of the same nitrile rubber are the freedom from fire and toxicity hazards.

Blends of nitrile rubber' latex with casein have been used to adhere vinyl sheeting and vinyl plastisol coatings to paper, nylon and rayon.

Phenolic resins may be blended with nitrile rubber latexes to give adhesives useful for bonding and impregnation of many surfaces.

Blends of nitrile rubber latexes with "vinsol" yield adhesives uses in the bonding of aluminium foil, asbestos board, card board and craft paper.

34.

Pressure Sensitive Adhesives

Introduction

Pressure sensitive adhesive products encompass typically webs of paper, plastic films or sheets of metal foils carrying on one side a coating layer of a solventless, solid adhesive composition that possesses sufficient tackiness or tack to permit such webs of paper, plastic or metal to be adherend to the surface of an object by merely contacting and momentarily pressing the adhesive layer carrying side of the web directly against the object surface. Generally in the technology of pressure sensitive adhesives, the physical properties known in the ark as tack, peel adhesion and creep resistance are paramount in determining the suitability of any given pressure sensitive adhesive composition to provide the necessary application properties and in service durability required of the pressure sensitive adhesive product.

The first property, tack, is in effect the instantaneous adhesion of the adhesive layer of the web to the surface of an object that is developed immediately after contacting the web with the surface. The second important property, peel adhesion, is the adhesion of the pressure sensitive adhesive product after the adhesive layer has been in contact with an adherent surface for sufficient period of time to reach a steady state or equilibrium with the .surface. For pressure sensitive adhesive products that are meant to be only temporarily adhered, such as masking tapes and descriptive labels, peel adhesion of one kg or less is usual. Conversely, the products that are to be permanently adherend, such as product trademark or institution lables, must exhibit peel adhesion of at least 1.5 kg with level of 2.5 kg or more being preferred. The third physical property utilized to define the suitability of pressure sensitive product for a given use is its creep resistance. Ideally, pressure sensitive adhesive products, whether removal or permanent are sought that exhibit no separation.

In readily, however, products withstanding fifty hours or more of stress are considersed to be superior. The pressure sensitive adhesive must be formulated so as to exhibt resistance to adhesive degrading environmental conditions such as elevated temperature, sunlight, organic solvents, moisture, acids and bases to which pressure sensitive adhesive product will be exposed in service.

Some of the typical examples are as follows :

Formulation

Ingredients	**Parts by Wt.**
1. Milled pale crepe	100
Poly-beta-pinene resin (m.p. 700C)	75
Petroleum oil	5
Polymerized trimethyl dihydroquinoline	2

Formulation

Ingredients	**Parts by Weight**
2. Milled smoked sheet rubber	100
Zinc oxide	50
Dehydrogenated rosin	75
Sym-di-beta-naphthyl-para-phenylene diamine	2
Lanolin	10

Formulation

Ingredients	**Parts by Weight**
3. Butadiene-styrene copolymer (70:30 ratio)	50
Milled smoked sheet rubber	50
Ester of hydrogenated rosin	50
Polymerized trimethyl dihydroquinoline	2
Petroleum oil	20

Formulation

Ingredients	**Parts by Wt.**
4.Polyvinyl ethyl ether	100.00
Hydrogenated rosin	50.00
Phenyl-alpha-naphthylamine	0.35
Polyethylene glycol diricinoleate	1.50

Adhesives of No. 1,2 & 3 are typical formulations for most general applications, whereas No. 4 is employed where unusual clarity and sunlight ageing are required. For high temperature masking tape application a pressure sensitive adhesive is usually necessary.

A typical pressure adhesive :

Formulation

Ingredients	**Parts by Wt.**
5.Crude rubber	50
GRS	50
Octyl phenol formaldehyde	20
ZnO	60
Diethylene glycol ester of dehydroabietic acid	110
Antioxidant	2

Control of the amount of cure is necessary for optimum performance. Insufficient cure will cause shear failures at elevated temperature. Over cure will result in the loss of some of the pressure sensitive tope properties.

6. Pressure sensitive acrylic adhesives are being used on many speciality tapes because of water white clarity and extremely good resistance to changes due to oxidation. A typical example is as follows :

Typical Pressure Sensitive Acrylic Adhesive :

Formulation

Ingredients	**Parts by Weight**		
	A	**B**	**C**
Fuse oil ester of acrylic acid	95	—	—
2-ethyl hexyl acrylate	-	75.00	80
Vinyl acetate	-	18.00	93
Acrylic acid	5	-	2
Maleic anhydride	-	2.00	-
Diacetone acrylamide	-	5.00	5
3- Methyloxy propyl trimethyl silane	-	0.05	-

7. A thermoplastic tackifying resin is prepared by the following method : Into a reactor are charged 200 parts of heptane and 6 parts of anhydrous aluminium chloride at a temperature of about 25°C while continuously stirring the mixture, 400 parts of a hydrocarbon mixture containing unsaturated hydrocarbons are slowly added to the reactor over a period of about 90 minutes. Temperature of the reactor is maintained at about 30°C for about 60 minutes. The hydrocarbon mixture has the following composition:-

Thermoplastic Tackifying Resin Adhesive

Formulation

Ingredients	**Parts by Wt.**
2 pentene	5 parts
Isoprene	45 "
Unsaturated hydrocarbon	50 "

After this polymerization, 25 parts of water, 8 parts of hydrated calcium hydroxide and 8 parts of clay are added to the polymerize and the agitation continued for about 120 minutes at 90°C. The mixture is then filtered to remove insoluble catalyst, calcium and clay. The filtrate is then steam distilled at a pot temperature of 235°C. The residual molten resin is poured from the reactor and cooled.

8. Adhesive Strip For Automotive Trim,

Formulation

Ingredients	**Parts by Weight**
Chlorinated rubber	200
Isobutylene-divinyl aromatic polymer	200
Hydrogenated wood resin	44
Tall oil fatty acids	8
Carbon black	140
Oil in carbon black	
Asbestos powder	320
Processing oil	475
Talc	320
Calcium oxide	46

The hydrogenated wood resin increases tackiness. The tall oil fatty acid acts as a wetting agent for the particulate materials. The line binds any water present. In the mixing procedure, the elastomers are charged into jacketed mixer and then hydrogenated rosin is added and mixed into a homogenous mass at 71°C. Then carbon black is added and mixed to a smooth consistency. Then the asbestos and about one fourth of the processing oil is added and mixed. Now the hydrated silica, another fourth of the processing oil, the talc and lime are mixed. The balance of the processing oil now is mixed in the mixture is cooled and discharged from the mixture. The composition is extruded through a die to form a tape.

9. E V A Trialkyl Cyanurate Copolymer Adhesive

Formulation

In to an agitator autoclave of stainless steel, the following substances are introduced: 400 parts by weight of vinyl acetate; 100 parts of butyl acrylate 600, parts of benzene, 280 parts of a stabilizer solution containing 10 % by weight of polyisobutyl vinyl ether, 4 parts of triallyl cyanurate dissolved in vinyl acetate, 4 parts of tert-butyl perpivalate, and 260 parts by weight of ethylene. The mixture is agitated, for 30 hours at 60°C. After cooling and depressurizing to normal, a dispersion is made.

10. Carboxylate Polymer Based Adhesives:

Formulation

Ingredients	**Parts by Wt.**
Maleic anhydride	7
Butyl acrylate	40
Ethylene-vinyl acetate copolymer	53
Glycerine ester of hydrogenated rosin	30
Coumarone-indene resin (m.p.1000C)	3
Coumarone-indene resin (Liquid)	10
Dioctyl phthalate	10
Antioxidant	05

The above mixer was blended in a molten state at 150°C for about 6 hours.

11. Fumaric Diester Vinyl Acetate Polymer :

Formulation

Ingredients	**Parts by Wt.**
Di-2-ethyl hexyl fumarate	64.0
Vinyl acetate	30.0
Monoisopropyl fumarate	5.0
Glycidyl methacrylate	1.0
Acetone	13.0
Petrol (B.P. 85°C)	53.4

The mixture is placed in a vessel of stainless steel which is provided with stirrer, reflux condenser, thermometer, and nitrogen feed which can be heated with steam. The mixture of the monomer is dissolved in the solvent while stirring and warmed to the reflux temperature (48°C). 0.2 parts by weight of dibenzoyl peroxide (75 % water) dissolved in a little acetone, is then added as initiator. After 11 hours of reaction petrol is added. After a total reaction time of 15 hours the copolymer is ready for use.

35.

Resin for Rubber Based Adhesive

Indroduction

Rubber based adhesives offer the greatest variety of properties of any generic class of adhesive. Relatively low strength system such as rubber cement, pressure sensitive tapes and self seal envelops, all of which are based upon rubber have become household items. Other types of rubber based adhesives have been developed which are used for high strength structural applications required by the air craft, automotive, and other industries. The unusually wide range of properties available in adhesives based on elastomers is due in part to (a) the variety of properties obtainable in natural and synthetic rubber (b) the many modifying materials such as tackifying resins, filleres plasticizers and curing agents which may be physically or chemcally incorporated into the elastomers. The many modifications possible for rubber based adhesives have played a major part in their spectacular market growth in recent years.

Adhesive Components

Rubber based adhesives may contain a wide variety of components materials such as elastomers, resins or tackifiers, fillers, plasticizers and softeners, antioxidants, curing agents and sequestering agents. In addition to the components cited above, aqueous adhesives based on latex rubber also employ a wide variety of other materials suh as protective colloids, emulsifier thickeners and emulsion stabilizers.

Types of Rubber Based Adhesives

Rubber based adhesives are produced in a number of different forms such as solvent cement, latex cements, pressure sensitive tapes, sealants, mastics and hot melts.

Solvent Cements

Solvent cements are generally produced by removing the freshly milled elastomers from the mill and dissolving it in solvent. This "cutting" of the rubber into a solvent is accomplished in low speed mixing equipment known as churns. For natural rubber and SBR, solvents such as toluene, hexane, naphtha, gasoline or "rubber solvent" may be used for nitrile. Polychloroprene and other polar rubbers, polar solvents such as MEK, MIBK or ethylene dichloride may be used, alone or blended with nonpolar types. This dissolved rubber may then be blended with a solution of additives such as resins, to form the finished cement. Alternatively, direct addition of the dry materials such as tackifiers may be made to the rubber solution.

Latex Cements

Natural rubber originates as a latex or water dispersed colloid collected as sap from certain species of tropical trees. Most synthetic rubbers are produced by emulsion polymerization and are, therefore, normally available in latex form. Those of greatest commercial interest are styrene butadiene, acrylonitrile-butadiene and polychloroprene types. Rubber latex is considerably less viscous than a 15 % solution of milled rubber in toluene. For this reason, latex systems have many advantages over the solvent type. Major applications for latex adhesives are for porous substrates such as textiles, paper and leather. An effective way to improve tack and adhesivesness of an elastomer in latex form is by the addition of water dispersed resins as tackifiers. Since latex system exhibits better "hold out" on porous surfaces, one coat of such an adhesive often suffices for good bonding. Latex adhesives furnish adequate strength for a large number of applications. Probably over three quarters of all shoes made employ latex cements at some steps in the manufacturing process. Latex adhesives are used on paper for labels, laminations, bags and books and textiles for impregnation and seam bindings.

Mastics

Mastics constitute special type of adhesives which may be either latex or solvent based. The unique quality of mastics is their extremely high viscosity. Most mastics contain natural rubber, SBR, reclaim or their blends. Tackifiers and fillers are widely used.

Mastics are used in large volume, chiefly in industrial applications and in the construction industry where low bond strengths are adequate for the purpose. They are employed to fasten floor ceiling and wall tiles, roll floor covering and in the automobile industry for installing insulation, silencer and lining pads. Mastics are usually applied to both surfaces to be bonded.

Pressure Sensitive Adhesives

Pressure sensitive adhesives constitute a significant segment of total rubber based adhesive industry. The best known example of this type of system consists of a flexible tape coated with a permanently tacky mass. These adhesives lack high strength because they must be soft to be tacky. Since they are so formulated, they are also temperature- sensitive and highly susceptible to creep or cold flow. Tape is available in rolls which must unwind easily. The adhesive coating must show quick adhesion to substrates.

The first commerical applications of pressure sensitive tapes were in surgical tape and in friction tape for electrical, plumbing and similar fastening applications. These pressure sensitive tapes today are offered with a wide variety of backing materials such as crepe paper, aluminium foil, fabric, cellophane, cellulose acetate, polyester film, polyethylene, polypropylene, plasticized poly (vinyl chloride), woven glass fiber cloth, etc.

A more recent development is the double faced pressure- sensitive film which features a removable release sheet instead of conventional backing materials. Another pressure-sensitive adhesive application is in the field of labelling. Here, coloured or printed lable stocks are applied to a substrate with pressure.

Hot-melt Adhesives

The class of adhesives which is applied in hot-melt form is growing rapidly in industrial importance. These thermoplastic bonding agents are composed of 100 % non-volatile materials, i.e. containing no water, solvent or other volatile carriers. They are solid at room temperature, but are fluid at elevated temperatures. After application, bonding and cooling hot melt adhesives return to a solid state and develop their ultimate strength. Hot melt pressure sensitive adhesives are ideally suited where fast production speeds relatively low raw material cost and the elimination of the necessity to remove or recover solvents is essential for the favourable economics of the manufacturing process.

Function of Resins in Rubber Based Adhesives

The desired contact between adhesive and adherend must be achieved on a molecular scale to effect the proper flow and wetting characteristics necessary for good adhesion. Tackifiers may enhance the adhesion of non polar elastomers by improving wettability, increasing polarity and altering the visco elastic properties of the adhesive mass. By reducing elastic recovery and facilitating plastic deformation, the tackifier may enable the adhesive mass to contact the surface more intimately, thus enhancing bond strength.

Tack

In adhesive technology, tack may be defined as the property of a mateial which enables it to form a bond of measurable strength immediately upon contact with another surface. Tack is thus "instantaneous" adhesion and differs from ultimate strength. The time requird for development of strength by means of tack is very short. Tack is a function of rheological properties as well as tensile strength or cohesion yield value, modulus of elasticity and rate of elastic recovery. Tack is sensitive to variations in temperatures, pressure rate of application and removal of pressure and contact time.

Function Of Tackifiers

Although natural rubber possesses tack characteristics, the bond strength developed by rubber alone is inadequate for many uses. Tackifiers in the form of resins are added to these systems to increase their tack properties. Tackifiers are represented by a variety of resins are shown in Table 35.1. The choice of resin influences the qualities of adhesion from the stand point of tack, tensile strength, colour retention and resistance of embrittlement through oxidation. Maximum tack is obtainable correlated inversely with softening point or viscosity of the tackifying resin. The higher the softening point, the lower the percent resin at which maximum tack is obtained.

Tensile strength, as measured by the yield stress of an adhesive composition, decreases with increasing tackifier concentration. The ultimate elongation of such blends increases very rapidly as the concentration of tackifying- resin increases from 50 to 75%.

Emulsion Adhesives

Blends of rubber and modifiers having the most useful properties in adhesives are normally too viscous to be handled and supplied in bulk. There are two broad families of rubber based adhesives- Solvent cements and emulsion adhesives, Solvents cements consist of solution of relatively simple blends of an elastomer with tackifying resins and plasticizers. They have also the advantage of being applicable to substrates which are sensitive to water. Emulsion adhesives generally contain the same ingredients, in emulsified or latex form, but in addition they usually contain surface active agents and a protective colloid to stabilize the emulsion on storage. Among the advantages of latex adhesives over solvent cements are low cost, reasonable viscosity at high solid content and freedom from air pollution problems, toxicity or fire hazards.

Resin emulsion may be prepared using the following formulations :

Composition of Resin Emulsion

Ingredients	**% by wt.**
Resin Solution (80% solids) Resin	40.00
Toluene	10.00
Oleic acid	0.25
KOH Solution (2.5% solids)	
KOH	0.25
Water	10.00
Diluents & Modifiers	
10 % ammonia caseinate solution	15.00
Water	24.50

Experimental adhesives can be prepared by adding the appropriate amount of resin emulsion to natural latex with gentle agitation.

TABLE - 35.1 - Tackifying Resins - Types & Properties

Type	Acid No,	Softening point
Gum rosin	165	78
Wood rosin	163	73
Tall oil rosin	170	80
Polymerized rosin	152	95
Hydrogenated rosin	161	68
Pentaester of rosin	12	111
Glycerine-hydrogenated rosin	8	83
Penta-hydrogenated rosin	12	104
Aliphatic petroleum hydrocarbon	0	95-122
Alpha pinene	0	10-135
d-Limonere	0	10-135
Beta pinene	0	10-135
Terpene phenolic	0	100-135
Coumarone- Indene	0	100
Mixed calcium/zinc resinate	0	-
High zinc resinate	0	-

36.

Rubber Adhesives

Introduction

When fabric materials such as nylon, vinylon, rayon or polyester synthetic fibres are used as a reinforcing member for rubber articles such as tyres of automobiles, trucks, airplane, bicycles belts, air cushions, hoses or rubber vibration insulators, it is necessary to firmly adhere rubber compounds to these synthetic fabric materials. The adhesive composition used for treating a large quantity of fabric materials is preferably non-inflammable and nonpoisonous. From the above point of view, it is convenient and economical to use water as the medium for an adhesive composition. It is also desirable that the adhesive composition be durable and have a long shelf life.

RFL Adhesives

Rayon and nylon cords are generally treated with RFL adhesives i.e. the resorcinol-formaldehyde latex dips. A comparision of typical formulation made by the "in situ" method with resorcinol is shown in Table-36.1.

Formulation

Ingredients		**Parts by Wt.**
Resorcinol	18.5	-
R-F resins	-3	31.5
Sodium hydroxide	11.0	9.5
Ammonium hydroxide	-	-
Water	645.0	644.0
Formaldehyde (37%)	21.5	16.0
Styrene - Butadiene Latex	243.0	239.0
Vinyl piyridine-styrene Butadiene Terpolymer	61.0	60.0
Type cord used in evaluation	Rayon	Rayon

Procedure

Measured quantities of Resorcinol Formaldehyde and caustic soda are reacted while stirring together in a flask fixed with a reflux condenser at 80°C for 1.5 hr. The solution is then cooled and neutralized with 6N acetic acid and aprecipitate settles out of solution. The precipitate is collected by a centrifugal separator, dissolved in acetone, evaporated and dried under reduced pressure, and crushed to a powder of resinous material. Resinous material is dissolved in ammonium hydroxide to obtain uniform clear solution. The resulting solution is mixed with 40% vinyl pyridine styrene butadiene terpolymer latex, stirred sufficiently and used as an adhesive material.

The nylon cord is dipped in the adhesive solution and is dried at 190°C for 5 min. The rubber composition A and B are prepared as shown in the following table:

TABLE - 36.1 - Rubber Composition

Ingredients	Parts by Wt	
	A	B
NR	80.00	20.00
SBR	20.00	80.00
Carbon black	40.00	40.00
Softner	10.00	10.00
Stearic acid	2.00	2.00
N-phenyl - B - Naphthylamine	1.50	1.50
2 - benzothiozolyl disulfied	0.75	0.75
diphenyl guanidine	0.75	0.75
Sulfur	2.50	2.50

Providing a strong bond between reinforcing component made of nylon fibre and rubber, first an elastomeric terpolymer is provided; it is composed of 43% ethylene, 43.8% propylene and 13.2% 5-ethylidene 2-norbornene. Such terpolymer can be made in solution by reacting the monomer mixture in tetrachloroprene in presence of a vanadium type coordination catalyst A liquid adhesive composition useful as a tyre cord adhesive is prepared by:

(a) mixing 190g of terpolymer with 3000 ml of benzene and 450 ml of isopropanol to form a 6% solution of the terpolymer in the solvent mixture.

(b) 1540g of terpolymer is dissolved in water at a temperature of 40°C in a high shear, high speed turbine stator type of mixer with 770g of water containing 1.2% of an emulsifying agent (sodium lauryl sulfate).

(c) removing the benzene and isopropanol.

(d) cooling the resulting latex to 23°C.

(e) forming a more concentrated latex and 0.1 part of % sodium alginate is added and allowing the composition to stand for 16 hours.

(f) mixing 62.26g of latex with 59.33g of distilled water and cooling it to 9°C.

(g) 2.840g of ammonium hydroxide is added.

(h) mixing with the resulting latex 28.88g of RF resin and adjusting the pH to 7.2. Then 158.4g of distilled water and 1.67% aqueous sodium hydroxide solution are added. Then slowly 24.84g of resorcinol cakes with 36.3g of aqueous formaldehyde solution are added and stirred for 6 hours. Then add 38.3g of carbon black. It is very useful as a nylon tire cord adhesive.

Aqueous Polyurea Adhesive

This adhesive system is particularly useful as bonding agent for nonwoven and woven, natural or synthetic fibres and fabrics; cards, rope plastics, metals and glasses.

1000g of polyoxyethylene glycol are added to 325g of toluene diisocyanate at 50°C. Isocyanate capped polyoxyethylene glycol is recovered.

Polyester Tyre Cord Adhesive

Polyester has become a strong competitor of nylon and rayon tire cords during the past decade. Some of the examples are shown below:

(1) Polyester fibre-rubber bonding with polynucleus halophenol compound:

Five moles of formaldehyde are added to 1 mole of bis (5-chloro-2 hydroxy phenyl) methane and subjected to condensation in aqueous alkaline solution. Subsequently, the reaction system is neutralized with acetic acid. The reaction product is recrystallized from aqueous methanol. 0.5 mole of this compound is dissolved in 500g of dioxane, mixed with a solution of 2.5 mols of resorcinol in 500g of water and allowed to react with heating under reflux for 4 hours. Then, the reaction mixture is added dropwise while stirring into a large excess of water to precipitate a yellowish brown solid, which is of polynucleus halo phenol compound. Sixty parts of this compound (Al), 30 parts of 28% ammonia and 210 parts of water are mixed t6 obtain a solution (solution Al).

11.00 parts of resorcinol, 9.7 parts of 37% formalin, 3.0 parts of a aqueous sodium hydroxide and 116.3 parts of water (1400 parts in total) are allowed to react with stirring at 25°C for about 6 hours to obtain an aqueous solution of thermosetting resorcinol formaldehyde resin (Bl). 140 parts of Bl are added to 280 parts of vinyl pyridine-styrene butadiedne copolymer rubber latex (Cl) and left standing for 24 hours at 25°C to obtain a liquid mixture (RFL-1).

300 parts of the solution (Al) and 200 parts of water are added to 420 parts of RFL-1 to obtain an adhesive composition. The adhesive of the polyester fibre to rubber in the above laminate is evaluated by means of the H-test

(2) Ethylene-Propylene-Diene Terpctymers:

This type of adhesive composition is especially useful for forming this reaction which reacts with 103g of ethylene triamine in 500ml of dry acetone. A noncross linked amino containing poly urea polymer is recovered and reacted with 555g of epichlorohydrin and the final adhesive is prepared.

(4) Polyamide-Rubber bonding:

The following example illustrates the process

Formulation

Ingredients	**Parts by Wt.**
vinyl pyridine rubber latex	100
Trimethylol phenol	5
Resorcinol-formaldehyde resin	5
Cone. Ammonium hydroxide (28%)	10 drops
Water	50

Part of the water is used to dilute the viscous trimethylol propane and another for ammonium hydroxide. Thereafter the diluted solution is mixed with vinyl pyridine latex.

(5) Styrene-butadiene-carboxylic acid latex and epoxy

There are many products that require rubber bonded to metal such as electrical components like rubber isolators, switch gear, hangers, shock absorbers and foot pedals. Bonding rubber to different substrates involves a variety of factors such as the polarity between the respective substrates, the composition of metal and the presence of lubricants specifically binding the rubber to steel has posed extremely difficult problem.

An aqueous composition is prepared according to the process by first making a latex of the following recipe:

Formulation

Ingredients	**Parts by Wt.**
Styrene	42.50
Butadiene	42.50
Water	93.00
Surfactant	1.25
Preservative	0.25
Catalyst	0.25
Chain terminator	1.00
Chelator	0.05

The emulsion is agitated at 60°C for 6 hours after which 10 parts of methacrylic acid and 200 parts of water soluble epoxy compound is added. A curable natural rubber tyre stock compound is prepared according to the following.

formulation

Ingredients	**Parts by Weight**
Natural rubber	100.00
Carbon black	50.00
Sulfur	3.80
Accelerator	1.00
Activator	12.00
Plasticizer	3.00
Antioxidant	2.00

The rubber is milled and the rest of the ingredients added and dispersed. The aqueous composition is"trushed on to one surface of the pieces of steel. The coating is dried and cured. Thereafter, strips of cure natural rubber stock compound are pressed tightly against the adhesive coat surfaces to form a rubber adhesive steel laminate. The laminate is heated at 100°C for 1 hour to cure the rubber. Testing is done by stripping the rubber from the metal. In a similar test where no adhesive is used, there is no adhesion at all between rubber and metal.

(6) Cobalt-Naphthalene Promoter

Adhesion of rubber to metal is improved by incorporating a cobalt salt. A suitable rubber stock may be prepared by mixing 30 parts of natural rubber, 25 parts of cis polybutadiene rubber, 67.5 parts of oil extended S-B-R, 60 parts of carbon black, 5 parts of zinc oxide, 1.5 parts of stearic acid, 10 parts of naphthenic petroleum hydrocarbon process oil, 1 part of an antioxidant To this add 0.7 parts of N-TBBS, 0.2 parts of diphenylguanidine and 2 parts of sulfur. Using the basic recipe, a stock may be prepared, containing various adhesion promoting additives noted in the following table:

TABLE -36.2- STOCK PREPARATION WITH ADHESIVE PROMOTERS

Particulars	Stock	
	A	B
Additive:		
Cobalt (7%)	-	
2-Methylol-2-nitropropane	1.5	
Resorcinol-acetaldehyde resin	1.0	
Test Results:		
Adhesive pull (kg)	16	27
Appearance rating	1	5

Rubber to Metal Bonding

Metal Surface Preparation

Clean metal surface is of vital importance for getting a good bond. The first treatment is degreasing. to remove oil or grease, If the parts are too greasy, they are autoclaved followed by vapour degreasing with chlorinated hydrocarbon solvents. Steel parts can also be treated with alkali solutions to remove grease. The metal surface is then sand blasted, scoured to remove rust etc. Chemical surface treatment like pickling etc., also results in better bonding.

Polymethylene Polyphenyl Isocyanate and Chlorinated Polyethylene

An adhesive is prepared by dissolving 10 parts of chlorosulfonated polyethylene and 10 parts of polymethylene polyphenyl isocyanate in co mbination with 43 parts of xylene and 104 parts of trichloroethylene. One part of p-dinitrosobenzene and 5 parts of carbon black are dispersed in the polymer solution. The versatility of the adhesives is tested in vulcanizable elastomers.

Chlorosulphonated Polyethyhlene, Nitroso compound and Polyisocyanate: A binder composition dispersed in inert organic solvents is shown below.

Formulation

Ingredients	**Parts by Weight**
Chlorosulfonated polyethylene	10
di-C-nitrosoaromatic compound	5
Polyisocyanate	20
Chlorinated rubber	10
Resol	5
Pigment	25
Tack compound	20

This process can advantageously be employed using the adhesion assistants and binders for vulcanizing vulcanizable rubber mixtures based on S-B-R, NR, PCP, BR, or metal substrates. The bonds obtained mark high adhesive strength and high stability against corrosive media and against commercial oils and fats. The composite bodies may be used in large variety of technical fields, especially in the automobile industry as flexible bearing, clutches, shock absorbers and sealing parts in the chemical plants.

Polyurethane for Rubber to Rubber Bonding

Aromatic Nitro Compounds as Additives:

The simple aromatic nitro compounds would be adequate adhesion promoters for adhering decorative rubber articles to various substrates. The adhesion test results reported hereafter are obtained on laminate olefinic rubber and ployurethane rubber, a cement in accordance with the process having been interposed between the two rubbers. The vulcanizable olefinic rubber sheets employed are prepared of the following formulation :

Formulation

Ingredients	**Parts by Weight**
SBR	60.0
Polybutadiene	40.0
Carbon black	70.0
Oil	44.0
Zinc oxide	2.0
Stearic acid	2.0
Wax	3.0
Sulfur	1.7
Accelerator	1.2
Antioxidant	1.2

Following the procedure outlined above, such sheets are baked, cured, buffed and are surface coated by cement. The adhesive coated sheets are formed into a laminate by the above described procedure with a polyurethane rubber composition of the following formulation:

Formulation

Ingredients	**Parts by Weight**
Liquid polyurethane rubber	100
Silicone oil	0.10
Methylene bis (o-chloro-p-aniline)	20.98
Dioctyl phthalate	20.00

A cement containing an adhesion promoter of the process is prepared of the following formulation:

Formulation

Ingredients	**Parts by Weight**
2.4-Dinitrophenol	0.75
Polyurethane rubber	3.00
Toluene diisocyanate	1.00
Toluene	3.00

Adhesion test strips are produced employing this cement to adhere the described olefinic rubber to the polyurethane. The test results are as follows:

Test Temp	*Adhesion Kg/in*	*Nature of Adhesion*
Room	110	100% rubber tear
70°C	52	95% rubber tear
85°C	38	10% rubber tear

Glass fibre Bonding

The importance of glass fibre cords in automobile tyres has risen dramatically. Its use is made possible by the discovery of a suitable adhesive system. Formulations of dips with high solids content with sufficiently low viscosity to facilitate penetration have been developed with dips of about 35% solids, cords having 'dip pick up' values of 30% may be produced. Such cords have shown good performance in radial tire construction. A formulation having good stability is shown below:

Formulation

Ingredients	**Parts by Weight**
Water	14.0
Ammonia (28%)	2.7
Formaldehyde (37%)	1.6
Vinyl pyridine terpolymer latex (41 %)	74.6
R-F resin (75%)	7.1

Direct Bonding

When a resorcinol-formaldehyde resin is intimately mixed with rubber, the surface properties of the calendered sheets have higher adhesion, and the physical properties are gready improved. This is due to the increased polarity of the rubber, which arises from the powerful hydrogen bonding characteristics of the resorcinol resin. This makes possible for bonds between rubber and various substrate materials as steel wire tyre cords fibre glass. When finely divided hydrated silica are added, the adhesive strength is increased. Following table shows a typical example:

Formulation

Ingredients	**Parts by Weight**
Natural Rubber	100.0
Carbon black	40.0
Oil	6.0
Zinc oxide	3.0
Stearicacid	2.0
Antioxidant	1.0
2-Morpholinothio benzothiazole	2.5
Sulfur	2.5
Resorcinol	2.5
Hexa	1.6

37.

Styrene Butadiene Rubber Adhesives

Introduction

Styrene-butadiene rubber (SBR) which found only limited applications in adhesives before, has now surpassed natural rubber in adhesive volume. The adhesive deficiencies of SBR, especially in the areas of tack and cohesive strength, have been overcome through resin compounding, SBR based adhesives offer good heat ageing and water resistance. It is a uniform product which is light in colour and low in cost. In addition, SBR disperses easily in hydrocabon solvents to form an excellent base for adhesives. The adhesive compounder is no longer dependent upon SBR designed for dry rubber compounding. The rubber manufacturers now provide the solution compounder.

Properties of SBR in Adhesives

SBR has a relatively low polarity compared to other synthetic rubbers and unlike natural rubber SBR does not develop surface peroxidal activity upon mastication. Poor tack in SBR can be overcome by (1) reducing the molecular weight (2) decreasing the viscosity (3) adding tackifiers. SBR is rarely used alone as an adhesive.

Formulation and Applications

(1) Pressure Sensitive Adhesives

SBR is mainly blended with tackifiying resins such as hydrogenated rosin esters, terpene phenolic resin and alpha-pinene polymers.

Formulation

Ingredients	Parts by Weight
SBR (54 mooney viscosity, 23.5% styrene)	100
Hydrogenated rosin ester	75
Antioxidant	2
Toulene	1003
SBR (77 mooney viscosity, 25 % styrene)	100
Terpene phenolic resin	100
Solvent	1000

The amount and type of tackifying resin used in SBR adhesive is very important SBR adhesive can be formulated to obtain improved heat and ultraviolet light resistance:

Formulation

Ingredients	Parts by Weight
SBR (54 mooney viscosity, 25 % styrene)	100
Thermoplastic polyolefin rubber	150

Phenolic resin	15
Sp-1056	5
Zinc resinate	5
Antioxidant	2
Toluene	50

Other elevated PSA can be prepared using sulfur and Butyl Eight as the curing agent as shown in the following formulation:

Formulation

Ingredients	**Parts by Weight**
SBR (77 mooney viscosity, 23.5% styrene)	100
Zinc oxide	40
Hydrogenated rosin ester	100
Mineral oil	10
Sulfur	3
Butyl Rubber	8
Antioxidant	2
Solvent	100
SBR (54 mooney viscosity, 23.5% styrene)	100
Polyterpene resin	70.0
Polybutene	15
Toluene	815

PVC Adhesive Tape

Formulation

Ingredients	**Parts by Weight**
SBR (50 mooney viscosity, 23.5 % styrene)	50
Natural rubber (crude smoked sheet)	50
Polyterpene resin	45
Phenol terpene resin	45
Phenolic resin	12
Alumina	10
Di-tert-amyl hydroquinone	2
Carbon black	10
Calcium carbonate	50
Heptane	640
Ethanol	10

Box Board Adhesive

Formulation

Ingredients	**Parts by Weight**
SBR (54 mooney viscosity, 25% styrene)	100
Polyolefin rubber	150
SP-1056	15
Zinc resinate	2
Superlite	5
Toluene	50

(2) Sprayable Adhesives

The application of adhesives to substrates such as paper, card board, wood, plastic and cloth can be conveniently done using spray adhesive. A typical formulation shows a blend of two SBR containing 27.3% styrene and 0.7% divinyl benzene and part of a cross linked SBR containing 27.6 % styrene and 0.4% divinyl benzene. The two rubbers are milled together for about 2.5 min at 30-75°C. The adhesive formulation used is the following:

Formulation

Ingredients	**Parts by Weight**
Crosslinked SBR	100
Dimerized rosin	100
Hydrogenated rosin ester	40
Stalite	2
Morpholine	1
Hexane	450-500
Methylene chloride	50

(3) Tyre Tread Adhesives

SBR polymers are useful in making tyre tread cament particularly when used with oil extended SBR tyres. The following recipe is an example:

Formulation

Ingredients	**Parts by Weight**
High mooney SBR	100.0
Kerosene	40.0
Petroleum softener	10.0
Carbon black	60.0
Zinc oxide	5.0
Sulfur	2.2
LE (Diphenylamine & acetone)	1.0
Santocure	1.2
DPG	0.3

One hundred parts of the above compound are dissolved, after the usual approximate mixing in a mill, into 900 parts of petroleum naphtha to form a cement solution.

(4) Sealants And Caulks

SBR has some good properties like satisfactory tack is relatively low in cost and can be compounded easily. A typical starting formulation in the following.

Formulation

Ingredients	**Parts by Weight**
SBR (25% styrene)	12.0
Polymerized rosin	19.0
Methyl ester of hydrogenated rosin	2.0
Aromatic plasticizer	2.0
Soft clay	17.0
Fibrous talc	26.0
Xylene	12.0

(5) Automotive Putty

Unsupported tapes of putty like consistency based on oil extended SBR have been found to give good bonds to oily metal surfaces. An illustrative formulation is:

Formulation

Ingredients	**Parts by Weight**
Oil extender SBR	70.0
Phenolic resin and hexamine	75
Petroleum distillate	50
Zinc dust	100
Tetramethyl thiuram monosulfide	1.2
Diorthotoluyl guanidine	1.2
Sulfur	2.0
Calozal	10.2

(6) Panel and Flooring Adhesives

Formulation

Ingredients	**Parts by Weight**
SBR (23.5% styrene, divinyl benezene cross linked)	40
SBR(45 mooney viscosity, 43% styrene)	60
Clay	130
Calcium carbonate	130
Hydrogenated rosin ester	75
Terpene phenolic resin	52
Antioxidant	2
Solvent	

(7) Heat Resistant Adhesives

Formulation

Ingredients	**Parts by Weight**
SBR (23.25% styrene, 0.5% divinyl benezene)	35.0
SBR (45 mooney viscosity, 43% styrene)	35.0
Polychloroprene	9.5
Zinc oxide	3.5
Accelerator	0.3
Antioxidant	1.5
Magnesium silicate	13.0
Stabilized rosin	6.0

The above mixture is blended for 35 min at 110°C. On cooling 65 more parts of stabilized rosin plus 30 parts of a hydrogenated methyl ester of rosin are added. On dissolving the mass in 250 parts of rubber solvent, a permanently tacky adhesive is obtained.

Heat resistant adhesives can be formulated from SBR using the alfin catalyst system with SBR as the sole elastomer. The formulation is shown below:

Formulation

Ingredients	**Parts by Weight**
SBR (15% styrene)	30
SBR (60% styrene)	70

Magnesium oxide	4
N-phenyL=1Naphthylamine	2
Alkyl phenol polymer	50
Hexane	200
Toluene	200

(8) Spreading And Laminating Adhesives

Formulation

Ingredients	**Parts by Weight**
SBR	100
Sulfur and accelerator	1-20
Wood rosin	150-200
Solvent	200

Millatl 25-200°C

The milling gives a partial cure. After cooling, solvent is added to give the desired consistency.

(9) Tyre Cord Adhesives

Good tyre cord adhesives can be prepared using a rubbery SBR copolymer which has been polymerized in the presence of nitrogen containing heterocyclic modifying agent of the vinyl pyridine class, which gready increases the ozone and heat resistance of the latex adhesives. Odier tyre cord adhesives can be prepared based on the use of phenol formaldehyde rosin as in the example below:

Formulation

Ingredients	**Parts by Weight**
Resorcinol	10.93
Distilled water (20% solids)	5.23
37 % formaldehyde	1.35
10 % sod hydroxide	8.00
Rubber latex (41.4% solids) (vinyl pyridine-diene-styrene)	50.00
Rubber latex (41 % solids) (SBR)	60.00
Rubber latex (70% solids) (SBR)	24.00
Rubber latex (63% solids) (ester modified SBR)	20.00

(10) Tufted Carpet Adhesives

Formulation

Ingredients	**Parts by Weight**	
Natural rubber	25	100
SBR	75	
Whiting		200
Barium sulphate		10
Clay		10

Sulfur	
Zinc oxide	10
Accelerator	
Dispersing agent	
(Karaya gum)	As required

(11) Packaging Adhesives

SBR latex finds application as packaging adhesives. They do not have particularly good wet'tack properties and must be compounded with tackifying resins like ester gum. They offer good stability and oxidation resistance. A folding carton sideseam adhesive is shown below :

Formulation

Ingredients	**Parts by Weight**
SBR latex	40.0
Vinsol emulsion	10.0
Resin emulsion	30.0
ARRCO EO	19.5
Lanolubric	0.4
Penta chloro phenol	0.1

(12) Fabric Adhesives

SBR latex compound can be used for bonding sheet materials together such as two or more fabrics, fabrics to paper and fabrics to leather. Typical combining cement formulation is shown below:

Curing Type:

Formulation

Ingredients	**Parts by Weight**
SBR latex	100
10% potassium caseinate	2
Dispersion	4
Diothiocarbonate	3
Water	6
Thickener	As required
Non-Curing Type:	
SBR latex	250
10% potassium caseinate	20
50% Butyl zimate dispersion	4
Thickener	As required

Both the above formulations are applied by wet combining process.

38.

Soybean Adhesives

Introduction

A variety of adhesives of natural origin have been and, in some cases continue to be used by the wood industry. These natural adhesives represent alternate adhesives systems that can be derived from non-pertroleum sources. The plywood industry is a major consumer of adhesives within the forest products and is histrorically the major consumer of soybean adhesives.

The exact chemical composition of soybean varies with the variety that is grown and the growing conditions. On average, soybeans contain approximately 40%protein, 20% oil, 35% carbohydrates and 5% other constituents. The oil and protein are both important chemical constituents for commercial purpose.

The protein component is the most important constituent in the manufacture of adhesives. Soybean flour contains less than 55% protein, soybean concentrate contains from 65% to 89% protein, and soybean protein isolate contains more than 90% protein. Bulk soybean flour used as a source of wood adhesives typically contains 44% to 50% protein.

Formulation of Adhesives

Soybean protein adhesives are applied from an aqueous solution and are cured primarily by gelation and drying. Chemical reactions are of secondary importance in the curing process except in relation to lending water resistance to the final bond. Because soybean adhesive systems are aqueous and generally of low solids contents requiring loss of large amounts of water during cure, their use is restricted to applications involving porous adherends, such as wood and paper.

Soybean proteins like other proteins, have a complex three dimentional structure that is dependent on hydrogen bonding and disulfide cross links between the individual amino acid side groups, for protein to function as an adhesive. The internal cross links must be broken and the highly polar side groups on the amino acids made available for interaction with a polar adherend like wood. The distruption of the internal cross links is accomplished by dissolving the protein.

The processing temperature and the specific surface area of the soybean flour influence its solubility area ranging from 3000 to 6000 cm ^{2}/g.

Equally important, the solubility of soybean protein in water is a function of pH. The insoluble protein is usually solubilised at a pH substantially above the isoelectric point. Because the proteins are amphoteric, pH more acidic than the isoelectric point can also result in solubilization. Acidic solutions have not been used as wood adhesives mostly because acids degrade wood. However, proteins undergo hydrolysis at basic pH. Hydrolysis can affect the useful life of the adhesives as well as bond strength and water resistance. Several distinct steps are necessary to formulate useful adhesives from soybean flour; wetting, shearing, defoaming and dispersing. The soybean flour is usually mixed with sufficient water to make smooth dough free of dry lumps. Additional water is then added slowly with efficient mixing to form a mixture of thick consistency. If this second addition of water is added at once, the dough tends to break into lumps, making it nearly impossible to obtain a final smooth mixture to prevent or reduce foaming, a small amount of pine oil or other defoaming agent is usually added early in the mixing process. The defoamer is often mixed with dry soybean flour prior to blending to reduce dust formation. Next, slaked lime plus water, sodium hydroxide solution and sodium silicates are usually added to the smooth mixture in that order with short periods of mixing between each addition. The sodium hydroxide disperses the protein. The calcium hydroxide forms calcium proteinates that improve the water resistance of the adhesive and alters its consistency. The sodium silicate increases the water holding capacity, levels the viscosity, and prolongs the useful life of *the* formulated adhesive. A fifth optional mixing step involves the incorporation of cross linking agents during formulation of the adhesives. Cross linking of the adhesive during cure improves the water resistance of the bond that is formed.

Viscosity is an important property that governs the adhesive behaviour of soybean glues which varies over a wide range depending upon the application. Low viscosities are used for gluing highly adsorbant substances such as paper; higher viscosities (5,000 to 25,000 cp) are required for laminating adhesives.

Soybean adhesives can be applied by almost any conventional system, including roll applicators, extruders, sprayers and curtain coaters. These adhesives have been applied as dry powders, desired moisture being taken from the adherends. It can be cured by either hot or cold pressing.

Water Resistance

Dry soybean glues lines are either completely or partially reversible, resulting in loss of strength. Soybean adhesives are much less durable than PF adhesives. Spray dried or vacuum pan dried animal blood is often mixed with the soybean adhesives to improve the water resistance of hot processed panels. Blood is substituted for a few % to more than 50% of the soybean content. Admixture with animal blood also decreases the hot pressing cure time. Several sulfur based compounds such as carbon disulfide, polysulfide, ethylenc trithiocarbonate, thiourea and potassium xanthate and tanning agents like metal salts of copper, aluminium, chromium and zinc are added to soybean adhesives to improve their water resistance.

Protein Modification

Protein adhesives are known that provide good adhesives strength even inaqueous enviornments.These adhesives even cure in presence of water. Common protein like gelation can be chemically modified so that it functions as a biomedical adhesive curing in a moist enviornment by a mechanism similar to the curing of a natural barnaclecement. It appears that barnacle adhesives cure by crosslinking of phenolic amino acids (tyrosine) by action of a poly phenoloxidase enzyme (PPO). Studies show that lysines in gelation by reductive alkylation using 2,3 and 3,4 dihydroxy benzaldehyde produce side chains that can cross link in the presence of PPO. Because lysins and tyrosine make up a significant portion of the amino acids in soybean proteins, similar strategies might be used with soybean adhesives.

Microbial Degradation

In addition to the lack of water resistance, another objection to soybean adhesives has been the lack of resistance to mold and fungi growth, especially on exposure to high humidity. A variety of preservatives have been tried. This includes chlorinated phenols, pentachlorophenols, sodium pentachlorophenate, chloro-2- phenylphenol, tributyl tin oxide, copper-8-quinolinolate. These can be added at the dry end of adhesive formulation. Usually preservatives added are from 1 to 5% of the dry weight of the adhesive with the larger quantity being most effective.

Applications

Soybean protein glues, as mentioned above, are suitable for interior grade plywood and softwood panelling, and are also used as a component of blood albumen soybean adhesives for interior plywoods based on softwood. Where maximum bond strength is not required, e.g. for applications such as paper and softwood lamination, cardboard base fabrication and particle bonding, the glue may be extended with fillers such as clays and wood flour, to reduce cost.

Examples

For good adhesive properties the protein is required to be properly dispersed. This requires that the pH of the solution should be high, i.e. 11 or even higher. Thus various alkaline materials e.g. sodium or potassium hydroxide, tri-sodium phosphate (TSP) etc. are incorporated but this causes staining of the cellulose adherends, such as paper and wood etc. Thus it is preferable to use weak bases as calcium hydroxide, mono-sodium phosphate or borax for this purpose. Simple alkaline dispersions of soybean flour in water are adequate adhesives but the addition of slightly soluble calcium or magnesium salt such as calcium hydroxide improves water resistance. Addition of liquid of readily soluble grade of sodium-silicate increases the water-holding capacity, levels the viscosity and makes the useful life longer. Thus a standard method of preparation is as follows :-

Formulation

Ingredients	Parts by Weight
Soybean potein	100
Water, 300C	400
Calcium hydroxide	15
Sodium silicate, 400 Be"	25
Sodium hydroxide, 35% aqueous	15

Calcium hydroxide contributes to the formation of an irreversible gel. Addition of sulphur compounds such as carbon disulphide, ethylene thiocarbonate, thiourea and potassium xanthate increases cross-linking, thereby improving the water resistance, viscosity and resistance to hydrolysis. Copper, chromium and zinc salts also perform this function.The following formulation is thus more water resistant and viscous and is suitable for handing wood veneers :-

Formulation

Ingredients	Parts by Weight
Soybean flour	30
Water	120
Sodium hydroxide, 18% solution	13
Carbon disulphide	4
Calcium hydroxide	3
Sodium silicate	14
Copper sulphate	1
Water	5

Epoxy resins may also be used as soybean glue modifiers but the product becomes costly and difficult to control. Formaldehyde donors, and higher aldehydes etc., are also very good crosslinking agents for soybean glues, they improve water resistance, glue life, curing and consistency. Such additives are dimethylol urea, glyceraldehyde, hexamine, urea-formaldehyde resin etc. But solutions of formaldehyde and para-formaldehyde cannot be used due to premature gelation. These additives are incorporated in quantities up to 0.1 to 1% on dry glue weight. Premature gelation in the case of formaldehyde may be prevented by small percentages of amount of sodium sulphite. An example of such formulation is as follows :

Formulation

Ingredients	Parts by Weight
Soybean flour 100 mesh	100
Sodium phosphate	10
Sodium fluoride	5
Calcium hydroxide	7.10
Calcium carbonate	50.00
Copper sulphate	0.50
Water	510.00
Formaldehyde-ammonia	5.10

All the solids are ground to 100 mesh and dissolved in water to which the reaction product of formaldehyde and ammonia is added giving glue a consistency which remains unchanged for 6 hours. Within 24 hours after the gluing of wood a shear strength of 25 to 35 Kg/cm^2 is obtained in the dry state and 15 to 18 Kg/ cm^2 in the wet state.

Usually the steps involved in making of soybean adhesives are as follows: wetting, shearing, defoaming, dispersing, denaturing and inhibition. First the soybean flour is mixed with water, then sheared using efficient mixer to eliminate lumps. A suitable defoamer, usually pine oil, is then added to give proper dispersion of the protein and bring out its adhesiveness to the maximum crosslinking or denaturing agents are then added, followed by the addition of mold inhibitors e.g. penta-chlorophenol, copper naphthenate, coper -8 - 9 uinolinolate and tributylene oxide etc. in quantities up to 1 to 5% of dry glue weight. An example is given below :

Interior Plywood Glue

Formulation

Ingredients	**Parts by Weight**
Soybean flour	97.00
Pine oil	3.00
Hydrated lime	12.00
Sodium hydroxide, 50% solution	14.00
Sodium silicate	25.00
Carbon disulphide	1.25
Carbon tetrachloride	0.50
Penta chlorophenol	4.25
Water	344.00

Soybean flour is mixed with 175 parts water at 200°C and to this pine oil is added and mixed for 3 minutes until smooth, 145 parts water are further mixed followed by hydrated lime and 24 parts water. Sodium silicate is then mixed followed by carbon disulphide solution in carbon tetrachloride and finally the inhibitor is added. The whole thing is mixed for 10 minutes. The glue is ready for use and its working life is about 6 to 10 hrs. depending on the storage temperature.

Phenol based inhibitors dissolve in aqueous alkaline glue dispersions, through the formation of their double salts; hence for this purpose 1 % additional alkali per 5% inhibitor is required

As mentioned before, where maximum level of bonding strength is not required, the cost may be reduced by extending the formulations with films such as clays, shell flours, wood flour etc. These low cost adhesives are suitable for applications like softboard lamination, paper overlay gluing, aggregate binding, box book manufacture etc. One of such formulation is given below:

Cheaper Glue for Soft Board Lamination

Formulation

Ingredients	**Parts by Weight**
Soybean Flour	38
Bentonite clay	38
Polyvinyl acetate resin	15
Starch	5
Dimethylol urea	1
Pine oil	2
Borax	1

This dry glue is mixed until smooth at 200°C with 200 parts water. To this, 7 parts hydrated lime in 150 parts water with 6 parts 50% caustic lye is incorporated followed by 15 parts sodium silicate and 6 parts caustic lye (50%). To this 1.25 parts carbon disulphide in 0.50 part carbon tetrachloride is mixed till smooth.

This glue is suibable for both hot and cold-press applications.

Strong alkalies, like caustic soda, are not incorporated in dry glue formulation due to their hygroscopic nature but are included later on while mixing with water etc. Or otherwise, salts like sodium fluoride, sodium phosphate or sodium carbonate are used together with calcium hydroxide in the dry glue formulation which while dissolving in water yield caustic and insoluble calcium salts. This procedure gives one-package dry formulation. Addition of casein to soybean glue imparts extra tack and assemble time tolerance. Such glues are suitable for applications for which casein and soybean glues are normally used; e.g. lumber lamination, flush door gluing and furniture assemble etc. This blending reduces the cost of casein glues. One such formulation is as follows :-

Formulation

Ingredients	**Parts by Weight**
Soybean flour	57
Casein	15
Hydrated lime	12
Woodflour	5
Sodium carbonate	3
Pine oil	3

Dry glue is mixed with half its weight of water and after it becomes smooth, further water (l/4th of dry glue wt.) is added. For heavier glue, amount of water may be reduced.

Addition of dry soluble animal blood gives glues of improved water resistance and hot-press curing speed.When blood is incorporated the quantity of water in the formulation is increased. These blended glues are used for bonding hot press plywood. Animal glues are also sometimes used as modifiers for soybean glues, mainly to impart tack and flow properties, but water resistance is reduced, though the dry bond strength is excellent.

Addition of phenol-formaldehyde resins to soybean glues yields hot-press interior plywood glues. These glues have quick setting properties of soybean glues and permanency from phenolics. These blends are less reactive and more sensitive to stock moisture content than equivalent glues made from soluble blood.

Hot Press Interior Plywood Glue

Formulation

Ingredients	**Parts by Weight**
Soybean flour	50
China clay	30
Walnut shell flour	20

500 parts phenol-formaldehyde resin (40% solids), 3 parts pine oil are mixed with 100 parts of the above dry glue mix. This mix is mixed with 400 parts of water at 20°C, into this 40 parts of sodium silicate (50% solution) is incorporated and the whole is mixed for about 5 minutes till smooth. This adhesive is ready for immediate use with a working life of about 24 hours.

Method of Application

Soybean glues may be applied to various adherents by any of the conventional methods and equipment. Cold and hot methods of pressing techniques may be employed. Coverage of soybean glue varies from about 0.15 to 0.3 Kg./m^2. Practically all soybean adhesives harden by cold pressing to yield satisfactory cured bonds in wood laminates. Laminates involving paper cure quickly either hot or cold press due to rapid dehydration. As the setting process is by elimination of water, the moisture content of wood should not exceed 20%. For cold press plywood 4-12 hr. clamping at 70-100 N/cm^2 pressure is required while for hot press plywood clamping, for 3 to 10 minutes at 100-140°C temperature and pressure of about 100 to 150 N/cm^2 is required.

In the case of soybean glues, one thing of much importance is that the flour or meal used as the raw material should be un-treated; and also the temperature of the material right from the seed stage to the final glue stage should not exceed 75°C, to preserve the solubility of the soybean proteins.

39.

Starch Adhesives

Introduction

Starch is a natural polymer, a polysaccharide. It is abundant, relatively in expensive and relatively stable in quality and price. As a polymeric polyhydroxy compound, starch yields adhesives with excellent affinity to polar substrates, such as cellulose. As a result of its origin, structure, hydrophillic character, and ease of dispersion, starch is water sensitive and brone to attack by microorganisms. These drawbacks can be controlled by chemical modifications.

Starch occurs in roots and seeds of higher plants, from which it may be recovered by dry or wet milling processes. Typical commerical starches are listed in Table-39.1.

Table-39.1 COMMERCIAL STARCHES

Starch	Corn	Wheat	Rice	Tapioca	Potato	Sago
Source	Seed	Seed	Seed	Root	Root	Pith
Granule Size	5-26	3-35	3-8	5-35	15-100	10-70
Gelatinization :						
Temp.°C	62-72	58-64	68-78	49-70	59-68	60-67
Amylose (%)	28	25	19	20	25	26
Amyulose (DP)	480	-	-	1050	850	-
Amylopectin (DP)	1450	-	-	1300	2000	-

The common starches contain about 20-30% amylose and 70-80% amylopectin.

The degradation products of starch may be classified into the following four categories, which are used for making adhesives.

1. Unmodified starches
2. Acid modified starches or thin boiling starches
3. Oxidised starches
4. Dextrins

Unmodified Starches

Chemicallly starch has the same constitution as cellulose, *i.e.* $(C_6 H_{10} O_6)_n$. The size and shape of starch granules vary, depending upon their origin. The starch based adhesives show poor resistance to weathering, moisture and temperature changes. Under damp conditions, biodegradation is a hazard, which can be improved by incorporate preservatives. They can be used for dry interior user only. Addition of sodium hydroxide increases the resin of staining timber substrates.

Simple soda starch adhesive

Formulation

Ingredients	**Parts by Wt.**
Water	150
Starch	100
Caustic lye, 36° Be'	25
Water	25

The above content is agitated for 1 hour at 20°C until a glassy mass is obtained. If the temperature rises too high due to excess caustic soda, then starch may break down into dextrin. The caustic soda is added in lots until complete swelling of starch granules is obtained and a gelatious rubbery mass is formed. If the temperature is too low, the activity of caustic soda is reduced and the time of mixing too prolonged.

Borax is added as an alkaline medium increasing the viscosity of starch solutions. It is used in low concentrations e.g. 1 to 2 parts per 100 parts of starch. Use of borax improves the adheisve properties of low grade starches. In this case the following mixture is added to above formulation :

Soda starch adhesive with borase

Formulation

Ingredients	**Parts by Weight**
Water	550.00
Borax	0.14
Hydrochloric acid, 220 Be'	5.00
Water	50.00

Urea, dicyandiamide may be added to lower the viscosity and to increase the solid content.

High Strength Adhesive

The following adhesive is used for wood gluing and foil to paper gluing etc.

Formulation

Ingredients	**Parts by Weight**
Starch	100.0
Sodium hydroxide	3.2
Urea	24.0
Water	300.0

In this case urea is added along with caustic soda. A mixture of potato and maize starch gives the best adhesive water boiled and the starch is added with continuous stirring.

Paper Giue

Formulation

Ingredients	**Parts by Wt.**
Starch	40
Water	10
Calcium chloride	34

At first Calcium chloride is dissolved in water and starch is added to it slowly until a unifrom paste is formed. The paste is then dried and ground. Mixing is done for 2 hours at 20°C.

Tapoica Starch Wood Adhesive

Formulation

Ingredients	**Parts by Weight**
Tapoica starch	320.00
Water	500.00
Sodium bicarbonate	0.65
Sodium hydroxide, 26° Be'	80.00
Formaldehyde, 20 %	6.00
Turkey Red of ammonium salt	0.65

Sodium bicarbonate is dissolved in water, and the starch is added slowly with constant stirring. Sodium hydroxide is diluted with equal quantity of water and is added slowly. Temperature is maintained below 20°C. Stirring is continued for 12 hours. In the end formaldehyde and Turkey red oil are added.

Label Adhesive for Vitreous Enamel & Porcelain

Formulation

Ingredients	**Parts by Weight**
Starch	5
Zinc oxide	1

Mix the ingredients and grind in a ball mill. Add sufficient water before using to make a paste of desired consistency.

Paper To Glass Adhesives

Formulation

Ingredients	**Farts by Wt.**
Tapioca starch	125
Glycerin	10
Water	150
Zinc chloride	2

Mix thoroughly and heat to boiling stirring vigorously. If tapioca is in lumps, the mixture should soak overmight before heating.

Office Use Adhesives

Formulation

Ingredients	**Parts by Wt.**
Starch	100
Calcium chloride	47
Zinc chloride	36
Hot water	370

The two chlorides are mixed in 70 parts of water and heated to 65°C. Starch is then added slowly with constant heating and stirring. A clear jelly is obtained. To this, 300 parts of hot water are added. A denser, opaque and cheaper adhesive is obtained by using sodium silicate.

Denser, opeque & cheaper adhesive

Formulation

Ingredients	**Parts by Weight**
Tapioca star	100
Caustic soda, 36° Be (with equal amount of water)	30
Sodium silicate, 35° Be'	40
Hydrochloric acid, 22° Be'	33
Formaldehyde	5
Water	500

Starch is suspended in water, diluted caustic is stirred into it Hydrochloric acid is added to neutralise the alkali partly, and to it 150 parts more water is added. Finally formaldehyde is mixed. This adhesive is somewhat akaline, hence is not suitable for some applications. Alum may be added to neutralize the remaining alkalinity. It also increases the viscosity of die final product.

Watt Paper Paste

Formulation

Ingredients	**Parts by Wt.**
Water	220.00
Starch	120.00
Calcium chloride flakes	140.00
Water	550.00
Borax	1.20
Formalin (30%)	1.80

Water and starch are mixed at 20°C and then each is added and mixed for 2 hours. Water, borax, formaldehyde mixture is then added slowly.

Cheap Diluted Adhesive

This adhesive is quite cheap and also meets a number of industrial requirements.

Formulation

Ingredients	Parts by Wt.
Water	950.00
Sodium hydroxide	0.45
White soap	0.50
Tapioca starch	80.00
Sodium fluoride	2.00
Formaldehyde	5.00
Water	3.00

Starch is mixed with water, caustic soda and soap. It is heated to 85°C. Sodium fluoride, formaldehyde and water are mixed for about 15 minutes. Stability of the paste is enhanced by the addition of small amount of caustic and soap.

Non-weather Proof Corrugated Board Adhesive

This adhesive has quite low water to starch ratio, hence addition of calcium chloride is necessary to increase the translucent character and stability. As soap and sodium fluoride are precipitated by each, these are not incorporated.

Formulation

Ingredients	Parts by Wt
Water	854.00
Bentonite clay	10.00
Corn starch	80.00
Caustic soda	13.00
Corn starch	505.00
Borax	17.00
Formaldehyde	2.70

Water Resistant Corrugated Paper Box Adhesive

In this case urea-formaldehyde is added to increase the weather proofing qualities of the adhesive.

1st Mixture

560 litres of water are taken in a tank and heated up to 60°C. Then 50 kg of corn starch are added with stirring. Then 15 kg of caustic soda dissolved in water is added slowly with constant stirring. Add cold water to this mixture to make the total volume of 1250 liters.

2nd Mixture

1820 litres of water is heated to 40°C and 500 kg of corn starch is added. To this 45 kg of urea-formaldehyde resin are added and stirred vigorously till all the components are dissolved.

Final Mixture

1st mixture is added to the 2nd mixture with gentle agitation. Viscosity is adjusted by adding hot water.

Acid Modified or Thin Boiling Starch Adhesive

Unmodified starch gives highly viscous pastes at comparatively low solids. It is necessary for some applications to have high solid adhesives, at the same time the viscosity has to be suitable. Cooking of starch paste with acid below gelatinization gives an acid modified starch of reduced viscosity. These starches are known as acid modified or thin boiling starches. By varying the time, temperature, amount of acid and its kind, various types of starches of different thining and fluidity are obtained. Thin boiling starches are used for surface sizing of paper, textile, wrap sizing and laundry starches.

A simple starting fos nulation is given below :

Formulation

Ingredients	**Parts by Wt.**
Thin boiling cassava starch	200
Water	205
Caustic soda	20
Water	30

Caustic soda is dissolved in water and added slowly until a viscous semi-fluid consistency is obtained.

Water Resistant Seam Gums

Formulation

Ingredients	**Parts by Wt.**
Thin boiling starch	700.00
Soap	3.80
Urea-formaldehyde	105.00
Water	2000.00
Trisodium Phosphate (TSP)	10.00

TSP is added after cooking and cooling.

Library Paste:

Formulation

Ingredients	**Parts by Wt.**
Thin boiling starch	100.00
Corn syrup regular 43°Be'	15.00
Preservative	0.30
Water	220.00

Heat the mixture to 90"C for minutes and pack hot. It takes 2 to 7 days for paste to set up depending upon the cooling. Oil of winter green is sometimes added to provide characteristic odour. It has 40 per cent solids, and sets up to a stiff paste after being cooked. During application when prressure is applied with a finger or a brush, the paste softens sufficiently, so that it will apply smoothly.

Lay Flat Paper Laminating Adhesive

Formulation

Ingredients	**Parts by Weight**
Water	130.00

Thin boiling starch	100.00
Sulphonated castor oil 75 %0.	540
Hydrochloric acid 10 %	1.30
Sodium nitrate	40.00
Calcium chloride	40.00
Formaldehyde	0.50

Cartons or Bags Adhesive

Formulation

Ingredients	**Parts by Weight**
Water	135.0
Thin boiling starch	100
Corn syrup regular 43° Be'	25.00
Nonionic surfactant	0.25
Preservative	0.25
Cook to 90°C, hold for 20 minutes, to 55°C and add emulsion	100.00

The above adhesive is used to bond cartons or bags together, so that a number of them can be handled on a pellet, without danger of loading, slipping and sliding off. Emulsion is added to give good shear strength, but gives a brittle bond in tension. Thus bags and boxes can be separated from each other without tearing paper, when the bags or boxes are lifted upwards with a jerking motion.

Oxidised Starch Adhesives

Oxidised starch is usually made by wet treatment with sodium hypochlorite, hence it is sometimes called "chlorinates starch" also. Other oxidising agents used are hydrogen peroxide, sodium perborate and potassium persulfate. Oxidation to produce carboxyl groups in starch has two effects, which materially change the resulting paste properties. The starch becomes extremely hydrophilic and has a much reduced tendency to retrograde and reassociate in solution. The first property decreases its tendency to penetrate or migrate into a paper sheet, when used as a size of paper, while second property, i.e. reduced gel tendency causes them to be more stable to viscosity changes than the boiling starches.

Pastes of oxidised starches have improved clarity and their gelatinization temperature is lower than that of unmodified starch. Oxidised starches are used in quality adhesives for surface sizing of high grade paper and for paper coating. Oxidised starches may be further modified during formulation by additional oxidation at pH 10 or more. Extensive oxidation produces a very plastic, rather than viscous product.

Coating Colour Oxidised Starch Adhesive

Formulation

Ingredients	**Parts by Weight**
Water	70.00
Sodium metaphosphate	0.80

Soda ash	0.2
Calcium carbonate	40.00
Clay	160.00
Oxidised starch (Cooked in 96 parts of water)	32.00
Pine oil	0.24
10% soap solution	10.00

Wood Veneer Adhesive

Formulation

Ingredients	**Parts by Weight**
Oxidised starch	84.00
Barium peroxide	0.50
Soda ash	0.10
Whiting	5.00
Urea	10.00

These ingredients are mixed dry and added to 120 parts of water. It is heated to 70°C and after making it uniform, 2.5 parts of NaOH dissolved in 7.5 parts of water is also added.

Good Glue

Formulation

Ingredients	**Parts by Weight**
Water	500.00
Sodium bicarbonate	0.65
Oxidised starch	320.00
Hydrogen peroxide	10.00
Sodium hydroxide 36° Be'	80.00
Water	80.00

Turkey Red oil ammonium salt 0.65, oxidised starch, hydrogen peroxide and sodium bicarbonate are mixed at room temperature. The diluted caustic is then added and the mass is stirred for 12 hours.

Dextrin Based Adhesives

The dextrins come second in importance among the basic materials of cold adhesives. They are not only cheaper than natural gums, but also almost equally soluble in water. Dextrins are the degradation products of starches. This transformation is effected generally by heating the starch with a diluted acid or also by simple roasting of starch at high temperature. Dextrins are of three types as given below:

1. White dextrins
2. Canary or yellow dextrins
3. British gums

Properties

Dextrins are generally sold in powder form. The characteristics of the dextrins are dependent upon the origin of the starch, from which they are prepared and the technique of the conversion. The percentage of glucose formed is usually held to a minimum, because glucoses tend to increase hygroscopicity and decrease adhesiveness, clarity of paste and stability. Corn starch dextrins show poor paste clarity as compared to potato dextrins, but have good adhesive properties.

Dextrins do not have as good strength as the starch adhesives, though they are more soluble and set rapidly. Solubility of the dextrins in cold water depends on their glucose content, i.e. if more will be the glucose content higher will be solubility.

Dextrins break down on heating in the same way as starch, and therefore, as little heat as possible, for as short a time as possible, should be used in preparing dextrin adhesives. A simple dextrin adhesive used as photo paste is given below:

Dextrine adhesive for photo-paste

Formulation

Ingredients	**Parts by Weight**
White Dextrins	24.00
Water	24.00
Ginger grass oil	0.10

Dextrin is dissolved in water with a gentle heat and the oil is then stirred in.

Dextrins are slightly acidic and in acidic solution clearer adhesives are obtained, but the adhesive strength is reduced. Addition of alkali darkens the solution, but makes it more viscous and sticky.

For this purpose borax and caustic soda are added. Excess of caustic may have the reverse effect of reducing viscosity. Borax increases the density of adhesive reducing the drying time, and also it improves the stability, while reducing the cost. Sodium bisulphite masks the odour, bleaches, and act as preservative. One such formulation is given below:

Borax added dextrin adhesive

Formulation

Ingredients	**Parts by Wt.**
Dextrins	390
Water	500
Borax	46
Caustic Soda 36° Be'	6
Sodium bisulphite	4

At first half of the total water is mixed with dextrins and stirred vigorously. Then rest of water is added and the mixture is heated to 85°C. Sodium bisulphite is then added.

Quick Setting, Machine Adhesive For Sealing Wrappers

Formulation

Ingredients	**Parts by Wt.**
Yellow Dextrins	40.00
Water	50.00
Borax	40.00
Sodium hydroxide	2.00
Phenol	0.10
Turkey Red oil	0.50

Dextrin is dissolved in 45 parts of water. The borax is added with stirring. Sodium hydroxide is dissolved in 5 parts of water, and to it, dextrin is added with rapid stirring. The phenol and red turkey oil is then added. Wrapping paper is relatively impervious to the adhesive but in spiral tubes the paper is more absorbent and therefore the adhesive must be a litde denser. A modified formula is given below which contains tapioca starch, pardy replacing dextrins. This gives cheaper adhesives, giving less brittle film.

Denser dextrine adhesive

Formulation

Ingredients	**Parts by Wt.**
White dextrins	180
Water	600
Turkey Red oil	2
Light yellow dextrins	150
Tapoica starch	60
Borax	46
Sodium hydroxide	6
Sodium bisulphite	4

A thick paste of dextrins and starch is made with 300 parts water, to this turkey red oil is added followed by 280 parts water. It is heated to 85° C stirring. When the mass is gelatinised, borax is added, followed by sodium hydroxide dissolved in 20 parts water. The temperature is maintained at 85° C. Sodium bisulphite is added finally and the mass is stirred until it has completely dissolved.

Natural Cone Adhesive For Coloured Papers :

Formulation

Ingredients	**Parts by Wt.**
Light dextrin	630.00
Water	370.00
Turkey Red Oil ammonium salt	1.30
Sodium hydroxide 36° Be'	3.00
Formaldehyde (30%)	6.30

The mixture of water, dextrin and red turkey oil is heated to 80° C. Just enough sodium hydroxide is added to neutralize the acidity of dextrin, determined by litmus. Formaldehyde is added last.

Library paste

Formulation

Ingredients	**Parts by Weight**
White dextrin	280
Potato strach	280
Water	196
Glycerin	84
Phenol	2
Formaldehyde 30 %	3
Sassafras oil	1

A smooth paste is obtained with dextrin, starch and half of the water. Remaining water is then added and heated to a steam bath until smooth. Glycerin, phenol, formalin are then added.

Addition of soluble calcium salts produces a fatty paste. Both glycerine and calcium chloride make the adhesive slow drying which is desirable for highly calendered papers, that are slow to wet out. The following white paste is of that type.

Slow drying white paste

Formulation

Ingredients	**Parts by Weight**
Potato dextrin	100
Water	150
Calcium nitrate	10
Phenol	2

Calcium nitrate is dissolved in water heated to 75°C. Slowly dextrin is added with stirring, when every thing dissolved phenol is added.

Clear-White Highly Concentrated Adhesive

Formulation

Ingredients	**Parts by Weight**
Water	340.00
Turkey Red Oil 90%	1.30
Lithopone varnish grade	0.33
Dextrins soluble	660.00
Sodium bisulphite	3.30
Formaldehyde	6.60

Sodium bisulphite is used as decolorise and deodorise. Lithopone makes the product almost clear white.

Tube winding Adhesive

Formulation

Ingredients	**Parts by Wt.**
Water	400
Canary dextrin, 98 % cold soluble	200
White dextrin, 175 % cold soluble	100
Fine size clay	15
Sulphonated castor oil	1
Heat to 60° C and add borax	20
Heat to 90° C for 30 min. cool to 60° C and add lye	12
Formaldehyde	1

Paper To Glass Adhesive-non Water Proof

Formulation

Ingredients	**Parts by Wt**
Water	40.00
Canary dextrin, 95% cold soluble	60.00
Heat to 900C and add corn syrup	300.00
Phosphoric acid	0.50

Viscosity is adjusted to 10,000 to 20,000 cps. Phosphoric acid improves wetting and adhesion to paper.

Kraft Paper Envelop Gum

Formulation

Ingredients	**Parts by Wt.**
Tapoica dextrin	60.00
Glucose	5.00
©TAB-A = Phosphoric acid, 80 %	1.00
Formaldehyde	0.20
Water	33.80

Water is heated and dextrin is added slowly with stirring at 85° C till it is free from lumps. Glucose is added and cooled to 75° C. Finally formaldehyde and phosphoric acid are added.

Envelop Gum For Envelop Remoistenable Front Seal

Formulation

Ingredients	**Parts by Weight**
Water	159
Canary dextrin, 95 % cold soluble	300
Tributyl phosphate	1
Heat to 90° C for 30 min. and then cool to 60° C and add corn syrup	5
Water	

Case Sealing: Formulation Ingredients Water Tri butyl phosphate White dextrin, 45 % cold soluble Borax Heat to 950 C for 2 min. and cool to 60° C and add lye Formaldehyde pH is adjsuted between 9 and 9 : 4 by adding lye.

Water Resistant Multiwall Seam Gum

Formulation

Ingredients	**Parts by Wt.**
Water	1700
White dextrin	700
Soap	2
Urea-formaldehyde resin	70

The mixture is cooked at 90° C and cooled with water to about 2500 litres. Then ammonium chloride 14 kg. is added.

Gummed Label Adhesive

Formulation

Ingredients	**Parts by Wt.**
Water	600
Extra soluble dextrin	400
Turkey Red oil, 90 %	0.4
Formaldehyde, 30 %	120
Glycerin	40
Gelatin	20

Gelatin is soaked in 100 parts of water overnight and then heated to 80° C with stirring as the glycerin is slowly added.

Cork Label Adhesive

Formulation

Ingredients	**Parts by Wt.**
Dextrin	35
Gypsum	45
Fish glue	6
Casein	10
Soda ash	3

A homogenous mixture of dextrin and gypsum is made. Another mixture of fish glue, casein and soda ash is made. When adhesive is required, dextrin mixture is added in water, followed by other chemicals.

Denature Adhesive

Formulation

Ingredients	**Parts by Wt.**
1.Dextrin	1
Calcium	1
Casein powder	2

These are mixed and ground together. This is tasteless and resistant to saline.

Dextrins are aslo mixed with sodium silicate to form adhesives. The dextrins are made into a homogenous solution before other chemicals are added.

Formulation

Ingredients	**Parts by Wt.**
2. Water	90
White dextrin	30
Yellow dextrin	100
Glucose	20
Sodium silicate	25

Adhesive For Bonding Aluminium Sheets :

Formulation

Ingredients	**Parts by Wt.**
Dextrin	16
Sodium meta silicate	4
Glucose	2
Water	25

Envelop Gum-Remoistenable Front Seal :

Formulation

Ingredients	**Parts by Wt.**
Canary dextrin	25
Glycerin	5
Plasticizer	5
Water	5
Polyvinyl acetate emulsion	60

40.

Animal Glues

Introduction

Animal glue is an adhesive of great versatility with broad acceptance in industry. This natural polymer is an organic colloid derived from collagen-a protein constituent of animal skin, connective tissue, and bones, principally of cattle origin. Animal glues better known as Saresh in the market are more popular.

Its wide acceptance as an adhesive stems from its unique ability to deposit a tacky viscous film from a warm water solution, which on cooling a few degrees passes to a firm jelled state providing an immediate, moderately strong initial bond. Subsequent natural or forced air drying provides a permanent, strong, resilient bond between polar materials. Ease of preparation, ready application, good machining properties, relatively low cost and high-speed operations are characteristics of prime importance and interest in its use.

Animal glue is commercially available in a number of forms including the dry granulated products as hot glues, cold liquid glues for immediate use, and a wide selection of composition glues in cake or jelly form.

Chemical Composition

Animal glue is a protein derived from the simple hydrolysis of collagen which is a principal protein constituent of animal hide. The approximate chemical composition, of the glue is :

Formulation	**(%)**
Carbon	51.29
Hydrogen	6.39
Oxygen	24.13
Nitrogen	18.19
Total	100.00

Manufacture of Animal Glues

There are two types of animal glues-hide and bone.

Hide Glues

Hide glues are prepared by initial cleaning of the raw stocks by water followed by curing with milk of lime for the removal of non-glue proteins. The cured stocks are then lightly acidulated with acids such as hydrochloric, sulfuric and sulfurous, followed by careful removal of excess acid by additional washing with water. The treated stocks are transferred to cooking kettle, hot water is added and by a series of separate "Cooks" under carefully controlled schedule of time and heat, separate successive dilute glue solutions are drained from the cook kettle until the glue stocks are completely extracted of glue. The separate glue extraction liquors are then filtered, evaporated to 16 to 45 % glue solids, and in the newer installations are dried in noodle form on continuous dryers within 2 to 2 1/2 hr. using conditioned, filtered air.

Bone Glue

Bone glue, as the name implies, is processed from the collagen content of bones. Green bone glues are produced from fresh or "green" bone available as a by product of the packing industry. Bone glues prepared from solvent-extracted degreased bones are known as extracted bone glues . To prepare the modern bone glues, the bones are cleansed in water and /or dilute acids, charged to pressure tanks, and by a series of alternate steam pressure and hot water extractions, separate successive dilute glue solutions are removed from the bone stocks. The dilute glue liquors are then filtered or centrifuged for removal of free grease of fat followed by evaporation to high solids content Usually hide or bone glues are supplied in the form of thin pieces.

Properties

Animal glues are usually available as flakes, chips, powder or cake form, are well preserved against bacteria or mold infection for their intended industrial applications. These are odourless materials ranging in colour from light amber to brown. The density of animal glue is approximately 1.27, moisture content is about 10 to 14 %, Ash content between 2.25 to 4.00 %. Animal glues are soluble in water, insoluble in oils, waxes, organic solvents and absolute alcohol but may be emulsified in water-oil under proper conditions. One of the most interesting properties of animal glues solutions is that of passing from a liquid to a jelled state on cooling, again reverting to a liquid on reheating. This jellying property is of primary importance in many adhesive applications.

Precipitant for animal glue include absolute alcohol, tannic, picric and phosphotungstic acid and a saturated solution of zinc sulphate. Aluminium, ferric and chromic sulfates all thickens, coagulate and in some instances will precipitate glue from solution. Formaldehyde and formaldehyde donors added to glue solutions will provide an effective tonnage of the glue film.

Preparation of Glue Solutions

The direct addition of dry glue to hot water in a jacketed mechanically agitated mixer is recommended for fastest preparation. The hot water is preferably brought to 65 - 75° C bedore addition of dry glue. As the glue dissolves under heat, the temperature gradually drops to 60 - 65° C. Following this procedure batch preparations are common within 30 to 60 min.

An alternate procedure is to pre-soak the dry glue in cold water until swallon (30 to 45 min), and then transfer the swallon glue to jacketed melting tank with agitator, melting and stirring the glue into solution. This procedure is adopted mainly for small batches.

Galvanised iron and stainless steel mixing tanks are preferred. Electrically heated water jackets are usually preferred for small batches.

Liquid Animal Glues

Liquid animal glue adhesives for direct room temperature are preferred in many industrial applications. These products are prepared from hot animal glue solutions by the addition of gel depressant chemicals which in presence of water, arrest eliminate the natural gelling properties of the glue. On loss of water to the adherent and gradual drying, the physical action of gel depressant is eliminated and original unmodified properties of the animal glue take effect

Formulation & Applications

Animal glues have long been accepted as a standard products where economy, strength, permanence of bond, ease of use and versatility of prime importance are concerned. They usually contain preservatives, form suppressants, wetting agents and plasticizers like glycerin, sorbitol, glycols, sulphonated oils, fats and waxes. This is particularly used in book binding, luggage and set up paper box covering field.

Flexible Book Binding Glue

Formulation

Ingredients	Parts by Weight
Animal hide glue	30
Water	29
Glycerine	30
Preservative	1

Soak the glue in cold water for 2 hours and heat to 60° C with stirring using glycerine as the preservative.

Flexible Paper Box Glue

Formulation

Ingredients	Parts by Weight
Bone glue	45
Water	15
Glycerine	39
Preservative	1

Formic acid, phenol and formaldehyde etc. are the suitable preservatives.

Tin Can Label Glue

Formulation

Ingredients	Parts by Weight
Starch	100
Water	700
Gelatin	10
Sodium Silicate	100
Turpentine .	50

Starch and part of water, gelatin and remaining water are mixed separately and dissolved, they are then mixed together and then sodium silicate and turpentine are added.

Water Resistant Glue

Formulation

Ingredients	Parts by Weight
Animal glue	100.00
Water	225.00
Oxalic acid	5.50
Paraformaldehyde	10.00

Glue is dissolved in water and then other ingredients are added at about 40 to 45° C. Water resistance is developed slowly and reaches maximum in about 2 weeks.

Water Resistant Glue

Formulation

Ingredients	Parts by Weight
Glue	100.00
Potash alum	10.00
Acetic Acid	1.25
Denatured alcohol	1.25

Glue is dissolved in water. Then acid and denatured alcohol are added and stirred.

Wood Working Glue

Formulation

Ingredients	Parts by Weight
Animal Glue	100
Water	200
Urea	8
Glycerin	8

Addition of urea gives prompt remoistening and rapid setting. This glue is suitable for furniture, musical instruments and pencils etc.

Labels and Stamps Glue

Formulation

Ingredients	Parts by Weight
Animal glue	25
Trihydroxy ethylamine Abietate	50
Polymerized Terpenes	1
Water	170
Potassium hydroxide	1

Green bone glue is used in greatest volume for this adhesive. These animal glues possess the desired machining properties, quick, immediate tack with good tack life, and a speed and permanence of adhesion which are essential for this critical application.

Methods of Application

Animal glues are usually employed at 25 to 50 % concentration at 60° C . In this state it has a paint like consistency, and can thus be readily spread in the form of a thin continuous film. This film thickens on cooling permitting rapid development of desired tackiness and holds the adhesive at joint surface and this eliminates the danger of bleeding from the joint under pressure.

41.

Blood Albumen Glues

Introduction

The use of animal blood as an adhesive reaches backward into antiquity. Aztec Indians allegedly mixed animal blood with cement in their mortar, making possible the flat or plastered arch design that characterized many of their buildings. Some of these arches survive to this day, more as a monument to the adhesive strength of blood than the structural soundness of the arch itself. With the advent of World War II and a growing demand for water resistant 'interior' grades of plywood, blood glue assumes a place of prominence, assisted by substantial improvements in protein glue materials and technology. Although a several shift to synthetic resin adhesives for all grades of plywood has occurred in recent years, the consumption of blood glues is now expected to remain constant as petroleum resource problem influence the price and availability of resin constituents.

Solubility Categories

There are three general categories of dried blood used in adhesives. They are based on the severity of the drying treament. These are soluble, partially soluble, and insoluble. The preliminary steps before drying are the same in each case. Fresh liquid blood is collected in packing plants over a period of hours or even days. The fibrin or clotting substance is removed by mechanical agitation or acid precipitation, and preservative is generally added.

The first and most important category of dried blood adhesives is "soluble" blood which includes products of about 80 to 95% cold water solubility. This water-solubility value acts as a rough index for other useful properties of the dried blood, such as water requirement, soluble nitrogen content, and gel time, all of which are important to its overall adhesive behaviour. Soluble blood are carefully spray dried or vacuum dried at temperatures below the heat denaturing point of the blood protein. As with soyabean protein, the adhesive properties are closely related to solubility after processing.

The second category of dried blood is partially insoluble or denatured blood, which is understood to include water-solubilities from about 15 to 80% and covers a broad range of adhesive behaviour. Stable, unifrom dried bloods of intermediate solubility are the newest and probably the most important blood products to appear on the market since the development of soluble blood itself. The adhesive properties inherent in these products have been responsible for a steady increase in their volume and scope of application within the wood industry.

The third type of dried blood is totally insouble, and completely denatured. This material is generally intended for fertilizer rather than adhesive used, and is seldom prepared in any way for processing. At best, insoluble blood is a relatively poor adhesive base; it has seldom been utilized except as an organic filler contributing slightly to the adhesive properties of other active materials.

Properties

The source of animal blood has a large influence on its behaviour and adhesive properties. Blood differs considerably among species of animals, and also from one animal to another within a given species due to variations in age, condition, feed, etc. The commercial answer to this problem has been to dry blood stocks from different species of animals separately.and to blend large quantities of blood from a single species to yield bulk inventories of uniform properties.

All the soluble dried blood, are free-flowing medium density powders ranging in colour from dark red to almost black. As the degree of insolubility increases.the colour becomes more brown and the bulk density tends to drop. All dried bloods are hygroscopic and should be protected from moisture

As with soybean flour, the primary adhesive constituents in soluble dried blood are its proteins, serum albumin, and globulin. Blood actually contains other protein materials such as clotting compounds (fibrin) and red cells (haemoglobin). However, the fibrin is removed prior to drying and the hemoglobin is heavily complexed with metal ions, leaving mainly serum albumin and globulin available for adhesive purposes. A typical analysis for soluble dried beef blood is given below :—

TABLE -41.1- Analysis of Soluble Dried Beef Blood

Particulars	Value
Mesh size	05.6 % through 100 mesh
Water soluble protein	90.5%
Total nitrogen	14.7 %
pH	07.8 %
Moisture content	06.4 %

Blood protein molecules are highly polar and complex but heavily coiled or globular in form. Consequently, their many reactive groups are largely unavailable due to internal hydrogen bonding. Carefully dried blood protein dissolves readily in water to yield a moderately adhesive colloidal solution, but the full adhesive potential of its complex structure is developed only through alkaline dispersion.

Blood protein appears to become strongly adhesive at a lower pH than vegetable protein but several percent of a strong base such as sodium, potassium, or lithium hydroxide are ususlly necessary to develop its full adhesive potential.

Controlled applications of heat can·be employed to thicken a blood glue, alter its consistency, lengthen its working life, improve its cold bonding properties, or cure it irreversibly. This sensitivity to heat is mainly responsible for the popularity of blood glues, since it causes them to hot press rapidly and develop a high degree of water-resistance. Listed below is a glue based on soluble blood showing the use of hot water to coagulate the protein into a granular, high water content plywood adhesive.

High water content plywood adhesive

Formulation

Ingredients	**Parts By Wt.**
Water at 62° C	200.00
Soluble dried beef blood	80.00
Fine wood flour	18.00
Pine oil or equivalent defoamer	2.00
Mix 10 min	
Cold water	350.00
Pine oil or equivalent defoamer	2.00
Mix 2 min	
Hydrated lime in	7.00
Water atl 8-21 °C	14.00
Mix 2 min	
Sodium silicate solution	35.00
Mix 5 min	

This glue is ready to use when mixed and has a working life of about 4 to 8 hr., depending on storage temperature.

The following glue is also based on soluble blood. In this case, however, the blood has been denatured with dry heat to a low level of solubility (10 to 20%) prior to its use in the glue mix.

Glue based on soluble blood

Formulation

Ingredients	**Parts By Wt.**
Water atl 5-21 °C	300.0
Low solubility dried beef blood	75.00
Wood flour	21.00
Pine oil or equivalent defoamer	4.00
Mix 3 min or until smooth	
Water at 15-21 °C	330.00
Mix 2 min	
Hydrated lime in	10.00
Water at 18-23° C	20.00
50% Sodium hydroxide solution	16.00
Mix 10 min	
Sodium silicate solution	35.00
Mix 5 min	

This glue is ready for immediate use and has a working life of about 6 to 12 hr., depending on storage temperature. It is simpler to prepare and more reproducible than the hot water denatured blood glue, but it is still subject to viscosity variation due to mixer speed and efficiency.

Formaldehyde donors are an important class of denaturants for blood glues. Aldehydic compounds are useful for increasing the water-resistance, viscosity, working life, and water requirement of blood glues, while modifiying the consistency to any degree from gelations to completely granular. Compounds frequently used for this purpose are paraformaldehyde, formalin, dimethylol urea, sodium formaldehyde bisulfite, hexamethylenetetramine, tris-(hydroxy-methyl) nitromethane, monomethylol dimethylhydantion, and urea-or melamine-formaldehyde resins. Only small quantities (0.1 to 1.0 %) of these materials are required with sodiun hydroxide dispersions of blood protein to yield gross modifications. As the dispersing pH is reduced fron approximately 13 to 10, proportionately larger quantities of aldehyde are needed to yield corresponding effects. They are usually added after the blood is in solution, and most frequently after alkaline dispersion.

All phenolic resins seem to impart semiparmanent mold-resistance to blood glues when added in the quantities of 10% or more resin solids based on the weight of dry glue. The mold protection provided by these resins created a new grade of sheathing plywood for which the mold-resistance (and adhesion) are literally quaranteed for the structural life of the panel. Blood glues must be hot-pressed to gain the full measure of protection from phenolic resin, additives.

The following glues illustrate the combination of liquid phenolic resins with alkaline dispersed blood at the different levels for three separate purposes. The first is primarily a protein adhesive containing sufficient phenolic resin to impart mold-resistance and is typical of many commercial interior plywood glues.

Interior plywood glue

Formulation

Ingredients	**Parts By Wtt.**
Water at 15-21° C	175
Low solubility dried beef blood	50
Soluble dried beef blood	25
Fir wood flour	22
Pine oil or equivalent defoamer	3
Mix 3 min or until smooth	
Water all 5-210C	400
Mix 2 min	
Hydrated lime in	6
Water	12
Mix 1 min	
Sodium silicate solution	45
Mix 1 min	
50% sodium hydroxide solution	16
Mix 5 min	
50% solids phenolic adhesive Resin	27
Mix 3 min	

The second glue contains approximately equal weights of protein and phenolic adhesive resin solids, and is truly a hybrid glue. The protein constituent provides rapid cure under heat and pressure. The resin constituent is cured by latent heat in the laminate after removal from the press to provide a weatherproof, mold proof bond.

Weatherproof, moldproff bond

Formulation

Ingredients	**Parts By Wtt.**
Water at 37° C	75
Soluble dried beef blood	75
Fir wood flour	12
Wheat flour	10
Diesel oil	3
Mix 5 min	
Water at 370C	250
Pine oil	6
Mix 2 min	
Sodium silicate solution	150
Mix 10 min	
Cold water	150
40% solids phenolic adhesive resin	200
50% sodium hydroxide solution	50
Mix 5 min	

This glue is ready for immediate use, and it has a viscosity range of about 1500 to 3000 cps and a working life of about 24 hr. It can be used to produce plywood, flush doors, or other wood laminates of near exterior quality at pressing times substantially shorter than the resin constituent would otherwise permit

The third blood-resin adhesive is a conventional exterior plywood glue containing primarily alkaline phenolic resin with some soluble blood as its adhesive constituents. Adding 10% blood permits a 20% reduction in the pressing time of phenolic resin adhesives. Larger blood additions permit further, but not proportionate reductions in pressing time. For glues of this type to operate properly, the blood and resin solids together must develop sufficient cure of "green bond" in the press to resist internal steam pressure and moderately rough handling of the panels during removal from the press. The resin then completes a satisfactory latent cure in the hot-stacked panels. A typical glue mix is given below:

Hot-stached panel glue adhesive

Formulation

Ingredients	**Parts By Wt.**
Waterat21°C	190
Extender	70
Mix 2 min	
50% sodium hydroxide solution	40
Mix 1 min	
Sodium carbonate	18
Mix 15 min	
Diesel oil	3
Mix 1 min	

Dried soluble blood	30
Mix 5 min	
40% solids phenolic adhesive resin	500
Mix 5 min	

This glue is ready to use when mixed. It has a working life of about 8 to 16 hr. depending on storage temperature. Since this glue is primarily a resin adhesive, it operates at a considerable lower viscosity than regular blood protein glues, on the order of 1500 to 3000 cps a 21°C while developed primarily for plywood, it is a suitable weatherproof adhesive for other wood laminates to which penetrating heat and pressure can be readily applied.

Soluble dried blood is also added in moderate quantities to urea-formaldehyde hotpress resin glues, usually with other extenders such as wheat and nutshell flours, for improved water-resistance. Unlike phenolic adhesives, the blood does not permit a reduction in pressing time. This is apparently related to the type of blood dispresion, which in urea resin glues is neutral or slightly acid rather than strongly alkaline. This causes the formation of discrete swollen blood particles instead of a gelatinous colloid. Blood additions are especially useful for improving the bond strength and water-resistance of heavily extended urea resin glues. Assuming the darker color imparted by the blood is not a problem, these glues are excellent adhesives for hardwood plywood, solid-and hollow-core flush doors. Prefabricated structural units, lumber overlaying, and other uses where a strong, heat-cured water-resistant bond is required, especially involving hardwoods. A typical glue mix is given below:

Hardwood, plywood, solid & hottawcore flush door adhesive

Formulation

Ingredients	**Parts By Wt.**
Waterat21°C	120
Urea resin hot press catalyst	10
Mix 1 min	
Soluble dried beef blood	10
Wheat flour	100
Pine oil	1
Mix 5 min	
65% solids urea bonding resin	100
Mix 5 min	

This glue is ready to use when mixed and has a working life of about 8 to 16 hr. depending on temperature. Its viscosity is suitable for almost any method of application except spray. The wheat flour extension of the urea resin may be varied from about 25 to 150% depending on the cost-performance level desired, but the blood content with respect to resin should remain about the same.Conventional urea resin hot-press spreads and curing times should be used.

Dried soluble blood has found little use in melamine-and melamine-urea-formaldehyde resins, or resorcinol and phenol-resorcinol formaldehyde adhesive resins up to the present. The chemistry of these resins does not favour the development of useful blood dispersions; also, their cured properties already exceed the levels of water-resistance and reactivity which blood can impart

Blood-Soybean Flour Combinations

Certainly the largest single use for dried soluble blood during recent years has been water-resistant hot-press plywood glues, alone or in combination with other proteinaceous materials such as soybean flour. Glues of this type are the main stay of water-resistant softwood plywood production. Soluble blood and soybean flour make a particularly useful combination since each contributes properties in which the other is basically deficient Dispersed blood, although highly heat reactive and water-retaining, lacks good working properties and assemble time tolerance. Dispersed soybean flour has excellent working properties and assemble time tolerance but lacks hot-press curing speed and water-resistance. Together, these materials make an extremely useful series of low-cost, water-resistant, fast-curing, hot press adhesives suitbale for many wood gluing operations such as plywood bonding, stored heat lumber laminating, softboard and hard board laminating, flush door gluing, box manufacturing, and chipboard and treated paper overlay bonding. Examples of low and high blood content glues are given below:

Law blood content dry glue competition :

Formulation

Ingredients	**Parts By Wt.**
Soybean flour	72
Soluble dried beef blood	15
Wood flour	10
Pine oil or equivalent defoamer	3
Total	100

Mixing Directions :

Water at 15-21° C	200
Low-blood content dry glue	100
Mix 2 min or until smooth	
Water at 15-21° C	220
Mix 2 min	
Hydrated lime.in	8
Water at 15-21° C	16
Mix 1 min	
Sodium silicate solution	40
Mix 1 min	
50% sodium hydroxide solution	10
Mix 5 min	

High-Blood content dry-glue composition :-

Formulation

Ingredients	Parts by weight
Soluble dried-beef blood	70
Soybean flour	17
Wood flour	10
Pine oil or equivalent defoamer	3
Total	100

Mixing Directions :

Water at 15-21° G	160
High blood content dry glue	100
Mix 2 min or until smooth	
Water all 5-21° C	390
Mix 2 min	
Hydrated lime in	8
Water at 15-21° C	16
Sodium silicate solution	45
Mix 1 min	
50% sodium hydroxide solution	16
Mix 5 min	
Hexamethylenetetramine	2
Mix 3 min	

Both glues are ready to use when mixed and have a working life of about 4 to 8 hr., depending on temperature. Both glues meet the fast press times, wet spreads, and assembly time limits shown in the hot-pressing schedule that follows. Under certain conditions, these glues may be used cold-press; however, their cost is higher and performance generally poorer that blood glues developed specifically for cold-pressing.

Other hot-press glues may be formulated with blood-soybean flour ratios between 15:85 and 80:20. They all provide satisfactory dry adhesion, but water-resistance increases from marginal for the lower blood ratios to excellent for the high ratios. Because of the larger water requirement of blood compared with soybean flour, glue costs increase only about 25% over this range of blood contents.

Other Blood-Protein Combination

A number of animal and vegetable protein materials other than soybean flour may be combined with blood albumen to yield useful wood adhesive. Casein, animal glue, dried whole egg, fish meal, peanut flour, and cottonseed meal are examples. Some contribute additional tack and flow properties, whereas others contribute a particulate consistency similar to soybean flour. Except for casein, which has been used with soluble blood as a hot-press plywood glue in Europe for many years, none of these materials seem to offer any advantage over straight blood or blood-soybean adhesives in cost or performance.

Mold Resistance

The mold-resistance of heat-cured protein glues ranges from poor to good, depending on blood content. For exemple, glues containing primarily soybean flour and limited amounts of blood have no mold-resistance. Suitable mold inhibitors include the various chlorinated phenols and phenyl phenols, copper naphthenate, tributylin oxide, quinolinoleate and others. Unlike soybean adhesives, these fungicides should not be blended into dry glues containing substantial quantities of blood since they tend to react with its protein during dry storage.

As indicated earlier, phenolic adhesive resins also impart excellent mold-resistance to blood hot-press glues when added at the rate of about 10% resin solids, based on the weight of dry protein glue. This form of mold protection has the advantage of being very resistant to leaching from the cured glue film under wet service conditions since the resin itself becomes theremoset.

Application

As a result of more recent developments in protein adhesive technology, blood glues have emerged as superior cold-press plywood adhesives, even to the point of challenging soybean glues for their traditional "No-Clamp" cold-press markets on a strictly cost-performance basis. Most of these new glues derive their unusual cold-press properties from the use of partially soluble dried bloods, which alter their consistency after alkaline dispersion from slippery and gelatinous to granular and tacky by converting a portion of the blood into discrete sticky particles. In breaking up the colloidal character of dispersed soluble blood these particles accelerate the migration of water from the glue into adjacent dry wood, thus developing gel strength quickly enough to permit short cycle cold-pressing. These sticky particles of dispersed blood also help the glue film resist total absorption into wooden plies under pressure and prevent migration from areas of extreme pressure, both of which cause loss of bond strength through over penetration and starved glue joints.

An example of chemically modified type of blood cold-press glue is given below:

Blood cold-press glue

Formulation

Ingredients	**Parts By Wt.**
Water all 5-21° C	150
Dried soluble beef blood	75
Fir wood flour	22
Pine oil or equivalent defoamer3	
Mix 2 min or until smooth	
Water at 15-21° C	370
Mix 2 min	
Hydrated lime in	7
Water at 15-21° C	21
Mix 1 min	
Sodium silicate	50
Mix 1 min	
50% sodium hydroxide solution	16
Mix 5 min	

Water at 15-21° C	135
37% formalin	2
Mix 3 min	
40% solids phenolic adhesive resin	10

This glue is ready to use when mixed and has a working life of 4 to 8 hr., depending on temperature. It derives its high water requirement (6.84) and cold-press consistency from the combined denaturing effects of formaldehyde and phenolic resin solids on a normal alkaline dispersion of soluble blood. Both denaturants contribute to water-resistance, and the resin adds moderate mold - resistance. It is precipitated in place rather than thermoset as the glue line cures

All the cold-press blood glues are excellent adhesives for plywood, flush doors, hardboard and softboard laminating, treated paper over-laying, common lumber laminating and box shook manufacturers.

42.

Casein Glues and Adhesives

Introduction

Casein is milk protein, obtained from skimmed milk by precipitation with sulphuric, hydrochloric or lactic acid, to a pH of about 4.5. 100 kgs. of milk usually yields about 3 kgs. of casein. The precipitated casein is filtered, washed thoroughly, ground and screened to get 20 mesh or finer product for glue manufacture. Commercial casien contains about 80-90 per cent of protein, 1-4 per cent ash, 0-1-3 per cent of butter fat, 7-10 per cent moisture, 0-4 per cent lactose and 0-3 per cent acids expressed as lactic acid. The composition and amounts of impurities depend on, among other factors, the method of manufacture. Reunet casein is not, as it is, suitable for glue manufacture due to high ash content.

Properties

Casein is an off white powder. Its molecular weight is about 13000-19,000. It is insoluble in water at its isolectric point pH 4.6; the solubility increasing acidity or alkalinity, in the latter it is more readily soluble. Fixed alkalies like sodium hydroxide remain in the glue line as sodium caseinate, a soluble salt while calcium hydroxide, on which water-resistant wood glues are based, forms insoluble calcium caseinate in the glue line. Similar insoluble caseinates are formed by zinc, chromium and aluminium salts etc. Casein powder has a shelf life of above 1 year at 20°C.

Casein adhesives are unsuitable for outdoor use although they are more resistant to temperature changes and moisture than other water-based adhesives. Resistance to dry heat up to 70°C is good, but under damp conditions the adhesives lose strength and are subject to biodeterioration.Their resistance to orgnic solvents is generally good. Casein adhesives are often compounded with materials such as latex and dialdehyde starch to improve durability. Strong alkaline nature of mixed casein adhesives often affects the bonding of timber with high resin or oil content by virtue of a saponification action on poorly wetting surface contamination. Resultant bonds may be stronger than those obtained from synthetic resins. Hard woods are subject to staining. Gap-filling properties are good. Alkaline nature of casein glues precludes the use of copper or aluminium mixing vessels.

Like animal glues, casein glues have fairly good bond strength and those containing sodium hydroxide have even better resistance to water than animal glues; also they recover their original strength on redyeing. The fact that casein glues do not gelatinise makes them much easier to handle.The most serious drawback of casein for use in adhesive is the presence of fatty matter which has a very adverse effect on the tensile strength of joint made.

Classification of casein glues and adhesives

Water-resistant Casein-lime Glue

Water-resistant casein glue sets to a gel as the result of a slow chemical reaction, sodium caseinate gradually converted to calcium caseinate. Some of the calcium hydroxide in the formula has produced sodium hydroxide from a sodium salt also in the formula, dissolving the casein. The chemicals are dry mixed with casein as a ready mix powder and shipped to the user as a complete prepared glue for dispersing in water.

Calcium hydroxide when present in excess, shortens the working life but increases the water resistance of the glue line. Addition of sodium silicate (silica: soda ratio 3:1) increases the working life of the glue, at all levels of alkalinity. A simple formula using lime and alkali is given below. It has good water resistance, good working life about 7 hours.

Water resistant caseim-lime glue adhesive

Formulation

Ingredients	**Parts By Wtt.**
1. Casein	100
Water	150
Sodiu hydroxide	11
Water	50
Calcium hydroxide	20
Water	20

A sodium silicate containing casein glue formulation is given below: Cupric chloride works as an inhibitor. Cupric sulphate may also be used in place of cupric chloride. Other preservatives are esters of P-hydroxy benzoic acid, chlorinated phenols, phenyl mercuric acetate.

Formulation

Ingredients	**Parts By Wt.**
2. Casein	100
Water	150
Hydrated lime	20
Water	100
Sodium silicate	70
Cupric chloride	2
Water	30

Ammonium hydroxide may be used in place of sodium hydroxide in casein glues, but more water will be required to attain the same viscosity; working life will be reduced unless the proportion of lime is also reduced; this will adversely affect the water resistance.

As usual, wood flour, cellulose etc. are used as extenders in casein glues; they also reduce the penetration into the adherent.Ignorganic fillers are usually avoided as they make the glue line abrasive to wood working tools. Casein glues may be thickened by adding sodium sulphite, sugar or sodium hexametaphosphate. Thinning extends the working life of the glue. Casein adhesives of low alkalinity are sometimes thinned and stabilised by including 20% urea or 10% dicyandiamide, based on casein. Casein itself is usually treated with 1% non drying oil before introducing chemicals in making prepared glues, this retards action of chemicals on the casein and promotes easy welling of glue in mixing. Drying casein glue lime is ususally brittle.To make it slightly flexible glycerol, glucose, agar-agar, dimethyl-glycol phthalate, sorbitol sulphonated oils, rubber latices or resin emulsions are added, sometimes sodium flouride is added in place of sodium hydroxide.

The following emulsion type formulation is suitable as adhesive for plywood, leather and fabrics.

Emulsion type casein glue adhesive far plywood, leather & fabric

Formulation

Ingredients	**Parts by weight**
Polyvinyl isobutyl ether (medium viscosity)	100.00
Casein	18.00
Stearic acid	0.60
Boric acid	1.80
Salicylic acid	1.80
Ammonia 25%	6.90
Water	130.50
2, 6-Ditertiary butyl P-cresol	0.30
N-Heptane	27.00

A hot solution of casein, water (48 parts) and ammonia (1.8 parts) are mixed with stearic acid, water (15 parts) and ammonia (3 parts). An 80% polyvinyl isobutyl ether solution in heptane is warmed to 50°C and added with agitation to the above mixture. A solution of boric acid, salicylic acid, remaining water, 2,6-ditertiary butyl p-cresol and remaining ammonia is then finally added to it.

Casein Blend Glues

Casein blends with blood are dry powder glues for cold pressing plywood. The blood constituent in casein glue constributes quick setting, thus reducing clamp time, and both dry and wet strengths are improved. These glues are used in the construction of flush doors, boxes, furniture and other wood assembly work where dark colour imparted by the blood is accepted. Blend glues may compromise mixtures of casein with soyabean meal. This type of belnd is a way to the reduction of the cost

Lime free Casein Adhesives

Casein solution not involving lime may be used as adhesives for adherends other than wood. These are prepared by dissolving casein with sodium salts, which provide a sufficiently medium alkali to dissolve the casein. Commonly used sodium salts are borax soda ash, trisodium phosphate, and others. Casein in solution in strong alkalies, such as sodium hydroxide, and ammonium hydroxide, also have the adhesive value. Organic amines dissolve casein and there is some small use of alkyl amines, ethanolamines and morpholine as the solvent for casein adhesives. To give limefree casein adhesives some measure of water resistance, formaldehyde or formaldehyde donor in the form of resin or hexamethylene tetramine may be added. More commonly, an oxide or salt of zinc, aluminium or chromium are added to improve water resistance. A formulation is given below used for plywood:

Formulation

Ingredients	**1 (part)**	**2 (parts)**
Casein	100.00	100.00
Sodium phosphate	-	4.00
Urea	15.00	15.50
Water	460.00	480.00
Formaldehyde	7.50	8.00

Following formulation contains ammonia. It is a liquid waterproof glue.

Formulation

Ingredients	**Parts by weight**
i. Casein	12.0
Water	12.0
ii. Water	70.0
Ammonia	3.0
Caustic soda	1.5
Phenol	0.5

Casein is first swelled in water, and then the second group of ingredients are added. It is heated upto 60°C and stirred for complete dissolution. Ammonia volatilises off on drying of paste. The following casein glue is quite cheap and suitable for ordinary application. It is a dry power based on borax.

Dry Powder Formulation

Ingredients	**Parts**
Casein	100
Borax	16

Instead of borax, 20 parts of sodium carbonate may be used. The dry glue is made into a paste ready for use by dissolving it into 5 to 6 times its weight of water.

Applications

Ready mixed glues are prepared by mixing the powder into cold or tap water. The constituents are added in definite order at definite time intervals. Glue preparation normally takes about 20 to 60 minutes. Ready mixed glues are easy to prepare and to apply casein glue wood joints are normally made by cold pressing but hot pressing at moderate temperature is sometimes used.

Casein Adhesives for Bonding Paper

1. Foil to Paper Laminating

An ammonical solution of casein is blended with latex of S-B or polychloroprene type to produce a flexible bond in the aluminium foil-to-paper lamination, for many end uses. The laminate must be free from colour, odour and toxic materials. Aluminium foil is also occasionally bonded to glassine, rubber, fibre glass, asbestos, vulcanized fibre, masonite, plastic sheeting and tissue paper. Following are the examples :-

Formulation

Ingredients	Parts
SBR	40
1, 2, bis phenoxyethane	100
Water	368
Casein	8

This adhesive is tack free and blocking when dried. When exposed to heat the solid plasticizer melts, giving a PSA having a tack life of about 15 min.

This type of adhesive is used for bonding vinyl sheeting and vinyl plastisol coating to paper, nylon and rayon. Casein in fairly large amount is miscible with nitrile rubber lattices. Borated casein is made by mixing casein 20 parts per 100 parts of borax and preservative made upto 12%.

Formulation

Ingredients	Parts
Nitric rubber (medium nitrile)	80
Borated casein	20

2. Casein Paste For Labelling

Casein pastes for labels have a position of some importance in providing moisture-resistant paper-to-glass or paper-to-metal bonds. The bond requires moisture resistance at low alkalinity by reaction of casein with metallic salts, a degree of resistance, for instance to permit beer and soft drink bottles to be immersed in ice water without losing the label. Paper labels can be applied to tin cans with a composition of casein and rosin.

3. Other Paper Bonds

Wet tack and a good degree of moisture resistance account for a small use of casein adhesive in the seaming of paper bags, in spiral or convolute winding of paper for cups, cartons and tubes and in book binding.

The adhesive which holds the seam of a cigarette together may be an alkaline solution of casein comprising wax to provide moisture resistance. This is one of the oldest uses of casein adhesive. To adhere waxy paper to surfaces an alcohol soluble derivative of casein may be used. As an adhesive for cellophane a water-alcohol solution of casein may be used.

Casein Adhesive for Binding Dissimilar Materials

Among these assemblies are : metal to wood, cork to metal, cork to wood, linoleum to wood, caremic tile to wood, plastic sheeting to wood, stone to wood, plastic heet to glass and vinyl to plywood. Casein latex may be the primer for a final glue line of phenolic adhesive in bonding metal to wood. Metal to plywood laminate is especially useful where greater stiflhers and resistance is desired. Here elasticity of bond is provided by combining latex with caesin.

Combination of casein with other adhesives improves degrees of softness or hardness.

43.

Fish Glues

Introduction

Fish glue, as the namé indicates, is obtained as the by-product of the fish skin industry, was the first liquid glue that reached commercial importance and was the forerunner of all household glues. Even with the many synthetic adhesives of to-day, there are specialized applications which require the unique properties found in fish glue. Here are a list of properties which make fish glue particularly unique:

1. Supplied as a liquid adhesive.
2. Completely water soluble.
3. Good adhesion to metal, rubber, glass, cement, cork, wood and paper.
4. High initial tackiness.
5. Can be used as remoistenable adhesive, similar to contact adhesive.
6. Insoluble in organic solvents.
7. Will not soften at high temperatures upto 260° C.
8. When used as a metal coating it can be baked to provide a tough and tenacious film that is highly resistant to corrosion.
9. When dry fish glue is hard enough to be sanded. It is not gummy,
10. Because of its water solubility, it can be used as an in-process or temporary adhesive.
11. Fish glue can be made water resistant and soluble in water.
12. Fish glue can be compounded to be thermoplastic and heat bondable.
13. Special grades can be used in photographic emulsions and coatings.

Manufacturing Process

Fish glue is derived from fish skins. The skins are thoroughly washed to remove any salt or extraneous matter. When they are completely freshened, the skins are cooked in water for a given time and temperature. The resultant broth is drained from the residue and concentrated in an evaporator to the finished glue solids of approximately 45%. Since the fish glue is a protein, special precautions must be taken to ensure cleanliness, as bacteria and resultant enzyme will quickly breakdown and degrade the glue. After evaporation is completed, an odorant is added to the finished glue to give a characteristic scent, and a bacteriocide is also added to give storage protection. Properly protected fish glue, stored at room temperature, will have a shelf life of atleast 2 years.

Properties

A typical fish glue has the following properties :-

Colour	Lightcaramel
Mild, Characteristic of the odorant added	
Viscosity	4000-7000 cps
Solids	43-50%
Temperature range	0°Cto260°C
Shear strength	3200 psi
Weight/Litre	0.9kg

Upon cooling to 44° C or below, liquid fish glue sets to gel. This is completely reversible, as it will revert to a liquid with no change in properties upon being warmed to room temperature. Dry films of fish glue are relatively brittle. They can be plasticized with glycerine or glycol to yield flexible films. Dried fish glue is insoluble in oraganic solvents. Although fish glue is very water soluble, it can be made water insoluble by the addition of polyvalent ion salts such as ammonium sulphate, ferric sulphate or chrome alum.

Applications & Formulations

Fish glue has good adhesion to many surfaces. In any bonding application using wet adhesive, one side must be porous to allow the adhesives to dry out. Two non-porous surfaces can be bonded by using fish glues as a remoistenable adhesive. Both sides are coated and allowed to dry. One side is then reactivated with a thin film of water and the surfaces pressed together. The wet adhesive has high initial tackiness or quick tack. This develops very rapidly on porous surfaces and lends itself to many card board and paper bonding applications. For less porous surfaces such as wood, the glue has a relatively long open time.

Rubber-to-Steel

In the manufacture of cans, each can is pressure tested to determine leakages. A rubber gasket is bonded, using fish glue, to the pressure testing apparatus and makes the temporary pressure seal. When the gasket wears out, it can be stripped off with the assistance of a wet putty knife. A new gasket, previously coated with fish glue, is lightly remoistenable, applied, and is ready for use. There is little down time, and no flammable solvents are used.

Strawboard-to-Steel

Embossing dies require a steel female die and a strawboard male die. The strawboard, or counter die, must be held in exact register to its respective female die. Fish glue assures good adhesion and exact registration by preventing the counters from slipping or sliding. Even heated dies will not move, since the fish glue is heat resistant to 2600 C. No flammable solvents are used, either.

Rubber-or Cork-to-Plywood

Glass frit or stain is compounded with fish glue by ball milling. The resultant water soluble stamping paste is applied to unfired porcelain by automatic rubber stamping equipment. During firing, 'the fish glue burns off at approximately 538°C. The temperature increases to the melting point of the frit, the colour is permanently fused into the porcelain.

Paper-to-Steel

Make-ready on either rotary or flat bed presses is easily done with fish glue, Paper, or, card board sheets can be adhered readily to steel. The bond is resistant to inks and solvent used for clean up. After the run is completed, hot water will soften the fish glue, allowing for easy removal and clean up.

Another application is in the gluing of labels to solvent cans. Since the solvent will not attack the glue, the labels will withstand solvent slippage. If water resistance is required, 5% glyxol can be added to fish glue before coating. After drying the bond will develop good water resistance in 24 hours.

Straight Line Gluing

Fish glue can be applied by rollers in straight line gluing operations. In the manufacture of printing forms, the glue sets quickly because of porous nature of the paper. Padding compounds can be made by the addition of glycerin which plasticise the glue and gives a very flexible bond.

Excellent Adhesive Formulation

Ingredients	Parts By Wt.
Fish glue	100.00
Water	0.22
Benzoic acid	0.22
Methylated spirit	0.75
Sassafras oil	0.15
Boiling water	8.00

Water Proof Fish Glue

Formulation

Ingredients	Parts By Wt.
Fish glue	100
Water	10
Alcoholic solution of gum rosin	100
Methylated Spirit	35

Alcoholic solution of gum rosin such as rosin, ester gum, lac enhances water resistant properties.This type of glue is used for setting jewellery, fixing precious stones to glass and metals.Carefully added small quantities of hydrochloric acid, acetic acid, berzoic acid, tartaric acid etc. remarkably enhance the adhesive properties.

Fish glue may be added to hot animal glue at a slow rate to prevent cooling, the latter below its gel point; this is particularly useful for making gummed tapes. Addition of fish glue to polyvinyl acetate emulsions improves the cold flow and creep resistance, heat resistance, initial tack, glue penetration and resistance to aliphatic solvents. Fish glues are incorporated in latex adhesive for shoe industry to improve wet tack and adhesion.

A special high grade clarified fish glue known as photo-engraving glue is making items such as blue print paper, tracing cloth, letter press printing plates and etched name plates etc.

44.

Suppliers of Plant & Machineries

ADHESIVE TAPE MACHINERY

Moscow Machine Tools
C-293
Mukund Ngr. Ghaziabad,
Uttar Pradesh-201001
India
TEL : +91 (0) 120 24731630
FAX : +91 (0) 120 24793507
E-mail:
moscowindia@yahoo.co.in

Machinkraft Equipment
337 3rd Rd., Sindh Hsg. Soc.
Aundh
Pune, Maharashtra-411007
India
TEL : +91 (0) 20 25887464
FAX : +91 (0) 20 25880353
E-mail:
info@machinkraftequipment.com

Jangir Co.
19/73
West Moti Bagh
Old Rohtak Rd.
Delhi, NCT of Delhi-110007
India
TEL : +91 (0) 11 23652201

C Trivedi & Co.
A-1/16
Phase-II, GIDC Est.
Vatva
Ahmedabad, Gujarat-382445
India
TEL : +91 (0) 79 25830552
FAX : +91 (0) 79 25830553
E-mail: ctrivedi@ctrivedi.com

Natraj Industries
Plot No. 65
Sect. 6
Faridabad, Haryana-121006
India
TEL : +91 (0) 129 25241403
FAX : +91 (0) 129 25243403
E-mail:
hitesh@del3.vsnl.net.in

Goldmann Automatics Pvt. Ltd.
1 Vardhman Indl. Est.
Village Rd.
Bhandup (W)
Mumbai,
Maharashtra-400078
India
TEL : +91 (0) 22 25618805
FAX : +91 (0) 22 25643997
E-mail: goldmann@vsnl.com

Frigmaires Engineers
Janta Indl. Est.
Gala No. 8, Opp. Phoenix Mill
Senapati Bapat Marg
Lower Parel
Mumbai,
Maharashtra-400013
India
TEL : +91 (0) 22 24945624
FAX : +91 (0) 22 22187750
E-mail: fe@vsnl.com

SP International
Ground Flr., 9
Sona Udyog Indl. Est.
Parsi Panchayat Rd.
Andheri (E)
Mumbai,
Maharashtra-400069
India
TEL : +91 (0) 22 28322554
FAX : +91 (0) 22 26437045

CHEMICAL PLANT MACHINERY

Anand Reinforced Systems
Plot No. 44
IDA
Opp. BEL
Mallapur, Hyderabad,
Andhra Pradesh-501507
India
TEL : +91 (0) 40 27157316
FAX : +91 (0) 40 27159618
E-mail:
ars26@rediffmail.com

Vascon Engineering Equipments
C-31/1
Indl. Est.
(Nr. SBH, Opp. RMSC Stockyard)
Sanathnagar
Hyderabad,
Andhra Pradesh-500018
India
TEL : +91 (0) 40 23708586
FAX : +91 (0) 40 23708586
E-mail:
vasconengg@yahoo.com

Chemtech Industrial Equipments
D-3
IDA, Phase-V
Jeedimetla
Hyderabad,

Andhra Pradesh-500855
India
TEL : +91 (0) 40 23097963
FAX : +91 (0) 40 23190528

Raja Industries
C-210
Phase-II
Mayapuri
New Delhi, NCT of
Delhi-110064
India
TEL : +91 (0) 11 25400521
FAX : +91 (0) 11 25407196

Technofab Engg. Ltd.
502, Eros Apts., 56
Nehru Place
New Delhi, NCT of
Delhi-110019
India
TEL : +91 (0) 11 26411931
FAX : +91 (0) 11 26221521
E-mail:
techfab.tfebd@axcess.net.in

TR Sharma Engg. Works
A-156
Hari Ngr.
New Delhi, NCT of
Delhi-110064
India
TEL : +91 (0) 11 25405328
FAX : +91 (0) 11 25403754
E-mail:
paintmachinery@yahoo.com

Balkrishna Boilers Inds.
Plot No. 14
Jay Khodiyar Indl. Est.
Nr. Subhash Est.
Ramol Rd.
Ahmedabad, Gujarat-380026
India
TEL : +91 (0) 79 25855883
E-mail: info@balkrishn.com

Shri Momai Fabricators Engineers
C/57
Lakulesh-II
B/h Sardar Est.
Ajwa Rd.
Vadodara, Gujarat-390019
India
TEL : +91 (0) 265 2565566
FAX : +91 (0) 265 2569816
E-mail:
iyer@shreemomai.com

Ahmedabad Industrial Engineers
402
`Shantam' Cmplx.
Gurukul Rd.
Memnagar
Ahmedabad, Gujarat-380052
India
TEL : +91 (0) 79 27433061
FAX : +91 (0) 79 27420131

Vivek Chem-Fabs
Plot No. 71
Sect. 27A, 15/1 Mile Stone
Mathura Rd.
Faridabad, Haryana-121003
India
TEL : +91 (0) 129 25274848
FAX : +91 (0) 129 28843308

Anas Associates
Plot No. 99
Indra Cmplx. Kheri Rd.
Faridabad, Haryana-121002
India
TEL : +91 (0) 129 2296786

Kay Iron Works Pvt. Ltd.
Village Jorian
Radour Rd.
Yamuna Nagar,
Haryana-135001
India
TEL : +91 (0) 1732 279821
FAX : +91 (0) 1732 225142
E-mail:
kayiron@nde.vsnl.net.in

Amir Tanks & Vessels Pvt. Ltd.
84-85-B
Sect. F
Sanwer Rd.
Indore,
Madhya Pradesh-452015
India
TEL : +91 (0) 731 2422849
FAX : +91 (0) 731 2422936
E-mail:
nadkarni@sancharnet.in

Pharmaceutical Machinery Manufacturing Works
47/B
Laxmibai Ngr.
Indore,
Madhya Pradesh-452006
India
TEL : +91 (0) 731 2410963
FAX : +91 (0) 731 2410071
E-mail:
pharmamach@satyam.net.in

Shree Heat-Tech Engineers Pvt. Ltd.
Plot No. W-361
Rabale MIDC
Navi Mumbai,
Maharashtra-400701, India
TEL : +91 (0) 22 27692614
FAX : +91 (0) 22 27690354
E-mail:
rashree@bom3.vsnl.net.in

Grovers Pvt. Ltd.
3F4, Shankardham
Sundervan Cmplx.
Off Lokhandwala Cmplx.
Andheri (W)
Mumbai,
Maharashtra-400053
India
TEL : +91 (0) 22 26314574
FAX : +91 (0) 22 26313014
E-mail:
vivek@groversequip.com

Saiman Engineers Pvt. Ltd.
D/3
Hari Bhakti Indl. Est.
Old Ghod Bunder Rd.
P.O. Mira
Thane, Maharashtra-401104
India
TEL : +91 (0) 22 28458206
FAX : +91 (0) 22 28458466
E-mail:
saimanengg@hotmail.com

TS Enterprises
E-416 Rd. No. 14
VKI Area
Jaipur, Rajasthan-302013
India
TEL : +91 (0) 141 22330613
FAX : +91 (0) 141 22330243
E-mail:
dsaboo@rediffmail.com

Chetan Enterprise
No. 6 Nehru Ngr.
Old Mahabalipuram Rd.
Kottivakkam
Chennai, Tamil Nadu-600041
India
TEL : +91 (0) 44 24925547
FAX : +91 (0) 44 24925030
E-mail:
dhaman_a@hotmail.com

Allfab Engineers
B-1
Indl. Est., Phase-III
Guindy
Chennai, Tamil Nadu-600032
India
TEL : +91 (0) 44 22346132
FAX : +91 (0) 44 24891601
E-mail:
lakshmii@md2.vsnl.net.in

Virat Tank & Vessels
A-36, Bldg. No. 3
Laghu Udyog
I B Patel Rd.
Goregaon (E) Mumbai,
Maharashtra-400063
India
TEL : +91 (0) 22 28735305

Aspick Engg. Pvt. Ltd.
D-5 Indl. Est.
Guindy
Chennai, Tamil Nadu-600032
India
TEL : +91 (0) 44 22341399
FAX : +91 (0) 44 22349801
E-mail: aspick@kmr.net

Dukes Enterprises
No. 5
Thiru-Vi-Ka Indl. Est.
Ekkattuthangal
Chennai, Tamil Nadu-600097
India
TEL : +91 (0) 44 22324619
FAX : +91 (0) 44 22324619

Anand Dis-Brew Engg. Works
5
Rajinder Ngr. Indl. Area
Mohan Ngr.
Ghaziabad,
Uttar Pradesh-201007
India
TEL : +91 (0) 120 24627318
FAX : +91 (0) 120 24629210
E-mail:
anand_disbrew@yahoo.co.in

Uttam Sucrotech Ltd.
C-42-43, Meerut Rd.
Indl. Area
Ghaziabad,
Uttar Pradesh-201002
India
TEL : +91 (0) 120 2713210
FAX : +91 (0) 120 2714201

STORAGE TANKS

Enfab Industries Pvt. Ltd.
C-2, Shanthi Niwas
Mettuguda
Secunderabad, Andhra Pradesh-500017
India
TEL : +91 (0) 40 27824343
FAX : +91 (0) 40 27830010
E-mail:
enfabs@hd1.vsnl.net.in

Buildworth Pvt. Ltd.
G S Rd.
Dispur
Guwahati, Assam-781005
India
TEL : +91 (0) 361 2340352
FAX : +91 (0) 361 2341411
E-mail: bwpl1@sancharnet.in

Mech Engineers
920-A
Phase-II, Indl. Area
Ramdarbar
Chandigarh,
Chandigarh (UT)-160002
India
TEL : +91 (0) 172 2652417
FAX : +91 (0) 172 2652417

Shefa Engineers Pvt. Ltd.
D-162
Phase-I
Okhla Indl. Area
New Delhi,
NCT of Delhi-110020
India
TEL : +91 (0) 11 26811883
FAX : +91 (0) 11 26810986
E-mail:
shefa@del3.vsnl.net.in

Mass Kinematics Pvt. Ltd.
Alleluia Menezes Bldg., 3rd Flr. Opp. MES Inspection Bunglow Altinho Panaji Goa,
Goa-403001 India
TEL : +91 (0) 832 2437864
FAX : +91 (0) 832 2228091
E-mail:
kinemat@goatelecom.com

Arvind Anticor Ltd.
"Arvind"
Jasodanagar Char Rasta
Nr. Vatva GIDC
Ahmedabad, Gujarat-382445
India
TEL : +91 (0) 79 25891941
FAX : +91 (0) 79 25830287
E-mail:
arvindanticor@hotmail.com

Adarsh Fabricators
Plot No. 212
Sect. 24
Faridabad, Haryana-121005
India
TEL : +91 (0) 129 25234689
FAX : +91 (0) 129 25233028
E-mail: adarsh@sify.com

Swati Storwel Pvt. Ltd.
44 & 45 Sect.-1
Indl. Area
Parwanoo,
Himachal Pradesh-173220
India
TEL : +91 (0) 1794 232570
FAX : +91 (0) 1794 232770
E-mail:
chemi1@nde.vsnl.net.in

Hexagon Engineers Ltd.
No. 93/2
Margosa Rd. 12th Cross
Malleswaram Bangalore,
Karnataka-560003
India
TEL : +91 (0) 80 23440056
FAX : +91 (0) 80 23466747
E-mail:
hexagon6@engineer.com

Bhagheeratha Electricals & Structurals Ltd.
5th Flr.
KSHB Office Cmplx.
Panampilly Ngr.
Kochi, Kerala-682036
India
TEL : +91 (0) 484 2312387
FAX : +91 (0) 484 2321077
E-mail:
beslkoch@giasmd01.vsnl.net.in

Febchem Engineering Works
Plot No. A/2
Sect. A, Indl. Area Sanwer Rd.
Indore,
Madhya Pradesh-452003
India
TEL : +91 (0) 731 2720467
FAX : +91 (0) 731 2723087
E-mail: febchem@yahoo.com

Bright Pharma Machinery
37-A
New Empire Indl. Est.
Kondivita Rd., J B Ngr.
Andheri (W) Mumbai,
Maharashtra-400059
India
TEL : +91 (0) 22 28214341
FAX : +91 (0) 22 28210190
E-mail: b
rightpharma@hotmail.com

Higien Products (I)
G T Rd.
Goraya, Punjab-144409
India
TEL : +91 (0) 1826 262301
FAX : +91 (0) 1826 262627
E-mail: higien@vsnl.net.in

Chetan Enterprise
No. 6 Nehru Ngr.
Old Mahabalipuram Rd.
Kottivakkam
Chennai, Tamil Nadu-600041
India
TEL : +91 (0) 44 24925547
FAX : +91 (0) 44 24925030
E-mail:
dhaman_a@hotmail.com

Ved Engg.
B-38 Sect. 60
Noida, Uttar Pradesh-201301
India
TEL : +91 (0) 118 24580507
FAX : +91 (0) 118 24580815
E-mail:
vaidant@del3.vsnl.net.in

BOILERS : INDUSTRIAL

Bharat Heavy Plate & Vessels Ltd. A Unit Of Bharat Yantra Nigam Ltd.
PO BHPV
Visakhapatnam,
Andhra Pradesh-530012
India
TEL : +91 (0) 891 2517381
FAX : +91 (0) 891 2517626
E-mail:
bhpv.ec@rmj.sprintrpg.ems.vsnl.net.in

Nitasha Envirotech Pvt. Ltd.
1062-63 Phase-II
Indl. Area
Chandigarh,
Chandigarh (UT)-160002
India
TEL : +91 (0) 172 2656700
FAX : +91 (0) 172 2652998
E-mail: nitasha1@glide.net.in

National Furnaces
21/731
Bakshi House
Faiz Rd.
Karol Bagh
New Delhi,
NCT of Delhi-110005
India
TEL : +91 (0) 11 23637605
FAX : +91 (0) 11 23510557
E-mail:
natfur@rediffmail.com

Enmax Systemz
Block C - 60B
Kalkaji
New Delhi,
NCT of Delhi-110019
India
TEL : +91 (0) 11 26447880
FAX : +91 (0) 11 26473243
E-mail:
enmax@satyam.net.in

Balkrishna Boilers Inds.
Plot No. 14
Jay Khodiyar Indl. Est.
Nr. Subhash Est.
Ramol Rd.
Ahmedabad,
Gujarat-380026
India
TEL : +91 (0) 79 25855883
E-mail: info@balkrishn.com

Vivek Chem-Fabs
Plot No. 71
Sect. 27A, 15/1 Mile Stone
Mathura Rd.
Faridabad, Haryana-121003
India
TEL : +91 (0) 129 25274848
FAX : +91 (0) 129 28843308

Ambica Engg. Works
16/A, 1st Main,
Modi Hospital Rd.,
W.O.C Road, 2nd Stage.
Bangalore,
Karnataka-560086
India
TEL : +91 (0) 80 23495370
FAX : +91 (0) 80 23496120
E-mail:
ambica_e_w@vsnl.com

Asian Boiler Engineers Pvt. Ltd.
130-A
Golanji Hill Rd.
Sewree
Mumbai,
Maharashtra-400015
India

TEL : +91 (0) 22 24131630
FAX : +91 (0) 22 24139624
E-mail:
abengg@bom3.vsnl.net.in

Enmas Andritz Pvt. Ltd.
4th Flr., Guna Bldg. Annexe,
443 Anna Salai
Teynampet
Chennai, Tamil Nadu-600018
India
TEL : +91 (0) 44 24338050
FAX : +91 (0) 44 24322412
E-mail: eal@vsnl.com

Bharat Yantra Nigam Ltd.
15/1 Thornhill Rd.
Allahabad,
Uttar Pradesh-211001
India
TEL : +91 (0) 532 2622769
FAX : +91 (0) 532 2622901
E-mail: bynl@hotmail.com

Lalsons Machines Pvt. Ltd.
A-45 Phase-I
Mayapuri Indl. Area
New Delhi,
NCT of Delhi-110064
India
TEL : +91 (0) 11 25143223
FAX : +91 (0) 11 25147483

Ambica Engg. Works
16/A, 1st Main,
Modi Hospital Rd.,
W.O.C Road, 2nd Stage.
Bangalore,
Karnataka-560086
India
TEL : +91 (0) 80 23495370
FAX : +91 (0) 80 23496120
E-mail:
ambica_e_w@vsnl.com

Saraswati Industrial Syndicate Ltd.
A-4 Sect. 24
Noida, Uttar Pradesh-201301
India
TEL : +91 (0) 120 24524071
FAX : +91 (0) 120 24542072
E-mail: exports@isgec.com

The Indian Sugar & General Engg. Corp. Process Divn,
A-4 Sect. 24
Noida,
Uttar Pradesh-201301
India
TEL : +91 (0) 120 24524071
FAX : +91 (0) 120 24542072
E-mail:
corpcomm@isgec.com

CT Boiler Pvt. Ltd.
7/1B
Motilal Nehru Rd.
Kolkata,
West Bengal-700029
India
TEL : +91 (0) 33 24641005

EVAPORATORS

Surya Industrial Equipments
D-109 Phase-I
IDA Jeedimetla
Hyderabad,
Andhra Pradesh-500055
India
TEL : +91 (0) 40 23096355
FAX : +91 (0) 40 23098163

Pas Construction & Engineering Company Pvt. Ltd.
803, Madhuban, 55
Nehru Place, New Delhi,
NCT of Delhi-110019
India
TEL : +91 (0) 11 26419122
FAX : +91 (0) 11 26463981
E-mail: pasakr@vsnl.com

Mazda Ltd.
Mazda House, 650/1
Panchvati 2nd Lane
Ambawadi
Ahmedabad,
Gujarat-380006
India
TEL : +91 (0) 79 26431014
FAX : +91 (0) 79 26565605
E-mail:
mazdaad1@sancharnet.in

Delphi Automotive Systems Ltd.
Phase-I 240
Udyog Vihar
Gurgaon, Haryana-122016
India
TEL : +91 (0) 124 26439600
FAX : +91 (0) 124 26439618
E-mail: delphic@vsnl.com

Murhopye Scientific Co.
B-11 Metagalli Indl. Est.
Mysore, Karnataka-570016
India
TEL : +91 (0) 821 2582235
FAX : +91 (0) 821 2581235
E-mail: murhopye@eth.net

Febchem Engineering Works
Plot No. A/2
Sect. A, Indl. Area
Sanwer Rd.
Indore,
Madhya Pradesh-452003
India
TEL : +91 (0) 731 2720467
FAX : +91 (0) 731 2723087
E-mail:
febchem@yahoo.com

Shree Heat-Tech Engineers Pvt. Ltd.
Plot No. W-361
Rabale MIDC Navi Mumbai,
Maharashtra-400701
India
TEL : +91 (0) 22 27692614
FAX : +91 (0) 22 27690354
E-mail:
rashree@bom3.vsnl.net.in

Sri Rudran Instruments Co.
56 Vaikundapuram 2nd St.
Nungambakkam
Chennai, Tamil Nadu-600034
India
TEL : +91 (0) 44 28172803
FAX : +91 (0) 44 28175843
E-mail: srico@satyam.net.in

Seba Engineers Pvt. Ltd.
D-26 Indl. Area
Bulandshahr Rd.

Ghaziabad,
Uttar Pradesh-201009
India
TEL : +91 (0) 120 24703703
FAX : +91 (0) 120 24703703

Saraswati Industrial Syndicate Ltd.
A-4 Sect. 24 Noida,
Uttar Pradesh-201301
India
TEL : +91 (0) 120 24524071
FAX : +91 (0) 120 24542072
E-mail: exports@isgec.com

STIRRERS : CHEMICAL

Enfab Industries Pvt. Ltd.
C-2, Shanthi Niwas
Mettuguda
Secunderabad,
Andhra Pradesh-500017
India
TEL : +91 (0) 40 27824343
FAX : +91 (0) 40 27830010
E-mail:
enfabs@hd1.vsnl.net.in

Magnum Industries
IDA Mallapur
Hyderabad,
Andhra Pradesh-500076
India
TEL : +91 (0) 40 27172495

Kwality Traders
91 Bhagat Singh Mkt.
New Delhi,
NCT of Delhi-110001
India
TEL : +91 (0) 11 23347333
FAX : +91 (0) 11 23346939
E-mail:
thermo-meter@yahoo.co.in

ChemiProcess Engineers
14 Laxmi Co-op. Indl. Est.
Nagarwel Hanuman Mandir Rd.
Amraiwadi
Ahmedabad,
Gujarat-380026
India
TEL : +91 (0) 79 22748168
FAX : +91 (0) 79 22748001

Vividh Hi-Fab
987/10C, GIDC
Makarpura
Vadodara, Gujarat-390010
India
TEL : +91 (0) 265 2641101
FAX : +91 (0) 265 2642953
E-mail: vividh@icenet.in

Febchem Engineering Works
Plot No. A/2
Sect. A, Indl. Area
Sanwer Rd.
Indore,
Madhya Pradesh-452003
India
TEL : +91 (0) 731 2720467
FAX : +91 (0) 731 2723087
E-mail:
febchem@yahoo.com

Bright Pharma Machinery
37-A
New Empire Indl. Est.
Kondivita Rd., J B Ngr.
Andheri (W)
Mumbai,
Maharashtra-400059
India
TEL : +91 (0) 22 28214341
FAX : +91 (0) 22 28210190
E-mail:
brightpharma@hotmail.com

Diamond Fabrications (India) Pvt. Ltd.
S-133 MIDC
B/h Century Inka
Bhosari
Pune, Maharashtra-411026
India
TEL : +91 (0) 20 27120141
FAX : +91 (0) 20 27120642
E-mail: enquiry@dfipl.com

Chetan Enterprise
No. 6
Nehru Ngr.
Old Mahabalipuram Rd.
Kottivakkam
Chennai,
Tamil Nadu-600041
India
TEL : +91 (0) 44 24925547
FAX : +91 (0) 44 24925030
E-mail:
dhaman_a@hotmail.com

National Engg Industries Ltd.
2/2
Shashi Bhusan Basak Lane
Kolkata,
West Bengal-700036, India
TEL : +91 (0) 33 25578652
FAX : +91 (0) 33 25288458
E-mail:
neiupmt@yahoo.com

ADHESIVE APPLYING MACHINERY

Orbit Equipments Pvt. Ltd.
1 Venkat Reddy Cmplx.
Tarbund
Secunderabad, Andhra Pradesh-500009
India
TEL : +91 (0) 40 27817296
FAX : +91 (0) 40 27813877
E-mail:
orbiteqp@hd2.dot.net.in

ITW Dynatec
Flat No. 1 F3
S S Plaza
North Kamala Ngr.
Hyderabad,
Andhra Pradesh-500062
India
TEL : +91 (0) 40 27128510
FAX : +91 (0) 40 27141438
E-mail:
dynatecindia@rediffmail.com

Mahisa Electronics
H-204
Ansa Indl. Est.
Saki Vihar Rd.
Saki Naka
Mumbai,
Maharashtra-400072
India

TEL : +91 (0) 22 28523690
FAX : +91 (0) 22 28523690
E-mail: kshah@mahisa.com

ADHESION TESTER

ISA Impex Pvt. Ltd.
56
Defence Cly., 100 Feet Rd.
Indiranagar
Bangalore,
Karnataka-560038
India
TEL : +91 (0) 80 25280747
FAX : +91 (0) 80 25280706
E-mail: isaimpex@vsnl.com

Productive Technologies Pvt. Ltd.
C-56
Jhandewalan Flatted
Factories Cmplx.
New Delhi,
NCT of Delhi-110055
India
TEL : +91 (0) 11 23636708
FAX : +91 (0) 11 23636824
E-mail: proteq@vsnl.com

Precision Standard Testing Equipment Corp.
C-117
FF Cmplx., Phase-III
Okhla Indl. Area
New Delhi,
NCT of Delhi-110020
India
TEL : +91 (0) 11 26915846
FAX : +91 (0) 11 26834850
E-mail: presto@vsnl.com

Solarman Engg. Project Pvt. Ltd.
6/14 Indl. Area
Kirti Ngr.
New Delhi,
NCT of Delhi-110015
India
TEL : +91 (0) 11 25934705
FAX : +91 (0) 11 25457941
E-mail:
solarman_engg@yahoo.co.in

Kamal Metal Industries
Subhash Indl. Est., (202)
Ramol Rd.
Ahmedabad,
Gujarat-380026
India
TEL : +91 (0) 79 25855880
FAX : +91 (0) 79 25855921
E-mail:
kmigroup@yahoo.com

Ducom
SB-113
1st Stage
3rd Cross
Peenya Indl. Est.
Bangalore,
Karnataka-560058
India
TEL : +91 (0) 80 28396665
FAX : +91 (0) 80 28394438
E-mail: ducom@vsnl.com

Lumetronics
B-44
Giriraj Indl. Est.
Mahakali Caves Rd.
Andheri (E)
Mumbai,
Maharashtra-400093
India
TEL : +91 (0) 22 28202170
FAX : +91 (0) 22 28360730
E-mail: info@lumetron.com

Prolific Engineers
D-91
Sect. 2, Noida,
Uttar Pradesh-201301
India
TEL : +91 (0) 120 24524251
FAX : +91 (0) 120 24522648
E-mail:
prolific@hclinfinet.com

ADHESIVES MIXER

Chemac Equipments Pvt. Ltd.
M J D'Souza Compound
Safed Pool, Sakinaka
Mumbai,
Maharashtra-400072
India
TEL : +91 (0) 22 28510777
FAX : +91 (0) 22 28516986
E-mail:
chemac@bom4.vsnl.net.in

Machinkraft Equipment
337
3rd Rd., Sindh Hsg. Soc.
Aundh Pune,
Maharashtra-411007, India
TEL : +91 (0) 20 25887464
FAX : +91 (0) 20 25880353
E-mail: i
nfo@machinkraftequipment.com

Sathe Engineering Company Pvt. Ltd.
E-198/199
Kavinagar Indl. Area
Ghaziabad,
Uttar Pradesh-201002
India
TEL : +91 (0) 120 24700252
FAX : +91 (0) 120 24700316
E-mail:
sathe@del3.vsnl.net.in

Dhopeshwar Engineering Pvt. Ltd.
A-16, CIE
Balanagar, Hyderabad,
Andhra Pradesh-500037
India
TEL : +91 (0) 40 23771579
FAX : +91 (0) 40 23772450
E-mail:
dhopesh@hd2.dot.net.in

Skylab Engineers & Fabricators
3/1, Revabhai Indl. Est. 1
Opp. Bhimnath Hotel
CTM Cross Rd.
Ahmedabad, Gujarat-380026
India
TEL : +91 (0) 79 25857829
FAX : +91 (0) 79 25850005
E-mail:
skylabeng_fab@yahoo.com

Schurtek Engineers
18,Mistry Indl. Cmplx.
Cross Rd.-A
MIDC

Andheri (E)
Mumbai,
Maharashtra-400093
India
TEL : +91 (0) 22 28325903
FAX : +91 (0) 22 28351358
E-mail:
schurtek@bom3.vsnl.net.in

ADHESIVES DISPENSERS

Sumitron Exports Pvt. Ltd.
27, Comm. Centre, 1st Flr.
Phase-I
Naraina Indl. Est.
New Delhi,
NCT of Delhi-110028
India
TEL : +91 (0) 11 25796783
FAX : +91 (0) 11 25796353
E-mail: sumitron@vsnl.com

Loctite India Pvt. Ltd. A Henkel Company
28 Spencer Rd.
Frazer Town
Bangalore,
Karnataka-560005
India
TEL : +91 (0) 80 25579851
FAX : +91 (0) 80 25579852
E-mail:
marketing@loctite.co.in

Mahisa Electronics
H-204
Ansa Indl. Est.
Saki Vihar Rd.
Saki Naka
Mumbai,
Maharashtra-400072
India
TEL : +91 (0) 22 28523690
FAX : +91 (0) 22 28523690
E-mail: kshah@mahisa.com

TAL Manufacturing Solutions Ltd. A TATA Enterprise
TELCO Premises
Chinchwad
Pune, Maharashtra-411033
India
TEL : +91 (0) 20 27402345
FAX : +91 (0) 20 27476465
E-mail: ynath@telco.co.in

ADHESIVE PUMPS

Jayambe Engineering Enterprise
90-91/5, GIDC Indl. Est.
Opp. Ambica Ngr. Odhav
Ahmedabad,
Gujarat-382415
India
TEL : +91 (0) 79 22876187
FAX : +91 (0) 79 22971187
E-mail:
jeepumps@wilnetonline.net

Fluid Tech Systems
Rajkeshri Indl. Est.
Nr. Bharat Party Plot
National Highway No. 8
Amraiwadi
Ahmedabad,
Gujarat-380026
India
TEL : +91 (0) 79 22891694
FAX : +91 (0) 79 22974142
E-mail: rotofluid@icenet.net

Hydro Power Corporation
258 GIDC Indl. Est.
Makarpura
Vadodara, Gujarat-390010
India
TEL : +91 (0) 265 2642741
FAX : +91 (0) 265 2642741
E-mail:
hydro@hypopump.com

Corres Flow Engineers
1/20
Kailash Indl. Est., Jay
Chemical St.
B/h Hindustan Marbles
Odhav
Ahmedabad,
Gujarat-38241, 5India
TEL : +91 (0) 79 22874219
FAX : +91 (0) 79 22891459

C Bole & Co.
61
Narayan Dhuru St.
Mumbai,
Maharashtra-400003
India
TEL : +91 (0) 22 23429641
FAX : +91 (0) 22 23424040
E-mail:
monexengg@hotmail.com

Aqua Air Engg. & Services
4, Pramod House
Kadamwadi Lane, Marol
Pipeline
Andheri (E)
Mumbai,
Maharashtra-400001
India
TEL : +91 (0) 22 28241985
FAX : +91 (0) 22 28241985
E-mail:
tmharris@satyam.net.in

Promivac Engineers
3575, PNB Bldg.
Netaji Subhash Marg
Daryaganj
New Delhi,
NCT of Delhi-110002
India
TEL : +91 (0) 11 23281082
FAX : +91 (0) 11 23275160
E-mail: promivac@vsnl.net

GUMMING MACHINERY

Super Fine Pack Machine (I)
Kothi No. 1168
Sect. 19
Faridabad, Haryana-121001
India
TEL : +91 (0) 129 25417783
FAX : +91 (0) 129 25423702

Bright Pharma Machinery
37-A
New Empire Indl. Est.
Kondivita Rd., J B Ngr.
Andheri (W)
Mumbai,

Maharashtra-400059
India
TEL : +91 (0) 22 28214341
FAX : +91 (0) 22 28210190
E-mail:
brightpharma@hotmail.com

Kamal Export Industries
Datta Bhavan
Kashinath Dhuru Rd.
Dadar (W)
Mumbai,
Maharashtra-400028
India
TEL : +91 (0) 22 24221555
FAX : +91 (0) 22 24373474
E-mail: kei@vsnl.com

Ravi-Kiran Industries
213
Mittal Indl. Est. No-2, Marol Naka, Andheri (E) Mumbai,
Maharashtra-400059
India
TEL : +91 (0) 22 28506569
FAX : +91 (0) 22 28506135
E-mail: ravikiran@vsnl.com

Dianamark
Bible House, 5-2-13/4
Opp. Jabbar Cmplx.
Hyder Basti
Secunderabad, Andhra Pradesh-500003
India
TEL : +91 (0) 40 27532548
FAX : +91 (0) 40 27536451
E-mail:
dianamark@hotmail.com

COATING MACHINERY

Coatec India
F-79 Phase-VII
Indl. Area
SAS Ngr.
Chandigarh, Chandigarh (UT)-160055
India
TEL : +91 (0) 172 2253435
FAX : +91 (0) 172 2253439
E-mail:
coatecindia@hotmail.com

Artek Enterprises Pvt. Ltd.
45 Deepak Bldg.
13 Nehru Place
New Delhi,
NCT of Delhi-110019
India
TEL : +91 (0) 11 28618378
FAX : +91 (0) 11 26216934
E-mail: arteke@vsnl.com

Bharti Engineers
WZ-2181A, 2nd. Flr.
Raja Park Chowk
Rani Bagh
Delhi, NCT of Delhi-110034
India
TEL : +91 (0) 11 27197114
FAX : +91 (0) 11 27198943
E-mail:
bharti@del3.vsnl.net.in

Ravi Sales Corporation
WZ-2181
Raja Park Chowk
Rani Bagh
New Delhi,
NCT of Delhi-110034
India
TEL : +91 (0) 11 27197114
FAX : +91 (0) 11 27198943
E-mail:
bharti@del3.vsnl.net.in

C Trivedi & Co.
A-1/16
Phase-II, GIDC Est.
Vatva
Ahmedabad, Gujarat-382445
India
TEL : +91 (0) 79 25830552
FAX : +91 (0) 79 25830553
E-mail: ctrivedi@ctrivedi.com

Sud & Waren Pvt. Ltd.
Plot No. 72
Indl. Area
Sect.6
Faridabad, Haryana-121006
India
TEL : +91 (0) 129 25248464
FAX : +91 (0) 129 25246141
E-mail: sud@nde.vsnl.net.in

Expert Industries Ltd.
274-C
KIADB Indl. Area
Bommsandra
Bangalore,
Karnataka-562158
India
TEL : +91 (0) 8110 232690
FAX : +91 (0) 8110 232037
E-mail:
expert@expertindia.com

Boolani Engineering Corporation
7 & 8
Unique Est.
Off Veer Savarkar Rd.
Mumbai,
Maharashtra-400025
India
TEL : +91 (0) 22 24302826
FAX : +91 (0) 22 24229875
E-mail: plastic@vsnl.com

Premier Engineering Works (Regd.)
1 Jodh Ngr.
Sultanwind Rd.
Amritsar, Punjab-143006
India
TEL : +91 (0) 183 2483501
FAX : +91 (0) 183 2398702
E-mail:
prengg@jla.vsnl.net.in

Fancy Prahladka India Pvt. Ltd.
55B Kali Temple Rd.
Kolkata,
West Bengal-700026
India
TEL : +91 (0) 33 24555182
FAX : +91 (0) 33 24555182
E-mail:
pioneerpackaging@vsnl.com

Dianamark
Bible House, 5-2-13/4
Opp. Jabbar Cmplx.
Hyder Basti
Secunderabad,
Andhra Pradesh-500003
India

TEL : +91 (0) 40 27532548
FAX : +91 (0) 40 27536451
E-mail:
dianamark@hotmail.com

LABEL PRINTING APPLYING MACHINERY

Bevcon Wayors Pvt. Ltd.
Ground Flr., Kavya Delux Apts.
Madhuranagar
Hyderabad,
Andhra Pradesh-500038
India
TEL : +91 (0) 40 23732628
FAX : +91 (0) 40 23733626
E-mail:
bevconwayors@hotmail.com

GS Bhamra & Sons
Plot No. 3
Cement Rd.
Upper Anand Parbat
New Delhi,
NCT of Delhi-110005
India
TEL : +91 (0) 11 25767214

Saraswati Business Pvt. Ltd.
A-15 Saraswati Vihar
Pitampura
Delhi, NCT of Delhi-110034
India
TEL : +91 (0) 11 27913726
FAX : +91 (0) 11 27910291
E-mail: sales@zedpack.com

SS Industries
9/53
Kirti Ngr. Indl. Area
New Delhi,
NCT of Delhi-110015
India
TEL : +91 (0) 11 25935340
FAX : +91 (0) 11 25404799

Ankit Machinery
8 Tirupati Est.,
Opp. Bombay Housing
Nr. Rangshala Compound
Bapunagar
Ahmedabad, Gujarat-380024
India
TEL : +91 (0) 79 22745481
E-mail:
amflex@wilnetonline.net

Balajee Pharmaceutical Engineers
10 Techno Est.
CTM
Ahmedabad, Gujarat-380026
India
TEL : +91 (0) 79 22870850
FAX : +91 (0) 79 25730280
E-mail: bms@balajee.com

KPJ Enterprises
5/3 Assisi Ngr.
P L Lokhande Marg
Chembur
Mumbai,
Maharashtra-400043
India
TEL : +91 (0) 22 25510217
FAX : +91 (0) 22 28260293
E-mail: paul_john@vsnl.net

Sree Krishna Strapping & Labels Pvt. Ltd.
New No. 48 (Old No. 20/1)
North Crescent Rd.
T Ngr.
Chennai, Tamil Nadu-600017
India
TEL : +91 (0) 44 28252414
FAX : +91 (0) 44 28284964
E-mail:
skgmds@satyam.net.in

L&M Automatics
60/7
Old Dal Mandi
Kanpur,
Uttar Pradesh-208001
India
TEL : +91 (0) 512 2208001
E-mail:
lm_automatics@rediffmail.com

45.

Suppliers of Raw Materials

SODIUM HYDROXIDE

DCM Shriram Consolidated Ltd.
5th & 6th Flr.
Kanchenjunga Bldg.
18 Barakhamba Rd.
New Delhi,
NCT of Delhi-110001
India
TEL : +91 (0) 11 23316801
FAX : +91 (0) 11 23318261
E-mail: dscl@dscl.com

Atul Ltd. Bulk Chemicals & Intermediates Divn.
P.O. Atul
Atul, Gujarat-396020
India
TEL : +91 (0) 2632 2330261
FAX : +91 (0) 2632 2330241
E-mail: hq@atul.co.in

Ambala Silicate Udyog
141 Vikas Vihar
Ambala, Haryana-134003
India
TEL : +91 (0) 171 2540041
FAX : +91 (0) 171 2541892
E-mail:
sodiumsilicate@usa.net

Bihar Caustic Ltd.
Ghanshyam Kunj
Gorwa Rd. P.O. Rehla
Palamau,
Jharkhand-822124
India
TEL : +91 (0) 6184 222585
FAX : +91 (0) 6184 287205

The Travancore-Cochin Chemicals Ltd.
P.O. Box 4004
Udyogamandal P.O.
Ernakulam, Kerala-683501
India
TEL : +91 (0) 484 2551011
FAX : +91 (0) 484 2532420
E-mail:
tccudl@kelnet07.xlweb.com

Century Rayon A Divn. Of Century Textiles & Industries Ltd.
159, Industry House
Churchgate Reclamation
Mumbai,
Maharashtra-400020
India
TEL : +91 (0) 22 22027570
FAX : +91 (0) 22 22025109
E-mail: cenbom@vsnl.com

Haritha Chem India
15 Sellaperumal St.
Kossapalayam
Pondicherry,
Pondicherry-605013
India
TEL : +91 (0) 413 2225380

BORAX

Sisco Research Laboratories Pvt. Ltd.
2F
Satam Indl. Est., 'C' Wing
Chakala
Andheri (E), Mumbai,
Maharashtra-400099
India
TEL : +91 (0) 22 28203882
FAX : +91 (0) 22 28380998
E-mail: srl@bom3.vsnl.net.in

Chempro Exports India
1st Flr., Pushpawati Bldg.
No. 1, 568
Chira Bazar, Girgaon Rd.
Mumbai,
Maharashtra-400002, India
TEL : +91 (0) 22 22051551
FAX : +91 (0) 22 22199160
E-mail:
chempro@bom3.vsnl.net.in

Haritha Chem India
15 Sellaperumal St.
Kossapalayam
Pondicherry,
Pondicherry-605013
India
TEL : +91 (0) 413 2225380

Ram Agro Chemical Industries Ltd.
196/6 Govindappa Naick St.
Parrys
Chennai,
Tamil Nadu-600001
India
TEL : +91 (0) 44 25248913
FAX : +91 (0) 44 25323095

Allipo Chemicals
49 GIDC
Makarpura
Vadodara, Gujarat-390010
India
TEL : +91 (0) 265 2642908
FAX : +91 (0) 265 2642708
E-mail: allipo@satyam.net.in

UREA-FORMALDEHYDE RESINS

Gupta Plastics
42 DLF Indl. Area
Kirti Ngr.
New Delhi,
NCT of Delhi-110015
India
TEL : +91 (0) 11 25417831
FAX : +91 (0) 11 25195721
E-mail: pawan@garg.org

Atul Ltd. Polymers Divn.
Atul PO
Atul, Gujarat-396020
India
TEL : +91 (0) 26328 233204
FAX : +91 (0) 26328 233639
E-mail: po@atul.co.in

Nuchem Ltd. Chemicals Division
54, Indl. Area NIT
Faridabad, Haryana-121001
India
TEL : +91 (0) 129 25234541
FAX : +91 (0) 129 25233895
E-mail:
chemdiv.@nuchem.com

Plastic Resins & Chemicals
Thottada
Kannur, Kerala-670007
India
TEL : +91 (0) 497 2820867
E-mail:
farmaclt@md4.vsnl.net.in

Gom Industries Ltd.
Plot No. 42
Sect. A, Indl. Est.
Sanwer Rd.
Indore,
Madhya Pradesh-452015
India
TEL : +91 (0) 731 2721064
FAX : +91 (0) 731 2722852
E-mail: gom@gomindia.com

DEXTRIN

Anoopam Adhesives
Plot No. 159
Zone B-04, Phase-I
GIDC
Vithal Udyognagar,
Gujarat-388121
India
TEL : +91 (0) 2692 235121
FAX : +91 (0) 2692 236496
E-mail:
karmayo70@rediffmail.com

Barmalt (I) Ltd.
Jharsa Rd.
Gurgaon, Haryana-122001
India
TEL : +91 (0) 124 26381401
FAX : +91 (0) 124 26380201

Premier Chemical Industries
47 Temple St.
Chickpet Cross
Bangalore,
Karnataka-560053
India
TEL : +91 (0) 80 22874507

Sisco Research Laboratories Pvt. Ltd.
2F Satam Indl. Est., 'C' Wing
Chakala
Andheri (E)
Mumbai,
Maharashtra-400099
India
TEL : +91 (0) 22 28203882
FAX : +91 (0) 22 28380998
E-mail: srl@bom3.vsnl.net.in

Bharat Starch Industries Ltd.
N-75
Connaught Circus
New Delhi,
NCT of Delhi-110001
India
TEL : +91 (0) 11 23313195
FAX : +91 (0) 11 23325289
E-mail: bsil@nda.vsnl.net.in

GLYCERIN

Jocil Ltd.
P.O. Box 216
Arundelpet
Guntur,
Andhra Pradesh-522002
India
TEL : +91 (0) 863 2290190
FAX : +91 (0) 863 2290090
E-mail:
jocil@jocil.xeevga.xeemail.ems.vsnl.net.in

Nahar Industrial Enterprises Ltd.
1107, Ashok Est. Bldg.
24 Barakhamba Rd.
New Delhi,
NCT of Delhi-110001
India
TEL : +91 (0) 11 23311069
FAX : +91 (0) 11 23311009

Godrej Soaps Ltd. Chemicals Unit
Burjorjinagar, Plot No. 3
Village Manerao, Taluka: Valia
Bharuch, Gujarat-393135
India
TEL : +91 (0) 2642 272354
FAX : +91 (0) 2642 272355

Aegis Chemical I ndustries Ltd.
Baldota Bhawan, 117
M K Rd.
Churchgate
Mumbai,
Maharashtra-400020
India
TEL : +91 (0) 22 22046438
FAX : +91 (0) 22 22002602
E-mail:
aegisbom@@vsnl.com

Raj Agro Mills Ltd.
Nr. Civil Airport
V.P.O. Pawa
G T Rd.
Ludhiana, Punjab-141020
India
TEL : +91 (0) 161 2844423
FAX : +91 (0) 161 2844811

E-mail:
raml@del3.vsnl.net.in

NEOPRENE RUBBER

Indo Rubber Corp.
No. 2, 1st Flr.
Perianna Maistry St.
Chennai, Tamil Nadu-600001
India
TEL : +91 (0) 44 25260966
FAX : +91 (0) 44 25214744
E-mail: indorubber@eth.net

Rusko Industrial Products
22
Mooker Nallamuthu St.
Chennai, Tamil Nadu-600001
India
TEL : +91 (0) 44 25224097
FAX : +91 (0) 44 25224097
E-mail:
ruskorubber@hotmail.com

Caravan Engineers
Plot No. 38
Poona Small Scale Indl. Co-op Est. Ltd.
Gultekdi
Pune, Maharashtra-411037
India
TEL : +91 (0) 20 24269444
FAX : +91 (0) 20 24261746
E-mail:
caravan1@.vsnl.com

Palus Elastomer Processors Pvt. Ltd.
Plot No. 10
Palus Indl. Est.
Sangli, Maharashtra-416310
India
TEL : +91 (0) 2346 226069
FAX : +91 (0) 2346 226082

TOLUENE

Kochi Refineries Ltd.
P.O. Box No. 2
Ambalmugal
Ernakulam, Kerala-682302
India
TEL : +91 (0) 484 2780261
FAX : +91 (0) 484 2720855

Benzo Chem Industries Pvt. Ltd.
Madhu Kunj
Opp. Prabhadevi
Shankar Ghanekar Rd.
Mumbai,
Maharashtra-400025
India
TEL : +91 (0) 22 24370553
FAX : +91 (0) 22 22041255
E-mail:
gcpl@bom3.vsnl.net.in

Garnet Chemical Corp.
Plot 89
Rd. 3, Hindu Cly.
Dadar (E), Mumbai,
Maharashtra-400014
India
TEL : +91 (0) 22 24164745
FAX : +91 (0) 22 24164745
E-mail:
garnetcorp@vsnl.com

Shalimar Chemical Industries Pvt. Ltd.
107, 1st Flr.,
Sahakar Bhavan, 340/48
Narsi Natha St. Mumbai,
Maharashtra-400009
India
TEL : +91 (0) 22 22340340
FAX : +91 (0) 22 23425478

Narmada Chematur Petrochemicals Ltd.
National Highway No. 8
P.O. Narmadanagar
Bharuch, Gujarat-392015
India
TEL : +91 (0) 2642 247160
FAX : +91 (0) 2642 246497
E-mail: jidesai@
narmada-chematur.com

METHYLMETHACRYLATE

Gujarat State Fertilizers & Chemicals Ltd. Polymers Unit
P.O. Petrofils
Vadodara, Gujarat-391347
India
TEL : +91 (0) 265 2373341
FAX : +91 (0) 265 2372794
E-mail:
gafcpu@gsfcho.xeebdq.xeemail.com

ZINC OXIDE

Chowdhry Rubber & Chemical Co.
1403
Pan Mandi, Sadar Bazar
Delhi, NCT of Delhi-110006
India
TEL : +91 (0) 11 23673373
FAX : +91 (0) 11 27534153
E-mail:
anshdeep@del3.vsnl.net.in

Zed Chemicals Pvt. Ltd.
Plot No. P/152
Ramni Vas Gopal Bhuvan
Navgrah Mohollo
Mangal Bazar
Vaghodia, Gujarat-390001
India
TEL: +91 (0) 26682 2452174

Chowdhry Industries
30.8 KM Stone
MIE
Delhi-Rohtak Rd.
Bahadurgarh,
Haryana-124507
India
TEL : +91 (0) 1183 2367560

Daman Metallic Oxides
Bhatia Niwas, Room No. 5,
1st Flr. 233/235
Samuel St.
Mumbai,
Maharashtra-400003
India
TEL : +91 (0) 22 23413306
FAX : +91 (0) 22 23424682

Silverchem
D-18 (III)
Site No. 1
Panki Indl. Area
Kanpur,
Uttar Pradesh-208001
India
TEL : +91 (0) 512 616590
E-mail:
rohitbrij@rediffmail.com

CALCIUM CARBONATE

AAV Minerals & Chemicals Pvt. Ltd.
63
Najafgarh Rd.
New Delhi,
NCT of Delhi-110015
India
TEL : +91 (0) 11 25418936
FAX : +91 (0) 11 25466838

20 Microns Ltd.
307-308, 3rd Flr.
Arundeep Cmplx.
Race Course (S)
Vadodara, Gujarat-390007
India
TEL : +91 (0) 265 2330714
FAX : +91 (0) 265 2335755
E-mail:
enquiry@20microns.com

Gujarat Clay Mills Pvt. Ltd.
Microfine House
Qureshi Ngr.
Kurla (E), Mumbai,
Maharashtra-400070
India
TEL : +91 (0) 22 25228688
FAX : +91 (0) 22 25230932

Kalinga Carbonates Ltd.
Chandaka Nuclear Indl. Cmplx.
Sect. B
Village & P.O. Patia
Bhubaneshwar,
Orissa-751031
India
TEL : +91 (0) 674 255172

Elfotech Electro Chemicals Ltd.
No. 81
II Cross, Opp. Chanakya Apts.
B/h Balaji Theater
Sithankudisai St.
Pondicherry,
Pondicherry-605013
India
TEL : +91 (0) 413 2242398
FAX : +91 (0) 413 2242986

ANTIOXIDANTS

ICI India Ltd.
10th Flr., DLF Plaza
DLF Qutub Enclave 1
Gurgaon, Haryana-122001
India
TEL : +91 (0) 124 26358400
FAX : +91 (0) 124 26359849

Speciality Organics Pvt. Ltd.
49-B
Sect. B, Mandideep,
Madhya Pradesh-462016
India
TEL : +91 (0) 755 2721392
FAX : +91 (0) 755 233605
E-mail:
speorgpl@bom6.vsnl.net.in

Camlin Ltd.
Camlin House
J B Ngr.
Andheri (E)
Mumbai,
Maharashtra-400059
India
TEL : +91 (0) 22 28360302
FAX : +91 (0) 22 28366579
E-mail: art@camlin.com

High Polymer Labs Ltd.
803, Vishal Bhavan, 95
Nehru Place
New Delhi,
NCT of Delhi-110019
India
TEL : +91 (0) 11 26431522
FAX : +91 (0) 11 26474350
E-mail: hpll@hpl-group.com

Singh Plasticisers & Resins (I) Pvt. Ltd.
117B
Arjun Ngr.
Safdarjung Enclave
New Delhi,
NCT of Delhi-110029
India
TEL : +91 (0) 11 26194641
FAX : +91 (0) 11 26169709

PHENOLIC RESINS

ABR Organics Ltd.
A-3, Madhava Apts.
2-2-23/41/4 & 5, Bank Cly.
Bagh Amberpet
Hyderabad,
Andhra Pradesh-500013
India
TEL : +91 (0) 40 27619059
FAX : +91 (0) 40 27610362
E-mail:
info@abrorganics.com

Gupta Plastics
42
DLF Indl. Area
Kirti Ngr.
New Delhi,
NCT of Delhi-110015
India
TEL : +91 (0) 11 25417831
FAX : +91 (0) 11 25195721
E-mail: pawan@garg.org

Dharamnath Plastic Industries
Plot No.5301
Phase-VI
GIDC Est.
Vatva
Ahmedabad,
Gujarat-382448
India
TEL : +91 (0) 79 25841487

Dua Polymers
Plot No. 226
Sect.24
Faridabad, Haryana-121005
India
TEL : +91 (0) 129 25237454
FAX : +91 (0) 129 25233718
E-mail:
duapolymers@yahoo.com

Cosmos International
D-119
Sect. 10
Noida,
Uttar Pradesh-201301
India

TEL : +91 (0) 120 24557397

MAGNESIUM OXIDE

Vass Pharmachem Pvt. Ltd.
D-1, Nilkumbh
C G Rd.
Ahmedabad, Gujarat-380006
India
TEL : +91 (0) 79 26463707
FAX : +91 (0) 79 26423931
E-mail:
vasapharma@hotmail.com

Dineshchandra Industries
Narang,4th Flr., 330
Narshi Natha St.
Masjid Bunder
Mumbai,
Maharashtra-400009
India
TEL : +91 (0) 22 23427804
FAX : +91 (0) 22 23433228
E-mail:
dineshchandra@vsnl.com

Indian Chemical & Minerals
1/97
Fairlands
Thappukkadu
Salem, Tamil Nadu-636016
India
TEL : +91 (0) 427 2441824
FAX : +91 (0) 427 2339380
E-mail:
maheshksharma@vsnl.com

Rajasthan Chemical & Mineral Industries
61/210
Canal Rd.
Kanpur,
Uttar Pradesh-208001
India
TEL : +91 (0) 512 2360279
FAX : +91 (0) 512 2294445
E-mail:
saffar1@sancharnet.in

Hansflon Plasto Chemical Pvt. Ltd.
B 1/45
Safdarjung Enclave
New Delhi,
NCT of Delhi-110029
India
TEL : +91 (0) 11 26885796
FAX : +91 (0) 11 26888473
E-mail:
hansafln@nda.vsnl.net.in

HEXANE

Bharat Petroleum Corporation Ltd.
Bharat Bhavan, 4 & 6
Currimbhoy Rd.
Ballard Est.
Mumbai,
Maharashtra-400001
India
TEL : +91 (0) 22 22618281
FAX : +91 (0) 22 22616793
E-mail:
okesy@bharatpetroleum.com

Shalimar Chemical Industries Pvt. Ltd.
107, 1st Flr., Sahakar Bhavan, 340/48
Narsi Natha St.
Mumbai,
Maharashtra-400009
India
TEL : +91 (0) 22 22340340
FAX : +91 (0) 22 23425478

FILLERS CHEMICAL

Gujarat Clay Mills Pvt. Ltd.
Microfine House
Qureshi Ngr.
Kurla (E)
Mumbai,
Maharashtra-400070
India
TEL : +91 (0) 22 25228688
FAX : +91 (0) 22 25230932

ROSIN

India Rosin Industries
F-18
Sipcot Indl. Cmplx.
Gummidipoondi,
Tamil Nadu-601201
India
TEL : +91 (0) 4119 222156
FAX : +91 (0) 4119 25240339

Dujodwala Products Ltd.
812/813,
Tulsiani Chmbrs., 212
Nariman Point
Mumbai,
Maharashtra-400021
India
TEL : +91 (0) 22 22824089
FAX : +91 (0) 22 22841284
E-mail:
power@bom3.vsnl.net.in

Dungra Chemicals Pvt. Ltd.
Medows House, 3rd Flr.
Nagindas Master Rd.
Fort Mumbai,
Maharashtra-400023
India
TEL : +91 (0) 22 22666153
FAX : +91 (0) 22 22654154
E-mail:
dungra@bom5.vsnl.net.in

Jay Kay Dye Chemical Corp.
27/201
Motilal Ngr. No. 3
Goregaon (W)
Mumbai,
Maharashtra-400090
India
TEL : +91 (0) 22 28729509
FAX : +91 (0) 22 28211749

Hariharathmaja Chemical Works
Thottekkat Compound
D H Rd.
Ernakulam, Kerala-682016
India
TEL : +91 (0) 484 2352847
FAX : +91 (0) 484 2303005

Cutch Oil & Allied Industries (1949) Pvt. Ltd.
310, Hari Chmbrs., 58/64
S B Singh Rd.

Mumbai,
Maharashtra-400023
India
TEL : +91 (0) 22 22673174
FAX : +91 (0) 22 22679877
E-mail:
gellants@cutchoil.com

Effluent Equipments
D-95
Focal Point
Rajpura, Punjab-140401
India
TEL : +91 (0) 1762 2411113
FAX : +91 (0) 1762 2411122
E-mail:
eeq95@effluentindia.com

The Eimco-KCP Ltd.
Ramakrishna Bldgs.
P.O. Box 5644, 239
Anna Salai
Chennai, Tamil Nadu-600006
India
TEL : +91 (0) 44 28555171
FAX : +91 (0) 44 28555863
E-mail:
ekcp@md2.vsnl.net.in

THICKENERS

Hardayal Engg. Works Pvt. Ltd.
S-5, 6 & 7
G T Rd. (S)
Ghaziabad,
Uttar Pradesh-201001
India
TEL : +91 (0) 120 24840678
FAX : +91 (0) 120 24840678
E-mail:
hardayal@ndf.vsnl.net.in

GELATINE

Sterling Gelatin A Divn. Of Sterling Tea & Industries Ltd.
Sandesara Est.
Atladara
Padra Rd.
Vadodara, Gujarat-390012
India
TEL : +91 (0) 265 2321512
FAX : +91 (0) 265 2357502
E-mail: stil@wilnetonline.net

Bhopal Glues & Chemicals Pvt. Ltd.
Jinsi
Bhopal,
Madhya Pradesh-462008
India
TEL : +91 (0) 755 2257000
FAX : +91 (0) 755 2553924
E-mail: glues@vsnl.com

CJ Gelatine Products Ltd.
C Jairam Compound
Tokersi Jivarajwadi, A Donde Marg
Sewri (W)
Mumbai,
Maharashtra-400015
India
TEL : +91 (0) 22 24131609
FAX : +91 (0) 22 24133193

India Gelatine & Chemicals Ltd.
77 Mittal Chmbrs.,
7th Flr., 228
Nariman Point
Mumbai,
Maharashtra-400021
India
TEL : +91 (0) 22 22021874
FAX : +91 (0) 22 22845522
E-mail:
igcl@bom3.vsnl.net.in

Raymon Gelatine
91-92, Atlanta, 209
Backbay Reclamation
Nariman Point
Mumbai,
Maharashtra-400021
India
TEL : +91 (0) 22 22835116
FAX : +91 (0) 22 22026813
E-mail:
raymon@bom5.vsnl.net.in

Shaw Wallace & Company Ltd.
Tolstoy House, 15-17
Tolstoy Marg
New Delhi,
NCT of Delhi-110001
India
TEL : +91 (0) 11 23714216
FAX : +91 (0) 11 23319351

STARCHES

Bharat Starch Industries Ltd.
N-75
Connaught Circus
New Delhi,
NCT of Delhi-110001
India
TEL : +91 (0) 11 23313195
FAX : +91 (0) 11 23325289
E-mail: bsil@nda.vsnl.net.in

Dhariyal Chemicals
2, Prakruti Apts.
Nr. Parimal Rly. Crossing
Paldi
Ahmedabad,
Gujarat-380007
India
TEL : +91 (0) 79 26638117
FAX : +91 (0) 79 26635224
E-mail:
dhariyal@hotmail.com

Goodrich Agrochem Pvt. Ltd.
146-R Model Town
Karnal, Haryana-132001
India
TEL : +91 (0) 184 2266843
FAX : +91 (0) 184 2265157
E-mail:
goodrich_agrochem@rediffmail.com

Rai Agro Industries Ltd.
A-8
DLF Indl. Area-1
Faridabad, Haryana-121003
India
TEL : +91 (0) 129 2276550
FAX : +91 (0) 129 2276884
E-mail:
raiagro@mantraonline.com

Saidex Industries
#23 2nd Main Rd.
Vyalikaval
Bangalore,
Karnataka-560003

India
TEL : +91 (0) 80 23348982
FAX : +91 (0) 80 23348982
E-mail: saidex@vsnl.com

CASEIN

Sisco Research Laboratories Pvt. Ltd.
2F
Satam Indl. Est., 'C' Wing
Chakala
Andheri (E)
Mumbai,
Maharashtra-400099
India
TEL : +91 (0) 22 28203882
FAX : +91 (0) 22 28380998
E-mail: srl@bom3.vsnl.net.in

Classik Casein
178/10,
Chandreshwar Bhavan
4th Flr.
Sion Main Rd.
Sion (W)
Mumbai,
Maharashtra-400022
India
TEL : +91 (0) 22 24071318
FAX : +91 (0) 22 24092718

Indus Chemie
174, Samarat Bhavan
R. No. 3, Gujarat Society
Sion (W)
Mumbai,
Maharashtra-400022
India
TEL : +91 (0) 22 24071318
FAX : +91 (0) 22 24092718
E-mail:
classikcasein@hotmail.com

Guntur District Milk Producer's Co-Op. Union
Feeder Balancing Dairy
(Vadlamudi)
Guntur,
Andhra Pradesh-522003
India
TEL : +91 (0) 863 2232981
FAX : +91 (0) 863 258248

ACRYLIC ACID

Anil Chemicals Ltd.
J-18 MIDC Area
Chikalthana
Aurangabad,
Maharashtra-431210
India
TEL : +91 (0) 2432 282895
FAX : +91 (0) 2432 283227

Indus Chemie
174, Samarat Bhavan
R. No. 3, Gujarat Society
Sion (W)
Mumbai,
Maharashtra-400022
India
TEL : +91 (0) 22 24071318
FAX : +91 (0) 22 24092718
E-mail:
classikcasein@hotmail.com

Pidilite Industries Ltd. A Parekh Group Company
Ramkrishna Mandir Rd.
Off Marol Vasanji Rd., P.O. Box 17411
Andheri (E)
Mumbai,
Maharashtra-400059
India
TEL : +91 (0) 22 28387240
FAX : +91 (0) 22 28384989

Indian Petrochemicals Corporation Ltd. A Govt. Of India Undertaking
P.O. Petrochemicals
Vadodara, Gujarat-391346
India
TEL : +91 (0) 265 2373144
FAX : +91 (0) 265 2373163
E-mail:
pac@wilnetonline.net

Precious Chemicals
88, Gandhinagar Cly.
Karelibaug
Vadodara, Gujarat-390001
India
TEL : +91 (0) 265 2422716
FAX : +91 (0) 265 2270373
E-mail:
sureshapatel@icent.com

ETHYLENE OXIDE

Dipsi Chemicals Pvt. Ltd.
68/A, Nariman Bhavan,
6th Flr. Nariman Point
Mumbai,
Maharashtra-400021
India
TEL : +91 (0) 22 22026173
FAX : +91 (0) 22 22079085
E-mail:
didesu@bom5.vsnl.net.in

SMZS Chemicals Ltd.
S M House, 11
Sahakar Rd.
Vile Parle (E) Mumbai,
Maharashtra-400057
India
TEL : +91 (0) 22 28208445
FAX : +91 (0) 22 28208451
E-mail:
smzs@bom4.vsnl.net.in

Sunshield Chemicals Ltd.
Janki Niwas
N C Kelkar Rd. Dadar
Mumbai,
Maharashtra-400028
India
TEL : +91 (0) 22 24313265
FAX : +91 (0) 22 24307094
E-mail:
sunshild@bom4.vsnl.net.in

Unitop Chemicals Ltd.
Sony Apts.
Opp. St. Jude's High School
Jarimari
Andheri (E)
Mumbai,
Maharashtra-400072
India
TEL : +91 (0) 22 28510275
FAX : +91 (0) 22 28513247
E-mail: ucl@vsnl.com

Rushabh Chemicals Ltd.
3
Parul Ngr. Shopping Centre
Sola Rd.

Ahmedabad, Gujarat-380061
India
TEL : +91 (0) 79 27475509

Shree Vallabh Chemical
6
Mandir Cmplx.,
Opp. Hiramoti Mkt.
Mani Ngr.
Ahmedabad, Gujarat-380008
India
TEL : +91 (0) 79 25464613
FAX : +91 (0) 79 25465326
E-mail:
shivaninon@icenet.net

PLASTICISERS

Pumax Chemicals Pvt. Ltd.
50, H.A.C.P. Cly.
Ground Flr. Opp. Vikrampuri
Secunderabad,
Andhra Pradesh-500009
India
TEL : +91 (0) 40 27810247
FAX : +91 (0) 40 27848157
E-mail:
pumax@satyam.net.in

Aquolac Group of Companies
70
Najafgarh Rd.
New Delhi,
NCT of Delhi-110015
India
TEL : +91 (0) 11 25467534
FAX : +91 (0) 11 24618606
E-mail: aquolac@vsnl.com

Shital Chemicals Pvt. Ltd.
"Shital"
B/h ONGC
Sabarmati
Ahmedabad,
Gujarat-380005
India
TEL : +91 (0) 79 27503001
FAX : +91 (0) 79 27503005

Nuchem Ltd. Chemicals Division
54, Indl. Area
NIT
Faridabad, Haryana-121001
India
TEL : +91 (0) 129 25234541
FAX : +91 (0) 129 25233895
E-mail:
chemdiv.@nuchem.com

Agrichem
112-D
Govt. Indl. Est.
Charkop
Kandivili (E)
Mumbai,
Maharashtra-400067
India
TEL : +91 (0) 22 28683097
FAX : +91 (0) 22 28682642
E-mail: agrichem@vsnl.net

DEFOAMING AGENTS

Genuine Chemical Industries
R-16
Bombay Mkt.
Umarwada
Surat, Gujarat-395010
India
TEL : +91 (0) 261 612200
E-mail:
dbg@worldgatein.com

Auchtel Products Ltd.
142/C, 2nd Flr., Victor House
N M Joshi Marg
Lower Parel
Mumbai,
Maharashtra-400013
India
TEL : +91 (0) 22 24933975
FAX : +91 (0) 22 24939755

Lord Chemical Industries
Opp. Khalsa College
Mohui Park
Amritsar, Punjab-140001
India
TEL : +91 (0) 183 2228070
FAX : +91 (0) 183 2211803
E-mail:
kapur_vinay@hotmail.com

Ennor Muds & Chemicals
A-12
Anna Nagar (E)
Chennai,
Tamil Nadu-600102
India
TEL : +91 (0) 44 26265792
FAX : +91 (0) 44 26261168
E-mail:
ennor@md2.vsnl.net.in

Bharti Engineers
WZ-2181A, 2nd. Flr.
Raja Park Chowk
Rani Bagh
Delhi, NCT of Delhi-110034
India
TEL : +91 (0) 11 27197114
FAX : +91 (0) 11 27198943
E-mail:
bharti@del3.vsnl.net.in

CAUSTIC SODA

DCM Shriram Consolidated Ltd.
5th & 6th Flr.
Kanchenjunga Bldg.
18
Barakhamba Rd.
New Delhi,
NCT of Delhi-110001
India
TEL : +91 (0) 11 23316801
FAX : +91 (0) 11 23318261
E-mail: dscl@dscl.com

Atul Ltd. Bulk Chemicals & Intermediates Divn.
P.O. Atul
Atul, Gujarat-396020
India
TEL : +91 (0) 2632 2330261
FAX : +91 (0) 2632 2330241
E-mail: hq@atul.co.in

Ambala Silicate Udyog
141 Vikas Vihar
Ambala, Haryana-134003
India
TEL : +91 (0) 171 2540041
FAX : +91 (0) 171 2541892
E-mail:
sodiumsilicate@usa.net

Bihar Caustic Ltd.
Ghanshyam Kunj
Gorwa Rd.
P.O. Rehla
Palamau, Jharkhand-822124
India
TEL : +91 (0) 6184 222585
FAX : +91 (0) 6184 287205

The Travancore-Cochin Chemicals Ltd.
P.O. Box 4004
Udyogamandal P.O.
Ernakulam, Kerala-683501
India
TEL : +91 (0) 484 2551011
FAX : +91 (0) 484 2532420
E-mail:
tccudl@kelnet07.xlweb.com

PIGMENT DISPERSIONS

Devarsons Industries Ltd.
443, GIDC Indl. Est.
Nr. Water Tank
Odhav
Ahmedabad, Gujarat-382415
India
TEL : +91 (0) 79 22871092
E-mail:
devarson.coldyes@gnahd.global.net.in

Colour-Chem Ltd.
Ravindra Annexe
194
Churchgate Reclamation
Mumbai,
Maharashtra-400020
India
TEL : +91 (0) 22 22022161
FAX : +91 (0) 22 22029781

Kromatik & Insulants Pvt. Ltd.
D-8 Indl. Est.
Mogappier (W)
Chennai,
Tamil Nadu-600058
India
TEL : +91 (0) 44 26243432
FAX : +91 (0) 44 26359220
E-mail:
ratna@md3.vsnl.net.in

Dhupar Chemicals Pvt. Ltd.
7/82 Tilak Ngr.
Kanpur,
Uttar Pradesh-208002
India
TEL : +91 (0) 512 2290258
FAX : +91 (0) 512 2290254
E-mail:
finishes@sancharnet.in

Mat-Sol Industries
2308/201
Sapna Mkt.
Gali Hingabeg
Tilak Bazar
Delhi, NCT of Delhi-110006
India
TEL : +91 (0) 11 23985360
FAX : +91 (0) 11 23953491
E-mail:
matsol@rediffmail.com

BORIC ACID

Chempro Exports India
1st Flr., Pushpawati Bldg.
No. 1, 568
Chira Bazar
Girgaon Rd.
Mumbai,
Maharashtra-400002
India
TEL : +91 (0) 22 22051551
FAX : +91 (0) 22 22199160
E-mail:
chempro@bom3.vsnl.net.in

Haritha Chem India
15 Sellaperumal St.
Kossapalayam
Pondicherry,
Pondicherry-605013
India
TEL : +91 (0) 413 2225380

Ram Agro Chemical Industries Ltd.
196/6
Govindappa Naick St.
Parrys
Chennai,
Tamil Nadu-600001
India
TEL : +91 (0) 44 25248913
FAX : +91 (0) 44 25323095

Allipo Chemicals
49 GIDC
Makarpura
Vadodara, Gujarat-390010
India
TEL : +91 (0) 265 2642908
FAX : +91 (0) 265 2642708
E-mail: allipo@satyam.net.in

FORMALDEHYDE

Assam Petrochemicals Ltd.
Lamb Rd.
Ambari
Guwahati, Assam-781001
India
TEL : +91 (0) 361 24246
FAX : +91 (0) 361 2547643

Cibatul Ltd.
P.O. Atul
Valsad, Gujarat-396020
India
TEL : +91 (0) 2632 283204
FAX : +91 (0) 2632 283639

Nuchem Ltd. Chemicals Division
54, Indl. Area
NIT
Faridabad, Haryana-121001
India
TEL : +91 (0) 129 25234541
FAX : +91 (0) 129 25233895
E-mail:
chemdiv.@nuchem.com

Polyformalin Pvt. Ltd.
Baneji Rd.
Kacherypady
Kochi, Kerala-682018
India

TEL : +91 (0) 484 2301679
E-mail:
polyformalin@sify.com

Rock Hard Petro Chemicals Industries Ltd.
102-A, Alankar Point, 5
Rajgarh Kothi
A B Rd.
Indore,
Madhya Pradesh-452001
India
TEL : +91 (0) 731 2491185
FAX : +91 (0) 731 2492679

HARDENERS : EPOXY RESIN

Atul Ltd. Bulk Chemicals & Intermediates Divn.
P.O. Atul
Atul, Gujarat-396020
India
TEL : +91 (0) 2632 2330261
FAX : +91 (0) 2632 2330241
E-mail: hq@atul.co.in

Ciba Speciality Chemicals (I) Ltd.
Bldg. No. 40
Off Aarey Rd.
Goregaon (E)
Mumbai,
Maharashtra-400063
India
TEL : +91 (0) 22 28403221
FAX : +91 (0) 22 28403306

Anabond Ltd.
3-A
3rd Flr.
Adyar Bridge Rd.
Adyar
Chennai, Tamil Nadu-600020
India
TEL : +91 (0) 44 24917529
FAX : +91 (0) 44 24919105
E-mail: anabond@vsnl.com

Bengal Poly Resins Pvt. Ltd.
1st Flr., 27
Bentinck St.
Kolkata,
West Bengal-700001
India
TEL : +91 (0) 33 22480229
FAX : +91 (0) 33 22430751

JK Paper Co.
19
Gagan Vihar
Trans Yamuna
Delhi, NCT of Delhi-110051
India
TEL : +91 (0) 11 25717773

PHOSPHORIC ACID

Zodiac Chem
1/5068
Balbir Ngr.
Gali No. 2
Shahdara
Delhi, NCT of Delhi-110032
India
TEL : +91 (0) 11 22286711

Gujarat Alkalies & Chemicals Ltd.
P.O. Petrochemicals
Vadodara, Gujarat-391346
India
TEL : +91 (0) 265 2372681
FAX : +91 (0) 265 2372130
E-mail:
nksachar@gujaratalkalies.com

Ketan Chemical Corp.
208, Sahakar Bhawan
340/48
Narshi Natha St.
Mumbai,
Maharashtra-400009
India
TEL : +91 (0) 22 23448181
FAX : +91 (0) 22 23444680
E-mail:
ketanchem@maharashtradirectory.com

ETHYL ACETATE

Ghaziabad Organics Ltd.
C-73
Malviya Ngr.
New Delhi,
NCT of Delhi-110017
India
TEL : +91 (0) 11 6239896

Gayatri Minerals & Chemicals
34-A
Shastrinagar
Nizampura
Vadodara, Gujarat-390002
India
TEL : +91 (0) 265 2781284
FAX : +91 (0) 265 2780228
E-mail:
info@gayatrionline.com

Ankit Acid Pvt. Ltd.
201, Trimurti Arcade
Nr. Sarvodaya Hospital
LBS Marg
Mulund (W)
Mumbai,
Maharashtra-400086
India
TEL : +91 (0) 22 25115113
FAX : +91 (0) 22 25148486

AMMONIUM CHLORIDE

Indiana Chem-Port
349
GIDC Est.
Makarpura
Vadodara, Gujarat-390010
India
TEL : +91 (0) 265 2642067
FAX : +91 (0) 265 2644717
E-mail:
indiana@wilnetonline.net

Om Chemicals
511/B
Fule Galli
M Vadgaon
Belgaum,
Karnataka-590005, India
TEL : +91 (0) 831 2482978
FAX : +91 (0) 831 2442271
E-mail:
om_chemicals@rediffmail.com

Sisco Research Laboratories Pvt. Ltd.
2F
Satam Indl. Est., 'C' Wing
Chakala
Andheri (E)
Mumbai,

Maharashtra-400099
India
TEL : +91 (0) 22 28203882
FAX : +91 (0) 22 28380998
E-mail: srl@bom3.vsnl.net.in

SULPHUR

Ashish Sulphur Dyes Pvt. Ltd.
213, Laxmi Plaza
Laxmi Indl. Est.
Link Rd.
Andheri (West)
Mumbai,
Maharashtra-400053
India
TEL : +91 (0) 22 26912953
FAX : +91 (0) 22 26399288
E-mail:
asd11@bom5.vsnl.net.in

Oreintal Carbon & Chemicals Ltd.
A-14
Indl. Area No. 1
South Side of G T Rd.
Ghaziabad,
Uttar Pradesh-201001
India
TEL : +91 (0) 120 2741246
FAX : +91 (0) 120 2741249

Oriental Carbon & Chemicals Ltd.
31, 4th Flr.
N S Rd.
Kolkata, West Bengal-700001
India
TEL : +91 (0) 33 22206831
FAX : +91 (0) 33 22207063
E-mail:
occl.cal@rme.sprintrpg.cms.vsnl.net.in

BUTYL ACETATE

Ghaziabad Organics Ltd.
C-73
Malviya Ngr.
New Delhi,
NCT of Delhi-110017
India
TEL : +91 (0) 11 26239896

Anis Rasayan & Chemicals Pvt. Ltd.
721
Lalbhai Contractor Cmplx.
Opp. Parsi Library
Nanpura
Surat, Gujarat-395001
India
TEL : +91 (0) 261 23478998
FAX : +91 (0) 261 23461860
E-mail: anis@ad1.vsnl.net.in

Ankit Acid Pvt. Ltd.
201, Trimurti Arcade
Nr. Sarvodaya Hospital
LBS Marg
Mulund (W)
Mumbai,
Maharashtra-400086
India
TEL : +91 (0) 22 25115113
FAX : +91 (0) 22 25148486

NITRILE RUBBER

Indo Rubber Corp.
No. 2, 1st Flr.
Perianna Maistry St.
Chennai, Tamil Nadu-600001
India
TEL : +91 (0) 44 25260966
FAX : +91 (0) 44 25214744
E-mail: indorubber@eth.net

Apar Industry Ltd.
Apar House, Bldg. No. 5
Corporate Park
Sion-Trombay Rd.
Chembur
Mumbai,
Maharashtra-400071
India
TEL : +91 (0) 22 25242371
FAX : +91 (0) 22 25246326
E-mail:
aisbmby@bom3.vsnl.net.in

Bombay Oil Seals Co.
Sanghavi Est., Opp.
Nityanand Ngr.
Nr. Bombay Suburban
Electric Supply
LBS Marg
Ghatkopar (W)
Mumbai,
Maharashtra-400086
India
TEL : +91 (0) 22 25002040
FAX : +91 (0) 22 25001630
E-mail:
boscomum@vsnl.com

EPOXY RESINS

Crystal Polymers & Additives Ltd.
1-8-144/152, AVA Sangam Bldg.
P G Rd.
Secunderabad,
Andhra Pradesh-500003
India
TEL : +91 (0) 40 27814887
FAX : +91 (0) 40 27845994

JK Paper Co.
19
Gagan Vihar
Trans Yamuna
Delhi, NCT of Delhi-110051
India
TEL : +91 (0) 11 25717773

Arcoy Industries
606
Abhijeet Cmplx.
Mithakhali Six Roads
Ellisbridge
Ahmedabad, Gujarat-380006
India
TEL : +91 (0) 79 26425300
FAX : +91 (0) 79 26561331
E-mail:
arcoy@ad1.vsnl.net.in

SULPHUR DIOXIDE

Chemtron Science Laboratory
EL-47
Electronics Zone
Mahape, TTC Indl. Area
MIDC
Navi Mumbai,
Maharashtra-400709
India
TEL : +91 (0) 22 27619306

FAX : +91 (0) 22 27682758
E-mail: csl@bom3.vsnl.net.in

Toshniwal Instruments Pvt. Ltd.
]8, Mohatta Bhavan
Off Dr. E Moses Rd.
Worli
Mumbai,
Maharashtra-400018
India
TEL : +91 (0) 22 24923979
FAX : +91 (0) 22 24936166
E-mail:
toshniwal@bom3.vsnl.net.in

TCP Ltd. Chemical Divn.
10, Karpagambal Ngr.
Nageshwara Park
Sathagiri Bhawan
Mylapore
Chennai, Tamil Nadu-600004
India
TEL : +91 (0) 44 24991358
FAX : +91 (0) 44 24991777

FUMEDSILICA

Bhagwat Rasayan Udyog
562
Sect. 16A
Faridabad, Haryana-121001
India
TEL : +91 (0) 129 25288517

Dineshchandra Industries
Narang,4th Flr., 330
Narshi Natha St.
Masjid Bunder
Mumbai,
Maharashtra-400009
India
TEL : +91 (0) 22 23427804
FAX : +91 (0) 22 23433228
E-mail:
dineshchandra@vsnl.com

Gujarat Silicon Pvt. Ltd.
Amarnath House, Mitha Galli
Nr. Teen Darwaja
Grain Mkt.
Jamnagar, Gujarat-361001
India
TEL : +91 (0) 288 2676702
FAX : +91 (0) 288 2755086
E-mail: gujsil@vsnl.com

CARBON BLACK

Carbon India
152-153, Ajmeri Gate
Delhi, NCT of Delhi-110006
India
TEL : +91 (0) 11 23236666
FAX : +91 (0) 11 23237383

Consolidated Petrotech Industries Ltd.
Plot No. 1
GIDC Est. (Palej)
Ahmedabad,
Gujarat-392220
India
TEL : +91 (0) 79 22159

Cabot India Ltd.
NKM International House, 6th Flr., 178
Babubhai M Chinai Marg
Mumbai,
Maharashtra-400020
India
TEL : +91 (0) 22 22027846
FAX : +91 (0) 22 22850406

SHELLAC

Ranchhoddas & Sons
24/A, Swastik Chmbrs., 23/24
Carnac Rd.
Mumbai,
Maharashtra-400001
India
TEL : +91 (0) 22 22625419
FAX : +91 (0) 22 22623405

DKR Shankar Sah & Co
105
Iyah Mudali St., P.O. Box 2443
Chintadripet
Chennai,
Tamil Nadu-600002
India
TEL : +91 (0) 44 2834849
FAX : +91 (0) 44 25341022

AM Jordan Pvt. Ltd.
29
R N Mukherjee Rd.
Kolkata,
West Bengal-700001
India
TEL : +91 (0) 33 22484917
FAX : +91 (0) 33 22430572

TITANIUM DIOXIDE

Cochin Minerals & Rutile Ltd.
P.O. Box No. 73, VIII/224
Mkt. Rd.
Alwaye, Kerala-683101
India
TEL : +91 (0) 484 2626789
FAX : +91 (0) 484 2625674
E-mail:
sachexim@vsnl.com

Kolmak Chemicals Ltd.
21-A
Shakespeare Sarani
Kolkata,
West Bengal-700017
India
TEL : +91 (0) 33 22477512
FAX : +91 (0) 33 22406476
E-mail:
tioxide@cal2.vsnl.net.in

EI DuPont India Ltd.
DLF Plaza Tower, 8th Flr.
Phase-I
DLF Qutab Enclave
Gurgaon, Haryana-122002
India
TEL : +91 (0) 124 26540900
FAX : +91 (0) 124 26540889

ALUMINA

Industrial Ceramics
Plot No. 24B
Phase-III, IDA
Jeedimetla
Hyderabad,
Andhra Pradesh-500055
India
TEL : +91 (0) 40 23095174

FAX : +91 (0) 40 23736641
E-mail:
piyushanu@rediffmail.com

Orient Abrasives Ltd.
1212, Chiranjiv Tower, 43
Nehru Place
New Delhi,
NCT of Delhi-110019, India
TEL : +91 (0) 11 26462225
FAX : +91 (0) 11 26443859
E-mail: abl@del3.vsnl.net.in

Ace Manufacturing & Marketing
Survey No. 1786
Village: Gothda
Taluka-Savli
Vadodara, Gujarat-391770
India
TEL : +91 (0) 2667 222902
FAX : +91 (0) 2667 222309

IRON OXIDE

Coral Chemicals Pvt. Ltd.
805, Akashdeep Bldg., 26A
Barakhamba Rd.
New Delhi,
NCT of Delhi-110001
India
TEL : +91 (0) 11 23310413
FAX : +91 (0) 11 23323348
E-mail: binay@del2.net.in

Massawi Mikrotech Minerals Pvt. Ltd.
Plot No. 114
GIDC, Phase-II
Naroda
Ahmedabad, Gujarat-380001
India
TEL : +91 (0) 79 22813056
FAX : +91 (0) 79 22840776

Tainwala Enterprises
44, Ginni Niketan
Robertson Rd.
Frazer Town
Bangalore,
Karnataka-560025
India
TEL : +91 (0) 80 25484050
FAX : +91 (0) 80 25483337

CALCIUM OXIDE

Deepika Minerals & Chemicals
C-38
Opp. Samipur Badli, Suraj Park
New Delhi,
NCT of Delhi-110042, India
TEL : +91 (0) 11 27853074
FAX : +91 (0) 11 27105246
E-mail:
gulshan01@hotmail.com

Balco Chemicals
859/4/D
GIDC
Makarpura Indl. Est.
Vadodara, Gujarat-390017
India
TEL : +91 (0) 265 2561275
FAX : +91 (0) 265 2648102

Singhbhum Calcining Plant
44 B
Phase-II
Adityapur, Jamshedpur,
Jharkhand-832109
India
TEL : +91 (0) 657 2409625
FAX : +91 (0) 657 2229873

WAX

Ecoshine Wax
1796
Sect. F
DSIDC Ltd. Indl. Area
Narela
Delhi, NCT of Delhi-110040
India
TEL : +91 (0) 11 27781028
FAX : +91 (0) 11 27428096
E-mail:
ecoshinewax@rediffmail.com

Gujarat Waxes
701
Shapath
Opp. Rajpath Club
National Highway No. 8
Ahmedabad,
Gujarat-380015
India
TEL : +91 (0) 79 26750890
FAX : +91 (0) 79 26770971
E-mail:
gujaratwax@hotmail.com

Asiatic Petrochemicals
2
Sneh Nagar Main Rd.
Indore,
Madhya Pradesh-452001
India
TEL : +91 (0) 731 269546
FAX : +91 (0) 731 2468950

SILICA

Bharti Engineers
WZ-2181A, 2nd. Flr.
Raja Park Chowk
Rani Bagh
Delhi, NCT of Delhi-110034
India
TEL : +91 (0) 11 27197114
FAX : +91 (0) 11 27198943
E-mail:
bharti@del3:vsnl.net.in

Resources International
Sesa Ghor, 2nd Flr.
Entrance III, Patto Plaza
Panjim
Goa, Goa-403001
India
TEL : +91 (0) 832 2229933
FAX : +91 (0) 832 2229911
E-mail:
email@resourcefulgroup.com

Hindustan Mineral Products
Ahmedabad Highway
Village Bhamaiya
Godhra (PMS)
Godhra, Gujarat-389001
India
TEL : +91 (0) 2672 240340
FAX : +91 (0) 2672 242605

STEARIC ACID

Jocil Ltd.
P.O. Box 216
Arundelpet Guntur,
Andhra Pradesh-522002
India
TEL : +91 (0) 863 2290190
FAX : +91 (0) 863 2290090
E-mail:
jocil@jocil.xeevga.xeemail.ems.vsnl.net.in

Chowdhry Rubber & Chemical Co.
1403
Pan Mandi
Sadar Bazar
Delhi, NCT of Delhi-110006
India
TEL : +91 (0) 11 23673373
FAX : +91 (0) 11 27534153
E-mail:
anshdeep@del3.vsnl.net.in

Rajkot Soap Factory
37, Opp. Samrat Hotel
Karanpara
Rajkot, Gujarat-360001
India
TEL : +91 (0) 281 2224352
FAX : +91 (0) 281 2385272
E-mail:
pasand@maharashtradirectory.com

MALEIC ANHYDRIDE

Adarsh Chemicals & Fertilizers Ltd.
Udhna
Surat, Gujarat-394210
India
TEL : +91 (0) 261 2677233
FAX : +91 (0) 261 2677251
E-mail:
adchem@winnetonline.com

Mysore Petrochemicals Ltd.
401/404
Raheja Centre, 214
Nariman Point
Mumbai,
Maharashtra-400021
India
TEL : +91 (0) 22 22840714
FAX : +91 (0) 22 22040747
E-mail:
igpetro@bom3.vsnl.net.in

Shubham Dyes & Chemicals
1/26
Roop Ngr.
Delhi, NCT of Delhi-110007
India
TEL : +91 (0) 11 22933200
FAX : +91 (0) 11 22944202
E-mail:
shubhcam@nda.vsnl.net.in

POLYBUTENE RESINS

Gujarat Petro Synthese Ltd.
National House, 6
Tulloch Rd.
Mumbai,
Maharashtra-400039
India
TEL : +91 (0) 22 22022031
FAX : +91 (0) 22 22022135

Gujarat Petro Synthesis Ltd.
77/11
Phase-I
GIDC Est.
Ahmedabad, Gujarat-380023
India
TEL : +91 (0) 79 830224

PI Polymers A Divn. Of P.I. Industries Ltd.
237
GIDC
Panoli, Gujarat-394115
India
TEL : +91 (0) 2646 272105
FAX : +91 (0) 2646 272313
E-mail:
mgupt.piilpnl@narmada.net.in

WHITE OIL

Pioneer Petrochem Pvt. Ltd.
31/35
Rohtak Rd.
Punjabi Bagh
New Delhi,
NCT of Delhi-110026
India
TEL : +91 (0) 11 25191511
FAX : +91 (0) 11 25439529

Ankini Petrochem Ltd.
18, 2nd Flr.
Shree Krishna Centre
Mithakhali Six Rd.
Navrangpura
Ahmedabad,
Gujarat-380009
India
TEL : +91 (0) 79 2401706
FAX : +91 (0) 79 26426489
E-mail:
ankpetro@ad1.vsnl.net.in

Appro Lubes Pvt. Ltd.
Vinod Cmplx., No. 25
J C Rd.
Bangalore,
Karnataka-560002
India
TEL : +91 (0) 80 22237102
FAX : +91 (0) 80 22237102
E-mail:
contact@approlubes.com

TALC

Gayatri Fillers Pvt. Ltd.
406
Sahjanand Cmplx., B/h AEC
Naranpura
Ahmedabad,
Gujarat-380013
India
TEL : +91 (0) 79 286704
FAX : +91 (0) 79 286376
E-mail:
gayatrimicro@icenet.net

Associated Minerals Corporation
Katchery Rd.
Giridih, Jharkhand-815301
India
TEL : +91 (0) 6532 222205
FAX : +91 (0) 6532 222335
E-mail:
asomin@rediffmail.com

Indian Chemicals
Bypass Plot No. 428/2/1
New Jail Rd., Badwai
Karond
Bhopal,
Madhya Pradesh-462038
India
TEL : +91 (0) 755 2742146
E-mail:
indian_chemicals@yahoo.com

CLAY

Agarwal Minechem Industries
277, Satyam Tower, A-2
Paschim vihar
New Delhi,
NCT of Delhi-110063
India
TEL : +91 (0) 11 25577755
FAX : +91 (0) 11 25688008
E-mail:
agminechem@mailcity.com

20 Microns Ltd.
307-308, 3rd Flr.
Arundeep Cmplx.
Race Course (S)
Vadodara, Gujarat-390007
India
TEL : +91 (0) 265 2330714
FAX : +91 (0) 265 2335755
E-mail:
enquiry@20microns.com

Cutch Oil & Allied Industries (1949) Pvt. Ltd.
310, Hari Chmbrs., 58/64
S B Singh Rd.
Mumbai,
Maharashtra-400023
India
TEL : +91 (0) 22 22673174
FAX : +91 (0) 22 22679877
E-mail:
gellants@cutchoil.com

SURFACTANTS

Intra Consolid (I) Ltd.
C-3/3064
Vasantkunj
New Delhi,
NCT of Delhi-110070
India
TEL : +91 (0) 11 26890334
FAX : +91 (0) 11 26895042

Aico Agencies Pvt. Ltd.
75
Outside Raipur Gate
New Cloth Mkt.
Ahmedabad, Gujarat-380002
India
TEL : +91 (0) 79 22166482
FAX : +91 (0) 79 22145207
E-mail: aico@ad1.vsnl.net.in

El DuPont India Ltd.
DLF Plaza Tower, 8th Flr.
Phase-I
DLF Qutab Enclave
Gurgaon, Haryana-122002
India
TEL : +91 (0) 124 26540900
FAX : +91 (0) 124 26540889

BENTONITE

Nava Durga Chemicals & Minerals Pvt. Ltd.
MCH, Q. No. EWS 1-56
West Parsigutta
Hyderabad,
Andhra Pradesh-500048
India
TEL : +91 (0) 40 27600558
FAX : +91 (0) 40 27600558

Agarwal Minechem Industries
277, Satyam Tower, A-2
Paschim vihar
New Delhi,
NCT of Delhi-110063
India
TEL : +91 (0) 11 25577755
FAX : +91 (0) 11 25688008
E-mail:
agminechem@mailcity.com

Ashapura Mineral Co.
Plot No. 236-69
GIDC Est. (Chitra)
Ahmedabad, Gujarat-364004
India
TEL : +91 (0) 79 26232

GYPSUM

An Ultrafine Mineral
307/20
Siddhivinayak
Opp. Vivek College,
Siddharthnagar
Goregaon (W)
Mumbai,
Maharashtra-400062
India
TEL : +91 (0) 22 26902279
FAX : +91 (0) 22 26902279
E-mail:
satish_138_in@yahoo.com

Mehta Overseas
59
Bank Cly.
Raika Bagh
Jodhpur, Rajasthan-342006
India
TEL : +91 (0) 291 2512203
FAX : +91 (0) 291 2512203
E-mail:
naveen.mehta@vsnl.com

Ennor Muds & Chemicals
A-12
Anna Nagar (E)
Chennai,
Tamil Nadu-600102
India
TEL : +91 (0) 44 26265792
FAX : +91 (0) 44 26261168
E-mail:
ennor@md2.vsnl.net.in

CYCLOHEXANOL

Gujarat State Fertilizers & Chemicals Ltd.
P.O. Fertilizernagar
Vadodara, Gujarat-391347
India
TEL : +91 (0) 265 2372451
FAX : +91 (0) 265 2372966
E-mail:
mail@gsfclimited.com

AROMATIC OIL

Crown Lubricants
34/35
Gandhi Rd.
Puzhal
Chennai, T
amil Nadu-600066
India
TEL : +91 (0) 44 26590171
FAX : +91 (0) 44 26591271
E-mail: crownlub@eth.net

Hindustan Petroleum Corporation Ltd.
Hindustan Bhavan
P.O. Box No. 155
8
Shoorji Villabhdas Marg
Mumbai,
Maharashtra-400001
India
TEL : +91 (0) 22 22618031
FAX : +91 (0) 22 22611822
E-mail: info@hindpetro.com

Sah Petroleums Ltd.
406/407
Embassy Centre
Nariman Point
Mumbai,
Maharashtra-400021
India
TEL : +91 (0) 22 22301911
FAX : +91 (0) 22 22875751
E-mail: ipol@vsnl.com

ISOPRENE

Hindustan Lever Ltd. Chemicals Divn.
ICT Link Rd.
Chakala
Andheri (E)
Mumbai,
Maharashtra-400099
India
TEL : +91 (0) 22 28329471
FAX : +91 (0) 22 28225708

El DuPont India Ltd.
DLF Plaza Tower, 8th Flr.
Phase-I
DLF Qutab Enclave
Gurgaon, Haryana-122002
India
TEL : +91 (0) 124 26540900
FAX : +91 (0) 124 26540889

RESORCINOL

Alchem
1661 Suthar St.
Nanpura
Surat, Gujarat-395001
India
TEL : +91 (0) 261 2425709
FAX : +91 (0) 261 2431317
E-mail:
anupam.rasayan@pobox.com

Associated Petrochem Pvt. Ltd.
49-6 Km
Delhi-Rohtak Rd.
Sampla, Haryana-124501
India
TEL : +91 (0) 1262 27019003
FAX : +91 (0) 1262 27022591
E-mail:
thymolindia@hotmail.com

Sneh Dyechem Ltd.
Plot No. B-1
BDA, Koh-E-Fiza
Bhopal-Indore Rd.
Bhopal,
Madhya Pradesh-462001
India
TEL : +91 (0) 755 2541635
FAX : +91 (0) 755 2545615

ZINC DUST

Forage Chemical Industries
A-33, Antop Hill
Warehousing
ACME Co. Rd. Wadara (E)
Mumbai,
Maharashtra-400037
India
TEL : +91 (0) 22 24111762
FAX : +91 (0) 22 24183639
E-mail: forage@sify.com

The Metal Powder Company Ltd.
Maravankulam
Thirumangalam,
Tamil Nadu-625706
India
TEL : +91 (0) 4549 2882490
FAX : +91 (0) 4549 220689
E-mail:
mepco@pronet.net.in

XYLENES

Kamal Organic Chemicals
S-7, Jayashree Apts.
Prathana Samaj Rd.
Vile Parle (E)
Mumbai,
Maharashtra-400057
India
TEL : +91 (0) 22 26107313

WOOD ROSIN

India Rosin Industries
F-18
Sipcot Indl. Cmplx.
Gummidipoondi,
Tamil Nadu-601201
India
TEL : +91 (0) 4119 222156
FAX: +91 (0) 4119 25240339

Dujodwala Products Ltd.
812/813, Tulsiani Chmbrs.,
212 Nariman Point
Mumbai,
Maharashtra-400021

India
TEL : +91 (0) 22 22824089
FAX : +91 (0) 22 22841284
E-mail:
power@bom3.vsnl.net.in

COPPER SULPHATE

Arun Udyog
B-3/7
Paschim Vihar
New Delhi,
NCT of Delhi-110063
India
TEL : +91 (0) 11 25687718
FAX : +91 (0) 11 25268326
E-mail:
metkam@ndf.vsnl.net.in

Allipo Chemicals
49 GIDC
Makarpura
Vadodara, Gujarat-390010
India
TEL : +91 (0) 265 2642908
FAX : +91 (0) 265 2642708
E-mail: allipo@satyam.net.in

The Mysore Coffee Curing Works Ltd.
P.O. Box No. 1
K M Rd.
Chickmagalur,
Karnataka-577102
India
TEL : +91 (0) 8262 220371
FAX : +91 (0) 8262 220064

HYDRATED LIME

Deepika Minerals & Chemicals
C-38
Opp. Samipur Badli,
Suraj Park
New Delhi,
NCT of Delhi-110042
India
TEL : +91 (0) 11 27853074
FAX : +91 (0) 11 27105246
E-mail:
gulshan01@hotmail.com

Balco Chemicals
859/4/D
GIDC
Makarpura Indl. Est.
Vadodara, Gujarat-390017
India
TEL : +91 (0) 265 2561275
FAX : +91 (0) 265 2648102

ZINC CHLORIDE

Allipo Chemicals
49 GIDC, Makarpura
Vadodara, Gujarat-390010
India
TEL : +91 (0) 265 2642908
FAX : +91 (0) 265 2642708
E-mail: allipo@satyam.net.in

Orbit Fine Chem Pvt. Ltd.
482 Indl. Area Phase I
Panchkula, Haryana-134109
India
TEL : +91 (0) 172 2568482

Kalidas Sheet Metal Industries Pvt. Ltd.
P.O. Box 252
Broadway Lane
Kochi, Kerala-682031
India
TEL : +91 (0) 484 2369060

HYDROCHLORIC ACID

Chlorochem Industries
A-29
Lajpat Ngr.-II
New Delhi,
NCT of Delhi-110024
India
TEL : +91 (0) 11 26848872

Bahubali Chemical Industries
No. 4, "The Emperor",
1st Flr.
Fatehgunj Main Rd.
Vadodara, Gujarat-390002
India
TEL : +91 (0) 265 2791449
FAX : +91 (0) 265 2793607
E-mail:
nikunjchem@satyam.net.in

SODIUM BICARBONATE

DCW Ltd.
3rd Flr., "Nirmal"
Nariman Point
Mumbai,
Maharashtra-400021
India
TEL : +91 (0) 22 22871914
FAX : +91 (0) 22 22028838
E-mail: ho@dcwltd.com

Tuticorin Alkali Chemicals & Fertilizers Ltd.
553
Anna Salai, Teynampet
Chennai, Tamil Nadu-600018
India
TEL : +91 (0) 44 24345276
FAX : +91 (0) 44 24348044
E-mail: tacmsd@vsnl.com

Micro & Macro Agencies Pvt. Ltd.
4th Flr., 11
Clive Row
Kolkata,
West Bengal-700001
India
TEL : +91 (0) 33 22426014
FAX : +91 (0) 33 22426014

117. MANUFACTURE OF TIN CONTAINERS
118. MANUFACTURE OF STORAGE TANKS, PRESSURE VESSELS, HEAT EXCHANGERS
119. MARK II HAND PUMPS
120. MARUTI WORKSHOP CUM - SERVICE STATION
121. MECHANICAL JACKS
122. METAL CUTTING DIE DESIGN
123. METAL CUTTING OF AND GRINDING WHEELS (ABBRASIVE CUTTING WHEELS)
124. METAL HOOKS & CLIPS
125. METAL SEPARATION (COPPER, TIN, LEAD) FROM SPENT WASH ACID
126. METALLIC RING JOINTS
127. METALLIC GASKET (SPIRAL WOUND)
128. MICROVEE & ABSOLUTE FILTER
129. MICROWAVE OVEN
130. MILD STEEL INGOTS
131. MINI STEEL PLANT
132. MODERN VEHICLE WORKSHOP
133. MOPED
134. M.S.HINGES
135. M.S.INGOT AND HR. STEEL STRUCTURALS
136. M.S.INGOT BY INDUCTION FURNACES
137. M.S.PIPES
138. M.S. WELDING ELECTRODE
139. MUFFLERS & SILENCERS FOR THREE WHEELERS
140. NAIL CUTTER WITH FILER & MANICURE
141. NICHROME WIRE
142. NICKEL LINED SCREENS
143. NON-FERROUS ALLOY ROLLING
144. NON-FERROUS FORGING
145. NON-FERROUS FOUNDRY
146. NON PRESSURE
147. INCANDESCENT LAMP
148. NUMBER COMBINATION LOCKS FOR LUGGAGES
149. NUTS & BOLTS
150. PAPER COATED ALUMINIUM AND COPPER WIRE
151. PETROMAX CONTAINER
152. PHOTO ETCHING OF STAINLESS STEEL PLATES
153. PIPE GALVANIZING PLANT
154. PISTON RING-AUTOMOBILE
155. PLANT PROTECTION EQUIPMENTS
156. PLATINUM LABORATORY APPARATUS
157. PRESSURE COOKER & ALUMINIUM UTENSILS
158. PRESSURE COOKER (ALUMINIUM)
159. PRESSURE DIE CASTING
160. PRINTED ALUMINIUM COLLAPSIBLE TUBES
161. PRINTED TIN CONTAINERS
162. PRINTING PRESS (CYLINDER MACHINE)
163. PUMPS FOR CHEMICAL INDUSTRY (SPECIAL)
164. RAILWAY SLEEPERS (M.S.)
165. RAZOR TWIN BLADE
166. R.C.C SPUN PIPES
167. RECONDITIONING OF M.S. DRUMS/BARRELS
168. RE-ROLLING COPPER AND BRASS SHEET AND RODS
169. RE-ROLLING MILLS
170. RESIN COATED SAND
171. RESIN CORED SOFT SOLDER WIRES
172. ROLLING MILL (BY INDUCTION FURNACE) & MANUFACTURE OF BARS, ANGLES, SQUARES, TUBES AND OTHERS
173. ROLLER BEARING & FORGING
174. ROLLING OF STAINLESS STEEL PATTA
175. RUBBER INSULATED PLIERS (HAND TOOLS)
176. RUBBING COMPOUND FOR AUTOMOBILES
177. SCIENTIFIC LABORATORY EQUIPMENTS
178. SCOOTER ASSEMBLING
179. SECONDARY LEAD EXTRAC -TION BY SCRAP BATTERY PLATES,PIPES & SHEET
180. SEAMLESS M.S. TUBES & PIPES
181. SELF TAPPING STEEL SCREW
182. SEWING NEEDLES
183. S.G. IRON & ALLOY STEEL
184. SHEET METAL PRODUCTS, (FERROUS/NON-FERROUS)
185. SHIP/MARINE CONTAINER
186. SHOCK ABSORBERS
187. SHOE EYELETS
188. SHOT AND GRITS BY AUTOMIZATION PROCESS
189. SHOVELS
190. SILICO MANGANESE ALLOYS
191. SILENCERS (MUFFLERS) EXHAUST & TAIL PIPE FOR ALL TYPES OF VEHICLES
192. SINTERED BEARING
193. SINTERED BUSHES
194. SINTERED METAL PRODUCTS
195. SOFT AND HARD FERRITES
196. SPANNERS
197. SPARK PLUGS
198. STEEL PLANT (ELECTRIC ARC FURNACE BASED- EAF)
199. SPHERIODAL GRAPHITE CAST IRON
200. SPRAY DRYER
201. STAINLESS STEEL HINGES
202. STAINLESS STEEL SHEET ROLLING TO PRODUCE STAINLESS STEEL UTENSILS
203. STAINLESS STEEL UTENSILS
204. STAPLE PINS,PAPER PIN, GEM CLIPS ETC.
205. STEEL CASTINGS
206. STEEL CHAIN
207. STEEL FOUNDRY
208. STEEL FURNITURES AND ELECTRICAL APPLIANCES
209. STEEL PLANT (MINI)
210. STEEL RODS AND COILS FROM SCRAPS
211. STEEL ROLLING MILL
212. STEEL STRIPS (COLD ROLLED) SILICON WITH GRAIN RIENTED FOR ELECTRIC USE
213. STEEL TRANSMISSION LINE TOWERS & ROLLING MILL TO PRODUCE STEEL SECTION
214. STEEL FURNITURES AND ELECTRICAL APPLIANCES
215. STEEL WIRE DRAWING AND GALVANIZING
216. STEEL WOOL
217. SUBMERGED ARC WELDED PIPES
218. SUBMERSIBLE PUMP MANUFACTURING
219. SUPER ENAMELLED COPPER WIRE
220. THREE WHEELERS
221. TIE-ROD ENDS
222. TIN CONTAINERS
223. TOOLROOM AND SHEET METAL PRODUCTS
224. TRACTOR TRAILERS
225. TRANSMISSION POWER FITTING
226. TUBULAR POLES
227. SUPER ENAMELLED COPPER WIRES
228. TUBULAR POLES FOR ELECTRICAL TRANSMISSION (BY FABRICATION PROCESS)
229. TUBULAR POLES OF M.S. & HIGH TENSILE STEEL
230. VACUUM CLEANERS
231. VACUUM FLASK (STAINLESS STEEL)
232. VALVES FOR REFRIGERA TION AND AIR-CONDITION
233. VEHICLE WELDING & PAINTING
234. VENETION BLIND
235. WASHING MACHINES (AUTOMATIC & COMPUTERISED)
236. WATER CONTROLLER (AUTOMATIC)
237. WATCH STRAPS/CHAINS/ BRACELETS/BELT BRASS & STAINLESS STEEL
238. WATER COOLERS
239. WELDED WIRE MESH
240. WELDING ELECTRODES
241. WICK STOVES
242. WIND MILL WINDOW FRAME (FERROUS & NON-FERROUS)
243. WRIST WATCH

359. DI ETHYL OXALATE
360. DI METHYL ORTHOPHTHALATE
361. DI-METHYL PHTHALATE
362. DICLOFENAC GEL
363. DIOCTYL PHTHALATE (DOP)
364. DI PHENYL GLYCERINE
365. DI PHENYL OXIDE
366. DINITRO-CHLORO BENZENE
367. DISTILLED WATER
368. DODECYL BENZENE SULPHONATE
369. DUSTLESS CHALK
370. EDTA & ITS SALTS
371. ELECTROLESS NICKEL PLATING ON PLASTICS
372. ENDOSULFAN
373. EPOXY RESIN BASED COMPOUND
374. ETHYL ACETATE
375. EHTYL ETHER
376. ETHYL ALCOHOL (POTABLE LIQUOR)
377. ETHYL HEXANOL
378. EXTRACTION OF ESSENTIAL OILS BY SUGAR CRITICAL FLUID (CARBON DIOXIDE) METHOD FROM FLOWERS, HERBAL & SPICES
379. FERRIC ALUM
380. FERRO CHROME LIGNO SULPHONATE
381. FERRO MANGANESE
382. FERRO SILICONE
383. FERRO VANADIUM FROM VANADIUM SLUDGE
384. FERROUS SILICATE
385. FERROUS SULPHATE
386. FERTILIZER FROM ANIMAL BLOOD & LEATHER WASTE
387. FLUORESCENT TUBE LIGHT POWDER
388. FOAMED PVC COMPOUNDING & ITS PRODUCTS
389. FORMALDEHYDE
390. FRACTIONAL DISTILLATION OF D.M.O (DEMENTHOLIZED OIL)
391. FRACTIONAL DISTILLATION OF ESSENTIAL OIL & MEDICINAL PLANT EXTRACT
392. FRICTION DUST (LIQUID & POWDER) FROM CNSL
393. FRUIT FLAVOURS
394. FURFURAL FROM RICE HUSK
395. GARLIC ACID
396. GASKET SHELLAC COMPOUND
397. GEAR OIL
398. GIBBERELLIC ACID
399. GLASS PUTTY
400. GLYCERINE
401. GOSSYPOL (POLY PHENOL) FROM COTTON SEED OIL
402. GUAR GUM POWDER
403. HAIR FIXER (HAIR GEL TYPE)
404. H - ACID
405. HENNA PASTE MAKING
406. HEPTAL DEHYDE
407. HIGH CARBON FERRO CHROME
408. HYDRATED CALCIUM SILICATE BRICK
409. HYDRATED LIME FROM SEA SHELL
410. HYDROCHLORIC ACID
411. HYDRO FLUORIC ACID
412. HYDROGEN PEROXIDE (BY AUTO-OXIDATION PROCESS)
413. ICE PACKS (SOLUTIONS TYPE, WHITE GEL TYPE, VIOLET SEMI SOLID POLYMER TYPE)
414. IMPROVING DROP POINT PARAFFIN WAX FROM 45-50°C TO 75-80°C
415. INDUSTRIAL ALCOHOL
416. INTEGERATED COMPLEX OF EASTER & ALLIED PRODUCTS (D.O.P, D.B.P, ETHYL ACETATE WIRE ENAMEL & CABLE JELLY)
417. IMFL (WHISKY) & COUNTRY LIQUOR
418. IRON OXIDE FOR MAKING FERITTE
419. IRON SULPHIDE
420. JUTE BATCHING OIL
421. KESH KALA TEL (HAIR DYE LOTION) (VASMOL 33, BLACK NITE TYPE)
422. L-LYSINE MONOHYDROCHLORIDE
423. LACTIC ACID FROM WHITE SUGAR BY FERMENTATION PROCESS
424. LDPE GRANULES FROM VIRGIN (LDPE RESIN)
425. LEAD EXTRACTION FROM BATTERY SCRAP
426. LEAD OXIDE (A) LEAD MONOXIDE
(B) LEAD TETRA OXIDE
(C) GREYLEAD OXIDE
427. LIQUID GLUCOSE & ITS BY PRODUCTS
428. LIQUID OXYGEN BOTTLING PLANT
429. LIQUID SHOE POLISH
430. LIQUID FLOOR POLISH
431. LUBE OIL VISCOSITY IMPROVED FOR P.P.G/P.E.G.
432. LUBRICANTS ASHLESS 100% COMBUSTION
433. MAGNESIUM CARBONATE AND MAGNESIUM BICARMONATE
434. MAGNESIUM HYDROXIDE POWDER
435. MAGNESIUM SILICATE
436. MAGNESIUM SULPHATE
437. MALACHITE GREEN
438. MALEIC ANHYDRIDE
439. MANGANESE SULPHATE
440. MANUFACTURING OF CARBON MONO-OXIDE WATER GAS
441. MENTHOL BOLD CRYSTALS FROM FLAKES
442. MENTHOL CRYSTAL & MENTHA OIL
443. MERCURIC OXIDE
444. METAL PRE-TREATMENT CHEMICALS
445. METHANE GAS BY SODIUM ACETATE & SODA LIME
446. METHYL ACETYL RICINOLATE
447. METOL
448. METOL FROM HYDROQUI-NONE & METHYLAMINE
449. MICANITE
450. MICRO NUTRIENT MIXTURE
451. MINERAL WATER
452. MINERAL WATER AND PET BOTTILNG PLANT
453. MINERAL WATER IN BOTTLES, GLASS AND POUCHES
454. MINI CEMENT PLANT (BY ROTARY KILN PROCESS)
455. MIXED FERTILIZER
456. MOSQUITO & FLIES REPELLENT AGARBATTI (INCENSE STICKS)
457. MONO CHLORO ACETIC ACID
458. MONOCROTOPHOS (TECHNICAL)
459. MOSQUITO COIL
460. MOSQUITO COIL & MAT
461. MOSQUITO MAT
462. MOTHER TINCTURE & BIO CHEMIC MEDICINES
463. NAPHTHALENE & PHENYL (INTEGRATED UNIT)
464. NATURAL MINERAL WATER BY REVERSE OSMOSIS PROCESS
465. NICKEL PLATING BRIGHTNER (PRIMARY OR CARRIER BRIGHTNER & SECONDARY BRIGHTNER)
466. NICKEL SULPHATE
467. NICOTINE FROM TOBACCO WASTE
468. NICOTINE SULPHATE FROM TOBACCO WASTE
469. NITRO BENZENE
470. NITRO CELLULOSE SANDING SEALER/LACQUER
471. NITRO MUSK
472. NITROGEN & OXYGEN GAS PLANT
473. NON-IONIC SURFACTANT (WETTING AGENT)
474. NO-CARB PASTE
475. OCTANOL
476. ORTHO NITRO PHENOL
477. OXALIC ACID FROM MOLASSES
478. OXALIC ACID FROMRICE HUSK
479. OXALIC ACID FROM TREE BARK
470. OXALIC ACID FROM WASTE VEGETABLES
471. OXYGEN GAS PLANT
472. OXYGEN GAS PLANT (AIR SEPERATION METHOD)
473. PARA-AMINO BENZOIC ACID
474. PARA-AMINO PHENOL
475. PARA TOLUENE SULPHONIC ACID
476. PECTIN FROM RAW PAPAYA
477. PERFUME (LEMON & OTHERS)

CRUDE NAPHTHA
570. TRIMETHYL AMMONIUM CHLORIDE
571. TRIPHENYL PHOSPHITE (T.P.P)
572. ULTRAMARINE BLUE (LIQUID)
573. UREA FORMALDEHYDE & MELAMINE FORMALDEHYDE POWDER
574. UNDECYLINIC ACID
575. VINYL ACETATE MONOMER
576. VITAMIN C
577. VITAMIN E
578. WASTE WATER TREATMENT PLANT FOR INDUSTRIAL SECTOR IN INDIA (ONLY MARKER SURVEY)
579. WIRE DRAWING LUBRICANT
580. WIRE ENAMEL
581. XANTHATES
582. YELLOW DEXTRIN
583. ZINC CHLORIDE
584. ZINC OXIDE
585. ZINC PHOSPHATING BY COLD PROCESS
586. ZINC SILICATE
587. ZINC STEARATE
588. ZINC SULPHATE
589. ZINC SULPHATE MONOHYDRATE
590. ACID BLACK
591. AURAMINE'O'
592. AZO DYES STUFF
593. DYE & DYE INTERMEDIATE
594. DYE INTERMEDIATES
595. MALACHITE GREEN
596. METHYLENE BLUE
597. PHTHALOCYANINE BLUE
598. PHTHALOCYANINE BLUE & GREEN
599. REACTIVE DYES
600. SULPHUR BLACK DYE
601. VAT DYES
602. WATER CHILLING PLANT
603. WADDING OIL (100%) FOR WADDING OF COTTON HOSIERY CLOTH IN THE DYEING PROCESS
604. WHITE OIL
605. WAX FLOOR POLISH

ELECTRICAL, ELECTONICS, COMPUTERS AND INFOTECH/IT PROJECTS

606. AIR CONDITIONING
607. ALUMINIUM ALLOY CONDUCTOR
608. ALUMINIUM CABLE
609. ALUMINIUM ELECTROYTIC CAPACITORS
610. AUDIO CASSETTE ASSEMBLING & RECORDING
611. AUDIO CASSETTES DUPLICATING RECORDING
612. AUDIO CASSETTES & AUDIO STUDIO
613. AUDIO CASSETTES PLANE & RECORDED
614. AUDIO MAGNETIC HEADS
615. AUDIO MAGNETIC TAPE
616. AUDIO/VIDEO CASSETTES
617. AUTO BULB/LAMPS
618. AUTOMATIC VOLTAGE STABILIZER
619. BATTERY PLATES
620. BACK OFFICE (Rs. 5000/-)
621. B/W TV & COMPUTER MONITOR PICTURE TUBE
622. BREAD BOARDS
623. CALL CENTRE
624. CAMERA (35 MM)
625. CAPACITORS
626. CARBON ELECTRODE USED FOR BATTERY CELL
627. CARBON POTETIOMETERS
628. CEILING FAN
629. CERAMIC INSULATOR
630. CHILDREN INFOTECH TRAINING INSTITUTE (Rs. 5000/-)
631. CHOKE AND PATTI
632. CHOKE AND STARTER
633. CHOKE USED FOR FLUORESCENT LAMPS
634. COLOUR TELEVISION
635. COLOUR AND BLACK & WHITE TELEVISION
636. COMPACT DISC
637. COMPACT DISC PLAYER (AUDIO/VIDEO)
638. COMPUTER EDUCATION INSTITUTE
639. COMPUTER ASSEMBLY
640. COMPUTER HARDWARE
641. COMPUTER KEYBOARD
642. COMPUTER PERIPHERALS
643. COMPUTER PRINTERS
644. COMPUTER RIBBON
645. COMPUTER RIBBON REINKING OR REFILLING
646. COMPUTER STATIONERY
647. COMPUTER STATIONERY &

IMPORTED HARDWARE PARTS
648. COMPUTER TERMINALS
649. COMPUTERISED WASHING MACHINE (AUTOMATIC)
650. COMPUTER SOFTWARE
651. CONDENSER FOR MOTOR USING MPP FILM
652. CONTENT DEVELOPMENT CENTRE (EOU) (Rs. 5000/-)
653. CONTROL PANEL BOARD
654. COOLING COIL FOR AIR CONDITIONERS
655. COPPER STRIP COIL FROM SCRAP
656. CORDLESS TELEPHONES
657. CYBER CAFE
658. CYBERKIOSK (Rs. 5000/-)
659. DATA PROCESSING CENTRE (Rs. 5000/-)
660. D.C. MICRO MOTORS
661. D.G.SETS
662. DISH ANTENNA AND CABLE T.V. NETWORK EQUIPMENT
663. DISTRIBUTION TRANSFORMERS & REPAIRS
664. DOMESTIC ELECTRICAL APPLIANCES- ROOM COOLER, WASHING MACHINE, WATER HEATER, ELECTRIC ROOM HEATER
665. E-SCHOOL
666. E-COMMERCE/BUSINESS
667. ELECTRIC ENERGY METER
668. ELECTRIC FANS
669. ELECTRIC HORN FOR AUTOMOBILE
670. ELECTRIC LAMP/GLS (INCANDESCENT LAMP)
671. ELECTRIC MIXER
672. ELECTRIC MOTORS UP TO 10 HP. REWINDING OF ALL TYPES OF MOTORS WATER PUMPS
673. ELECTRIC MOTOR WINDING (FOR FAN, MIXIES, ETC.)
674. ELECTRIC STEAM IRON
675. ELECTRICAL APPLIANCES
676. ELECTRICAL FIXTURES
677. ELECTRICAL STAMPING
678. ELECTROLYTIC CAPACITORS
679. ELECTROMAGNETIC RELAY
680. ELECTRONIC BALAST/CHOK
681. ELECTRICAL CHOKE
682. ELECTRONIC DIGITAL WATCHES
683. ELECTRONIC DIGITAL WEIGHING MACHINE
684. ELECTRONIC FIRE ALARM
685. ELECTRONIC GAS STOVE LIGHTERS
686. ELECTRONIC PRESSURE INDICATORS, ELECTRICALS, ELECTRONIC LIQUID LEVEL INDICATORS, ELECTRONIC TEMPERATURE INDICATOR, DIGITAL TACHOMETER
687. ELECTRONIC TELEPHONE INSTRUMENTS
688. ELECTRONIC TOYS
689. ELECTRONIC WATCHES & CLOCKS
690. FAX MACHINES
691. F.H.P MOTORS
692. FLOPPY DISKETTES
693. FLUORESCENT LAMP STARTER
694. FLUORESCENT TUBULAR

Above all the Detailed Project Reports are available at *"ENGINEERS INDIA RESEARCH INSTITUTE"*. 4449, Nai Sarak (D), Main Road Delhi - 110 006
●Ph : 91-11-23918117, 2391 6431, 23840361, 31082370 ●Fax : 91-11-2391 6431
●E-Mail : eirisidi@bol.net.in

LAMPS WITH INTRODUCTION TO MERCURY VAPOUR LAMP
695. FRANCHISEE COMPUTER EDUCATION CENTRE (Rs. 5000)
696. GAS DETECTOR (L.P.G)
697. GENERATOR SET & PUMP SETS
698. GENERATOR (BATTERY OPERATED)
699. GIS SERVICE CENTRE (GEOGRAPHICAL INFORMATION SYSTEMS)
700. HARDWARE FITTING FOR TRANSMISSION LINE OVERHEAD LINE MATERIAL
701. HEADERS FOR TRANSISTOR ICS SEMI CONDUCTOR
702. H.T & L.T INSULATORS
703. H.T & M.V INDUSTRIAL CUBICAL SWITCH BOARD
704. INFORMATION MOVING DISPLAY (L.E.D TYPE)
705. INSURANCE CLAIM PROCESSING CENTRE (EOU) (Rs. 5000/-)
706. INTEGRATED CIRCUITS
707. INTERNET BASED STOCK TRADING (Rs. 5000/-)
708. INTERNET SERVICE PROVIDER (I.S.P.)
709. JELLY FILLED TELEPHONE CABLES
710. LAP TOP COMPUTERS
711. LEAD ACID BATTERIES
712. LEAD ACID BATTERY PLATES AND ASSEMBLING OF BATTERY
713. LEGAL TRANSCRIPTION & SECRETARIAL SERVICES CENTER (EOU)(Rs. 5000/-)
714. LIGHT EMITTING DIODES (L.E.D)
715. LINEAR ICS TRAINER KIT
716. LOUD SPEAKER
717. L.T TRANSFORMER REPAIRING
718. MEDICAL TRANSCRIPTION CENTRE
719. METAL FILM RESISTORS
720. METALLISED POLYPROPYLENE, POLYESTER FILM CAPACITOR
721. MICA BASE ELECTRONIC COMPONENTS
722. MICA PAPER WASTE PAPER FROM MICA WASTE
723. MICRO PROCESSORS TRAINER KITS BASED ON MICRO PROCESSORS
724. MINI COMPUTER (PERSONAL COMPUTER)
725. MINIATURE CIRCUIT BREAKER (M.C.B)
726. MINIATURE WATCH BATTERIES (BUTTON CELL)
727. MIXER/GRINDER (MIXI)
728. MONO CHROME COMPUTER MONITOR
729. MOTOR START ELECTROLYTIC CAPACITOR
730. MULTI LAYER P.C.B
731. MULTIPLE RELAY FOR LOW VOLTAGE
732. NEON INDICATOR
733. NEON SIGN MANUFACTURE
734. OPTICAL FIBRE CABLES
735. ON LINE SHOPPING MALL (Rs. 5000/-)
736. OPTO MECHANICAL & ELECTRICAL EQUIPMENTS
737. PHOTO COLOUR LAB
738. PICTURE TUBE (B/W)
739. PLAIN PAPER COPIER
740. PLASTIC FILM CAPACITORS
741. POLYESTER CAPACITORS
742. PORTABLE GENERATOR SET
743. PORTAL
744. PORTABLE TELEVISION(TV)
745. POWER CAPACITORS
746. POWER INVERTERS
747. POWER PLANT
748. POWER TRANSFORMERS UP TO 600 KVA
749. PRINTED CIRCUIT BOARD
750. PVC WIRES & CABLES
751. RE-CONDITIONING OF PICTURE TUBE
752. RESIN CAST CT & PT (1 KV)
753. SEMI CONDUCTOR DEVICE
754. SEMI CONDUCTORS FOR TRANSISTORS & DIODES
755. SETTING UP OF A VIDEO STUDIO
756. SMOKE DETECTORS
757. SOLAR CELLS
758. SOLAR MODULES
759. SOLAR PHOTO VOLTAIC SYSTEM
760. SOLDER FLUXES
761. SOLAR WATER HEATING PANELS
762. STEEL FURNITURE & ELECTRICAL APPLIANCES
763. STEREO AMPLIFIERS
764. STEREO CASSETTE RECORDERS/PLAYERS
765. STREET LIGHT FITTINGS SURGE SUPPRESSOR
766. TANTALUM CAPACITORS
767. TEFLON COATED ELECTRIC CABLE
768. TELEMEDICINE (DISTANCE HEALTH CARE) (Rs. 5000/-)
769. TELEPHONE CORD/CABLE
770. TELEPHONE (PUSH BUTTON TYPE)
771. TELEPHONE (PUSH BUTTON & CORDLESS)
772. TELEVISION (CTV & B/W)
773. TELEVISION (3-D)
774. TELEVISION DEFLECTION COMPONENTS
775. TELEVISION SIGNAL BOOSTERS
776. TELEVISION TUNERS
777. TRACTION BATTERIES
778. TRAINING INSTITUTE OF MEDICAL TRANSCRIPTION
779. TRANSFORMER FOR B/W TV
780. TRANSFORMER FOR VOLTAGE STABILIZER & E.H.T
781. TRANSMISSION POWER LINE FITTING
782. TRANSMISSION TOWER FITTING
783. TV AUDIO EQUIPMENT CABINETS & THEIR ASSEMBLING UNIT
784. UN-INTERRUPTED POWER SUPPLY (U.P.S)
785. VARIABLE FREQUENCY
786. VARIABLE VOLTAGE A.C. DRIVE
787. VIDEO CASSETTES (COMPLETE MANUFACTURING & ASSEMBLING)
788. VIDEO CASSETTES RECORDER (V.C.R)
789. VIDEO FILM STUDIO
790. VOLTAGE REGULATOR FOR AUTOMOBILES
791. VOLTAGE STABILIZERS
792. VOLTAGE STABLIZER & T.V. GAIN BOOSTER
793. WAX AND CHEMICAL COATED, BRAIDED TINSEL WIRE
794. WEBSITE DESIGN & E-MAIL REGISTERING
795. WELDING ELECTRODES
796. WIND ENERGY POWER PROJECT (10 MW)
796A WIRES (METAL)

FOOD, AGRO FOOD, PROCESSED FOOD, AGRO PLANTATION, CULTIVATION, FARMING, DAIRY/MILK, TOBACCO/PAN MASALA, BREWERY & DISTILLERY, EDIBLE OILS, EOU FOOD PRODUCTS AND ALLIED PRODUCTS

797. ALCOHOLIC BEVERAGES & VENEGAR FROM COCONUT WATER
798. ALCOHOL DRINKS FROM ETHYL ALCOHOL BY MIXING OF VARIOUS FLAVOURS
799. ANTI SCALE COMPOUND FOR ADDING INTO SUGAR JUICE BOILING
800. APPLE JUICE CONCENTRATED & DEHYDRATED FRUIT & VEGETABLES
801. ARTIFICIAL FISH MEAL FOR POULTRY FEED
802. AUTOMATIC BISCUIT PLANT
803. BABY CEREAL FOOD AND MILK POWDER
804. BACTERIA FOR CANE JUICE
805. BAKER'S YEAST
806. BAKERY INDUSTRY
807. BANANA PUREE
808. BEER & WINE
809. BEER PLANT (BREWERY)
810. BIDI
811. BIDI & CIGARETTE
812. BISCUIT PLANT

813. BREAD (AUTOMATIC PLANT)
814. BLACK PEPPER (SPICES)
815. BREAD AND BISCUITS
816. BREEDING FARM
817. BROILER CHICKEN
819. BUTTON MUSHROOM CULTIVATION & PROCESSING
820. CANNING OF RASAGULLAS IN METAL CANS
821. CAFFEIN FROM TEA WASTE
822. CANNING OF FRUITS & VEGETABLES
823. CASEIN AND BY-PRODUCTS
824. CASHEW FRUIT JUICE FROM CASHEW FRUIT APPLE
825. CASHEWNUT KERNEL EXTRACTION FROM CASHEWNUT FRUIT
826. CASHEWNUT SHELL LIQUID & KERNEL PROCESSING
827. CASHEW FENI
828. CATECHEU (BY CHEMICAL PROCESS)
829. CATTLE FEED FROM TAPIOCA
830. CHEWING & BUBBLE GUM
831. CHICKEN/SHEEP MEAT PROCESSING
832. CHOCOLATE (MILK)
833. CIGARETTE AND BEEDIES
834. COCOA BUTTER FROM COCOA MASS
835. COCONUT PRODUCTS & BY PRODUCTS PROCESS COMPLEX
836. COLD/SOFT DRINKS
837. COLLECTION OF MILK AND MILK MAKING POWDER
838. COLLECTION OF MILK AND PACKING IN POLYTHENE POUCH (1/2 KG.1 KG. & 2 KG.)
839. CONDENSED MILK (SWEETNED)
840. CONFECTIONERY INDUSTRY (TOFFEE & CANDY, SEMI-AUTOMATIC PLANT)
841. COUNTRY LIQUOR FROM MOLASSES
842. CIGARETTE
843. DAIRY FARM AND DAIRY (MILK) PRODUCTS (PASTEURISED MILK, BUTTER, GHEE, PANEER)
844. DAIRY FARM TO PRODUCE MILK & PACKING IN POUCHES (50%) & CAN(50%)
845. DAIRY FOR MILK PROCESSING
846. DAIRY FARM (BUFALO)
847. DAL (PULSE) MILL UNIT
848. DEHYDRATION OF CARROT & GARLIC
849. DEHYDRATION & CANNING OF FRUITS & VEGETABLES
850. DEHYDRATION OF FIGS
851. DEHYDRATION OF FRUITS AND VEGETABLES
852. DEHYDRATED ONIONS AND ONION POWDER
853. DRY ICE BY BREAKING OF AIR
854. DRYING OF RED CHILLIES, HALDI, DHANIA, AND GREEN PEAS
855. EGG POWDER (40,000 EGGS PROCESSING PER DAY)
856. EXPORT OF PROCESSED FOODS AND MARINE PRODUCTS
857. FISH CANNING & POUCHING
859. FISH FARMING (PRAWN & OTHER MARINE PRODUCTS)
860. FISH MEAL
861. FLOUR MILL AND MUSTARD OIL
862. FOOD COLOUR & ORASTED GROUNDNUT GRAM PEAS, ETC IN POUCHES
863. FROG LEGS PROCESSING
864. FROZEN MEATS PROCESSING
865. FOOD FLAVOURS (WHISKY) VODKA, GRAPE, BUTTER SCOTCH)
866. FOOD PRODUCTS COMPLEX (DEHYDRATED ONIONS, GARLIC POWDER & FLAKES, CATTLE FEED, TOMATO POWDER, TOMATO PRODUCTS, CANNED FRUITS & VEGETABLES, TOMATO PURE, GROUN NUT OIL, REFIND OIL, DEHYDRATED GRAPES, BANANA POWDER & WAFFERS)
867. FRUIT JUICE, JAM, JELLIES & ALLIED PRODUCTS
868. FRUIT JUICE, PICKLES PROCESSING AND CANNING
869. FRUIT JUICE MAKING & PACKING IN PLASTIC CONTAINER/POUCHES
870. FRUIT PROCESSING (JAM & JELLIES)
871. FRUIT PULP & JUICE CONCENTRATES
872. FRUIT & VEGETABLE DRYING (FREEZE DRYING METHOD)
873. GOAT & SHEEP FARMING
874. GRAM DALL/PULSE MILL
875. GRAPE DEHYDRATION
876. HARD BOILED CANDY (TOFFEE & CANDY)
877. HERBAL CIGARETTES
878. HONEY PROCESSING & PACKAGING
879. ICE CREAM OF DIFFERENT FLAVOURS
880. ICE CREAM STABILIZER
881. ICE MAKING PLANT
882. INDIAN MADE FOREIGN LIQUOR (I.M.F.L)
883. INSTANT FOOD (IDLI MIX, DOSA MIX, GULAB JAMUN MIX)
884. INSTANT FOOD (INSTANT FOOD & FAST FOOD PARLOUR)
885. INSTANT NOODLES
886. INSTANT TEA
887. INSTANT TEA FROM BLACK TEA
888. INTEGERATED STARCH BAKING POWDER/YEAST INDUSTRY
889. IODIZED SALT
890. IODIZED SALT (ORDINARY MOISTURE-LESS/FREE FLOWING IN PLASTIC BAGS AND CONTAINERS)
891. JAM, JELLIES, FRUIT JUICE & ALLIED PRODUCTS
892. KATHA AND CUTCH
893. KHANDSARI SUGAR
894. KHANDSARI SUGAR & IMFL
895. LACTIC ACID FROM WHITE SUGAR BY FERMENTATION PROCESS
896. LACTOSE & BY PRODUCTS PROCESSING FROM MILK
897. LIQUID GLUCOSE AND ITS BYE PRODUCTS
898. MACRONI AND VERMICILLI
899. MALT EXTRACTION FROM BARLEY
900. MANGO PROCESSING (MANGO PULP, JUICE & SLICES)
901. MAYUR BRAND TYPE CHEWING TOBACCO
902. MINERAL WATER
903. MILK PRESERVATION & MARKETING TO WHOLE SELLERS (INPOUCH PACKING BY UHT TECHNOLOGY)
904. MILK PROCESSING AND PACKAGING OF MILK PRODUCTS
905. MILK PRODUCTS (CASEIN, LACTOSE, GHEE & WHEY POWDER)
906. MILK TOFFEE
907. MINI FLOUR MILL
908. MINI SUGAR PLANT
909. MISRI (PEARL SUGAR CANDIES)
910. MODERN RICE MILL
911. MURABBA
912. MUSTARD OIL EXTRACTION & REFINING
913. MUTTON TALLOW
914. NAMKEEN INDUSTRY (BHUJIA, CHANA CHUR ETC.)
915. NAMKEEN & SWEETS
916. NON-BASMATI RICE FROM PADDY
917. OLEORESIN, ESSENTIAL OIL, DYES & POWDER OF SPICES
918. OLEORESIN EXTRACTION FROM DIPTERO-CARPUT TURMINATUS AND PINUS KHASYANA
919. OLEORESIN EXTRACTION FROM CHILLI
920. PAN MASALA AND POUCH

1059. BUFFALO HORN TIP, HOOF
1060. BANQUET HALL
1061. BUTTON
1062. CALCINED PETROLEUM (C.P) COKE
1063. CANVAS SHOES
1064. CANVAS SHOES, JUNGLE BOOTS
1065. CARBON BRUSH, BRUSH HOLDER & SLIP RING
1066. CEMENT SHEETS WITH COIR FIBRE & OTHER SEGMENTS
1067. CERAMIC TILES (GLAZED) BY DOUBLE FIRING/HEATING
1068. CHILDREN RECREATION CENTRE
1069. COAL BRIQUETTES
1070. COLD STORAGE & ICE
1071. COLD STORAGE FOR FRUITS AND VEGETABLES
1072. COMPRESSOR (HERMETIC) FOR AIR CONDITIONER
1073. COSTUME JEWELLERY/ IMITATION JEWELLERY
1074. DECORATIVE LAMINATED SHEET (SUNMICA)
1075. DIAMOND CUTTING & EXPORTS
1076. DRINKING STRAW FROM PROPYLENE
1077. ENGINEERING COLLEGE
1078. ENTERTAINMENT CLUB
1079. FASHION TECHNOLOGY INSTITUTE
1080. FAST FOOD PARLOUR
1081. FAST FOOD (INSTANT FOOD & FAST FOOD PARLOUR)
1082. FIRE EXTINGUISHERS (SODA ACID TYPE)
1083. FISH NET
1084. FLORICULTURE (CUT FLOWER ROSE) WITH GREEN HOUSE
1085. FLOOR COVERING SHEET
1086. FILM STUDIO (VIDEO)
1087. FLUSH DOOR, CHIP BOARD, WOOD WOOL & OTHER INSULATING BOARDS
1088. GAS DETECTORS OF L.P.G
1089. GEMS MANUFACTURING
1090. GLASS BOTTLE BY SCRAP
1092. GOAT & SHEEP FARMING
1093. GOLD ELECTROPLATING
1094. GOLD JEWELLERY (E.O.U)
1095. GOLD PLATED SILVER JEWELLERY & CUTLERY
1096. GRANITE SLAB AND TILES
1097. GREEN HOUSE
1098. HARD CHROMIUM PLATING
1099. HEALTH CLUB AND BEAUTY PARLOUR CUM HAIR SALOON WITH SONA BATH
1100. HEALTH CLUB CUM BEAUTY PARLOUR TRAININGINSTITUTE
1101. HORN TIP,HOOVE BUTTON
1102. HOSPITAL
1103. HOSPITAL (100 BEDS)
1104. HOSPITAL (200 BEDS)
1105. ICE MAKING PLANT
1106. IMITATION AND COSTUME
1107. JEWELLERY (NECKLACE, EARRINGS EAR TOP ETC.)
1108. INITMATE SCENT CHEMICALS FROM ALL TYPES OF FLAVOUR
1109. INVESTMENT CASTING
1110. JUTE, COIR, GLASS ROPE/ SUTLI
1111. JUTE TWINE
1112. L.P.G BOTTLING PLANT
1113. L.P.G REGULATOR (DOMESTIC PURPOSE)
1114. LAMINATED PARTICLE BOARD & HARD BOARD
1115. LAMINATED SAFETY AND TOUGHENED GLASS
1116. LEASING & HIRE PURCHASE
1117. LICHEN (CHARILA)
1118. MANILA ROPES
1119. MEDICAL COLLEGE
1120. MATCH UNIT FROM WAXED PAPER
1121. MEDIUM DENSITY FIBRE BOARD
1122. MELAMINE CROCKERY
1123. MINERAL WATER
1124. MINI CEMENT PLANT
1125. MIRROR SILVER, GOLDEN, PINK, BLACK & SMOKES
1126. MODERN ADVERTISING AGENCY WITH DTP & FILM STUDIO
1127. MOTEL/SMALL HOTEL
1128. MULTI COLOUR PRINTING
1129. MULTI STOREY COMMERCIAL COMPLEX ALONGWITH RESIDENTIAL AND DELUX FLATS FOR FOREIGN TOURISTS & REVOLVING RESTAURENT AT THE TOP
1130. MULTIPLE LAMINATION INDUSTRY
1131. MUSHROOM GROWING AND PROCESSING (BY DEEP FREEZING METHOD)
1132. NEWS PAPER PRINTING
1133. NICKEL LINED INDUSTRIAL SCREEN
1134. OFFSET COLOUR PRINTING PRESS (SIX COLOUR)
1135. OFFSET PRINTING PRESS
1136. P.C.C ELECTRIC POLES
1137. PHOTOGRAPHIC DEVELOPER & FIXER
1138. PVC EXTRUSION PROFILE (DOOR & WINDOWS)
1139. POP-CORN
1140. PHOTO ETCHING OF S.S.
1141. PRE STRESSED CEMENT CONCRETE PIPES
1142. PILFER PROOF CAPS
1143. PILFER PROOF CAPS AND CROWN CAP
1144. POUCH MAKING & GRAVURE PRINTING (ROTO PRINTING)
1145. POULTRY & FISH FARMING (INTEGERATED UNIT)
1146. PRINTING OF TIN SHEETS
1147. READYMADE GARMENTS
1148. RESTAURANT
1149. ROSE PLANTATION AND ROSE OIL EXTRACTION
1150. ROTOGRAVURE PRINTING
1151. SAFETY BELTS
1152. SAFETY MATCHES
1153. SHOE LACES
1154. SILK COCOON CULTIVATION (GROWING OF SILK COCOON WARM)
1155. SILK SCREEN PRINTING FORMULATIONS FOR PLASTIC, PAPER & CLOTH
1156. SPIKENARD (JATAMANSI)
1157. STENCIL COATING SOLUTION
1158. SUGAR CANDY (MISRI)
1159. SUGAR CANE PLANTATION
1160. SUGAR CANE JUICE PRESERVATION
1161. SURAT ZARI
1162. SYNTHETIC SHOES & SOLES
1163. TEA PACKAGING INDUSTRY
1164. TENNIS BALLS
1165. THREE STAR HOTEL
1166. TRAVELLING AGENCY
1167. TRAYS, TROLLEYS FOR HOSPITAL WITH SCRATCHLESS COATING
1168. WAX EXTRACTS (TANNING POWDER)
1169. WIRE ROPE SLINGS
1170. WOOD WOOL SLAB
1171. WOODEN CANE FURNITURE WITH EXPORT POTENTIAL
1172. WOODEN FURNITURE
1173. WOODEN PANEL INCLUDING KILN SEASONING
1174. WOODEN FURNITURE
1175. WATCH CASE BUFFING
1176. WATCH DIAL
1177. WRIST WATCHES
1178. WATCHES (ELECTRONIC)
1179. ZEDOARY (KACHUR)

EDIBLE OILS, ESSENTIAL OILS LURICATIING OILS, GREASES, VEGETABLE OILS, WAXES, CAMPHOR, PERFUMES & PERFUMERY COMPOUNDS AND REFINED OILS ETC.

1180. AROMATIC PERFUMERY COMPOUND
1181. AEROSOL
1182. AGARBATTI PERFUMERY COMPOUND
1183. BEES WAX MANUFACTURE
1184. CAMPHOR
1185. CARDANOL FROM CASHEW NUT SHELL LIQUID
1186. CASTOR OIL
1187. CASTOR OIL DERIVATIVE OLEORESINS
1188. CHILLI OIL
1189. CITRONELLA OILS
1190. CLOVE OIL
1191. CONCENTRATE OF ROSE JASMINE & LILY ETC.
1192. COLOURED FLAME CANDLE

Price Rs. 4320/- for each "Detailed Project Report" Payable in advance through Draft/Cash/M.O. in favour of *"ENGINEERS INDIA RESEARCH INSTITUTE"*. 4449, Nai Sarak (D), Main Road Delhi - 110 006 *OR Ask by V.P.P.* • Ph : 23918117, 2391 6431, 23840361 •Fax : 91-11- 2391 6431 •E-Mail : eirisidi@bol.net.in • WebSite : www.startindustry.com

1193. CANDLES (SEMI-AUTOMATIC)
1194. CORN OIL (MAIZE OIL)
1195. DEHYDRATED CASTOR OIL
1196. EUGENOL FROM CINNAMON LEAF OIL
1197. EXTRACTION OF ESSENTIAL OIL (CARDAMON, JEERA, AJOWAN, GINGER OILS ETC. & PACKAGING OF GROUND SPICES)
1198. EXTRACTION OF JASMINE ESSENCE
1199. EXTRACTION OF ESSENTIAL OILS BY SUPER CRITICAL FLUID METHOD FROM FLOWERS, HERBS & SPICES
1200. EUCALYPTUS OIL
1201. EXTRACTION OF OIL FROM OIL SEED EXPANDEREXTRUSION TECHNOLOGY)
1202. FAT LIQUOR SULPHATED OIL
1203. FLAVOURS FOR FOOD
1204. GARLIC OIL & POWDER
1205. GINGER OIL, SANDALWOOD OIL AND NAGARMOTHA OIL
1206. GINGER OIL
1207. GINGER OIL & GINGER DUST
1208. INTEGERATED WAX COMPLEX
1209. IONONE FROM LEMON GRASS OIL
1210. JASMINE & LILLY FLOWER OIL
1211. LEMON GRASS OIL
1212. LIQUID PARAFFIN
1213. LUBE OIL & GREASE
1214. LUBRICATING OIL
1215. MENTHOL CRYSTALS
1216. MENTHOL OIL & CRYSTAL
1217. MICRO CRYSTALLINE WAX
1218. MUSTARD OIL (EDIBLE OIL)
1219. OIL FROM ARTEMISIA HERBS
1220. PALM OIL CRUSHING UNIT
1221. PAN MASALA
1222. PARAFFIN WAX
1223. PARAFFIN WAX FROM SLACK WAX
1224. REFINED OIL-SUN FLOWER OIL, GROUNDNUT OIL, STAFF FLOWER OIL & COTTON SEED OIL
1225. REFINED VEGETABLE OIL
1226. RECLAMATION OF USED ENGINE OIL
1227. RICE BRAN OIL (R.B.O)
1228. ROSE OIL EXTRACTION
1229. SMOKE LESS CANDLE
1230. SPICE OIL & OLEORESINS
1231. SOLVENT EXTRACTION PLANT (OIL CAKE BASED)
1232. SYNTHETIC ALMOND OIL
1233. SYNTHETIC TALLOW
1234. SYNTHETIC GHEE
1235. VEGETABLE OIL EXTRACTION & REFINING
1236. WADDING OIL (100%) FOR WADDING OF COTTON HOSIERY CLOTH IN DYEING PROCESS
1237. WAX EMULSION FOR TEXTILE
1238. WAX FLOOR POLISH

PAINT, ENAMEL, SOLVENTS, THINNERS, INKS & VARNISH

1239. ACRYLIC EMULSION PAINTS
1240. ALUMINIUM PAINT
1241. AUTOMOBILE PAINTS
1242. BALL POINT PEN REFILL INK
1243. BITUMINIOUS ROAD EMULSION
1244. BITUMEN
1245. BITUMINIOUS FELTS FOR WATER & DAMP PROOFING
1246. BITUMINIOUS ROAD EMULSION RAPID MEDIUM & SLOW SETTING
1247. BUFFING & POLISHING
1248. CEMENT PAINT FOR WHITE & GREY CEMENT

1249. DISPERSANT
1250. DRY DISTEMPER
1251. DRY DISTEMPER & CEMENT PAINT
1252. DUPLICATING INK BLACK FOR GESTNER DUPLICATOR
1255. EMULSION PAINTS (WATER BASED)
1256. HAMMERTONE PAINT
1257. INSULATING VARNISH & WIRE ENAMEL
1258. IRON OXIDE PIGMENTS
1259. INSULATING VARNISH (POLY VINYL BUTYRAL BASED, FFC GRADE)
1260. LIME COLOUR (CEMENT COLOUR)
1261. SYNTHETIC RED OXIDE FOR FLOORINGS
1262. SOLVENT & THINNERS
1263. MARKING INKS (WATER PROOF)
1264. METAL NAPHTHANATE (AS DRIER FOR PAINTS)
1265. N.C.PUTTY
1266. OFFSET PRINTING INK
1267. OIL BOUND DISTEMPER PAINT
1268. PAINT BRUSHES
1269. PAINT REMOVERS
1270. PAINT INDUSTRY
1271. PAINT & VARNISH
1272. PICTURE VARNISH
1273. POWDER COATING PAINT
1274. PRINTING INKS (OFFSET, FLEXO & ROTO GRAVURE)
1275. PRIMER PAINT & ENAMEL PAINT
1276. PUTTY & WATER PROOFING PAINT
1277. PRINTING INKS (FLEXO-GRAPHIC INK)
1278. PUTTY (METAL CASEMENT)
1279. RED OXIDE PRIMER (ANTI CORROSIVE)
1280. REFRECTORY PAINT (GRAPHITE BASED)
1281. SCREEN PRINTING INKS
1282. SILK SCREEN PRINTING INK FORMULATION FOR PLASTIC, PAPER, CLOTH
1283. STAMP & PAD INK
1284. STOVING PAINT
1285. SPIRIT SOLUBLE MALEIC RESIN
1286. TEXTURE PAINT
1287. THINNERS AND ITS ALLIED PRODUCTS
1288. TONER INK
1289. VARNISH THINNER (SOLVENT)
1290. VACUUM METALLIZING LACQUERS
1291. WOOD PRIMER

PHARMACEUTICAL, DRUGS, AYURVEDIC/HERBAL COSMETICS & MEDICINES, HOMOEOPATHIC MEDICINES, DISPOSABLE SYRINGE, DENTAL COLLEGE & FINE CHEMICALS ETC.

1292. AROMATIC PILLS
1293. ASPIRIN
1294. AYURVEDIC PAIN BALM OINTMENTS
1295. AYURVEDIC CHURAN AND TABLETS
1296. AYURVEDIC TABLETS (HAJMOLA TYPE)
1297. AYURVEDIC/HERBAL PHARMACY
1298. AYURVEDIC SHERBATS
1299. AYURVEDIC PRODUCTS
1300. BULK DRUGS (E.O.U)
1301. BLOOD BAGS
1302. CALCIUM GLUCONATE
1303. CAPSULE, TABLET & INJECTION WITH MODERN INSTRUMENTS
1304. CASHEW FENI
1305. CHLOROQUINONE PHOSPHATE (BULK DRUGS)
1306. CLINICAL THERMOMETER
1307. DENTAL CLINIC

Above all the Detailed Project Reports are available at *"ENGINEERS INDIA RESEARCH INSTITUTE"*. 4449, Nai Sarak (D), Main Road Delhi - 110 006
● Ph : 91-11-23918117, 2391 6431, 23840361, 31082370 ●Fax : 91-11-2391 6431
●E-Mail : eirisidi@bol.net.in

1308. DENTAL COLLEGE
1309. DENTAL GRADE EUGENOL
1310. DEXTROSE MONOHYDRATE, LIQUID GLUCOSE
1311. DEHYDRATED ONION & ONION POWDER
1312. DEXTROSE POWDER (ANHYDROUS FROM STARCH)
1314. DEXTROSE SALINE SOLUTION
1315. DISTILLERY (I.M.F.L)
1316. DISPOSABLE NEEDLES FOR SYRINGES
1317. DISPRIN
1318. DISTILLED WATER
1319. EMPTY HARD GELATINE CAPSULES
1320. FILLING & PACKING OF CAPSULES
1321. GLUCOSE - D - POWDER
1322. GLYCERINE
1323. HERBAL COSMETICS
1324. HERBAL SHAMPOO
1325. HERBAL HAIR OILS (AYURVEDIC)
1326. HOMOE & BIO-MEDICINES WITH MOTHER TINCTURE
1327. HOMOEPATHIC MEDICINES
1328. HYPODERMIC NEEDLES
1329. I.V. FLUIDS
1330. IBUPROFEN
1331. INFUSION & TRANSFUSION SETS (I.V. SET)
1332. INJECTABLE FOR PHARMACEUTICALS
1333. INJECTION AMPOULES PACKAGING BOX
1334. INTEGERATED SURGICAL COTTON
1335. ICE MAKING PLANT
1336. ICE & COLD STORAGE
1337. LACTOSE & BY PRODUCTS PROCESSING FROM MILK
1338. LICHEN (JATAMANSI CHARILA)
1339. LIQUID GLUCOSE AND ITS BY-PRODUCTS
1340. L-LYSINE MONOHYDRO CHLORIDE
1341. LIQUID GLUCOSE FROM POTATOES
1342. MEDICAL COLLEGE
1343. NICOTINE FROM TOBACCO WASTE
1344. OINTMENT-AYURVEDIC (YELLOW & WHITE)
1345. PHARMACEUTICAL AND FOOD GRADE GELATINE
1346. PHARMACEUTICAL INDUSTRY (TABLETS, CAPSULES, LIQUID, GEL, OINTMENT POWDER INJECTABLE)
1347. PHARMACEUTICAL UNIT (EOU) WITH FORMULA TIONS, INJECTABLES, ETC. PYRIDINE & DERIVATIVES
1348. SALT (IODIZED SALT)
1349. SALINE & INJECTION WATER
1350. SALINE WATER & DEXTROSE SOLUTION (I.V.FLUID IN PLASTIC BOTTLES)
1351. SORBITOL
1352. STARCH (MAIZE)
1353. SURGICAL ADHESIVE PLASTER
1354. SURGICAL BANDAGES
1355. SURGICAL GLOVES
1357. SURGICAL COTTON
1358. SURGICAL COTTON AND BANDAGE
1359. SYNTHETIC CAMPHOR POWDER
1360. TABLETS & CAPSULES
1361. TISSUE CULTURE
1362. TINCTURE FROM RECTIFIED SPIRIT
1363. TRIMETHOPIME
1364. VETERENARY MEDICINES (ONLY FORMULATIONS)
1365. VITAMIN 'C', SORBITOL' ANHYDROUS DEXTROSE, STARCH

PULP, PAPER, STRAW/GREY BOARD, KRAFT PAPER, PACKAGING, PAPER CARRY BAGE, PAPER FROM AGRO WASTE & STATIONERY ETC.

1366. AMMONIA PAPER
1367. AUTOMATIC BOOK BINDING
1368. ADHESIVE (FEVICOL TYPE)
1369. ALL PIN & GEM CLIPS
1370. CARBON PAPER
1371. CARD BOARD
1372. CARBON LESS PAPER
1373. CELLPHANE PAPER
1374. COMPUTER FORMS & SECURITY PRINTING PRESS
1375. CORRUGATED BOARD & BOX (PRINTED & LAMINATED)
1376. CORRUGATED BOARD AND BOXES FROM FROM CARD BOARDS
1377. CORRUGATED CARTONS FROM PLAIN PAPERS
1378. CORRUGATRED PACKING & MATERIAL (BULB & TUBES PACKING)
1379. DESK TOP PUBLISHING
1380. DEFOAMING AGENT FOR PAPER PLANT
1381. DRINKING STRAW PAPER
1382. D.T.P CUM OFFSET PRESS
1383. EGG TRAYS
1384. EXERCISE NOTE BOOK, REGISTER AND PAD
1385. FLEXOGRAPHIC INK
1386. GREETING CARD BY OFFSET PRESS
1387. HAND MADE PAPER FILTER PAPER
1388. HARD BOARD
1389. INJECTION AMPOULES PACKAGING BOXES
1390. INSULATIING PAPER
1391. KRAFT PAPER
1392. KRAFT PAPER FROM BAGASSE
1393. LAMINATED PACKAGING PAPER WITH PRINTING
1394. LAMINATION & COATING ON PAPER
1395. M.G. PAPER FROM WASTE PAPER
1396. MILL PAPER FROM WASTE PAPER
1397. MILL BOARD FROM RICE & WHEAT STRAWS
1398. MILL BOARD FROM WASTE PAPER
1399. MINI PAPER PLANT FROM SISAL
1400. MINI PAPER PLANT
1401. MULTI WALL PAPER SACKS
1402. NEWS PAPER FOR CHILDREN
1403. NEWS PRINT PAPER FROM RICE STRAW BAGASSE
1404. NEWS PAPER CHILDRENS
1405. NEWS PRINT PAPER
1406. OFFSET AND TREADLE TYPE PRINTING PRESS
1407. MILL BOARD BASED ON RICE STRAW
1408. PAPER AND BOARD FROM STRAW
1409. PAPER & PAPER PRODUCTS
1410. PAPER ENVELOPES
1411. PAPER CARRY BAGS
1412. PAPER BOARD CARTON
1413. PAPER CONES FOR LOUD SPEAKERS
1414. PAPER FROM AKRA
1415. PAPER FROM BAGASSE WITH CORRUGATED BOARD & BOXES
1416. PAPER FROM BAMBOO
1417. PAPER GLASSES FOR BEVERAGES
1418. PAPER FROM RICE HUSK & WHEAT HUSK
1419. PAPER FROM TREE BARK, EUCALYPRUS WOOD
1420. PAPER PRODUCTS
1421. PAPER PLANT (WHITE WRITING & NEWS PAPER FOR PULP & WASTE PAPER)
1422. PAPER PLATES, PAPER GLASS
1423. PAPER CONES & TUBES
1425. PAPER PLANT WITH DTP & PRINTING & PUBLISHING UNIT
1426. PAPER BASED PHENOLIC SHEET
1427. PAPER CUP FOR ICE CREAM
1428. PAPER TUBES SPIRAL WINDING COMPOSIT CONTAINER
1429. PAPER LABLE FOR BEER BOTTLES
1430. PARTICLE BOARD & BLACK BOARD WITH SANDING & LAMINATION OF PARTICLE BOARD
1431. PARTICLE BOARD FROM RICE HUSK
1432. POUCH FILLING & MAKING FOR TOMATO SAUCE
1433. POUCH MAKING &

GRAVURE PRINTING
1434. PROCESSING OF PAPER FOR FEEDING IN COMPUTER
1435. PULP FROM BAMBOO & WOOD
1436. PAPER FILES
1437. PLAYING CARDS
1438. ROSIN SIZING AGENT (FOR PAPER PLANT)
1439. SAND PAPER
1440. SANITRY NAPKINS
1441. SILICON COATED PAPER
1442. STENCIL PAPER
1443. STRAW BOARD AND GREY BOARD
1444. STRAW BOARD & MILL BOARD
1445. STRAW BOARD AND PAPER BOARD
1446. TISSUE PAPER FACIAL
1447. TISSUE MOIST TOILETERY CLEANSING TISSUE AND RELATED PRODUCTS
1448. TISSUE PAPER ROLLS
1449. TETRA PACK FOR MILK PACKAGING, GHEE & OTHER LIQUIDS
1450. TOILET PAPER ROLLS
1451. TOILET PAPER & NAPKINS
1452. WAX COATED PRINTED PAPER
1453. WET FACE FRESHNER TISSUE
1454. WHITE WRITING & PRINTING PAPER
1455. WRITING & PRINTING PAPER (PAPER MILLS)

PLASTIC, B.O.P.P, ACRYLIC, DISPOSABLE PLASTIC PRODUCTS, PET PRODUCTS, P.V.C, H.D.P.E, P.P, L.D.P.E., P.U, A.B.S, THERMOFOARMING, MASTER BATCHES, & POLYMER AND RUBBER PRODUCTS, TYRE, TUBE, ADHESIVE, SHEET, COIR & MANY OTHERS

1456. ABS GRANULES FROM ABS SCRAPS FROM OLD T.V. CABINETS, WHITE GOODS ETC.
1457. ACRYLIC BEADS
1458. ACRYLIC COPOLYMER EMULSION
1459. ACRYLIC LATEX
1460. ACRYLIC SHEET
1461. ACRYLIC SHEET & MOULDED PRODUCTS
1462. ACRYLIC TEETH
1463. AUTO TUBES
1464. AUTO FLAPS FOR TRUCKS & BUSES
1465. AUTO TYRES & TUBES
1466. BABY BOTTLES (PLASTIC) WITH WHITESILICON RUBBER NIPPLES
1467. B.O.P.P. FILM
1468. B.O.P.P. PRESSURE SENSITIVE SELF ADHESIVE TAPE
1469. BABY NIPPLE (SILICON)
1470. BABY NIPPLE (BIG SIZE)
1471. BALLOON PLASTIC ADVERTISING
1472. BLISTER FILM PVC
1473. BLISTER PACKAGING & POUCH PAKAGING
1474. BLOW MOULDING PLASTIC CONTAINER
1475. COATING ON METALIZED POLYESTER FILM/METALISED PAPER/ ALIMINIUM FOIL
1476. COATING ON PLASTIC (ELECTROLYSIS) & GLASS
1477. COIR FOAM (RUBBERISED)
1478. COLOUR COATING ON PLASTICS
1479. COLOUR MASTER BATCHES FOR VARIOUS PLASTICS
1480. CYCLE TYRES AND TUBES
1481. DISPOSABLE PLASTIC CUPS GLASSES, ETC.
1482. DISPOSABLE PLASTIC SYRINGES & NEEDLES
1483. DISPOSABLE PLASTIC SYRINGES
1484. DOUGH MOULDING COMPOUND (D.M.C)
1485. EPOXY RESIN
1486. EXPANDED POLYESTRENE MOULDING (THERMOCOLE)
1487. F.R.P AUTO,SCOOTER ROOFS & CEILINGS
1488. F.R.P PRODUCTS (HELMET, WASHBASIN SHEETS, ROOFING SHEETS)
1489. FIBRE REINFORCED PLASTIC (HIGH PRESSURE MOULDING WITH SMC BMC AND DMC)
1490. FIELD RUBBER CONVERTED TO THE 60% LATEX RUBBER
1491. FLEXIBLE P.U. FOAM
1492. FORMALDEHYDE CROCKERY & OTHER ITEMS
1493. FORMALDEHYDE RESIN (UREA, PHENOL,MELEMINE)
1494. GASKET SHEET
1495. GUM BOTTLE (PVC)
1496. GLASS BEADS
1497. HDPE COATED PAPER SACK
1498. H.D.P.E. BAGS
1499. H.D.P.E. CONTAINERS (BLOW MOULDING)
1500. H.D.P.E. CONTAINER, POLY JARS BY INJECTION MOULDING (FOOD GRADE)
1501. H.D.P.E. JERRY CANS
1502. HDPE MANUFACTURING FROM ETHYLALCOHOL
1503. H.D.P.E PIPE AND FITTINGS
1504. H.D.P.E. PIPES
1505. H.D.P.E PRINTED BAGS
1506. H.D.P.E TWINES AND ROPES
1507. H.D.P.E. & L.D.P.E PIPES AND FITTINGS
1508. H.D.P.E/PP BOX STRAPPING
1509. H.D.P.E/PP WOVEN SACKS USING PLAIN LOOMS
1510. HOLOGRAM STICKERS-3D
1511. H.M BAG PLANT WITH PRINTING UNIT
1512. HAWAI CHAPPALS (RUBBER)
1513. I.V PLASTIC BOTTLE
1514. ICE CREAM CUP (PLASTIC)
1515. INJECTION MOULDED AUTO COMPONENTS
1516. INJECTION & BLOW MOULDED PLASTIC PRODUCTS
1517. INJECTION MOULDED PLASTIC PRODUCTS
1518. INTEGERATED COMPLEX ESTER'S & ALLIED PRODUCTS (D.O.P,D.B.P, & ETHYL ACETATE, BUYTL ACETATE, WIRE ENAMELS, JELLY CABLE COMPOUND)
1519. L.D.P.E. (LOW DENSITY POLY ETHYLENE) GRANULES FROM VIRGIN (L.D.P.E. RESIN)
1520. INTEGERATED SURGICAL RUBBER GOODS INDUSTRY
1521. INJECTION MOULDED PLASTIC BALLS
1522. L.D.P.E FROM ETHYL ALCOHOL
1523. LDPE MOULDED PRODUCTS
1524. LAMINATION OF COEXTRUSION MULTILAYER FILM IN ROLL FORM
1525. LATEX RUBBER
1526. LATEX RUBBER CONDOM
1527. MASTER BATCHES (COLOURED, P.V.C, L.D.P.E, H.D.P.E, ETC.)
1528. MELAMINE FORMALHYDE RESIN
1529. MOULDED LUGGAGE
1530. MULTI-LAYER (3 LAYER BAGS)
1531. MULTI-LAYER (3 LAYER) FILM WITH LAMINATION & PRINTING
1532. OIL SEAL
1533. PET BOTTLE/CONTAINERS
1534. PET BOTTLES FROM PRE FORM
1535. PET BOTTLE & MINERAL WATER
1536. PET PRE-FORM FROM PET RESIN
1537. PET PRE-FORM CUM PET BOTTLES
1538. PET PRE-FORM PET BOTTLES CUM MINERAL WATERS
1539. POLY CARBONATE RESIN
1540. PTFE COMPONENTS
1541. PU/PVC SOLE FOR SPORT SHOE BY IMPORTED M/C.
1542. PVC BATTERY SEPARATOR
1543. P.V.C COMPOUNDS (FRESH)
1544. P.V.C COMPOUNDS (SCRAP)
1545. P.V.C ELECTRICAL INSULATING TAPE
1546. P.V.C. EXTRUSION PROFILES
1547. P.V.C FITTINGS
1548. P.V.C FLEXIBLE FUSIBLE POWDER HEAT FUSIBLE POWDER
1549. P.V.C GRANULES (FOR

Above all the Detailed Project Reports are available at *"ENGINEERS INDIA RESEARCH INSTITUTE"*. 4449, Nai Sarak (D), Main Road Delhi - 110 006
• Ph : 91-11-23918117, 2391 6431, 23840361, 31082370 • Fax : 91-11-2391 6431
• E-Mail : eirisidi@bol.net.in

INSULATION & SHEETS GRADES)
1550. P.V.C GRANULES FROM PVC SCRAPS (WITH POLLUTION CONTROL)
1551. P.V.C HOSES
1552. P.V.C LEATHER CLOTH
1553. P.V.C FLEXIBLE PIPES
1554. P.V.C PIPES AND FITTINGS
1555. POLYTHENE BAGS (PRINTED)
1556. PVC PLASTICS FILM SHEET SOFT/RIGID
1557. PVC RESIN AND COMPOUND
1558. PVC RULAR
1559. PVC STABLIZERS (SINGLE PACK SYSTEM)
1560. PVC WIRE AND CABLES
1561. PAPER BASED PHENOLIC SHEET FOR ELECTRICAL
1562. PHENOL FORMALDEHYDE RESIN
1563. PHENOLIC RESIN
1564. PLASTIC BEADS FROM PLASTIC SCRAPS
1565. PLASTIC BUTTONS
1566. PLASTIC CANS
1567. PLASTIC COLLAPSIBLE TUBE
1568. PLASTIC CORRUGATED SHEET & BOXES
1569. PLASTIC FILM AND SHEETS WITH PRINTING FLEXO & ROTO/LDPE/HDPE/PP/HM/PVC
1570. PLASTIC FILTER MASTER BATCH & OTHER MASTER BATCHES FOR VARIOUS PLASTICS
1571. PLASTIC JERRY CANS
1572. PLASTIC GRANULES OR POWDER FROM PLASTIC SCRAP
1573. PLASTIC INJECTION MOULDED T.V. CABINETS
1574. PLASTIC ITEMS MANUFAC TURE FROM POWDER MELAMINE
1575. PLASTIC GOODS
1576. PLASTIC PIPES & TARPAULINES
1577. PLASTIC SHEET FROM SCRAP
1578. PLASTIC PLANT (BLOW MOULDING & INJECTION MOULDING)
1579. PLASTIC PRODUCTS (GOLD, SILVER, NICKEL)
1580. PLASTIC TOYS
1581. POLYESTER BEADING
1582. POLYESTER FILM
1583. POLYTHENE BAGS & AUTOMATIC PRINTING
1584. POLYTHENE PRINTED BAGS
1585. POLYURETHANE FOAM AND ITS PRODUCTS
1586. PROPYLENE FILM (PRINTED) & BAG MANUFACTURING
1587. PLASTIC MATS
1588. RAINBOW COLOUR ON PVC FILM & SHEET
1589. RED MUD PVC PIPES AND FITTINGS
1590. RE-RUBBERISED OF SOLID TYPE
1591. RESIN COATED SAND REXINE
1592. REXINE CLOTH & ALLIED PRODUCTS
1593. RUBBER ADHESIVE
1594. RUBBER AUTO PARTS
1595. RUBBER BELTING
1596. RUBBER MOULDING UNIT INCLUDING LINING RUBBER SHEETING
1597. RUBBER RECLAIMING
1598. RUBBER ROLLERS FOR TEXTILE MILLS & PAPER INDUSTRIES
1599. RUBBER & PLASTIC SHEETS, MATS & FLAPS
1600. RUBBER SHEET AND ALLIED HOSPITAL RUBBER GOODS
1601. RUBBERIZED PVC GASKET
1602. RUBBERISED COIR
1603. RUBBER COMPOUND FOR AUTOMOBILES
1604. SAFETY BELTS
1605. SILVER AND GOLD PLATING ON PVC AND NYLON-6
1606. SILICONE RUBBER NIPPLES/ TEATS
1607. SPECTACLE FRAMES (PLASTIC)
1608. SPUNGE RUBBER
1609. SURGICAL EXAMINATION GLOVES
1610. SYNTHETIC PEARL COATING ON POLYSTYRENE BEADS
1611. SYNTHETIC RUBBER ADHESIVE
1612. TEFLON MANUFACTURING
1613. TEFLON TAPE
1614. TEFLON TAPES & CABLES
1615. THERMOCOLE SHEET AND MOULDED PRODUCTS EXPANDED POLYESTERENE EXTRUSION PROFILES
1616. THERMOFORMED PACKAGING (BLISTER PACKAGING & POUCH PACKAGING)
1617. THERMOPLASTIC POLYURETHANE
1618. THERMOFORMED CUPS, PLATES & GLASS WITH HIPS SHEET
1619. THERMOCOLE
1620. THERMOCOLE BASED DISPOSABLE GLASS, CUPS & PLATES
1621. TOOTH BRUSHES
1622. TOY BALLOON, DECORA TIVE & INDUSTRIAL BALLOONS
1623. TREAD RUBBER
1624. TYRE RETREADING (HOT)
1625. TYRE RETREADING BY COLD PROCESS
1626. TYRE TUBES & FLAPS
1627. TYRE & TUBES
1628. UNSATURATED POLYESTER FOR REXINE
1629. V-BELT AND FAN BELT
1630. VINYL ASBESTOS AND PVC WALL PAPER
1631. VITON (FLUORO ELASTOMER)

SOAP, COSMETICS & PERFUMS

1632. ACID SLURRY, SYNTHETIC DETERGENT POWDER
1632. ACID SLURRY
1633. AGARBATTI SYNTHETIC, PERFUMERY COMPOUND
1634. AFTER SHAVE LOTION
1635. ANTISEPTIC CREAM
1636. BETA IONONE
1637. BLEACHING POWDER
1638. BLUE DETERGENT POWDER
1639. CLEANING POWDER (VIMTYPE)
1640. COLD CREAM
1641. COLOURED FLAME & PERFUMED CANDLES (RED, BLUE, GREEN FLAME)
1642. COSMETIC INDUSTRY (MODERN)
1643. COSMETIC INDUSTRY (SHAMPOO, SPRAY PERFUME, TALCUM POWDER
1644. DETERGENT POWDER (ARIEL TYPE)
1645. DETERGENT POWDER (NIRMA TYPE) FULLY AUTOMATIC PLANT
1646. DETERGENT WASHING POWDER
1647. FISH OIL SOAP
1648. GLYCERINE TRANSPARENT SOAP
1649. HAIR REMOVING CREAM
1650. HERBAL COSMETICS
1651. HERBAL SHAMPO & CREAM
1652. HERBAL/AYURVEDIC COSMETICS
1653. INCENSE POWDER, INCENSE STICKS & INCENSE CAKE
1654. OPTICAL WHITENERS
1655. ROSE OIL EXTRACTION
1656. SHAMPOOS (COCONUT OIL BASED COLD PROCESS)
1657. SHAVING CREAM
1658. SINDUR (KUMKUM)
1659. SOAP COATED PAPER
1660. SPRAY DRIED DETERGENT POWDER
1661. STAIN REMOVER
1662. TALCUM POWDER (FACE & TOILET POWDER)
1663. TOILET AND HERBAL SOAP
1664. TOOTH PASTE & POWDER
1665. WASHING DETERGENT POWDER AND WASHING SOAP
1666. WASHING POWDER LIQUID DETERGENTS, LOTION & SHAMPOO

ENTERTAINMENT CLUB WITH 4 STAR HOTEL
1779. HOSPITALS
1780. ICE CREAM PARLOUR
1781. INTERNET SERVICE PROVIDER (I.S.P.)
1782. MEDICAL COLLEGE
1783. MEDICAL COLLEGE, HOSPITAL & RESEARCH INSTITUTE
1784. MEDICAL TRANSCRIPTION CENTRE
1785. MENTAL RETARDATION HOSPITAL & CEREBRAL PALSY
1786. MOTEL/SMALL HOTEL
1787. MULTISTOREY COMMERCIAL COMPLEX
1788. MULTISTOREY RESIDENTIAL COMPLEX
1789. NURSERY SCHOOL
1790. NATURE CARE CENTRE
1791. NURSING HOME
1792. ONLINE SHOPPING MALL (RS. 5000/- REPORT)
1793. PORTAL
1794. REHABILITATION CENTRE FOR AGED & NEEDY PERSONS
1795. RESIDENTIAL CUM COMMERCIAL COMPLEX
1796. RESTAURANT
1797. RESTAURANT WITH PUB
1798. SCHOOL (PRIMARY)
1799. SCHOOL (HIGHER SECONDARY)
1800. THREE STAR HOTEL
1801. TOURIST CLUB
1802. TRAINING INSTITUTE FOR MEDICAL TRANSCRIPTION
1803. VIDEO FILM STUDIO
1804. WARE HOUSE
1805. WEBSITE DESIGN & E-MAIL REGISTERING

AGRO BASED INDUSTRIES

1806. COAL BRIQUETTES FROM AGROWASTE
1807. FURFURALFROM RICEHULL
1808. MUSHROOM CULTIVATION & PROCESSING (BUTTON)
1809. MUSHROOM GROWING & PROCESSING WITH AIR CONDITIONING
1810. MUSHROOM CULTIVATION & PROCESSING UNIT DEHYDRATION & PACKAGING OF OYSTER & PADDY STRAW MUSHROOMS
1811. ORGANIC MANURE
1812. PAPAYA CULTIVATION
1813. PAPAYA & TOMATO CULTIVATION
1814. PROCESSING & UTILISATION OF COCONUT
1815. PROCESSING OF SHEEP HAIR TO PRODUCE WOOL

BAKERY, CONFECTIONERY & FOOD PRODUCTS

1816. AGROLACTOR SOYA MILK
1817. APPLE FRUIT JUICE WITH CANNING BOTTLING
1818. AYURVEDIC SHARBAT
1819. BAKERY UNIT (PASTRIES, BREAD, BUNS, CAKE, TOFFEE ETC.)
1820. BAKING POWDER
1821. BANANA & ITS BY PRODUCTS
1822. BANANA POWDER
1823. BANANA WAFERS
1824. BANANA CULTIVATION
1825. BEER INDUSTRY
1826. DEHULLING OF JAUN FOR BEER
1827. BEER & WINE
1828. BEER, ALCOHOL, IMFL
1829. BESEN PLANT
1830. BISCUIT PLANT
1831. BREAD & BISCUIT PLANT
1832. BOTTLING PLANT COUNTRY LIQUOR FROM RECTIFIED SPIRIT
1833. BRANDY
1834. BREAD RUSKS
1835. CANNED FRUITS & VEGETABLES
1836. CANNING & PRESERVATION OF MEAT
1837. CANNING & PRESERVATION OF VEGETABLES
1838. CANNING OF MANGO PULP & MANGO SLICES
1839. CARBONATED BEVERAGS
1840. CASHEW FENI
1841. CASHEW NUT (DRIED & FRIED)
1842. CATTLE BREEDING
1843. CATTLE BREEDING & DAIRY FARM TO PRODUCE MILK
1844. CATTLE FEED FROM TAPIOCA
1845. CHEWING GINGER & AMLOKI
1846. CHEWING GUM
1847. CHILLI SAUCE
1848. CHILLI POWDER
1849. CHOCOLATE
1850. CIDER PLANT
1851. COCOA POWDER
1852. COCOA BUTTER & COCOA POWDER
1853. COCONUT SHELL POWDER
1854. COCONUT WATER
1855. COCONUT SWEET (WATERY)
1856. COCONUT MILK POWDER (DEHYDRATED)
1857. COCONUT PRODUCTS & BY PRODUCTS (INTEGRATED PLANT)
1858. COLD DRINK
1859. CURRY POWDER
1860. DAIRY FOR MILK PROCESSING (GHEE, BUTTER & PANEER)
1861. DAIRY PRODUCTS
1862. DAIRY PRODUCTS MILK PACKAGING IN POUCH (GHEE, BUTTER, ETC.
1863. DAIRY FARM TO PRDUCE MILK WITH PACKAGING (COW)
1864. DAIRY FARM TO PRDUCE MILK WITH PACKAGING (BUFALLOE)
1865. DAIRY FARM & MILK PRODUCTS
1866. DAL MOTH, CHANACHUR & BHUJIYA
1867. DEHYDRATION OF FRUITS & VEGETABLE
1868. DESICCATED COCONUT POWDER FROM COCONUTS
1869. DEHYDRATION & CANNING OF FRUITS & VEGETABLES
1870. DRY FRUIT ROASTING & PACKAGING
1871. DRYING OF RED CHILLIES, HALDI, DHANIYA, PEAS & GROUND NUT
1872. EGG POWDER
1873. FISH CANNING IN TIN & POUCHES
1874. FISH DEHYRATION (DRYING OF FISH)
1875. FISH MEAL
1876. FISH PROCESSING (BEAST FREEZING PROCESSES)
1877. FLAVOURS FOR FOOD INDUSTRIES
1878. FLOUR MILL (ROLLER)
1879. FROZEN MEAT
1880. FOOD DEHYDRATION (FRUITS & VEGETABLES)
1881. FRIED & ROASTED GROUND NUT, GRAMS, PEAR ETC.
1882. FRUIT JUICE MAKING & PACKAGING IN PLASTIC CONTAINER
1883. FRUIT JUICE IN TETRA PACK (DRINKS)
1884. FRUIT JUICE, SQUASHES, SAUCE & KETCHUP, JAM, JELLY, VINEGAR ETC.
1885. GARLIC FLAKES
1886. GARLIC POWDER
1887. GHEE & BUTTER
1888. GINGER (PULVERISED)
1889. GINGER GLAZING & PRESERVATION
1890. GINGER STORAGE
1891. GINGER PROCESSING
1892. GINGER OIL & GINGER DUST
1893. GINGER POWDER (DRY) & OLEORESIN
1894. GRAPE DEHYDRATION
1895. GRAPE CULTIVATION
1896. GRAPE JUICE
1897. HONEY PROCESSING & PACKAGING
1898. ICE CREAM & ICE CANDY
1899. ICE CUBE
1900. INVERT SUGAR
1901. IDLI MIX, DOSA MIX SAMBHAR MIX, VADA MIX, GULAB JAMUN MIX
1902. INSTANT COFFEE & INSTANT TEA

1903. INSTANT NOODLES
1904. INSTANT SOUPS
1905. IODIZED SALT FROM CRUDE SALT
1906. JAM CHUTNEY PICKLES & SQUASHES
1907. KATHA MANUFACTURING
1908. LECITHIN (SOYA BASED)
1909. LEMON & ITS PRODUCTS
1910. MACARONI MANUFACTURING
1911. MACARONI, SPAGHETTI, VERMICELLI & NOODLES
1912. MAIZE & ITS BY PRODUCTS MALTING PLANT
1913. MANGO PAPPAD (AAM PAPPAD)
1914. MANGO POWDER RIPE
1915. MANGO POWDER
1916. MANGO PROCESSING & CANNING (MANGO PULP)
1917. MEAT PROCESSING (CHICKEN MUTTON)
1918. MEAT PROCESSING (BUFFALO)
1919. MENTHOL BOLD FROM MENTHOL FLAKES
1020. MILK POWDER
1921. MILK POWDER & GHEE
1922. MILK POWDER, GHEE & SPICES
1923. MILK PRESERVATION & MARKETING TO WHOLE SELLERS
1924. MILK PRESERVATION & MARKETING TO WHOLE SELLERS (IN POUCHES)
1925. MILK TOFFEE MANUFACTURES
1926. MINERAL WATER
1927. MINERAL WATER IN POUCHES
1928. MINI FLOUR MILL ATTA MAIDA, SUJI & WHEAT BRAN
1929. MITHAI/HALWAI (SWEET & NAMKEEN)
1930. MUTTON PROCESSING
1931. PAN MASALA (MEETHA, SADA, ZARDA) MAKING & PACKING
1932. PAN MASALA AND POUCH MAKING
1933. PANEER (CHEESE)
1934. PAPAD & BARIYAN
1935. PAPAD PLANT
1936. PEPSICOLA IN POLYTUBES
1937. PETHA PACKAGING
1938. PICKLES
1939. PIGGERY/MEAT/CHICKEN PROCESSING
1940. PINE APPLE JUICE CANNING
1941. POTATO & ONION POWDER
1942. POTATO & ONION FLAKES
1943. POTATO CHIPS
1944. POTATO GRANULES
1945. POUCH FILLING FOR SAUNF SUPARI ILAICHI ETC.
1946. PRESERVATION OF RAWS MANGO JUICE
1947. PROCESSED CHEESE & MARINE PDTS.
1948. PULP FROM TARMARIND
1949. READYMATE PROCESSED FOOD
1950. RICE & CORN FLAKES
1951. RICE BASMATI (TRADING)
1952. RICE POLISHING & PACKAGING IN POUCH
1953. ROASTED/SALTED/MASALA/ CASHEW NUTS ALMONDS & PEA NUT
1954. ROLLER FLOUR MILL

INFOTECH/IT PROJECTS

1955. MEDICAL TRANSCRIPTION
1956. E-COMMERCE
1957. CYBERCAFE
1958. INTERNET SERVICE PROVIDER (ISP)
1959. COMPUTER EDUCATION CENTRE
1960. PORTAL (WEBSITE DESIGN)
1961. CALL CENTRE

TERMS AND CONDITIONS

FOR INDIA

1. Please ask for Quotations of Each *Market Survey Cum Detailed Techno Economic Feasibility Report.* Payable in advance through Draft/M.O./Cash in favour of 'ENGINEERS INDIA RESEARCH INSTITUTE', Delhi. Delivery by Regd.post within 2 Days. (Postage Free)

2. Ask for the Hi-Tech Projects Monthly magazine. Each Magazine covers many Project Profiles for selection of Industry.

FOR OVERSEAS

1. Please ask for Quotations in US $ of Each *Market Survey Cum Detailed Techno Economic Feasibility Report.* Payable in advance through Draft/M.O./Cash in favour of 'ENGINEERS INDIA RESEARCH INSTITUTE', Delhi. (Payable in India) Delivery by Regd.post within 4 Days.

2. Ask for "Hi-Tech Projects" Monthly magazine. Each Magazine covers many Project Profiles for selection of Industry.

ENGINEERS INDIA RESEARCH INSTITUTE

Add: 4449, Nai Sarak (D), Main Road, Delhi - 110 006 (India)
Ph:. 91-11-23918117, 23916431, 23840361, 98114-37895
Fax: 91-11-23916431 E-Mail : eirisidi@bol.net.in
Website:www.eiriinia.org
Also at : 4/27, Roop Nagar, Near Roop Nagar No. 1 School, Delhi - 110 007 (India) Ph:. 23840361

JUST PUBLISHED-NEW BOOKS

HAND BOOK OF PERFUMES WITH FORMULATIONS

This book covers Creating a Perfume, Flower Perfumes & Formulation, Fantasy Perfumes & their Formulation, Colognes for Men, Olfaction & Gustation, Raw Materials of Perfumes, Classification of Odours & Odourants, Packaging of Perfumes, Testing of Perfumes, Aerosol Spray, Aromatic Perfumery Compounds, Scent & Perfume, Spray Perfume, Perfumes for Soap, Detergent & Agarbatti etc. Suppliers of Raw Materials.

HAND BOOK OF PERFUMES & FLAVOURS

The book covers Perfume, Formulary of Perfume, Formulary of Flavour, Chemicals Specifications for Perfume & Flavour Components, Natural Odours Simulated with Aromatic Chemicals, Simulated Flower Scents, Simulated Marine Scents (Algae), Plant & Equipment Suppliers, Suppliers of Raw Materials, Manufacturer / Exporters / Suppliers of Perfumes. Project profiles has also included for the benefits of the new entrepreneurs.

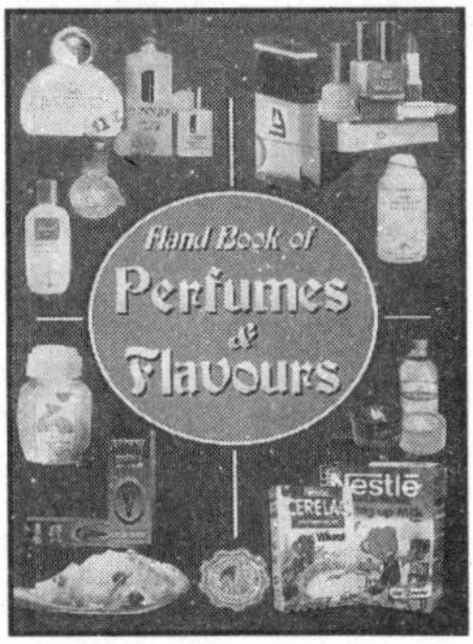

AGRO BASED PLANTATION CULTIVATION & FARMING HAND BOOK

The Book Covers Goat Farm, Floriculture (Cut Flower), Tissue Culture, Tea, Banana Cultivation, Piggery Farm, Dairy Farming, Bee keeping, Mushroom Cultivation and Processing, Teak Tree Plantation and many more. Project Profiles and Suppliers of Equipments etc.

COSMETICS PROCESSES AND FORMULATIONS HAND BOOK (WITH HERBAL COSMETICS TECHNOLOGY & FORMULAE)

Raw Materials used in Cosmetics, Equipments Details, Packaging of Cosmetics, Various Herbal and other Cosmetics manufacturing Technology, Project Profiles, Suppliers of Herbs, Raw Materials and Machinery etc.

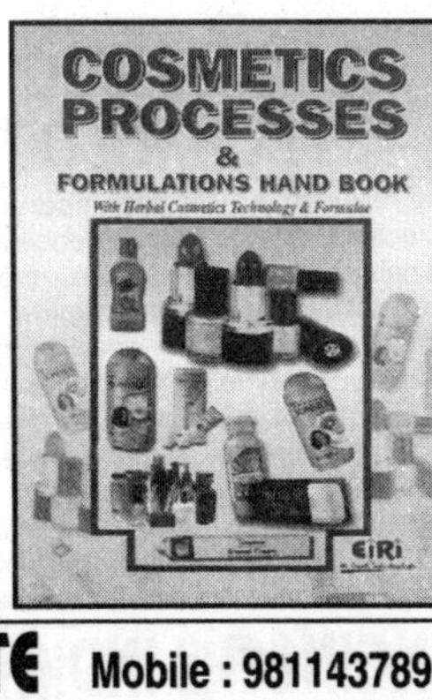

ENGINEERS INDIA RESEARCH INSTITUTE **Mobile : 9811437895**

4449, Nai Sarak, Main Road, Delhi - 110 006 (INDIA) Ph./Fax : 91-11- 23918117, 23916431, 23840361

JUST PUBLISHED-NEW BOOKS

HAND BOOK OF HERBS, MEDICINAL & AROMATIC PLANTS CULTIVATION

Book covers Aloe Vera, Ashwagandha, Babchi, Belladonna, Buckwheat, Coleus, Costus, Costus, Cowhedge, Datura, Digitalis, Discorea, Duboisa, Foxglove, Geranium, Guggal, Hop, Henna, Isabgol, Liquorice, Lemon Grass, Long Pepper, Neem, Parrot Tree, Perivinkle, Primrose, Pyrethrum, Rauvolfia, Roselle, Roselle, Rutin Bearing Eucalyptus, Rose, Senna, Steroid Bearing Solanum etc.

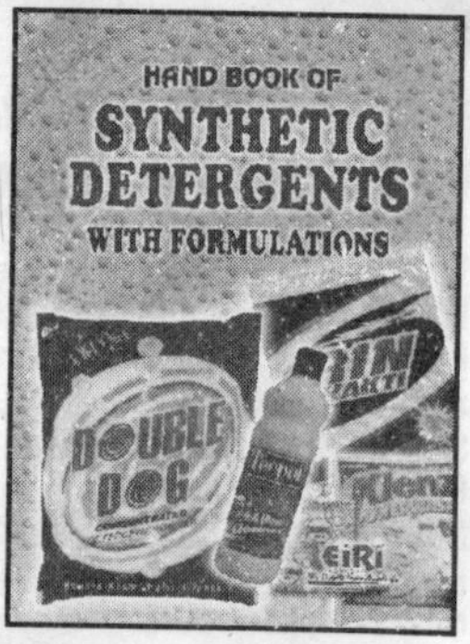

HAND BOOK OF SYNTHETIC DETERGENTS WITH FORMULATIONS

Group of Synthetic Detergents, Synthesis of Detergents, Manufacture of Synthetic Detergents with Formulae, Testing of Detergents and Soaps, Project Profiles, Suppliers of Machinery and Raw Materials, Acid Slurry, Sirf Excel Type Detergent, Ariel Type Detergent, Dry Mix Process, Dry Clean Unit and much more others.

PROFITABLE SMALL SCALE MANUFACTURE OF SOAPS & DETERGENTS

The Book is a unique book on soaps & detergents. All the necessary informations to produce soap & detergents have been covered including raw materials, soap manufacture on tiny scale, equipments for tiny/cottage scale soap industry, soap from non edible oil, soap from soap stock, Manufacturing of medicated soap, Shaving soap, shaving creams, synthetic detergent powder, detergent cake and powder, Enzyme detergent powder, Project Profiles on various Soap and Detergent projects, Suppliers of Plant and Machinery and raw materials etc.

TECHNOLOGY OF TEXTILES

The new edition of the book is covering latest technology including dyeing, bleaching, drying, spinning and weaving, gel spinning processes, melt spinning, denim production, properties and applications of super absorbent polymers, mechanical structures problems of staple yarn, advantage multi phase weaving, improving dye uptake of natural fibres, mill vs. powerloom fabrics, processing of lyocell fibres, antibacterial fabric, pre treatment and dyeing of fibre blends with elastane, non apparel applications of weft knitted fabrics, aquatex, the ultimate in finishing of upholestry, making silk fabrics wrinkle free, processing technology for cotton garments, project profiles on readymade garments, necktie, hosiery, socks knitting, powerloom, cotton yarn etc., equipments suppliers, cotton fabrics suppliers etc. are also given.

ENGINEERS INDIA RESEARCH INSTITUTE Mobile : 9811437895

4449, Nai Sarak, Main Road, Delhi - 110 006 (INDIA) Ph./Fax : 91-11- 23918117, 23916431, 23840361